The Inland Campaign for Vicksburg

MODERN WAR STUDIES

William Thomas Allison
General Editor

Raymond Callahan
Heather Marie Stur
Allan R. Millett
Carol Reardon
David R. Stone
Samuel J. Watson
Jacqueline E. Whitt
James H. Willbanks
Series Editors

Theodore A. Wilson
Founding Editor

THE INLAND CAMPAIGN FOR VICKSBURG

Five Battles in Seventeen Days,
May 1–17, 1863

Timothy B. Smith

University Press of Kansas

Parts of Chapter 16 appeared in a previously published volume as Timothy B. Smith, "'A Victory Could Hardly Have Been More Complete': The Battle of Big Black River Bridge," in Steven E. Woodworth and Charles D. Grear, eds., *The Vicksburg Campaign: March 29–May 18, 1863*, 173–193 (Copyright © 2013 by the Board of Trustees, Southern Illinois University).

Published by the University Press of Kansas (Lawrence, Kansas 66045), which was organized by the Kansas Board of Regents and is operated and funded by Emporia State University, Fort Hays State University, Kansas State University, Pittsburg State University, the University of Kansas, and Wichita State University.

Library of Congress Cataloging-in-Publication Data

Names: Smith, Timothy B., 1974– author.
Title: The inland campaign for Vicksburg : five battles in seventeen days,
May 1–17, 1863 / Timothy B. Smith.
Description: Lawrence, Kansas : University Press of Kansas, 2024 | Series:
Modern war studies | Includes bibliographical references and index.
Identifiers: LCCN 2023033991 (print) | LCCN 2023033992 (ebook)
ISBN 9780700636556 (cloth)   ISBN 9780700636563 (ebook)
Subjects: LCSH: Vicksburg (Miss.)—History—Civil War, 1861–1865. | Vicksburg (Miss.)—
History—Siege, 1863. | Mississippi—History—Civil War, 1861–1865—Campaigns. |
United States—History—Civil War, 1861–1865—Campaigns. |
Grant, Ulysses S. (Ulysses Simpson), 1822–1885—Military leadership.
Classification: LCC E475.2 .S654 2024 (print) | LCC E475.2 (ebook)
| DDC 973.7/344—dc23/eng/20230929
LC record available at https://lccn.loc.gov/2023033991.
LC ebook record available at https://lccn.loc.gov/2023033992.
British Library Cataloguing-in-Publication Data is available.

Printed in the United States of America

10 9 8 7 6 5 4 3 2 1

The paper used in this publication is acid free and meets the minimum requirements of the American National Standard for Permanence of Paper for Printed Library Materials Z39.48-1992.

In memory of my grandparents

Leon and Mary Kate
and
Bogan and Cordie

CONTENTS

MAPS

ILLUSTRATIONS

PREFACE

The curious workings of memory and preservation have made Vicksburg a case study in perception. Obviously, many visitors and buffs are familiar with the Vicksburg National Military Park, established in 1899 as part of the golden age of battlefield preservation. Most visitation to Vicksburg-associated sites comes there, right off of Interstate 20 as it is. But probably the most popular portion of the campaign, if less visited, is the phase of five battles in seventeen days when Union Major General Ulysses S. Grant moved from his crossing point of the Mississippi River south of Vicksburg northeastward to the state capital and then westward to bottle up the city itself. It has all the classic objects of tension, drama, fighting, and surprise to make a great story, and how it all played out is fascinating beyond degree. Fortunately, the Conservation Fund, American Battlefield Trust, the state of Mississippi, and the National Park Service have led in the process of acquiring and marking many of these outlying campaign sites and battlefields, making them accessible to visitors who want to see more than just the assault and siege lines at Vicksburg itself. Unfortunately, even now these outlying battlefields are so remote that individual visitors on their own still have trouble even finding them, much less extrapolating what happened where.[1]

But the Inland Campaign for Vicksburg from May 1 to May 17, 1863, is often misunderstood in popular memory. From the debate over Grant's supply line or lack thereof to the swiftness of it in general, historians have had different schools of thought and come to differing conclusions, not all of them based on the evidence. In fact, there has not been a single, stand-alone academic investigation of this portion of the campaign as yet, certainly not one that delves deeply into the primary manuscript sources to ferret out the various nuances of the campaign.

For instance, the discussion of Grant's supply system had been woefully overlooked and explained only with generalities. Obviously, his own contradictory statements made in Grant's memoirs did not help. But it is clear that

Grant did not fully cut loose from his supply base; in fact provisions were arriving at the head of the army throughout the campaign. What is ironic is that even that was not enough to sustain the army, and neither was the famed foraging off the land. The crisis hovering over the Army of the Tennessee by the time it reached the four battles in six days in mid-May was much more acute than normally perceived.[2]

Likewise, the swiftness of the Union advance was not the famed blitz-krieg it is so often touted as. There were certainly days when Grant moved quickly—"a sort of whirlwind at times," one Federal described it—and over-all Grant's movements were certainly fast enough to befuddle his Confederate opponents. But as historians William Shea and Terry Winschel argue, "the pace of the Union advance was not particularly fast." In fact, Winschel argued that this form of warfare was "Blitzkrieg, U. S. Grant Style" rather than the typical German offensive most often associated with World War II. While there were indeed periods of intense movement and fighting, there were larger stretches of nonmovement and stillness in both armies through-out the seventeen days. But it produced what was needed for the Federal high command: just enough swiftness to keep Grant's opponents off balance and to maintain his own strength, even if it was close. Lincoln described the "slows" in reference to other Union commanders, but Grant's movements at Vicksburg showed he had no such ailment.[3]

If there is debate on some of the finer points of Grant's Inland Campaign, few with any ounce of an open mind dispute the brilliance of it, and no one can argue with the results. In the final tally, Grant arrived victorious at the exact place he sought: the high ground east of Vicksburg, where he had access to both the city and an open and unchallenged supply route via the Missis-sippi and Yazoo Rivers to the north. It was the very ground Grant had wanted for months now, and finally he could begin the process of actually capturing Vicksburg. And while some can quibble with Grant's methods, it is clear that the movement was brilliant and dazzling. Winschel, in fact, describes the Inland Campaign as "boldness personified and Napoleonic in its concept." If caveats are given, such as the nature of the Confederate resistance or the abil-ity of the Confederate commanders Grant faced, it is nevertheless clear that the Inland Campaign was the stuff of military legend. As such, there is ample reason why modern military manuals and doctrine use the campaign as an ex-ample of how to operate successfully. Even General-in-Chief Henry Halleck himself, certainly no fan of Grant, gave it the ultimate praise by comparing it "most favorably" with Napoleon's operations in the Ulm Campaign in 1805.[4]

While there has been no volume dedicated solely to this phase of the ac-tion, there are various treatments in larger campaign studies, most notably

Edwin C. Bearss's three-volume *The Vicksburg Campaign*. Likewise, there are a few individual examinations of some of the various battles, including my own *Champion Hill: Decisive Battle for Vicksburg*. Chris Mackowski's *The Battle of Jackson, Mississippi, May 14, 1863* is another, but the other battles are woefully lacking in treatment other than the larger campaign studies. There is definite room for Mackowski-type treatments of battles including Raymond and Big Black River Bridge, small though they were, and Port Gibson is deserving of a larger, more detailed tactical study.[5]

But with this current series (a five-volume examination of the entire campaign) being an operational-level campaign study, the emphasis is not necessarily on the tactical action except to provide the same basic level of coverage as the rest of the Inland Campaign. As a result, readers will not find in-depth battle studies for any of the five May battles, and should peruse *Champion Hill* and *The Battle of Jackson* for more detail on those engagements. Likewise, other topical facets of the operations have been highlighted in other books such as *The Decision Was Always My Own: Ulysses S. Grant and the Vicksburg Campaign* or *The Real Horse Soldiers: Benjamin Grierson's Epic 1863 Raid through Mississippi*, the latter of which details the raid that was winding down even as this phase of the campaign was beginning but nevertheless had an immense impact on the operations. Hopefully, more tactical studies will appear in the future on the other battles.[6]

But in a larger sense, these collective seventeen days were profoundly important, as they obviously were the determining factor of Grant reaching Vicksburg and opening up his new line of supply so desperately needed. And it was a closer-run thing than normally thought, as only a few minor changes in some of the parameters could likely have changed the whole process to a different construct. Any changes could have brought monumental differences in results, and unlike earlier Union attempts to reach Vicksburg that were limited and fairly low risk with the potential of high reward, this gamble was high risk/high reward and was the final, no-turning-back attempt. Yet Grant prevailed and reached Vicksburg and was then ready to start the next process in the campaign: actually taking the city itself. But in the whole nine-month-long campaign, there was no more tension- and drama-filled period than these seventeen days when Grant's Army of the Tennessee marched through the wilds of Mississippi to victory after victory, tearing the heart out of the state of Mississippi and the Confederacy.

Many people have aided me in the process of completing this volume. The staff at the various archives were extremely helpful in my research. Several historians read the manuscript for me and provided critical feedback; John Marszalek and Terry Winschel provided many useful corrections and edits to the narrative. The staff at the University Press of Kansas, including Joyce Harrison, Kelly Chrisman Jacques, and Derek Helms, were all wonderful to work with again, and copy editor Jon Howard did his usual superb polishing on the manuscript. My family means more to me than anything except God, and Kelly, Mary Kate, and Leah Grace make life meaningful. I have dedicated this book to the memory of my grandparents, who passed away long ago but left many wonderful memories of an era long past.

PROLOGUE

"An Army Marches on Its Stomach"

"Amateurs study tactics," it is said, "[but] professionals study logistics." Put another way, many historic figures were said to have pronounced that "an army marches on its stomach." No matter the idiom, the basic argument is that an army from any time in history has to be supplied well to function properly and to win battles, campaigns, or wars. While such phrases sometimes unfairly dismiss the study of strategy or tactics, the basic meaning cannot be missed: supplies are a major concern for moving armies and nations at war.[1]

In no part of any campaign could that be argued more than in the first seventeen days of May 1863, after Major General Ulysses S. Grant crossed to the east bank of the Mississippi River with his Army of the Tennessee bound for Vicksburg. The results of both his own campaign and the response from his counterpart defending Mississippi and especially Vicksburg, Lieutenant General John C. Pemberton, were solidly based on logistics and the means and ability to supply their respective armies with food, equipment, and ammunition enough to wage a struggle for the treasured city and the larger prize, the Mississippi River. While heavy on strategy, speed, and tactical acumen, the Inland Campaign from the crossing at Bruinsburg to the ramparts of Vicksburg itself was one largely of logistics. "The whole of his [Grant's] strategy pivoted on the question of supply," historian J. F. C. Fuller wrote, particularly now with a Confederate army between his own force and "his base of supply at Memphis."[2]

In the most basic terms, John Pemberton had a growing crisis on his hands logistically as he defended Vicksburg, which was fast becoming his main area of focus. His move on May 1 to the river city from his normal headquarters at Jackson, the state capital, was plain enough amid the unfolding crisis; "I command the department from here," he informed his commanders that day. Obviously, the military defense consisting of earthen fortifications ringing Vicksburg as well as heavy batteries along the river were important, as were the outlying areas that could provide maneuvering room for a mobile portion of his army. But if the troops either out meeting the enemy or huddled inside Vicksburg could not be fed, supplied, and provided with ammunition, it would all be useless, and Vicksburg would be doomed.[3]

Pemberton had conceived as much and presumed Grant's campaign for Vicksburg would come down to a confrontation at the city's defenses themselves, perhaps even in a siege. For months, Pemberton had accordingly been gathering all the supplies his meager framework of transportation could collect. If it came down to it, Pemberton could huddle inside the strong Vicksburg defenses and wait there, still closing the Mississippi River to normal enemy traffic until help could arrive from the outside. But he had to have plenty of supplies inside the garrison to do so.[4]

By the end of April 1863, Pemberton had succeeded in shipping a huge allotment of goods to Vicksburg. Some 526,468 rations of bacon were on hand on that day, as were two and a half million rations of rice. There was also around two hundred and fifty thousand rations of flour and meal each, with over seventy-five thousand of lard. Huge amounts of other supplies, in the millions of rations, were also on hand, including over nine million of salt and three or four million of peas and sugar as well as half a million in molasses. There was also a cattle herd pasturing around Edwards Station, although the commissary officers debated exactly how many there were, some saying as many as four thousand. A better guess was probably around fifteen hundred at around three hundred pounds each, which calculated to about four hundred and fifty thousand rations of beef.[5]

Yet a major concern for Pemberton and his supply situation was the artery to receive more resources: the Southern Railroad of Mississippi. Goods could conceivably be brought in over the dirt roads by wagon, but for larger shipments in the size needed to subsist an army of tens of thousands inside Vicksburg for weeks and weeks, the railroad had to be utilized well. Unfortunately, it was already overburdened and in terrible shape, often washed out and frequently enduring accidents and stoppages due to faulty machinery or bridges. One traveler noted that the line "was in a most dangerous state . . . it was completely worn out." A Mississippian noted in her diary at one point, "the cars run off the track and killed seven men and wounded 20." Nevertheless, the railroad was Pemberton's main channel to get communications out and supplies in, the Mississippi River having been severed to the north and south of Vicksburg by the Federal navy.[6]

The Yazoo River corridor into the Mississippi Delta was likewise a secondary option and was utilized nonstop in shipping mostly corn into Vicksburg, but this means was not nearly as feasible as the railroad. For one, the few vessels on the river system and its tributaries could not keep up with the demand, and many of them were involved in shipping troops and deflecting Federal incursions, some being plied with cotton and guns to make "cottonclads." More problematic was that Confederate possession of the Yazoo River extended downstream only to Snyder's Bluff, where the big guns closed the river to Federal traffic. Below that, the Union navy had free range. That meant that Confederate Yazoo River steamers loaded with goods had to stop at Snyder's Bluff at the least and transfer the goods by wagon the final dozen or so miles into Vicksburg, which put the varying state of the simple roads again in play. Perhaps even more of a factor was that Federal expeditions had advanced into the Delta frequently over the previous few months and had damaged much of the area's infrastructure, and what the enemy did not destroy Mother Nature did with the heavy flooding that ruined a lot of the harvests. Perhaps most obvious, the Yazoo Valley, fertile though it was, simply could not grow ammunition that the Confederate army needed to defend Vicksburg.[7]

Consequently, the Southern Railroad became Pemberton's only choice of getting major supplies in, especially ammunition. But it was vulnerable, as Colonel Benjamin H. Grierson's recent raid through the state had shown. The line was down for a week around Newton Station after Grierson passed through, but there were even more vulnerable points Pemberton had to defend. One was the Pearl River bridge at Jackson, although even if that span was destroyed, the rail line could still connect with the Mississippi Central Railroad and the New Orleans, Jackson, and Great Northern Railroad that lay west of the Pearl River. They had been lopped off themselves to the north and south and did not connect with the greater Confederacy, so their possession was still not all that was needed, but they nevertheless connected to larger parts of Mississippi that could provide supplies. As a result, the loss of the Pearl River bridge would be disastrous but endurable. Conversely, damage to the closer-in Big Black River bridge, a mere eleven miles from the depot in Vicksburg, would probably be fatal. Loss of that structure would deprive Vicksburg of any outside connection whatsoever.[8]

Yet the Federals did not have to damage the big bridges to cut the rail line. Depending on where Grant marched after crossing the Mississippi River, merely putting his army astride the rail line at any point would stop all traffic and halt any new provisioning of Vicksburg. One of Pemberton's major fears, and indeed the prediction of many a soldier in Grant's army, was that the Federals would sweep northward to cut the railroad with the army before moving westward to confront Vicksburg itself. And Grant was contemplating just such a thing, with Charles Dana, a special observer reporting from the ground to the War Department, informing Washington as early as April 6 that "the landing [is] to be made at or about Grand Gulf, and the army is to operate on the southern or eastern shore of the Big Black, where the land is elevated and the roads good, threatening both the bridge across the Big Black and Jackson. . . . The enemy will be compelled to come out and fight." Pemberton accordingly had to be mindful of the possible need to advance outside Vicksburg with a mobile portion of his command to deflect Grant's army away from the critical rail line.[9]

Pemberton realized as much, and he kept the railroad busy in the days after Grant landed east of the Mississippi River, bringing more and more supplies into Vicksburg while Grant was still miles to the south preparing for his advance. Over the course of the first two weeks of May, Pemberton's commissary officers brought into Vicksburg nearly four hundred thousand additional rations of bacon, two-thirds of it from Jackson and the rest from Meridian, both significantly sitting on the Southern Railroad. In addition, a million and a half rations of rice came in from Jackson, as did nearly that many of salt. Smaller quantities of corn, lard, meal, peas, and vinegar also arrived via the railroad from both places, as did soap and candles, the main reason for the smaller quantities of those being that Pemberton had already gathered large stocks of corn and other items inside Vicksburg during the spring. Additional rations of bacon, salt, sugar, meal, rice, and molasses in the tens of thousands were also staged at various depots on the Southern Railroad east of Vicksburg, mostly at Bovina just ten miles to the east, but others in smaller quantities were also landed at Edwards and Bolton across the Big Black River. Pemberton was obviously attuned to his logistical situation as May developed.[10]

The exact opposite situation confronted Grant as he began his trek northward toward Vicksburg. In fact, Grant had by far the more difficult logistical situation of the two. While Pemberton had a reasonably secure supply line into Vicksburg and to his army, safe until the enemy broke it, Grant did not. Rather, the reasonably safe portion of his supply line extended southward by river from Union-held territory (Memphis) only to Milliken's Bend on the Mississippi River opposite and upstream from Vicksburg. As he had been doing for months now, Grant could bring in any sort of supplies he needed there and even down to Young's Point, or up the first few miles of the Yazoo River for that matter, but there the safety ended. To get supplies to his army now that it was across the Mississippi River at Bruinsburg, south of Vicksburg, he had to ferry those supplies, including equipment and ammunition, southward by wagon along the bayou roads in Louisiana and the well-worn trail his army had blazed in late March and April. The route from Milliken's Bend to Richmond, along Roundaway Bayou to Smith's Plantation, thence around Bayou Vidal to the Holmes Plantation and from there around Lake St. Joseph to Hard Times, was nearly seventy miles and was grueling with bad roads, frequent pontoon bridges that could wash away any day, and Confederate guerrillas, not to mention the alligators and snakes amid other types of vermin. But that was the easy part. Once at Hard Times, the supplies had to be ferried over the river by boat and then carried forward to the inland army by whatever conveyance could be had, as most of the wheeled vehicles of the army remained west of the river initially. Worse, as Grant's troops pushed forward, the distance to take those supplies grew with every step trod in the Mississippi wilderness.[11]

Grant consequently depended on a delicate and very nearly nonexistent supply line rather than the secure line of communication most military theorists advised. But Grant was adapting, much of it toward the Clausewitzian fashion he had been employing now for a while in going against the book, primarily the military theories of Henri Jomini. The Swiss theorist advocated clear and safe lines of supply, which this was anything but. The Prussian Carl von Clausewitz, in contrast, promoted a more foraging-based supply strategy taken from Napoleon himself as he surged across Europe not always with secure lines of supply back to France. He instead set up local supply dumps to which he could gather supplies in the surrounding region for forwarding to his units in the field: "Warfare based on requisition and local sources of supply is so superior to the kind that relies on depots, that the two no longer seem to be the same instrument," Clausewitz argued.[12]

Grant had every intention of setting up these forward supply dumps, first at Grand Gulf, and then hoping by increments to shorten the long route back to Milliken's Bend. In fact, he had initially intended on taking Grand Gulf and making it his base of supplies, from which to bring up to the army everything he needed. But Grand Gulf had proved far too strongly defended to be assaulted amphibiously, and Grant chose to land farther downriver at Bruinsburg. That gave him an uncontested landing, largely because Bruinsburg was south of Bayou Pierre and the first crossing of that substantial stream was far inland near Port Gibson. As a result, opposing Confederates had to detour far off the direct route from Grand Gulf to Bruinsburg to contest the landing, they acting on the very definition of exterior lines while Grant moved along the direct line, the shortest path between two points and the definition of interior lines of communication.[13]

Yet Grant's crossing at Bruinsburg also had its disadvantages despite forcing the Confederates to go out of the way to get to his new crossing point, thereby allowing Grant to beat them to it. Crossing below Bayou Pierre now meant that to take Grand Gulf and get back on the original plan of having it be his base, he now had to not only defeat the enemy concentrating against him south of the bayou but also to make the same detour inland to get across the formidable waterway. Now Grant was on exterior lines while the enemy had the advantage of interior lines of communication.

Grant envisioned other bases as well that would eventually shorten his supply line even more. Taking Grand Gulf would cut off the entire lengthy move south of Bayou Pierre, but he still had the Big Black River between him and Vicksburg, which offered the same disadvantages. Initially, if the Confederates responded, they had to go out of their way to get across the river far inland, Hankinson's Ferry being the first major crossing point upstream from the Big Black River's mouth at Grand Gulf (Thompson's Ferry being much less ideal). But as Grant moved forward, he would then, like before, have to move inland to get across as well. Much better suited was setting up a depot at Warrenton, which was above both Bayou Pierre and the Big Black River and would offer unfettered access for supplies to reach Grant's army without going on roundabout routes east of the Mississippi River. Since Warrenton was also south of Vicksburg, however, many of the same miles and miles of travel would still be necessary in Louisiana to get supplies across the river even at Warrenton. That said, Grant also had his officers devising plans to shorten that route west of the river as well.[14]

The absolute best-case scenario would be for Grant to eventually reach the high ground east and north of Vicksburg at Snyder's and Haynes' Bluffs on the Yazoo River, "the ground I so much desire," he admitted. Once that was taken, which Grant had admittedly been trying to do for months now first in the Mississippi Central and Chickasaw Bayou efforts and then in the Yazoo Pass and Steele's Bayou expeditions, Grant would have an outlet for provisions, as the navy could easily get supplies up the now undefended Yazoo even if Confederates still held Vicksburg. Then, there would be no more long routes by wagon through Louisiana to positions south of Vicksburg, which were followed by long wagon movements northward to reach the ever-advancing army. Rather, transports could simply unload at the Yazoo River landings and the goods be taken directly to the army confronting Vicksburg. It was certainly the ultimate logistical goal, which would solve Grant's supply conundrum even without taking Vicksburg. But it was a long way from Bruinsburg to Snyder's Bluff, and Grant would probably have to fight much of his way there. One perceptive Union soldier knew as much as he jumped off on this new campaign: "When we left Bruinsburg where we landed this morning we drew 3 days rations with nothing but crackers & Coffee that was all and expect us to steal or starve as there is not a team of Mules or Horses below Vicksburg and we will not have any more until we make communication with our men on the Yazoo River."[15]

Fighting his way northward first to a secure supply situation and then on to take Vicksburg would involve days if not weeks, and that intervening period was the critical time for Grant and his army. If he fought too many battles and ran out of ammunition faster than he could bring it up along his lengthy line of communication, Grant could be easily defeated. If his men ran out of food or equipment, their ability to fight hard would be severely diminished. If he stopped a movement too long and exhausted the supplies in the local area his men would begin to go hungry. It was definitely a gamble to make such a sprint northward to acquire the connection to the Yazoo River, but it had to be done. There was no other option left at this point.

In the meantime, Grant would depend on two things to supply his army. One, a lesson he later said he learned earlier in the war, was to live as much as he could off the land. While withdrawing in northern Mississippi after the disastrous twin raids by Major General Earl Van Dorn and Brigadier General Nathan Bedford Forrest destroyed his supply center and the railroad leading to it from the north, Grant noted, "our loss of supplies was great at Holly Springs, but it was more than compensated for by those taken from the country and by the lesson taught." But living off the land was dangerous, especially if moving slowly; a stationary or creeping army could vacuum up all the supplies in a given area in no time. Without moving on, the army would soon be devoid of supplies if that was the only source.[16]

But as proof that this could be done, Napoleon had depended largely on the land to provide goods in a complicated system of depots and foraging expeditions that provided fairly well for his major campaigns through Austria and Prussia (1805–1806). But if Grant was depending on that type of resource material here in America, he was walking a fine line of disaster. Historians estimate that the population density of France (and consequently other nearby European nations through which Napoleon campaigned) was about 140 people per square mile in the first couple of decades of the nineteenth century. By 1860, that density had risen to 176 in France, 142 in Austria, and 159 in Prussia per square mile. But there was nothing like those density numbers in the southern United States in 1863.[17]

Conversely, in 1860, the population density of the Confederacy (the eleven states that seceded) was about eleven people per square mile, and that number included the slaves in those respective states. That number is skewed downward somewhat, however, because of major regions that were nearly uninhabited, such as Texas (as a whole a mere two and a half people per square mile) and Florida (even less—just barely over two). In fact, if those two states were removed, the rest of the Confederacy had a much higher density. Just taking out Texas raised the population per square mile in the rest of the Confederacy to a little over sixteen, and removing Florida raised it even more, to higher than eighteen per square mile. Yet those figures are also still somewhat skewed lower because of additional barely occupied regions in the Mississippi Delta, East Tennessee and western North Carolina, northern Georgia, western Virginia, and northwestern Arkansas. The density would likely be in the twenties in the majority of the Confederacy, certainly along rivers and rail lines where most of the transportation routes and cites were located.[18]

An examination of individual locations in the Confederacy bears this out. In 1860, Virginia (including the western part that broke away in 1863) had a population density of around twenty-four people per square mile. As would be expected, more southern and western states had lower rates, with Georgia—where Major General William T. Sherman would later live off the land in his March to the Sea—standing at a little under eighteen and Mississippi—where Grant was about to enter the wilderness—at just above sixteen. Again, those numbers are skewed a little low given vast regions of all three states that had a very small population. In Virginia, for example, Wirt County in the mountains of what would later become West Virginia was as low as under sixteen, while Augusta County in the Shenandoah Valley, where armies would feed off the land, sat at twenty eight and a half people per square mile. Similarly, in Georgia, Rabun County in the northeastern mountains had a population density of a mere eight and a half, while Miller County in the far southwestern corner was even lower at a little over six. But along the line Sherman took to Savannah on his famed march, Baldwin County had a density rate of thirty-four people per square mile.[19]

In Mississippi, where the lower rates of the Delta would skew the overall numbers for the state downward, county-level density rates give a better projection of just how much Grant could depend on the inhabitants for supplies. In northern Mississippi, where Grant said he learned he could do such a thing, Marshall County had a population density of nearly thirty-five in 1860, with Lafayette, just to its south and containing Oxford (where Grant said he came to this conclusion) at just about twenty-four. Those numbers were similar to what Grant would find in the southwestern portion of the state as he crossed the Mississippi River at Bruinsburg. Claiborne County, where he crossed, had a density of thirty-one, while Warren just to the north and containing Vicksburg itself stood at thirty-four and a half. If Grant ranged at all eastward to outflank Vicksburg, he would enter Copiah County with a density of twenty and a half as well as Hinds with a density of thirty-seven, although in the latter case the numbers were somewhat skewed upward because of the presence of Jackson, the state capital. Few in Jackson grew large numbers of food crops, and accordingly the rural regions outside the capital would have a lower density than the overall county numbers indicated.[20]

Consequently, when Grant crossed the river and began his campaign northward, he could count on finding food at a similar rate Sherman would find in Georgia later in the war but less than what would be available in the Eastern Seaboard states. But the really significant result was that population density here in the United States even in 1860 was a mere fraction of what Napoleon had found in the early 1800s in Europe—around a fifth of the density in fact. While armies were smaller, although probably not a fifth smaller to correlate with the drop in density, still thousands of men marching through any given area dependent on food taken from the countryside was a tricky business. And Grant would be doing so in the spring, normally known as "starvation time," when many of the supplies gathered the previous fall were beginning to run out; Sherman, of course, marched through Georgia during the fall harvest period. Moreover, springtime was notoriously wetter than falltime, which could slow an army and make it less able to move quickly to new scavenging areas not already swept by the army's foragers. The bottom line was that Grant was stepping off into a near wilderness that was much less inhabited than what Napoleon had found and less well stocked than what Sherman would find farther east. The result was a major risk that only time would tell if it would work. But it was simply a continuation of Grant's movement away from the Jominian concepts of war toward more of a Clausewitzian style. Henry Ward Beecher, in fact, succinctly summed it up when he eulogized Grant: "If he neglected the rules of war, as at Vicksburg, it was to make better rules, to those who were strong enough to employ them."[21]

More significant, while food, particularly meat and forage, could be had for man and beast from the surrounding area, not all that was needed for an army could be gleaned so readily from the countryside. Bread would be much harder to come by in the quantities needed, and hardtack would be a major item to be transported. Likewise, everything the army shot had to be hauled to it or carried inland initially. Ammunition would be even scarcer if Grant had to fight much at all. As a result, Grant planned on a second major aid: to have regular wagon trains rolling out of his bases of supplies, whether that be Bruinsburg initially or Grand Gulf (if and when it was secured) or even Warrenton. Certainly, when he reached the Yazoo River the task of supplying the army with ammunition from the landings would be easier given the shorter and more secure distance. But he had to make it there first, and in the meantime—supplied only with what he could find on the way and what could be hauled overland in Louisiana, across the river, and then up to the army—Grant would be in a fight against time to reach the Yazoo River before his supplies ran out. Perhaps Bruce Catton described it best when he wrote of Grant's plan to "cut his supply lines and gamble that he could fight his way to a decision [or the Yazoo River] before starvation set in." Otherwise, he might reach that "culminating point" that Clausewitz had warned an offensive commander about, when he reached his point of overextension.[22]

A correspondingly Clausewitzian Confederate commander might just counterattack at that critical moment, as Clausewitz advised, and if so all bets were off in this very different Inland Campaign that was about to begin. But only time would tell if Pemberton could make the similar leap to the Clausewitzian mindset to take advantage of Grant's delicate logistical situation.

The Inland Campaign for Vicksburg

1

"I Have to Overcome Obstacles to Reach Him"

To May 1

The little insignificant river landing at Bruinsburg, Mississippi, suddenly became alive with activity on April 30, 1863. Once a thriving landing with connections to some of the most important people of the region and nation, at times even Andrew Jackson himself and Aaron Burr decades before, Bruinsburg had by 1863 dwindled to a mere few huts and buildings that were no longer significant in any way. But it was not the buildings or people that interested the Federal Army of the Tennessee that morning. It was rather the landing itself and the good road that led up into the hills and northeastward to Port Gibson.[1]

Ulysses S. Grant was understandably nervous as he peered from the pilot-house of the ironclad USS *Benton* that morning. The gunboat slowly nudged into the bank at Bruinsburg, crammed with Indiana soldiers who quickly spilled ashore to see if there would be any Confederate resistance. Fortunately for Grant they found none, but his concern was not completely gone. A more reasonable explanation for the easy landing was that the Confederates held the high bluffs inland, much as they had done at Chickasaw Bayou back in December. The road inland would be of no use if the army could not get out of the river bottom.[2]

But alas, there was no enemy defense there either. Consequently, Federal brigades led by the 11th Wisconsin began to spill up the narrow road to the hills, taking possession of the high ground east of the river. The only delay was "occasioned by a battery in climbing the steep ascent," one Federal explained. Meeting the Union soldiers at the top of the bluffs was Windsor Plantation, the stately mansion of Smith Coffee Daniell's widow, Catharine.

There, the Federals rested before moving on later that day, bound for Port Gibson and ultimately to Vicksburg. It was the beginning of a new phase of the campaign, one Illinoisan declaring it "the final movement for the investing and capture of the great stronghold." But in reality, it was just another step in the complex effort to reach the hill city of Vicksburg.[3]

In the most contextual terms, the effort to capture Vicksburg boiled down to two very different parts. One, perhaps the easiest in most cases but probably the more difficult here at Vicksburg—largely because of terrain—was to get into a position to attack the city. In most battles or campaigns, getting into position was the easy part, such as with Grant at Shiloh, where the enemy came to him. But here at Vicksburg it was different, and Grant spent a good six or seven months just trying to reach the outskirts of Vicksburg so that he could attack it. Because of the tall riverfront bluffs to the west, the Mississippi Delta to the north, and the inaccessibility of the southern and eastern approaches, Grant had found it terribly difficult even to reach that high ground. "I am very well but much perplexed," he had recently admitted to his wife, Julia, adding, "heretofore I have had nothing to do but fight the enemy. This time I have to overcome obstacles to reach him."[4]

Obviously, once he got to Vicksburg, which he had not yet done, Grant would have to shift to the second phase of actually taking the city. That might involve any number of efforts, such as direct assault or even a siege. But Grant was a long way away from that at this point. Between Bruinsburg and Vicksburg lay miles of river-, creek-, and bayou-crossed land that at times was very difficult to operate on. Plus, there was a defending Confederate army somewhere out there that would no doubt resist to the greatest degree possible. Worse, resistance meant delay, and delay meant a possible dearth of supplies. Grant had to move quickly to get to Vicksburg if this latest effort would succeed. He had exhausted all other possibilities, and this one, certainly once across the river, was the final effort, succeed or fail. If this was Plan G in the continual adaptation of new ideas to reach Vicksburg, once across the river there was no Plan H. Grant would either get to Vicksburg, bottle up the enemy army there, and open up a secure supply line, or he would likely be defeated, perhaps captured, and maybe even killed. No wonder he was nervous upon setting out into the wilds of Mississippi.[5]

Landing at Bruinsburg was accordingly not anything that different than what had already occurred, and it was not anything new in the old effort just to get to Vicksburg. But it was by far the most risky of the phases, when Grant would be on his own in enemy territory without a secure supply line and without the possibility of quick reinforcement if something went wrong.

Grant himself later expressed his thoughts when he reached the high ground that put him into a position to continue:

> When this was effected I felt a degree of relief scarcely ever equaled since. Vicksburg was not yet taken it is true, nor were its defenders demoralized by any of our previous moves. I was now in the enemy's country, with a vast river and the stronghold of Vicksburg between me and my base of supplies. But I was on dry ground on the same side of the river with the enemy. All the campaigns, labors, hardships and exposures from the month of December previous to this time that had been made and endured, were for the accomplishment of this one object.[6]

The road to Bruinsburg—all those campaigns, labors, and hardships Grant mentioned—began much earlier and much farther away from the tiny community on the banks of the Mississippi River. In fact, what led to Grant's crossing here in late April was the result of a Union advance along the river from both directions. With the Mississippi River an obvious strategic icon, as it had been in previous wars as well, operations on and near the waterway began almost as early as the war itself. "Vicksburg is the key," President Abraham Lincoln argued early in 1862, adding, "the war can never be brought to a close until that key is in our pocket."[7]

The major Union thrust came from the north. Over the course of a year and a half, Federal armies pushed hard, fighting many bloody battles to reach a point where Vicksburg itself could be approached. Operations centered not surprisingly on the Mississippi River itself initially, but the Confederate bastion at Columbus, Kentucky, stopped all thought of the Federals proceeding southward on that route. Rather, Ulysses S. Grant and his naval soulmate, Flag Officer Andrew H. Foote, talked their departmental commander, Major General Henry W. Halleck, into unleashing them on a bypassing expedition to the east. Conveniently, the Tennessee River flowed parallel with the Mississippi only a hundred miles to the east (although in an opposite direction), and that river allowed the better-equipped Federals to utilize the transportation arteries that were the major rivers and penetrate into the Confederacy. Foote's victory at Fort Henry and Grant's subsequent capture of Fort Donelson in February 1862 carried huge implications beyond Grant's famous declaration that "no terms except unconditional and immediate surrender can be accepted"; creating the hero Grant, blotting out an entire Confederate field army of some fifteen thousand men, and eventually causing the capture of

Nashville were hugely important developments in the Union war effort. But no larger progress came than when naval gunboats initially, and then transports laden with thousands of army soldiers later, trudged southward up the Tennessee River to the meeting area of Alabama, Mississippi, and Tennessee. Camping at Pittsburg Landing on the west bank of the river, Grant's goal then was the railroad junction at Corinth, Mississippi, some twenty-two miles to the southwest. He had only to await the arrival of Major General Don Carlos Buell's Army of the Ohio from Nashville, which followed up the Confederate withdrawal from that city, as well as departmental commander Halleck to launch the advance.[8]

The Confederate defenders responded before Grant could move. General Albert Sidney Johnston had overseen the retreat from Kentucky while his other wing withdrew from Columbus; since they were on opposite sides of the Tennessee River they could no longer support each other. Johnston had to reach a position where the two wings could combine, which was at Corinth in Mississippi. Johnston accordingly gave up all of Kentucky, much of Tennessee, Columbus, and Nashville while concentrating his forces at Corinth. But rather than await the Union advance, Johnston chose to attack, especially before the two Federal armies united. "I would fight them if they were a million," Johnston declared with a definite amount of hyperbole.[9]

Johnston's advance led to two days of heavy fighting on the banks of the Tennessee River at Shiloh in early April, but the bold gamble to strike while the enemy armies were separated did not work; Buell's arriving forces made a vast difference on the second day. Despite Johnston's declaration that "we must this day conquer or perish," Johnston died amid the fighting, leaving command to General P. G. T. Beauregard. The Confederate army ultimately withdrew to Corinth to prepare for the inevitable Union advance that came later in May. At that time, the combined Union armies, with another brought in as well—all now under Halleck—pushed forward and took Corinth in late May without much of a fight despite Beauregard's earlier declaration that "if defeated here, we lose the Mississippi Valley and probably our cause." Beauregard realized that he could not hold the place, and his next goal was to save the army even if he lost Corinth. It was fortunate he did so, because much of the saved army that could have been destroyed in a losing effort to save Corinth would become the core of the force that would defend the rest of the Confederacy's hold on the Mississippi River, including Vicksburg.[10]

At the same time, a less powerful Union advance up the Mississippi River occurred as well, spearheaded by the Union navy. Flag Officer David G. Farragut led his oceangoing vessels up the Mississippi River, accompanied by troops under Major General Benjamin F. Butler. These forces easily pushed

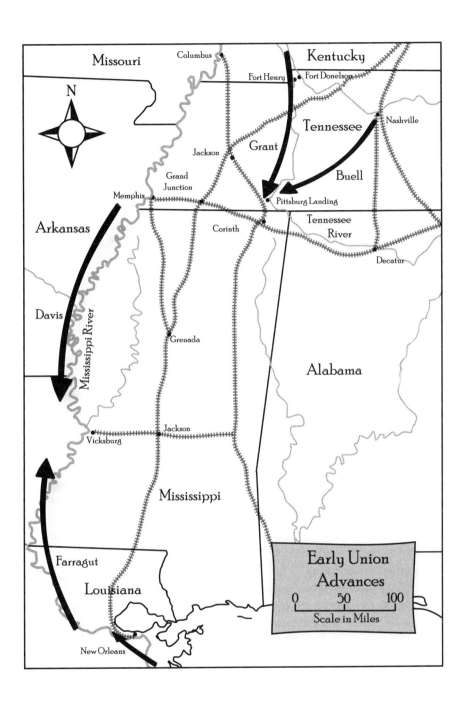

past the forts defending New Orleans, Forts Jackson and Saint Philip, and by late April New Orleans, along with the body of Albert Sidney Johnston buried therein, was in Federal hands. Confederate commanders withdrew northward to the next available line on which to stake a defense: the Southern Railroad of Mississippi. There, Brigadier General Martin L. Smith began to fortify the river city of Vicksburg to put "us in a condition to dispute with a fair prospect of success a farther advance." The Federals were not long in following.[11]

The breathtaking events of the spring nevertheless turned to a waiting game in the summer and fall. While Farragut and a small infantry command actually approached Vicksburg and the ships even passed the city, the force was far too small to be able to take possession of the city. They merely bombarded Vicksburg mercilessly while the infantry commander, Brigadier General Thomas Williams, tried to dig a canal that would divert the Mississippi River away from the city. It was not successful, and all could see that larger numbers would be needed from the Union's northern thrust to make any real difference. Lieutenant Colonel James L. Autry, one of the Confederate commanders at Vicksburg, in fact bluntly told the Federals that "Mississippians don't know, and refuse to learn, how to surrender to an enemy." He added that "if Commodore [David] Farragut or Brigadier General [Benjamin] Butler can teach them, let them come and try."[12]

The Union commander to the north, Henry Halleck, was not interested, however, despite Secretary of War Edwin M. Stanton's urging that "I suppose you contemplate the occupation of Vicksburg and clearing out the Mississippi to New Orleans." Instead of moving southward in an effort to open the Mississippi River and take Vicksburg, Halleck merely scattered his troops east and west to consolidate control of the railroads he had just acquired. The result was a loss in momentum, even after President Lincoln called Halleck to Washington in July to be his overall commander. He left the Union command structure in its current state when he left, which meant that no one had autonomy to command the department. Consequently, there was little push forward by the Union forces for months.[13]

The Confederates took the momentum and also the initiative. Beauregard soon fell out of favor even more with the Confederate president, Jefferson Davis, and did not last past June. In his stead in command of the army was General Braxton Bragg, who took much of his force and moved it to Chattanooga to protect that place; he then moved northward in an invasion of Kentucky in the fall. A Union crisis was averted at Perryville in early October when Bragg had to withdraw back into Tennessee, much like General Robert E. Lee had been forced to do in his own simultaneous invasion of the north resulting in the Battle of Antietam.[14]

A corresponding advance from the Confederates left in Mississippi under Major General Earl Van Dorn got no farther than an attempt to retake Corinth in early October; Van Dorn retreated with heavy losses, but significantly, his army remained mostly intact to defend the Mississippi Valley and Vicksburg.[15]

This lull in major activity would likely remain the case until someone in the arena acquired the authority to do something. A Confederate command change with that potential came in early October when John C. Pemberton took control of the Department of Mississippi and East Louisiana. But as passive, indecisive, and administrative as Pemberton was by nature, that change would likely not foster the major transformation needed to institute significant operations in the Mississippi Valley. "No officer ever devoted himself with greater assiduity to his duties," one Jackson newspaper wrote. "Late and early he is at his office, laboring incessantly." In fact, Pemberton would remain on the defensive for the rest of the campaign, seeking to parry threats rather than to make them; the isolated offensive events that would emerge would come primarily as defensive actions in the larger context.[16]

That was not the case on the other side. When Halleck departed for Washington, he left the west's senior commander in his original district command rather than pushing him upward to fill his vacated position. That left Ulysses S. Grant senior in the west but with no more authority than he had before. And now with his superior hundreds of miles away and hearing from many more subordinates than before, attention to Grant was thus diluted and the result was months of inactivity and a defensive stance that ate at Grant's natural aggressive temperament. Grant later wrote of the "two and a half months of continued defense over a large district of country, and where nearly every citizen was an enemy ready to give information of our every move."[17]

But when Halleck finally relented and in mid-October 1862 gave Grant the position he should have gained in July, Grant went straight to work. Taking command on October 25, he ordered a movement the very next day, starting operations against Vicksburg. "With small re-enforcements at Memphis," Grant wrote Halleck the day after he took formal command, "I think I would be able to move down the Mississippi Central road and cause the evacuation of Vicksburg and to be able to capture or destroy all the boats in the Yazoo River." But being so new in this elevated position and desiring to please his powerful boss in Washington, Grant planned a campaign that was almost straight out of the manuals of the day, certainly in line with Halleck's own treatise, *Elements of Military Art and Science*. To gain the high ground east of the city, Grant planned a well-secured advance down the Mississippi Central Railroad, complete with supporting columns and a secure supply line. From there, he could launch his attack on Confederate Vicksburg.[18]

But the plan did not work in this particular environment. One problem was distance and geography; Grant had to cross multiple rivers that stretched perpendicular across his line of advance, and the Confederates managed to burn bridges so that rail traffic, upon which Grant depended so heavily, was delayed. With winter now coming on, that was a recipe for disaster. Likewise, isolated Confederate offensive activity was also a factor, with cavalry raids deep in Grant's rear hitting both his forward supply base at Holly Springs as well as the rail line feeding that base, the Mobile and Ohio. The damage was severe enough to cause Grant to stop his advance. "Fall back with your entire command to the north side of the Tallahatchie, the troops retiring by the same route they advanced on," Grant advised one of his officers, Major General James B. McPherson. He added, "keep your transportation as well to the front as much as possible and instruct your commissaries to collect all the cattle fit for beef they can and corn-meal from the mills. Destroy all the mills within reach of you and the bridges after you are done using them."[19]

Political effects also took their toll. With rumors of Major General John A. McClernand raising troops for his own advance down the Mississippi River to take Vicksburg, Grant sent a portion of his force back to Memphis under his friend Major General William T. Sherman to lead the effort before Mc-Clernand arrived. Usurping some of McClernand's very own troops, Sherman became a second prong of the advance, although not supporting columns in the sense that each could be at the other's rescue in a matter of hours or even days. In fact, it took Sherman three weeks to get back to Memphis and down to Vicksburg to make his attack. In the meantime, the defensive Pemberton utilized well the railroads at his disposal and even the rivers to some degree and shifted troops to the newly threatened point, defeating Sherman at Chickasaw Bayou on December 29. "I reached Vicksburg at the time appointed, landed, assaulted, and failed. Re-embarked my command unopposed," Sherman reported simply. Both of Grant's advances failed miserably, and worse, McClernand showed up in the midst of it all. It was time to rethink the traditional ways of doing things.[20]

The first order of business was to take care of the McClernand issue. After the Illinoisan overplayed his hand a bit and made an attack on Arkansas Post, in the direct opposite direction from Vicksburg, Grant gained authority to relieve or replace McClernand as commander of the expedition to capture the city. "Two commanders on the same field are always one too many," Grant quipped, "and in this case I did not think the general selected had either the experience or the qualifications to fit him for so important a position." Grant took overall command himself and moved southward to Young's Point, almost directly across the river from Vicksburg. McClernand fumed but eventually took his place in the army's hierarchy commanding the senior corps, along with Sherman and McPherson.[21]

With the command situation straightened out for now, Grant began to process how to reach the vicinity of Vicksburg. A broad river stood in his way, and access was blocked by the big guns at Vicksburg. There was no way he could go up the bluffs from the west or get past them easily to operate south of the city. The northern approach was likewise covered with fortifications all the way up the Yazoo River to Snyder's Bluff, where big guns closed that artery. The only conceivable area from which to approach Vicksburg was from the east, but Grant simply could not reach that point, especially in the high water of the ensuing winter months.[22]

Grant accordingly began several odd operations that were so far against the normal way of doing things that they constituted a new way of war. Grant first tried to restart work on Williams's old canal from 1862, but the effort to change the course of the mighty Mississippi River failed. "Our canal here don't amount to much," Sherman admitted. "It is full of water, but manifests no disposition to change the channel. It is a very small affair, and we can hardly work a barge through it for the stumps." So also failed a haphazard and longer route west of the river through Lake Providence, also intended to offer a way through to bypass Vicksburg.[23]

To get to the high ground east of Vicksburg, Grant also started two novel expeditions in the Mississippi Delta. One hinged on flooding the Delta enough to allow passage through an old waterway known as Yazoo Pass, which would allow access into the intricate Delta river systems and eventually lead into the Yazoo River. Following the Pass and the Coldwater, Tallahatchie, and Yazoo Rivers southward would place troops on that high ground east of Vicksburg above the Confederate guns at Snyder's Bluff. But many a wary glance occurred as regiment after regiment dove into the Mississippi wilderness over what one Federal described as "a kind of overland steamboat, mud puddle route unheard of but in the philosophy of modern warfare." He added, "can you imagine the consternation which our advent into this unexplored part of Dehaney will create amongst the bullfrogs & Alligators whose peaceful dreams have hither to been undisturbed since this map of clay was sent on its voyage around the sun." Not surprising, the effort failed when the wily Confederates managed to place a small fort on some of the only dry ground in the region at Greenwood; Fort Pemberton brought the expedition to a halt.[24]

Similarly, Grant tried to reach the same high ground on the Yazoo River by

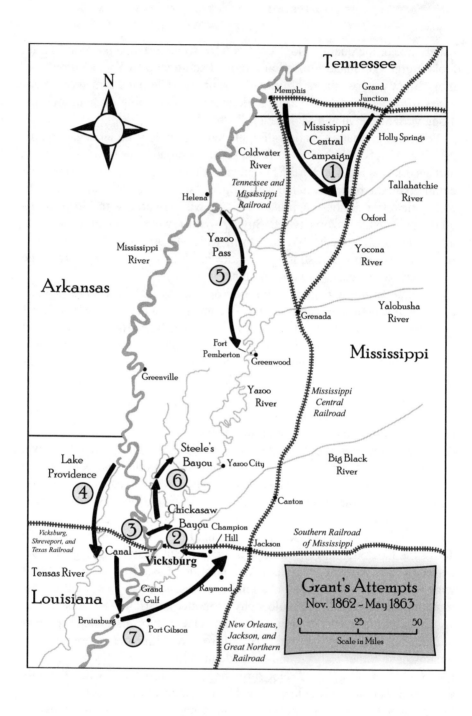

N

Tennessee

Memphis   Grand
              Junction

Mississippi
Central
Campaign
①   Holly Springs

Coldwater
River

Tallahatchie
River

Tennessee and
Mississippi
Railroad

Helena

Oxford

Yazoo
Pass
⑤

Yocona
River

Mississippi
River

Arkansas

Grenada

Yalobusha
River

Mississippi

Fort
Pemberton   Greenwood

Greenville

Yazoo
River

Mississippi
Central
Railroad

Steele's
Bayou   Yazoo City

Big Black
River

Lake
Providence
④

⑥

Canton

Chickasaw
Bayou   Champion
③   / Hill
Vicksburg,
Shreveport, and   Canal   ②
Texas Railroad   Vicksburg

Southern Railroad
of Mississippi

Jackson

Tensas River

Louisiana

Grand
Gulf   Raymond

Bruinsburg   Port Gibson
⑦

New Orleans,
Jackson, and
Great Northern
Railroad

Grant's Attempts
Nov. 1862 – May 1863

0   25   50

Scale in Miles

way of Steele's Bayou, which entered the Yazoo far downstream from Snyder's Bluff, where the Federals still controlled the river. Passage through the small Delta waterways such as Black Bayou, Deer Creek, and Rolling Fork would yield access to the Sunflower River, which entered the Yazoo above the big guns at Snyder's. Grant described it as an effort "to find a practicable passage to the Yazoo River without passing the enemy's batteries at Haynes' [Snyder's] Bluff, . . . to enable me to land most of my forces east of the Yazoo, at some point from which Haynes' Bluff and Vicksburg could be reached by high land." Rear Admiral David Dixon Porter took most of his big ironclads on the route and nearly wound up losing them when Confederates blocked the path. With help from hard-marching Union infantry under Sherman himself, the gunboats managed to back out of the treacherous waterways to safety. But so ended yet another experiment in failure.[25]

For months, Grant tried to find any way he could to get to the eastern high ground around Vicksburg, but each attempt failed. High water and bad weather were the major culprits, although John Pemberton was able to parry each threat with Confederate forces operating on interior lines of communication, which meant he was able to get troops to threatened points before the Federals could spring the traps. The administrator Pemberton showed good flexibility as the campaign plodded along on a chessboard hundreds of miles deep and wide; movements were therefore slow, allowing Pemberton time to react. But as the efforts moved in closer to Vicksburg, as with Steele's Bayou, Pemberton found it more and more difficult to react quickly and in fact barely got troops to that area to head off the Federal thrust inland. The closer the campaigning came to Vicksburg, the less lead time Pemberton had and his natural indecision therefore become a major factor.[26]

By late March, Grant had figured out as much, but how to get to the city and begin taking it was still in question. He contemplated for a moment an all-out assault up the Yazoo River but quickly decided that would be far too costly even if it was successful, which was not a given. "After the reconnaissance of yesterday," he wrote Admiral Porter, "I am satisfied that an attack upon Haynes' Bluff would be attended with immense sacrifice of life, if not with defeat." There had to be some other way, but the only other conceivable approach was long, risky, and fraught with danger. In fact, if he chose this route and failed, there probably would not be another chance.[27]

In what historian Bruce Catton has described as "one of the two or three important decisions of the Civil War," Grant made the critical choice to move southward past Vicksburg so that he could operate from that direction. The

simple plan, once south of the city and across the river, was to march northward to that ideal high ground east of Vicksburg. In fact, Grant frequently
wrote that, once on the other side of the river, the campaign would be all but
over. He wrote Julia his innermost thoughts: "Foot once upon dry land on
the other side of the river I think the balance would be of but short duration."
Later he added that "once landed on the other side of the river I expect but
little trouble." Even closer to crossing time he wrote, "possession of Grand
Gulf too I look upon as virtual possession of Vicksburg and Port Hudson and
the entire Mississippi River." Getting south of Vicksburg would be the hard
part, Grant assumed.[28]

Moving to the south would indeed be fraught with troubles, not the least
of which would include being "in violation of all the principles of the art of
war," Grant explained. But it was in essence the only option Grant had left.
In those terms, it was a relatively simple situation. Because of political and
media pressures, he could not risk returning to Memphis and trying an overland route again as Sherman and even Porter wished to do; it would be seen
as a defeat once more. With all options to the west and north likewise tried
and determined unrealistic, the southern plan was all that was left. Yet it had
its own problems, namely getting the army south of Vicksburg, supplying it
there, and then getting it across the river. For the latter, the navy would be
positively essential, and that meant getting the vessels past the Vicksburg batteries. "From the moment of taking command in person," Grant admitted, "I
became satisfied that Vicksburg could only be turned from the south side."[29]

First and foremost, the navy had to cooperate. Gone were the days earlier
in the war when the army could order the inland river vessels to do what it
wanted. Now that the ironclads and lesser gunboats had been placed under
naval control, there was no more ordering but rather asking. Fortunately for
Grant, despite Admiral Porter being most desirous of going back to Memphis, the naval commander was very much open to risking his gunboats in
a passage of the formidable Vicksburg batteries. But his agreement came
with a warning: "I am ready to co-operate with you in the matter of landing
troops on the other side, but you must recollect that when these gunboats
once go below we give up all hopes of ever getting them up again. If it is your
intention to occupy Grand Gulf in force it will be necessary to have vessels
there to protect the troops or quiet the fortifications now there." He cautioned:
"If I do send vessels below it will be the best vessels I have, and there will be
nothing left to attack Haynes' Bluff, in case it should be deemed necessary
to try it."[30]

That said, Admiral Porter made his run on the near-moonless night of
April 16. With seven ironclads and three transports, with several barges

lashed to the sides carrying coal and provisions, the navy made it past the Vicksburg batteries despite the fire increasing the farther they went. Yet only the unarmored steamer *Henry Clay* succumbed. Porter wrote that "every fort and hill-top vomited forth shot and shell, many of the latter bursting in the air and doing no damage, but adding to the grandeur of the scene." Grant now had a flotilla south of the city, but given the ease of passage he decided to send more vessels six nights later. These were entirely unarmored transports, six of them and a ram also with barges tied alongside. Manned by infantry, all but one made it safely past in this second attempt despite the "disagreeable music," although many were shot up considerably. Ironically, Grant's flagship at Shiloh, the *Tigress*, did not survive. Nevertheless, in the words of Pemberton staff officer Major Robert Memminger, "the character of the defense of Vicksburg, as expressed by General Pemberton, was changed."[31]

With transports and gunboats now south of Vicksburg in force, Grant felt confident in his ability to cross the river. He was so confident in fact that he had started the shift southward a couple of weeks earlier. "The order for marching was hailed with pleasure by all," Luther Cowan wrote home, "for the soldiers had become quite tired of lying in camp, cleaning up grounds, and of hearing the anticipated investment and capture of Vicksburg talked of so much." Another soldier noted that "the concentration of Grant's Army . . . below means something, which may speak for itself before the end of next month." Under McClernand's careful eye, Federals shifted southward from Milliken's Bend in late March to Richmond and thence on down along Roundaway Bayou to near New Carthage. High water stopped the advance along the river at that point, and a ferry system would be required to move troops farther. Some troops were ferried on down to Somerset Plantation, but Grant's soldiers were at the same time also opening an inland road around Bayou Vidal now that the level of the water was falling in mid-April. That road led all the way to the Perkins's Plantation at Somerset. But to get all the way southward to Hard Times opposite Grand Gulf, the initial target for crossing, another land route had to be opened around Lake St. Joseph. By late April a land route of some seventy miles was nevertheless open, ready for the army to march to the crossing point.[32]

Several problems still remained, however. One was that crossing at Grand Gulf required neutralizing the Confederate defenses there, including the big guns in two different forts. The navy was unable to do so on April 29, so Grant had to adapt and move farther down the river. "The enemy fought his upper battery with a desperation I have never yet witnessed," Porter admitted, "for though we engaged him at a distance of 50 yards, we never fairly succeeded in stopping his fire but for a short time. It was remarkable that we did not disable his guns, but though we knocked the parapets pretty much to pieces, the guns were apparently uninjured." The naval vessels and transports nevertheless ran the Grand Gulf batteries that night and were ready by the next morning to load the army at Disharoon's Plantation for the trip across. But being that far down meant the landing would have to come south of Bayou Pierre, which meant an inland march would be required to get across the formidable bayou. In fact, the first crossing point of Bayou Pierre was nearly fifteen miles inland near Port Gibson. While Bayou Pierre would likely create a shield for Grant as he crossed, as the Confederates would have to go out of the way as well to get south of the waterway to confront the landings, crossing south of the bayou still presented more length in a Union march that was already becoming very extended.[33]

A bigger problem was that the Confederates, if they detected the southward slide, could resist the landing either at the river itself or along the range of hills a mile or so inland. Resisting at the riverbank was probably not an option due to the overwhelming superiority of the Union naval guns, but there certainly could be a defense inland, much like the Confederates had waged at Chickasaw Bayou. President Lincoln had earlier declared this as a day of fasting and prayer, and the tired soldiers sweeping up the bluffs no doubt cherished any help they could get. Still, Grant displayed his nervousness when explaining that "I deemed it a matter of vast importance that the high ground should be reached without resistance." In large part due to numerous diversions that were taking almost all Confederate attention north and east of Vicksburg, primarily Colonel Benjamin Grierson's famed raid, there was not a Confederate to be seen as Grant's troops pushed ashore and up the winding road to the hills. One Federal noted that "we were now on the bluffs on equal footing, a long sought for position."[34]

It was an impressive feat, and Grant's hardy soldiers knew as much. One Indianan wrote home that "the transfer of the army is admirable," adding that "officers from the Potomac say they have seen nothing like it—They aver that it would have been impossible to have moved the Army of the Potomac as we have moved as we have moved a 100 miles crossed the largest river of the continent and without an ounce of baggage or rations except what the men have carried on their backs." Others merely marveled that the enemy had not contested the move inland at the range of hills, staff officer Lieutenant Colonel James H. Wilson writing in his diary, "hills steep, covered with dense growth of forest trees; road enters through a defile which could have been easily defended."[35]

Yet as much of a victory as it was, there were still problems looming, one Federal humorously labeling his letter as from "Camp of Confusion." At this

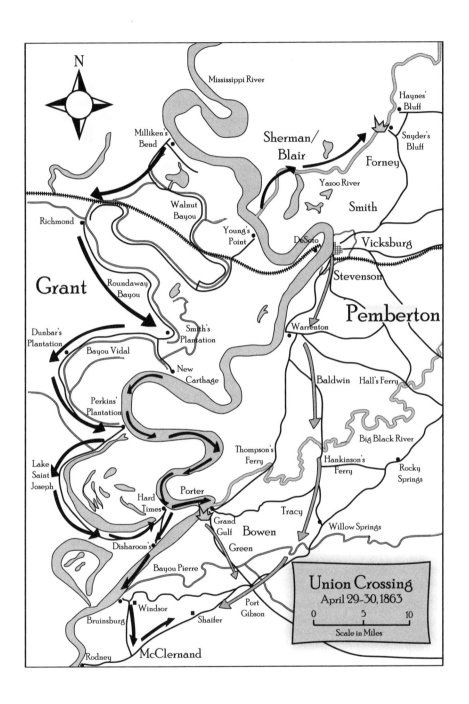

point, the biggest problem was feeding the army. Grant's supply and communication line now stretched from Bruinsburg across the Mississippi River
and back up the winding path around Lake St. Joseph, Bayou Vidal, and
Roundaway Bayou to Richmond, Louisiana, where it then went to Milliken's
Bend. And then it stretched more safely back up to Memphis and Northern
held territory. "I have been more troubled to know how to supply you with
ammunition," Grant admitted to McClernand, "until water communication is
established, than on any other subject." Medical supplies were also a major
concern. It was nowhere near the secure supply line that theorists such as
Jomini or Halleck recommended, but Grant had few options at this point.
Worse, as the Army of the Tennessee began its march inland toward Port
Gibson, that line of communication would only grow in length.[36]

Still, by sundown on April 30, Grant was across the river with some four of
McClernand's divisions, with at least one more of McPherson's waiting to be
moved across. Others were likewise moving southward toward Disharoon's
for the trip across; one Federal declared this the "start [of] the real siege." The
invasion of Mississippi had begun, and Grant now had his high ground east of
the Mississippi River. But he was not quite yet in position to begin the process
of taking Vicksburg. That citadel still loomed twenty-five miles north of Port
Gibson, the first crossing point of Bayou Pierre. The Federals would have to
move across that intermediate area before they could reach Vicksburg, and
everyone counted on the Confederates making that as difficult as possible.[37]

While Ulysses S. Grant was adapting his way into the movement below
Vicksburg, John C. Pemberton was falling for every feint and trick Grant
provided. On the defensive where he was most comfortable, Pemberton actually performed fairly well throughout the first five months of the campaign.
But the success he had in parrying each Union thrust was more attributable to
the odd environment, geography, and timing than anything else, along with
a heavy dose of superior conduct from his subordinates. It had been Forrest
and Van Dorn, acting on recommendations and orders from others instead
of Pemberton, who led the raids that ended the Mississippi Central advance.
Brigadier General Stephen D. Lee had commanded the defense at Chickasaw Bayou. Over the course of the winter months from January to March,
Pemberton's subordinates, namely Major Generals Carter L. Stevenson and
William W. Loring, had conducted the defense while Pemberton never once
went personally to the scenes of action. He instead commanded from his
headquarters in Jackson. Yet being in command of the department, Pemberton was entitled to some if not all of the credit. He pushed the right buttons

and pulled the right levers at the right times, even if others were conducting the operations on the various scenes.[38]

Still, a pattern of defense was emerging, wherein Pemberton was able to fairly easily parry the threats at long distances that required long periods for the enemy to implement. As operations drew closer and closer to Vicksburg, however, events started moving faster, and Pemberton, for example, just barely got assets into position to thwart the Steele's Bayou expedition much closer to and on the same side of the river as Vicksburg than the other operations. And as the ultimate enemy move, perhaps out of desperation, came south of Vicksburg, it came so close that Pemberton did not have time to react sufficiently.[39]

The nearness of the Mississippi River crossing, just thirty straight-line miles south of Vicksburg, was not the only factor in Pemberton's increasingly delayed response, however. Even while marching southward in Louisiana and sending vessels past Vicksburg, which should have been a telltale sign of where the campaign was going, Grant had diversions out to the north and east to take Pemberton's attention. In mid-April, Benjamin Grierson's famed cavalry raid left Tennessee and for the next two weeks traveled the length of Mississippi, finally reaching safety in Baton Rouge on May 2—"a dash" one Confederate called it. Nearly all his activity, especially during the critical last week of April, was north or east of Vicksburg. And there were diversions to this major diversion as well, including movement of troops out of Corinth in coordination with the famed Mule March through Alabama as well as troops operating out of La Grange and Memphis, Tennessee, in northwestern Mississippi. These planned feints for the main diversion effectively took Confederate attention in northern Mississippi in opposite directions, to the northeast and northwest, which allowed a seam down the middle that Grierson effectively utilized to begin his raid. At the same time, Grant had brigades and ultimately a division under Brigadier General Frederick Steele operating again around Greenville, Mississippi, and Deer Creek north of Vicksburg. Then, right as Grant prepared to cross the river in late April, he sent Sherman on a diversion north of Vicksburg as well, back up the Yazoo River to his place of defeat the previous December near Chickasaw Bayou. Sherman forced the Confederates to react whether they really thought he was fully intending to get to Vicksburg or not: "We was ordered out to meet them," one Mississippian explained, adding that it resulted in "three nights & two days of lolling about in the rifle pits." Regiments moved from south of town to reinforce the area north of Vicksburg, and one Georgian wrote home that it "is thought here they will attack us both above and below and in the center all at the same time." Consequently, there was a lot going on north and east of Vicksburg, and Pemberton's head was literally spinning as he watched Federals circling about him and his department. "The enemy press me on all sides," Pemberton dolefully admitted.[40]

In all the chaos, much of it coming closer and closer to Vicksburg, Pemberton missed the most significant movement west of the Mississippi River. "Reported, but not yet confirmed, movement under McClernand, in large force, by land west of river and southward. Much doubt it," he informed Richmond. He instead concentrated on, indeed became obsessed with, Grierson's movement, which was a direct threat to his department, particularly Vicksburg and the rail line that supplied it. Pemberton had been as nearly obsessed with gathering supplies for Vicksburg, and Grierson's Raid threatened that effort while the danger Grant posed was still at that time far across the Mississippi River. Pemberton consequently focused on catching Grierson, the vast majority of his messages between April 24 and 29 dealing with the raid. In fact, Pemberton often personally sent messages even to officers of such low rank as major or captains in an effort to coordinate the defense and chase.[41]

All the while, even as Grant passed vessels downriver past Vicksburg, Pemberton mostly misread the indications. "It was impossible to obtain any reliable information of the enemy's movements, rumor placing him in various places at the same time," Pemberton admitted. He understood the threat to the south in mid-April, especially with the navy's actions, and even sent more troops southward to Grand Gulf, but so many other threats were appearing everywhere else at the time as well. In fact, warned repeatedly by his division commander down at Grand Gulf, Brigadier General John S. Bowen, that the Federals were concentrating there, Pemberton had just as many warnings of threats around Vicksburg itself. Most notably, Major General Carter Stevenson, tasked with defending the city and up to Snyder's Bluff, argued that "there is no information in my possession which induces me to believe that the larger force is not above us. I respectfully submit my opinion that no re-enforcements be taken from Vicksburg for Grand Gulf until it is ascertained definitely that the main force of the enemy is opposed to it." And with Grierson appearing at Newton Station on the Southern Railroad almost out of nowhere, especially since Pemberton had been assured Grierson had been turned around and was headed back to Tennessee, it seemed Federals were literally everywhere. For the next week, until April 29, Pemberton's attention was fixated anywhere but south of Vicksburg.[42]

Admiral Porter's attack at Grand Gulf on April 29 shook Pemberton out of his fog, but it was too late. And he was still not sure about the other enemy sightings: "To concentrate my whole force south and east of Big Black for the support of General Bowen against a landing at Grand Gulf, or any point south of it not yet apparently even threatened, would, I think, have been unwise, to say the least of it." But Grant crossed the river at Bruinsburg the very next day. And with Bruinsburg being thirty straight-line miles south of Vicksburg, Pemberton could not react that quickly, especially with the need for the troops he did send to march a lengthier route inland to get across both the Big Black River and Bayou Pierre. Grant later noted that "in order to intercept us they had to go by Port Gibson, the nearest point where there was a bridge to cross upon. This more than doubled the distance from Grand Gulf to the high land back of Bruinsburg." As a result, Confederates were out of position to meet the landing either at the riverbank or the high hills where the river valley ended. There was not even so much as cavalry available to picket the river, as John Bowen's mounted troops, Colonel Wirt Adams's Mississippi Cavalry, had been peeled off its picket duty to go after Grierson. Grant landed un-molested as a result, and Federals in corps strength flooded into Mississippi before Pemberton could react. "Before he could determine which was the real attack, and which were mere diversions," Pemberton's engineer Major Samuel Lockett noted, "General Grant had perfected his arrangements."[43]

The damage was done, and now Pemberton could only try to contain the flood. He had a small amount of troops nearby under Bowen, who was tasked also with maintaining a defense at Grand Gulf. Pemberton likewise sent ad-ditional troops, but given the distances their arrival in time would be doubtful, and even if they arrived in time to confront the Union surge they would be terribly worn out. But even as Pemberton started more troops southward, he significantly never left Jackson to go himself to coordinate the effort. Bowen was in charge below, and he assured Pemberton, "I will fight them the other side of Port Gibson."[44]

Instead, Pemberton went to Vicksburg. It was a clear indication of his thought process, including where he believed he needed to be and what he perceived as being most important as "the great fight has now commenced on the Mississippi," as one of his soldiers explained. Vicksburg was not just the key for Lincoln; it was also almost literally the last ditch for John C. Pemberton.[45]

2

"I Am Pushing Forward"
Predawn May 1

The small town of Port Gibson, Mississippi, population 1,453 souls in 1860, was an important place in its own right even before civil war came to Mississippi. As county seat for Claiborne County, only 892 of its residents were white, 538 being slave and also boasting a large population of free blacks, twenty-three in total. Port Gibson held the rank of sixth largest city in the state (behind Natchez, Vicksburg, Columbus, Jackson, and Holly Springs in that order) with the third-highest free black population; only Jackson and Natchez overshadowed it in that regard. Seemingly isolated and not on any major trading avenues, Port Gibson was nevertheless a factor even before war.[1]

While not on a river or major railroad itself, which made all the other larger towns important transportation hubs, Port Gibson's nearness to both was what made it important. Just a mere ten miles inland from the Mississippi River, landings at Rodney and Bruinsburg gave access to the town. And while Bayou Pierre was not anything like the Mississippi River or even the Big Black or Yazoo Rivers to the north, it still offered waterborne access at times. Likewise, the town emerged near where the famed Natchez Trace crossed the lower fork of Bayou Pierre. Most notably, Grand Gulf was only seven miles away, and by the time war came in 1861 there was a small local railroad that ran between the two, even crossing Bayou Pierre just west of town. Inland though it was, Port Gibson had fine connections to the outside world. No wonder one Federal soldier who viewed the settlement described it as "large and rich."[2]

The people of Port Gibson were indeed well-off, many owning plantations out in the country. One soldier described it as "one of the wealthiest, as well as one of the most beautiful towns in the State. It stands on a level plain, the streets are broad and regularly laid out, and some of the buildings are handsome and costly." The town itself boasted several churches, hotels, and schools. The three brand-new and beautiful suspension bridges that crossed Bayou Pierre, one on the main channel west of town and the other two on the forks to the north and northeast, were examples of such finery, not only offering an ornamental and artistic flair to the crossings but also aiding in trade and commerce. So also did the shortline railroad that crossed Bayou Pierre at the suspension bridge across the main channel and ran toward Grand Gulf on the Mississippi River. And the town also boasted a famous figure in the war. The son of Peter Van Dorn had attended the United States Military Academy at West Point and had served many antebellum years in the army out West, where he was once dreadfully wounded in action against the Comanche. When war started, Earl Van Dorn became an early Confederate general who unsuccessfully commanded armies at Pea Ridge and Corinth before winning his fame on the cavalry raid on Holly Springs. He and much of Pemberton's cavalry were then shipped eastward to Middle Tennessee, where Van Dorn had a rendezvous with both destiny and a jealous husband just mere days after Grant crossed the river near his old hometown. Killed by a bullet to the back of the head, Van Dorn would eventually be brought back to Port Gibson to be laid to rest.[3]

Yet as war came to the county and its seat and many boys rushed off to wage it, the fighting literally came to the town in early May 1863. Because of the Federal landing below Bayou Pierre, and because the first available crossing points of that substantial stream were all the way eastward nearly at Port Gibson itself, possession of the town became paramount for both sides. Those brand-new suspension bridges across the bayou would be the most important, but holding the town effectively gave possession of those structures.[4]

As a result, both armies had to move through the bottleneck that was Port Gibson to reach the Federal landing area south of Bayou Pierre or, conversely for the Federals, to break out of the locale south of the bayou. Port Gibson was the neck of the hourglass through which all forces had to squeeze, and all Confederate units heading southward to confront this Federal incursion passed through or near the town even if crossing on the railroad or suspension bridges slightly to the west. Knowing the ground much less well, Federal commanders assumed the only crossings were at the town itself, and so John McClernand, leading his corps inland on the afternoon of April 30, informed his commander Grant that he was pressing ahead. Labeling his note "on the road to Port Gibson, Miss.," he added, "I am pushing forward the Thirteenth Army Corps, with the hope of seizing the bridge across Bayou Pierre, near that place."[5]

The result was mass chaos among the inhabitants as their little town became the focal point of the growing campaign. One Confederate described how "in the streets all was confusion. Men with pale faces running hither and thither, some with arms and seeking a command, women sobbing on every side, children in open eyed wonder clinging to their weeping mothers not understanding the meaning of it all, and negroes with eyes protruding like open cotton bolls were jostling each other and every body else and continuously asking about 'dem Yankees.'" He went on that "the ladies cheered us through their tears, and besought us to drive the invaders from their homes." One particular lady prayed as the troops moved through, saying she felt like they were her own sons heading into battle.[6]

And as fate would have it, battle was not long in coming.

Time was so much of the essence that the major Federal movement inland began even that afternoon on April 30; one Ohioan noted that they "started after the secesh." McClernand explained of the night march that "I thought the result justified the risk, although I was convinced that if disaster or defeat followed I would be ruined." Division after Union division, some twenty thousand men by Grant's estimate in the four divisions of the XIII Corps and one of the XVII Corps, consequently began their trek along the narrow roadways of Claiborne County ultimately eastward toward Port Gibson and those important bridges that would be necessary for the leap across both branches of Bayou Pierre. Obviously, it could be done without the bridges, but not quickly and decisively. McClernand knew that if the enemy had time to destroy them the movement would be halted temporarily, so he pushed on in a night march—something very rare for the Civil War. After speeches from Illinois governor Richard Yates and Congressman Elihu Washburne, the troops set out.[7]

Leading the way was Eugene Carr, the senior brigadier general in the XIII Corps and second in rank to McClernand in that unit. The New Yorker was an old soldier even though still relatively young, having served in the old army in the cavalry as well as in that arm in the trans-Mississippi, where he added more wounds to his prewar record. Yet there was some confusion as Carr pushed his two brigades down the road from Windsor to Bethel Church and then eastward on the Rodney Road. Some of the units forewent their rations in an effort to push ahead: "Without waiting to get any supper we pushed rapidly forward." An Indianan noted, "the general said we had done without anything to eat for a week & we could do it again if there was any chance for a fight." Leading the way was Colonel Charles L. Harris's brigade, the 21st Iowa in the lead, but about 10:00 p.m. Harris had a sudden bout of cramps in the intestines, something certainly not uncommon among such unhealthy areas, but they were bad enough that Harris had to turn over command to the next ranking officer, Colonel William M. Stone of the 22nd Iowa. Following behind was Brigadier General William P. Benton's brigade. Having mostly left all stock and wheeled vehicles behind, Carr himself rode "a great big ugly poor mule, his sword and belt hanging on the horn of his saddle."[8]

But confusion was all around. Besides the mix-up that saw a delay in issuing rations to the troops at Bruinsburg even before moving up into the hills, other logistical misunderstandings also appeared for the invading Federals. Not the least of them was the open understanding that those very rations, three days' worth issued to Carr's division, "were to last for five," as Carr explained it. "The boys began to throw away their extra clothing and put crackers in their knapsacks," Isaac Jackson of the 83rd Ohio explained. Which road to take was another issue: the Bruinsburg Road up the banks of Bayou Pierre, or the more inland path to the south, the Rodney Road. Obviously, the more inland road became the preferred route to stay clear of any flooded creeks from the recent torrential downpours in late April, although engineers were out to create the least resistance in crossing the many creeks that still meandered across the inland road. Despite the issues, the division pulled away from Windsor around four o'clock that afternoon and despite the change in command made steady progress throughout the night eastward toward Port Gibson. But it was hard going, as the road was narrow and the night dark. Carr himself described the journey as "a tiresome night's march," and many soldiers commented on the change from the flat soggy bottomland of Louisiana to the hills of Mississippi: "We soon found that marching up and down the Mississippi hills, even if they were not very high, was far different and more tiresome than the level ground on the West side, and we soon became very much wearied."[9]

Also at issue was the future supply problem, with the army crossing as it did with very few wheeled vehicles; those that did accompany the army were for the necessary ammunition. Grant quickly issued orders that whatever vehicles could be found along the route and nearby were to be commandeered to carry ammunition and any provisions brought along. A search revealed an assortment of wagons and carriages, Grant later writing that "a motley train it was. In it could be found fine carriages, loaded nearly to the top with boxes of cartridges that had been pitched in promiscuously, drawn by mules with plough-harness, straw collars, rope-lines, etc.; long-coupled wagons, with racks for carrying cotton bales, drawn by oxen, and everything that could be found in the way of transportation on a plantation, either for use or pleasure."[10]

Stone nevertheless led the Federals along, a scent of haste running through the higher command even while the common soldier probably wondered why there was such a rush; certainly, marching all night was not normal, so there must be something important up ahead. Stone understood, admitting that "my instructions were to reach Port Gibson at as early an hour as possible, and occupy the several bridges across Bayou Pierre at that place." But he also described the path and surrounding country: "The road over which we marched passed through a country much broken by gorges and ravines, and thickly covered with tall timber, underbrush, and cane, so peculiar to the Southern country." An Illinoisan agreed, writing that "the whole night's march was like a dream. . . . Mile after mile of sunken road—up hill & down—now rustling across an angle of leafy woods, now toiling across the ridges of a heavily plowed field the long column winds on."[11]

No one expected any major Confederate resistance, especially out here not only beyond the Big Black River from Vicksburg but even across Bayou Pierre from Grand Gulf. Still, taking no chances, Stone had some of his Iowans out front as guards and skirmishers just in case. The 21st Iowa still led the brigade despite the command change, and four companies ranged out front as an "advance guard" to make sure the head of the column was secure. Taking no chances, Stone also had a howitzer from Captain Henry H. Griffiths's 1st Iowa Artillery with them. Two of the Iowa companies (A and B) under Lieutenant Colonel Cornelius W. Dunlap served as actual skirmishers in the lead while the other two (D and F) under the regiment's major, Salue G. Van Anda, remained just behind on the road with the howitzer while the rest of the brigade marched in column behind. Colonel Samuel Merrill of the 21st Iowa was proud to relate that "we had the honor of being the leading column of this great army." But it was tense, an Iowan right behind the lead regiment admitting that "winding around the hills in a narrow roadway in the woods, expecting an ambush every minute, was too serious to justify a spirit of levity. . . . Even the regimental evangelist who had written a poem, two idylls, and refrain within the last two or three days was hushed into silence."[12]

But Stone's Iowans were only the tip of the spear, because Benton's brigade followed, and behind that were three more divisions of McClernand's XIII Corps pressing swiftly eastward toward Port Gibson. Each had crossed the river in turn, drawn rations, and made the steep climb up to the high ground around Windsor before departing on their own march in the lead brigade's wake, all up the same narrow road past Bethel Church. Immediately behind Carr was Brigadier General Peter Osterhaus's division of two brigades under Brigadier General Theophilus T. Garrard and Colonel Lionel A. Sheldon.

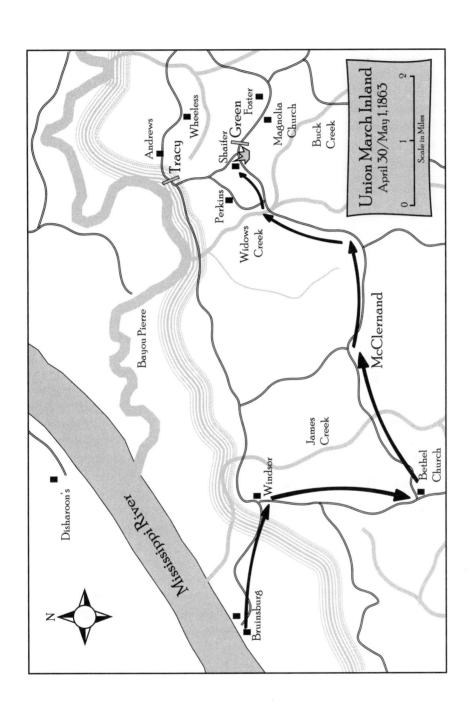

Union March Inland
April 30/May 1, 1863

Scale in Miles
0   1   2

N

Mississippi River

Disharoon's

Bruinsburg

Windsor

Bayou Pierre

James Creek

Bethel Church

McClernand

Widows Creek

Perkins

Tracy

Andrews

Wheeless

Shaifer

Green

Foster

Magnolia Church

Buck Creek

These were the troops that had led the way southward on the western side of the Mississippi River, fighting and wading their way around the bayous and flooded terrain to reach the eventual crossing point. Behind Osterhaus came Brigadier General Alvin P. Hovey's division also of two brigades under Brigadier General George F. McGinnis and Colonel James R. Slack, these troops hailing originally from the Helena garrison but now joined with the XIII Corps. Hovey simply explained that "we continued our march through the night."[13]

Finally, in the rear of the corps came Brigadier General Andrew J. Smith's two brigades under Brigadier General Stephen G. Burbridge and Colonel William J. Landram. The division crossed the river last, and after gaining six day's rations that were to be used at two-thirds rate so they would last nine days, the troops set out behind the others about eleven o'clock that night, Burbridge leading the way. Landram led his brigade forward in Burbridge's rear an hour later, taking up the march after midnight. Colonel Theodore E. Buehler of the 67th Indiana related that his men "marched steadily all night," an artilleryman in the Chicago Mercantile Battery elaborating that they traveled "over bluffs and hills, through valleys and dales, over ditches, bridges and everything else that came in our way." An Ohioan related that the troops "marched toward Port Gibson without halting."[14]

But McClernand's troops were not all that were moving inland. As the weary soldiers of McClernand's XIII Corps trudged on through the night, McPherson's XVII Corps was beginning its river crossing, Brigadier General John A. Logan's division leading, followed by others. "Seven gunboats and four transports crossing troops as fast as possible," one Wisconsin artilleryman wrote in his diary. An unfortunate collision of boats deep in the night resulted in the complete loss of a battery and perhaps more important a transport, but the crossing continued. And Sherman's XV Corps was likewise moving toward an eventual crossing, although some parts were still as far back as Milliken's Bend and even on the feint up the Yazoo River. But they would soon be heading south to cross as well.[15]

It was by all accounts a "long and tedious night's march," as Colonel Samuel Merrill of the 21st Iowa described it, of course it being the most tedious to his regiment because it was the leading Union unit marching into Mississippi. Others also described the "tedious, tiresome, and exhausting [march], because of the heavy burdens and the frequent halts on the road." Silence was mandatory, and one Iowan explained that "the frogs and beetles were the only disturbers of the night vigils." Making the tension worse, eventually there was Confederate resistance up ahead. Around midnight, even as the tail end of McClernand's corps in the form of Landram's brigade of Smith's division was just pulling out of the Bruinsburg area, shots erupted in the still night some twelve road miles to the east near Magnolia Church. The troops in the rear could easily hear the ruckus up ahead deep in the night as it was, and all knew the chances of reaching the Bayou Pierre bridges without resistance were now slim.[16]

The reason there was confrontation deep in the night was because Confederate Grand Gulf commander Brigadier General John Bowen had managed to shift troops at the last minute south of Bayou Pierre. "The move by Bruinsburg undoubtedly took the enemy much by surprise," a gloating Grant informed Washington a couple days later. In fact, he sent word back home to Galena with Congressman Washburne to "tell my friends in Galena that I considered the biggest half of my work in taking Vicksburg done when I landed my army safely at Bruinsburg and got a foothold on the Mississippi shore." But the Confederates did not cooperate by rolling over. As Grant and Admiral Porter attacked Grand Gulf on April 29 and found it too strong to take, Bowen had to surmise the enemy's next moves. A clear indication came when Porter's flotilla as well as the transports moved south of Grand Gulf that night, strongly foreshadowing that the campaign was moving to the south, below Bayou Pierre. Where the enemy would land was still in question—perhaps Rodney, perhaps farther north—but it was clear by the night of April 29 that the area of confrontation was moving south.[17]

That brought innumerable problems for Bowen. One issue was that he had a grand total of almost no troops in that area. He had concentrated his division, two brigades under Brigadier General Martin E. Green and Colonel Francis M. Cockrell, at the big guns at Grand Gulf, where all managed to repel the attack. But concentration north of Bayou Pierre meant no troops to spare down below that major watershed. And worse, what troops there were down there had been recently moved eastward in an effort to catch Benjamin Grierson's cavalry meandering across the state. Pemberton had pulled Colonel Wirt Adams's Mississippi Cavalry, the very unit guarding the landings south of Bayou Pierre, eastward to gobble up Grierson. Although some of Adams's troopers managed to catch the Illinois cavalry and fight them a short time, most notably at Union Church on April 28, they never really were able to stop them and by this point on the night of April 30 Grierson was making his way southward toward Baton Rouge. But Adams was still in chase, meaning the landings south of Bayou Pierre were totally uncovered.[18]

Another problem was that, given the unique geography of the area, getting troops down to face the new threat would take time. Bayou Pierre was a wide and substantial watercourse for the first few miles before it reached the Mississippi River, it narrowing only farther up in the hills nearer to Port Gibson. But it was still substantial even there, despite breaking into two forks, requiring bridging (the new suspension bridges) to get across easily. As a result, any shift of troops southward below Bayou Pierre required them to move eastward nearly all the way to Port Gibson to get across. In effect, any Confederate forces marching from Grand Gulf to meet the Federals wherever they landed on the Mississippi River would require a lengthy dogleg around by Port Gibson rather than moving in a straight line, obviously the shortest distance between two points.[19]

Bowen realized as much, and although acknowledging the need to keep troops at Grand Gulf to continue its defense, he also had to send a force southward as well to meet this newly developing threat. With only a select few troops of his own division to face the danger, Bowen sent the only other general officer he had, Brigadier General Green, with about a thousand troops south to Port Gibson and thence out toward the Mississippi River landings. With Green, who had only about five hundred of his own troops, was the 6th Mississippi and a section of Hudson's Mississippi Battery also known as the Pettus Flying Artillery. Green actually left more of his brigade behind to cover Bayou Pierre in case of a naval expedition up it, as well as at points on the Big Black River. For that matter, Cockrell's regiments were also somewhat scattered to cover more areas, most notably along Bayou Pierre (1st Missouri) as well as the Mississippi River front south of Grand Gulf down to Bayou Pierre (2nd Missouri). Nevertheless, the majority of the brigade continued to man Grand Gulf itself.[20]

As a result, Green was soon isolated south of Bayou Pierre. But by this point, clear indication that the landing was occurring at Bruinsburg had come in, so that at least pinpointed where the threat was. But then cropped up yet another problem: two roads led from the Bruinsburg area toward Port Gibson—the Bruinsburg Road closer to Bayou Pierre and the Rodney Road farther south. Which the enemy would take, or both, was not known, but Bowen had to cover each one. Green accordingly moved southwestward on the road leading out of Port Gibson to where the Bruinsburg and Rodney Roads joined. There, not having sufficient force to cover both, he waited for more troops and information, sending pickets out on each road. At the same time, he pushed forward himself to reconnoiter on the Rodney Road and find a suitable place to make a defense if the enemy came from that direction: "I went forward to reconnoiter the country and choose location for the battle."[21]

Wary of a new attempt to silence Grand Gulf's batteries, Bowen also appreciated the crisis growing south of Bayou Pierre and accordingly went himself to locate the best place of defense even as Grant's troops were flooding ashore at Bruinsburg on the afternoon of April 30. "I went out in person and established Green in his position," Bowen related, then returning to Grand Gulf to coordinate the defense. Fortunately, the position Bowen chose was the exact one Green had determined to hold in his own reconnaissance earlier that day, out near a small community church named Magnolia, which one soldier explained "gets its name on account of so many Magnolia trees." Green related that "I went forward several miles examining different locations, and was best pleased with the one near [Magnolia] Church." Bowen concurred. Green's major defense would be on the Rodney Road, up which it seemed hordes of Federals were moving. Indeed, heading Bowen's way on that very road was his old friend from St. Louis, Grant, along with other friends and acquaintances from the old army such as Eugene Carr, Peter Osterhaus, and James McPherson. But it would be no friendly reunion.[22]

Green could concentrate his defense on the Rodney Road because more troops soon arrived to cover the other one. Fortunately, although far too late, Bowen's commander Pemberton was also realizing the situation. In response more to the attack at Grand Gulf than the farther Union movement southward, Pemberton began funneling troops southward to Bowen's support, although in addition to being far too late being also far too little. Still, Pemberton had started southward an Alabama brigade of Major General Carter Stevenson's division under Brigadier General Edward D. Tracy, and the brigade marched through the night of April 29 across the Big Black River at Hankinson's Ferry to Port Gibson. One soldier in the 31st Alabama noted that they set out: "I recon to hunt their gun boats." Bowen related that the Alabamians arrived "jaded from a forced march and without provisions. I ordered them to halt near town, to collect stragglers, cook rations, and after a short rest to report to Green, who would point out their position."[23]

Though exhausted, Tracy's Alabamians soon arrived and were given the defense of the Bruinsburg Road. Bowen had ordered the troops to rest and cook rations, but Colonel Isham W. Garrott of the 20th Alabama related that "before the cooking was done . . . the order to march was given, and the troops proceeded down the bayou to a point 5 or 6 miles in front of Port Gibson, where we were formed in line of battle on the night of the 30th, the brigade having marched 40 miles in twenty-seven hours." The men thereafter got what rest they could, sleeping on their arms. Consequently, Confederate forces were on the move deep in the night just as the Federals were, but all knew a fight was coming. William Roberts of the 31st Alabama scribbled in his diary, "guns ordered to be in trim. Old loads removed."[24]

And there were others on the move as well. Pemberton had started yet another brigade southward, Brigadier General William E. Baldwin's of Major General Martin L. Smith's division, also from Vicksburg. Baldwin's Mississippians and Louisianans took the similar route as Tracy ahead of them, moving across the Big Black River at Hankinson's Ferry on the steamer *Charm* and, with orders from Bowen, moving toward Port Gibson. These troops likewise marched hard and were extremely fatigued, moving deep in the night as well but making it only to the suspension bridge over the north fork of Bayou Pierre at Grindstone Ford by midnight on April 30. There, Baldwin called a halt to rest, but at the least they were in the area for whatever would happen when the sun rose.[25]

Green was the man most on the spot, however, and deep in the night he placed his weary but confident troops in their positions. On the Bruinsburg Road, Tracy's Alabamians took a position near a big bend in Bayou Pierre at the Bayou Pierre Presbyterian Church. There, they covered the northern route toward Port Gibson. A little over a mile to the south, Green's troops also went into line "on the crest of a hill running diagonally across the road." He sent forward skirmishers and pickets about a mile, toward the Abram K. Shaifer farmhouse that sat on the north side of the lane. In these positions, Confederate officers ordered their tired soldiers to sleep as much as they could: "Sleep on their arms and be ready for action at a moment's warning." But Green knew there would not be a lot of sleep had, because the Federals were nearing by the minute. Still, he assumed no major confrontation would erupt until daylight.[26]

But there was already a blunder made that would prove enormous in the battle to come. Despite Green's and Bowen's agreement on where to place the lines, neither Green's nor Tracy's brigades fully defended the large creek system of Widows and Buck Creeks, which both roads crossed. That was not so much an issue, as there were plenty of ridgetops to defend in this cut-up countryside. But what was hugely important was that neither brigade fully defended the one crossover road between the two main roads east of Widows Creek; it ran from the Shaifer House on the Rodney Road to the William Andrews place on the Bruinsburg Road. Failure to secure that road well within Confederate lines meant the Federals would have access to it, which meant they could swiftly and easily move troops back and forth with interior lines and support the different forces on the two roads. And once the Federals occupied even one end of the crossover road, that meant the two Confederate forces on the two roads would be operating on exterior lines without a quick means of supporting one another. In fact, troops would have to go nearly all the way back to Port Gibson to enter the opposite road and then march back out to the battlefield. It was a disaster already in the making.[27]

Gunshots suddenly shattered the stillness of the night as April 30 bled into May 1: "Pretty blue-eyed May!," one Iowan reflected. Martin Green had just ridden into the Shaifer yard where the women were hastily packing household items. He assured them there was no hurry as the enemy would be daylight in arriving. Then shots erupted, causing the women to move even faster. But Mrs. Shaifer was no stranger to military matters; she was the older sister of Colonel (later general and governor) Benjamin G. Humphreys, who commanded the 21st Mississippi in Virginia.[28]

Colonel Stone had continued to lead his brigade forward, the companies of the 21st Iowa still out front as skirmishers, until they began to ascend the tall ridge out of Widows Creek near the Caleb Perkins house. Farther ahead on the left of the road sat the small farmhouse of the Shaifer family, with Magnolia Church farther to the east on the right side of the road. More important, also up ahead was the Confederate battle line of Martin Green's brigade, studded with the Mississippi artillery. One Arkansan described how they could hear the enemy approaching: "It was so still we could hear every command given." It was a recipe for battle, the only oddity being that it was deep in the night, only a little after midnight in fact. "In the vast dead and middle of the night," an Iowan explained, "a shot was heard—then another, and then a volley of musketry." It was then that McClernand explained the Iowans were "accosted" by the waiting Confederates. One sleepy soldier in Carr's division admitted that "I was not well and could not keep awake on the night of [the] 30th until music commenced; then I lost all desire for sleep."[29]

The leading Iowans stumbled on the advanced pickets of Green's brigade a little after midnight, both Bowen and Carr, neither of whom were actually there at the moments of the first shots, stating it was actually at 1:00 a.m.; Green himself reported it was around 12:30 a.m. Captain William D. Crooke and Company B of the 21st Iowa were the first to take fire, but the Iowans managed to return it despite the shock deep in the night. Nevertheless, leading brigade commander Stone immediately reacted to those opening shots, which he placed "about three-quarters of a mile from Magnolia Church" and "in an angle of the road." Stone placed the four Iowa companies on each side of the road while at the same time ordering Colonel Merrill of the 21st Iowa to bring up the rest of his regiment. Stone then pushed forward in the darkness, meeting slight but determined resistance from the enemy pickets positioned between the Shaifer House and Magnolia Church. "I became satisfied that we had not yet reached the immediate vicinity of the enemy's main force," Stone declared.[30]

But Stone soon did: "As our skirmishers reached the head of the lane in front of Magnolia Church they received a tremendous volley of musketry from the enemy, strongly posted on the right and left of the church." Stone was convinced this time, and he sent word back quickly for the entire brigade to move forward into line. "It was like shoving your nose into a hornet's nest," a following Iowan of Stone's brigade reflected. William Benton's pursuing brigade likewise moved forward and deployed, Charles Wilcox of the 33rd Illinois writing that "we came upon the enemy in force who *saluted* us with several rounds of grape and cannister." In the meantime, the one howitzer at the front also took position in the line, but by this time the Confederates opened with several guns, convincing Stone "at once that we had reached the place where the battle of the night was to be fought."[31]

Green's trans-Mississippians gave as good as they got, with the artillery doing most of the fighting. There was only one battery, Hudson's Mississippi Battery, although Colonel Merrill of the leading 21st Iowa adamantly declared there were as many as seven Confederate batteries firing on his men — certainly an embellishment of the horrific monster confronting him in the dark. Still, one of his Iowans described the artillery fire as "like thunder and earthquake." Green related that the artillery, "though in a very warm place, succeeded in driving the enemy's battery from its position. This, however, was soon replaced by another, which opened upon us with great fury. . . . The enemy's shells and balls fell thick around them, wounding many; yet they stood by their guns and kept up a regular fire." There was also fire from the infantry, and Green explained that "at times the musketry was very warm, extending the whole length of our line."[32]

With more obviously on his hands than he bargained for, Stone sent to the rear for additional artillery. The lone howitzer of the 1st Iowa Battery under Sergeant William R. Leibert was already in action "with great spirit and apparent accuracy," Stone noted, but he wanted the full battery up, and being nearby it was soon on site and in action. A now-arrived Carr also wanted the accompanying 1st Indiana Battery as well, it being in line back with William Benton's following brigade. Benton wrote that the order was no more than issued when the Indianans approached "at a full run, arriving on the ground in a few minutes." Soon, both batteries were in place on the ridge in rear of the Union line and began to open up on the Confederates ahead, one Federal writing of the sparks, sounds, and rumble all being noticeably different in the dead of night than during more normal battle hours. Stone himself explained that "the extreme darkness, the screaming and bursting of shells and the rattle of grape through fences and timber, conspired to render the scene presented by this midnight battle one of the most terrific grandeur." The Confederate response, though outnumbered, was just as astounding, and Stone admitted "the artillery duel was one long to be remembered by those who witnessed it.

The fire of the rebel batteries, on account of their knowledge of the ground, was quite accurate, and many of our men and horses were disabled by them." One of his Iowans declared simply, "the difficulties to be encountered in a strange country can better be imagined than described."[33]

Yet just as quickly as the fighting erupted, it ended when the moon set without either side gaining an advantage. The artillery fought for an hour or two, but then both sides reduced their fire as ammunition was at a premium for both here in the deep wilds of Mississippi where there would be little chance of resupply any time soon. This night fighting, while accomplishing the immediate goals for each side—stopping the Federal advance for the Confederates and locating and keeping in place the Confederate defensive line for the Federals—nevertheless accomplished little else. While each side declared they drove the opposing artillery away by about 3:00 a.m., neither side admitted to falling back. Rather, both sides realized it would be much better to stop the fighting and await daylight when a real battle could take place once everyone could see what was happening. Stone admitted he found "myself in the face of the enemy, in a position carefully selected, with a perfect knowledge of the ground." Division commander Carr was sympathetic and allowed the delay for rest as much as anything. He noted that, when the troops disengaged and lay down, it was "our first rest since 3 o'clock the preceding morning."[34]

Accordingly, the noise withered as both sides stood down. Stone related that "the enemy's batteries were driven from the field and silenced," but he significantly declined to advance against the allegedly withdrawing enemy. Rather, the Federals lay down on their arms to await a renewed assault or dawn. "We laid down upon our arms, but not to sleep," Major Joseph B. Atherton of the 22nd Iowa related, "as we were in momentary expectation of a renewal of the combat." Others were convinced as well. McClernand wrote that Carr's division "rested upon its arms at Shaiffer's plantation during the short remnant of the night," but all knew what lay ahead. "Our men lay down upon their arms to await the coming dawn," Stone added, "when they were to meet the rebel infantry face to face in bloody combat."[35]

Sounds of the night fighting ranged all up and down the Mississippi Valley, prompting those in higher command to concentrate on these events. Federals in the column winding their way toward the front heard the ruckus; division commander Hovey, behind Osterhaus, related that the cannonading was easily heard and "the column pressed forward." Lieutenant Joseph G. Strong in the 28th Iowa in Hovey's division explained that "we could hear the boom of artillery in our advance. We quickened our pace." Similarly, Colonel Friend S. Rutherford of the 97th Illinois back in A. J. Smith's division wrote that his column then began to move forward "with a double-quick." Back at the river with McPherson's crossing corps, division commander Colonel John B. Sanborn explained that "the rapid reports of artillery from the east side of the river announced that the advance of the army had come upon the enemy, and the soldiers were eager for the fray." McPherson himself had just congratulated Logan's division and promised them a good night's rest, but the sound of the guns caused him to change the plan and order them forward immediately. Once on the road, an artilleryman in Logan's division quipped that the firing to the east "convinced us that somebody was getting furloughs. We rushed ahead."[36]

All these troops began to stack up as daylight approached, one deployed Federal of Carr's division writing that "we laid down upon our arms, awaiting the tardy coming of daylight." Hovey rode through his arriving and deploying troops, shouting "boys, prepare your breakfasts soon, for we go into battle in half an hour." His arriving Union brigades soon went into line behind Carr's nervous troops, ready to advance as soon as the sun appeared to the east.[37]

Yet by this time there was another concern, as a road left the main Rodney Road at the Shaifer House and meandered to the north all the way to the Bruinsburg Road, upon which the Confederates of Tracy's brigade were deployed. The Federals down on the Rodney Road quickly surmised that there were more of the enemy to their north, who had deployed and moved forward as a result of the artillery fight to the south. Carr quickly placed troops on that connecting road as well while awaiting the arrival of yet another division, Peter Osterhaus's, which would be sent to tangle with whatever was in that direction. Until then, a small force of only four companies of the 33rd Illinois under Major Leander H. Potter would suffice. And sure enough, soon after being placed in position by McClernand staff officer Lieutenant Colonel Henry C. Warmoth, the Illinoisans began to skirmish with the Confederates the farther they went northward, one Federal writing that "the enemy opened fire upon him with his cannon." Still, Potter of the 33rd Illinois managed his skirmishers well until Osterhaus's veterans could arrive.[38]

Such confusion begged the attention of the high command of both armies. Division commander Carr was the ranking officer for the Federals until closer to dawn, when McClernand himself arrived and made his headquarters at the Shaifer House. Originally intending to sleep overnight back in the palatial confines of Windsor, the Daniell mansion, McClernand had left at 2:00 a.m. when sounds of firing could be heard from the east and moved all night, arriving about daylight. Brigade commander William Benton explained that

"Major General McClernand came dashing to the front, asking a thousand questions as to the position and strength of the enemy, the roads, and the general topography of the ground, and, with matchless energy, proceeded to verify every statement by a personal investigation." Grant was also pushing forward but was farther to the rear, and two of the corps commanders were still back at or west of the Mississippi River as well. It seemed this would be McClernand's fight, especially early on.[39]

The same was true for the Confederates—even more so. Pemberton himself would not shift to the crisis point like Grant but would instead make his way into Vicksburg itself this very day. With no corps system in the Confederate army and only division commanders, that left Bowen, Pemberton's youngest and newest division commander, in charge of the most concerning of all the crisis points on this day. Sure, Sherman was feinting at Chickasaw Bayou and Grierson was riding southward, and there was even concern as far up as Yazoo Pass, but this was the hammer blow that would break the Vicksburg defenses and a "bewildered" Pemberton simply left it to arguably his most inexperienced division commander. But Bowen was not on site either, he having returned to Grand Gulf the night before. That left Martin Green, a brigade commander, in charge of potentially the only chance Pemberton had of stopping the flood of Federals invading his department. And Green and Bowen had erred in placing their lines east of the connecting road at the Shaifer House, allowing the Federals access to it and interior lines while Bowen would have no such luxury.[40]

Obviously, the difference in weight in terms of general officers congregating around Magnolia Church was one thing, but it was indicative of a larger problem for Pemberton: higher-level officers normally commanded more and more troops. That certainly was the case as McClernand's entire XIII Corps of four divisions (eight brigades of nearly fifteen thousand men) were all ashore east of the river and moving toward Port Gibson, with McPherson's XVII Corps likewise starting to cross. Grant would in total put across the river as much as twenty-three thousand troops these first couple of days. But all the Confederates managed to get on site by dawn on May 1 were two small brigades and an attached regiment, the 6th Mississippi. A couple of other brigades were en route (Baldwin's and eventually part of Cockrell's from Grand Gulf), but even then four small brigades would likely be no match for an entire Federal corps plus some. It was developing into an unequal contest, but the mere fact that Grant managed the movements so that it turned out that way was significant. Perhaps even more of a cause was how John Pemberton so mismanaged the situation to cause it to develop this way.[41]

Nevertheless, the last of the piercing darkness began to fade away as dawn slowly neared and all knew there was a fight coming. It was May Day, May 1. Ironically, nearly nine hundred miles to the northeast, another army had just crossed another river and was also heading toward combat as another out-numbered defender likewise sought to blunt that advance. But Confederate commanders in Virginia had reacted better than Pemberton had in Missis-sippi, and the climactic battle at Chancellorsville would be very different than what was developing here in the similar wilderness of Mississippi.[42]

3

"A GOOD DAY FOR A FIGHT"

May 1 Morning

"The country in this part of Mississippi stands on edge, as it were," Ulysses S. Grant wrote years later when completing his memoirs, "the roads running along the ridges except when they occasionally pass from one ridge to another. Where there are no clearings the sides of the hills are covered with a very heavy growth of timber and with undergrowth, and the ravines are filled with vines and canebrakes, almost impenetrable. This makes it easy for an inferior force to delay, if not defeat, a far superior one." The battlefield was certainly not the choicest place to fight and was, logically, part of the reason the Federal commanders delayed their advance until daylight; it would be confusing enough even when light allowed a commander to see. "The country is the most broken and difficult to operate in I ever saw," Grant concluded.[1]

The battlefield of Port Gibson (also termed Magnolia Church, Magnolia Hill, or Thompson's Hill) was indeed confusing, more so than most others. The isolation of it, then and now, lent itself to wilderness-like terrain, certainly akin to the heavily wooded battlefields at Shiloh, Chickamauga, or the famed Wilderness in Virginia that would see heavy fighting in 1864 and ironically was scene to a major battle this same day of 1863 at Chancellorsville. While having nowhere near the numbers involved as those more famous battles, Port Gibson nevertheless had the added attribute of the rugged terrain that none of the others contained to any great degree, Snodgrass Hill at Chickamauga or Dill Branch Ravine at Shiloh notwithstanding. Grant's claim that the land stood on edge was a very apt description. One Federal simply termed it "an awful place to fight."[2]

The reason for such undulating geography was because of two creek systems that ate through the famed loess hills in the area. Obviously, the dominant water feature was Bayou Pierre to the north, but two systems that ran roughly northward into Bayou Pierre some three and a half miles apart cut up the land in terrific fashion. The dominant creek system delineating the western edge of the battlefield was Widows Creek, with its major tributary Buck Creek. Widows Creek began about five miles south of Bayou Pierre with numerous wet-weather tributaries that fed the main channel, causing many ravines in the table land above. Flowing due northward in a fairly straight line, the creek crossed the Rodney Road less than a mile west of the Shaifer House, which stood on the tall ridge looming over the eastern side of the creek valley. It also crossed the Bruinsburg Road farther along its path downstream (northward), much closer to Bayou Pierre.[3]

More important to the battlefield, Widows Creek's tributary Buck Creek flowed into Widows right at the Rodney Road crossing, having flowed around two and a half miles from southeast to northwest. The feeder branches of Buck Creek likewise ate away at the ridge to the north and east, tearing it up terribly in huge ravines and valleys. The tall ridge north and east of Buck and Widows Creeks was the ridge on which the Shaifer House as well as Magnolia Church sat, and it was where the Confederates first held their position. In his earlier reconnaissance to pick the best spot for defense available, Green had chosen well in terms of terrain if not the road network, and Bowen had agreed when he saw it himself. Tracy's position on the Bruinsburg Road was likewise on the ridge that led down to the valley of Widows Creek.[4]

Directly east across the ridge on which the Shaifer House and Magnolia Church sat was the other creek system, the northern and northeastern sides of this ridge falling off into the Centers Creek watershed. That creek flowed into Bayou Pierre farther upstream, closer to Port Gibson itself, and meandered from its headwaters about three miles to the south roughly due north. But there were even more branches to this system, including named tributaries such as the Irwin and White Branches as well as the main channel that veered more southwest. The feeder branches, no less than seven major ones not including multiple smaller ones, likewise cut up the terrain even more, creating ridges and ravines much like a more than five-fingered hand. The Bruinsburg Road crossed the main channel of Centers Creek just two miles out of Port Gibson, but the main channel stayed north of the Rodney Road, which crossed the southernmost tributaries, namely White and Irwin Branches.[5]

Given the heavy nature of the ravines and valleys and the corresponding lack of farmable land, the tops of the ridges only being cleared, there were understandably only a few residents in the area. Abram K. Shaifer of course lived on the ridge were the Rodney Road climbed out of Widows Creek, and other families lived along the main road, including the Fosters, Bucks,

Willises, and Parkinsons. Others lived along the Bruinsburg Road, the Andrews, Wheelesses, and Clarks. Many in the community worshiped at the small Magnolia Church nearer the Shaifer residence.[6]

This was not the sort of place any of the Union commanders would choose to fight a battle, but Green and Bowen placed their defense here for just such a reason. One Federal admitted that "the rebs had the advantage in evry posable way." Accordingly, it was a wise decision to call off the night fighting and wait for daylight so that at least some semblance of organization could be had amid all the chaotic terrain. But once that daylight came, the aggressive John A. McClernand wasted no time in moving forward. And Bowen knew full well by this point that it was McClernand in front of him, prisoners already captured indicating the presence of "three or four" divisions under the Illinois general. And others were arriving as well. Bowen was perhaps in a tighter spot than he knew.[7]

"The morning of the first of May broke upon us brightly and beautifully," Illinoisan Luther Cowan wrote home, and "reminds us more of a midsummer morning at home than the poetic 'Morn of Sweet May Day." And with the dawn John McClernand knew he had a fight on his hands, but that is exactly what he wanted. Except possibly here. He much preferred to get possession of the bridges over the various Bayou Pierre crossings before waging a fight, but when that was done the aggressive McClernand would welcome a battle wherein he could finally show these West Pointers that politicians could fight too. Yet it seemed that the Confederates were not going to allow him that luxury, and given what it was McClernand likewise welcomed a fight here. Even Eugene Carr was upbeat, riding by the 42nd Ohio and declaring that it was "a good day for a fight."[8]

Yet the terrain troubled McClernand, what he could tell in the dark illustrating the cut-up nature of the ravines and ridges. But what especially bothered him was that he had never seen the full extent of the terrain in daylight. All he could rely on at this point was hearsay, such as when he explained that "coming up about day-dawn in the morning, I learned from a fugitive negro that the two roads diverging at Shaiffer's led to Port Gibson, one to the right by Magnolia Church, and the other to the left, passing near Bayou Pierre." The slave furthermore told him that the roads were nowhere more than two miles apart but the land was "diversified by fields, thick woods, abrupt hills, and deep ravines." As Benton described, McClernand verified all he heard "by further inquiry and by personal reconnaissance." Of course, Confederates had been confronted on both roads as well, and the corps commander soon determined, in his words, to "advance my forces upon the cord of the rude ellipse formed by the roads."[9]

But a couple of problems were not yet solved to be able to do that. One was that the next division in line had not arrived, that being Peter Osterhaus's. Carr's two brigades were already in line on the Rodney Road and could not be moved, with only mere companies on the crossroad starting at the Shaifer residence leading over to the Bruinsburg Road. Until Osterhaus arrived nothing further could be done. Osterhaus did arrive momentarily, however, right before sunup, at which time McClernand sent the first brigade under Brigadier General Theophilus T. Garrard forward on the crossover road, the other still ascending the long ridge up from Widows Creek. "After the smoke of the previous engagement and the glimmering of the rising sun had ceased to blind our view," McClernand explained, "I ordered General Osterhaus to move his division on the road to the left." He wanted to place heavy troops on that road, which he assumed would be less defended than the one he was on, and at the same time to "make a diversion in favor of my right, prepatory to its attack upon the strong force understood to be in front." McClernand hoped the ruckus Osterhaus caused would aide Carr in his attack to the south, and so he delayed Carr in his advance until Osterhaus's full effort could take effect. Osterhaus dutifully pushed past the Shaifer House with Garrard's troops and moved on up the connecting road, "passing the yards and outhouses of Shaifer's," Osterhaus explained. As his second brigade under Colonel Lionel A. Sheldon arrived at the Shaifer House, McClernand motioned it to the north as well.[10]

Garrard had not gone far northward on the crossover road when he encountered the Confederate line astride the lane itself, just in front of where it joined the Bruinsburg Road. There was a high ridge at that point, the divide between the feeder branches of Widows Creek to the west and those leading to Centers Creek to the east and Bayou Pierre itself to the north. Osterhaus described a clear field leading to the ridge on which the Andrews houses and other buildings such as the slave cabins sat; many of the slaves nearest the battle line were frantically getting themselves and possessions out of the way. But getting to the ridge was the problem, as the road traveled over a narrow causeway that Osterhaus described as "a very narrow strip of land with deep ravines on both sides forming only a backbone of from thirty to eighty feet wide, thus affording an excellent defile for defense." The divide between the tributaries of Centers Creek to the east and Widows Creek to the west hosted the road itself, and the ridge ran all the way to the bluffs overlooking a wide bend on Bayou Pierre. Tracy's Alabama brigade held the high ground at the

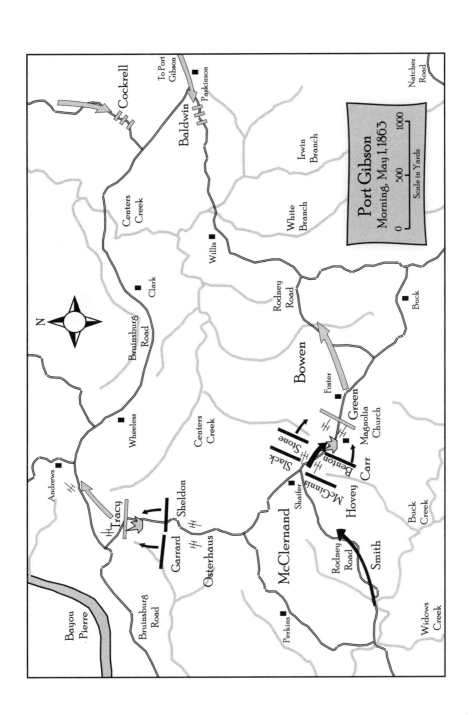

Port Gibson
Morning, May 1, 1863

Scale in Yards
0   500   1000

N

Cockrell

To Port
Gibson

Baldwin

Parkinson

Centers
Creek

Willis

Irwin
Branch

White
Branch

Rodney
Road

Buck

Clark

Bruinsburg
Road

Bowen

Foster

Green

Magnolia
Church

Natchez
Road

Wheeless

Centers
Creek

Slack

Stone

Benton

Carr

McGinnis

Hovey

Buck
Creek

Andrews

Tracy

Garrard

Sheldon

Osterhaus

McClernand

Shaifer

Rodney
Road

Smith

Bayou
Pierre

Bruinsburg
Road

Perkins

Widows
Creek

junction of the roads as well as the ravines to the south nearer the causeway; there, he prepared to resist the Federal onslaught.[11]

Tracy's Alabamians had barely taken their position when firing deep in the night alerted them to trouble. More activity came around daylight, along with frantic messages from Green down on the Rodney Road that he needed more infantry and artillery, "strenuously urging that if the left was not sustained the right would be cut off from all chance of retreat . . . and . . . that . . . he could not sustain his position on the left for fifteen minutes unless re-enforced." Tracy "reluctantly" sent Green the 23rd Alabama and two of Captain John W. Johnston's Botetourt (Virginia) Artillery guns about daylight; Johnston was actually the nephew of General Joseph E. Johnston.[12]

The deletion left Tracy only three regiments to put in line. The remaining Virginia guns took position in the center on the high hill near some "negro houses," with the 30th Alabama supporting them and becoming the center regiment. The 20th Alabama went in on the right, part of the line being at an oblique angle rearward to take advantage of the nature of the ground and the ravine that led off down into Widows Creek. But only several companies were in regular line, four being tasked with extending the 20th Alabama's line farther all the way to Bayou Pierre, some eight hundred yards to the right rear. Two companies "were posted at very long intervals" while two more went into skirmish formation to make up more ground. It was obvious that the right was insecure, but Tracy hoped these Alabama companies would hold the line there, or at the least give ample warning if trouble came from that direction. Finally, the 31st Alabama went into position on the left of the 30th Alabama and the guns, "in a gorge or ravine grown up with reeds, bushes, and some few small trees." The 31st Alabama was the flank regiment, Green's own forces being a mile or so to the southeast, until the 46th Alabama marched in around 8:00 a.m. from a grueling trek; the regiment, all 160 of them, went into position on the left of the 31st Alabama, extending the line somewhat.[13]

Garrard's Federal brigade slowly approached this Confederate line, and Osterhaus quickly positioned Captain Charles H. Lanphere's 7th Michigan Battery about a mile and a quarter from the Confederate guns to the rear but considerably closer to the enemy infantry in the ravines near the causeway. Garrard's brigade took a position near a cornfield, creeping forward all the way to a rail fence, all the while becoming engaged at longer distances. The 118th Illinois on the right and 120th Ohio on the left formed the bulk of the brigade, with the 67th Indiana and 7th Kentucky also in line supporting the artillery and the 49th Indiana out in front of the line as skirmishers; at times, the 7th Kentucky was also out front. The advance was slow and chaotic, many of the regimental commanders reporting numerous halts for thirty minutes or even an hour before word came to creep forward again. In the meantime, all also reported a heavy artillery duel between the Federal gunners of the 7th Michigan Battery, augmented by the later-arriving 1st Wisconsin Battery, and their foes of the Botetourt (Virginia) Artillery up ahead, at times the Federal infantry lying down so the gunners could fire over their heads. Captain Lanphere reported that his men worked "under a most galling fire from the enemy's artillery." Osterhaus himself brought up the big Wisconsin guns as reinforcements, he having ridden to the rear only to find them stopped and making coffee. "I can wait no longer, boys; come mit me!" he shouted. In fact, Lieutenant Charles B. Kimball reported that some of his 1st Wisconsin Battery had to relieve some of the Michiganders on the front line at times, the rest of the battery fighting in sections farther to the left.[14]

Obviously, some way had to be found to get at the enemy so well defended, Osterhaus explaining that the causeway was "the only approach to a military position on the hill." The first push against the Confederate line came in the center, where the 30th Alabama held the road and soon began pouring volleys into the slowly emerging enemy. The movement "soon developed the fact that all the ravines and gullies in front of them were full of the enemy's infantry," Osterhaus related. The Alabamians also supported the Virginia guns, which brought additional ordnance down on them. Enemy skirmishers also crept ever closer, and sharpshooters managed to take out several of the cannoneers as well as horses of the battery. "The contest here soon became warm and bloody," related one of the Alabamians. But it had hardly even begun.[15]

Still, Garrard fought on, the guns of Lanphere's Battery doing most of the heavy work. In fact, the battery occasionally advanced even under the intense fire, doing so by sections at hundred-yard increments. As one section would cover the advance forward, the other would surge ahead. When it had taken a new position, the rearward section would follow up under cover of the advanced guns. The infantry followed the advancing artillery as well.[16]

Soon, Sheldon's following brigade also arrived and went into position first behind Garrard's troops but then moved forward to the right on the east side of the road, the 42nd Ohio on the left connecting with Garrard's troops but a little forward. Osterhaus was afraid his line might be flanked from the east and sent the brigade that direction, although Sheldon soon found no enemy but terrible terrain: "A close inspection of the ground through this, occupied by Colonel Sheldon, made it apparent that there was no immediate danger, the ground being exceedingly rough," Osterhaus reported. He called the brigade back to the left, the center of Garrard's line. The 1st Wisconsin Battery attached to the brigade also moved forward to take position near the front and support the Michigan cannoneers already in action, eventually driving the Confederate guns back up to the top of the ridge with the other pieces. Back nearer the connecting road, the 42nd Ohio managed to get into such a firefight that they required aid from Garrard's right regiment, the 118th Illinois, which moved forward to the right to support the Ohioans. One of the Illinoisans subsequently termed it "very warm work." The 120th Ohio also shifted right and wound up in front of the 42nd Ohio, when Colonel Marcus Spiegel advanced and drove the Confederate skirmishers from the nearby ravine. Spiegel admitted that in the twenty or so minutes he fought across the low ground he was "[un]able to do him much harm, he being completely under cover on the opposite bank of the ravine." The other two regiments, the 118th Illinois and 42nd Ohio, probed forward as well toward the compact Confederate line but were unable to make any progress in moving it. There was some concern about friendly fire with the regiments mashing together, but little actually took place.[17]

Yet matters were disintegrating in the Confederate line as the fighting swelled outward from the 30th Alabama. In particular, the 20th Alabama to the right became heavily engaged, as did, particularly concerning, the extended companies on the right connecting with Bayou Pierre. If the Federals turned the flank the entire line would be compromised. Perhaps worse in the meantime, the two forward Virginia guns were also taking heavy fire and losing men, the pieces nearly being disabled. Fortunately at the exact right time, two other guns of the battery arrived and soon replaced the fought-out pieces, providing fresh gunners and ammunition to battle the overpowering Federal artillery of two full batteries. But these guns also soon became the chief target of the Union gunners and were similarly so damaged that they too were ordered to the rear: "It seemed impossible for them to remain longer on the field without being sacrificed," explained Colonel Isham W. Garrott of the 20th Alabama. Still, the infantry held and blunted several of the Federals' muted advances.[18]

Worse for Tracy's Alabamians, the Federals were starting to organize an all-out advance. East of the road, Colonel Spiegel's 120th Ohio followed the retreating Confederate skirmishers into the wooded ravine and there was able to pinpoint the Confederate line on the opposite side. Spiegel ordered an advance. He explained that his Ohioans "quickly drove them from the bank to the knoll, where they rallied and made a stand, which only increased the determination of my brave boys." The Ohioans rushed forward and "drove them pell-mell from behind the knoll," but that was as far as Spiegel was willing to go. "I did not deem it prudent to pursue them farther," he related, "being at least 300 yards in advance of any of our troops."[19]

More than just the Ohioans advanced in the assault, however. The 16th

Ohio and 22nd Kentucky also moved forward on the left of the 42nd Ohio, which also restarted its forward advance. The 114th Ohio was also pushed forward from its battery-guarding duty in the general movement. Unfortunately, by this time the regiments of Garrard's and Sheldon's brigades were so intermixed that it was difficult to determine who was where. Colonel Sheldon, in fact, explained that at one point the 42nd Ohio had to be withdrawn from the lip of a ravine because, unbeknownst to him, the 69th Indiana of Garrard's brigade was in front and susceptible to the Ohioans' fire across the ravine.[20]

All the while, the Alabamians overlooking the ravines and causeway slowly fell back, first the skirmishers and then even the main line. The Confederate withdrawal was not fatal, but it was nevertheless concerning, especially with what else was transpiring. Tracy's Alabamians, without their ordnance train, were starting to run low on ammunition, very much a concern. Likewise, the Virginia guns, only four left on the right wing, were soon so crippled that they incrementally had to be removed to the rear, taking away a prime force that had been pounding the Federals all morning. The slight withdrawal of the Confederate right wing came on top of these developments, not a retreat per se but a reshuffling of the line along the top of the plateau that widened as the ridge between Widows and Centers Creeks approached Bayou Pierre. In fact, the left of the Confederate line, the 31st Alabama, basically maintained its position while the right withdrew a short distance, Colonel Isham Garrott of the 20th Alabama describing the right-wing companies falling back a mere two hundred yards, but enough to reconfigure the Confederate line from one facing southward astride the crossover road to one now facing more southwestward astride the Bruinsburg Road itself. But it still occupied the same high ground as before, with a still insecure hold on Bayou Pierre itself on the right flank. Nothing, of course, secured the left flank except the wilds of the Centers Creek bottoms.[21]

That right flank was growing more concerning, however, especially as Bayou Pierre took a great turn and caused more of a gap between the Confederate right and the valley. Nothing remained but to shift forces to the right and center pressed so heavily by the continually following Federals. Fortunately, little concern existed for the left, where the 46th Alabama had taken position. Orders soon went out as a result for half the regiment, small though it was, to move northward to reinforce the 30th Alabama in the center while the other half moved all the way to the right to support those elongated companies of the 20th Alabama still holding the flank. Colonel Michael L. Woods quickly had his Alabamians in their new lines, just in time to meet more Federal advances. Colonel Garrott in fact described how the 46th Alabama took a position in a road cut and "bravely met their attack, and held them at bay." The flank was safe for now, but for how long was the question. In addition, Sergeant Francis G. Obenchain of the Virginia artillery led the two working guns here on the right back into action, taking position on a commanding knoll six hundred yards behind the new Confederate front. Captain Johnston had been "borne from the field completely exhausted," leaving Obenchain in command.[22]

The biggest concern over here on the right, however, was the loss of the commander, Edward Tracy. About 8:00 a.m., as he commanded along the front line, Tracy took a bullet to the upper chest and neck region, falling forward and only managing to mutter "O Lord!" The command fell to Colonel Garrott of the 20th Alabama, who reported that Tracy "fell near the front line, pierced through the breast, and instantly died." That left the entire right wing of the Confederate defense without a general officer in command, and Garrott knew little to nothing of the overall plan, only what he had overheard from Tracy as the morning crisis began to unfold.[23]

At a loss of what to do, Garrott sent a messenger over to the Rodney Road for instructions. In the meantime (it took several hours for the messenger to make the roundabout route back nearly to Port Gibson and return), Garrott kept fighting. "I knew nothing of the plan of battle," he lamented, but resolved that "the enemy was in our front, and I knew of no order to retire." His Alabamians had been forced back slightly, but Garrott managed to hold his new position against what can only be described as the methodical and less-than-overwhelming Federal advance of Osterhaus's division. Growing more and more nervous, Garrott sent a second messenger, his regimental adjutant John S. Smith, to request reinforcements and ammunition. Smith would not return until midafternoon.[24]

Finally, around 11:00 a.m., word arrived from Bowen himself. But it provided little more context for the suddenly promoted Garrott: "Our position was to be held at all hazards." Unknown to Garrott, however, Bowen was sending help, but he had a similarly growing crisis down on the Rodney Road to attend to in the meantime.[25]

"At 6:15 a.m., when sufficient time had elapsed to allow Osterhaus' first attack to work a diversion in favor of my right," McClernand later explained, "I ordered General Carr to attack the enemy's left." So began the major fighting on the Rodney Road around the Magnolia Church line even as Osterhaus slowly plodded along to the north. But it was a confused stuttering of advances, made more so by the gathering troops along the roadway from

Bruinsburg and the already gathering wounded in the rear. One attendant was, in fact, ordered to remove his hospital farther to the west, where it was set up actually in a more exposed position on the side of a hill, resulting in his own wounding.[26]

Yet McClernand had only two brigades in line on the Rodney Road, although Osterhaus's division was moving along the narrow connecting road to the north. Fortunately for McClernand, two more divisions were even then winding their ways eastward, Alvin Hovey's two brigades set to arrive at the Shaifer House any minute now and then A. J. Smith's still on the road to the west but slated to arrive shortly as well. And behind that was presumably the van of the XVII Corps, John Logan's division of three brigades. Consequently, while McClernand had a lot of firepower building up, it was not exactly like he had overwhelming force up front at the very moment he began his attack.[27]

In fact, only the two brigades of Carr's division sat astride the road near the Shaifer House as yet, Benton's on the right or south side of the road and Stone's on the left. But they were not even fully in line as yet, Charles Wilcox of the 33rd Illinois writing that "we have not all got our positions yet, but the battle commences in earnest." Even so, McClernand hurled Carr forward toward the Confederate line that sat in plain view now that the sun was up, just a quarter of a mile to the east atop the system of ridges that fed off to the east into Centers Creek and to the west into Buck Creek. High atop the centermost ridge right along the road sat the dominant location of the battlefield: "Upon one of these hills, in plain view, stood Magnolia Church," McClernand explained.[28]

The Confederate line consisted of Martin Green's partial brigade augmented by the 6th Mississippi. Portions of Green's original brigade had been doled out in various directions, and he had moved south of Bayou Pierre with only the 15th Arkansas, the 12th Arkansas Battalion, and a portion of the 21st Arkansas. The Mississippians and artillery battery had also arrived to augment his numbers, which he needed badly. It was of course Hudson's Mississippi Battery that mostly conducted the nighttime firefight, the infantry units also keeping skirmishers and pickets well to the front of the Magnolia Church line, even at first all the way to the Shaifer House where the first shots rang out. Slowly during the night and after daylight, however, the pickets had been continually driven eastward by the slowly advancing Federals. Green explained that "at daylight the enemy could be seen reconnoitering in force every direction."[29]

Soon the Federals did more than reconnoiter and skirmish. With orders to move forward, Benton shoved his Illinois and Indiana regiments forward off from behind the protective ridge near the Shaifer House and down into the great ravine to its south. He had been all along his line: "Gen. Benton comes along the line and orders us to fix bayonet for he's going to charge," one soldier explained. With a company from each regiment out front as skirmishers and the 33rd Illinois exploring the ravines south of the road, one of them writing that "[I] hope I may never be in such a tight place again," Benton's main line consisted of the 8th and 18th Indiana while the 99th Illinois formed as a reserve; one Indianan admitted that "we drew up in line of battle the bullets whistled over us thick & fast." The huge gaping chasm that Benton faced began at the road and grew larger as it fed into Buck Creek to the south, but his Federals plunged downward into the wilderness and then up the other side in an amazing feat of military maneuvering. McClernand himself described it as "woods, ravines, and a light canebrake," but it was much worse than that. Carr reported the ravine contained "obstacles almost insurmountable, consisting of ravines with precipitous ascents and descents, covered with tangled thickets and dense canebrakes." Making it worse was the Confederate fire; one Illinoisan described "how the shells and shot whiz around me." Attending the brigade was Captain Martin Klauss's 1st Indiana Battery repositioned on the more level ground on the left of the road; one Iowan noted he saw Mc-Clernand himself "swinging his hat, cheering them, indicating that they were doing some damage to the enemy."[30]

The path was a little better to the north side of the road where Stone's Iowans and one Wisconsin regiment moved forward as well, they mostly encountering an open field that allowed a better view as well as artillery support although the 22nd Iowa faced a thick canebrake that one member declared was "literally mown down with bullets." But Carr held them back momentarily, intending that Stone be the bait and Benton be the main force that would extend around the enemy's left and turn it. "I kept the enemy employed with my second brigade and the two batteries on the left of and in the road," Carr related, "while I sent the First Brigade . . . through ravines, canebrake, and timber to the right of the road, to press on his left flank." Stone himself verified Carr's thinking, writing that Carr directed him to "hold my infantry in readiness to charge the enemy's lines when the decisive moment should arrive." The movement produced the desired results. "An obstinate struggle ensued," McClernand reported.[31]

Confederate brigade commander Green agreed, writing that "between 6 and 7 o'clock the enemy's skirmishers again moved forward and engaged mine. This soon brought on a general engagement by both artillery and infantry." Green had only the three partial units of Arkansas troops on his left and the Mississippians on the right, but a problem was already developing beside the fact that Green was outnumbered by huge proportions, a measly four regiments and an artillery battery up against an entire division that was growing by the minute by the addition of others. Bowen in fact related that "they continually received fresh troops." Now, having been in action much of the night and now again heavily after daylight, the Mississippi cannoneers were beginning to run out of ammunition. Finally, Green realized he had to have help and sent word to Tracy up on the Bruinsburg Road to send anything he could. Pressed far less heavily by Osterhaus's methodical advance, which actually led Grant to later quip that Osterhaus "was not faring so well," Tracy sent Green the 23rd Alabama and a section of the Botetourt (Virginia) Artillery. But given the distances and route that had to be taken nearly all the way back to Port Gibson, they would be some time in arriving. Perhaps the most notable arrival, however, was John Bowen himself, who appeared on the Rodney Road line around 7:00 or 8:00 a.m. to check on Green and his defense of the Magnolia Church position. He immediately knew it was not a good situation. In fact, his horse was soon wounded in the thigh, one of four he would mount that day, and the animal's switching tail continually peppered the general with blood, making observers wonder if Bowen himself was hit.[32]

And it only grew worse as more Federals arrived. Soon, Hovey himself rode up and "reported his division to be on the ground," McClernand explained. Not knowing what lay ahead and how much force would be needed here or with Osterhaus on the Bruinsburg Road, McClernand ordered Hovey to go into column of brigades at the Shaifer House ridge and await the arrival of the last division of the corps, Smith's, at which time Hovey would be sent forward wherever he was needed. McClernand did not want to be caught without a reserve if anything went wrong on either road, and Hovey had his troops lie down in their positions to keep them under cover from the Confederate fire that was continually falling in the area. But when Smith momentarily arrived as well, around 7:00 a.m., McClernand felt confident enough to send Hovey into the action with Carr, Osterhaus reporting no trouble on his front. And if there was, Smith was now close enough to help there. "The four divisions of my corps were now upon the field," McClernand explained, "three of them actually engaged, and the fourth eager to be." Yet Smith would have to wait his turn, remaining in line in "the fields in front of Shaiffer's house." Smith effectively served as the reserve for both wings as well as covering the center between the two roads.[33]

With orders to support Carr "without the least delay," Hovey's Federals accordingly moved forward even as Benton and Stone were engaging the Confederates at Magnolia Church. In fact, Hovey went into action much like Carr had, with one brigade on each side of the road. Brigadier General George

McGinnis's Indiana brigade with one attached Wisconsin regiment plowed off into the same ravine Benton was struggling through, Hovey describing it as "a deep and rugged ravine . . . and filled with vines, cane, deep gulches, and exceedingly difficult of passage." One of his soldiers described it as "the roughest country God made." McGinnis was even more descriptive, writing that "we advanced about three-fourths of a mile over a surface of country which under any other circumstances would have been pronounced impassable. High hills, in many places almost perpendicular, deep ravines, thickly covered with cane and vines, interfered very much with our advance." And worse, Benton was loudly calling for help for his exposed right flank; in response, the 24th Indiana surged ahead to solidify that wing. It did so, McGinnis describing "a short but very sharp engagement," after which the Indianans returned to their own brigade.[34]

James Slack's mixed brigade of Indiana, Iowa, and Ohio troops, including one woman disguised as a man in the 24th Iowa, similarly moved to the north in rear of Stone's Iowans, although some of the units remained on the roadway in flank formation for easy movement. Slack's route was so comparably easy in fact that his rearward brigade arrived at its assigned position about the same time that McGinnis's brigade did in front of the division, with part of McGinnis's right still struggling through the deep recesses of the ravine. Slack, just as Stone ahead of him, had a much easier time than Benton's and McGinnis's troops south of the road. The brigade eventually fanned out to the left, where the 47th Indiana held the extreme left and blunted a Confederate advance in that direction.[35]

It was fortunate that McClernand hurried Hovey forward because his troops were sorely needed. Benton and Carr had found that the Confederate line, only a brigade even though Benton declared he fought three of them, extended beyond the right flank of the division and thus was in danger of turning the Federal line. As a result, Benton shifted his brigade to the south as he advanced, opening up quite a "considerable gap" between his left and Stone's right near the road. Benton described how after driving the enemy skirmishers back toward the church, "I ordered a change of front forward on tenth company, which was accomplished most handsomely, at a double-quick, over the most difficult ground." He added, "so promptly and splendidly was the movement executed under a galling fire of shell and musketry, that I was at a loss which most to admire, their valor or the efficiency of their drill." But the forward move put the Federal lines now only within a hundred and fifty yards or so of the Confederate position, artillery and all, and McClernand related that "the shout of the enemy [was] distinctly heard about this time." In fact, Benton's complete line now held the 18th Indiana, 99th Illinois, 33rd Illinois, and 8th Indiana, left to right, with Colonel Henry D. Washburn's 18th Indiana resting near Magnolia Church, his left almost touching it. His regiment also faced the Confederate battery to the east, but Benton explained how his troops stood firm, "giving him volley for volley with interest." An Illinoisan said it was a "continual howl of musketry."[36]

The Confederate line was indeed stronger at this point, the Alabamians and a section of the Virginia Battery having arrived by around 8:30 a.m. The newcomers filed into line east of Magnolia Church near the Foster House under a heavy fire, the Alabamians going into line on the right of the Mississippians, making them the right of the entire Rodney Road line. The Virginia artillery took a strong position on high ground, and soon even a section of the Hudson Mississippi Artillery that had run out of ammunition managed to replenish its limbers and reenter the fight. Terrain of course aided the primarily stationary Confederates, their defensive stance not being affected by the huge ravines the Federals had to negotiate to get to their line. Still, Green reported the odds were "at least eight to our one, and double our number of pieces of artillery."[37]

With word from Benton that he needed help especially on his now vulnerable left, McClernand quickly ordered Hovey to plug the gap. He did so with the left of McGinnis's brigade and the right of Slack's unit. Hovey himself had ridden forward along the road and met Slack and Colonel Robert A. Cameron of the 34th Indiana of McGinnis's brigade nearby under the cover of the brow of the hill. Lieutenant Colonel William H. Raynor commanding the 56th Ohio of Slack's brigade also wandered up to the meeting. Hovey had been advised of the Confederate battery to the front by Captain Klauss of the 1st Indiana Battery and immediately began to ponder an attack. But he had no communication with McGinnis, still struggling through the ravine to the south. "Here I attempted to communicate with General McGinnis, who was in the rear of his brigade, but the ground was impassable for my aides on horseback, and my voice could not be heard on account of the noise around him." Hovey would have to make do with Slack's troops and only the left of McGinnis's brigade.[38]

Yet it took time for all these maneuvers to take place amid such inhospitable terrain, especially south of the road. Meanwhile, large swaths of time went by as McClernand impatiently pushed ahead with his front lines not knowing what all he would encounter; indeed, the terrain had been his major enemy to this point, and it was only after a while that Green's Confederates became an issue with the threat to his right flank. Stone in fact explained that he merely moved forward gradually across a ravine and opened fire on the enemy across a field, although one of his Iowans admitted that "I have now been in battle and it is not fun to hear balls sing around, about as many as you could imagine." Benton himself looked longingly to the rear for aid, writing that "at length the anxiously looked for succor came."[39]

Much of the problem lay with the Confederate artillery up ahead, both the section of the Botetourt and the Hudson batteries. But the infantry was also becoming a concern. With Bowen himself now on the field, he ordered the 6th Mississippi to advance against one of the Union batteries on the north side of the road. The Mississippians moved forward with a shout across the Foster cornfield, as did the 23rd Alabama to their right, led by Bowen himself. Hampered by their own concerns about being flanked to the south, however, the Arkansans on the left of the Magnolia Church line did not take up the advance but merely remained in position. But the Mississippians and Alabamians did not go far. They were soon stopped by the growing Federal numbers, particularly the 47th Indiana on the far Union left flank, and they returned to their original position in line. But the saucy advance had caused even greater concern in the Union ranks.[40]

With the Confederates even now advancing in some areas, the gap growing between Benton and Stone, and the renewed Confederate artillery causing concerning casualties, Hovey motioned toward the enemy artillery and told his officers "it must be taken." This was the crisis point. "To terminate a sanguinary contest which had continued for several hours," McClernand reported, "General Hovey ordered a charge, which was most gallantly executed." Carr later took umbrage to McClernand's statement, but both divisions moved forward. Benton himself, of Carr's division, related that "some one, unknown to me, gave the order 'charge,' which was executed with the wildest enthusiasm, the men of my brigade vying with their friends of Hovey's division who should first reach the enemy." There was also conflict even among Hovey's commanders, as Hovey initially advised Colonel Cameron of the 34th Indiana of McGinnis's brigade, the left regiment in the brigade that made better time farther up the ravine nearer the road, to take the battery. Colonel Slack "claimed the honor for his command," Hovey explained, but adding that "I settled the matter by directing Colonel Cameron, Thirty-fourth Indiana Regiment, to make the charge." As a bone to Slack, he also ordered Raynor and the 56th Ohio to support it. Slack was to be ready to move forward with his entire brigade as well if needed.[41]

In particular, Colonel Cameron's 34th Indiana leaped a fence and rushed ahead with bayonets fixed, the 56th Ohio right with them as well as three companies of the 28th Iowa supporting them. Brigade commander Slack related that his Ohioans "rushed up to the very muzzle of the rebel guns." Others moved ahead too, including a portion of the 11th Indiana as well as several other units Hovey could not determine. Units of Benton's brigade charged as well, including the 18th Indiana and 99th Illinois, Benton having told Colonel George W. K. Bailey of the latter regiment, "now Col. Bailey, you have the center of the brigade as now formed and I expect you to see that battery is captured." Yet Green's Confederate fire was hot and halted the advance momentarily, and the men went to ground for a couple of minutes as the Confederates pelted them with small arms and artillery fire. "The fire became intense and concentrated," Hovey admitted, and Colonel Cameron ordered his men to ground just behind the brow of the hill. Once the following 11th Indiana and 46th Indiana surged ahead, however, the Indianans sprang forward again. After watching his advance stall, Hovey himself bellowed "'forward' as loud as I could." The troops sprang up and moved on, quickly reaching the Confederate line that was only a matter of a hundred yards or so ahead. "Again the bright bayonets of the Twelfth Division were glittering in the sun; again a wild shout, a shout of triumph, reverberated through the hills," Hovey crowed.[42]

The greatest advance came generally along the Rodney Road where Hovey's units pushed forward into the gap between Carr's brigades, but Carr's regiments to the left and right also picked up on the advance and contributed as well. Unfortunately, the rivalry over who led and executed the charge continued long afterward, with Carr's soldiers giving ample credit to Hovey's troops while Carr himself claimed the attack was "with their assistance." However, Hovey minced no words about his own division's lead: "The honor of the charge belongs to the Twelfth Division." In truth, both were involved, but the fighting amid the most difficult terrain many of these soldiers had ever seen was so confusing that it was almost impossible to determine who was who and who did what. For his part, McClernand staff officer Henry Warmoth explained that "Hovey is the hero."[43]

In response to the charge, Green's Arkansans, Mississippians, and Alabamians began to melt away from the line, pushed in the center as well as continually being outflanked to the south, or Confederate left. One Iowan joyously bragged that "the Confederates had taken all the medicine that their systems could assimilate—and then evaporated." As the Confederates fled, they left behind the section of Virginia artillery, the horses all down and there being no way to remove the guns. "These men had stood manfully to their guns," Green explained, "until at least half their number were either killed or wounded, and were compelled to leave their guns for want of teams to bring them off, all their horses except two being killed."[44]

While Stone's troops poured in a heavy fire from the left of the road assisted by some of Slack's regiments now up and to the Confederate line, the Federals of McGinnis's and Slack's brigades as well as Benton's advanced ever farther, driving back the infantry who left the two guns. The 56th Ohio claimed to have captured the battle flag of the Confederate battery, Colonel Raynor keeping it himself. But it was not all Hovey's troops. Private Amos Nagle of the 99th Illinois of Benton's brigade captured the flag of the 15th Arkansas with four battle names emblazoned upon it: "Oak Hill, Elkhorn, Corinth, and Hatchie Bridge." One of the members, presumably Nagle, carried it "in his bosom during the day." The 99th Illinois also aided in capturing the two guns along with the 34th and 46th Indiana of McGinnis's following brigade, Captain William H. Charles of Company H of the 18th Indiana arriving first and the men of the 11th Indiana turning around one of the captured guns and discharging the piece into the backs of the fleeing Confederates. Colonel Daniel Macauley of the 11th Indiana rightly reported that there were "a number of claimants for the honor."[45]

Despite the argument, which would carry on long afterward with Carr complaining that McClernand gave Hovey's troops more credit than they deserved, the assault was successful. Benton was right that "herein is glory enough and to spare for both divisions." Hundreds of Confederates fell captive, as did the two battle flags and two cannons, three caissons and their six mule teams, and the attendant artillery ammunition. Carr claimed that "this success was the result of the splendid fighting of the whole division, which provided the opportunity." Yet Hovey declared "that any organized body of troops from any other division participated in the capture is, I think, contrary to the position of the corps at the time and the truth of history."[46]

By the time Green's Confederates melted away from the Magnolia Church line, one Iowan describing that they were now "in the footrace of the war," Grant himself was on the field and examined both wings of the developing position. "About this time I heard that Major General Grant had come up from Bruinsburg, and soon after had the pleasure of meeting him on the field," McClernand explained. In fact, both entered the fray, one Wisconsin soldier writing that both Grant and McClernand were "present, and they were in the thick of the battle like the rest of us." McClernand was probably less enthused than he wrote, however, desiring to fight the battle on his own. Grant seemed less that satisfied as well, relating that he found both McClernand and Illinois governor Richard Yates, with Congressman Washburne along as well, giving speeches to the victorious Federals; McClernand biographer Richard Kiper quipped that "the politician in the Illinois Democrat would not die." After Grant and McClernand rode the line that had been re-formed on the Magnolia Church ridge, to the cheers of the Federal soldiers, Grant prodded the Federals along, realizing the battle was not finished and that the Confederates would likely take a new line on the dominant ridges to the east. McClernand himself reported that "I ordered Generals Carr and Hovey to push the enemy with all vigor and celerity." A flinching Washburne and Yates remained with Grant for a time, Grant telling the latter calmly, "Governor, its too late to dodge after the ball has passed."[47]

The Confederate high command was in much worse shape. Green had been told all morning that William Baldwin's brigade was on the way to his aid, and he continually gave concerned glances eastward along the road hoping to see the head of the brigade marching up. Bowen explained that "courier after courier had been sent for General Baldwin, but his troops were utterly exhausted that he could not get up in time to prevent this [retreat]." In fact, leaving Green to defend the Rodney Road at Magnolia Church for just another hour, Bowen himself rode rearward to hurry Baldwin along. But time ran out.[48]

The Federals eventually lurched into motion and drove the withdrawing Confederates rearward over a mile to the Centers Creek watershed, some of the troops marching by the flank in the road itself. The ground lay littered with dead and wounded, as well as the detritus of battle, muskets being numbered "by the hundred." But evidence quickly came that there was indeed a new enemy line to the front. There, along the banks of Centers Creek and its tributaries, another round of fighting would emerge in the afternoon.[49]

4

"Bowen Is Hard Pressed"

May 1 Afternoon

"A furious battle has been going on since daylight just below Port Gibson," John C. Pemberton informed Jefferson Davis in the early afternoon on May 1. He had been getting regular updates from Bowen throughout the morning by telegraph from Port Gibson, and he sent Bowen's 1:20 p.m. message on to Richmond almost verbatim, including that Tracy had been killed, some of the Virginia guns had been captured, and that Bowen was outnumbered "trebly." Indeed, he would be outgunned fifty-eight to sixteen in the battle. Pemberton added context at the end of his own message, however, begging that reinforcements be sent to him and looking ahead to when the Federals would move on the railroad feeding Vicksburg and perhaps even take Jackson, the state capital. It was a dire situation.[1]

Bowen had sent additional messages throughout the morning. Around daylight, he had informed Pemberton that "prisoners taken this morning say [John A.] McClernand is in command; that three or four divisions are landed." The prisoners admitted to as many as twenty thousand troops oncoming, although Bowen declared "I disbelieve the report." At 9:00 a.m., Bowen sent a follow-up that stated "I am vastly outnumbered." He indicated he hoped to hold his position until Baldwin arrived, which it turned out he could not do. His 1:20 p.m. message to Pemberton, sent on to Richmond, indicated the growing disaster, Bowen adding "the men act nobly, but the odds are overpowering."[2]

Obviously, word was out about this major fight even while it continued on, and both sides' chains of command reacted, even all the way to Richmond. But there was a major difference in the high commands' response on each side. While Grant and the majority of the rest of the Union commanders traveled with the army and were present at this critical event, Pemberton did not, choosing to remain away from the fight and at his most prized possession itself, Vicksburg. In fact, Pemberton completed his move to the river city that day as a result of the events of the day before, although much of the department's bureaucracy remained in Jackson and would only over time move into Vicksburg itself. Some confusion necessarily erupted, as even Pemberton's chief of staff remained in Jackson temporarily and there was some difficulty in coordinating messages and orders.[3]

Pemberton nevertheless continued to pepper Richmond with updates throughout the afternoon as he got them from Bowen, and Secretary of War James A. Seddon responded only that reinforcements would be starting that way soon, particularly from General P. G. T. Beauregard's department in South Carolina. Even the less-than-helpful General Joseph E. Johnston in Tennessee wired a caution that "if Grant's army lands on this side of the river, the safety of Mississippi depends on beating it. For that object you should unite your whole force." Obviously, Johnston was behind time and a master of the obvious, and his advice was easier said than done. Indeed, Pemberton had more to look out for than just the events at Port Gibson, threatening though they were. Grierson's cavalry was still out there somewhere, although best indications were that they had left the immediate area and were heading for Baton Rouge. Pemberton called off some of the pursuers and sent them toward Port Gibson to "operate against enemy there." He also continually received frantic messages from northern Mississippi commander Brigadier General Daniel Ruggles, but Pemberton paid them little attention and told Ruggles he could not help: "I have no re-enforcements to send you." Closer in, the major threat continued at Snyder's Bluff, although it was looking by this point less and less like a major offensive. Still, it was a major concern in Pemberton's mind, just as Grant hoped.[4]

Pemberton reacted to each threat, at times grasping at anything that could help. He even penned a message to Lieutenant General E. Kirby Smith across the Mississippi River: "Cannot you do something to operate against them on your side of the river?" He also kept the governor of Mississippi, John J. Pettus, well informed. Yet the departmental commander also acted tangibly, although again too little and too late. While he had to maintain forces at Vicksburg, he also started more reinforcements southward, including pulling in troops from Meridian to the east. He managed to start three brigades southward on May 1 itself, regiments from Brigadier Generals Abraham Buford's and Lloyd Tilghman's brigades from the Big Black River bridge and Jackson area as well as a brigade from Carter Stevenson's division manning the Vicksburg defenses. He also called northward a brigade under Brigadier General John Gregg from Port Hudson. To command these additional troops and Bowen himself, who was still only a brigadier general just recently put in command of a division of two brigades (Green's and Cockrell's), Pemberton sent his mobile major general William Loring southward as well. "Hurry on troops with all possible haste," Pemberton told Loring in a later message. "Bowen is hard pressed."[5]

Loring started gathering his troops for the move, but Pemberton's state of mind was rattled and Loring was the beneficiary. The original message telling him to move and detailing the troops involved and jumping-off points for them amazingly included no mention of where to go. In informing Pemberton he could move by noon, Loring had to ask for elaboration: "Your telegram says via Vicksburg, but does not say where to go." Pemberton responded with more detail about the move to Port Gibson and Loring's assumption of command once there, careful to note that Bowen would retain command of his division. Pemberton's nervousness also became evident in messages sent directly to those involved in the move, such as Tilghman. Several messages went to the brigade commander that included wordage such as "move at once," "hurry on your two regiments as rapidly as possible," "with greatest dispatch," and "go the most direct route." He also included biting statements such as "I expected your two regiments to be on the march, by dirt road, from Edwards Depot before this" and "as ordered several times to-day . . . this is peremptory, and will be obeyed at once." Obviously, Pemberton's state of mind on this critical May 1 was not good. Loring nevertheless began the trek southward, obviously with no hope of making a difference this day but perhaps he could on the next.[6]

In contrast, Grant traveled with the army itself, taking care of the larger departmental duties en route and even getting involved in some of the tactical action as well. On the march eastward on the night of April 30 and during the day on May 1, Grant did not neglect the larger context, such as ordering his chief quartermaster Lieutenant Colonel Judson D. Bingham to "prepare two tugs to run the blockade, with two barges each in tow." He wanted the barges loaded with rations and oats, all of it fortified with hay. Grant needed more supplies south of Vicksburg, and the roundabout route was long and slow. He would try the Vicksburg batteries again.[7]

Grant also commanded the army in person, although he left a lot of the tactical decisions in the ravines to McClernand. Aggravating as McClernand was, there was no doubt about his bravery. McClernand was even then in the thick of the fighting right along with his staff, one of whom declared that "the bullets whistled like the wind." But Grant kept overall authority and even at times gave orders for artillery on the left. As to reinforcements, McClernand "sent repeated messages to me" for additional help on the Rodney Road, but

Grant went himself and could not see the need for them in such harsh terrain. "I had been on that as well as all other parts of the field, and could not see how they could be used there to advantage." Nevertheless, McClernand was at the front and fairly demanded Logan's division of McPherson's trailing XVII Corps as well as McPherson's other nearby division now under a colonel of all things, John Sanborn, who was not even on site yet; one of the junior brigade commanders, Colonel Samuel Holmes, actually directed the present brigades in the rear of the Union army. Grant would split the difference and send these reinforcing XVII Corps units into action on both wings.[8]

So unlike Pemberton, who was not on the battlefield itself, Grant was. But there was another difference: Grant had entered the Mississippi wilderness, out of which little news would be forthcoming to Washington any time soon. In fact, Grant would not send his first message back for a couple more days. While Bowen was in telegraphic communication with Pemberton and Pemberton with Richmond, the closest telegraphic station Grant could utilize was back at Memphis. He would thus have the luxury of no one figuratively peering over his shoulder as he conducted his Inland Campaign, but it could also be a detriment that he was so out of touch that little to no help outside of his own making could get to him if matters went sideways. He just had to make sure that did not happen, and once more contrary to his counterpart Pemberton, there seemed to be little panic in Grant's mind as he cast off into what could only be described as a significant gamble with his army.

John Bowen was in crisis mode. He left Green's line near Magnolia Church around 10:00 a.m. to look after the rest of his defense and especially to find Baldwin's reinforcing brigade and hurry it forward. Repeated messages had gone rearward for the troops to hurry, and finally Bowen went himself to make sure the advance was as rapid as it could be. "Leaving orders with Green to hold the position for an hour," he noted, "I rode back and urged forward Baldwin's brigade, then arriving, to his support." Baldwin's troops had made it as far as Grindstone Ford the night before and had moved on southward at dawn this day, the sounds of firing growing to the southwest quickening their steps. One 46th Mississippi soldier wrote of crossing the suspension bridge: "We were falling down and against the railing, because of the swing our footsteps gave it." The requests for haste arrived "in quick succession," Baldwin noted, and he pushed his troops right through Port Gibson and on out the Rodney Road. Colonel Claudius W. Sears of the 46th Mississippi explained that the regiment "went through town as rapidly as possible—people brought out water for us as we passed." William Pitt Chambers of the same regiment noted that, although it seemed to be a beautiful town, "I had not time to observe anything."[9]

Yet disaster struck while Bowen was gone: Green had been forced back. "I returned just in time to see the position lost," Bowen admitted. He had no choice but to create a new line, which he did with Baldwin's troops, one Mississippian writing that "we had barely formed line when the enemy opened fire on us with artillery and small arms." But fortunately, yet another partial brigade was also on the way; Francis Cockrell was similarly nearing the battlefield, having left Grand Gulf six miles distant at eight o'clock that morning, and he momentarily arrived with three more regiments. "I now had all the force at my command on the field," Bowen rationalized, except three regiments and two battalions on duty elsewhere such as Grand Gulf and Bayou Pierre. But this was such a crisis that he later also ordered most of them toward the field of battle.[10]

Such paltry numbers were problematic, especially with so divergent lines on two different roads. The biggest threat seemed to be on the Rodney Road, but Bowen was also getting word from the Bruinsburg Road that the Federals were pushing there as well and that ammunition was running low, Tracy's ammunition train not having yet arrived. His death made the situation there even more precarious. Bowen consequently shuffled his entire defense to reinforce the right up on the Bruinsburg Road and to make sure there was a general officer there while at the same time putting his freshest troops at the main threat area on the Rodney Road. He thus pulled Green's tired brigade out of position and sent it up to the Bruinsburg Road to reinforce Tracy's command now under Colonel Garrott, making Green the senior officer on that front. At the same time, Bowen also sent one of Cockrell's reinforcing regiments up there as well. On the Rodney Road, Bowen positioned Baldwin's four regiments as well as the other two of Cockrell's, Colonel Sears of the 46th Mississippi bellowing, "fix bayonets, boys! And if they come bleed 'em!" With all comparatively fresh troops here on the Rodney Road, hopefully they would be able to stem the tide until dark.[11]

Accordingly, Martin Green led his Arkansans with the attached Mississippians, Alabamians, and the 6th Missouri of Cockrell's brigade back to the forks in the Rodney and Bruinsburg Roads nearly back at Port Gibson before heading out westward on the Bruinsburg Road to solidify Garrott's line. Help was indeed needed there and quick, as Garrott was facing at least two brigades with more moving to join them. Garrott had already withdrawn his right slightly to a western-facing line across the Bruinsburg Road rather than the southward-facing line astride the crossover road from the Shaifer House, but now he pulled back even farther when Federal pressure corresponded to his move and began to push even more. Indeed, numerous Federal reports indicated the right swing the various units made, causing Garrott to withdraw once more behind several larger ravines on both ends of a new line, everywhere except the high ground on which the road ran. Garrott related that he "ordered [them] to retire with their commands and take a new and strong position behind the crest of the ridge." The Alabamians took particularly heavy fire as they crossed the open ridge in retreat, but most made it to re-form the lines while a few officers and men were wounded or captured. Among them was Lieutenant Colonel Edmund W. Pettus commanding the 20th Alabama now that Garrott was commanding the brigade; Pettus was also brother of Mississippi governor John J. Pettus. Green arrived just as Garrott was forming his new line and, after Garrott explained the situation, "declined to make any change." Rather, Green quickly shuffled his reinforcing columns, exhausted though they were, into line to the left: "I did [so] as speedily as the wearied condition of my men would admit." Under a heavy fire, the 6th Missouri went into position at the double-quick near a cornfield on the left of the 31st Alabama, and Green's full brigade, including the 6th Mississippi and 23rd Alabama, continued the line to the south on the left of the 6th Missouri.[12]

Osterhaus's Federals followed up the Confederate withdrawal, taking advantage of the high knolls the Alabamians had utilized before with artillery. Garrard's brigade, although jumbled a little bit, essentially moved through the ravines south of the Bruinsburg Road, the connecting ravines at times being separated by only a ridge that Osterhaus described as "at some places only a narrow ridge not more than from five to ten yards wide." Astride the road itself and to the left were mostly Sheldon's men, although the 120th Ohio was also on that flank. Once in place, the Federal infantry regiments had shifted to the right ninety degrees to come on line with the new Confederate position. They then probed ahead, few making anything close to an assault but skirmishing heavy enough to determine the enemy's identity. Colonel James Keigwin, for example, reported that "the Thirty-first Alabama, which was in line about 60 yards distant, opened fire upon us with small-arms." Keigwin caught the Alabamians as they withdrew to their major position around the Andrews house, but the advance stopped there. In fact, the fighting bogged down to lengthy firefights around this time, brigade commanders in the jumbled Union division actually alternating units in and out of the front line. Keigwin's own 49th Indiana was soon relieved by the 42nd Ohio after an hour-and-ten-minute firefight. Similarly, after the 120th Ohio made its attack on the knoll and drove the Confederate right back, Colonel Marcus Spiegel continued on but met stiff resistance when the Alabamians "rejoined the main body." He described the Confederates as "concealed behind logs, fences, and houses, and some perched upon the tops of trees." When his ammunition began to run out, the 69th Indiana came forward to relieve him and the Ohioans went to the rear to refill their cartridge boxes from the dead and wounded. Taken aback by the resistance and terrain, Osterhaus declared that "the large number of rebel infantry occupying every inch of ground in my front made the above deployment of my whole infantry force necessary."[13]

Stopped while confronting this new Confederate line, Osterhaus played on the enemy with artillery while he decided what to do. Nearby, the 69th Indiana began singing "Rally 'Round the Flag," to which one Confederate yelled, "we'll make you rally round your damned old flag." Desiring more knowledge of the enemy line, Osterhaus sent forward heavy skirmishers, which took some of the ground easily and "held every foot of ground thus gained." Bolstered by the initial success, Osterhaus decided to try an all-out assault in the center where the 42nd and 16th Ohio and 22nd Kentucky lay just on and south of the road. These were the same troops that had assaulted across the corduroy bridge at Chickasaw Bayou several months before, so they knew how to advance under fire. But the surge soon confirmed a solid Confederate line. The Federals moved "against a most terrific fire to the very edge of the first ravine," Osterhaus explained, "but it would have demanded too great a sacrifice of life to have persisted in this attack and I therefore withdrew the regiments behind a swell of ground, leaving only a line of skirmishers on the ground gained." There had to be another way to force the enemy back: "The great strength of the Rebel position was potent," Osterhaus admitted.[14]

More heated fighting erupted at specific places, largely the result of Green's order immediately upon taking position to "press the enemy, knowing that unless we could drive him back we must fall back to prevent being cut off." Grandson of Henry Clay, Colonel Eugene Erwin accordingly led his 6th Missouri forward in an attack and retook the two crippled guns of Johnston's Battery lost earlier in the morning. Taking a strong position on a ridge, Erwin maintained his position against less than a strong Federal response for an hour and a half of long-range skirmishing. Unfortunately, no one else followed, Green himself admitting that "the other portion of the line, although the troops fought hard, could not advance the lines."[15]

Later in the afternoon, Erwin again continued his advance to another ridge, prompted both by Green's order and by a seeming flanking maneuver on the far right. Erwin decided on his own to attack to take pressure off the flank and ordered the Missourians to move forward where he met a host of Federals. By this time running out of ammunition and sorrowfully finding that neither Garrott's Alabamians to his right nor Green's Arkansans to his left had moved

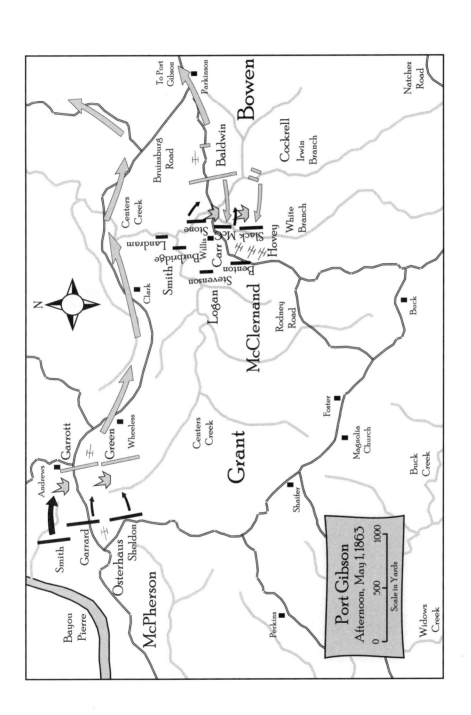

Port Gibson
Afternoon, May 1, 1863

Scale in Yards
0   500   1000

forward with him, despite repeated calls to do so, Erwin ordered his Missourians to make a show of attack by loudly proclaiming "fix bayonets." But at the same time he ordered them to file by the flank out of the desperate situation. Each company gave a volley as they proceeded to the rear and formed another line, but Erwin soon gave the order to "face by the rear rank and retire at double quick, which they did in good order." He had to abandon the two recaptured guns, but the safety of his command was paramount; still, he reported that "with one regiment I charged the whole left wing of the Federal army," and he lamented that "had Tracy's brigade joined me in the charge, instead of withdrawing at that time, we would have completely routed their left wing."[16]

Colonel James Keigwin's 49th Indiana specifically met the Missourians as they made an advance of their own on the 6th Missouri's position, the regiment having returned from its rearward break. Keigwin led his Indianans through one branch of a ravine easily but then met another that "I found from the depth and roughness . . . that I would have to pass it without any order." He commanded his men to move forward at the double-quick with a yell and "from the noise that was made I am sure that every officer and soldier obeyed the command." As the Indianans topped the ridge near some buildings the Missourians arrived as well, but Keigwin noted that "we were about one minute too fast for them." The Missourians fled and Keigwin noted that, as Erwin's troops scampered across the cornfield, "we poured the lead into their backs, much to our amusement and their sorrow."[17]

As the afternoon unfolded, the nervousness of the Confederates became acute, especially with the sound of fighting on the Rodney Road far in their left rear by now. Green himself realized that "we were at least 1 ½ miles in advance of the other portion of the army." But by far the biggest determinate of the afternoon came when yet another Union brigade arrived on the Bruinsburg Road, Brigadier General John E. Smith's of Logan's division. The troops had marched forward all morning from Bruinsburg, hearing the fighting to the front: "All the time we could hear the heavy roar of artillery and as we gained the summit of the hills back from the river, the quick, spiteful crack of the musketry could be distinguished at intervals." An Illinoisan who could clearly hear the guns up ahead admitted that "for the first time we realized that we were in the vicinity of war, the roar of musketry being continuous also the artillery—we were hearing the guns of both armies." Only two of the division's brigades arrived, however, due to chaos back at Bruinsburg during the crossing as well as the blocked-up single road west of Shaifer's House. In fact, Grant wrote that Logan began to deploy "as soon as the last of the Thirteenth [Corps] was out of the road." Logan went with one brigade to McClernand's support while corps commander McPherson went with Smith's to aid Osterhaus. McClernand had offered Osterhaus more troops throughout the day, and the division commander declared he had about all he needed given the terrain: "He declined them until more urgent occasion should arise." They were indeed about all he needed given his tepid advance, and Logan himself described in his report that when Smith went into line Osterhaus "was being closely pressed by a heavy force of the enemy." The perception in the Federal high command was completely reverse of what it was on the ground. Nevertheless, around 2:00 p.m. Smith formed his brigade in two lines near the left of Osterhaus's jumbled brigades, the 20th and 31st Illinois and 23rd Indiana up ahead and the 45th and 124th Illinois two hundred yards in rear. The Indianans pressed forward as skirmishers and tangled with the Confederate companies holding the right near Bayou Pierre, driving them back periodically to a high ridge where the Alabamians "essayed a formidable stand." Luther Cowan of the 45th Illinois noted that despite their moving forward with a shout that "made the heavens and earth ring again," the terrain, canebrake, and Confederate defense made the situation unpleasant. "It looked rough," he noted, later adding "it looked rather tough."[18]

Osterhaus had by this time become convinced that only a flank attack on the Confederate right near Bayou Pierre itself would move the enemy, and so he waited for the arrival of Smith's troops. But it took a good two or three hours from initial conception amid discussion with Lieutenant Colonel James H. Wilson of Grant's staff, who agreed, to final placement of Smith's troops. And then as Smith's brigade arrived on the field, Smith and perhaps McPherson as well decided to attack straight up the road like Osterhaus had been trying to do all afternoon. Knowing it would not work, Osterhaus let them try nevertheless, adding "the men advanced gallantly, but of course had to give way as soon as they came within range of the enemy's missiles." At that point, a couple of the new regiments were detailed to move to the extreme left flank to make the attack there. By midafternoon they were arriving and ready to go into action, Grant himself spurring them onward under heavy fire. "The bullets flew like hailstones," one Illinoisan admitted.[19]

With orders to "advance the left, and, if possible, outflank the enemy," Smith chose this opportune time to order a charge, and the entire brigade surged forward toward the Alabama companies in skirmish formation. One Illinoisan described how the "brushes were very thick and meney hills." The five regiments easily overpowered the Confederate defense, though it was not a total breakthrough given the lay of the land and terrain impediments.

Indeed, McPherson himself was with Smith and explained that "this movement was perfectly successful, though the impracticable nature of the country (full of deep ravines and canebrakes) retarded the movement more than I could have wished, and prevented us from reaping the full fruits of the victory." McClernand even intimated in his report that Smith's advance failed "to carry the enemy's position." Yet it was enough to cause Green to realize his defense was at an end. According to one Illinoisan, the Confederates "soon began to run from their hiding places like rats from an old barn, and then you ought to have heard our boys yell, and see the rebels run."[20]

In fact, Osterhaus claimed that, with most of the attention in the Confederate line focused on the flank attack to the north, Osterhaus and his own division made a corresponding advance along the road, Osterhaus himself leading the way. "I lead the charge personally," he reported, and "the charge was a complete success; in a few minutes these brave men climbed over all obstructions with their victorious hurrahs, driving the broken lines of the enemy before them." Numerous regiments then slid across the narrow neck of land along the road and fanned out to create new lines past the initial ravines, driving the Confederates back in the process.[21]

The pressure on the Confederate right flank was simply too much, added to the continually building force against the main Confederate line. Green explained that he had held his position "for some hours," but orders from Bowen arrived to "hold my position until near sunset, and by that time, if I could not advance, to retire." Green knew he could not hold the right as he had been doing with mere companies all day and consequently ordered his wing of the army to prepare to withdraw. He wanted the entire line to utilize a covering ravine and march by the left flank up the Bruinsburg Road, with two additional guns of Johnston's Battery going back into action in the rear to "divert his attention from our movements." In the chaos and fog of battle, however, the order went to the right of the line before it did the left, which complicated the movement when the left should have moved out first. Green lamented that he would have disengaged completely without the enemy knowing it had the orders worked as he had planned, but the Federals picked up on the chaos and pressed ahead. Fortunately, Erwin's 6th Missouri was still out front in its debacle, and although nearly surrounded and captured, the Missourians nevertheless provided some rearguard force to allow both Green's and Garrott's brigades to scamper away. The artillerymen tried to "drag the pieces off by hand, but had to leave them," Bowen explained in reference to the two recaptured Virginia guns, and Erwin then brought his Missourians out as the rear guard. Erwin's 6th Missouri, Green noted, "was the last regiment to leave the field."[22]

As afternoon emerged, the situation west of Port Gibson was getting worse for the Confederate defenders. And then yet another problem presented itself about this time. With so many Federals arriving, they continually fanned out to the north and south, those to the north eventually connecting in the valley of Centers Creek with the force down on the Rodney Road. Those to the south were, perhaps more important, nearing the Natchez Road (modern Natchez Trace), which if gained would give the Federals an open road into Port Gibson and into the rear of the Confederate force. Such a move would be easy, as Bowen had no troops whatsoever defending that road. Somehow Bowen had to keep the enemy from moving farther southward around his left flank while at the same time withdrawing if forced to do so at the same pace on each of the roads he was manning. If either defense faltered, it would leave the other in danger of being turned and even cut off and captured. Each had to fall back incrementally together to assure a mutual defense, but Bowen also wanted to hold as long as he could, until night if possible, so that more time would be allowed to provide a defense and to react to this obviously concerning invasion.[23]

Even amid the chaotic withdrawal of Green's troops, Baldwin took position amid the parallel-flowing (north and south) branches of Centers Creek, the White and Irwin Branches. He placed the 17th Louisiana on the left of the road in a patch of woods amid broken ravines while the 31st Louisiana went into line across the road on the north side, although detached from the 17th Louisiana by one of the valleys feeding into Centers Creek. The 4th Mississippi filed into line south of the 17th Louisiana, its right also in the patch of woods but the majority of the regiment facing an open field. The final regiment, the 46th Mississippi, went into position as the reserve some six hundred yards to the rear to cover one of the batteries that Cockrell's brigade had brought from "the ditches" at Grand Gulf, Baldwin having no artillery with him. Two guns initially went into action (those not captured earlier in the day), but some of Cockrell's guns also went into position here later on, although all fired slowly because of a lack of ammunition. One 46th Mississippi soldier nevertheless explained that "we gave them some grape and canister to think on." Shortly thereafter, Cockrell's Missourians also filed into line to the left of the 4th Mississippi. There, the new Confederate force, hidden among the ravines for cover instead of on the bare ridgetops, awaited the growing Union legions surging down the Rodney Road.[24]

And quite a force it was. As the minutes and hours moved on from morning to afternoon, the Federals of Eugene Carr's and Alvin Hovey's divisions surged ahead along the Rodney Road across the ridge on which Magnolia Church stood and through the connecting ravines to the east; the church itself quickly became a hospital for the wounded. Up ahead, the Federals found the valley of several tributaries of Centers Creek, the main channel being to the north but White and Irwin Branches spreading southward through huge ravines. It was on the other side of the first one that John Bowen fashioned a new defense, and Colonel William Stone's Iowans led the advance into this new fight. "I saw at once that the enemy had been strongly re-enforced and were determined to make another stand," Stone explained. He added that "their position was well chosen, on a high hill covered with timber and commanding the entire ground over which we were compelled to approach." McClernand declared the new Confederate position was "stronger than the first."[25]

The other Federals followed up after a short break "to enable all to rest and procure water," brigade commander McGinnis explained, some said as many as two miles but more like a little under a mile to the bold bluffs along White and Irwin Branches. Both of Carr's brigades moved ahead, Stone's in the lead again to the left of the road where it eventually encountered stiff opposition; Stone in fact related that "we sustained alone the concentrated fire of their infantry and artillery." One Indianan noted that "we found them again, ready to show fight." Stone continued that "finally other brigades and batteries became engaged as well, and the battle raged with terrific fury along our lines." But his Iowans fired back, most of them anyway. After the fight one realized his gun had not been working despite repeatedly charging cartridges down the barrel. It had as many as six rounds when he discovered it, and he was accordingly "greatly frightened when the matter was explained to him." Benton's troops likewise followed portions of Hovey's division forward, moving by the flank along the road itself. While not on the first line, Benton still fed regiments into position when needed. Hovey likewise pressed ahead under orders from Grant himself and pushed both McGinnis and Slack forward as well as one of A. J. Smith's arriving brigades under William J. Landram. Hovey noted his troops "immediately marched across a ravine in the direction the enemy had taken." Even as these troops pushed out over the wide plateau between Buck and Centers Creeks, they came under fire from lingering Confederates holding as long as possible, even fighting in the ravine itself, but they eventually ran up on the main Confederate line situated across the first creek.[26]

Action picked up all along the line as the mingled Federals pushed ahead. And a new wing of this Rodney Road force opened up on the far left as advance elements of A. J. Smith's division of McClernand's XIII Corps and John Logan's division of the XVII Corps began to arrive and were fed into the fields between the two main forces on the two roads. One of Logan's brigade commanders, in fact, explained that he was put into line "filling up a space between the left and right of General McClernand's line," in other words the forces on the two roads.[27]

Indeed, there were soon far too many Federals arriving to get them all in battle. A. J. Smith's division had arrived after daylight, Stephen Burbridge's brigade first followed by William Landram's, and had been held in reserve. The two brigades followed behind the advancing front lines, often champing to get into action. When orders arrived for Colonel Friend S. Rutherford of the 97th Illinois to act at his own discretion, cries from the ranks ensued: "To the front; to the front!" Yet the troops remained in rear although under fire, Colonel Theodore Buehler of the 67th Indiana in Burbridge's brigade writing that he was for a while in "a rather uncomfortable place, the balls whizzing in unpleasant proximity to our ears." Ultimately, the division moved forward "across the battle-field of a few hours previous and re-established line of battle as before in rear of the advance." Ultimately, Landram moved to the left, where he became engaged across the branches of Centers Creek while Burbridge, on McClernand's order, moved first to the right upon the threat from the Missouri regiments but then back across the battlefield to support Landram, who was in action on the left. Several soldiers fell out in the heat of the day compounded by the march the night before, and Burbridge himself described how it "was very exhausting from the necessity of rapidly shifting ground with part or the whole of the brigade, as the weak points of our lines successively presented themselves." Still, a portion of Burbridge's brigade likewise engaged on the left, Colonel Buehler describing his Indianans "charging up the hill in gallant style."[28]

Even the troops of a different corps began to arrive. James McPherson's lead division under John A. Logan moved across the river at Bruinsburg late on April 30, Logan himself crossing on May 1 and catching up, although one of the brigades was materially delayed when the two steamers collided in the night and took down an entire artillery battery. Brigadier General Elias Dennis's trailing brigade was thus delayed, and it reached the field only near dark on May 1, being led by a staff officer Logan left to guide it. But the other two brigades arrived around noon, in time to enter the fight. "Heavy and rapid firing had been heard for several hours," McPherson explained, "indicating[] clearly that a battle was in progress, and the men moved forward with promptness and alacrity, notwithstanding the intense heat, anxious to take part in the contest." But with that temperature many fell by the wayside, one Ohioan declaring that "half the Co. gave out from heat." Some even reported deaths due to sunstroke during this period of hot weather in May. Hearing where best to put the troops, McPherson led Smith's brigade up to support Osterhaus on the Bruinsburg Road and sent the other into the mael-strom on the Rodney Road. While McPherson went with Smith's troops to the north, division commander Logan accompanied Brigadier General John D. Stevenson and his troops. McPherson's other division under Colonel John B. Sanborn was on the way but would not arrive in time to engage, although one Illinoisan was aghast at the battlefield when they did arrive. "I saw my first man killed in battle," he wrote years later; "the top of his head was shot off. It gave me a feeling I have never forgotten."[29]

John D. Stevenson's brigade of Illinois, Missouri, and Ohio troops thus entered the fight north of the Rodney Road, going into line in support of Bur-bridge's brigade. One 8th Illinois soldier remembered "we were almost dead with heat & fatigue," but Logan described the section as "a vacancy in Gen-eral McClernand's line." Stevenson's troops took the front line when called upon, the 81st Illinois moving up on Burbridge's left and eventually the 8th Illinois as well. Colonel James J. Dollins of the 81st Illinois noted that "the whistling of the shots over us was indeed sublime and musical, but not a man of us was hurt." When claims of fatigue emerged, the 7th Missouri likewise entered the line, all on Burbridge's left.[30]

Yet nowhere amid the newly established Federal thrust was there more concern than on the far right, where the main effects of a new Confederate blow landed. Over on the right of the Rodney Road force, Slack's Federals had similarly probed toward the Confederate line. Benton's troops remained in rear to support the division's batteries on the ridge, but two regiments of Slack's brigade, the 47th Indiana and 56th Ohio, pressed on with skirmishers in front all the way to and across the ravine. There, they met the main Confed-erate line upon pressing up the slope. "Immediately upon their rising the hill," Slack explained, "the action became general." These regiments met murder-ous Confederate fire and halted, Lieutenant Colonel John A. McLaughlin ex-plaining that the enemy were "in a position favorable to taking us upon the right flank and in our rear." The troops then turned and marched by the flank out of the ravine, all the while forced back by the Confederates. "We were soon compelled to retire from our position" Slack admitted, "by re-enforce-ments of the enemy in large numbers approaching over the crest of a hill to our right and rear." Slack ordered a new line formed on the slope to try and hold out until help could come.[31]

This major Confederate advance came under the guidance of Bowen him-self. Concerned with the Federal movement in that area and especially toward the Natchez Road, he personally led the two Missouri regiments of Cock-rell's brigade to the left of the line some three hundred yards past Baldwin's troops and pushed them forward in an attempt to roll up the Union right flank. "Between 12 and 1 o'clock I attempted, with two of Colonel Cockrell's regiments, to turn the enemy's right flank," Bowen reported, "and nearly succeeded." The Missourians formed in column of regiments in the valley of Irwin Branch, the 5th Missouri in front and the 3rd Missouri in rear, although once down in the valley the lead regiment shifted to the left and "unmasked" the other, both of which moved forward abreast of each other. "We thought that we could do this with ease and so we were started," one Missourian admitted, but it quickly became obvious it would be much harder than they thought. Most problematic was a large field and a dense canebrake in the valley they had to cross. "Under the personal direction of General Bowen," Cockrell explained, "these regiments dashed upon and engaged the enemy at very close range for some forty minutes and drove back in confusion the line first engaging us." In fact, Bowen wrote that three lines of Federals met them: "The first was routed, the second wavered, but the third stood firm."[32]

The Confederate advance understandably caused much concern in the Federal ranks. Hovey himself rode toward that direction and immediately began to pick up on concern coming from regimental commanders and staff officers. McGinnis himself told of a developing move of the enemy toward their right "with the probable intention of flanking us." McGinnis had sent several companies to secure the flank and then the entire 34th Indiana, but word soon arrived from a staff officer that artillery was also seen moving in that direction. Indeed, very soon shells started falling among the Federals from the Confederate battery positioned near the ravine, Hovey inspecting the unexploded ordnance and determining it to be 12- and 24-pound howitzer ammunition. With the battery was "a large force of infantry, marching partly hidden by the woody ravine." Hovey quicky responded by massing all four batteries available to him on the ridge to the rear, something he would do often in battle, and firing almost point-blank into the ravine itself where the Confederates massed. The 2nd and 16th Ohio, Battery A, 1st Missouri, and Battery A, 2nd Illinois Artillery, some just arriving from their hard march eastward from Bruinsburg, added the firepower of twenty-four guns on the critical right flank.[33]

The Confederates nevertheless hit the right of Slack's line and the newly positioned 34th Indiana, now at right angles to Slack's men so that McGinnis and Slack had a refused flank to meet the advance. The main fighting occurred down in the ravine itself, some of the men taking position "in the bed of a creek." It was here that Cockrell's Missourians surged ahead and tried to turn the Union right. Slack reported that "these lines had not more than been formed when three rebel regiments . . . came down at a charge, with terrific yells, and could not be seen, because of the very thick growth of cane, until they reached a point within 30 yards of my line."[34]

Fortunately for the Federals on the beleaguered right flank, help was on the way. McGinnis sent forward the 24th Indiana and 29th Wisconsin of his brigade to add weight to the push, but they arrived too late and had to help halt the retreat. McGinnis described the Confederate line as "strongly posted on the opposite side of a deep ravine." The combined effects of Slack's and McGinnis's advancing Federals here on the right told on the Confederate defenders, but their advance could not break through, McGinnis himself describing the stand-up fight from the ravine itself and even as the troops pushed onto the bluff as raging "without any intermission whatever for an hour and thirty-seven minutes." Hovey simply noted, "here these gallant regiments met with severe loss."[35]

Slack's and McGinnis' Federals opened up a heavy fire nonetheless, Lieutenant Colonel McLaughlin of the 47th Indiana reporting that "the pieces of our men became so heated from rapid, continuous firing as to make it impossible for them to continue firing longer with safety to themselves." With the aid of the artillery in rear and the dense cane in front, Slack broke the Confederate attempt anyway; he reported his men opened "a most terrific and jarring fire, which arrested their charge and threw them into some confusion, but they soon recovered." But there was no getting through the cane under fire, and according to one Confederate Missourian, "after we had been there a while, our colonel came along the line and told us to go back one at a time." But that did not mean the fighting ended. Cockrell's Confederates withdrew to their original line but maintained it for a couple more hours, Bowen himself riding among them and exclaiming, "I did not expect that any of you would get away, but the charge had to be made, or my little army was lost." Slack explained that "it was a fair, square fight of regiment against regiment, of about equal numbers and equally armed." McClernand himself met Slack on the field and "complemented me very highly for gallantry, efficiency, & bravery," saying he was pushing for Slack's promotion.[36]

Still, there was much lingering tension even as the Confederate attack stalled and then broke rearward. Indeed, the Confederates were giving as good as they got, the colonel of the 29th Wisconsin, Charles R. Gill, requesting of McGinnis permission to be relieved "for a short time." McGinnis agreed but had no other regiments to send forward, his others being engaged elsewhere. There were other regiments of other brigades and divisions nearby, however, and upon request Benton sent forward the 8th Indiana. "Although they were short of ammunition," McGinnis approvingly wrote, "they went in with a will and rendered the necessary relief, and fought gloriously and victoriously during the remainder of the engagement." One of the Indianans related that "Benton told him to take the old 8th down & show the 29 Wisconsin how to do it." He added, "so away we went on the double quick."[37]

For his part, Bowen was disappointed at the result: "After a long and desperate contest, we had to give up the attempt." But he saw some good come of it, adding that "I am of opinion, however, that this attack saved the right from being overwhelmed, and kept the enemy back until nearly sunset." And he was not giving up. Later in the afternoon, Baldwin reported that Bowen "directed me to make an effort to advance and try their strength." It was between 3:00 and 4:00 p.m.[38]

Baldwin pieced together a plan in which the 46th Mississippi moved forward to the main line between the 17th and 31st Louisiana, and all would then move ahead together. The 4th Mississippi on the left moved forward first because of the field on their front, but the Mississippians quickly met the combined firepower of numerous batteries that had accompanied the nine Union brigades of five divisions that had assembled on the Rodney Road. Baldwin intended the Mississippians to "dash across the space to the woods beyond, and seize and hold the position." In fact, Baldwin related that the Mississippians "commenced the movement as directed, and started across the field under a heavy fire of musketry, but before the other regiments could be placed in motion it was compelled to retake its position, having found, as reported, two brigades of infantry opposed to its left." Worse ground was in front of the other regiments, Baldwin writing that the area in front of the 17th Louisiana "was so much cut up by ravines and other irregularities of ground that no line of battle could be formed, and companies were compelled to act independently." Similarly in front of the 46th Mississippi "the ground was too much intersected by hollows, woods, and deep ravines to admit of simultaneous action." The Mississippians moved forward across the creek anyway but "were met by a terrible fire of grape, canister and musket shot" and were soon ordered back. Baldwin quickly came to the conclusion that "an attempt to move forward would result in the destruction of the entire command without accomplishing the object," and so he sent word to Bowen, who "directed me to relinquish the attempt." The Mississippians were sent back to their reserve position, William Pitt Chambers writing that "we left our dead across the creek, but brought most of the wounded away." Nevertheless, later when the 17th Louisiana needed support on the right, four companies of the 46th Mississippi moved up on the right side of the road. There was also some small movement of the 4th Mississippi, mainly rearward when Confederate artillery rounds fell among their ranks. One Indianan later claimed to have captured the regiment's flag in the confusion.[39]

Throughout the fading afternoon, similarly small but probing Federal movements also took place, including a thrust near the road where one regiment of Stephen Burbridge's brigade of A. J. Smith's division moved through a gap in the woods to exploit an advantage: "The firing continued at irregular intervals along the line for some time afterward, but the indications plainly proved that they were only covering a rapid retreat." Orders similarly arrived for Benton's entire brigade to move to the left to support Osterhaus, but just as quickly Grant countermanded the order. Benton's Federals remained on the Rodney Road, although they occasionally moved again, one time immediately after "the men had just lighted their camp-fires to prepare some supper."[40]

But the overwhelming numbers of Federals ultimately told, as by that time McClernand had a grand total of six brigades in three divisions plus Logan's single brigade on the Rodney Road, far too many for all to get into the action. The artillery that accompanied them, despite delays in getting to the field, also soon congregated and overpowered the Confederate defense. Bowen himself lamented that "I hoped I could hold it until dark," but "I was reluctantly compelled to fall back." He did so even as Green was pulling back on the Bruinsburg Road to the north. The small Confederate force that had put up such a daylong fight was now in full retreat toward Bayou Pierre and the critical bridges across it.[41]

"It was a terrible Mayfestival," one German in the 23rd Indiana wrote home, but it was finally over. "The shades of night soon after closed upon the stricken field," John McClernand explained, "which the valor of our men had won and held, and upon which they found their first repose since they had left D'Schron's Landing, twenty-four hours before." There was no corresponding rest for the wearied Confederates. Each wing of Bowen's little army soon withdrew near dark, Bowen having issued orders that all cross Bayou Pierre at the railroad and suspension bridge. Green's troops led the way "about half an hour before sundown," followed by Garrott's Alabamians and then Cockrell's Missourians from the far left. The brigades crossed at the railroad bridge and suspension bridge and took a position to hold the crossing point of Bayou Pierre, burning the railroad bridge and what one Confederate described as "one of the finest suspension bridges I ever saw." Baldwin remained in rear to cover the withdrawal, but upon marching toward the bayou he observed the railroad bridge on fire in the growing twilight and assumed it was the suspension bridge—his way across. He therefore moved through Port Gibson and crossed the lower branch of the bayou there, destroying that bridge and setting fire to the one at Grindstone Ford farther north before heading west to rejoin Bowen's command at the railroad bridge. The path through Port Gibson was, Baldwin reported, "the route I had come in the morning."[42]

It was a chaotic retreat for Baldwin's troops, one Mississippian describing how their rations sent out from Vicksburg finally arrived in town and that the people "had them prepared for us; but we marched through town without making any halt." And they were not the only ones moving northward. He added that "whole families were flying, they knew not where, while delicately nurtured ladies, implored us by endearing epithets, to save them from the hands of the foe. My eyes filled more than once as I marched by seemingly unheeding these tearful appeals." He gave five dollars to a slave boy for three hens and during a halt once across the bayou cooked one of them: "It was certainly the *toughest* chicken I ever tried to eat."[43]

In the midst of leading the fight himself throughout the afternoon, Bowen continued to report his situation to Pemberton, who responded that reinforcements under Loring and ammunition were on the way but "you had better whip them before he reaches you." At 3:00 p.m. Bowen updated his commander that "I still hold my position. . . . They are pressing me hard on the right. My center is firm; the left is weak." He added, "When can Loring get here?" Later around dark he indicated that he was falling back across Bayou Pierre, saving all the provisions he could, although some would have to be burned. He also added that once the enemy took the town all communication would be cut by telegraph. That brought a panicked response from an obviously out-of-touch Pemberton, who at one point wrote, "is it not probable that the enemy will himself retire to-night?" He also took exception to Bowen falling back behind Bayou Pierre, writing that "you said this evening you would fight him on the other side of Bayou Pierre. Why have you changed your mind? . . . You ought to attack before he can greatly increase his strength." Perhaps Bowen just rolled his eyes at the response, thinking Pemberton should come and do it himself if he wanted it done.[44]

The results of the day's fighting were not totally evident right away, however, although in retrospect it is clear that the battle "secured Grant's beachhead on Mississippi soil," according to historian Terry Winschel; it also doomed Grand Gulf. But the soldiers at the time had trouble seeing through the confusion, not even knowing if the next day would bring a second day of battle. One Alabamian related that it was "not a great victory achieved by either side." For his part, Grant knew he had his old friend Bowen in a tight spot and ordered McClernand to "push the enemy, with skirmishers well thrown out, until it gets too dark to see him." Skirmishing continued as dark shrouded the field, although the Federals found it hard to advance on the now combined road toward Port Gibson; Colonel Daniel Macauley of the 11th Indiana noted that he "awaited a chance to get in, there being here but one road, and it filled with troops at a halt." The Federals continued the advance nevertheless, John Stevenson of Logan's division describing how even closer to Port Gibson the Confederates made a stand: "My line was instantly formed, and the fire returned, which caused the enemy to again retreat precipitately." One of his soldiers similarly described "scratching our way through one of the thickest canebrakes I ever seen." The Federals left off the pursuit nearer the town, a thankful Baldwin writing that "they allowed us to continue our march undisturbed." By then, almost all had stopped the advance and sought any rest they could find: "Our men sank exhausted upon the ground. They had marched all night and fought all day under a burning sun, and without having had a mouthful to eat since the previous evening." Charles Wilcox of the 33rd Illinois related that "we return to the field, stack our arms on the line of battle and lie down to sleep, and oh, how thankful we are, for we have slept but about four hours within the last sixty." But an Iowan explained that no fires were allowed, griping that "nothing is as cheerless as a bivouac without a fire."[45]

Still, the Federals were jubilant. The "rebs rather got whipped," explained one Ohioan in his diary; another termed it "a good thrashing." An Illinoisan informed his wife "we have met the scoundrels and thrashed them well." Wilcox added, "we don't know our whole success, but we know this, that we drove the enemy in every close contact." Colonel Marcus Spiegel of the 120th Ohio related that his regiment "had nothing more to do than to exult, cheer, and be merry, and that I assure you was done." Hovey again claimed that "the honor of repulsing the enemy at this point unquestionably belongs to the batteries of the Twelfth Division." McClernand similarly crowed that Port Gibson was "one of the most admirably and successfully fought battles in which it has been my lot to participate since the present unhappy war commenced." German division commander Peter Osterhaus nearly picked up one of his colonels and yelled to his troops: "Vell, boys, I dells you vat it is: you do as vell tomorrow as you does today and we whip dem repels undil they can't eat sauerkraut!" Perhaps the happiest man in the Union army was Job Yaggy of the 124th Illinois: "I picked up a pair of new drawers which the rebels had left and put them on."[46]

But it is clear that the Federal advance, with such harsh terrain, had been limited and sporadic. Brigades jumbled together and stacked up rather than moving forward against what could only be described as light Confederate resistance. That an entire corps and another partial division could not sweep away sixteen small Confederate regiments with only a handful of artillery pieces perhaps said more about the gun-shy Federal command (especially Osterhaus on the Bruinsburg Road) than the terrain itself, although the latter was certainly an issue. McClernand himself gave note to the "insurmountable obstacles in the nature of the ground and . . . exposure to the fire of the enemy." Grant likewise explained the delay, writing that the terrain was "the most broken country I ever saw. The whole country is a series of irregular ridges, divided by deep and impassable ravines, grown up with heavy timber, undergrowth, and cane. It was impossible to engage any considerable portion of our forces at any one time."[47]

Union and Confederate surgeons alike worked together on the battlefield to tend to the resulting carnage, not always agreeing on the best procedures. Brush arbors went up to house the wounded. At times, mystifying results were also mind-boggling, one steward reporting the arrival of a dead Iowan: "Could find no mark on him, shock to the heart, likely." Casualties for the Federals totaled 875, including 131 killed, 719 wounded, and 25 missing. The vast majority were in McClernand's XIII Corps, with Carr, Hovey, and Osterhaus having two or three hundred casualties each. Confederate losses totaled 384 according to Bowen, certainly a low number. But the battle was significant, although not in the manner of deciding anything per se. There was still a long road to Vicksburg for the Federals, across two major waterways in fact. And resistance would no doubt increase the closer they came, certainly more so than the paltry four small brigades Pemberton managed to get into action south of Bayou Pierre. Rather, the significance of the battle was that the Federal landing, unopposed at the river itself and then at the bluffs inland, was finally resisted ten or fifteen miles eastward, where it was too late. And the resounding Union victory, although of tepid nature despite Pemberton himself describing it as "disastrous in its results," solidified the toehold Grant now had on the east side of the Mississippi River. John McClernand himself admitted that, "if not a decisive battle" itself, it set the stage for the forward movement and the coming campaign farther into the wilds of Mississippi.[48]

And that would come quickly: even as Grant called off the fighting that night ("further pursuit in the dark was not deemed prudent or advisable"), Grant's orders to McClernand at dusk on May 1 were to "renew the attack at early dawn." He hoped to get the bridges across Bayou Pierre intact, later admitting that "crossing a stream in the presence of an enemy is always difficult." But it would be worth the end result, one Illinoisan scribbling in his diary that "in a few days Vicksburg too must succumb to the valor of the Grand Army under the command of the invincible *Grant*."[49]

5

"I Suppose Grant Knows Where He Is Taking Us"

May 2

Colonel William M. Stone of the 22nd Iowa was in a reflective mood as he wrote out his report of the fighting the day before at Port Gibson. He noted that the enemy "were gathered from several States, and were led by a general who fought us at the memorable battle of Shiloh, over one year ago." Stone had actually been at that fight, not as a member of the 22nd Iowa but of the 3rd Iowa. "We met them again upon more equal terms," he continued, "and in a contest as fierce as Shiloh, considering the numbers engaged."[1]

But Stone had an even more unique perspective as he looked not just behind but also in larger context to the path ahead. He had actually been captured at Shiloh and run through Mississippi as a prisoner. "One year ago I passed through the State of Mississippi a prisoner of war," he recalled, "on my way to a Southern prison. Now I am marching with a victorious army, with my former captors fleeing before us, seeking shelter beyond the reach of our heroic columns. Such is the change that has come over the cherished plans and bright visions of the men who are endeavoring to destroy the nationality of our people."[2]

Yet the spring campaigning in 1863 took even larger form than just at Port Gibson or Stone's contextual approach, as important as that fighting was the day before. With the victory at Port Gibson on May 1, Grant was east of the river for good. No longer could the army be hurled back into the water or hamstrung by that obstacle. Defeat could still come, but if so it would likely be in a regular pitched battle, not with the river affecting it in any way except perhaps in the movement of supplies. Grant even quipped of his army to Julia that "before they are beaten they will be very badly beaten." The emphasis was accordingly on the future, not the past.[3]

There were other operations ongoing as well, including those tangential to the main Vicksburg effort. Benjamin Grierson would arrive in Baton Rouge this day, concluding his monumental and significant raid through the heart of Mississippi. It was this raid, of course, that had largely allowed Grant such an easy passage over the Mississippi River. Colonel Abel Streight's "Mule March" was also proceeding but, unlike Grierson's raid, heading for disaster. There was also skirmishing in Tennessee and western Virginia.[4]

But the most famous fighting this day took place at Chancellorsville outside Fredericksburg, Virginia. After pushing across the Rapidan River to the small crossroads of Chancellorsville, Major General Joseph Hooker stalled his advance and General Robert E. Lee acted. This was the famous day when Lieutenant General Thomas "Stonewall" Jackson made his march around the flank of the Union army. Attacking near nightfall, Jackson drove back the Union XI Corps in a stunning surprise attack that netted a lot of territory, mostly in Hooker's fearful mind. By the end of the near disaster, Hooker would be on the defensive for good and would soon withdraw back northward across the river, handing Lee one of the most stunning victories of the war.[5]

Yet this success came at a severe cost. Amid the chaos and confusion of the darkening landscape, Jackson perhaps unwisely scouted ahead of his lines and fell terribly wounded on his return, the result of confused friendly fire. He would live through the initial wounds, despite having his left arm amputated; amid the initial shock to the army, Lee admitted that "he has lost his left arm; but I have lost my right." Worse for the Confederates, other major commanders such as Major General Ambrose P. Hill were also wounded in the fighting, at one point leaving Jackson's entire corps under the command of cavalryman Major General J. E. B. Stuart. Adding the fact that Lee had divided his army multiple times to pull off the victory, he was nevertheless in a very dangerous spot. Only Hooker's fear and timidity saved a potential disaster in the making for Lee, and the net result was a victorious though severely battered Confederate army holding the line to Richmond.[6]

That same timidity and confusion was also seen in the expanding Mississippi operations on this May 2, although news of the Virginia battle would be days in arriving out West. But the chaos rested on the opposite side out in Mississippi. South of Vicksburg, a confident Union general, opposite from in Virginia, planned his advance while his timid and confused Confederate counterpart, anything but Lee-like in Virginia, would dawdle to near disaster. But the major difference was that, unlike the soon-calming actions in

Virginia, those overshadowed events in Mississippi were just starting to gather momentum as Grant began his movement across Bayou Pierre and northward toward Vicksburg.[7]

Very much unlike his counterpart in Virginia, Ulysses S. Grant pushed on deeper into Confederate territory on May 2. "I suppose Grant knows where he is taking us to," one Ohioan lamented in his diary that day, "for we don't." Grant's forces, four divisions of McClernand's XIII Corps and one of McPherson's XVII Corps, had halted around dark the day before well short of Port Gibson itself; fires were not permitted being so close to the enemy. But they were on the move early the next morning, pushing forward into town and more important to the various crossings of Bayou Pierre. Yet the advance was complicated partly because of Confederate resistance and partly because of Federal nervousness, several mentioning a false alarm during the night in which many thought the Confederates were still there and on the attack. "At 3 o'clock this morning the pickets discharged their pcs and rushed into camp," one Federal wrote. "It proved, however, to be a false alarm." More significant was the fact that Bayou Pierre split into two major branches as it neared Port Gibson, the town sitting just south of the southernmost fork. There were as a result numerous places for a Confederate defense, perhaps even on the lower fork at the town itself. Then there was another branch just as substantial to the north, making multiple crossings necessary.[8]

Grant pushed forward nonetheless on the morning of May 2 after what McClernand termed "the fugitive enemy," making the final trek into a now-evacuated Port Gibson. "We commenced hunting for the enemy," one Illinoisan explained. The road was littered with items thrown away by the retreating Confederates, Colonel Theodore E. Buehler of the 67th Indiana remarking that with his troops "finding arms and clothing scattered in every direction, it soon became evident that the rebels had left for a healthier clime." Also up ahead, according to one Ohioan, was a group of women led by the mayor's wife who wanted to formally surrender the town; the mayor had been wounded in the fighting and could not perform the duty himself. McClernand noted that his troops, Smith's division leading "and followed by the rest of my corps, triumphantly entered Port Gibson." Stephen Burbridge's brigade was first into town, he writing that "I had the pleasure of raising the Stars and Stripes to their wonted place of honor." The flag accordingly flew high atop the county courthouse. Colonel Joshua J. Guppey of the 23rd Wisconsin noted that his had "the honor of being the first regiment which entered the city, and which gave the first cheer for our national flag, raised over it by General Burbridge."[9]

As soon as McClernand arrived and took possession of Port Gibson, he sent a staff officer back to inform Grant. Lieutenant Colonel Henry Warmoth rode to the rear but could not find Grant; he wandered around the battlefield a while before heading back to Port Gibson by another route, still looking for the commander. By the time he found Grant he was back in Port Gibson itself, where he humorously delivered his message: "Genl. Grant, I am sent by Genl. McClernand to inform you that we have Port Gibson." Warmoth added, "he was surrounded by a good many officers. It was thought very funny." But not all was humorous, as Grant was apparently seething at some of McClernand's antics from the day before. The speeches were one thing, but Grant's order to conserve as much artillery ammunition as possible, given the tense supply situation, allegedly garnered a response from McClernand that "he was the one fighting the battle and would use whatever ammunition he believed was appropriate." On top of the rations issue on April 30, Grant was getting more and more disgruntled with McClernand.[10]

But Grant now had Port Gibson, with a lot of McClernand's help whether he liked it or not. "It is a beautiful little town," one Federal scribbled in his diary, William T. Rigby of the 24th Iowa noting that the clock on the Presbyterian church in town, with the hand pointing heavenward, struck 8:00 a.m. as they passed that morning. Many of the people, along with the influx of refugees escaping from Grierson's Raid to the east, had left town, and the 45th Illinois sang the "Battle Cry of Freedom" as they moved through the empty streets. Contrary to popular belief that Grant burned every village he went through except Port Gibson, which was later labeled "too beautiful to burn," Grant rarely burned any of the towns his troops passed through. Grant, in fact, later wrote that the local people "all seem to stay at home and show less signs of fear than one would suppose. These people talk a greatdeal about the barbarities of the Yankees but I hear no complaints where the Army has been of even insults having been offered." One Federal even related that the citizens of Port Gibson "was very clever while we stayed there accommodated us in every way that they could." That said, as more regiments poured in Grant had to check McClernand's troops, one Federal admitting that the "boys jerked every thing they wanted from the stores." Grant wrote the corps commander to "place Guards immediately about the town and require troops to be kept near their colors. The men are now running riot in the most disorderly manner." One Illinoisan admitted that the "citizens would like very much to have us leave as soon as convenient." He then observed: "The war is sitting a little more heavily on the chivalry now than it ever has; we are not guarding their property and driving their negroes home as much as we 'was.' The boys have great times taking bacon, sugar, molasses, and whatever they can get from the old secesh, while they stand around begging like culprits to be left alone." Other places were also taken over, including a printing office for "getting out blanks," or paroles for those captured. Soldiers signed notes from the bank, and those who were "a private of yesterday [and] a bank president to-day," one Ohioan noted, stashed the banknotes for future use when "it is not at all likely that it will be refused by the inhabitant along the route." In the hotel where many of the wounded were collected was, according to another Federal, "the Rebel Gen. Tracy's corpse on the floor in the hospital, covered with a sheet."[11]

Beautiful though Port Gibson was, Grant's more important concerns were the bridges over Bayou Pierre, mainly the one just north of town itself, which McClernand's troops quickly found on fire. Members of the 67th Indiana rushed to the site but "once reaching it were saluted by a few shots from rebel pickets on the other side." The Indianans tried to extinguish the flames, but "after a few hours of futile labor, they were ordered to desist." All the Federals could do was watch "the fine suspension bridge" as it burned and fell into the muddy waters of the bayou. Brigade after brigade thus stacked up in town as the rebuilding process began: "We were formed into column in the streets and lay down to rest," one Indianan explained. Unfortunately, one Federal scared up a skunk in town that "began to circulate its perfumery promiscuously, making the men jump up and gasp for breath and scattering them in every direction and almost every man set up the yell which passed from one Regiment to another all through the Division which astonished the natives or as the general expressed it next morning he thought the Devil had broke loose amongst us."[12]

With the floor of the suspension bridge completely burned out, work soon began on building another crossing, the engineers at work covered by skirmishers sent out to deflect attention. Grant's engineer, James H. Wilson, who had overseen the Yazoo Pass expedition, took the lead in rebuilding the bridge, Grant writing that Wilson was "going into the water and working as hard as any one engaged." Assisting him were Logan's division engineer, Captain Stewart R. Tresilian, and the division's pioneer corps under Captain William F. Patterson. "Not needing a permanent structure," Wilson explained, "it was determined to construct a raft bridge." Work began about twenty yards upstream from the suspension bridge, and he added that "buoyant materials in abundance were obtained by tearing down the buildings, cotton gins, &c., in the vicinity." Wilson asked McClernand repeatedly for infantry to do the literal heavy lifting, and although promised, it was hours before they arrived around noon. And at least one Ohioan explained that a trial run with an artillery piece and four mules tipped over the initial structure and all went into the bayou. Strengthening then occurred. Still, by four o'clock that afternoon, after troops worked for several hours, the new structure—168 feet long, including corduroyed approaches—was complete and ready for the Federals to utilize in leaping the south fork of Bayou Pierre, which was actually only about five feet deep and with a "very gentle current." A proud Tresilian noted that there was "not one stick of timber to commence operations with until some houses in the vicinity were torn down and carried by the men over a distance of 100 yards." The army then started moving across, with Grant himself sitting his horse on the bank watching, urging "men, push right along; close up fast, and hurry over." More tense moments came when artillery batteries crossed and submerged parts of the bridge at times with the heavy guns. Yet eventually "the entire army crossed with perfect safety," producing a scene, of all scenes to pick from, that made the cover of the June 13 issue of *Harper's Weekly*. In the meantime, other troops fanned out to the outskirts of town to defend against any marauding Confederates, Stephen Burbridge explaining that "I was ordered to take my brigade to the hills back of the town, as there were symptoms of the enemy coming in on our rear."[13]

There were other diversions going on as well by this time. McClernand led the way into Port Gibson with Smith's and Carr's divisions, the latter gaining a brand-new, just-arrived Brigadier General Michael K. Lawler to take over the Iowa brigade ("a good brigade and well officered," he wrote) that had changed hands frequently over the last two days. McPherson's troops followed. Logan's division had engaged in the battle the day before, but Sanborn's division was likewise east of the river now and proceeding northeastward, although command issues still plagued it. The commander who had led it into Yazoo Pass, Brigadier General Isaac F. Quinby, had fallen ill, and since that time Colonel John Sanborn, one of the brigade commanders, had led the division. Sanborn reported his division's arrival to Grant personally, but Sanborn would not remain in command long. Grant knew Sanborn was a good commander, but he was "senior of the twelve colonels in the division," and having a colonel in command of a division was problematic. Grant quickly brought in Brigadier General Marcellus M. Crocker from commanding a brigade in John McArthur's XVII Corps division to take command, he doing so at noon on May 2. Sanborn returned to command of his brigade, although Crocker himself was sickly. But Grant noted that "his weak condition never put him on the sick report when there was a battle in prospect, as long as he could keep on his feet."[14]

Worse for Sanborn was the arrival of visitors to his meager mess. He later related how, as the brigade waited for servants to prepare the meal, up came Crocker with his staff, without food. They joined in, but right in the middle of it also arrived McPherson and his staff, also without food. Then Grant and his staff arrived as well, Sanborn hosting all of them. Somehow, the cooks managed to provide enough food for all.[15]

Also concerning Grant at this time was the sudden arrival of his twelve-year old son, Fred, whom he had left back at Bruinsburg with the hopes that he would stay with the navy until he could get to an occupied (and safe) Grand Gulf. In fact, Grant had asked Major General Lorenzo Thomas to keep him there, but Fred "join[ed] a party in chasing a rabbit on the land, and I took advantage of that permission to push my investigations over the hills." He eventually fell in with another seeming orphan, Charles Dana, and Fred spent a wild day wandering around the gut-wrenching battlefield, lying down to sleep as "the most woe-begone twelve-year-old in America." Neither he nor Dana had horses until they came across two old dilapidated ones, Grant recalling that "the first time I call to mind seeing either of them, after the battle, they were mounted on two enormous horses, grown white from age, each equipped with dilapidated saddles and bridles." Fred soon went his own way, but Grant offered a captured horse to Dana despite the owner arguing that it was his personal property, not the Confederacy's. Grant quipped that he had several horses "wandering somewhere about the Southern Confederacy" and that the officer could have one of those in return if he found one, but as for this horse, "I think he is just about the horse Mr. Dana needs." Dana later related that "whenever I went out with General Grant anywhere he always had some question to ask about that horse." Grant was more concerned about Fred, however, and was not at all happy with him moving inland. "In after years," Fred related later, "he often told the story of my following him on the battlefield of Port Gibson with more interest and satisfaction than he manifested to me at that time." As for his own personal transportation, Grant crossed without a horse as well but fortunately came across A. J. Smith at Bruinsburg, who had managed to capture a couple of animals. He gave one to Grant, and he rode the animal with only simple tack for the next few days. "I had no facilities for even preparing a meal," Grant noted, later saying he carried with him only a toothbrush across the river. The newspaper correspondent Sylvanus Cadwallader, who traveled with the army, noted that the reports of his "having no baggage but a toothbrush, are so literally true that no exaggeration is possible."[16]

From "a little house of the village" Grant saw to these administrative and personal issues, but his biggest concern was up at the head of the army. At the front, Grant ordered McPherson to send brigades different directions to locate additional crossing points while the bridge-building process continued. Mainly, Grant wanted "a strong brigade" to move three or four miles up the bayou to a ford, guided by "the black boy sent herewith." He added, "let the brigade push across the bayou and attack in flank the enemy, now in full retreat through Willow Springs, demoralized and out of ammunition." To make sure the job was done right, he stipulated, "General John E. Smith with his brigade, will execute this order."[17]

Smith did so, followed by another brigade of the division—Brigadier General Elias Dennis's, who was a temporary commander while the regular brigadier, Mortimer D. Leggett, was absent up north. The two brigades moved up the bayou four miles "under the guidance of a negro," James H. Wilson explained, and crossed at Askamalla Ford before heading back along the opposite bank. One Illinoisan described how they were "halted, ordered to strip off our clothing and wade the stream, which we did." Little skirmishing erupted, the Confederates knowing what was happening and already having fallen back behind the north fork of the bayou. Still, Smith's presence in force between the two forks was a positive development as all waited for the bridge to be rebuilt so the divisions could start their way northward. Even better, Smith's troops found nearly four tons of bacon near where he stopped on the main road north to Willow Springs near Lucknow, the plantation home of Confederate Colonel Benjamin G. Humphreys of the 21st Mississippi, even then engaged at Chancellorsville in Virginia. Smith admitted, "this proved a valuable acquisition to our limited supplies," and a common soldier was candid enough to admit that it "was a great releaf to our soldiers for the most of us was giting very short of rations as we had drawed no rations since we left the river and in the fight nearly half the men lost their haversacks." In addition, one particularly fortunate Ohioan found "a coffee pot full of gold and silver." But not everyone was happy with the hard march, one Ohioan remarking a little too loudly when Colonel Manning F. Force gave the order to move on, "he must be a hard-hearted man." Force recalled that he heard him "think aloud."[18]

In the meantime, Federal troops also moved to the west of Port Gibson, they being John D. Stevenson's brigade of Logan's division. Logan himself was along as well, moving to the main Grand Gulf Road while units of Carr's division reached the railroad bridge across the bayou below where the forks split. Also along on that trek was Fred Grant, Logan having invited him: "Come, my boy, and I will show you the prettiest fight you will ever see." Grant also ordered McClernand to send part of his corps westward, as some of the force moving that direction had "run into an Alabama regiment." He

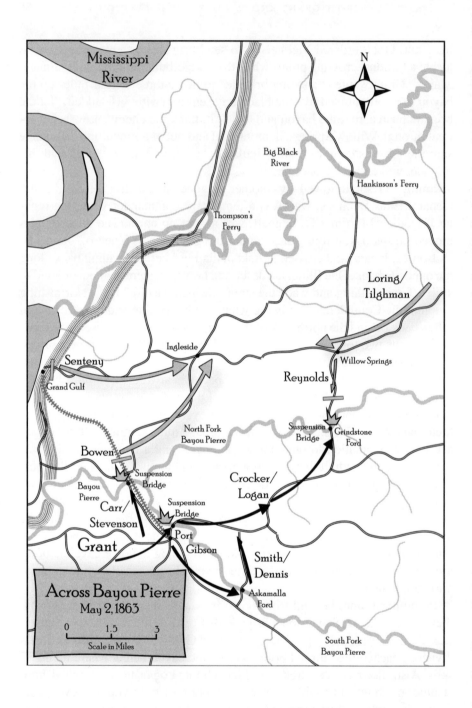

Across Bayou Pierre
May 2, 1863

0   1.5   3
Scale in Miles

was concerned that "the enemy may be practising a sharp game to get in our rear, with a force to distroy all we have." Once at the bridge site, the 7th Missouri of Stevenson's brigade fanned out and took a position on the edge of the bank to perhaps move across or, as Grant said, to "occupy his attention" while the main force moved to the east. The Confederates of Cockrell's brigade had burned the railroad bridge as well, but as Carr's following Federals arrived he threw skirmishers across "on the burning ruins of the railroad bridge, and found that the enemy had retreated." As a result of all the maneuvering, Grant soon had at least three good crossing points on the combined bayou or south fork.[19]

Still, once the bridge at the town became operational the major remaining impediment was the north fork of the bayou, which Grant pressed on toward in the "excessive heat," one Indianan related. The newly arrived division of the XVII Corps now under Marcellus Crocker led the way and "marched 8 miles to [the] north fork of Bayou Pierre." Proceeding northward on one of the main roads leading toward Willow Springs, the Federals found another nice new suspension bridge aflame at Grindstone Ford, "a fine structure" in McPherson's description. Colonel Force, leading the 20th Ohio, noted that his skirmishers reached the bayou even as "a scouting party of the enemy was in the act of destroying the bridge." This time the troops "and a few negroes from the plantation nearby" were able to put out the fire despite it damaging the structure, at the cost of one man "who fell into the river, and is supposed to be killed." By this time nightfall had come, but Grant himself was on site and ordered work commenced and continued all night to have it ready for crossing the next morning. Skirmishers from Colonel George B. Boomer's brigade and even some artillery somehow forded the stream and held the opposite shore while the pioneers worked. In the meantime, Grant also ordered units to guard the roadways to the rear, mainly those between the two forks of the bayou, covering both the crossing at the railroad bridge on the main road to Grand Gulf as well as the new bridge at Port Gibson. After all, this route was still the pathway for reinforcements and supplies, so Grant wanted no chances taken even as he planned to surge on ahead and get across the last remaining barrier to an advance, the north fork of Bayou Pierre.[20]

"I think [the] enemy has landed nearly his whole force on this side," a worried John Pemberton informed Jefferson Davis on May 2. But the news quickly got worse. He added that Bowen had fought all the day before south of Bayou Pierre, Pemberton reminding the president that "you know the country about Port Gibson and approaches to Vicksburg and Jackson." But the last he had heard from Bowen was the evening before, Bowen's 5:30 p.m. message that he was falling back behind Bayou Pierre. The news caused a flurry of activity, including removing records from Jackson and shifting the department office totally to Vicksburg, including furniture and office supplies. Pemberton also dissolved court-martial cases to meet the crisis head-on.[21]

The obvious question in Vicksburg was where Bowen was behind Bayou Pierre. If he was north of Port Gibson, between Bayou Pierre and the ferries on the Big Black River, then communication should still be available with Vicksburg and he could simply retreat along that line of communication and supply in safety. But if Bowen had fallen back to Grand Gulf, "which is reported," Pemberton added, he saw innumerable problems. He labeled Grand Gulf as "a *cul de sac*," hemmed in by Bayou Pierre to the south, the Mississippi River to the west, and the Big Black River to the north. The only way in and out was east, and if Bowen fell back to Grand Gulf that would leave nothing to stop a Federal movement to the Big Black River to cut that escape route; Bowen would be hemmed in and have to surrender. That is why holding the Federals south of the north fork of Bayou Pierre was so important. If Bowen had gone to Grand Gulf, Pemberton informed Davis, "he must endeavor to cross Big Black, destroying his guns and stores." Ironically, it was the very same situation Pemberton himself was in, only with Confederate Western Theater commander General Joseph E. Johnston telling him to get out of the trap that was Vicksburg.[22]

With such spotty information, Pemberton scrambled to make sense of everything, some rumors even pointing to a Confederate victory the day before: "We got the best of it," one Georgian wrote home, another Confederate stating more accurately that General Tracy had fallen and Bowen had four horses shot from under him. In addition, Pemberton was still receiving reports of Grierson's trek, Major General Franklin Gardner at Port Hudson affirming that the "enemy's raid has successfully passed to Baton Rouge." Pemberton rightfully worried about communication with Port Hudson if Bowen was forced back, telling Gardner that "Bowen is hard pressed." Additional news of more Federal raids in northern Mississippi also arrived.[23]

Pemberton had to make some quick decisions, but being indecisive by nature he called a council of war whereby it was determined to give up Grand Gulf if it was not already taken. He sent word to Bowen of the decision. Obviously, Bowen's troops, important as they were, constituted only a fraction of Pemberton's total command, so he also kept the larger picture in mind. He similarly contemplated abandoning Port Hudson, but he was determined to defend Vicksburg. He asked Davis to send at least a million rounds of ammunition, "principally caliber .69," and he also began to concentrate his troops for the coming fight. "The battle will probably be fought outside of Vicksburg," he informed the president. "I am concentrating all I can."[24]

The assurance of concentration was somewhat misleading, however. Pemberton was already sending troops southward to aid Bowen, although in pitifully small fractions. In all, he sent a mere two regiments at first under Major General William Loring and Brigadier General Lloyd Tilghman, mainly to cover Bowen's withdrawal if he was still at Grand Gulf or to reinforce him if he was around the Big Black ferries. "Proceed at once to Port Gibson" were Loring's orders. Later, when word came that the Federals were crossing Bayou Pierre east of Grand Gulf, Tilghman's orders were to "move as rapidly as possible to Grindstone Ford [on the north fork] and hold it at all hazards." Either way, Grand Gulf was untenable and would have to be sacrificed; Pemberton just hoped that the troops would not be included in the offering. In fact, the crisis was so acute that Pemberton started other troops southward as well, eventually the entirety of Carter Stevenson's division: Colonel Alexander W. Reynolds's Tennessee brigade even crossed the Big Black River but became mixed up and did little fighting, while Brigadier Generals Thomas H. Taylor's and Seth Barton's troops remained north of the river. Nevertheless, historians such as Ed Bearss have reflected that the Confederates missed a golden opportunity to pounce on isolated parts of the XVII Corps at this point. Pemberton's determination to remain in Vicksburg obviously removed a central head directing affairs.[25]

Pemberton's more accurate meaning of concentration was department-wide. "I shall concentrate all the troops I can," he assured Davis, "but distances are great." He nevertheless began to call in all troops in his department who could conceivably be spared, ordering them to the Vicksburg and Jackson area rather than Grand Gulf or Port Gibson. By this point, Pemberton had given up on a defense farther south and decided to make his stand along the railroad running from Vicksburg to Jackson. In mentioning the evacuation of Grand Gulf and even of Port Hudson, Pemberton argued that "the whole force [should be] concentrated for defense of Vicksburg and Jackson." He added that his special concern was "to keep railroad communications, on which our supplies depend." He had an average of thirty days' supplies at Vicksburg and wanted more, but continual railroad problems, including derailments, cut into efficiency.[26]

The heavy concentration toward Vicksburg and Jackson began on May 2 and 3 and saw troops from all across Pemberton's department redeploy to the area. And on this matter even Pemberton and Johnston agreed, Johnston writing from Tullahoma, Tennessee, "if Grant crosses, unite all your troops to beat him. Success will give back what was abandoned to win it." But Johnston's message was old, outdated, and tinged with ire. Obviously, Grant had already crossed, and the time to meet him per Johnston's ideas had been on May 1 or earlier nearer to Port Gibson. Pemberton had tried and failed, although it was not much of a concentration. At the same time, Johnston most likely meant giving up Vicksburg temporarily to win the success via concentration, something he had been urging all along. Pemberton chose not to do so.[27]

But Pemberton did concentrate nearer to Vicksburg, especially along the rail line to Jackson. He was acutely concerned for the railroad bridge over the Big Black River, so nearby Edwards Station became an obvious staging area. He began to call in troops from north and east, including all guards along the Mississippi Central Railroad north of Jackson. Soon, Brigadier General Winfield S. Featherston's entire brigade situated near Grenada was called into Vicksburg by forced march, one of his Mississippians complaining that "he has no humanity about him, his head is as flat on top as an African negro's and he's as mean as the devil wants him to be." Those troops east of Jackson also began to move westward, including Brigadier General Abraham Buford's brigade at Meridian, Buford being told to "urge the citizens to arm themselves" in order to defend the railroads from reported new Union raids from the north. But Buford was needed worse to the west, Pemberton telling him personally to "bring all your force immediately to Vicksburg. Use all possible haste." Even unarmed exchanged prisoners of war were rounded up and arms sought for them.[28]

Yet Pemberton's immediate concern was to salvage Bowen's troops even if he could not rescue Grand Gulf itself. In sending Loring and Tilghman southward, Pemberton told them that Bowen "is represented as having fallen back to Grand Gulf, and the road is open to enemy." He accordingly warned the two generals to be on the lookout for an approaching Federal force, especially once across the Big Black River. He authorized them to fall back behind that river to use it for a defense if necessary, but his real goal was to extricate Bowen from the cul-de-sac if he was still in it. But that was the problem: Pemberton could not contact Bowen despite repeated messages, ultimately telling him that "you must endeavor to cross Big Black, abandoning Grand Gulf, and destroying guns, ammunition, and stores."[29]

Finally, mercifully, Bowen responded, although the message only arrived at Pemberton's headquarters early on May 3. But it was exactly what Pemberton wanted to hear. Bowen reported that he had initially fallen back toward Grand Gulf, one of his Alabamians describing how they "fell back a mile or two day over to day rambled around as near the battle field as possible." But Bowen added that Grant was bridging Bayou Pierre and moving to cut him off along the Jackson Road. "Should they reach the junction before me," he wrote, "I will be completely cut off and invested." Given that he was out of supplies and that Grant's army "is at least five times as large as my command," Bowen had already determined to withdraw northward but "put off doing so" until Loring could arrive. Loring and Tilghman, having moved south through Rocky Springs and depending on citizens for information as to what was going on, fortunately soon showed up at Bowen's position on Bayou Pierre west of Grand Gulf itself about 11:00 p.m. on May 2, having scattered the troops they brought with them farther forward to keep open the escape route, namely sending Tilghman's two regiments (15th and 26th Mississippi) to Grindstone Ford itself. "Upon my laying all the facts in my possession before them," Bowen continued, "they are of opinion that my only hope is in the proposed move." Since Loring outranked Bowen, he took overall command once Bowen ordered the troops northward (Loring "declined to assume command of the troops"), advising Pemberton to communicate with him via Rocky Springs along the road to Jackson. Hopefully, Loring and Bowen could get ahead of the surging Federal army before the trap shut and make it to safety. "My only fear is that I may be too late," Bowen admitted.[30]

The work of destruction soon began at Grand Gulf itself during the night of May 2, all while Bowen marched his command of several brigades northward toward the junction with the main roads to Vicksburg and Jackson. He explained how "the time for each command to move being fixed as to avoid any delay or confusion when the several commands from their respective positions should meet on the main road." The movement somehow went off like clockwork. Joining the column on the way were those who had been left at Grand Gulf itself. While initially keeping most of his command from Port Gibson at the railroad bridge across Bayou Pierre, Bowen had left Lieutenant Colonel Pembroke S. Senteny's 2nd Missouri in Grand Gulf, and they withdrew from the fortifications there during the night. But the Missourians destroyed as much as possible before leaving, including spiking the guns that remained and blowing up three different magazines that held ammunition (heard all the way up the river by Sherman's troops) as well as "our tents and a great quantity of our baggage committed to the flames." A few men remained to burn the stores there, but soon Grand Gulf was evacuated and no longer an asset to the Confederates. "We had heavy hearts I assure you," one Missourian lamented, "for we found Grand Gulf the most pleasant place we had ever camped."[31]

Yet with the evacuation of Grand Gulf began another, more problematic effort: escape from behind the surging Federal thrust that all knew was a movement in their rear to capture them. And that is where the smaller scale concentration of troops under Loring and Tilghman became critical, Loring

having left the railroad around Edwards earlier and moved southward, ultimately going all the way to Bowen's position near the railroad bridge with
Tilghman. Also joining the command below was Brigadier General Stephen
D. Lee, who was placed in charge of the Alabama brigade that Edward Tracy
had fought so hard at Port Gibson, dying in the process.[32]

As Loring withdrew, he now being the senior commander on site (Bowen
reported that Loring kept "me with him as a staff officer"), he knew his only
chance was to clear the various crossroads to Hankinson's Ferry before the
Federals arrived from below the north fork of Bayou Pierre. The force consequently marched with gusto, one Mississippian writing that, despite starting
slowly and hearing the magazines at Grand Gulf exploding behind them, "the
command 'close up' was wholly unnecessary." An Alabamian admitted that
they retreated "in quick time though in good order."[33]

Fortunately for the Confederates, there was a holding force to protect
them as they marched. As Grant's divisions moved forward to cut off this
very movement, they would meet Loring's Confederates blocking the routes
northward. Tilghman had brought a couple of regiments with him, and he
and Loring left them near Willow Springs as they moved on to Grand Gulf.
Colonel Arthur E. Reynolds commanded them while the generals were gone,
but soon the withdrawing Grand Gulf garrison arrived on the main road north
during the night and began to file northward to and across the river at Hankinson's Ferry. "We did not stop from the time we started until we crossed on
the pontoon over Big Black River," one Missourian noted. To add force to the
rear guard, Tracy's Alabama brigade, now under Stephen D. Lee, moved to
hold the Willow Springs area while Reynolds's regiments, soon back under
Tilghman, moved westward to hold another critical crossroads at Ingleside.[34]

Meanwhile, back in Vicksburg and almost completely out of touch with the
critical race occurring south of the Big Black River, Pemberton saw to administrative issues, something with which he was much more comfortable. His
commander at Vicksburg, Carter Stevenson, reported a lack of ammunition,
an arriving lot of a hundred and seventy-two thousand cartridges only adding a mere "9 rounds per man for this district." (This explains Pemberton's
message to Davis about more ammunition.) Pemberton also began to order
more supplies into Vicksburg, including cattle still out toward Port Gibson
on the east side of the Big Black River. To make what rations he did have go
further, he also ordered a cut for the Vicksburg garrison: "The meat ration
will be henceforward reduced to one-half pound of bacon and three-quarters
of a pound of beef. Peas and rice must be issued in lieu of the diminution."
Carter Stevenson could certainly see the coming trouble, at one point on
May 2 mentioning "especially as our roads are now subject to interruption."[35]

Comfortable though he was with administrative efforts, Pemberton still realized the dire situation unfolding. Illustrating the critical nature of the threat from below, to which he was already responding by concentrating his troops nearer to Vicksburg, Pemberton also advised others to prepare. To his aide Robert W. Memminger, still in Jackson, he wrote that "the enemy has or is crossing his whole force. It is very likely he will move on Jackson. Be prepared to remove all records eastward." Even more dire, Pemberton also wrote Governor Pettus: "I think it would be well to remove the State archives from Jackson. The enemy has or is crossing nearly his whole force. It is likely he will move on Jackson." Pemberton also ordered others to remove any government machinery eastward into Alabama. But he was not totally giving up on holding Jackson, writing his commander there, Brigadier General John Adams, "I intend to make some intrenchments about Jackson." He also began to order all roving bands of cavalry, no matter how small, to congregate at Raymond to stall a Union advance toward Jackson and to work on the enemy's rear.[36]

It was certainly crisis time at Vicksburg. Major Samuel Lockett, Pemberton's chief engineer, did not like the looks of things and admitted to his wife amid all the bustle, "things are once more looking very squarely." A lower-level Confederate added in his diary: "This is truly an important time in our history."[37]

Quite a lot of Northern brainpower was spent on repairing the north fork Bayou Pierre bridge during that busy night of May 2, including that of Grant's engineer Wilson as well as XVII Corps engineer Captain Andrew Hickenlooper. The latter also mentioned that Grant's staff officer Lieutenant Colonel John A. Rawlins was similarly there helping in addition to Logan's division engineer Captain Tresilian. Most of the damage was on the far side of the bridge, where a few of the crosspieces had been burned in two, but Wilson was able to fabricate a new floor over improvised struts to make it crossable. Infantry soldiers were also detailed to help with the work, namely the 4th Minnesota of Sanborn's brigade, although they were once again late in arriving at 11:30 p.m. All the while, portions of the cavalry force, including Captain John S. Foster's 4th Independent Company Ohio Cavalry, spent the night between the forks "bringing in the stragglers belonging to the Third and Seventh Divisions of the corps."[38]

But getting across Bayou Pierre was not Grant's only concern. By this point he was in contact with his old friend Bowen, who requested "a suspension of hostilities between our forces for the period of twenty-four hours, and extend the usual privilege of burying my dead and looking after my wounded." Bowen at some point apparently also conversed in person with McPherson, his old West Point classmate; only a formal note went to Grant himself. Two Confederate officers brought the message under flag of truce, but Grant was not amiable. Obviously, Bowen needed that much time to ensure his escape, but Grant wisely denied it and kept moving. He wrote his old friend and neighbor from the St. Louis days, "although always ready to extend any consistent courtesy to alleviate suffering I cannot comply with your wish in this matter." He went on: "[A] dispatch now in my possession shows that you are expecting reinforcements and additional munitions of war. I deem therefore the request unreasonable and one you could not expect me to comply with." Bowen's dispatch had been found in the telegraph office in Port Gibson when the town fell to Grant's forces. Grant had left a provost guard at Port Gibson to keep the peace and find out all they could while he moved on, some of the 11th Wisconsin going back to the battlefield to bury the dead even two days later and others searching the houses of Port Gibson and finding a "good menny guns and Powder."[39]

Also of concern was that Grant still had numerous divisions back on the road to or from Bruinsburg and even in Louisiana all the way to Milliken's Bend. While virtually all of McClernand's XIII Corps was now in Mississippi, only two of McPherson's XVII Corps divisions were. Elements of the third division under Brigadier General John McArthur would not cross any time soon, and some never, so that McPherson mainly began pushing inland with only two of the three divisions in his corps. Likewise, Sherman's entire XV Corps was still strung out back to Young's Point and Milliken's Bend, Steele's and Tuttle's waiting word to move forward and Major General Frank P. Blair, Jr.'s division just returning this very morning from its foray up the Yazoo River as a diversion. It would take some time to get the corps southward in Louisiana and across the river.[40]

Sherman was still diverting attention to the north as late as the night of May 1, in fact, claiming that "our division has had perfect success, great activity being seen in Vicksburg, and troops pushing up this way." Sherman wanted the effort continued until nightfall, adding, "by prolonging the effort, we give Grant more time." But the division was to hurry back to the Mississippi River during the night, as orders had arrived for the XV Corps to likewise move southward to cross the river and join the others. Sherman had actually already ordered Steele's and Tuttle's divisions down to Perkins's Plantation while Blair remained at Milliken's Bend and Richmond for the time being "to cover this end." One of Blair's soldiers noted correctly in his diary that "we are about the rear guard of the entire Army."[41]

Sherman himself had received the orders to move southward, he informing Blair that he would go in person the next day, May 3, to Richmond and
then take the same old route the rest of the army had trudged southward
along Roundaway Bayou, Bayou Vidal, Lake St. Joseph, and to Hard Times.
Steele's and Tuttle's brigades prepared immediately, one Illinoisan scribbling
in his diary, "the recent movement of two army corps from this place, tells us
that stirring times are close at hand." Those two divisions would be the first to
go, Sherman allowing Blair a little rest after the diversion of the last few days
as well as to occupy the now nearly deserted area west of Vicksburg. "If the
enemy supposes we have evacuated the peninsula, they may be foolish and
rash," Sherman alerted Blair. While resting, he wanted Blair to comb through
the invalid camps and put anyone able to do so to work, so that Blair's troops
could prepare for the movement south as well: "This will leave your regiments for real soldier duty."[42]

Yet in the midst of all the planning, there were a couple of really overarching concerns. One was exactly where Sherman would cross the river.
Obviously, Bruinsburg was still an option, most of two corps having now
crossed at that point. But crossing there would require a lengthier march by
way of Port Gibson, when there was a much shorter route available if Grand
Gulf could be occupied. In fact, Grant's overarching goal after getting across
Bayou Pierre in force was to take possession of that place. Union occupation
would certainly allow Sherman to land there, cutting off numerous miles the
corps would have to march and lessening the time it would need to get up to
the front and support the rest of the army in case a battle developed.[43]

Perhaps as important, if not more so, was the potential for Grant's supply
line to be significantly lessened with the possession of Grand Gulf. Any supplies that reached the army prior to taking that place would have to go by the
Bruinsburg route, which added great degrees of difficulty due to the lengthy
route and country roads. But offloading supplies at Grand Gulf itself would
cut off the need to go via Port Gibson and also open up the better roads that
connected to Vicksburg and other points to the north.[44]

But just getting supplies even to Grand Gulf to keep up with the needs of
the army would be difficult enough, so Grant also concentrated on streamlin-
ing the route west of the Mississippi River. In fact, in Sherman's orders to his
corps to move, he mentioned the need for "extraordinary efforts to push forward supplies, both for our own corps and General Grant's army; but the officers and men of the whole army should be impressed with the real difficulty
of supplying so large an army of men and horses by such a road." Sherman's
main opposition to this southerly roundabout plan all along had been the supply situation, and obviously nothing had changed in his outlook.[45]

Seeing to this Louisiana section of the supply line mainly fell, at least temporarily, to Frank Blair even while the XV Corps engineer Captain William L. B. Jenney worked out the scientific aspects of shortening the route. Grant had first issued orders for his commander in that area, Brigadier General Jeremiah Sullivan, to "give special attention to the matter of shortening the line of land transportation from above Vicksburg to the steamers below. As soon as the river has fallen sufficiently, you will have a road constructed from Young's Point to a landing just below Warrenton, and dispose of your troops accordingly. Everything depends upon the promptitude with which our supplies are forwarded." Sullivan simply forwarded the order to Blair, writing that "I have no troops with whom to execute this order. Major General Blair having assumed command at this point, and having control of all the forces, is, therefore, the proper officer to execute the provisions of this order." Sherman had already figured out as much, and for the time being he ordered Blair to guard the road all the way back to Richmond and down to New Carthage, where hopefully steamers could transport the supplies. Cavalry was especially wanted to patrol the roads and defend the vital artery, and Blair was even to see that wagon trains were guarded mainly by "the men left behind belonging to regiments in the advance, with orders to report to their respective commands for duty." To help, in addition to sick and others on detail, McClernand had also left the 60th Indiana and 96th Ohio of Smith's division back across the river at Perkins's Plantation, causing a ruffle between brigade commander Burbridge and division commander Smith. Some said the reason was the lack of leadership in the regiments and others the lack of ammunition, one Ohioan admitting that the entire regiment had a mere eighty rounds total.[46]

Beyond the division and district commanders who provided the troops for the route and workers to shorten it, the real work of supplying goods and ammunition on the western side of the Mississippi River fell to staff officers, mainly Chief Quartermaster Lieutenant Colonel Judson D. Bingham and Chief Commissary Lieutenant Colonel Robert Macfeely. War Department observer Charles Dana had good things to say about each, writing Secretary of War Edwin Stanton that Bingham was "one of those I spoke of as accomplishing much with little work. He is an invalid almost, and I have never seen him when he appeared to be perfectly well; but he is a man of first-rate abilities and solid character, and, barring physical weakness, up to even greater responsibilities than those he now bears." He similarly described Macfeely as "a jolly, agreeable fellow, who never seems to be at work, but I have heard no complaints of deficiencies in his department. On the contrary, it seems to be one of the most efficacious parts of the great machine." Lieutenant Stephen C.

Lyford of Sherman's staff handled much of the ordnance supply. These three became especially important in funneling all the required goods southward west of the river so they could be crossed and sent to the army wherever it was.[47]

Yet getting those goods to the army east of the river was also a problem. Everything seemingly hinged on taking Grand Gulf, even the long-debated plan of holding tight there for a while and sending a corps southward to cooperate with Major General Nathaniel Banks at Port Hudson. Banks was, ironically, writing even that day, "if you can forward by the Black River the corps mentioned in your dispatches, we can expel the enemy from Louisiana." But everything seemed now to depend on acquiring Grand Gulf, which crossing the north fork of Bayou Pierre would outflank. Confederate defenders remaining there could easily be tucked into a trap that would end only one way, so their obvious choice if Federals spilled across Bayou Pierre toward Willow Springs would be to evacuate. In fact, one Missourian at the railroad bridge between Port Gibson and Grand Gulf noted that they had "heard their drums all day," and the fact that some were actually in rear of their current position was concerning to say the least. But who in the Federal camps knew what John Bowen was doing, and much of the Union decision-making process would depend on Confederate movements in response to this huge Federal incursion into Mississippi.[48]

6

"The Road to Vicksburg Is Open"

May 3

Napoleon Bonaparte conducted one of his most amazing campaigns in mid-1805 when he marched clear around the unsuspecting Austrians, commanded by Karl Mack von Leiberich, concentrated near the European city of Ulm. The "unhappy General Mack," as he had been termed, refused to come out and fight while Napoleon's corps marched across the French, German, and Austrian countryside, crossing the Danube and getting into the rear of the city and forcing its surrender on October 20, 1805. It was classic Napoleon: quick, decisive, and unrelenting. War theorists from Jomini to Clausewitz have long hailed maneuver as a central tenet of military success, and the modern United States military touts the idea of maneuver as one of its key nine principles of war. Napoleon certainly showed its worth at Ulm and on numerous other campaign chessboards.[1]

Just such a type of warfare could also describe Ulysses S. Grant. He was quick to turn flanks rather than assault outright, although some of those did occur as well. But Grant was primarily a maneuvering general, as seen in his attempts to get in rear of and cut off the enemy forces at Fort Donelson, in the Tennessee River Campaign, at Chattanooga, and ultimately in the Overland and Petersburg Campaigns in Virginia later in the war. But there is no better example of such Napoleonic-style activity than in the Vicksburg Campaign, where Grant almost reproduced Napoleon's Ulm maneuver complete with a river and a surrender. While not all of Grant's efforts to turn flanks and maneuver resulted in such drastic surrenders of whole forces, it is significant that, among three of the major surrenders of armies in the Civil War, Grant was the impetus for each.[2]

As complex as the Vicksburg Campaign was, there were varying levels of such attempts at maneuver. On the lowest of the operational levels, raids such as Van Dorn's on Holly Springs, Forrest's in West Tennessee, and Brigadier General Cadwallader Washburn's in rear of the Confederate army on the Tallahatchie River, all in December 1863, certainly fit the description. Larger efforts such as Sherman's movement to Chickasaw Bayou behind the Confederate army at Grenada was a larger example, as were several of the various bayou expeditions in the wet winter of 1863. But Grant's final attempt to reach Vicksburg by moving south of the city, crossing the river, and marching up to cut off its supply line from the east had all the markings of Napoleonic strategy. Grant was of course by this time heavily invested in that attempt and had made a successful crossing of the river and lodgment in Mississippi. Time would tell if he would be as successful in the full venture as Napoleon was at Ulm, including a mass surrender.[3]

Yet at this stage of the campaign there was an exact duplicate of the larger effort being carried out, if smaller in scale. Grant's effort to surge forward across both branches of Bayou Pierre was largely to turn the significant Confederate position at Grand Gulf and hopefully to force the surrender of the garrison. If he could get across the bayou branches and reach the Big Black River in rear of Grand Gulf, he could seal the escape route for the Confederate garrison and hopefully walk into Grand Gulf, his anticipated new supply base, without a fight. But he would have to be quick, as Bowen's Confederates were already marching out of the trap set within the larger trap that made up this final attempt to reach and take Vicksburg. Small though it was in comparison to the larger effort, this attempt to cut off and capture a significant portion of the Vicksburg defenders near Grand Gulf was nevertheless an important stepping stone that at the least would hopefully gain for Grant Grand Gulf and, in a best-case scenario, whittle down the number of Confederates he would have to deal with later at Vicksburg itself. Whether it would be totally successful would remain to be seen, but a culmination of this isolated part of the campaign, one way or the other, would likely come even this day, May 3.[4]

With so much at stake for each side, dawn on May 3 brought renewed movement in both armies; the various Union divisions in particular soon began their movements with high hopes of making a major statement this day. The Union occupation of Port Gibson was significant enough, as was the crossing of the lower branch of Bayou Pierre. A toehold was now firmly held east of the Mississippi River, one Federal describing how "Grant now had two army corps firmly planted on the high ground leading to the rear of Vicksburg; for this he had planned, and his army had marched, and waded, and sailed, for six months." And better yet, that foothold was enough to make Grand Gulf untenable, as Bowen quickly figured out. But Grant did not know of the evacuation quite yet as May 3 dawned, and so he wanted to provide the final push to isolate the Confederate stronghold. Moving across the northern branch of Bayou Pierre would easily do that, placing Federals north of that stream and within easy distance of the Big Black River itself. As Grand Gulf sat between Bayou Pierre and the Big Black River, any Confederates remaining there would be cut off and easily captured. As a result, Grant pushed forward across Bayou Pierre early that morning, hoping to capture Grand Gulf's garrison but at the least take the place itself.[5]

The main push came at Grindstone Ford, where Grant had engineers and pioneers hard at work repairing the bridge. "By working all night," Grant wrote McClernand just after daylight, "the bridge at this crossing was got ready for the troops at sunrise." An Iowan declared that "the bridge grew up, like the gourd of the prophet, in one night." Union troops poured across early that morning, one Illinoisan admitting that "it swung some and looked scary, as we passed over the charred timbers, but the cables were all right." Yet no one knew quite what they would find once across. John E. Smith noted that as he advanced "we reached the residence of an intelligent planter, who assured us that there was no enemy in the vicinity, they having all passed the day before." At almost that very moment, a Confederate battery from the ridge beyond opened up on his column. Word from local slaves conversely advised that the Confederates had been reinforced during the night. It looked as though Grant would get across, but at what cost no one was certain.[6]

McPherson's troops nevertheless pushed on after the "flying rebs," the advance between the forks of the bayou marking the first time McClernand's XIII Corps had not led the army since back in March. And there was a small fight just north of the bridge. Logan's division led the march and soon met Arthur Reynolds's two Confederate regiments "advantageously posted on a commanding ridge" near the Willow Springs Post Office. Artillery fire rang out, but McPherson brought Crocker's entire division forward and slowly pushed away the slight Confederate resistance. McPherson reported both the enemy and fortifications ahead, but once the Confederates evaporated one Grant staff officer irritatingly noted, "found neither rifle-pits nor enemy." Logan quipped that "the enemy, however, profiting by the lesson we had given him on May 1, fired only a few shots from a gun of small caliber and pursued his hasty retreat." One of Crocker's Indianans explained that they were "met by a furious fire of shot & shell which made it seem probable that the rebels were determined to make a stand," but after a delay in getting artillery up "it turned out that the enemy had left." Soon, the Federals occupied Willow Springs: "The cross-roads at the post office were gained," McPherson noted.[7]

After dispatching the small body of Confederates—Reynolds's two regiments left behind when Loring and Tilghman moved on to Grand Gulf and at this critical point the only force defending the vital door to the cul-de-sac—McPherson pushed onward through Willow Springs, both his and Logan's escort cavalry companies and others sweeping ahead and eventually netting 154 Confederate prisoners that fell behind. But the terrain was so choppy—"mountainous, and full of trees and bushes"—one German Indianan wrote, that not all could be rounded up easily: "We cannot find all of them." One Confederate who did willingly come into Union lines was a boyhood friend of McClernand's staff officer Henry Warmoth, who explained that "he was glad to see me and wanted to quit and go home. He . . . gave us a great deal of information. I ordered him paroled." Nevertheless, McPherson reached the crossroads by 9:00 a.m. From there, one division, Logan's, moved westward on the Grand Gulf Road toward Ingleside Crossroads while the other, Crocker's, headed northward toward the Big Black River and Hankinson's Ferry, the direction the small Confederate force had apparently retreated. But by this time elements of Bowen's force from Grand Gulf had also arrived and those Confederates north of Willow Springs, Reynolds's two regiments, had actually moved westward toward Ingleside, leaving the main road defense to the arriving Grand Gulf force—namely Lee's Alabama brigade and Cockrell's Missourians. These two brigades went into position and made another more determined stand at Kennison Creek. In describing the stifling of "an advance of some fourteen regiments, with large amounts of artillery," however, Loring gave the credit to Reynolds and his two regiments: "[Reynolds] prevented the success of the flank movement."[8]

McPherson admitted that the enemy seemed "disposed to contest the ground with great pertinacity." One Indianan explained that the earlier process below Willow Springs "was repeated," but this time the Confederates fought: "The enemy's shell burst over our heads and struck all around us." Crocker deployed Sanborn's brigade astride the road, the 59th Indiana out front at skirmishers; in line in rear was the 4th Minnesota on the right and 48th Indiana on the left. Because of the resistance that Sanborn described as "a long line of skirmishers, and formed a few regiments of infantry and put in position a battery of artillery," Crocker soon added George Boomer's brigade on the right, the 5th and 10th Iowa extending the skirmish line in that direction. To the left went Samuel Holmes's troops, the 10th Missouri as skirmishers backed by the 80th Ohio and 17th Iowa. A 10-pound Parrott rifle from one of the batteries also took position up front, and the entire division began to creep forward to and across the creek but not up the opposite hill where the Confederate line lay.[9]

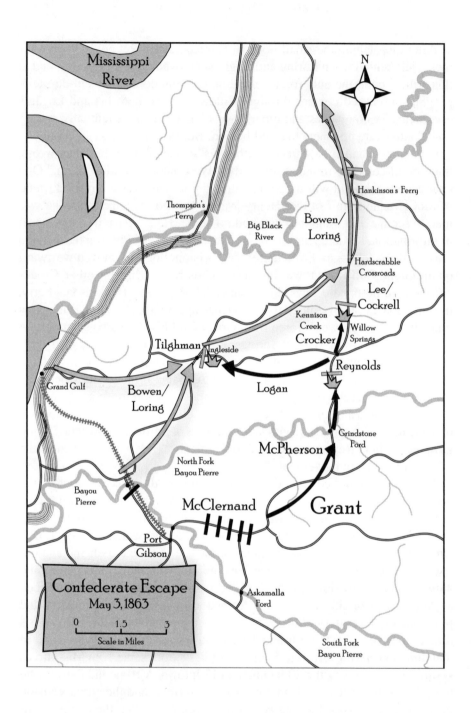

Mississippi
River

Thompson's
Ferry

Big Black
River

Bowen/
Loring

Hankinson's Ferry

Hardscrabble
Crossroads

Lee/
Cockrell

Kennison
Creek

Willow
Springs

Crocker

Tilghman   Ingleside

Reynolds

Grand Gulf

Bowen/
Loring

Logan

McPherson

Grindstone
Ford

North Fork
Bayou Pierre

Bayou
Pierre

McClernand

Grant

Port
Gibson

Askamalla
Ford

Confederate Escape
May 3, 1863

0   1.5   3
Scale in Miles

South Fork
Bayou Pierre

One Federal commander admitted the small Confederate enemy was "checking our advance." The ground itself was horrible, McPherson adding that "the face of the country was very much broken, with almost impassable ravines filled with trees and a dense undergrowth, and narrow, tortuous roads, offering great facilities to the enemy to cover his retreat, and of which he availed himself to the best advantage." As the day unfolded, however, Crocker pushed, and the timely arrival of Logan's division, which had marched westward after Tilghman's two regiments but turned northeastward upon McPherson's order ("[we] marched in every point of the compass," one Illinoisan admitted), emerged on the Confederates' right flank and caused them "to move precipitately toward the ferry." Logan had encountered Tilghman's two regiments near Ingleside, but they likewise held long enough for the entire Confederate force to get past the critical crossroads before themselves falling back. Crocker noted that "their retreat from our front was doubtless greatly hurried by that advance of the division of General Logan on their right flank," threatening Hardscrabble Crossroads that led to the ferry. One of his soldiers put it more bluntly: "Looked like a bloody trip but Genl Logan came in on their Right flank and they . . . get out of there so we were saved the trouble of burying some dead Yankees & Rebs too." One Illinoisan explained that the Confederates "left for more healthy parts," but it was soon clear that the Confederate defense at Kennison Creek had held long enough for the Grand Gulf force to escape to the rear across the Big Black River. Grant simply termed the fighting as "slight skirmishing all day" and later referred to it as "a skirmish nearly approaching a battle."[10]

Logan wrote his wife that "the enemy are now flying before us." In pursuit was Dennis's brigade of Logan's division, Colonel Manning F. Force's 20th Ohio in the lead. Force later told how he was standing with McPherson, Logan, and Dennis—his corps, division, and brigade commanders—when McPherson turned to Logan and ordered: "General Logan, you will direct General Dennis to send a regiment forward with skirmishers well advanced, rapidly toward the ferry." Logan turned to Dennis and ordered: "General Dennis, you will send a regiment forward with skirmishers well advanced, rapidly toward the ferry." Dennis turned to Force and continued: "Colonel Force, you will take your regiment forward with skirmishers well advanced, rapidly toward the ferry." Force pushed all the way to the river, where "a working party of the enemy were in the act of destroying the bridge," Logan reported. Force drove the Confederates away and crossed over the partially destroyed pontoon bridge, also described as "a bridge of flat boats" and "three floats or barges," capturing some tools and preventing the destruction of the bridge; also captured were "General Bowen's pistols, which were picked up by a private of the regiment." The general had laid them down to help destroy the bridge and had to leave in such a hurry that he left them. Bowen and his Confederates had knocked holes in the sides of the boats, but the Federals quickly nailed boards over the holes and kept them afloat. But neither division went any farther despite Logan's engineer Captain Stewart R. Tresilian repairing the "badly scuttled" bridge, McPherson writing that "it being now nearly dark, and the enemy driven across the Big Black, the pursuit was discontinued and the troops disposed in the best defensive position for the night." Still, McPherson had managed to cap the cul-de-sac that ended at Grand Gulf. By that time, however, the Confederates had withdrawn from it and were safely to the north and east.[11]

It was not exactly an Ulm-worthy conclusion, but Grant would take it nonetheless.

If McPherson's troops were the latch that held the door across the cul-de-sac closed at Hankinson's Ferry, McClernand's XIII Corps was the door itself that blocked access into or out of the Grand Gulf enclave. Obviously, the Federals missed the opportunity to hem in the Confederate Grand Gulf force, but now the door became just as important in creating a safe haven for the rest of the Federal army to cross the Mississippi River and supply itself from Grand Gulf. Accordingly, much of McClernand's corps followed McPherson's advance, intent on reaching and holding Willow Springs. From there, Federal columns could probe across or up the Big Black River or even northeastward toward Jackson. As McClernand moved forward, he left Carr's division in rear as a reserve and guard—Lawler's brigade "in quiet occupation" at Port Gibson itself to watch both the crossing near the railroad line and the new bridge at the town while the other, Benton's, remained on the road northward between the two forks of Bayou Pierre. Benton took the opportunity of the break to brag on his men: "Genl Benton made us a speech last night braged on us how we had stood up to the work and in marching[.] Talked very nice and we gave him a hearty cheer and said we was ready for more of it." Another related that Benton "said we were all heroes covered all over with glory and a lot more such stuff." McClernand cautioned Carr that "the object, of course, is to watch the line of the Bayou Pierre." At the same time, he informed Grant that morning that "the balance of my corps is on the way to Willow Springs, or to any point you may desire to have them halted." The plan moving forward was still undecided, although McClernand knew there would be a halt once across the main impediments to take possession of Grand Gulf, to allow Sherman's corps to arrive, and perhaps even to send a corps southward to join Banks. Willow Springs was the perfect place to halt and make crucial decisions.[12]

The Federals enjoyed the break, the first they had had in days. Some talked of swimming frequently in Bayou Pierre and reading in their leisure time. But there was always a tinge of fear, one Indianan admitting "we are in the heart of Dixie at last." And it was not just Confederates they feared. One Federal told of a couple of men breaking into beehives and spreading infuriated bees all over, sending officers of all ranks scrambling: "The stars, eagles, leaves and bars were no more respected by them than the chevrons of the 'non-comish' or the unadorned uniform of the private."[13]

An ironic occurrence happened while the Federals made their camps at Willow Springs. The local plantation owner of Ashwood was Alfred Ingraham, one Federal describing him as "Professor Ingraham." McClernand staff officer Henry Warmoth added that he had a "splendid house. He is a splendid man." McClernand moved forward himself and soon made his headquarters at the plantation house, which was not odd in the least. What was odd, however, was that Ingraham's wife, Elizabeth, was none other than Major General George G. Meade's sister, Meade of course the soon-to-be commander of the Army of the Potomac at Gettysburg. Evidently, Ingraham himself was also a friend of General Carr. Despite being related to such a high-ranking Federal, Mrs. Ingraham was staunchly Confederate, referring to the Federals as "our enemies." But she knew how to keep her property safe, and when McClernand asked to make his headquarters there she noted it was "graciously granted, for the protection is very desirable." The Ingrahams had already suffered enough, one son having been killed at Corinth. They also had "a pretty daughter, but she wasn't home, she had skedaddled, afraid of the Yankees." And their suffering was not over. Meade himself later wrote that his sister and family had been "reduced to actual want" and identified the cause as Federal plundering that was "not only un-necessary but unauthorized."[14]

As the rest of McClernand's XIII Corps advanced across Bayou Pierre to Willow Springs, McClernand began to grow more and more concerned, however. He was taking a position north of formidable creeks, and Grant had already informed him that the enemy was reinforcing on his front. More problematic at this point was the supply issue. McClernand complained often about his supply situation as he moved forward, first from Port Gibson, then at "Willow Ford," and then from Willow Springs itself. On the march, he wrote Grant that "my corps will be out of rations to-morrow. I am, as you are aware, without means of transportation. I ask that you will cause rations to be sent out immediately." He added that one of his own officers was in the rear "collecting what articles of subsistence he can" but that "the troops in advance left scarcely anything." As he moved on to Willow Springs itself, McClernand encountered McPherson's train, which sent him into another frenzy. "I am closed up in the rear of the long train attached to the Seventeenth Army Corps," he wrote, backhandedly giving his disdain that McPherson had managed to gather a supply train of any size while his corps had none, as he had earlier informed Grant. He asked that the train be ordered to the side to allow his troops to pass, that is if Grant wanted his corps in supporting distance of McPherson in case of a fight. And indications looked possible, McClernand adding that his (outdated) intelligence was that the Confederates had gathered near the Bayou Pierre railroad bridge, thinking the Federals would move that way directly to Grand Gulf. McClernand labeled the move via Grindstone Ford and north of Bayou Pierre as "the flank movement now being expected." Obviously, the Confederates had indeed been there, but they had long since departed northward.[15]

As a result, McClernand did not press onward quite yet. As McPherson had already probed ahead, McClernand situated his other three divisions now on site in defensive array to hold the roads and creek crossings in the area, Osterhaus on the Jackson Road at the crossing of Willow Springs Branch, Hovey at the junction of the Vicksburg and Jackson Roads, and Smith at the junction of the Vicksburg and Grand Gulf Roads. His orders were to "be so disposed as to enable them to be handled with facility and to support each other," and he ordered his commanders to especially watch for Confederate movements from the Jackson Road or from the east, the only directions McPherson's troops had not pressed forward.[16]

The result was some down time that the near-famished Federals took full use of to feed themselves. Their rations issued at Bruinsburg were gone by this point, and there was pitifully little being issued to them as yet. The only other alternative was to find what they ate, and a massive foraging effort consequently soon began. One Illinoisan described how "we are bivouacked in line of battle, and live upon what we can forage." Another enumerated his unit's haul the next day despite the heat, writing that they "brought in 6 horses, 4 mules, a wagon, 27 hams, and 5 niggers." He also noted that "negroes are flocking to our lines with mules, horses, and wagons," which aided the foraging capability of the still nearly wagonless army across the Mississippi River.[17]

As the Federals settled in near Willow Springs and began probing northward toward the Big Black River in the remainder of May 3, despite how the "day was very warm and roads awful dusty," McClernand was already thinking ahead. With the movement southward to join Banks still a possibility, he nevertheless kept his attention pointed northward. He had scouts out to examine the road network, informing Grant that the path leading northward came within two miles of the Big Black River at Hall's Ferry, where gunboats and steamers could possibly also navigate. It was feasibly a key point for future efforts.[18]

But Grant was more worried about another key point: Grand Gulf. In fact, it was the main goal now, one Federal accurately describing from Port Gibson how "we had thought to take Grand Gulf but they have such strong batteries that we couldn't land and therefore had to come to this place and come up on the back side of them." But it turned out that Grant would not need force to actually capture Grand Gulf, as it was already in Federal hands, courtesy of the United States Navy. Grant had alerted Porter on the morning of May 1 from the Port Gibson battlefield of the possibility of Grand Gulf being mostly evacuated because "Bowen himself is here," adding, "therefore I wish you would send up and attack the batteries as soon as possible." It actually took a couple of days for the necessary coordination to occur, and Grant originally planned to send McPherson's two divisions to Grand Gulf to cooperate with Porter on May 3. "I think to-morrow at 10 O'Clock my advance may be looked for at the Gulf. Would it not be well to have most of the Gunboats there at the same time?," Grant wrote Porter. Consequently, despite taking Grand Gulf under fire on May 2, Admiral Porter had weighed anchor on the morning of May 3 "for the purpose of attacking them again, if the Confederates had not retreated." With him were the ironclads *Lafayette*, *Carondelet*, *Mound City*, and *Pittsburg*. In a bit of seeming disappointment, Porter informed Secretary of the Navy Gideon Welles that "the enemy had left before we got up, blowing up their ammunition, spiking the large guns, and burying or taking away the lighter ones." Porter could not wait to inspect the defense that had stopped his flotilla on April 29 and reported in detail about them, writing that "the works are of the most extensive kind, and would seem to defy the efforts of a much heavier fleet than the one which silenced them. . . . Grand Gulf is the strongest place on the Mississippi." Still, Porter was glad to have possession now, four days late, writing that it was even fitting for the navy to capture it: "We had a hard fight for these forts, and it is with great pleasure that I report that the Navy holds the door to Vicksburg." But there was not much left, one Federal describing how "the town that was formerly here is completely destroyed, nothing remaining but cisterns and chimneys to indicate the former habitation."[19]

Just glad that Grand Gulf was in Union hands by whatever branch and in whatever shape, Grant made plans to quickly go there himself. But he would not waste troops on the effort now that it was firmly in Federal hands, so after starting part of the way with a brigade of infantry he left them behind and chose to simply ride there himself with a mere twenty or so cavalry of Captain Foster's 4th Independent Company Ohio Cavalry. Accompanying him were also staff such as John Rawlins and engineer Wilson, whom Grant loved to chide for his boyishness: "Wilson, there's a fallen tree you haven't jumped yet." Also along was Charles Dana and son Fred. It was a dangerous movement, riding alone with just a small escort, and any wayward Confederate still unfound in the cul-de-sac that Grand Gulf had become could land a severe blow on the Union high command. McClernand for one worried over Grant's move to Grand Gulf, writing that "had you not better be careful lest you may personally fall in with the enemy on your way to Grand Gulf?" But Grant was confident enough, explaining that slaves, contrabands, and prisoners taken stated that the "last of the retreating enemy had passed that point."[20]

Grant went anyway, as he said to make "the necessary arrangements for changing my base of supplies from Bruinsburg to Grand Gulf." Dana in fact described how all the way he kept making "inquiries on every side about the food supplies of the country we were entering. He told me he had been gathering information on this point ever since the army crossed the Mississippi, and had made up his mind that both beef and cattle and corn were abundant in the country." Consequently, once at Grand Gulf onboard the flagship *Louisville* (Porter having departed earlier that day with the *Benton* and other vessels), Grant wrote Halleck in Washington of his progress, bragging on his troops: "Composed of well-disciplined and hardy men, who know no defeat, and are not willing to learn what it is. This army is in the finest health and spirits." He also reported the current news he had received at Port Gibson of Grierson's famed raid, writing that it "has been the most successful thing of the kind since the breaking out of the rebellion. . . . I am told the whole State is filled with men paroled by Grierson." He later added: "Grierson has knocked the heart out of the State."[21]

Heavier on Grant's mind was the critical supply situation, and with Bingham, Macfeely, and Lyford in charge of the flow west of the Mississippi River, Grant immediately put another of his staff officers in charge of the operations east of the river. Despite having resigned on April 27 to return to his law practice and see to personal family issues, Colonel William S. Hillyer was still with the army; this was no time to leave, Grant being "so anxious for me to stay with him," Hillyer wrote his wife. He had been with Grant for years now, and even upon crossing the river on April 30 Grant issued orders that Hillyer was "assigned to the duty of Superintending the transportation and supplies to the Army below Grand Gulf." He had great discretion, Grant adding that "he is authorized to take charge of all transportation both land and water and generally to exercise such authority in the name of the

General Commanding as he may think necessary for the purpose of keeping the Army promptly supplied." Grant had then left Bruinsburg for the army, telling Hillyer to catch up with him. Hillyer asked where headquarters would be, and Grant humorously replied, "Well, I don't exactly know till I've consulted Pemberton." Once Grand Gulf fell to the Federals, Hillyer moved his operation there and continued to oversee the movement of supplies through the bottleneck that was Grand Gulf. He worked mainly through corps- and division-level staff officers, and Captain Edward Tittmann of Osterhaus's division took charge of the supply situation at Grand Gulf itself. Being in the rear, Hillyer assured his wife that "you need have no apprehensions about my safety here—I am put on special duty to superintend the transportation of supplies and ammunition to the Army and will not be in the fight." But he did write that "I am pressed beyond my capacity—I never had so much responsibility on my shoulders before."[22]

Once at Grand Gulf, Grant likewise took care of some personal matters, writing Julia that he had won a great battle and adding, perhaps unwisely, word of his son Fred's participation. "Fred is very well, enjoying himself hugely. He has heard balls whistle and is not moved in the slightest by it." Certainly, that was what every mother wanted to hear, especially with Julia already having a terrible time up North amid her family, who were all secessionists; despite her protestations that she was not Southern-minded, "no matter how earnestly I denied it, they would exclaim: 'It is right for you to say you are Union, Julia, but we know better, my child; it is not in human nature for you to be anything but Southern.'" Grant also related that Congressman Washburne as well as Governor Yates were with him at Grand Gulf, both "immensely delighted."[23]

But while there, Grant also made several key decisions in addition to changing his underclothes. He later noted that "I had not been with my baggage since the 27th of April and consequently had had no change of underclothing, no meal except such as I could pick up sometimes at other headquarters, and no tent to cover me." One Iowan described him as "without a tent and laid out with the men." Grant added: "The first thing I did was to get a bath, borrow some fresh underclothing from one of the naval officers and get a good meal on the flagship." Then he turned to military matters and the major decisions he had to make.[24]

The main issue was, now that he had Grand Gulf, whether to detach a corps and send it to Banks in Louisiana. That seemed to be the desire of Halleck in Washington (who was still urging this move as late as May 11, although it was delayed in transmission) as well as Banks. But Grant saw too much opportunity now to give up the momentum, and in reality it was an easy decision. "I shall not bring my troops into this place [Grand Gulf]," he informed Halleck on May 3, "but [will] immediately follow the enemy, and, if all promises as favorable hereafter as it does now, not stop until Vicksburg is in our possession." Some later said Grant disobeyed a direct order, which Halleck denied; Halleck's biographer John F. Marszalek argues that "after all, Halleck repeatedly told his generals that since they were on the battlefield, they had the final say." Making the decision easier, at Grand Gulf Grant received word that Banks would not be in a position to attack Port Hudson for several days or even weeks, and rumors also existed that Confederate reinforcements were on the way.[25]

With momentum on his side, Grant simply could not wait. He consequently wrote Banks that after "gaining a foothold at Grand Gulf" he would not be sending the corps. "Meeting the enemy, however, as I did south of Port Gibson, I followed him to the Big Black, and could not afford to retrace my steps." He added: "Many days cannot elapse before the battle will begin which is to decide the fate of Vicksburg." To perhaps turn the tables, he then actually called on Banks to send him troops: "It is impossible to predict how long it [the fighting at Vicksburg] may last. I would urgently request, therefore, that you join me or send all the force you can spare to co-operate in the great struggle for opening the Mississippi River."[26]

Charles Dana, the War Department's spook with Grant's headquarters, also informed Washington of the plan, writing the next day: "General Grant intends to lose no time in pushing his army toward the Big Black Bridge and Jackson, threatening both and striking at either, as is most convenient. As soon as Sherman comes up and the rations on the way arrive, he will disregard his base and depend on the country for meat and even for bread. Beef-cattle and corn are both abundant everywhere." He added: "General Grant is of the opinion that Pemberton will endeavor to bring on the decisive battle within the next ten days." It is not certain whether Dana's message brought more calm or nervousness to Washington when it arrived, probably the latter.[27]

With the decision made, Grant then had to worry about Washington's response. He later wrote how "I knew well that Halleck's caution would lead him to disapprove of this course; but it was the only one that gave any chance of success." In a classic example of asking for forgiveness rather than permission, he figured that "the time it would take to communicate with Washington and get a reply would be so great that I could not be interfered with until it was demonstrated whether my plan was practicable." In calculating the time it would take for messages to get to Washington and back, he later admitted, "I remember how anxiously I counted the time I had to spare before that response could come." He guessed he had a little over a week of freedom. "You can do a great deal in eight days," Grant speculated.[28]

With the idea of moving on to Vicksburg now solidified, Grant's main concern remained supplies; he even had to ask Porter to take custody of the prisoners captured at Port Gibson "owing to the lack of provisions with my command in the field." He admitted to Halleck that he would have to live off the land somewhat: "The country will supply all the forage required for anything like an active campaign, and the necessary fresh beef. Other supplies will have to be drawn from Milliken's Bend." He added that "this is a long and precarious route, but I have every confidence in succeeding in doing it." Grant also immediately fired off a message to Sherman, who was beginning to make his way southward toward Hard Times for a crossing now at Grand Gulf. After giving him the details of the fight at Port Gibson ("Our victory was complete. We captured 500 prisoners, four guns, killed General Tracy, and a large number of the enemy"), he came to the main message. "My base is now at this place," he told Sherman, "and, in executing your orders for joining me, you will govern yourself accordingly." He then gave specific orders: "I wish you to collect a train of 120 wagons at Milliken's Bend and Perkins' plantation. Send them to Grand Gulf, and there load them with rations, as follows: One hundred thousand pounds of bacon, the balance coffee, sugar, salt, and hard bread." That was for the other two corps. "For your own use," he added, "on the march from Grand Gulf, you will draw five day's rations, and see that they last five days." To make sure Sherman understood the importance of this effort, he added: "It is unnecessary for me to remind you of the overwhelming importance of celerity in your movements."[29]

Grant was in fact so concerned about the supply situation that he altered the normal ways of army bureaucracy to provide them. In writing to one of the corps quartermasters, Grant's staff officer Rawlins added that "you will issue to the troops of your command without provision returns for their subsistence during the next five days, three rations, keeping an accurate account of the same in order that the issues may be covered by proper authority hereafter." Grant himself ordered the same thing on May 5: "The Comy [Commissary] of Subsistence in charge of Stores at Grand Gulf will load all teams presenting themselves for rations with promptness and dispatch regardless of requisitions or provision returns[.] There must be no delay on account of either lack of Energy or formality on the part of the C.S. [Commissary of Subsistence] at Grand Gulf."[30]

Transportation, of course, would be the main issue, as only a few wagons made the initial passage with the army and any subsequent movement across the river took up large space on transports. One Federal declared their transportation was cut from thirteen wagons per regiment to just one, another saying his regiment was allotted two. Grant had foreseen the problem and ordered that initially upon crossing the river "Army Corps Commanders, will direct their Chief Quartermasters, to seize for the use of the Army in the field, during the ensuing campaign, such wagons and teams, as may be necessary for transportation, belonging to the inhabitants of the country through which they may pass." The result was a literal hodgepodge of vehicles. But it was a start until more wagons could be ferried over the river.[31]

With the need of additional supplies, Grant also tried the old system of passage of the Vicksburg batteries. His chief quartermaster Bingham back at Milliken's Bend worked to secure the two tugs with barges strapped alongside that Grant had ordered, intent on making the run as early as the night of May 2. But getting everything ready was a problem. Bingham requested help from Steele's division to load the stores, but "none were furnished." He talked with Sherman to make sure there would be land units nearby in case the vessels were stopped, and Sherman "advised me to wait until the next night (3d)," because it would take him some time to get into position. Finally, despite picking "the four largest and best barges that I could obtain," only two were fit for service by then, so Bingham opted to send only one tug, the *George Sturgess*, and two barges. Bingham's quartermaster workers and a few contrabands were "compelled to work night and day until the barges were ready," and he sent them on their way that night.[32]

The result was a disaster. Confederates that had backfilled the deserted Union-occupied areas began firing on the mass even from the Louisiana shore, and then the Vicksburg batteries opened up. The tug was hit almost immediately and burst into flames, as did the barges. Lieutenant James Marquess of the 27th Missouri, who had volunteered for the run, described how a Confederate shell "exploded and blew her up, and set the tug and both barges on fire. . . . All the damage was done immediately." The barge on the port side was already sinking anyway, and the one on the starboard side soon began to as well. The crew jumped aboard whatever would float and "quarter was asked," although it took a while for the Confederates to halt their fire and send out skiffs to rescue the soggy blockade runners. Among the captured were several newspaper reporters, prompting Sherman, no lover of journalists, to quip that they "were so deeply laden with weighty matter that they must have sunk" and that "in our affliction we can console ourselves with the pious reflection that there are plenty more of the same sort."[33]

Grant's options for getting supplies southward were consequently dwindling, although Quartermaster Bingham was successful in getting a barge loaded with coal past the batteries a few nights later. Ironically, an effort from the past also reappeared and offered at least some good news. Grant's chief engineer Frederick Prime noted that a "small steamboat . . . [*Victor*] did pass through the canal and the bayou, and is now in use below New Carthage." All that work earlier in the winter had paid at least minimal dividends.[34]

All the while, the common soldiers knew what was happening. Edward Wood of the 48th Indiana wrote home incisively in early May from the Big Black River: "[We are] preparing for the grand assault upon the stronghold of Vicksburg and I think with a fair prospect of success. All the canal digging, passes & cutoffs by which it has been attempted for six months past to get in the rear of Vicksburg have been abandoned and the whole of Grant's army is being rapidly concentrated near this point by the route we came." And he and others were confident despite the hardship: "We have subsisted almost entirely on the country. Corn meal & fresh meat beef pork & mutton have furnished our living and pretty scant it has been at that. And yet our men do not complain—they are elated with the successes that attended the landing on this side, the enemy having fallen back before them and they are eager to push forward to new victories."[35]

By May 3, despite continual firing at each other across the Big Black River at Hankinson's Ferry that caused one Federal to lament that he "got little to no sleep last night for the two pickets fireing so much at each other," the issue had solidified again to where the two sides could take a break. Grant on site was anxious to move on, he even leaving Grand Gulf deep in the night on May 3 to proceed to the head of the army at Hankinson's Ferry, where he made his headquarters at the Samuel Bagnell House between the ferry and Hardscrabble. But he just could not push the divisions forward quite yet. "The enemy is badly beaten," Grant assured Sherman, "greatly demoralized, and exhausted of ammunition. . . . All we want now are men, ammunition, and hard bread. We can subsist our horses on the country, and obtain considerable supplies for our troops." He also added a clear indication of his plans: "The road to Vicksburg is open." But he first had to make sure of his supply situation and allow the men some rest from the recent heavy activity. In advising McClernand the next day that "Grand Gulf is now the base of supplies," he wrote that "there will be no general movement of the troops before the cool of the evening if at all to day."[36]

That was in direct contrast to Pemberton, who was not on the field itself but remained at Vicksburg. The result in the gap in communication was predictable, Pemberton still not having heard from Bowen during the night of

May 2. "Nothing has been heard from General Bowen since 5.30 last evening," he told Loring at one point, adding, "my anxiety to hear is very great,
and I hope you will keep me constantly and regularly informed of your position and current events."[37]

Not being on site of course took from Pemberton the ability to quickly
make the key decisions, and he willingly gifted Loring with that duty. Not
fully knowing even by the morning of May 3 what was happening, he told
Loring to use his own discretion about how to extricate Bowen. "The difficulty of subsisting a large army between the Big Black and Bayou Pierre
Rivers is very great, and to subsist one of the size of your army cannot be
done for any great length of time." That said, if Loring was able to hold the
Bayou Pierre crossing temporarily, Pemberton told him to do so. That would
allow Bowen time to escape. But Pemberton then made his major decision
that he could make from his detached position. "If, however, you find that
the position on Bayou Pierre cannot be held, and you must fall back, you will
fall back across the Big Black River." Pemberton advised Jefferson Davis as
much on May 3, writing that Grand Gulf was lost but that was not critical:
"It lost most of its importance by the crossing of troops below." The plan
forward would be to use the Big Black River to defend Vicksburg, he adding
that "I shall concentrate all my troops this side of Big Black. The question
of subsistence and proximity to base, and necessity of supporting Vicksburg,
have determined this."[38]

Ironically within the lagging communications that day, both Bowen and
Loring had requested verification as to where to make the defense. Loring
first intended to man the Jackson Road and indicated he would make his stand
near and headquarters at Rocky Springs, where Pemberton was to communicate with him. But Pemberton soon decided that he could not stop a Federal
movement northeastward toward Jackson, and so accordingly he began to
make plans for that city's fall despite an effort to defend against such a ca-
lamity. But the real prize was Vicksburg, and Pemberton decided that the best
place to defend a Union approach on that place was at the Big Black River.
Accordingly, he ordered his commanders to the south to make their stand
there, inside the protective shield that the river provided. "You will take position on river at railroad bridge, striking the river at that point or such other as
may be most convenient," Loring's return orders read.[39]

Orders to move inside the shield of the Big Black River necessitated other
questions, however, and the lag in communication because of Pemberton's
absence again brought danger resulting from chaos. In fact, Assistant Inspec-
tor General and former Secretary of the Interior Jacob Thompson related to
one of the generals that "the lieutenant general commanding will not come

out to-day, owing to present condition of things at office." Loring informed Pemberton that morning that "the command is now rapidly passing the Big Black," and he desired further orders. "Shall the army move with dispatch to Vicksburg, or shall it hold the Big Black? I would like to know your wishes with reference to the future movement of the army." Similarly, Bowen asked point-blank: "Shall I move to Vicksburg or to Edwards Depot? Answer to Rocky Springs." Needing to make a decision, the indecisive Pemberton responded that both would be done. He would hold the various ferries and bridges along the "line of the Big Black" proceeding northward, including Thompson's, Hankinson's, Hall's, Crocker's, and Baldwin's, but the majority of the army would concentrate farther north around the railroad bridge, Pemberton's lifeline to the outside world.[40]

Pemberton accordingly sent his engineer, Major Samuel H. Lockett, to fortify these ferries that suddenly "became points of great strategic importance." Lockett assigned an engineer to each. But the terrain was against a Confederate defense west of the Big Black River, as at most ferries the high hills butted up against the east side, with an alluvial plain as much as a mile wide on the western side of the river at each. That made fortifications right up at the river impossible on the western side and would allow enemy artillery on the higher hills east of the river to command the crossings. Lockett thus settled for *têtes de pont*, or fortifications on the opposite side of the river that were guarded, which he noted were required "or [else] to relinquish the idea of taking the river as a line of defense." The most famous example of this was at the Big Black River railroad bridge, where Lockett put special effort into fortifying. He also removed the machinery from a steamboat, the *Dot*, and laid it crosswise of the river at the railroad bridge to facilitate more traffic.[41]

Fortunately for Pemberton, his subordinates did not fail him and by later that afternoon on May 3 Loring was nearly across the Big Black River and informed Pemberton not to send any messages via Rocky Springs but "by a road north of the Big Black." He also informed him that he managed to save and get across the river at the "boat-bridge," as Carter Stevenson described it, some one hundred thousand pounds of bacon. But Stevenson also added that Loring was unable to get the cattle across: "It was just too late." That said, a portion of Bowen's bacon stationed between the forks of Bayou Pierre was not removed and fell into Grant's hands, which he used to feed his already hungry troops. A Federal also related that he and his fellow Illinoisans "captured a large drove of beef cattle."[42]

So despite his determination to remain inside Vicksburg and command from there, Pemberton was concentrating his army for a defense. "As soon as possible," he wrote Carter Stevenson, "I desire to concentrate the army, with a view to operations against the enemy." He similarly informed Governor Pettus that "I must concentrate my whole army to beat Grant's." Pemberton had let the enemy steal a march on him and get a foothold in Mississippi, but he was reacting now, although tardy, to concentrate his forces perhaps even for a fight. If his bold words were true, he eventually intended to fight with that concentrated army, although at this point there was no mention of any offensive use of the troops, just purely defensive. Indeed, how and where Pemberton would fight, if the indecisive general even would, might determine the campaign and thus the fate of Vicksburg.[43]

7

"RATIONS NOW ARE THE
ONLY DELAY"
May 4–6

In the Finger Lakes region of New York State sit numerous small towns bearing iconic names such as Utica, Cayuga, Auburn, and Amsterdam. Nearby are even more general names less associated specifically with that state, places such as Port Gibson, Bolton, Bovina, and Raymond. But this region is not sole proprietor of these historic names. Likewise, in the southwestern region of Mississippi, of all places, can also be found small towns with the exact same names. It is no coincidence that while migration patterns normally ran east and west, with the vast majority of people settling in Mississippi coming from the slave states to the east such as Alabama, Georgia, South Carolina, and North Carolina—and bringing their "property" with them to like-minded areas—the non–slave state that had the most nativity of Mississippians in the 1860 census was actually New York. When these New Yorkers migrated to Mississippi, they brought with them their place-names and instituted their own little corner of home in the wilds of southwestern Mississippi.[1]

Local histories provide verification. Utica, Mississippi, for example, was a name offered in 1837 by the town's postmaster, Ozias Osborn. He hailed originally from Utica, New York. Cayuga, a Native American name from that tribe, was similarly named some said by Osborn as well and others by a different settler from that region. One early writer explained that four Haring brothers came to the area from New York decades earlier, Cornelius settling and prospering in Port Gibson. Eleazer Haring settled farther northward in the county, "and it was he who gave the familiar New York names, Utica and Cayuga, to the Hinds County localities." Unfortunately, their brother Chester was not so prosperous; he was killed in a duel in Natchez. A third hamlet of Auburn also gained that distinctive New York name, many said likewise dubbed by Osborn. Whoever named them, the New York influence is clear.[2]

Individuals stories bore out the same. Newspaperman Sylvanus Cadwallader told of returning to the army at Hankinson's Ferry after a couple days at Grand Gulf getting his dispatches out. He rode through territory teeming with civilians, at one point seeing "a group of children that had just been dismissed from school on account of the approach of our army." He related that "as soon as the children saw me they took to the fence corner thickets, like a covey of quail, and it required considerable persuasion on my part to induce them to come out of hiding and answer some friendly questions." It turned out that the teacher was nearby on the school steps and "begged for the privilege of a few minutes conversation." Cadwallader described how "she came from central New York, a year before war was declared between North and South, and was never able thereafter to get through the lines on her way homeward." She admitted that the Southern people had been more than generous to her despite her loyalty, but she took this opportunity to make her getaway. Warned that there was nothing but soldiers back to Grand Gulf and then northward, she went anyway with a special pass from Grant himself.[3]

Another example was Sarah Fitch Poates, who lived farther north near Bolton. She had likewise come southward from New York to teach school, but she became more Southern-leaning in her views when she married a Mississippian, even calling the Federals "rascals." Later in the war, she declared upon Lincoln's reelection that he would be "our torment" for another term. Yet she missed New York terribly and wished to see her mother, her plight made worse by her homeplace standing at times between fighting forces, her slaves taken or run away, and her husband conscripted into the Confederate army.[4]

It is ironic that the very area Grant was getting ready to march through was a little snapshot of New York. It is even more ironic that many had moved there for a better life; brigade commander Colonel James Slack related to his wife, "[I] find a great many Northern people here, located for their health." Now they faced destruction. Nevertheless, no matter who lived in the area, Grant needed it to fulfill his purpose of reaching Vicksburg by the best route, even if it did put native Northerners at greater risk. But all knew what kind of tide was rolling toward them, and accordingly many left the area, one Iowan remarking that "the small villages were all deserted by the inhabitants. Even the negro-cabins showed little signs of life." Those who remained "looked as if they had swallowed a large dose of vinegar and cod liver oil." Another wrote his wife ("Dear Woman") that "the old planters flea at our approach like the chased deer before the hounds leaving everything behind that they can't take along most of the old niggers woman & children corn & thousands of lbs. of bacon and molases sweet potatoes etc." But it did not have to be that way, as generally the evacuated homes were more susceptible to foraging and destruction while those who remained generally gained a guard and were treated civilly. "Courtesy was invariably met with courtesy," one Iowan explained.[5]

"I think we are on the high road now to take Vicksburg," XVII Corps commander James B. McPherson wrote his mother from Hankinson's Ferry on May 4. Certainly, a firm foothold had been secured east of the Mississippi River. But despite the decision to press on toward Vicksburg, Ulysses S. Grant had to wait to do so. Timing was important, but moving too fast could be just as detrimental as moving too slow. In the back of his mind, of course, was the original plan—along with the likely assumption on the part of everyone else involved from Banks to the south to Halleck in Washington—that he would secure his position at Grand Gulf and send help to Louisiana to take Port Hudson once and for all before beginning renewed operations against Vicksburg. But Grant had too much of a golden opportunity facing him to do that, and he had already decided to push on.[6]

But there first had to be a wait for supplies and reinforcements to arrive; those rations issued at Bruinsburg had long since disappeared, and whereas at least one Federal noted while stopped near Willow Springs that "we are feasting fine at this time," only a few days would exhaust the area's food provisions. Indeed, many others were reporting "rations entirely exhausted" or "drawed one and a half crakers for a days ration Drawed no meat or sugar & coffee. Jayhawked some beef." Another added, "nothing to eat but confiscated beef," and sassafras in abundance replaced coffee. An Indianan mentioned "two crackers issued to each man." But at least one Illinoisan made the best of it, writing home that "we have been on short rations too but I believe it has been an advantage for eating too much in this hot country and drinking too much of the stagnant water is very unwholesome." Yet steady streams of supplies and ammunition were already coming into Grand Gulf and needed only to be sent forward to the army. Plus, Sherman was on the way, even making a quick trip across to Grand Gulf ahead of his troops, meeting Charles Dana in the process. It would take a couple days to get it all together, but Grant realized the best way to advance was to do it in the most prepared way, and a couple more days would not hurt in the long run. After all, he had eight days. Consequently, the men remained stationary for a couple more nights, one Illinoisan complaining that they "would have gladly sold our precarious birth-right for a mess of pottage or a pot of mush, but as a general thing, we succeeded in securing the necessaries of life."[7]

Accordingly, Grant issued orders for the Army of the Tennessee to wait, to bide its time now that the necessary leaping of Bayou Pierre had been accomplished and Grand Gulf was in his hands. There was little more that could be gained by a swift move than could be done in a couple days now that the Confederates from Grand Gulf had narrowly escaped from the cul-de-sac between all the rivers and bayous. There was likely nothing more to gain from pushing on swiftly, whereas there was much to reap by waiting. Once Sherman and the supplies were up, Grant could move forward at the peak of power. In the meantime, the politicians still with the army, Governor Yates and Congressman Washburne, made the best of their captive audiences.[8]

The present portion of the Army of the Tennessee consequently went into camps at their current positions, still capping the cul-de-sac at Grand Gulf but this time not so much to keep the Confederates in but to keep them out of the new base of supplies. Dana himself explained that "the army here is distributed across the peninsula, guarding every point." McPherson's two divisions under Logan and Crocker had ended their chase the evening before at Hankinson's Ferry, and there they went into camps, holding that very critical crossing and more important the bridge that the Confederates had not had time to destroy. That did not stop Confederate artillery from shelling the area the next morning and killing and wounding a few Federals, but Logan's batteries returned fire and drove the Confederates back; fortifications soon went up on each side of the river. Farther south, McClernand's four divisions held the major roads coming in from the north and east, mostly connecting at the critical point of Willow Springs, as well as on southward to Bayou Pierre and even at Port Gibson for a time. As a result, five divisions (Carr's was still below Bayou Pierre) held the mere seven-mile gap between Bayou Pierre and the Big Black River.[9]

The lull was welcome even if the reason was unknown. One Ohioan admitted that "after we have captured Vicksburg, and the history of Grant's movements is known, we shall then understand why we guarded Hankinson's Ferry so long." And one believed "Mr. Hankinson owed us something nice for taking such good care of his ferry for him." Still, troops that had been on the move constantly for days and even weeks welcomed a time of rest; corps commander James B. McPherson wrote his mother that "you have no idea my dear mother of the fatigues of such a campaign. I never was so completely tired out in my life as I was last night, for seven days I had not had more than three hours sleep out of twenty four and my men were equally fatigued." Officers, too, needed time to write their reports of the battle that occurred at

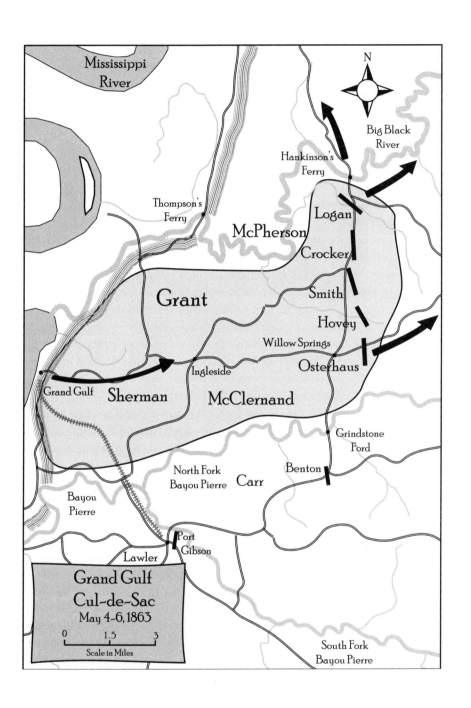

Mississippi
River

N

Big Black
River

Hankinson's
Ferry

Thompson's
Ferry

Logan

McPherson

Crocker

Smith

Grant

Hovey

Willow Springs

Osterhaus

Ingleside

Grand Gulf

Sherman

McClernand

Grindstone
Ford

Benton

North Fork
Bayou Pierre

Carr

Bayou
Pierre

Port
Gibson

Lawler

**Grand Gulf
Cul-de-Sac**
May 4-6, 1863

0   1.5   3

Scale in Miles

South Fork
Bayou Pierre

Port Gibson just a couple days earlier. Hovey wrote his report, James Slack writing his wife that "I have seen Genl Hovey's report. He gives me a very flattering compliment, and I think Genl McClernand will do the same thing." Perhaps the biggest benefit was camping so near ample water, and one Indianan termed the resulting bathing of the entire army after weeks of marching and fighting as the "Big Wash." An Ohioan even told of an amusing incident at Hankinson's Ferry in which some skinny-dipping Federals were suddenly fired upon by Confederates, and the swimmers "got out of that stream remarkably quick, and some did not stop to get their clothing, but flew for camp as naked as they were born."[10]

In the meantime, the army went to work gathering supplies. These came from two places, one being Grand Gulf and the steady amount of rations and ammunition being gathered there and particularly just across the river at Hard Times. Obviously, a bottleneck occurred where the goods had to be crossed over the river with the minimal water transportation available. Once across, however, what wagons that were available rolled to and from Grand Gulf to the army around Hankinson's Ferry and Willow Springs in relative safety because of the nearness and the protection offered by the cul-de-sac. But because of the similar lack of wagons on the east side of the Mississippi River even this late, provisions from Grand Gulf were slow in coming and short when they arrived. One Ohioan scribbled in his diary on May 5, "rations issued ½ crackers to each man." But he was vibrant nevertheless, adding that "men all in fine spirits anxious to follow the rebs." A rain during the night of May 4 also helped cool the weather, although it soaked the men, replenishing the creeks somewhat where before some had reported they "had to use water out of the standing holes that was in the Branch." Also helping was an arriving mail shipment and the opportunity to send letters home, even those informing loved ones of deaths; one Illinoisan advised those at home, "well we are in the state of Mississippi." Also helping was the arrival of knapsacks that some regiments had left at Port Gibson before the battle and other units' "camp equipage."[11]

Second, in addition to the wagons moving goods from Grand Gulf, Grant's men scoured the countryside gathering anything edible. He later explained that "beef, mutton, poultry and forage were found in abundance. Quite a quantity of bacon and molasses was also secured from the country, but bread and coffee could not be obtained in quantity sufficient for all the men." Added to that list of unobtainable items was of course ammunition. But the Federals did what they could, even putting many of the local mills in operation: "We expect to live on cornbread and whatever we can get until the teams come up," one Illinoisan explained. Grant pointed out that "every plantation, however, had a run of stone, propelled by mule power, to grind corn for the owners and their slaves. All these were kept running."[12]

Yet the buildup of supplies was slow, the army consuming nearly everything soldiers could find in the country and bring up from Grand Gulf in real time, leaving only a little to be built up into the three days' rations Grant required for moving forward. And the local population was not that helpful, many denying having anything. Some were indeed destitute, one complaining to an Iowan: "The girl was crying & told me that our men had taken every particle of Provision out of the house & that she had eaten nothing since the morning before." He added, "this is but one of many such cases that are occurring every day." A less concerned group of soldiers confronted a woman who denied having anything and tried to shoo them away by mentioning a guard on the way from McPherson. The men "very politely told her that take would do to tell Marines but we was hungry and had no time to spare." He related that a slave woman watching them gather all they could remarked, "she neber see sich folks she said it was a sign dey had no raisin." Often, soldiers came back with way more than they needed or could carry in terms of non-food items, such as one Indianan writing of "many things of no profit to the soldier . . . fine dishes, bed quilts, womens clothes etc." One Illinoisan also humorously related the bad effects on other Mississippi occupants: "From some cause the poultry followed us into camp and was put to death for running the picket guard."[13]

Sylvanus Cadwallader editorialized on the effort, writing that "foraging upon the enemy was brought to the highest stage of efficiency. Army wagons by scores and hundreds were sent out daily from ten to fifteen miles, escorted by infantry details sufficient to protect them from any sudden foray of Confederate Cavalry." He continued: "They returned at nightfall groaning under the weight of impressed supplies, and increased by the addition to the train of every vehicle, no matter what its description that could bear the weight of a sack of grain, piece of salt meat, or pails full of butter, eggs, honey or vegetables." He noted that so much was found that "salt, sugar, coffee, and sometimes a small quantity of 'hardtack,' were the only issues then made from our supply trains coming from Grand Gulf." Yet it was all mostly for immediate consumption, and getting a stock of several days' provisions remained difficult for the army, now numbering at least twenty-five thousand with additional units arriving all along. Artillery and cavalry units had a more difficult time as well, needing food not only for themselves but also their horses.[14]

Confusion occurred as foraging parties from all commands crisscrossed the area. One Ohioan related an amusing incident in which he and six others conveyed three "baby wagons loaded with camp kettles filled with beef for the regiment." They moved at night outside the picket lines and encountered another party they thought might be Confederates. The enemy was known to be in the area, this Ohioan remarking that "we was living off the enemies country and so were they and it did not leave a big lot for us." The Ohioans scampered into a covered ditch and challenged the oncoming enemy, only to find out it was "a 69th Ind. Boy." There were six more of them behind as well, so they all banded together: "Then we had an army of 14 men and all loaded with broiled beef[.] Very dangerous." Sometimes actual confrontation occurred. One Indianan wrote of a teamster out foraging, filling a sack full of corn for his mules. A group of Confederates appeared, yelling, "Boys, heah is a d——yank in heah stealing ouah cohn. . . . Get out of heah." The teamster calmly replied, "gentlemen, please give me time to get a few more ears. My mules are nearly starved." The Confederates obliged, one marveling Federal surmising, "I suppose that they had never been called gentlemen before."[15]

The foraging at times became overdone, and orders from army headquarters as well as both McClernand's and McPherson's had to be issued to stop straggling and the pillaging of private dwellings. There was some enforcement, Major Luther Cowan of Logan's division in McPherson's corps reporting to his wife that "I was arrested yesterday by General McClernand for not arresting a man for pillaging a house a few days ago. I was released a little while ago—all right." He added, "I was in hopes they would court martial me and send me home, but no show yet." McPherson went so far as to mention his "pain and mortification" that he had to reiterate the articles of war for his troops and also had to reprimand his men for "promiscuous firing." He also ended the use of bands and drums except for the long roll, all commands to be given by bugle. Ever seeking an advantage, the troops thereafter made a lot of fun of what they referred to as the "pain and mortification order." And making matters more chaotic amid the foraging, there was a continual influx of slaves and "hangers on." Many had joined the marching columns, one Federal describing coming through Port Gibson: "As we marched through not many of the white people remained in the town but negroes of all ages and sizes were gathered along the road swinging their hats and rejoicing for they had already got the idea that they were free and many of them gathered up what they could carry and started to go with us, marching along side of the column of troops." Most slaves not "properly engaged as servants to officers" were turned over to the provost for "public service."[16]

Just because the forces remained in camp for the next couple days did not mean there was no movement, however. Both corps commanders sent out scouts and reconnaissances in their general areas to see what defenses the

Confederates had and what the likelihood of battle was when the army did move. In addition to the various cavalry units available, much of the scouting was done by the Signal Corps detachment that was "employed almost wholly in reconnoitering" due to terrain that was "unsuited to any extensive lines of communication by signals." Eventually, Captain J. W. De Ford worked out detachments for Grant's headquarters as well as the three corps commanders' headquarters, whereby "each corps commander was kept well informed as to his own command and General Grant as to the whole army." It was one such detachment up ahead of the army that Fred Grant and one of his father's orderlies tried unsuccessfully to capture one day, thinking they were Confederates; Fred later admitted, "not until we had gone too far to retreat, did the idea occur to us that the would-be captors might possibly become the captured."[17]

But the scouts on May 4 and 5 found little of anything besides "a number of horses, mules, wagons, and commissary stores, which were turned over to their respective departments, receiving receipts therefor." McClernand reported that even on the evening of May 3 "I reconnoitered ahead on the Jackson road . . . and found nothing." But he did pick up on accurate intelligence that the Confederates, "variously estimated from two regiments to 10,000 men, are reported by different spectators to have passed yesterday morning, on the Jackson road, to the forks of Vicksburg and Grand Gulf roads, and to have returned a short distance, and turned to the left to cross the Big Black, at the crossing of the Vicksburg road." It was an extremely accurate rendition of what the Confederates had done the day before.[18]

McClernand continued his reconnoitering on May 4. Part of Osterhaus's division moved forward on the Jackson road as many as six miles but again found nothing. The effort did not even find the trace of Confederates, McClernand informing Grant that "no portion of the enemy retreated on the road beyond General Osterhaus' present camp," they all having crossed the Big Black River at Hankinson's Ferry. But the scouting did turn up news of four steamers at Hall's Ferry another eleven or so miles up the Big Black, assets that McClernand began to think about capturing: these steamers might be very helpful in supplying the army up the Big Black. McClernand soon outfitted a cavalry, infantry, and artillery expedition to go secure the boats, he following five miles of the route himself, but the expedition proved fruitless. At the least, however, it confirmed that there was little to no Confederate resistance east of the Big Black River all the way up to Hall's Ferry, which was just twelve miles south of the Southern Railroad.[19]

More scouting occurred on May 5, with Osterhaus's cavalry moving east of the Big Black River and actually encountering a small Confederate band that McClernand described as "a corps of observation sent out to watch our approach." Osterhaus himself was along and ordered the 2nd Illinois Cavalry to attack what soon emerged as a more numerous Confederate force, but "his attack was so energetic and quick that the rebels could not find time to form. The lieutenant and his men were among them with drawn sabers and drove them for 5 miles." Several Confederates were captured, mostly from the 14th and 20th Mississippi that had been mounted. By May 6, McClernand had cavalry scouting all over the area, confirming that "the main force of the enemy on the east of Big Black has returned to Edwards Station, on the railroad and east of the Big Black." Without any resistance to speak of, Osterhaus expanded his base area with cavalry, sending a force all the way to Cayuga north of Rocky Springs, with cavalry scouts on all the roads to the northeast, some all the way toward Utica and Gallatin. Others went along the river itself, still after the Confederate steamers that had apparently fled northward, as well as a small detachment northward toward Edwards Station. These "corps of observation" were not intended to take territory or fight the enemy but merely to locate the Confederates and detect any movement toward the main camps of the various corps. But in doing so, they found the pathway straight toward the railroad east of the Big Black River undefended and even mostly unoccupied.[20]

At the same time, McPherson was also sending out his own scouting parties. On May 4, he detailed portions of two regiments of infantry, the 93rd Illinois and 26th Missouri of Boomer's brigade from Crocker's division, as "a party of observation." One regiment was to move northward along the east bank of the river, the other southward on the same side. The orders were to "advance under cover of the hills to avoid observation, while flankers will proceed cautiously, exploring every blind road, bridle-path, or crossing, with a view to discover what works, if any, the enemy may have erected on the banks of the river and what fordable places or ferries there may be, the officer in command keeping a running sketch of the route passed over."[21]

With nothing found on the May 4 scouts, McPherson landed on a bolder reconnaissance the next day, May 5. "You will immediately detail two regiments of infantry from Colonel Boomer's brigade and a section of artillery to proceed across Big Black," McPherson ordered Crocker, "in the direction of Warrenton and Vicksburg, on a reconnaissance." A squadron of troopers from the 6th Missouri Cavalry would precede the infantry and go farther. The purpose was "to examine the roads, find out, if possible, the points toward which the enemy retreated, his designs, &c. The object being simply a reconnaissance, he must not allow himself to become seriously engaged." Reports from contrabands indicated that the Confederates had fallen back as much as eight miles from the river crossing, so McPherson cautioned the infantry not to move over four or five miles and let the cavalry determine the rest.[22]

To make sure of the effort, McPherson went along himself, with his corps engineer Captain Andrew Hickenlooper in tow. Charles Dana, writing from Hankinson's Ferry on May 5, explained that "McPherson is going over this morning with a competent force to stir them up." He added that, once Sherman and the supplies were up, "the general advance up this peninsula will be resumed." Hickenlooper reported that McPherson himself moved some four miles across, Boomer pushing forward with the 5th and 10th Iowa four miles across the river, along with guns of the 6th Wisconsin Artillery, and the cavalry went even farther. Ultimately, they met Confederates of the 41st Georgia of Carter Stevenson's division.[23]

All the while, Grant used the lull in the forward movement to bring up more and more supplies for the army now about to pounce forward on the Confederates, he writing of the roads from Grand Gulf to Hankinson's Ferry and Willow Springs being "well beaten by the travel of our wagons." Within the cul-de-sac itself, wagons could move without much fear of marauding Confederates to resupply the army from Grand Gulf. It was a safe situation that would not always be available, especially as the army moved farther north and the supply lines became longer. The smart thing was to supply now for the upcoming moves, and many commanders reported the next few days were spent in "bringing up its supplies of ammunition and provisions." As soon as that was done, Grant would move.[24]

Despite one Pemberton staff officer scribbling in his diary "in status quo," there was no corresponding lull in the Confederate operations through the three days of seeming Union inactivity. Because of the movement inside the Big Black River shield, the need to reposition troops to meet the obvious coming threat that no one knew when or where would occur, and the preparation for any contingency, Confederate units had little rest during this interim period. Some of the troops, especially those who had been in continuous operation since before Port Gibson, were again called on to continue the defense of Vicksburg. Nerves were on edge all the while, especially when the telegraph station at Edwards Station went offline on the evening of May 5. Operators informed that "we have not been able to get Edwards Depot since 7:40 p.m. and cannot account for his absence. We are fearful that the enemy have taken possession of that point." Messages could still be transmitted to Jackson through Edwards, indicating that the line was not broken, but the operators recommended refraining from sending anything sensitive in case "they may have an [operator] there to intercept any important message." It turned out to be no such crisis, but it did plant the idea of the Federals moving toward Edwards Station firmly in Pemberton's mind.[25]

The chaos was widespread, and no more dramatic than in the state capital. The Jackson *Daily Mississippian* printed continual day-by-day updates of the nearing Union forces at both Port Gibson and Snyder's Bluff, but it also put a large chunk of its attention still on Grierson's Raid, indicating just what an effect it had in Mississippians' minds. Still, the editors surmised that "Grant is doubtless endeavoring to play the same game he did at Fort Donelson." A gas shortage in the city at the same time did not help the nervousness. An astounded Governor Pettus ordered his government to begin packing even as he began to set up a defense; he sent his family eastward to safety but remained to oversee the work in his capital. He called for "five hundred negroes" for a week "to fortify the city of Jackson," leaning on the "patriotism of the people" to lend them and warning that "the names of those who fail to respond to this appeal will be handed to me." The Jackson mayor and city government also called on the citizens to form their own companies for defense, but chaos increased as the days passed. One of the Northern newspaper correspondents taken on the river on May 3 and brought to Jackson reported:

> Great excitement prevailed in the Mississippi Capital at the time of our arrival, on account of the report that General Grant, at the head of his victorious army—he had then captured Grand Gulf—was marching on the town. At the street corners were knots of excited men, discussing the prospects of the future with more feeling than logic. To us, who had long been careful observers, it was evident they were at a loss what to do; and you can imagine we rather enjoyed the trepidation of the Rebels. We saw a number of vehicles of various kinds loaded with household furniture, and men, women, children, and black servants, all greatly excited, moving rapidly out of town. A panic of the most decided kind existed among all classes of society; but we had no difficulty in perceiving that the negroes of both sexes, young and old, enjoyed the quandary of their masters and mistresses. . . . The Mayor had put forth a gasconading hand-bill, designed as a placebo, which was posted in prominent parts of the capital, informing the citizens that there was not the least cause for alarm; calling the people of Mississippi to arms, to repel the barbarous invader from the soil he polluted with his footsteps, and all that sort of stereotyped rant and braggadocio for which the South has ever been famous.

But apparently, at least according to the reporter, the mayor was one of the first ones out of town.[26]

By May 5 Governor Pettus had seen enough and gave orders for all the government departments to be ready to move within "half an hour's notice." He also issued a proclamation calling on the people to form companies for a defense: "Recent events, familiar to you all, impel me, as your Chief Magistrate, to appeal to your patriotism for united effort in expelling our enemies from the soil of Mississippi." He continued: "Let no man capable of bearing arms with hold from his State his services," and he declared that those who did would "hereafter wear the disgraceful badge of the dastardly traitor who refused to defend his home and country." He wanted the citizens to meet and organize into companies, sending their "musket rolls" to the governor's office. "Awake, then—arouse, Mississippians, young and old, from your fertile plains, your beautiful towns and cities, your once quiet and happy but now desecrated homes, come and join your brothers in arms," he implored. But he was personally in crisis, sending his family eastward even as he received news of his brother's capture at Port Gibson days earlier.[27]

With the *Daily Mississippian* advising that "the darkest hour [is] just before day," the government began evacuating on May 6, Absalom M. West reporting to his wife that he and the governor planned to leave the city for Meridian that day and that "the people [were] in a perfect panic." Another observer agreed, writing that "the people [are] despondent and alarmed." The actual evacuation was just as bad. A clerk in the Treasury Department, Luther Baechtel, wrote in his diary that the Treasury Department train jumped track three times on the way to Meridian. But it had to be done, Pettus admitting that "the advance of heavy columns of the enemy upon the city of Jackson . . . , at a time when we had no adequate force for its protection, rendered it necessary, in my opinion, to remove the archives and public property of the State, as far as I was able, from Jackson."[28]

In this "confused state of public affairs," the state's treasury went to Mobile, Alabama, the judicial records to Selma, and the archives to Demopolis. The military equipment that could be removed went only to Meridian, and the state quartermaster general reported that "we have been quite fortunate in saving nearly everything with the exception of a few articles of camp and garrison equipage, and sacks, and some office furniture." A more pressing problem was the state penitentiary, the superintendent advising Pettus that there were a few inmates who were "unfriendly to our cause" and would likely join the Federals, they being "*Lincolnites* of the deepest dye." Pettus sent the belligerent prisoners to Wetumpka, Alabama, after contacting the governor of that state, and pardoned a few who said they would fight; the remaining ones, mostly too old to resist, were "turned out without pardon."[29]

Little activity other than in Jackson occurred east of the Big Black River, however, despite that being where the Federal army was located. There was some effort to organize small Confederate cavalry commands to hit the flanks and rear of the Federal army as it presumably moved toward Vicksburg, the orders reading to "press the enemy's rear as much as possible, cutting their supply trains." There was also a larger concentration of troops converging on Jackson, but there was little positioning of forces themselves in the area east of the Big Black River. While Pemberton kept his main force to the west of the river, he left the defense of the area to the east for the numerous reinforcements that were reportedly on the way.[30]

The main force that was operating in the area east of the Big Black River of course found Federals. Lieutenant W. L. Cromwell led a detachment of cavalry southward toward Willow Springs on May 4 but was blocked by the Federal divisions then holding the area. And he even endured friendly fire, which wounded four of his men. The next day, May 5, he confronted several of McClernand's probes in the area around Hall's Ferry, Cromwell admitting that he met the enemy's cavalry and "they charged and routed me." He nevertheless alerted Pemberton of his efforts and that "my horses are broken down." At the least, Cromwell furnished good intelligence that the enemy was nearby east of the river, and he was willing to continue his operations: "What are your orders," he queried as he ended his message.[31]

Aiding the Confederate defense east of the Big Black River, reinforcements from several areas were indeed on the way by the time Grant was across Bayou Pierre and about to head northward. One Confederate admitted to his wife that "I am fearful that we are going to be troubled to hold this place, but reinforcements are coming in on every train so when the fight does open it will be in ernest." Major General Simon Bolivar Buckner at Mobile sent the 2nd Alabama Cavalry to help. More substantial, Secretary of War James A. Seddon informed Pemberton that ten thousand men had been ordered to move to his department from South Carolina, then under the command of General P. G. T. Beauregard. The South Carolina commander balked at the order to send ten thousand, and Seddon admitted that possibly only five thousand would actually move, but Beauregard did send those five thousand in two brigades, plus two batteries, commanded by Brigadier Generals States Rights Gist and William H. T. Walker. Beauregard termed these two brigades his "best troops" and asked Pemberton to keep them together, preferably in a division under Gist, so that they would retain their autonomy and, despite being left unsaid, perhaps make it easier to send them back in bulk when the crisis in Mississippi was over. Beauregard later elaborated that these were "the best that could be spared, under two of my ablest generals," and added that his own son, Rene Beauregard, was making the trip as well, he being a lieutenant in one of the batteries. For Pemberton's part, he was thankful any troops were on the way but complained to Seddon in Richmond that "it is a very insufficient number. The stake is a great one. I can see nothing so important."[32]

Pemberton also used the authority he had within his own department to order more troops to the area. While communications with Franklin Gardner at Port Hudson were sketchy at best because of the Union army's presence in between as well as Grierson's destruction of the railroad south of Jackson, Pemberton nevertheless sent messages by courier part of the way. He ultimately ordered Gardner himself to move northward with two brigades numbering five thousand men together. Pemberton specifically wanted Brigadier General Samuel B. Maxey, but Gardner, who could not read the entire message in cipher and spent several days seeking clarification, eventually sent the two brigades. First a mainly Tennessee brigade under Brigadier General John Gregg moved northward, followed later by the brigade under Maxey. Gardner himself did not leave Port Hudson.[33]

Pemberton likewise continued to call in smaller bodies of troops in his own area, as well as supplies and stores for the final showdown at Vicksburg, if it came to that. Those called in earlier, such as Buford from Meridian, were still on the way but would be forwarded directly behind the shield of the Big Black River. Faraway points such as Fort Pemberton at Greenwood were almost totally given up, Waul's Texas Legion making its way to the crisis scene and thereby leaving only a token garrison behind. Pemberton also ordered his petulant district commander in northeastern Mississippi, Brigadier General Daniel Ruggles, to "send at once to this point every available man you can, except your artillery at Columbus and your cavalry in advance." He then added, "no excuse will be taken for not obeying this." A wise Ruggles soon forwarded to Vicksburg two regiments of Mississippi State Troops under state militia commander Brigadier General Jeptha V. Harris. In terms of supplies, Pemberton finally had to issue blanket orders from Vicksburg: "Impress all the bacon and beef you can get, and send it here at once."[34]

Outside his shrinking realm around Vicksburg, Pemberton also had to deal with his departmental commander in Middle Tennessee, Joseph E. Johnston. He had long been a thorn in Pemberton's side and had a knack for being late in orders and messages and uninformed about what was occurring in Mississippi. Some of that could have been Pemberton's fault, of course, but he was quite busy at the time dealing with the crisis in his department. Johnston, for instance, wrote on May 6: "Have heard nothing further from you of the previous battles, reported on 1st. What was the result, and where is Grant's army?" He followed with "let me know the location of your troops, number, and places, in cipher" as well as an order to put Brigadier General Alfred Cumming in command of a Georgia brigade in the place of Brigadier General Thomas H. Taylor, who would remain and serve Pemberton on his staff. Still, it was obvious that Johnston was pretty uninterested in what was happening in Mississippi, certainly not seeing it as the crisis that it was.[35]

Yet even with the work outside the Vicksburg area, it was abundantly clear that Pemberton's focus was on the river city itself. In fact, on May 5 Pemberton's assistant adjutant general Robert W. Memminger issued orders that "Headquarters Department of Mississippi and Eastern Louisiana is removed from Jackson, Miss., to Vicksburg. All communications will be addressed accordingly." Perhaps to better facilitate the movement of supplies into Vicksburg, the order also stipulated that for the time being the quartermaster, commissary, and ordnance departments would remain in Jackson.[36]

Pemberton's placement of troops likewise indicated his area of major concern. By May 4, all five of his divisions were tucked away inside the Big Black River. Loring and a few troops remained southward around Hankinson's Ferry to watch the enemy while Bowen's exhausted division, which had been conducting active operations for several days now, including the battle on May 1, moved northward to an encampment on Clear Creek just north of Bovina. One of John C. Moore's soldiers near Warrenton related that "in a few days after Bowen's defeat, some of his troops passed our camps worn down and exhausted from repeated forced marches." He added, "it always makes me feel bad to behold a retreating army." Bowen reported his arrival, writing that his men were "exceedingly broken down with the heat and long-continued fatigue, and will not be collected well together before to-morrow afternoon." One of his men agreed, writing that "this last day's march ranks one among our very hardest since the organization of the Brigade." Others were exhausted as well, Claudius Sears of the 46th Mississippi describing the trek back to Vicksburg as "a hot, dusty and inglorious march." A grateful Pemberton nevertheless wired Richmond that day "respectfully urging that he [Bowen] be promoted to the rank of major-general."[37]

But Pemberton did not have a lot of time for rest, not knowing that the Federal probes were merely that. In fact, as Union forces began to move northward, even approaching Edwards Station as well as across the Big Black River at Hankinson's Ferry, Pemberton began to deploy his divisions to keep the enemy at bay to the east. Plus, he had worries in other directions, with a portion of Major General John Forney's division still deployed northward along the Yazoo River to Snyder's Bluff as well as others southward to Warrenton, where there was obviously Union activity. Even on the river he was alert, especially after the failed Union attempt to get the tug and barges through on

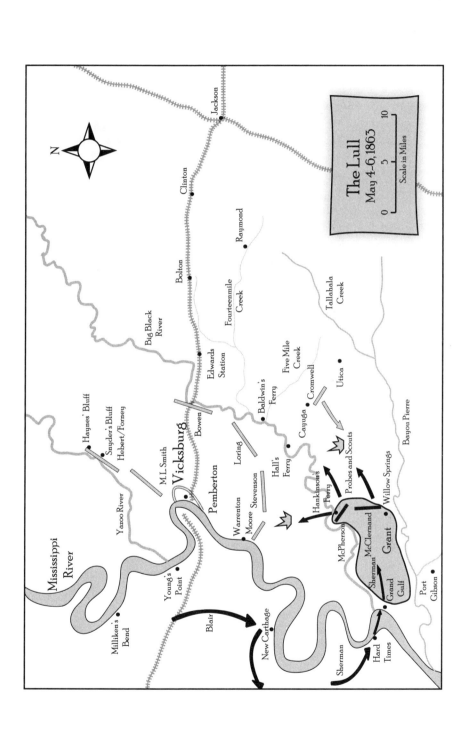

The Lull
May 4-6, 1863

0   5   10
Scale in Miles

the night of May 3. Pemberton reported that effort was unsuccessful and that twenty-four prisoners were rounded up, including "one correspondent New York *World*, two New York *Tribune*, and one Cincinnati *Times*."[38]

The river effort being what it was, Pemberton's attention remained fixated to the east, the obvious direction of trouble. As he read the Federal probes, Pemberton continued to convince himself that the main Union thrust would come at the railroad bridge. It was obvious that the right thing for any Federal commander to do would be to cut off Vicksburg's supply and communication lines, and Pemberton determined that was an area of immediate need. But the other avenues of approach could not be abandoned either, especially with Federals across the Big Black to the south.[39]

Accordingly, Pemberton began to shift his divisions to meet the growing threat, even using Bowen's exhausted brigades. The division being near Edwards and the railroad bridge, he ordered it to be ready to man those works by taking over for some of Loring's troops, although Loring was at this point still to the south: "Keep your self ready to move at a moment's warning to take Loring's position at Edwards," he notified Bowen. Loring's troops, still concentrating, would shift to the south to watch the ferries in that direction after strengthening the works around the railroad bridge for Bowen's troops: "I wish to change your position to support Stevenson." Meanwhile, Stevenson's division around Vicksburg would shift farther south and watch the approaches all the way down around Redbone Church and toward Hankinson's Ferry and over to Warrenton. It would provide eventually a manned line of nine brigades in Bowen's, Loring's, and Stevenson's divisions, left to right, along the Big Black River and over to the Mississippi at Warrenton. Meanwhile, Forney's two brigades would continue to hold north of the railroad on the Yazoo River and southward to Warrenton. Major General Martin L. Smith's brigades continued to man Vicksburg itself and act as a reserve.[40]

With the orders issued, the divisions began to move to their assigned positions on May 4. Loring was still down at Hankinson's Ferry with the rear guard but began the process of moving up toward Edwards to take command of his division as it shifted southward. He notified Pemberton from Hankinson's Ferry before leaving, however, that "I may be forced, whether I wish it or not, to give this enemy battle here." Pemberton's staff officer Jacob Thompson responded that "if you are satisfied the enemy is in force at Hankinson's Ferry, you must make your disposition to meet him. . . . If battle is imminent, the lieutenant-general commanding will come down himself." As May 4 developed and it became clear that the Federals were not interested in moving across the Big Black River in force that day, Loring left to take command of his division, themselves "prostrated by constant marching and want of sleep."[41]

The lull allowed Loring to turn over defense of the southern stretches of the Big Black River to Stevenson's arriving brigades, namely the Georgia one under Taylor slated to soon be under the command of Alfred Cumming. Loring recommended it move all the way to the river itself at Hankinson's Ferry to halt any more Federal movement. But Loring, as he made his way northward to his division, also decided it was time to give his larger thoughts, given Pemberton's obvious concern for the railroad bridge to the north. Loring had just left the southern ferries where there were numerous Federals and queried Pemberton: "Has it occurred to you that it would be a difficult matter for a large command of the enemy to march to the railroad without making preparations, and that they might move upon Warrenton by water?" Contrary to Pemberton's developing thoughts, Loring was betting on a crossing of the Big Black to the south and a Union advance due northward to Vicksburg. "You are better able, however, to judge of this," Loring added.[42]

As it turned out, Pemberton was indeed better able to judge, as Grant was thinking right along with Pemberton, not Loring. And through the night, to Loring's growing disgust, Pemberton's shuffling of divisions continued, Loring writing from Mount Alban that Bowen was moving, his own division was concentrating, and that "Stevenson and Taylor [are] in their positions." He added, "have no further information relative to enemy's movements other side Big Black." But more Federal moves early the next morning toward the railroad, McClernand's probes northward, sent Pemberton into a frenzy to defend the bridge. Loring was there by that time, Pemberton telling him that "you must hold the bridge."[43]

Amid the shuffling of commands, one Confederate writing that "our generals have been riding about fixing on the place where we shall meet Mr. Yankee," Carter Stevenson was also beginning to get agitated. Jacob Thompson lectured him that "the attention of the lieutenant-general commanding is drawn as much to the Big Black as in your direction, and unless he is kept constantly advised of every movement, he is unable to act with any satisfaction or certainty." Stevenson did not need the lecture but simply advised that his line was too lengthy to keep an eye on everything. By dawn on May 5, for instance, he had Stephen D. Lee's Alabama brigade at Hall's Ferry to the north, Alexander W. Reynold's Tennesseans near Hankinson's Ferry itself, and Seth Barton's Georgians at Warrenton. It was an L-shaped line of some fifteen miles covered by three brigades. "The line is too extended," Stevenson alerted Pemberton, "and with but three brigades, and having no cavalry, [I]

cannot properly watch it." As Stevenson's fourth brigade also took its position in rear as a reserve, he also requested supplies be sent down so the men
would be properly equipped. Pemberton did so, as well as ordering cavalry to
aid Stevenson in watching the various ferries.[44]

As the lull continued into May 5, Carter Stevenson tried a new tactic down
at Hankinson's Ferry. Like Loring, he believed that Grant would likely cross
there and push northward to Vicksburg, so he ordered the ferry and bridge
itself unmanned, drawing Reynolds's brigade back a bit to "give the enemy
a chance to show his force." Obviously, McPherson did so that day by crossing Boomer's troops, although with only a small force before returning south
and east of the river—"small parties" one Confederate staff officer described
them. But the crossing seemed to make Pemberton more aware of the threat
below, especially when word arrived that Federal cavalry had approached
to within a mile and a half of Redbone Church and were "advancing rapidly." Pemberton accordingly shifted in his thoughts a little, he writing later
on May 5: "When the enemy intends to make his advance in force against
Warrenton he will probably demonstrate heavily toward railroad bridge." To
help Stevenson's defense, he authorized Brigadier General John C. Moore's
brigade of Forney's division down at Warrenton to be temporarily attached to
Stevenson's command, giving him five brigades to defend the lower ferries
and Warrenton.[45]

Although the Federal probes westward and northward made Pemberton
take pause as to which way the telling blow would come, he continued to
implement his original plan on May 5. He ordered Bowen to take position at
the railroad bridge itself, in the works constructed on the east side, and to send
a regiment on to Edwards as an advance. Bowen sent Colonel Amos C. Riley's 1st Missouri Cavalry (dismounted). Further orders arrived for Bowen to
remove the hundred and fifteen thousand pounds of rice onboard the steamer
Bufort at the railroad bridge, it being one of the vessels scared northward
by McClernand's probes to Hall's Ferry. Bowen's troops soon arrived and
took command of the railroad bridge area, although he was also ordered
to send any cavalry with him southward to aid Stevenson's defense of the
ferries.[46]

All the while, Loring was moving his division from the railroad bridge to
Lanier's Plantation on the Baldwin's Ferry Road. Pemberton advised haste,
although he ordered, "move as directed, but don't withdraw that portion of
your command which has been at Edwards Depot until relieved by General
Bowen." But soon Loring's brigades concentrated at Lanier's and endeavored
to find out as much as possible what was happening across the Big Black
River. More details emerged by May 6 of Union thrusts to the north toward

the railroad bridge "in large force and in several columns," and Lloyd Tilgh-man led the effort to get good intelligence from the local citizenry as well as his own scouts. They watched from across the river at times, and the civilians in the area gave word of thousands of Federals moving northward. Tilghman reported that he would "converse with the man (Hacklu) living at the ferry, who is reported by Mr. Lanier as a reliable man. I have also directed him to try and see Mr. Newman, who lives near by." Word of happenings below also arrived, interestingly, from Lieutenant Colonel Edmund W. Pettus of the 20th Alabama, captured at Port Gibson. Most thought he had been killed, but he ambled in on May 6, having escaped captivity by rolling over into the water and swimming away. If nothing else, it was a good thing to have the Missis-sippi governor's brother back in the army, and Pettus quickly sent a telegram to his brother the governor apprising of his safety.[47]

Yet as May 6 developed and more and more reports of Federal activity at both Hankinson's Ferry and Hall's Ferry arrived, it started to look like the in-cursions were "a mere party of observation." Still, Carter Stevenson was not satisfied with his line even now that he had fallen back somewhat, he terming it nine miles in length but still "too long—9 miles—for one division." He and a couple of his brigadier generals rode the entire line that morning and determined where they could fall back to if necessary, although he planned to send additional scouts forward to uncover any new enemy probes.[48]

But there was clearly a growing indignation among the division command-ers, Stevenson included, that centered on their belief that Pemberton was not commanding adequately. Obviously, the confusion of whether the en-emy advance would come up the east side of the Big Black River or across the ferries to the south was enough to cause chaos, but Pemberton was not helping matters by remaining in Vicksburg. Indeed, the division commanders seemed to be getting irritated especially at his determination to remain be-hind, Stevenson writing on May 4, "will go in to-morrow to see you." Loring too wrote on May 6, "will come to Vicksburg." An observant staff officer, Lieutenant William Drennan, picked up on the growing chaos, later writing his wife: "There is quite a feud existing between Loring and Pemberton—so far as Loring is concerned[.] I heard several expressions of disrespect at Greenwood—and also at Laniers and then at Edwards—in fact it amounted to that degree of hatred on the part of Loring that Capt. [William] Barksdale and myself agreed that Loring would be willing for Pemberton to lose a battle provided that he would be displaced."[49]

This command turmoil could not have come at a worse time, as Grant was preparing to move forward. One Louisianan incisively wrote in his diary on May 5, "the crisis to decide the fate of Vicksburg has nearly arrived."[50]

Even amid the scouting forward in preparation for a general advance, nerves began to fray on the Union side as well, perhaps because of the wait or even because of the delicate position the army was still in. "We shall have a hot time of it now for about a month as we are moving to the rear of Vicksburgh," brigade commander John E. Smith wrote home. Stuck out in the middle of nowhere as they were, however, the matter of supplies was the biggest issue. McClernand repeated to Grant on May 4 his note from the day before, adding that "I infer that you did not receive the communication. I repeat the request that it contains," which was to provide rations for the XIII Corps. He again reminded Grant that he had no transportation: "The teams belonging to this corps are, as you are aware, behind, and cannot be brought here unless water transportation is afforded to bring them across the river." Showing his growing frustration, especially when it seemed the XVII Corps had ample transportation, McClernand added that "I have sent three officers successively to look after this matter," but nothing had been done. The growing thoughts of conspiracy against him continued to fester in McClernand's fertile mind, and he even wrote President Lincoln from Willow Springs on May 6 about his situation.[51]

McClernand's outrage grew as May 4 moved on, and he penned yet another complaint to Grant that as of yet "no trains or provisions have yet arrived from Grand Gulf." Then he added a specific charge of favoritism, writing that "the officer in charge of transports has given preference to the Seventeenth Army Corps in everything. The baggage of that corps is being sent forward, to the exclusion of ammunition and provisions for the Thirteenth Army Corps; priority is even given to forage over necessary supplies for the Thirteenth Army Corps." McClernand further noted that only three of his XIII Corps wagons were across the river and that "I am convinced that your order to send out provisions and ammunition with any teams that may be found at Grand Gulf has failed to challenge obedience." He added, "without necessary provisions and ammunition, of course, I cannot answer for results."[52]

By May 6, McClernand was in such an uproar that he fairly demanded action from Grant. He sent his commissary chief, Lieutenant Colonel Wesford Taggart—who was also in charge of foraging in the area, to see Grant personally at Hankinson's Ferry, telling him with the note sent along that he wanted "an order placing a hundred wagons of the Seventeenth Army Corps, or any wagons, at his disposal, for the purpose of bringing rations to the men of the Thirteenth Army Corps." McClernand added, "he will explain the necessity for it."[53]

McClernand was not just being disruptive, as his commanders were reporting to him the very problems he forwarded on up the chain of command. His chief quartermaster was none other than his double father-in-law (McClernand had married two of his daughters), Lieutenant Colonel James Dunlap. Also at work supplying the corps were two assistants, Captains John T. Allen and Michael C. Garber. Both informed McClernand of the problems. Field officers did as well. Osterhaus, for example, notified McClernand on May 6 that "the provisions have not yet arrived. My men are now 3 days without bread or meal, and have to subsist on fresh meat only and all together from the Doctors reports there is some diarrhea prevailing already from that kind of food." He added that "it would be a great relief to the command if the commissary stores could be brought on soon." In a different note the same day, he elaborated that "we find meat and beef enough to supply us: bread stuffs are the great difficulty, but a small steam corn-mill in the neighborhood, which was put in operation to day, besides the mule mill, will go far to help us along." But it was more than just food. Osterhaus also had entire regiments and batteries without enough ammunition and ordered three of them to "equalize"; it was also ordered that "the 49th Ind., 114th & 120th Ohio Infantry being short of ammunition will remain here and draw a further supply to fill them up to 80 rounds per man. The 1st Wisconsin battery will also remain." Osterhaus ended another message: "Anxiously awaiting the ammunition."[54]

The other issue was getting more troops up. While there was still one division of McPherson's XVII Corps west of the Mississippi River, there were also three of Sherman's XV Corps divisions, and Grant wanted them first. He realized he would need to keep some troops west of the river and would much rather have some or all of McArthur's division there than Sherman's three. As a result, he ordered Sherman to quickly move to Grand Gulf and up to the army even while at the same time bringing supplies and shortening the route for both to Grand Gulf. In fact, Sherman caught up with much of McArthur's division near New Carthage, one brigade at Smith's Plantation and another at Holmes's, but related that "I shall pass it."[55]

Sherman did his best in a difficult situation, one of his soldiers reporting half-rations on the march to the river and only one wagon per regiment. Not knowing much more detail than what Grant had told him earlier, Sherman could get little more from him now, as Grant had moved to the front of the army up near Hankinson's Ferry and was not available for quick correspondence. But Sherman guessed at what he wanted and would do, telling Frank Blair that "he [Grant] is evidently moving by the road on the east side of Big Black." He added that he would press ahead himself and try to contact Grant "wherever he may be." But into Sherman's correspondence also creeped doubt just like in McClernand's, Sherman also writing that "you know we have not wagons and boats to handle all the material needed by this army, but the whole success of this plan depends on its hardihood."[56]

Sherman went to work anyway, John Marszalek writing that all throughout the campaign "Sherman did everything Grant asked of him." In telling Blair that "some other way must be found to feed this army," he went on: "I wish you would cause our old road over to Biggs' to be examined." Sherman, and Grant, wanted the route southward reduced by whatever means possible now that the river was falling, opening up new possibilities: "This road must be shortened, else this army will be without food in two days," Sherman predicted. But until that was done, the same old roundabout route the rest of the army had used to Hard Times was still the one to trod. "Keep everywhere hauling stores forward, so as to reach the Mississippi at Carthage or Perkins,'" he told Blair. When several new brigadier generals arrived at his headquarters, Sherman fairly exploded. "What I want is mules. If they will send me the mules, they can keep the brigadiers."[57]

Sherman traveled the route himself, arriving at Smith's Plantation near New Carthage by the evening of May 3 and moving on to Perkins's Plantation the next day. "Road tolerably good," he wrote his commanders in the rear, "but lumpy, from old plow furrows and ruts. All the road would become awful in a rain." There was also the rubbish of the entire army that remained behind the line of march, including stragglers and those not at all interested in rejoining their units up at the front. Sherman himself ran into one such soldier whom he found ensconced at an abandoned mansion in Louisiana, sitting in a satin chair "with his feet on the keys of the piano." He found out it was one of McPherson's men, and after the soldier explained that he was "taking a rest," Sherman noted that "this was manifest and I started him in a hurry to overtake his command." By the evening of May 4 Sherman crossed over to Grand Gulf itself but did not find Grant, who "was supposed to be out about 24 miles." There, he learned of the results of Grierson's Raid, writing that "it was Grierson who made the cavalry raid down to Meridian, and he is supposed to be traveling toward Baton Rouge or Dixie." He added, perhaps still with some doubt, "it has produced a sort of panic South, and Grant's movements will complete it, some say."[58]

Sherman issued his orders on May 5. To Tuttle he wrote, "continue your march down, so as to reach Grand Gulf in good order." He still had fears about supplies and could not help but add that "I apprehend great difficulty in the matter of food, and caution you to give the subject your whole attention. . . . Every ounce of food must be economized." He mentioned making three days' rations last five and added that "we must caution all the men accordingly." To Steele, who was temporarily detained because of a court of inquiry (the division moved out under brigade commander John Thayer's command), he similarly cautioned "not [to] stop at Perkins', but march right along down the Mississippi to a point opposite Grand Gulf." He also included the warning to "arrive in good order and condition." Ironically, as Sherman's troops pressed southward, they ran into the Confederate prisoners from Port Gibson being sent northward. "All expressions and remarks made by either party while our captives were passing were made in a friendly tone," Illinoisan Henry Seaman explained, "as though good feeling had ever existed between them." Another Illinoisan even remembered the Confederates joking that "all fashionable Southern gentlemen took a trip North during the hot months." Also sent back to the hospitals on plantations west of the river, after initially being brought forward with the army, were the wounded from Port Gibson and the other actions. Destruction was rampant nevertheless, one Illinoisan in Tuttle's division remarking that all the plantations had been "plundered by the advance. Steele's division, ahead of us today, completes the destruction."[59]

Far in the rear, Blair's orders required more detail, simply because that division was disconnected and was so tied to the supply chain. Sherman told Blair likewise to "come forward to me at Grand Gulf" but to leave four regiments along the line (two at Richmond and two at Milliken's Bend), although they would soon be replaced and released by four regiments ordered southward from Memphis. Blair was to turn over command of the western side in Louisiana to Brigadier General Jeremiah Sullivan and move southward, "bringing along as much rations and stores as you can, for there is little or nothing down here." He finished with, "I wish you to come forward with all possible expedition."[60]

But as matters developed, Sherman later modified his orders to Blair at the tail end of the column, writing that the crossing would go much slower than he had hoped because "the steamboats here are poor concerns, except the *Forest Queen*, and the ferrying across will be a slow process." He added, "I would not be surprised if you would overhaul us before we are all across." As a result, he allowed Blair to take it slower along the sixty-three-mile route: "Road cannot be mistaken; better at this end than at yours. . . . But in case of accident follow us to Grand Gulf." Because of the delay, he added, "don't hurry your march too much, for I feel certain it will take some days to pass over the troops now here, and the wagons. Try and arrive in good, compact order, and with as much provision and ammunition left as possible." He ended with "I shall begin to look for you on the third day from this, unless we move far inland. . . . I will keep in mind where you are, and await your junction with anxiety."[61]

Accordingly, Sherman crossed that very night, May 6, along with the 13th Illinois, and Tuttle's and Steele's divisions began their crossing soon thereafter. One Illinoisan described how "[we] find here a great crowd of troops crossing the river as fast as three transports and two gunboats can carry them." Most of the stores the men could not carry had to be left west of the river, Sherman barking orders to "burn them; burn them" but refusing to sign such an order when put on the spot. After crossing, some of the men took time out to get a look at the Grand Gulf defenses they had heard so much about, some taking umbrage with all the seized Confederate cannons being labeled "Captured by Rear Admiral Porter." Yet the crossing was not easy, just as Sherman predicted, he later admitting that "at the river there was a good deal of scrambling to get across, because the means of ferriage were inadequate." The *Forest Queen* was available as were some of the gunboats, the *Louisville* and *Carondelet*, and a few of the shot-up transports that had passed Vicksburg's batteries back in April. David W. Reed of the 12th Iowa explained that his regiment crossed on the *J. W. Cheeseman*, "one of the boats that had passed the batteries, and showed, by riddled woodwork and smokestacks, the terrible fire to which she had been subjected." The crossing continued through the night regardless, and the next day and that night as well, even as Blair made his way methodically southward to Hard Times. The XV Corps had arrived, two divisions' worth at least, and was ready to head northward as soon as all were across. "There are now six divisions of our men across and operating east of Grand Gulf," Sherman told one of his commanders; "let us catch up as quickly as possible consistent with bringing our men there in good fighting condition." Now with some thirty-three thousand troops east of the Mississippi River, Grant had ample force to restart his movement northward toward Vicksburg.[62]

Yet as the XV Corps set out on its march even that night over the "eternally plunging or winding" road, the men were given five days' worth of hardtack and coffee and told to conserve it as much as possible; meat would be taken from the surrounding country. "With these limited supplies," David W. Reed wrote, "the command cut loose from communication with the outside world." Obviously, the hardtack did not last five days, and only a couple of days in Reed admitted that "the only resources left them was to steal rations from the army mule, and eat parched corn or go supperless to bed." At times, the men rounded up some stray cattle and drove them into camp for roasting during the night, but even that was hard to come by as Sherman's men marched through an area already pretty much swept clean of anything edible by the troops ahead of them. One Indianan noted his rations had been "reduced to cold mush and tea," an Illinoisan similarly writing that "we could not draw eneything but flour, that is *NO CRACKERS* we baked the flour in fried cakes." And to make it worse, few were impressed with Mississippi, one Iowan writing that he marched "20 miles over a very rough country. The roads very good however except the ups and downs and dust." He added, "I stood it well . . . [but] I call this a very poor part of the country."[63]

While grateful to have the XV Corps now crossing, Grant still kept a handle on the situation in the rear despite being out front and seemingly out of immediate contact with Sherman. On May 5, for instance, he asked Lieutenant Commander Elias K. Owen of the ironclad *Louisville*, commanding the remaining flotilla since Admiral Porter had moved southward into Louisiana, to keep a gunboat "in the mouth of Big Black River, to watch any movement of the enemy in that direction." He also wanted one "in front of Grand Gulf, to guard the stores, and to convey any steamer that may require it." Finally, he asked—and fairly ordered—Owen to send the "remaining iron-clads" up to Warrenton "to prevent them from sending troops across the river, to interrupt our lines from Milliken's Bend and Young's Point." In addition, there was still some activity even south of Bayou Pierre, some of the supply trains actually moving back to Bruinsburg to bring up what had been left there. A detail from Colonel George Boomer's brigade, then at Hankinson's Ferry, even had slight skirmishing with Confederates near Bruinsburg on May 6 until Colonel Clark Wright and the 6th Missouri Cavalry arrived to drive the enemy away. Grant showed some concern about the area: "When every thing in the forks of the river [Bayou Pierre] is cleared out and ferries distroyed," he ordered forward "everything between Bruinsburg and Port Gibson." Especially of concern was getting the wounded from Port Gibson's fight to a safe place such as Grand Gulf or back across the river to the plantations on the western side.[64]

Grant even sent word back to his XVI Corps commander Major General Stephen A. Hurlbut in Memphis to mobilize for this last great effort. In addition to ordering Bingham to request a hundred more wagons from Hurlbut, he had already ordered four regiments from Memphis southward. But on May 5, Grant sent word for Hurlbut to start the entirety of Brigadier General Jacob Lauman's division southward, which the XVI Corps commander did, writing, "and [I] only regret that I am not there to fight it." But he did request that "as I have a very strong interest in my old division, and know their preference, I respectfully ask of the major general commanding to attach them to General Sherman's corps, as they and I have the fullest confidence and largest acquaintance with him and his command." Unstated, of course, was that the request was a backward slap, not especially at McPherson but probably more so at McClernand. In addition, Grant asked Hurlbut to utilize his cavalry "as much as possible for attracting attention from this direction." But he was very careful to limit the negative aspects of the cavalry raiders in his still fairly benign view of the war in mid-1863. While ordering the cavalry to live off the country and to "destroy corn, wheat crops, and everything that can be made use of by the enemy in prolonging the war," he still limited their raiding, ordering the "keeping out of people's houses or taking what is of no use to them in a military way." He summed up by stating, "in other words, cripple the rebellion in every way, without insulting women and children or taking their clothing, jewelry, &c."[65]

But Grant's main concern was local—namely getting troops and supplies across the river to Grand Gulf, where Colonel Green B. Raum became the post commander with his 56th Illinois and 17th Illinois as garrison to load and unload goods. To superintend the effort, Grant kept his staff officer Colonel Hillyer in charge of the Grand Gulf supply base with orders to do what was necessary to get supplies in and distribute them to the army. But he cautioned Hillyer to depend solely on the route west of the river, as the latest attempt to move supplies by Vicksburg had failed. "We will risk no more rations to run the Vicksburg batteries," he told Hillyer. Instead, he wanted the road network west of the river cut down: "The river falling will enable us to contract our lines so as to give but 8 miles of land transportation to bring them from Young's Point to below Warrenton batteries." This would have the added effect of allowing those troops guarding the more lengthy supply line to concentrate and join the army east of the river, including the two brigades of McArthur's division and Blair's division that were already en route.[66]

Still, being at the front of the army at Hankinson's Ferry, with only periodic trips into Grand Gulf, Grant left the rear area without firm overall control; his staff had to take up the slack at times. Hillyer was the transportation supervisor at Grand Gulf, with authority to speak for Grant if necessary: "See that the Com.y at Grand Gulf loads all wagons presenting themselves for stores with great promptness. Issue any order in my name that may be necessary to secure the greatest promptness in this respect. . . . Movements here are delayed for want of ammunition and stores. Every delay is worth two thousand men to the enemy. Give this your personal attention." Grant even gave Hillyer authority to relieve officers if they were not doing their jobs. Others took on additional authority as well. Colonel Theodore S. Bowers at Milliken's Bend, struggling to keep the supply chain full on his end, even went outside the chain of command to get additional resources. Telling Hurlbut in Memphis that "recent attempts have demonstrated the impossibility of sending supplies by the Vicksburg batteries during these moonlight nights," Bowers described the problems in just getting supplies to Grand Gulf. It was at the time forty-four miles that supplies had to be "wagoned," and "it is feared that, with the present limited land transportation, it will be impossible to keep the army from suffering," especially now that Grant had moved inland. Bowers stated that each regiment had on average only two wagons apiece; "all other teams have been thrown into the general supply train, which is still inadequate." Bowers wrote that "General Grant is in the advance, and cannot be consulted on the subject of this letter, but the great importance of keeping the army supplied induces me to present these facts for your consideration." In sum, Bowers asked that Hurlbut send down "all teams that can possibly be spared from your command," to be sent back "as soon as the present emergency passes away."[67]

Other staff issues causing confusion about the shorter route west of the Mississippi River notwithstanding, certainly Grant would have approved the forethinking of his staff officers, amid the delay at Hankinson's Ferry as he was. And he also requested that Bingham send a quartermaster to the head of the army as well, specifically requesting Captain William Gaster. He had wanted to start the army northward as soon as possible, but now by the night of May 6 the delay was stretching into a third day. "Ferrying and transportation of rations to Grand Gulf is detaining us on the Big Black River," he informed Halleck on May 6. Similarly, "the only thing now delaying us is the ferriage of wagons and supplies across the river to Grand Gulf," Grant wrote one of his generals on May 6. "Rations now are the only delay."[68]

With what meager supplies that were arriving being distributed and Sherman starting to cross the Mississippi River the night of May 6, Grant ordered the advance of the army restarted. Although taking a little longer than expected, he was ready to proceed by May 7. "Everything here looks highly favorable at present," he wrote Stephen A. Hurlbut back in Memphis. "We hold the bridge across Big Black at this place, and have had troops within 7 miles of Warrenton. Also command the next crossing, some 15 miles higher up the river, from which another road leads direct to Vicksburg."[69]

Grant wanted McPherson to lead the way, issuing orders for the divisions to move the next morning, May 7. McPherson sent out the orders quickly on the evening of May 6, writing Logan, "you will move your division to Rocky Springs to-morrow at 10 a.m." McPherson had his corps engineer already out exploring in the previous days and sent him to guide Logan and select adequate camping areas. "The men will march with three days' cooked rations in haversacks, and you will take in the wagons of your division all the ammunition and rations you possibly can." To make sure the bridge at Hankinson's Ferry was guarded at the same time, Crocker was ordered to send a brigade to replace Logan's troops and remain there until the lead elements of Sherman's XV Corps, crossing the Mississippi River even then, arrived to take its place.[70]

In starting east of the Big Black River, Grant was of course hinting at his intended plan, which was not actually hard to figure out. Essentially, Grant had two options to approach Vicksburg, one being crossing the Big Black River and heading straight for the city from the south. The other was to move up the east side of the Big Black River to the railroad, cut that transportation route, and then head west to an isolated Vicksburg. Most thought the Confederates would cover the Big Black River crossings, but McPherson's probes had actually found it easy to cross, especially at Hankinson's Ferry and presumably too at Hall's Ferry to the north. Still, these probes had alerted Pemberton to the idea that Grant would flood across the river and head directly north toward Vicksburg via Warrenton. Confederate newspapers printed such surmisings.[71]

Grant winced at the former choice. He did not want to get his entire army caught in the upside-down triangle between the Mississippi River on the west, the Big Black River to the east and south, and Vicksburg and the railroad to the north. Being unable to maneuver if necessary in that small of an area might prove decisive. "The broken nature of the ground would have enabled him [Pemberton] to hold a strong defensible line from the river south of the city to the Big Black," Grant later wrote, "retaining possession of the railroad back to that point." Still, Grant let the various probes at the numerous crossings work in his favor, admitting that he let them "induce the enemy to think that route and the one by Hall's Ferry, above, were objects of much solicitude to me." It even worked on some of his own troops, one of whom reported how "all the skiffs in the country were got together and roads were cut to the water at various places."[72]

While Grant indicated that the move would be west of the Big Black River in what one Confederate called a "ruse," he actually intended to move to its east up the corridor to the railroad. "It was my intention here to hug the Big Black River as closely as possible with McClernand's and Sherman's corps, and get them to the railroad at some place between Edwards Station and Bolton." That was logical, and Grant had actually let it be known that was his plan all along. Charles Dana described Grant as early as May 4 planning to push "his army toward the Big Black Bridge and Jackson, threatening both and striking at either, as is most convenient." Sherman likewise wrote on

May 5 that "the enemy has escaped across Big Black River, and Grant will now probably strike in the direction of the Jackson Railroad." Word must have filtered out to the army as well either by choice or leak, as numerous soldiers began to report the plan as early as May 6. The genius was apparent; not only would he drive in between any gathering Confederate forces at Jackson and those in Vicksburg, but he would also cut Vicksburg's one lifeline to the outside world as well as perhaps bottle up its defenders for destruction.[73]

With the plan decided upon, a nervous Grant simply waited as rations were distributed on the evening of May 6 and the army prepared to lunge forward the next day. One Federal explained that they "got a few rations of salt pork and crackers which put new life in us for we had marched . . . without super or breakfast." Another noted that "we are wanting for rations and then we will drive them into their stronghold." Yet another was just as confident. "I expect we will have a big fight in a few days," one Missourian informed his wife on May 6, "in which I expect to be on the winning side." Perhaps an Illinoisan said it best while in camp near the river: "I think that if they get many more whippings as they got the other day that they would get enough of it."[74]

8

"I THINK HE KNOWS WHAT HE IS DOING"

May 7–9

"We still have the Southron R.R. open," commented a Louisianan in his diary on May 7, adding "we are looking for an attack here at any moment." But by the time the campaign for Vicksburg began to move again on May 7, the chessboard of war had shrunk significantly. And with that shrinkage came large ramifications, especially concerning the generals themselves. Grant had been hampered somewhat throughout the entire campaign by long distances and water everywhere. As a result, his movements had been slow and methodical and therefore unsuccessful. But as the area on which he and John C. Pemberton were playing this strategic game became more constricted, Grant seemed to thrive on the quick movements and adaptation necessary to wage war on a smaller field. It helped that Grant was on the offensive and dictating movements; he could pick and choose when and where he wanted to go.[1]

His counterpart Pemberton conversely never could quite adapt quickly enough in this smaller area of operations. He had managed to thwart Grant's first several attempts to get east of the river onto the high ground, mainly because it took so long for the operations sometimes stretching across several hundred miles to develop. That gave the indecisive Pemberton time to utilize his interior lines of communication and shift troops to meet the next threat. As the Federal expeditions came closer to Vicksburg, however, the time lag that Pemberton depended on lessened, and he found it harder to meet each thrust. The Steele's Bayou expedition, for example, was much closer in to Vicksburg, and Pemberton just barely managed to get troops in the way of that effort. It is telling that even Samuel Lockett, Pemberton's chief engineer, was at this time, May 8, writing his wife, "I think he knows what he is doing."[2]

Now that the operations shifted south of Vicksburg and within a mere thirty miles at most from the heart of the city, Pemberton had simply not been able to keep up and, distracted by numerous diversions, had let Grant slip across the river almost undetected and make a firm lodgment on that very high ground east of the river he had sought so long. And as Grant began to move northward in the days after Port Gibson, into "the verry heart of their country," one Missourian noted, the chessboard continually shrunk as Grant moved closer and closer to Vicksburg. Pemberton's reaction time correspondingly lessened even more.[3]

By May 7, Grant again put his troops in motion. "The great Battle for Vicksburg has commenced," one Georgian deduced. By this point, the chessboard had shrunk to a basic parallelogram that stood on end that was a mere fifteen or so miles wide by about twenty-five miles long, give or take a little given the winding nature of rivers and creeks that set the parameters. With the north fork of Bayou Pierre as the base to the south and the Southern Railroad of Mississippi forming the northern segment, the western leg ran along the course of the Big Black River some twenty air miles northeastward from the Hankinson's Ferry area to Edwards Station. About fifteen miles on average east of the Big Black River was a series of creeks that formed the eastern face of the parallelogram, although the distance across was less to the south, a mere ten miles, than it was farther north along the railroad, where it grew to around twenty miles. Still, a tributary of Bayou Pierre, White Oak Creek, flowed into the bayou just twelve miles east of Willow Springs from a northeasterly direction. And only five air miles to the northeast along its course entered a major tributary of White Oak Creek, Tallahala Creek. With its headwaters up near Raymond, just four or so miles to the southeast of the town in fact, Tallahala Creek flowed southwesterly for around seventeen air miles to its junction with White Oak Creek, providing a total eastern face of the parallelogram covered by major watersheds at around twenty miles. It would be within this elongated box, taller than it was wide, that Grant would move northward to the railroad on the east side of the Big Black River.[4]

The interior of the parallelogram became all-important, including several small towns and villages that were contained within: Utica, Cayuga, Rocky Springs, Auburn (Old and New), Raymond, Clinton, Bolton, and Edwards Station. But more important to the moving Federals as well as the defending Confederates were a series of smaller creeks that traversed the box, mostly east to west. Neither White Oak Creek nor Tallahala Creek had any major tributaries coming in from the west; most tributaries, as well as the main channel of White Oak Creek upstream from the Tallahala Creek confluence, ran from the east and the high ground that separated this watershed from the

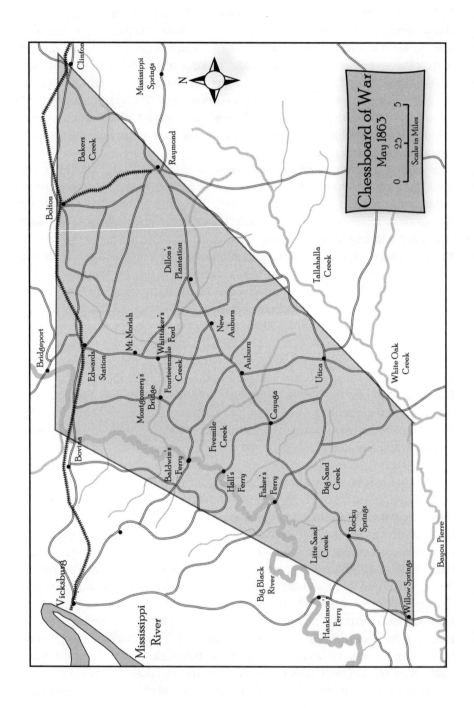

Chessboard of War
May 1863

0   2.5   5
Scale in Miles

Vicksburg

Mississippi
River

Clinton

Mississippi
Springs

Bakers
Creek

Raymond

Bolton

Bridgeport

Dillon's
Plantation

Mt. Moriah

Edwards
Station

Whittaker's
Ford
Fourteenmile
Creek

New
Auburn

Tallahalla
Creek

Bovina

Montgomery's
Bridge

Auburn

Utica

White Oak
Creek

Baldwin's
Ferry

Fivemile
Creek

Cayuga

Hall's
Ferry

Fisher's
Ferry

Big Sand
Creek

Big Black
River

Little Sand
Creek

Rocky
Springs

Hankinson's
Ferry

Willow Springs

Bayou Pierre

N

Pearl River tributaries to the east. But White Oak and Tallahala were major creeks in and of themselves and were not tributaries of the Big Black or Pearl Rivers, the two main watercourses in the area. Rather, they fed directly into Bayou Pierre in between, which itself ran into the Mississippi River near Bruinsburg.[5]

As a result, the creeks that traversed the high ground mainly between the Big Black River and Tallahala Creek were tributaries of the Big Black River, flowing westward into it rather than eastward into Tallahala Creek. While smaller creeks and branches inundated the entire area, the first of these major tributaries to reach across Grant's path was Big Sand Creek, only about two and a half miles north of Rocky Springs. With headwaters within a couple miles of White Oak Creek to the east, the Big Sand flowed basically westward across the parallelogram to the Big Black, entering the river between Hankinson's and Hall's Ferries. It also had a tributary, Little Sand Creek, that flowed from the Rocky Springs area itself into Big Sand Creek near its mouth.[6]

Although intermediate creeks such as Commissioner and McKee flowed part of the way across the area into the Big Black River watershed, by far the next major creek system to the north was Fivemile Creek, another five or six miles to the northeast and running parallel to Big Sand Creek. Its headwaters lay less than two miles from Tallahala Creek to the east and also ran basically westward, picking up several fairly large tributaries in the process and reaching the Big Black River near Baldwin's Ferry. While not an especially imaginative name, the title dated to the ceding of land from the Choctaw in 1820, where the boundary met the Big Black River at the site of what became known as Commissioner Creek. The next major creek to the north was five miles up, gaining that name, and another some fourteen miles up, gaining that name as well.[7]

Just another four to six miles to the north was that larger creek system, Fourteenmile Creek. Again with headwaters within a couple of miles of Tallahala Creek to the east, Fourteenmile Creek flowed basically westward just south of the town of Raymond and onward to the Big Black River, where it entered between Baldwin's Ferry and the railroad bridge to the north. Several large tributaries also fed Fourteenmile Creek from the north and south, including Turkey Creek around the main road to Jackson. One of Fourteenmile Creek's largest tributaries was Bakers Creek, which began over near Clinton and Jackson and flowed westward until it made a large curve to the south and entered Fourteenmile Creek south of Edwards Station. Bakers Creek reached all the way up to the railroad itself, at times even above it, making it the last major watershed Grant would have to deal with in gaining the rail line.[8]

Each of these creeks was good and bad in some ways. Flowing across the proposed line of Federal march, they would provide water to the Union troops who would probably find May in Mississippi quite hot; one Ohio colonel wrote home of already seeking shelter from "the burning sun." And yet each waterway could also be utilized by defending Confederates to hold a line to delay or even stop the Union advance—that is, if the Confederate commander Pemberton chose to do so. As of now, he had decided to concentrate his forces to the west of the Big Black River, using it as a shield that the Federals would have to break through to get to Vicksburg. Whether he would remain behind that shield in the days to come was anybody's guess.[9]

Still, as the armies began to move onto this smaller chessboard, all knew something was about to be decided. One Illinoisan incisively warned his family back home: "Old Grant is bound to take Vicksburg or get whipped, one or the other."[10]

"Soldiers of the Army of the Tennessee!," Grant began his congratulatory message on May 7, 1863, just as the army was jumping off for new efforts. In a rare exposition of congratulation and pomp, he mainly credited his troops with the victory at Port Gibson that allowed Grand Gulf to fall easily and the army to acquire "a firm foothold upon the highlands between the Big Black and Bayou Pierre, from whence we threaten the whole line of the enemy." But the order was not just congratulatory; it also called for finishing the work: "[A] few days' continuance of the same zeal and constancy will secure to this army the crowning victory over the rebellion. More difficulties and privations are before us. Let us endure them manfully. Other battles are to be fought. Let us fight them bravely. A grateful country will rejoice at our success, and history will record it with immortal honor."[11]

Grant began the process of threatening "the whole line of the enemy" that very morning as both corps began to move out northward. McPherson's two divisions at Hankinson's Ferry had orders to eventually move eastward to Rocky Springs, although only Logan's troops were to move at 10:00 a.m. this morning. Crocker's brigades were to move forward and man the bridge site when Logan departed and remain there until Sherman's troops, who began crossing the Mississippi River during the night, could arrive and take over. At that point, Crocker was to move to support Logan wherever he may be. Likewise, now with some rations having arrived late on May 6, McClernand was to move forward on the main road northward from Willow Springs also to Rocky Springs, where he would deploy and await the other troops to get into their positions. Sherman, of course, would also move forward and pass through Rocky Springs as well. Given the terrain, geography, and road network, and especially the Big Black River's surge to the east at this point, Grant wanted all troops to funnel through Rocky Springs before spreading out once more on a wide swath to approach the railroad on an even plane. Much like an hourglass, the divisions that were spread wide from Hankinson's Ferry to Willow Springs would all converge on a single narrow point at Rocky Springs before widening out once more to move northward.[12]

Each commander performed their mission that day, although supplies were still limited; even while moving forward, many units sent their wagons back on May 7 for a new load of provisions at Grand Gulf. As McPherson headed northward, for example, one of his Ohioans related that "men very much refreshed by their three days rest," although he added, "very short of rations." Brigade commander John B. Sanborn noted that "there being no transportation, the command was compelled to leave with only two days' rations on hand." Nevertheless, Logan's troops marched on time and reached Rocky Springs easily; one soldier described it as "consisting of several houses and a store or two." Crocker remained behind to cover the bridge and await Sherman's troops. The XV Corps commander was even then moving forward with his advance brigades, however, and would reach Hankinson's Ferry by May 8, allowing Crocker to move on to support Logan, although he did not march until the next day.[13]

McClernand also moved forward, actually again taking the point at Rocky Springs itself. "My whole corps is up to, or beyond, this point," McClernand notified Grant from Rocky Springs on May 7. In fact, the majority of the corps had advanced all the way up to Big Sand Creek. Osterhaus bivouacked that night astride the creek, with one brigade north of it and the other to the south. Carr's division came forward and took a position along the Big Sand to the right of Osterhaus's position, and Hovey then moved up to the left of Osterhaus, also along the creek. McClernand held A. J. Smith's division in reserve, camping that night back on the Little Sand just a couple miles to the rear. By nightfall on May 7, McClernand therefore had firm control of Rocky Springs and, more important, Big Sand Creek and its crossings, there having been no Confederate resistance at this defendable watershed. In addition, the free-flowing creeks even in this dry May weather provided the corps with ample water. But the men never got used to the critters that inhabited the region, camping outdoors as they did: "There is a good many Lizzards and other animamules down here that makes the boys hollow in the nights when they run over their legs or Boddies."[14]

When Logan's division of McPherson's XVII Corps marched into Rocky Springs as well, bivouacking in rear of McClernand's line that evening, that made five divisions in the general vicinity, with Crocker's still at Hankinson's

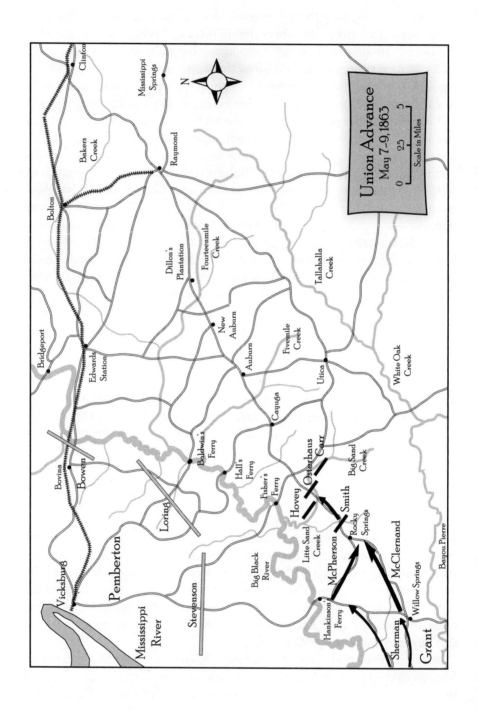

Union Advance
May 7-9, 1863

0   2.5   5
Scale in Miles

Ferry and Sherman's troops on the way to "relieve the last of the 17th [Corps]," Grant wrote. Grant himself moved forward as well, writing Halleck from Rocky Springs on May 8 that "all looks well." By this point Grant's camp equipage had come forward, which was actually not altogether much better than what little he had lived on previously. Dana described how "I get my meals in General Grant's mess, and pay my share of the expenses. The table is a chest with a double cover, which unfolds on the right and the left; the dishes, knives and forks, and caster are inside. Sometimes we get good things, but generally we don't. The cook is an old negro, black and grimy. The cooking is not as clean as it might be, but in war you can't be particular about such things." Fred was not so easygoing, writing that his father's movements "made his headquarters so uncomfortable, and his mess so irregular, that I, for one, did not propose to put up with such living, and I took my meals with the soldiers, who used to do a little foraging, and thereby set an infinitely better table than their commanding general. My father's table at this time was, I must frankly say, the worst I ever saw or partook of." Fred in fact seemed to wander around the army, at one point spending the night with several unfriendly officers on a farmhouse porch; they became much more friendly once they learned who the boy was, and Colonel Sanborn even "welcomed me kindly and loaned me part of his overcoat for a pillow." Sanborn himself explained that he awoke to an "intruder" punching his back with knees and elbows, to which he "made a great effort to expel the fellow" even while asking who it was. Sanborn related that a "boyish or childish voice" answered that it was Fred Grant: "I am cold." Sanborn sheepishly added, "a larger share of the robe was furnished and greater quiet followed."[15]

But even amid the renewed movement, McClernand was still not satisfied with the progress on several accounts. After Osterhaus sent the 2nd Illinois Cavalry and some infantry on ahead toward Hall's Ferry, a movement that led to a small skirmish, he himself probed forward nearly to the ferry. There, the corps' pickets spotted a Confederate artillery battery on the west side of the river commanding the crossing. A false alarm of a Confederate attack even sent many units into line of battle that afternoon. McClernand also gained word from "fugitive negroes" that Pemberton was fortifying and concentrating his army at Edwards Station to the north: "I think the enemy is in strong force."[16]

McClernand was also still not happy with the supply situation and chose this opportunity to again complain about favoritism even while he wrote Hillyer at Grand Gulf "help me." He notified Grant that Sherman had reportedly commandeered most of the streamers to get his troops across the Mississippi River "and thus longer delayed the wagons which I am relying on to bring adequate supplies of food and ammunition." He asked rhetorically: "Is it not important that the Army of the Tennessee should be fully supplied and put in the best fighting order? The political consequences of the impending campaign will be momentous."[17]

Of course, there were only a limited number of wagons to be had, many of them still on the opposite side of the river moving goods southward toward Grand Gulf; amazingly, some from east of the river were actually sent back to the west side. Others on the ground were concerned as well. One Federal worried over several issues, not the least of which was his pending promotion to lieutenant from private being delayed. "If I should fall in the taking of Vicksburg my dear family would only get a private's pension." But his major concern was food, adding that "we are rather short of rations [and] economizing to save transportation for it is a heavy job to wagon provisions for such a force as we have in this vicinity." Quartermaster Bingham was working hard on getting the route shortened to a day trip west of the Mississippi River and reported that supply trains were moving well on good roads "except for a few hours after the rain." He also advised Grant that, as soon as he amassed "fifteen or twenty" days' worth of supplies at Grand Gulf, he would send "a large number of teams to the front." There was a lack of steamers as well, but if Grant probably had to choose he would rather have Sherman's soldiers than a full allotment of rations with him. Still, Grant was working on the supply situation as best he could, including taking from the immediate area. McClernand confirmed that "I am still causing the country to be scoured," and other troops were also taking freely from the local civilians. McClernand even revised the idea of sending more steamers past the Vicksburg batteries, but Grant decided against that with the debacle on the night of May 3.[18]

At this point, Grant was still depending on wagons shuffling between Grand Gulf and his army, although they were many fewer than needed. One Indianan wrote in his diary on May 7, "still waiting for the supply train." It soon came, but he noted "after ten days on three day's rations we drew one day's rations." Still fairly within the protected cul-de-sac between Bayou Pierre, the Mississippi River, and the Big Black River, the teams were in little danger except perhaps by roving Confederate bands. Grant in fact wrote Sherman as late as May 8 that with "troops moving on the road I have not deemed it necessary heretofore to send escorts with trains passing back and forth." The wagons could move safely within the cul-de-sac, and even when Grant moved up to Rocky Springs and Big Sand Creek, which was at most about ten miles farther northward, there was still plenty of protection with Sherman moving forward. Grant in fact ordered McClernand that evening to "send all the teams you can spare, after putting three days' rations in the men's haversacks, back to Grand Gulf for rations and ammunition," and he also wanted a tabulation of how many rations he currently had and how many were on the way to his troops. Significantly, Grant then added that he wanted at least two men per wagon for protection and that "Sherman's forces being in rear, will protect our trains for one more trip, if they move promptly."[19]

In mentioning "one more trip," Grant was acknowledging that supply matters were about to change and that, once he moved on farther northward, away from Grand Gulf and the protected cul-de-sac, the meandering of supply wagons back and forth without specific protection would have to come to an end. He also ordered fortifications erected, mainly by contrabands sent back from the front, at Grand Gulf itself "to protect our stores at the landing"; the movement forward of the army made the risk at Grand Gulf itself that much greater. But the most dangerous part of the supply line would be between Grand Gulf and the army, and Grant admitted on May 9 that "I feel somewhat uneasy for our trains that are out now but hope they will get through all right." And he did not want to risk it again. "After that [the last shipment of wagons]," he wrote Sherman, "send no more but load them to have them ready until troops are coming to escort them." From now on it was likely that, if supply wagons rolled northward to the army, they would have to be guarded by specific units. To Hillyer himself Grant ordered to have "all other wagons you may have loaded up ready to forward when ever troops are coming up but do not send them out otherwise." He added about the return trip: "Hereafter I will send escorts whenever trains are going back. If possible so arrange as to send the greatest possible amount of hard bread salt and coffee with all forces of troops coming this way." He wrote the same day, evidently after hearing of Sherman's lack of wagons with his corps, that "I want as you suggest all the wagons brought from the other side of the river except what can be advantageously used there" and that "all wagons coming out to be loaded with Ammunition and Commissary Stores." In terms of ammunition, which could not be gleaned in the countryside, he ordered "100 rounds of ammunition for 50,000 men and 100 rounds for all Artillery in the field."[20]

But Grant was not about to let supply issues stop his momentum. Having himself moved up to Rocky Springs on May 7, he issued his orders for the next day from there. If McClernand was able to get the requisite supplies of the three days' rations per man, he was to move forward again to a line running east and west from Baldwin's Ferry to Auburn, both of which were north of Fivemile Creek. The lack of resistance in moving across Big Sand Creek made Grant think there would similarly be no Confederates at Fivemile Creek. He accordingly ordered McClernand to make the leap across to that watershed, one division going to Auburn itself on the main Jackson Road and the others spread out westward on a line to Baldwin's Ferry. McClernand would be on his own to decide the actual routes, Grant admitting that, while he knew there were direct roads to both places (Auburn and Baldwin's Ferry), "I do not yet know if there are intermediate roads." If only the two main roads existed, McClernand was to march two divisions on the two roads and fill in the middle "so as to bring them well up on the line connecting the two places." If there were intermediate roads in between, they were also to be utilized. The proposed movement obviously brought greater chance of contact with the enemy, Colonel Marcus Spiegel of the 120th Ohio writing home to his wife that evening, "we may have a Battle tomorrow; if so I will with the help of God do my duty."[21]

At the same time, McPherson was to move out as well, but eastward toward Utica. With the parallelogram getting somewhat wider the farther north the Federals went, Grant wanted to spread out his corps across the width of the land between the Big Black River and Tallahala Creek to cover the entire expanse on an east-west line. He advised McClernand that McPherson would "move on a road south of you, so as to be well up," and McPherson was to move out early from Rocky Springs on May 8 with Logan's division, Crocker's following when Sherman's troops arrived at Hankinson's Ferry. McPherson notified Crocker that he would leave a staff officer to show Crocker the turn he was to make to follow Logan instead of McClernand. Like McClernand, McPherson was to make sure his men had three days' "cooked rations" in their haversacks, he also sending wagons back and forth from Grand Gulf while in the remaining protection of the cul-de-sac.[22]

In planning for the move ahead the next day, Grant made a significant decision as to alignment. The movement from Bayou Pierre had resulted in McPherson manning the left and McClernand the right, but Grant changed the alignment when all units marched through the neck of the hourglass at Rocky Springs. As the corps moved forward the next day, McClernand would be on the left, next to the Big Black River, and McPherson on the far right as far as Utica. Sherman's arriving troops would fill the gap in the middle, a busy Grant ordering Sherman as early as May 7, "should I fail to direct it hereafter I want the bridge at this place [Hankinson's Ferry] totally destroyed when the last of your forces leave the place." Why Grant aligned the corps in this manner in pure conjecture, as he never revealed his thinking, but historians have surmised that he wanted his most inexperienced corps commander, McPherson, on the safest flank to the east. But it would seem that the safest place for the most inexperienced commander would be the center. Sherman, of course, had long railed against this entire plan, so perhaps Grant thought keeping him in the center would keep his most uninterested commander closed up. Having McClernand on the left—the position closest to the Confederate army and the most dangerous locale—was interesting to say the least, but it indicated fully that Grant had confidence in McClernand to do the job. Perhaps part of that confidence was that McClernand had by far the biggest corps in action at this point, four divisions of two brigades each compared to McPherson's and Sherman's two divisions of three brigades each. Maybe Grant wanted the largest corps on the most dangerous flank, or perhaps he wanted his most aggressive commander there. Alas, Grant never said what was behind his motives, but it is clear that the aggressive McClernand gained the dangerous left flank and the inexperienced McPherson the right.[23]

Despite the heavy-duty planning on Grant's part, however, the plan went off track on May 8, as none of the divisions moved forward. There was some confusion over the road network, prompting McClernand to ask for an explanation: "Is there not some mistake about this?" Grant had alerted him that the main road to Edwards Station northward left the Jackson Road a couple miles north of Cayuga between Big Sand and Fivemile Creeks, but there was no road there and McClernand queried "an intelligent negro" who had been traveling these roads for years; he said the road, along which the telegraph line ran and was thus known as Telegraph Road, departed to Edwards some seven miles above Cayuga, actually north of Auburn and Fivemile Creek. Osterhaus examined the road network and agreed as well. In addition, McClernand gained more intelligence from arriving Confederates deserters. Grant admitted the confusion and "change of route" based upon his engineers' evidence but added that, in the big picture, "I want your direction to be toward Edwards Station and intended my note only as information about the route."[24]

By far, the biggest issue causing the delay on May 8 was not confusion about roads but lack of supplies. Grant had hinged his orders on the prerequisite of having the three days' rations in hand before moving ("do not move until your wagons come up"), but few if any of the XIII or XVII Corps teams did. The War Department spook Charles Dana explained only on the evening of May 8 that "the ammunition and subsistence have begun to arrive from Grand Gulf," and McClernand reported that he was confident he could have the three days' rations handed out by the next morning, May 9, at which time he could move forward, just one day late. The teams had taken two full days to get to Grand Gulf, get loaded, and get back to the army. He also noted "sixty wagons, laden with ammunition, are reported to have left Grand Gulf at 2 p.m. They should also be here in the morning." In fact, McClernand's staff officer overseeing supply issues, Colonel Taggart, noted that he expected to have the corps fully supplied by the morning of May 9.[25]

Consequently, the supply and communication issues were already having an effect. Colonel Spiegel wrote home that "you must not feel uneasy if you do not get letters very frequent, for we are moving every day; no paper, no chance to send, neither have we received a mail for nearly two weeks." But it was worse in terms of supplies, as the present wagons were simply not able to keep the army fully stocked; even one of Sherman's men just coming up from Grand Gulf related in his diary they had only half-rations on May 8. Certainly, supplies were arriving continuously, but not in enough volume to fully supply the forces much less build up the requisite three days' rations at the same time. In fact, some commands had struggled to keep half the required amount, Osterhaus ordering back on May 4 that "the commanders of Regts and batteries will see that their men are provided with at least provisions enough to last 36 hours and if possible enough for 48 hours."[26]

It was a bad sign for what was to come: If Grant's army, within fifteen miles or so of Grand Gulf, could not keep fully supplied by trains and foraging, what would happen when it reached points twenty or thirty miles to the front? Time was of the essence, but it took time to get the rations out to the army on the restricted road network; Sherman even urged Grant to "make some uniform and just rule, and send somebody back to regulate this matter, or your road will be crowded and jammed unless it is done." Additionally, Confederates in unknown numbers were beginning to operate on the flanks and rear areas, threatening but certainly not stopping the trains moving forward. Colonel Clark Wright of the 6th Missouri Cavalry, tasked with defending the rear and right of the army, reported he had contact with small bands of Confederates, some even operating out of a reoccupied Port Gibson now that Grant's supply process shifted above Bayou Pierre. Yet Wright was unable to tell much about the enemy: "I am still unable to give reliable information of where the infantry are or where they come from." He surmised that some of the culprits could have been a part of the cavalry, perhaps even Colonel Wirt Adams's unit, that had been chasing Benjamin Grierson's raid.[27]

All the while, the transportation issues from Grand Gulf out to the army were becoming obvious as the main culprit for the problems. Back at Milliken's Bend, Grant's chief of commissary and subsistence, Lieutenant Colonel Robert Macfeely, reported that day that he was able to get supplies to Grand Gulf fairly easily in large numbers. Since May 2 (but not including the shipment of May 8 itself, as returns were not yet submitted), he had sent down to the Grand Gulf area more than three hundred thousand "rations of hard bread, coffee, sugar, and salt" and two hundred and twenty-five thousand rations of "salt meat," not to mention a hundred and thirty thousand of soap. "There has been no delay in sending forward stores from this place, the commissaries working night and day when there were any to be loaded." And the problems were not farther back either, as he noted that day he had two million complete rations there and another half-million en route down the Mississippi River from Memphis. Furthermore, the new and shorter road system west of the river from Young's Point would be operational in a couple days. Macfeely assured Grant, "I will use every exertion to keep your army supplied."[28]

Grant was glad that Macfeely had everything flowing on his end, although he continually sent word back to both Bingham and Macfeely that "I look to them to make their Departments efficient" and "remind them of the importance of rushing forward rations with all dispatch." He also continually urged the officers back along the line of supply to work on opening the new roads, which were to be "shortened by every possible means. Meanwhile all possible exertion should be made to keep the army supplied by the present route." And he detailed what he wanted again, mainly "hard bread, coffee, and salt . . . , and then the other articles of the rations as they can be supplied." He sent word directly to "Mackfeeley to send two rations of bread, salt & coffee to one of meat and sugar and to send no other rations until a full supply of these are on hand."[29]

But the problems lay in getting the goods across the Mississippi River to Grand Gulf and then up to the army. Evidently, McClernand's constant griping about favoritism was making some headway, Grant wanting, in addition to a report from Hillyer "about the number of rations on hand and sent forward from Grand Gulf," to know "how many teams have been loaded with rations and sent forward? How many have gone to the 13th Army Corps?" He later commented to Hillyer that "there has evidently been a great deal of pulling and hauling among Division [commanders] to get the advantage in transportation." Given the supply issues, Grant knew he had to live partially off the land itself, which provided ample meat and forage to a certain extent but was not the final solution and was growing less and less of a solution as each day passed. One Federal related to his parents that "I have seen scores of families with nothing to their name. . . . The army sweeps away everything you can think of, including mules and wagons." Yet not everyone was successful, Ohioan John Griffith explaining in his diary on May 8 that he "went on foraging expedition but came back tired and hungry without anything. Still short of rations." The longer the army remained nearly motionless, the less provisions were available because much of what had been available had already been scooped up.[30]

The supply situation, inadequate though it was, was nevertheless a major achievement to date. Grant asked Hillyer for a rundown on supplies ("I want to know as near as possible how we stand in every particular for supplies. How many wagons have you ferried over the river?"), and Hillyer asked his own people for the information, which was readily forthcoming. Captain Edward Tittmann, commissary for Osterhaus's division and in charge of the supplies at Grand Gulf, reported on May 7 that up to the day before he had "loaded at this place and sent to the front" mostly meat and bread, including 10,947 rations of pork, 2,400 of beef, and 37,033 of bacon. As the army could obtain that on the march, however, Grant was mostly interested in bread, and Tittmann had sent 78,041 rations of hardtack and 57,623 of flour. Other items in smaller quantities such as beans, sugar, coffee, and a whopping 168,000 rations of salt also went forward. But it left Tittmann pretty sparse rations at Grand Gulf itself, even with an arrival of goods on the *Moderator* on May 7: just 15,850 rations of meat and 10,000 of hardtack, although he had 54,000 rations of flour and a lot of beans and coffee, around 150,000 of each. Still, such massive numbers of especially beans, coffee, and salt would not last too many days with a growing army that was getting farther and farther away. The influx of goods across the river was helpful but certainly not adequate.[31]

And there was a major movement the other way as well, back toward Grand Gulf, largely composed of slaves who had flocked to the army. One Federal at Grand Gulf explained in the ensuing days that "we have recruited a regiment of Negro soldiers here this week." Interestingly, another Ohioan wrote in his diary on May 8 "there was 4 companies of negroes came in to our camp," and the next day added, "our men are busily engaged in getting up A negro Regiment." And that was in addition to all the wagons being sent back periodically from the army for more supplies. The roads to and from Grand Gulf were certainly getting their fair use in the early days of May 1863.[32]

Despite the delay and the foreboding supply situation, Grant planned to move onward the next morning, May 9. Modified orders went out for the divisions to perform the plan originally intended for May 8, just now on May 9. McClernand would move northward through Cayuga to and beyond Fivemile Creek while McPherson headed eastward to Utica, a relieved Crocker this time in the lead and Logan following. Crocker's participation was allowed because of Sherman's arrival at Hankinson's Ferry on May 8, Grant intending Sherman to move up the center between the other two corps. Crocker consequently moved forward to Rocky Springs that day, camping for the night "on the crest of a pine ridge." It was not ideal, this delay, but it was only for a day, and now the schedule seemed to be worked out and everything would again be on track—if, that is, the supplies arrived that evening and during the night.[33]

From faraway Richmond, Jefferson Davis could see plainly what was happening. "Am anxiously expecting further information of your active operations," he telegraphed Pemberton late on May 7. Then Davis reminded him of what Grant and his commanders knew all too well: "Want of transportation of supplies must compel the enemy to seek a junction with their fleet after a few days' absence from it." Davis knew the lay of the land and that the sparsely settled area could probably not support an army of Grant's size for long. The time for movement was fast approaching, and Clausewitz's concept of counterattacking the enemy at the culminating point, or where he reached the extent of his ability to sustain himself and was most vulnerable, was very much in play—thus Davis's use of the phrase "your active operations."[34]

But if Davis's intention was clear, it became lost in a muddle of other ideas both in this one message and others emanating from Richmond. Samuel Cooper, for instance, was writing the same day about putting Lieutenant Colonel Samuel W. Ferguson, who had done so well in the Steele's Bayou and Deer Creek operations, in charge of organizing cavalry to help defend northern Mississippi. Pemberton responded directly to him two days later, informing that "position unaltered . . . Enemy still on east side of Big Black." In recognizing the stalling-out of the Federal advance, Pemberton nevertheless mentioned plans for "active operations," although tellingly he did not use the term "offensive" operations.[35]

Likewise, Joseph E. Johnston was peppering Pemberton with messages totally outside reality. Over the course of a couple of days, Johnston advised contacting the Confederate commander across the river, Lieutenant General E. Kirby Smith, for help. Pemberton did so; he also worked on Beauregard for more troops, although the latter had trouble reading all of Pemberton's messages due to cipher confusion. But Johnston would soon become more of a factor as on May 9 Seddon ordered him to "proceed at once to Mississippi and take chief command of the forces, giving to those in the field, as far as practicable, the encouragement and benefit of your personal direction." Given the past relationship between Pemberton and Johnston and their inability to work together or hardly even to communicate, it was not an auspicious development. And Johnston himself wanted no part of it, safely ensconced in Middle Tennessee as he was. "I shall go immediately," he responded, "although unfit for field service." It was a classic case of lowering expectations from the start, and it would be a full four days before he arrived in Jackson.[36]

All sorts of other messages arrived as well from those outside Pemberton's immediate crisis area, including concerned reports from Jackson where Governor Pettus, having remained behind after the government fled, continued to build up the city's defenses. "Can we not have a few more troops here?" he queried, adding, "five hundred negroes on fortifications; soon finished." Tucked behind the Big Black River, there was little Pemberton could or would do for the governor, however, and he ordered his commander at

Jackson, Brigadier General John Adams, to "give orders to the chiefs of staff departments to move all valuable stores to the east as far as they can be conveniently moved, even if to Alabama." Adams did so, and he described the ongoing fortification effort: "Will have positions for sixteen guns, connected by rifle-pits, to the west of Jackson, resting on Pearl River, extending north and south, completed in one week." But, he added, "[I] have but two guns." And then Adams and Pettus became bogged down in bureaucracy, Adams noting that the governor "offers two State pieces. Shall I take them?" On his side of the bureaucratic logjam, Pettus was writing, "four State guns here. Direct General Adams to give requisitions for them." One wonders if this crisis was not a time to depend less heavily on paperwork, as Grant was doing, but perhaps these commanders learned as much from the administrative-minded Pemberton, who thrived on just such bureaucracy. In fact, Pemberton later responded, "[I] have instructed General Adams to take the guns, and ordered Major [Theodore] Johnston to issue rations to negroes on fortifications."[37]

Because of all the message traffic during this period from all over the Confederacy, Davis's admonishment for "active operations" was likely lost in the volume. But it was perhaps also muted by another command from Davis in that same message of late May 7. At the same time he was advising going on the offensive, Davis also wrote, "to hold both Vicksburg and Port Hudson is necessary to a connection with Trans-Mississippi." That was as clear as it got, and Pemberton further hunkered down to defend his prized possession, firing off a message to Franklin Gardner at Port Hudson: "Hold it to the last. President says both places must be held."[38]

As a result, Pemberton further built his strategy to coincide with the "hold . . . Vicksburg" part of Davis's message rather than the "active operations" portion. His actions bespoke as much, he tellingly writing Kirby Smith per Johnston's instructions to move "upon the line of communications of the enemy on the western side of the river. . . . To break this would render a most important service." But his explanation of why it was needed was the most telling: Pemberton explained his lack of cavalry did not allow him to "cut the lines of communication of the enemy with the Mississippi River or to guard and protect my own." Then he added, "my force is insufficient for offensive operations. I must stand on the defensive, at all events until re-enforcements reach me." Pemberton's mindset had obviously become totally defensive, with no plans as yet to go on the offensive. And that allowed the enemy to decide when and where the movements and fights would take place— certainly not a good omen for such an indecisive commander in the first place. Engineer Lockett explained that Davis's and Johnston's ideas "were very conflicting in their tenor, and neither those of Mr. Davis nor those of General Johnston exactly comported with General Pemberton's views."[39]

Accordingly, Pemberton did what he had been doing all along and was comfortable with: calling more troops inside his lair behind the Big Black River. Lockett noted he "then made the capital mistake of trying to harmonize instructions from superiors diametrically opposed to each other, and at the same time to bring them into accord with his own judgment, which was adverse to the plans of both." He elaborated on his view of this strategy: "Pemberton wished to take a strong position on the line of the Big Black and wait for an attack, believing that it would be successfully resisted, and that then the tables could be turned upon Grant in a very bad position, without any base of supplies, and without a well-protected line of retreat." For instance, when thoughts emerged of using Brigadier General Jeptha V. Harris's Mississippi State Troops brigade at Jackson, Pemberton firmly corrected: "General Harris' command will come here." He likewise called in all of Waul's Texas Legion from Fort Pemberton, hoping what little cavalry there was would aid him in his defense, even while likely recalling that it was Johnston's movement of most of Pemberton's cavalry to Middle Tennessee back in January that partially led to the crisis now upon him; one of Pemberton's staff officers described it on May 6 as the "greatest mistake that was ever made—depriving us of our cavalry in this Dept. as well take the arms off a man and expect him to defend himself." Pemberton could call back some of the small mounted forces operating east of the Big Black River, but until more arrived he was at a loss of what to do besides mounting infantry; one staff officer even replied to Loring that Pemberton was "fully aware of the fact that you need more cavalry, but that it is entirely out of his power to furnish you more now." Pemberton consequently looked longingly for the reinforcements then on the way, two brigades from Port Hudson, two from Beauregard in South Carolina, and even the exchanged prisoners from Arkansas Post, although there was debate as to where the reinforcements should go. Richmond even recommended sending forces from Braxton Bragg's army in Tennessee to Vicksburg, to be replaced with the exchanged prisoners. Nevertheless, a Union prisoner being shipped by rail eastward described "sidetracking frequently to allow trains that were loaded with Confederate troops, going west to reinforce the rebel army at Vicksburg, to pass us."[40]

Yet as the second week of May began, Pemberton started to get more and more pressure from within his own army for those active operations. The army's positions remained basically the same as before, although some tinkering proved beneficial as the days moved on. But with little movement of the enemy there was not a lot that needed to be changed. Stevenson remained on the right, with his four brigades and that of John C. Moore of Forney's division at Warrenton, although Moore had to pull back his camps to shield them from the frequent gunboat bombardment in early May. The other brigade of Forney's division, Brigadier General Louis Hébert's, was still up on the Yazoo River. Loring's division manned the line from Stevenson's left to Baldwin's Ferry with his three brigades and one of Martin L. Smith's in support, the other being in Vicksburg. Brigadier General John Vaughn's brigade of East Tennesseans was positioned north of the city to support Hébert's brigade at Snyder's Bluff, and also to be in supporting distance of Bowen's troops, which extended the line up to the railroad bridge across the Big Black River.[41]

But with the stuttered Federal movement northward at least to Rocky Springs, and the probes even farther, Pemberton gradually came to leave his more recent belief that the Federals would cross the Big Black River south of Vicksburg and head directly northward; he soon again viewed the most logical movement as being east of the river toward the railroad, his initial assumption. Pemberton now began to believe once more that the main blow would fall at the railroad bridge, and he alerted Bowen. As a result, the Confederate line gradually coalesced at a point farther northward than the lowest ferries, including Hankinson's. Stevenson had gradually fallen back from Loring's initial position holding the ferry on site and was by May 7 on a line between Warrenton and Baldwin's Ferry, at least eight miles north of Hankinson's Ferry. That of course allowed the Union probes across the river to extend northward, but there were no major movements by the enemy. Pemberton was accordingly content with allowing Stevenson to hold the lateral road between the main Warrenton Road southward and the Hall's Ferry Road, where Loring's line picked up near D. Whittaker's place. From there, Loring's division extended over to the Baldwin's Ferry Road at J. Whittaker's. It was still a lengthy line for Stevenson, as much as eight miles, while Loring's position astride both the Hall's Ferry and Baldwin's Ferry Roads was less lengthy, although Loring still complained about it; in addition, he had to watch the "private ferries" operating between the major ones on public roads, and one of Loring's staff officers reported that "the river can be bridged by the enemy, if he wishes, in a few hours at any point." Adding the territory north of Baldwin's Ferry still made Loring's line as much as six miles in length, and he reiterated his need for more cavalry "in taking care of the long line." But further indicating Pemberton's total defensive stance behind the Big Black River, Loring was to reinforce Bowen there when the Union advance on the railroad bridge occurred. There was no mention of offensive movements, just defensive.[42]

Given the developing situation and the lack of any offensive plan on the part of the departmental commander, who would not even come out of Vicksburg, several Confederate commanders began to complain about the inactivity. Colonel Claudius W. Sears of the 46th Mississippi jumbled the entire time of May 3–14 in his diary: "In camp without knowledge of the enemy—doing nothing—preparing for nothing while the enemy is marching up the Big Black in our rear."[43]

In particular, Loring had had enough and recommended a plan of offensive operations. But he sent it to Pemberton's assistant adjutant general, Robert W. Memminger, not Pemberton himself, which Pemberton biographer Michael Ballard believes was an indication of the growing animosity between the two generals. "I have not yet ventured a suggestion about the movements of the troops," Loring wrote Memminger late on May 9, "but will do so now, with your permission." In divining that the Federals would either turn toward Jackson or the railroad bridge, Loring offered his plan:

> Is it not, then, our policy to take the offensive before they can make themselves secure and move either way as it may suit them? Order your forces from Jackson to Raymond. The line from Baldwin's Ferry and below it, extending to Raymond, is, I am informed, a strong one; part of it I know from observation to be so. Direct Bowen's brigade upon the line. Let my division have pontoons ready and at any moment thrown across the Big Black at Baldwin's Ferry, Stevenson to guard the approaches with his division at Hall's Ferry and the other ferries, and be ready to cross to the rear of the enemy.

Essentially, Bowen was to move out and take defensive positions along Fourteenmile Creek while Loring and Stevenson crossed the Big Black and hit the Federals in the flank. It was similar to Robert E. Lee's plan at Second Manassas less than a year before, where Stonewall Jackson's corps had held the enemy in place with defensive positions while James Longstreet's troops hit the Federal flank. "I believe if a well-concerted plan be adopted, we can drive the enemy into the Mississippi, if it is done in time," Loring added. "They don't expect anything of the kind; they think we are on the defensive."[44]

Trouble was, the Federals were correct in their thinking—Pemberton was indeed on the defensive. But as more and more calls for moving over to the offensive came from his subordinate commanders, Pemberton began to budge. He at least entertained thoughts of going on the offensive, Carter Stevenson writing on that same May 9: "Shall I make the move against the enemy that you were contemplating this morning?" Stevenson did not elaborate on exactly what Pemberton was contemplating, but it was not a full-fledged advance, as he added, "if so, will five regiments be sufficient?" But Pemberton was at a minimum beginning to entertain offensive ideas, even if small in nature.[45]

But for now it was safe to say that Pemberton was still convinced that a defense behind the Big Black River was his best available option. As a result, the initiative remained firmly in Grant's hands — exactly where it had been all along.

If nerves were beginning to fray in the Confederate high command, the same thing was occurring east of the Big Black River among the Federal ranks, mainly because of more delay. The rations McClernand needed to equip his men and move forward on May 9 did not arrive until late the night before, although the high command took time to review the corps because of the delay; Osterhaus reported that he "had the honor of a review by Generals Grant and McClernand," and a staff officer noted that "the woods reverberated with their shouts of applause. Our army is in fine spirits." Grant had been reviewing his troops the day before as well, and on this day one Indianan noted in his diary: "Had the pleasure of seeing two Maj. Gens (McClernand & Grant) also many other officers of distinction, among whom *our own Osterhaus* always jovial and pleasant." An Illinoisan described how "we were out in line and he rode in front of us." The generals also rode Sherman's line, the eagle "Old Abe" of the 8th Wisconsin responding to doffed hats with "a shrill scream and a quick flap of his wings." Inspections also went on when not under review. Still, the XIII Corps commander continued griping about the lack of wagons for his corps, and he had not been overstating the case. In fact, it was only late on the night of May 8 that "a train with a limited quantity of ammunition and rations came up." McClernand notified Grant that it would take most of the day to "sort and issue the ammunition; also to issue the rations." McClernand initially hoped to have it done by the morning of May 9, at which time he would move out toward Fivemile Creek. In the meantime, he had sent a "reconnoitering party" ahead, which returned without incident. At the same time, a similar Confederate force moved southward as far as Cayuga, again without major confrontation.[46]

But McClernand would not move forward on May 9, distribution of the rations taking too long. Yet it eventually occurred, some reporting being issued hardtack by May 10. Consequently, only probes moved forward toward Cayuga and Fivemile Creek on May 9. The troops accordingly spent another welcome day in camp, resting from the long marches and constant movements of the past few weeks. One Federal elaborated extensively in his diary on lounging beneath a beech tree listening to a mockingbird as he "chatters, whistles, chirps, and makes every conceivable variety of notes; sometimes for half an hour, then he will fly away into some other part of the tree and sit quietly picking at his feathers and looking about, apparently eyeing his Yankee admirers with some suspicion (for I guess he is Secesh) for some time, when he will return to his old position from which he sings and sets up his lively singing again with all the assurance and gayety of a ballad singer in a theater." McClernand staff officer Henry Warmoth marked his twenty-first birthday in camp on May 9, he noting that "Genl. Benton sent me a bottle of whiskey" and that Carr's division band "serenaded me." Others took time to clean up a little, brigade commander John E. Smith informing his wife that "my clothes I have not had an opportunity to get washed since I left you." Colonel Marcus Spiegel of the 120th Ohio wrote his wife that day, describing how "for eleven days past we have had continual marching and Bivouacing. I have not seen my tent for 13 days, neither have I slept any wheres but out doors nor had my clothes off since that time." But another day of rest did wonders, he adding that "we are to day stopping and resting and I therefore took off my Drawyers, Undershirt and shirt and have my negro Boy washing it; I sit in the Shade until it tries [dries]."[47]

The continual delay was disappointing, but other corps of the army were able to move forward somewhat, making it seem to many in McClernand's divisions that Sherman and McPherson "passed us." One Indianan even noted when the 8th Wisconsin came along in the parched area without water that "we observed upon one man's shoulder, a full-grown American eagle; but he seemed to be weary of his long, hot ride, as his mouth was open and his wings drooped; and his woe-begone appearance resembled anything else than the proud 'American Eagle.'" The XIII Corps was not passed, but Sherman and McPherson were merely threading the hourglass at Rocky Springs to get on their new routes. McPherson's two divisions consequently broke camp that morning and moved, the corps commander still worried about his third division west of the Mississippi River. He wrote McArthur a quick note that morning before leaving Rocky Springs: "I am extremely anxious for you to come forward to the front with your command as soon as possible. We want every available man in the field when the battle comes off, which cannot now be long delayed." In fact, he admitted that "I have been trying to get you all forward since I first reached Perkins' plantation." McPherson even recommended coming on with a portion of the division if one or two of the brigades were still needed across the river but to come with what he could and to "bring with you what hard bread, coffee, &c., you can, and ammunition. Provisions, except meats, are very scarce." For his part, McArthur was trying to procure vessels to get his troops across to Grand Gulf, with little success.[48]

Despite McArthur's absence, McPherson moved eastward toward Utica with his two present divisions, supplied with "three fourths of three days rations." One Ohioan added that what flour they had been issued was nearly wasted when the order to march came before he was able to bake the dough. Crocker's division nevertheless reached Utica Crossroads and Meyer's Farm, although well short (about seven miles) of Utica itself, camping "in a thick underbrush." Logan followed and made camp a little later that evening: "Logan's division is just coming up," McPherson informed Grant at 7:30 p.m. But it had been a grueling march, Luther Cowan describing how "the dust very bad—sun very hot—men suffered badly." With McPherson was Wright's 6th Missouri Cavalry, which moved on and occupied Utica itself and scouted toward Tallahala Creek, engaging in some minor skirmishing. His orders were to "reconnoiter the enemy cautiously, and, if possible, find out his strength and intentions." McPherson sent others to the west toward Cayuga, and they also met and scattered a few Confederates. In fact, rumors were more numerous than Confederates, including one that Beauregard himself had arrived at Jackson. That said, McPherson informed Grant that, while all looked good, "the information that I have been able to obtain thus far is very indefinite." But he promised, "I may be able to get some more authentic information before morning; if so, I will send it to you immediately."[49]

Sherman also used the continuing lull in McClernand's movement to bring up his XV Corps, one of his Iowans describing the "rapid marches" to catch up. His lead division under Frederick Steele reached Hankinson's Ferry on May 8, replacing Crocker's troops, who had moved on with Logan's division to Rocky Springs and now toward Utica. "The dust which lay full three inches deep, was most disagreeable obstacle we encountered," explained Illinoisan Henry Seaman. At the same time, Tuttle's division moved eastward to Willow Springs "without transportation, [but we] loaded all the ambulances with what ammunition they could carry," Tuttle explained—although too fast to leave a brigade at a particular junction of the roads as Grant wished. Sherman responded that the order came too late for Tuttle to do so, as he had already pushed through, "but I will send orders for Tuttle to remain at Willow Springs, which will cover the same point." There, Tuttle's already famished soldiers "spent the forenoon in foraging, finding an abundance of beef cattle, sheep, hogs, corn, molasses, &c., and three mills in the neighborhood, which we immediately put in operation, grinding corn for the troops." That afternoon, orders came for Tuttle to move forward to Rocky Springs to replace McClernand's reserve division on Little Sand Creek, allowing Smith's division to join the other XIII Corps divisions on Big Sand Creek for the movement forward the next morning. Tuttle did so.[50]

Tuttle's arrival at Willow Springs brought more Federals to the Ingraham family residence, protected heretofore as the location of McClernand's headquarters. That protection vanished when McClernand left, and Sherman's troops had no such concern for Southern civilians, even sisters of Union generals. "Osterhaus gave him protection," one Illinoisan wrote, "but Tuttle won't come down with a single bayonet." The result was a total ransacking: "[A] fine library was disappearing fast, and every third man carried a smoked ham under one arm, and two or three volumes under the other." But Osterhaus was not always so caring either, he once cautioning his men: "You always brings me de livers and den I never knows notin about the killin of de animales." Another division commander, crusty old A. J. Smith, told a Mississippian on a mule complaining about the soldiers taking his goods: "Well, those men didn't belong to my division at all, because if they were my men they wouldn't have left you that mule."[51]

Sherman's arrival and integration into the movements of the army not only brought additional troops and supplies but also put Sherman's pessimism on site. Never a fan of this entire movement, Sherman continued to show his nervousness particularly about the supply situation. And he was not shy about giving his opinion, deep in the night of May 8 writing Grant his take on what was happening. He provided his view of what was occurring back at Grand Gulf, writing that "there are 500 wagons across the river, and with each is an officer pressing to have it cross over, as if the absolute safety of the army depends on that wagon." He went on that "Hillyer is doing his best, but each corps and division and brigade commander is there, urging forward his particular wagons, and the steamboat can only bring wagons in a particular ratio."[52]

Much more helpful to Grant was Sherman's notification that both McArthur and Blair were either at or soon to be at Hard Times, ready to move across, but he added that "it is useless to push out men here till their supplies are regulated, unless you intend to live on the country." The troops were indeed on the way. One of Blair's soldiers moving toward Grand Gulf noted on May 7 that they met Governor Yates on his return trip to Illinois. He "gave us a speech." Also there was the division's old commander, Brigadier General Morgan L. Smith, who had been dreadfully wounded at Chickasaw Bayou back in December. The general, still on crutches, arrived in an ambulance to the division drawn up in line with arms presented. One of the colonels helped him get down from the wagon and began to address him "with verbose congratulation," but the blunt Smith joked, "O hell! I didn't come out here to see you officers. How are you, boys?" The men immediately broke ranks and swarmed the popular general, who in his speech to them later took great pains to praise his replacement, Blair, who was known as a political appointee. Unfortunately for Blair's headquarters contingent, some of their wagons overturned on a bridge on the route and ejected copious amounts of whiskey bottles and beer kegs. The soldiers willingly helped clean up the mess.[53]

But Sherman went farther than just urging Grant to "issue some general order" or "make some uniform and just rule" regarding supply issues. He added: "Stop all troops till your army is partially supplied with wagons, and then act as quickly as possible, for this road will be jammed as sure as life if you attempt to supply 50,000 men by one single road." It was a definite check coming from Grant's most trusted subordinate. And it was not bad advice given the lack of food in the army at the time. One Ohioan scribbled in his diary: "Nothing to eat but cornmeal and fresh pork."[54]

But Grant would have none of it. He had never been afraid of going against Sherman, as his whole plan that had brought them to this very point illustrated. He listened and took advice for what it was worth, but Grant made his own decisions, even if Sherman himself did not agree. So it was in this case. Grant wrote back from Rocky Springs the next morning, dealing with the several points Sherman made. First, he admitted that "I do not calculate upon the possibility of supplying the army with full rations from Grand Gulf. I know it will be impossible without constructing additional roads," which the pioneers in fact did in the ensuing days. He went on: "What I do expect, however, is to get up what rations of hard bread, coffee, and salt we can, and make the country furnish the balance." He explained how the first troops over the river had few rations when they started inland: "We started from Bruinsburg with an average of about two days' rations, and received no more from our own supplies for some days. Abundance was found in the mean time. Some corn meal, bacon, and vegetables were found, and an abundance of beef and mutton." It had been done before, and Grant would stretch to the limit again; one of his Indianans mentioned "half rations for five days," and an Illinoisan grumbled that "we drew only flour again."[55]

More concerning was Sherman's recommendation to halt again until enough wagons and supplies arrived. Grant had basically been stopped for three days now, having made only small and incremental advances. His current position at Rocky Springs was just a little over five miles north of Bayou Pierre itself and only fifteen from Grand Gulf. "A delay would give the enemy time to re-enforce and fortify," he wrote in response. Plus, Grant's eight days were quickly ticking away, which the more Jominian Sherman could not understand. Grant assured Sherman that supplies were getting up soon and that Sherman's lack of adequate provisions from the surrounding area was simply because "you are in a country where the troops have already lived off the people for some days, and may find provisions more scarce, but as we get upon new soil they are more abundant, particularly in corn and cattle."[56]

As a result, Grant firmly told Sherman to bring Blair on over the river: "If Blair were up now, I believe we could be in Vicksburg in seven days. . . . Bring

Blair's two brigades up as soon as possible." He ended by writing that "the advance will move to-day to about 3 miles beyond Cayuga, and also on the Utica Road. Your division at Willow Springs should also move to this place." Grant wrote that message early on May 9, before the problems with McClernand's advance came to light and another delay occurred, but the sentiment was correct and McPherson did move. And all would move the next day.[57]

For his part, an exasperated Sherman rode forward from Hankinson's Ferry on the morning of May 9, all the way to Rocky Springs where he met Grant himself. "He is satisfied that he will succeed in his plan," Sherman wrote Blair, "and, of course, we must do our share." In ordering Blair's two present brigades forward (Brigadier General Hugh Ewing's being left back on the route temporarily), he informed Blair of the army's moves, the road network from Grand Gulf forward, and the plans for the next couple of days. "By the time we reach Auburn," he elaborated, "General Grant expects to discover in what manner the enemy intend to fight, and will then make new combinations accordingly." He also ordered Blair to forage freely on the citizens without damaging personal property: "Forage regularly by brigade, according to orders." Finally, he added, "I await your coming with intense anxiety, as I want your division always, with its batteries."[58]

Despite the reoccurring supply issues and Sherman's continued pessimism, Grant seemed finally ready to leap forward on the next day, May 10. He sent out more orders, the third night in a row for a forward movement of McClernand's XIII Corps to Fivemile Creek. "Move your command tomorrow on the Telegraph Road to Five-Mile Creek. Instructions have been given to Generals Sherman and McPherson to move so as to continue on the same general front with you." In addition, he added, "have all the lateral roads leading from your line of march carefully examined, to facilitate communication with the other corps in case of necessity." Similar orders went to Sherman and McPherson, who by nightfall the next day would hopefully also be forward of Fivemile Creek, only a little over ten miles south of the railroad Grant wanted so badly.[59]

Perhaps an omen of what was to come in the forward leap, some reported a "broad and vivid flash instantly followed by a tremendous and almost deafening explosion with a continuance of the flashing, but the detonations were more endurable." It was "the explosion of a monster meteor" that hit between Rocky Springs and Grand Gulf, and it highly scared those of less scientific mind and more otherworldly thoughts. Surgeon Silas Trowbridge, on his way to Hard Times with an orderly to inspect the medical facilities there, explained that "my orderly was a very superstitious young Swede, and although bold and intrepid in battle, was now filled with terror of the most overwhelming kind at beholding this grand and most magnificently beautiful exhibition of nature."[60]

Mother Nature's omen aside, few others knew Grant's future plans, Indianan Edward Wood writing "how long we shall remain in this vicinity or when Gen. Grant will be ready to strike the decisive blow of course it is impossible to say." But Grant was working that out, and one Illinoisan admitted "we look for warm work next week." With the move the next day ordered, Grant penned a quick note to Julia that night from Rocky Springs. "I am very well camping in the forests of Mississippi," he wrote, but he told her he was moving forward to Auburn the next morning and was expecting a fight soon. "Two days more," he wrote, "must bring on the fight which will settle the fate of Vicksburg." But he was confident: "No Army ever felt better than this one does nor more confidant of success. Before they are beaten they will be very badly beaten."[61]

9

"Mississippi Is More Seriously Threatened Than Ever Before"

May 10–11

Despite the major events in southwestern Mississippi that saw Grant barreling down toward either Vicksburg or the state capital, or both, the attention of both nations was not fixed on the Mississippi Valley. The huge battle at Chancellorsville had taken everybody by surprise, especially the outcome and the mode in which it was done. It was unheard of for a commander to divide his army more than once and then go on the offensive. And it was troubling to say the least for Northerners that the Army of the Potomac had fought no better than it did. But the realization soon set in that it was not necessarily the army's fault at all, despite the reports of the troubles the XI Corps experienced during Jackson's flank attack back on May 2. The army had not been allowed to fight, and that rested on the commander, Joseph Hooker.[1]

But by the time Grant restarted his advance from Big Sand Creek toward the north in Mississippi, Chancellorsville was a week past. Yet it still dominated the news because of one of the untold tens of thousands of casualties. The mysterious and almost mythical Stonewall Jackson had been dreadfully wounded on May 2; he lived through it despite an amputation and other smaller wounds. He was recovering nicely, news reports indicated, nearer to Richmond, and there were hopes of a full recovery.[2]

But then news broke in the East on May 10 that Jackson had taken a turn for the worse and actually died, some said of pneumonia and others more recently of complications from the wound and recovery. No matter the reason, Lee had lost his right arm permanently, and the Confederacy had to fight on without one of its most colorful and winning generals. The news broke the South's heart and enlivened Northerners' morale by simply realizing they would not have to deal with any more of Jackson's famed flank attacks. "We shall fear him no more," one Federal wrote. But Jackson was by no means the only death during this time, and not all were in Virginia either. One Confederate also noted another passing that early May: "Gen Vandorn is also dead but his death was different."[3]

As Americans watched the news unfold first of Jackson's death, then the public viewing in Richmond on May 12 when thousands filed by to look at the face of a hero, and finally at services in the coming days, it certainly took the limelight away from Grant's operations in Mississippi. After all, there had been little news out of that sector in terms of battles for over a week now, the last being the fight at Port Gibson, which, fierce and important though it was, simply did not match the titanic struggle at Chancellorsville. Preparations for Jackson's memorial services grabbed a lot of attention, and only the burial ended the immediate obsession with Jackson's death. A War Department clerk noted that "Jackson, the great hero, was the absorbing thought."[4]

All the while, Grant quietly moved his forces northward, not minding the lack of national attention. Many even in Grant's army, in fact, focused on the stunning news from Virginia that broke on May 13. But Grant had never been one for glory or honor anyway, and it was just fine with him that the only ones paying major attention now were the Confederates near Vicksburg. Still, a few perceptive soldiers in his own army realized what was happening. Brigade commander Brigadier General Mortimer D. Leggett wrote home on May 10 that "Grant is making glorious progress and with all manner of obstacles to surmount." Then he added high praise indeed: "He has overcome difficulties here that even Napoleon never dared encounter."[5]

Even as Americans' attention focused on the startling events in Virginia, Grant quietly pressed ahead in Mississippi. It was very Napoleonic in nature, three corps moving in tandem northward on different but parallel tracks, largely so he could glean from the countryside better. Having waited long enough with only stuttered starts, he finally began slipping his army northward for good on May 10, but still at excruciatingly slow increments, not exactly the full form of lightning warfare he had envisioned. His eight days were fast running out, but by this time he had a little more leeway in that Banks in Louisiana had written that he would not be able to cooperate until way over in May. Grant replied on May 10 again, explaining that "meeting the enemy, however, as I did, south of Port Gibson, I followed him to the Big Black, and could not afford to retrace my steps." With forces by May 3 all the way to Hankinson's Ferry and by May 7 at Rocky Springs, a full fifteen miles out from Grand Gulf, pulling back to Grand Gulf now would cancel all the forward progress made. In fact, it was only about the same fifteen air miles to Vicksburg itself from Rocky Springs. Grant was figuratively already halfway there, and to have pulled back would have resulted in the loss of momentum. "I could not lose the time," Grant wrote. And in order to change the dynamics of the desired cooperation, Grant added that "many days cannot elapse before the battle will begin which is to decide the fate of Vicksburg." He accordingly asked Banks to send him troops again![6]

And Grant was losing some momentum anyway, in the small leaps and much larger delays his army faced after the original May 7 jump-off date. But McClernand now seemed to have three days' rations up and on May 10 ordered his corps forward from its Big Sand camps to Fivemile Creek. If moving on the main Jackson Road, it was a good seven- or eight-mile leap, but according to Grant's latest placement of the corps, McClernand would shift to the left after the big bend of the Big Black River ended near Hall's Ferry. That would allow the XIII Corps to spill out into the larger area nearer the river and allow Sherman room to fill in the middle along the main Jackson Road. All the while, McPherson and the XVII Corps would detour to the right toward Utica and advance in the direction of Raymond. Grant's staff officer James H. Wilson was well out front reconnoitering the area and the roads, explaining that "it will be easy to communicate all along between the two roads meeting at Raymond." He also reported a civilian "probably well disposed and for the Union, at all events honest, says, no rebels this side of Fourteen Mile Creek."[7]

McClernand was indeed able to restart his advance on the morning of May 10, making the march easily and running into little or no Confederate resistance. By midmorning, he reported to Grant from Cayuga that "the head of my column is arrived at this place. Its advance guard is at Five-Mile Creek." He forwarded rumors that the Confederates were "crossing detachments of cavalry and infantry over Big Black . . . , but as yet are unauthenticated." Clearly, McClernand was still much more worried about his supply situation: "I beg to remind you again that my corps is supplied with a very small number of teams. . . . It is but just, both to you and myself, that this fact should be stated."[8]

More frayed nerves came with the restart, however, over and above Grant's correction of new brigade commander Brigadier General Michael Lawler for paroling prisoners he encountered. When Grant's staff officer Wilson arrived at McClernand's headquarters with orders to watch one of the Big Black River ferries, McClernand harshly retorted: "I'll be _____ if I'll do it—I am tired of being dictated to—I won't stand it any longer, and you can go back and tell General Grant!" Wilson did, but not before challenging McClernand

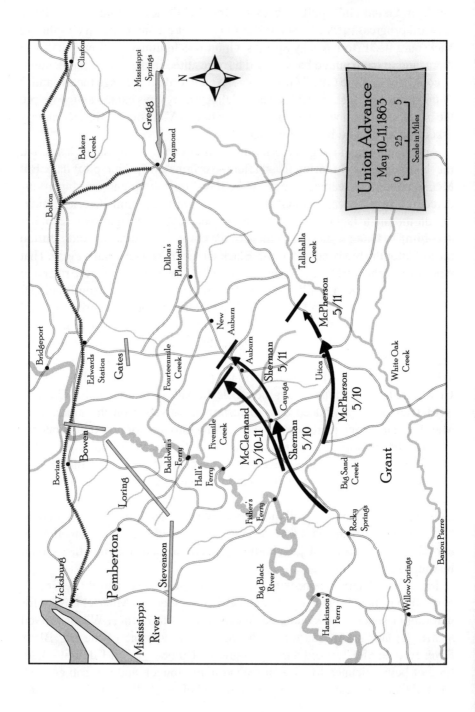

Union Advance
May 10-11, 1863

Scale in Miles
0   25   5

N

Clinton

Mississippi Springs

Gregg

Bakers Creek

Raymond

Bolton

Dillon's Plantation

Tallahalla Creek

Bridgeport

New Auburn

McPherson 5/11

Edwards Station

Gates

Fourteenmile Creek

Auburn

Sherman 5/11

White Oak Creek

Bowen

Baldwin's Ferry

Fivemile Creek

Cayuga

Utica

McPherson 5/10

Bovina

Loring

Hall's Ferry

McClerand 5/10-11

Sherman 5/10

Big Sand Creek

Pemberton

Stevenson

Fisher's Ferry

Rocky Springs

Grant

Vicksburg

Mississippi River

Big Black River

Hankinson's Ferry

Willow Springs

Bayou Pierre

to a fistfight for cursing at him: "Although you are a major general, while I am only a lieutenant colonel, I will pull you off that horse and beat the boots off of you!" McClernand backed down a bit and explained that he was merely "expressing my intense vehemence on the subject matter, sir, and I beg your pardon." A joke came of it; all such subsequent explosions of wrath around Grant's headquarters were thenceforth explained away as simply expressing their "intense vehemence on the subject matter."[9]

Taxing already frayed nerves even more, both McPherson and Sherman played their parts in the advance, but with more trouble. Neither hit the mark they were intended to during the advance on May 10, both complaining of the roads. Destroying the "boat bridge" at Hankinson's Ferry, Sherman's troops pushed off from there, Sherman describing how the "roads are very dusty; middle of day hot, but mornings and evenings cool." McPherson added that "the road is very dry and dusty following the divide between Big Black and north fork of Bayou Pierre." But the biggest problem was the lack of water, especially for McPherson on the far right. It was ironic that the very thing that had plagued Grant's campaign for months now became a cherished commodity. Grant had ordered McPherson to move "to water beyond Utica, provided you can find it within six or seven miles of that place." But McPherson's troops were moving through the highest areas of the neck of land he described, where the tributaries flowing eastward into Tallahala Creek were small and mostly dry. The headwaters of Big and Little Sand and Fivemile Creeks were a couple miles to the east and flowed westward to the Big Black River. Accordingly, McPherson operated in the driest region around. He informed Grant during the march on May 10, "there are no streams on the road, and the troops have suffered some for want of water." In fact, he did not make it all the way to where he wanted but did pass through Utica that day around noon before camping for the night at A. B. Weeks's plantation some two miles to the east and north. He admitted that "I had to be guided to-day in selecting camps somewhat by the chances of getting water." The common soldiers were not thrilled, of course, one writing that the men had only three-fourths rations and "officers nothing to eat. . . . The heat and sun and dust made the days march very hard. Water very scarce." Even passing through Utica brought no relief, Luther Cowan simply describing it as "about one-hundred houses—a miserable village." One Illinoisan described resting at a man's house who was cleaned out: "He was a bitter seceshionist and then wanted protection yet which made the Boys worse." A Wisconsin artilleryman mentioned the "frowning damsels in the windows and doors." Potentially worse was a near friendly-fire incident in which the 5th Iowa mistook the 6th Missouri Cavalry as the enemy; only a fortunate flag of truce resolved the matter.[10]

Sherman was also having problems getting his troops up, although less because of water and more because of distances involved. He pushed through the night but was not able to get much past Cayuga, although one of his excited soldiers related in his diary: "Seen Gen Grant Sherman Steel Tuttle Wood Buckland Mower and others." The troops also found a female college there: "There is several buildings here besides the nice brick college and we had good quarters but nothing hardly to eat."[11]

As a result, Grant had to stall yet another day in order to get his corps all on a line with Fivemile Creek, this time because of McPherson and Sherman instead of McClernand. He consequently ordered McClernand that evening, "you need not move to-morrow, except to better your position on Five-Mile Creek," although he was to secure the crossings and even probe ahead toward the next obstacle, Fourteenmile Creek. Grant added that he would remain at Cayuga that night and move on up to Auburn the next day as the corps realigned themselves. Orders were that Sherman would move forward to Auburn, taking possession of Fivemile Creek in the process, while McPherson moved farther past Utica and did the same farthest to the east: "Move your command forward also, so as to occupy something near the same east and west line with the other army corps." That would put all three corps in possession of and across Fivemile Creek, which would also provide the commands water in the meantime. McPherson responded from his Weeks's Plantation camps that "a forward movement of about 5 miles will bring me on an east and west line with Auburn." One of his soldiers quipped that the army was "running loose over half the State of Mississippi."[12]

But the campaign, despite ample rest, was beginning to wear on the soldiers. Although one Illinoisan marveled that "this morning we drew full rations of everything," that was the exception. Food in fits and spurts when it could be found or when it arrived from Grand Gulf was very much welcomed, but this was not adequate for full rations, which hurt physically. "We have been awaiting the arrival of the train and at night it came with our rations," one Missourian wrote in his diary, "and as we have not been having a full share it was quite welcome." But he did add, "cotton seeds and fleas, are our beds one as plentiful as the other." Mentally, it was problematic not knowing if or when another meal would be forthcoming. The basics of life were also missing, one Wisconsin soldier writing home that "we have not seen a tent since we left the Bend, the sun by day is very hot, and the nights are amazingly cold." But still the men kept a remarkably good attitude, John Jones continuing that "I have eaten more fresh meat this past month than ever before, mutton and beef. I think that this hot climate agrees first rate with me, I have never felt as healthy as I do at present."[13]

One Ohioan, Osborn Oldroyd, gave a particularly personal view of the soldier's life on the march. He described, for instance, how some

> take great care so to pack the hard-tack that it will not dig into the side while marching, for if a corner sticks out too much anywhere, it is only too apt to leave its mark on the soldier. Bacon, too, must be so placed as not to grease the blouse or pants. I see many a bacon badge about me—generally in the region of the left hip. In filling canteens, if the covers get wet the moisture soaks through and scalds the skin. The tin cup or coffee-can is generally tied to the canteen or else to the blanket or haversack, and it rattles along the road, reminding one of the sound of the old cow coming home.

Once on the march, he added:

> O, what a grand army this is, and what a sight to fire the heart of a spectator with a speck of patriotism in his bosom. I shall never forget the scene of to-day, while looking back upon a mile of solid columns, marching with their old tattered flags streaming in the summer breeze, and hearkening to the firm tramp of their broad brogans keeping step to the pealing fife and drum, or the regimental bands discoursing "Yankee Doodle" or "The Girl I Left Behind Me." I say it was a grand spectacle—but how different the scene when we meet the foe advancing to the strains of "Dixie" and "The Bonny Blue Flag."[14]

With the commands in camp on the night of May 10 and ready for the leap forward (Sherman and McPherson) across Fivemile Creek the next day, the commanders also saw to other matters. McPherson, still worried about his right flank, ordered his cavalry under Colonel Wright, the 6th Missouri Cavalry, on a special errand to the east. With reports of Confederates along Tallahala Creek, Wright was to break them up and drive them away and, if possible, to continue eastward to the New Orleans, Jackson, and Great Northern Railroad: "Make a dash over that way, and destroy the telegraph and railroad track, if . . . practicable." At the same time, he issued orders for his two divisions to move the next morning northward toward the Fivemile Creek headwaters. McPherson also organized a battalion of cavalry from several independent companies in the area and placed it under Captain John S. Foster, with orders to scout ahead of the corps the next day.[15]

Perhaps the biggest outcome of the rearward tidying-up was when Grant partially snapped at McClernand's continuing complaint about supplies and transportation. McClernand had performed his job that day easily and was not the cause of the delay, although he had been the days previous. Now, Sherman and McPherson were the causes, but Grant still lashed out at McClernand. The XIII Corps commander's reminder of too few wagons brought a scathing response from Grant, indicating his growing nervousness at the forward movements away from easy access to supplies at Grand Gulf, which in and of itself had actually not been so easy. But moving forward would create an even worse situation. Evidently in bad humor and tiring of McClernand's continued complaints, Grant wrote that afternoon:

> Your note complains of want of transportation. I have passed one and a part of another of your divisions, and am satisfied that the transportation with them, to say nothing of the large number of mules mounted by soldiers, would carry the essential parts of five days' rations for the command to which they belong, if relieved of the knapsacks, officers, soldiers, and negroes now riding. You should take steps to make the means at hand available for bringing up the articles necessary for your corps. Equal facilities have been given each of the army corps in all respects, no special order having been given to favor any one, except to give the first 30 wagons to the Thirteenth Army Corps.[16]

By May 10, John C. Pemberton had, with Stonewall Jackson's death, gained a spot among the lieutenant generals in the hierarchy of the Confederate high command, but that was of no concern and not even yet known out in the western Confederacy. And even had it been known, the rise in pecking order would have made little difference. In fact, there was a growing lack of confidence in Pemberton from many areas. His generals were getting nervous about the lack of offensive effort and his desire to remain on the defensive. And the political leaders of Mississippi were starting to chafe under his leadership as well. In addition to the Pemberton–Pettus correspondence and the Pemberton–Davis messages, Pettus and Davis kept up a regular communication, as did others from the state capital. Pettus mostly remained loyal to Pemberton, realizing he was the Confederate commander for his state and seeking to aid him all he could. But in doing all he could to provide State Troops and civilian support for Pemberton, Pettus made it plain to Davis just what was as stake: "Mississippi is more seriously threatened than ever before." Later, he warned that "no effort in the power of Federal Government will be spared to open the river this spring." Three days later he added, the "hour of trial is on us. We look to you for assistance. Let it be speedy." Certainly, a feeling of pending battle also ran through the army, one of Bowen's soldiers writing, "a bloody battle is daily expected to be fought at some point between Raymond & Big Black River."[17]

Nonelected leaders were more blunt and aimed almost directly at Pemberton. One Louisianan warned the War Department that "the people despair of defending the Mississippi Valley with such men as Pemberton and other hybrid Yankees in command." Most notably, the editors of the Jackson *Mississippian*, even while printing daily updates on the Federals' advance toward them as well as continuing its fascination with Grierson's Raid nearly a week after it ended, wrote Davis bluntly that "the people within this department—soldiers and citizens—do not repose that confidence in the capacity and loyalty of General Pemberton which is so important at this juncture." The editors assured the president that their paper had never "encouraged these apprehensions," but they made it just as plain that "fears are daily expressed by leading influential men that the valley may not be saved, and this feeling prevails to an alarming extent in army and among our people. Whether well founded or not, it must be obvious to you that the prevalence of such doubts at this time is extremely perilous." In offering a solution, the editors begged: "Send us a man we can all trust—Beauregard, Hill, or Longstreet—and confidence will be restored and all will fight to the death for Mississippi." Similarly, foundry owner Abram B. Reading of Vicksburg simply wired Davis: "Come to Vicksburg if possible. Your presence is needed."[18]

There was obviously little Davis could do, and he responded to the *Mississippian* editors frankly: "Your dispatch is the more painful because there is no remedy. Time does not permit the change you propose, if there was no other reason; but you will see that a new man would have everything to learn when immediate action was required." He added, "the distrust surprises me and is surely unjust. Try to correct it, for our country's sake." Davis understood that "immediate action was required" and therefore argued for keeping Pemberton. But the chance of getting that immediate action from Pemberton was not all that promising either. Perhaps it was for that very reason that Davis ordered Johnston to Mississippi the very next day. But if he hoped for any more immediate action from Johnston, he was likewise sorely mis-figuring.[19]

In fact, Pemberton remained sharply convinced that the entire Federal army was aiming at the Big Black River railroad bridge, not Jackson per se, and that his best strategy was to remain behind the river to fend off the advance. And the Federal movements throughout May 9 and on into the next day and the next seemed to bear him out, as McClernand leaped from Big Sand to Fivemile Creek and then probed on forward toward Fourteenmile Creek. The enemy seemed to be uncovering the various ferries and crossings below, with hardly any Federals remaining at Hankinson's Ferry and not many more up at Hall's Ferry. Lieutenant Colonel William N. Brown of the mounted 20th Mississippi who scouted the Hankinson's Ferry area with a few men in a canoe wrote that "I am still inclined to think the enemy have gone up the river." Colonel Thomas M. Scott of the 12th Louisiana, part of which actually crossed the Big Black River at Hall's Ferry, advised that "citizens and negroes report a heavy force of cavalry, artillery, and infantry moving up the Jackson road" and that "a brigadier general who dined yesterday at Mrs. Fisher's declared it to be their intention to take Jackson." Scott added, "I myself heard drums northeast of this place three hours since." Other reports put the number of Federals at around forty thousand. Action seemed to have moved up to the Baldwin's Ferry area, to which Pemberton gave special concern.[20]

Ignoring any of the offensive plans his generals had begun to push on him, Pemberton still planned to defensively meet the enemy at the railroad bridge. In a flurry of messages sent out to nearly all his commanders, Pemberton wrote Bowen, for instance, that "it is very probable that the movement toward Jackson is in reality on Big Black Bridge." Almost exactly worded messages also went to Loring, Stevenson, and recently arrived Brigadier General John Gregg in Jackson, to whom Pemberton added, "in which case you must be prepared to attack them in rear and on flank."[21]

The man on the spot at the focal point at the railroad bridge, Bowen, sought to understand intimately what Pemberton wanted done in that event, since the commander would not come out of Vicksburg. Bowen queried on May 10: "If the enemy advance in force, shall I give battle at Edwards Depot, or withdraw to the intrenchments, which will probably be finished this evening?" Pemberton quickly responded, "withdraw to intrenchments if they advance in heavy force." He was still intent on the river providing a defense.[22]

The other divisions were affected as well, and Pemberton ordered them concentrated more and more toward Bowen's position. With the Federal movement well past Hankinson's Ferry, Stevenson's heavy presence in that area and even Warrenton was no longer needed. Likewise, Loring's troops were no longer required in force down in the Hall's Ferry area. As a result, Pemberton ordered Loring to shift to the left toward Bowen and the railroad bridge, still covering Baldwin's Ferry at the same time, at which, according to Loring's brigade commander Lloyd Tilghman, enemy troops appeared "in pretty strong force" as early as May 11. One of Loring's Mississippians was glad for the move, writing that "it seamed that we had got in to a country full of hunny." Stevenson was also ordered to shift as well, keeping his left on Loring's right wherever it went and being prepared to move "at a moment's notice." The three divisions and added brigades from other divisions (Moore's, Waul's Legion, and Harris's Mississippi State Troops attached to Stevenson) were also gradually moving northward in response to the Federal surge in that direction, although in a confused manner with the division commanders complaining of contradicting orders and lack of support. It did not help when Pemberton sent Loring a second message to move closer to Bowen, explaining that the first had been written "in the dark" and that "this is written, fearing that you may not have been able to read the communication previously sent." Pemberton biographer Michael Ballard wonders if Loring saw another meaning of Pemberton doing things "in the dark" for some time now. In the confusion of the moves, Pemberton likewise became agitated at the lack of understanding his commanders had. His adjutant wrote both Loring and Stevenson that Pemberton "finds great difficulty in having his views comprehended, and wishes to see you at once personally." Perhaps Loring and Stevenson thought that some of the confusion might ease up if Pemberton would actually come out of Vicksburg.[23]

Nevertheless, as Pemberton became more and more convinced that the attack was aimed at the railroad bridge, he also began to formulate a coordinating plan to attack, but not with his army. Rather, it would be by forces from Jackson on what would then have to be the rear and flank of the Federal army. He ordered Colonel Wirt Adams on May 10 to take command of all cavalry in the area and to head to the Edwards and Raymond area to scout the enemy units in that neighborhood, keeping both Pemberton and his Jackson commander John Adams informed regularly. At the same time, he ordered John Gregg, recently arrived in Jackson with a brigade of mostly Tennesseans from Port Hudson, to move out as well: "Move your brigade promptly to Raymond." Gregg obeyed, the message arriving at 3:00 a.m. and the brigade moving two hours later with little to no warning to prepare. A full day of marching saw a tired brigade arrive by the night of May 11. One Raymond lady wrote that "I shall never forget the looks of those poor, tired, dusty, hungry soldiers who marched into Raymond." Pemberton wanted more to go with Gregg, however, and ordered John Adams to send any of Gist's brigade from South Carolina who had arrived as well, Adams responding that none had appeared except a few of Walker's brigade. Pemberton ordered them sent on behind Gregg, with all of Walker's troops to follow as soon as possible. Adams was to scout for him in the process even while "endeavor[ing] to cut his [Grant's] communications."[24]

Yet even as Loring and Stevenson were moving northward and the Jackson forces were moving to act on what was assumed to be the Union flank and rear, the focal point for Pemberton (and eventually Grant) was in fact the railroad bridge at the Big Black River. Even if Grant broke the railroad east of the river, he would still have to crack the Big Black River shield to get to Vicksburg. And that brought Bowen onto center stage.[25]

Bowen kept Pemberton aware of what he gleaned from scouts, especially as the Federals approached Fourteenmile Creek and the railroad. He confirmed the enemy were "camped from Rocky Springs to the college, north of Big Sandy. About 2,000 cavalry are gleaning the country of everything movable and sending it to their camp." Closer to his position, he added, "their cavalry moved as far as Fourteen-Mile Creek this afternoon, and were driven back 3 miles by Colonel [Elijah] Gates's scouts." Bowen prepared accordingly, his two brigades manning their specific positions, with Bowen describing how "every piece of artillery and every man has his place marked out" and "their places in them pointed out." Farther out at Edwards, of course, were the advance elements of the division, mainly Gates's 1st Missouri Cavalry dismounted, covering both the Whittaker's Ford and Montgomery's Bridge crossings of Fourteenmile Creek south of Edwards Station.[26]

Yet Bowen was in a predicament. If he remained at the railroad bridge, he could certainly cover that area well. But there were other ferries to his left and right that could easily allow a Federal crossing if not covered. Much like the various ferries to the south that needed to be manned as the Federals moved northward, and still watched even this late, those near the railroad line were now becoming critical. Especially so were the two nearest, Baldwin's to the south and Bridgeport to the north, as well as an intermediate one just three miles south of the railroad at Bachelor's Ferry. Pemberton notified Bowen to watch it as well, although Bowen had no idea of its existence until then.[27]

While knowing he could defend the bridge area in the entrenchments that he notified Pemberton would be finished that night, Bowen realized full well that "the position can be turned if the enemy pass Edwards and cross at Bridgeport Ferry." He consequently advised Pemberton that "my division is not sufficient to give battle at both points." Bowen would have to discern which would be the major location and move there, but therein was the real problem. Due to the flow of the Big Black River, which made a sharp swing from its southwesterly direction just past Bridgeport to a westerly flow and then as sharp a swing back to the south where the railroad bridge was, the river made a giant elongated S swing. Accordingly, for Bowen the trek from the railroad bridge to Bridgeport was about ten miles. But if the Federals reached Edwards Station, it was less than half of that to either: "While we have 9 or 10 miles to pass from one point to the other, the enemy march 3 or 4, from Edwards Depot." The unwritten result was that the enemy could be at either, or both, before Bowen could react in full. It was the definition of Bowen operating on exterior lines.[28]

The problem was real, as Pemberton knew full well, and Bowen's next recommendation was the germination of a move that Pemberton had long shunned: moving out from behind the shield of the Big Black River. But

Bowen had good arguments to do so. "If a force cannot be spared for that point," he wrote Pemberton, "could not my command, if supported at Raymond, move forward, and hold a position between Edwards and Fourteen-Mile Creek, fronting south, with our right near enough to Big Black to force them to cross at Baldwin's? Could we not thus preserve the entire railroad, as well as the bridge?" Also unstated was that holding Edwards Station would deprive the Federals of access to either the bridge or Bridgeport.[29]

It was a logical plan—except, that is, for moving outside the safety of the Big Black River. But at this point Pemberton started to waffle on his determination not to do so and began to entertain the idea. And, evidently, other plans for an offensive also began to enter his mind, he informing his staff still in the capital that "if the enemy moves on Jackson, I will advance to meet them, and must have subsistence provided at Jackson." It was not a foregone conclusion as yet, Pemberton still thinking that Grant would go to the railroad bridge. If he turned the other way toward Jackson, however, an advance might well be warranted.[30]

It was a lot for the normally indecisive Pemberton to deal with, essentially raising the idea of whether to "abandon the line of the Big Black." His inherent indecisiveness did not help, of course, and Grant consequently continued to maintain the initiative.[31]

"Fine May morning," one Federal wrote in his diary on May 11; "the birds are chirping this morning." Making it even better for the Federals, for once Grant's plans went off without any problem. McClernand solidified his possession of the Fivemile Creek crossings on the left and probed forward to see if there would be any resistance at Fourteenmile Creek anywhere from another three to six miles ahead, depending on the weaving nature of both watersheds. Meanwhile, Sherman and McPherson both moved onward to positions north of Fivemile Creek with easy marches that day despite one Federal in Logan's division of McPherson's corps reporting "roads very narrow, move slowly—day extremely hot—Men can't stand it very well." But they did, one Illinoisan in Stevenson's brigade writing that "although we are seeing some rough times we still have many things to cheer our hearts on our rugged way and though we march hard all day and a good portion of the night when we stop the bare ground appears an excellent bed & a cartridge box or pair of boots a good pillow." Another wrote of camping, "that is if, lying on the ground with a blanket over you can be called camping."[32]

Although not on the move to any great degree, McClernand was busy enough that day, writing Grant numerous times and evidently not worrying about the rebuke he had endured the afternoon before. And he offered more advice, but it was good advice this time, backed up by captured Confederate messages (Sherman also captured Confederate letters in the post office at Auburn) as well as "negroes coming in this morning." Ironically, given the subject of the confrontation earlier, his main concern were the ferries that were being uncovered as the army advanced northward; major ones such as Hankinson's and Hall's Ferries were all uncovered now that McClernand was across Fivemile Creek, but even smaller ones such as Campbell's and Fisher's between Hankinson's and Hall's Ferries and not on main roads were critical as well. McClernand wrote Grant on May 11, "I venture to make a suggestion . . . he will attempt to cross the Big Black in our rear, and isolate us by cutting our communications." He wanted to "shift our advancing columns farther to the left, resting our left flank upon the Big Black." It was logical, and Grant approved both: leaving forces at the ferries to the rear as well as McClernand shifting a division to the river itself in the next day's movement to Fourteenmile Creek. A misunderstanding occurred that might have caused a crisis, however, when the 95th Ohio, sent to guard Hall's Ferry, became lost: "The road the colonel was directed to take took him to Baldwin's Ferry." McClernand, of course, was on to something, as it was the exact plan Loring was pushing in the Confederate high command.[33]

Meanwhile, McClernand's divisions mainly stayed put at Fivemile Creek, only probes moving forward toward Fourteenmile Creek this day. Osterhaus moved forward to the forks of the Edwards Station and Raymond Roads with the 49th and 69th Indiana and one section of Lanphere's Battery, and from there cavalry moved ahead to Fourteenmile Creek looking equally for water and the enemy. But what they found was not promising. Cavalry sent out on both roads met Confederate resistance, the enemy on the road toward Edwards Station being "in too strong force to allow the party to proceed farther." Worse, he added, "negroes informed the officer in command that the enemy intended to offer obstinate resistance at that creek." The movement toward Raymond met Confederates as well, although in less force and with less resistance. Worse was that the forces found no water "but only a scanty supply" near New Auburn. It all convinced McClernand that the next day would be consequential: "There is little or no water between here and Fourteen-Mile Creek; so we will probably have to fight for the water of that stream."[34]

All the while, Sherman and McPherson moved forward without any resistance across Fivemile Creek on May 11 to be in line with McClernand, the 13th Illinois giving three resounding cheers for their old general when they passed Eugene Carr's headquarters of McClernand's corps; a similar episode occurred as Osterhaus reunited with some of the troops from his Missouri days. Sherman also visited old friends as he moved through Cayuga and to Auburn, where he camped for the night near "the pond of water." He visited the camp of the 48th Ohio that had been at Shiloh with him and told them he would like to have them back in his corps; three cheers went up from the regiment as the general departed. Despite the visitation, the marches were time-consuming and hot, one of Sherman's soldiers scribbling in his diary that night that he was "verry sore futed." Sherman himself scouted forward "a mile or so, and water is very scarce," he informed Grant. Indeed, one of his soldiers scribbled in his diary that very day, "the scenery along the way is roughly painted by the hand of nature."[35]

With some newly arrived rations issued, McPherson's XVII Corps also moved just a few miles up the Raymond Road to J. Roach's plantation, well beyond Utica and across the various branches of the headwaters of Fivemile Creek. But there were only a few rations issued, one Illinoisan describing how "I was offered 50 cts for three crackers by a man of an Oho Regt but I gave him one and John too, so he owes it to the next hungry man who comes to him looking for something to eat." That night near the Roach Plantation, he also described "a 'rich man' He pretended to be in favor of the union and talked much against the Southern Confederacy but after a while, the boys of course glad to hear him talk in our favor 'pitched in' eneway for thought 'if we don't take it the rebs will.'" He added that, in the process of plundering his home, "2 Secesh flags were found in his house which soon took all respect of his character and he was thought to be a TRAITOR."[36]

Grant himself remained at Cayuga throughout the day and night, although reconciling some of the corps strengths in the process. For instance, he informed McClernand that Sherman's six brigades had moved through Cayuga with "but four batteries, and all of them smooth-bore guns." If the XV Corps met much resistance, rifles would be very helpful, so he ordered McClernand to "retransfer the battery given to you from that corps, whilst at Milliken's Bend, and also to temporarily detach a section of 20-pounder Parrotts for the ensuing battle." In a classic case where nothing was easy, McClernand sent a different battery, wanting to keep the 1st Iowa Battery in his corps because it was one of only two in Carr's division, whereas Hovey's division, from which the other battery was sent, had four. "To have transferred Griffiths's would have involved a second transfer and consequent delay and confusion," McClernand wrote. Steele complained about the one originally sent, writing that "it was only four guns deficient in men and ammunition," and said that Griffith's Battery still had men from his infantry regiments detailed to it, adding that he would rather not have any battery than the one originally sent, "as it is not practicable for me to drill men and get ammunition for the one designated by Genl. McClernand."[37]

Farther outward, Colonel Wright's cavalry raid was also making good progress. He left McPherson's corps around six o'clock that morning and rode hard for some twenty-five miles to a point on the railroad just north of Crystal Springs, where his troopers began breaking the telegraph and rail line. He burned three bridges and broke the line at three distinct places over the course of a mile and a half. Amazingly, the troopers were back at camp that evening, having ridden fifty miles and performed the destruction in the process, but Wright noted that "my command is worn down by incessant labor for the last twenty days and nights, and would respectfully ask permission to rest men and horses for one day."[38]

With all his corps in line east to west above Fivemile Creek by the evening of May 11, Grant informing Halleck of the developments from Cayuga that evening, and not wanting to waste any more time, Grant issued his orders for the next day: "In accordance with my verbal instructions this afternoon," Grant wrote McClernand that evening at 8:15, McClernand was to move forward at daylight on the main Edwards Station Road toward Whittaker's Ford over Fourteenmile Creek and take possession of the creek and ground across it. At the same time, and in accordance with McClernand's request, he was to send a division farther west to hug the Big Black River itself, protecting that flank. He added, "move cautiously, but rapidly as convenient, and so that your entire corps will arrive on the Fourteen-Mile Creek simultaneously and in a compact line." And it was to be done in coordination with the other corps as well: "It is also important that your corps reach the creek at or about the same time that Sherman's does, he having to move only about 7 miles."[39]

McClernand issued his orders that evening: "Take up the line of march in the morning for Fourteen-Mile Creek." Hovey was to lead the way at 4:00 a.m., followed by Carr and then Osterhaus, all moving up the Edwards Station Road for what McClernand estimated as nine miles to the creek. A. J. Smith's division was to move more westward to Baldwin's Ferry and then northward toward Montgomery's Bridge, unless a shorter route could be had. In that event, Smith was still to make sure Baldwin's Ferry was covered and no Confederates could cross over in rear of the XIII Corps. McClernand then included much of the same language Grant had used, cautioning the various divisions to move promptly but cautiously and to arrive at the creek at the same time and in coordination with Sherman to the right. The orders filtered down the chains of command, Osterhaus alerting his division that "it is probable that we may meet the enemy tomorrow."[40]

Sherman received similar instructions that evening, with confirmation that McClernand would be coordinating his movement to the creek on his left and McPherson on his right. Sherman would leave his Auburn camp-sites and move up the main Jackson Road to Fourteenmile Creek at Dillon's Plantation.[41]

McPherson's orders were similar. He was to leave his Roach Plantation camps the next morning and move toward Fourteenmile Creek just south of Raymond, taking that town if possible, mainly for the stores that would hope-fully be located there but especially for the water of Fourteenmile Creek. The same concern for arriving simultaneously and keeping in supporting distance was included as well. McPherson issued his own orders, notifying Logan to lead the march at 3:30 a.m., followed by Crocker at 4:00 a.m., causing some resentment among Crocker and his division. Nevertheless, the entire army was moving on, one Ohioan noting in his diary that day: "Vicksburg is a doomed city."[42]

Yet as Grant ordered his corps forward, supplies were not surprisingly still a growing concern. "Weather fine. Health good. Rations short," one Iowan scribbled in his diary. Water was also scarce and was an obvious issue, but Fourteenmile Creek would provide that commodity the next day, where the various divisions would camp after hopefully taking the creek on all three axes of advance. But food was also an issue, although not as time-critical as water; soldiers could skip a day or two of food without the dire effects of missing two days of water. Ammunition was also a critical component, which could not be gleaned at all from the countryside unless captured, and the Confederates could be counted on to make sure that did not happen. McPher-son demonstrated the issues at this stage of the campaign, writing Grant on May 11: "I am impressing on my command the great necessity of economy in the use of rations, and am collecting all I can from the Country. In meats we can do well enough but it is very difficult to get hold of bread Stuffs." McPherson's command was utilizing all the wagons it could find but found them inferior: "They have most invariably broken down." He contextualized that "I left Milliken's Bend with 5 to a Regt. and some of these have never come across the River or at least have not reached their Regts. The Transpor-tation is barely sufficient to haul the Camp & Garrison Equipage Extra Am-munition & and other necessary supplies." While some of these issues were larger than they could remedy, Hillyer and Raum opened bakeries at Grand Gulf to change the flour into hardtack for the troops ahead in order to at least minimize the lack of bread to some degree.[43]

As a result, Grant cautioned McPherson especially that "at the latter place [Raymond] you will use your utmost exertions to secure all the subsistence stores that may be there, as well as in the vicinity." Then he added some of his fear that had begun to creep into his mind: "We must fight the enemy before our rations fail, and we are equally bound to make our rations last as long as possible." He reminded McPherson that "upon one occasion you made two days' rations last seven. We may have to do the same thing again. I look to you to impress the necessity of this upon your division and brigade commanders, and through them upon the troops."[44]

Grant's growing concern resulted from his movement out of the comparatively easy supply situation at Rocky Springs or even Big Sand Creek. There, still near the defendable cul-de-sac, trains could move almost with impunity back and forth to Grand Gulf, although continually inching forward opened some concern for marauding bands of Confederates, especially from the east. But up to May 7, Grant's commanders were able to send wagons back and forth safely, and Sherman brought his own while approaching. But even that proved somewhat concerning, as McClernand had to continuously delay because of the trouble of getting up supplies.[45]

But now as Grant moved forward, leaping big chunks of ground with every move, the chances of continual resupply were ended; one colonel even worried over the idea of sending letters across the expanding no-man's land back to Grand Gulf. Instead, Grant opted to seemingly cut loose from his base at Grand Gulf, at least in the traditional sense wherein various commands moved their own supplies to and from a base. Grant biographer Ron Chernow has called this Grant's "go-for-broke moment in the war." Now, the corps were much too far away for that to be done safely. But the army still had to be supplied with the goods that could not be gleaned from the area. "We will be in want of salt, bread, sugar, and coffee," Sherman admitted, adding that "we may safely trust to the country for meat." Illinoisan Henry Seaman consequently described a May 10 "general order coming from head quarters notifying us that we would be compelled to forage for all the meat we got here-after." Another Illinoisan explained that he "went into the fresh meat business." Obviously, all ammunition the army would shoot also had to be brought forward.[46]

It was not a complete cut with Grant's base of supply, however. Instead of the continual flow of wagons of each command back and forth, he opted to have larger wagons trains move out of Grand Gulf all at once, guarded by large amounts of troops that were slated to join the army anyway; he had some of McArthur's division of McPherson's XVII Corps and most of Blair's division of Sherman's XV Corps nearby, Blair's two present brigades having marched fifty-three miles in three and a half days to get to Grand Gulf by May 10. All the while, they marveled at the alligators in the bayous they crossed and marched beside: "The banks of the Bayou are strewn with dead Alligators that the Boys have killed."[47]

While continual regimental trains meandering back and forth would no longer occur, the next best thing was for massive wagon trains heavily guarded to move to the army. Grant so informed Halleck on May 11, writing that "as I shall communicate with Grand Gulf no more, except it becomes necessary to send a train with heavy escort, you may not hear from me again for several days." It was a risk to be sure, and it certainly flew in the face of all things Jominian concerning secure supply connections. And it obviously contradicted the maxims preached by Grant's boss Henry Halleck. But at this point there was nothing else to do. And the remaining campaign had to be done quickly and hopefully quietly, as even with the trains rolling in food would start to dwindle and every shot the army took would be that much less ammunition available. Certainly, Grant did not want to fight numerous battles before he reached a new base of supplies, hopefully outside Vicksburg on the Yazoo River. In fact, Sherman was already indicating he was having trouble, writing that he had sent some wagons back to Milliken's Bend to help in that area, knowing full well it "will be the reason of my being short of provisions and munition."[48]

Accordingly, Hillyer at Grand Gulf began to limit the smaller trains moving back and forth, one last one coming in to Cayuga on the early afternoon of May 11. Instead, Hillyer prepared the large trains to move forward with supplies Bingham had forwarded to Grand Gulf. Grant ordered only two wagons per regiment for "authorized camp and garrison equipage," two for supplies and ammunition, and one for regimental headquarters and medical supplies. He also allowed one wagon per brigade and division headquarters and one for division medical supplies. All other wagons except corps trains "will constitute a general supply train for the army." Adding another layer of oversight, Grant ordered Sherman's XV Corps quartermaster Lieutenant Colonel John Condit Smith to take charge of the "general supply train[s]" themselves once they left Grand Gulf. "I hope you will not regard this as an interference with your corps," Grant wrote Sherman, adding "[but] I know no one but him, now with the Army, and available, who is capable."[49]

And right on time, one of the trains left Grand Gulf on May 11 with a regimental guard and another, the largest, the next day, May 12, accompanied by Blair's division. Two brigades of that unit, Colonels Giles Smith's and Thomas Kilby Smith's, crossed the river on May 11, although Blair explained that "I had great difficulty in procuring transportation across the river." The brigades eventually did so on the gunboat *Louisville* and steamer *Forest Queen*, among other vessels. More troops were also coming into Grand Gulf, including one brigade of McArthur's division under Brigadier General Thomas E. G. Ransom with McArthur himself along as well, although he apparently moved on forward and joined the army even before his troops did.[50]

Two distinct and large wagon trains would accordingly leave Grand Gulf over the course of the next two days, the first that left this very day on May 11 composed of 183 wagons loaded "principally with food and ammunition," according to one of the guards. Despite being in Colonel Charles Wood's brigade of Steele's division that had crossed the river days earlier and was with the main army up ahead, Colonel George A. Stone's 25th Iowa conveyed this large train forward after crossing the river on May 10. The regiment had been left behind at Hard Times to get wagons across and to garrison the area until Blair's troops arrived. The Iowans crossed and took up the march late on May 11: "The train being very large we did not get started until 5 ½ P.M." Continuing the description of the march that afternoon, Iowan John Bell added: "The road is a continual succession of hills and vallies and is emphatically 'a hard road to travel.' The soil is yellow clay and the dust about 4 in. deep on an average." He continued: "Our march is very fatiguing—the continual halts caused by the delay necessary to get the teams up and down the hill were irksome and we did not get into camp until 12 o'clock A.M. Three wagons were upset during the day." In addition, "our march was about 13 miles and no water on the whole distance. Went to sleep on the ground without supper." Another Iowan noted in his diary that they were "guarding an immense wagon train loaded with provisions for Grant's Army who is fighting in the advance to get in the rear of Vicksburg. He has utterly cut loose from his base of supplies and we must take this train through."[51]

Even with these supplies beginning to move forward, it would take days to make the trip that was getting longer and longer the farther the Army of the Tennessee moved northward to "within striking distance of the railroad," Sherman explained to his wife. If Grant cut the rail line soon, that would mean a trip of some forty miles for the large and slow train to cover. Consequently, Grant reminded McPherson, "but withal there remains the necessity of economy in the use of the rations we have, and activity in getting others from the country."[52]

Without saying it out loud, Grant knew he was reaching the critical point of the campaign, in more ways than one.[53]

President Abraham Lincoln watched Ulysses S. Grant's campaign across the Mississippi River and toward Vicksburg with intense interest. Inwardly he thought Grant was making a mistake, but Lincoln kept quiet and later acknowledged that Grant had been right and he had been wrong. (Library of Congress)

The mastermind behind the Inland Campaign, Ulysses S. Grant pitted the need for speedy movements against the necessity of feeding his army. He chose the perfect balance and fought his way to Vicksburg in seventeen days, fighting and winning five battles in that span. (Library of Congress)

Grant's senior corps commander John A. McClernand led much of the way in the Inland Campaign, often performing the most difficult tasks. His troops fought heavily at the Battles of Port Gibson, Champion Hill, and Big Black River Bridge. (Library of Congress)

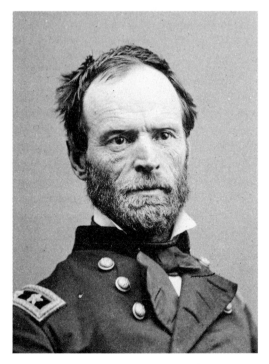

Originally on a diversion, William T. Sherman and his troops crossed the Mississippi River late but caught up with the rest of the army by the second week in May. He did not participate in many of the battles, Jackson being the exception, but Grant tasked him with destroying the effectiveness of the Mississippi capital as a staging area for Confederate efforts to aid the defenders of Vicksburg. (Library of Congress)

Grant's most inexperienced corps commander, James B. McPherson seemingly had the safest sector of the march inland. Yet his troops wound up participating in all the May battles except Big Black River Bridge. (Library of Congress)

One of Grant's hardest-fighting division commanders, Alvin P. Hovey of McClernand's corps fought well at both Port Gibson and Champion Hill. He was not afraid to tout his division's work either. (Library of Congress)

Politician John A. Logan, division commander in McPherson's corps, fought hard during the Inland Campaign. His troops were heavily engaged at Raymond and Champion Hill. (Library of Congress)

One of Grant's biggest concerns was feeding his troops as they moved toward Vicksburg, and he left staff officer William S. Hillyer behind to facilitate the movement of supplies up to the army. First at Bruinsburg and then at Grand Gulf, Hillyer oversaw the crossing of supplies over the river and then sent them forward to Grant's troops at the front. (Library of Congress)

Confederate president Jefferson Davis watched helplessly as his two generals in Mississippi worked at cross purposes in defending the state. Davis had a personal stake in the campaign, as he owned a lot of land in the Vicksburg area. (Library of Congress)

Despite being the Western Theater departmental commander, Joseph E. Johnston went to the crisis point in Mississippi only after Richmond ordered him to do so. Once there, he wanted nothing to do with the emerging debacle and declared himself too late to help. His unforced evacuation of Jackson the next day illustrated his disinterest. (Library of Congress)

Caught between two opposing superiors, Confederate Vicksburg commander John C. Pemberton made the dismal situation only worse with inefficiency and indecision. He and his commanders lost five battles in seventeen days, resulting in the Union army surrounding Vicksburg. (Library of Congress)

Much of the confusion around Vicksburg resulted from the senior Confederate division commander Carter L. Stevenson's faulty advice. Stevenson's troops engaged in only one of the May battles and were harshly handled at Champion Hill. (Library of Congress)

While out of the Vicksburg defenses to meet Grant, Pemberton left Martin L. Smith in command at Vicksburg itself. His troops would not be engaged to any degree in the May battles, but they would help defend the city when the Federals arrived. (Library of Congress)

John H. Forney was another Confederate division commander unengaged in the May battles. During Grant's advance, Forney's troops primarily defended the critical areas north and south of Vicksburg, including the vital staging area along the Yazoo River. (Library of Congress)

Pemberton's roving division commander William W. Loring went to the crisis point at Port Gibson early in the Inland Campaign and then engaged at Champion Hill. On the retreat, Loring led his division away from Pemberton's army to join forces with Joe Johnston in Jackson. (*Miller's Photographic History*)

Pemberton's most junior division commander, John S. Bowen conversely held the most important posts during the Inland Campaign. His troops fought hard at the Battles of Port Gibson, Champion Hill, and Big Black River Bridge. (Library of Congress)

Eventually part of Joe Johnston's force outside Vicksburg, John Gregg's brigade, originally from Port Hudson, fought nearly an entire Federal corps at Raymond. His Tennesseans and Texans fought hard but were overwhelmed by huge numbers. (Library of Congress)

Despite outranking a division commander, Lloyd Tilghman was still a brigade commander and was part of the anti-Pemberton faction in the army. His defense along the Raymond Road at Champion Hill covered that critical flank against timid Federal advances, but it cost Tilghman his life. (Library of Congress)

The critical crossing of Bayou Pierre came after the Battle of Port Gibson on May 1. This somewhat fictionalized newspaper version shows John Logan's troops crossing the bayou near one of the burning suspension bridges. (*Harper's Weekly*, June 15, 1863)

The heavy, close-up fighting at Raymond on May 12 is evident in this newspaper drawing of the action. (Library of Congress)

A Federal soldier drew this detailed view of the fighting at Jackson on May 14 along the Clinton Road. Samuel A. Holmes's Union brigade is approaching the Wright House just west of Jackson. (Library of Congress)

The heavy and at times hand-to-hand fighting at Champion Hill on May 16 is evident in this newspaper rendering of the battle. (Library of Congress)

10

"THE FIGHT FOR RAYMOND WAS TO TAKE PLACE AT THIS POINT"

May 12

"Raymond is a beautiful little town of about six hundred inhabitants," one observer noted in mid-May. But it was somewhat of an anomaly of its time. Situated in rural Hinds County, which it shared with the much larger and more cosmopolitan state capital at Jackson, Raymond nevertheless was one of the seats of the county. Several large Mississippi counties, including Hinds and Carroll, actually had two county seats with two courthouses and two sets of officials. Obviously, Jackson was much larger, in some six times bigger, but it also housed both the city and state governments as well as that section's county administration. Just fifteen miles to the southwest of Jackson, Raymond was a small but still well-established town, in fact becoming the "seat of justice" in 1829.[1]

While comparatively tiny—containing a mere 558 residents including 334 whites, seven free blacks, and 217 slaves—Raymond sat along some important corridors. Several roads branching in all directions led to various towns, the most important being Port Gibson, Utica, and Cayuga from the south, the direction an enemy army would travel, as well as to points farther north such as Edwards Station, Clinton, and Jackson. It also sat near the Natchez Trace to the west, and even prior to the war it had a rail connection to the Southern Railroad of Mississippi to its north; the line ran only about seven miles but had apparently gone defunct by the time the war began. Still, as a local crossroads and seat of half the county government, Raymond was an important small town, the stately two-story courthouse in the center of the square proving as much; one Federal even described it as "a rich town."[2]

It was from the high cupola atop the courthouse on the morning of May 12 that former Confederate congressman turned general John Gregg, having been sent to Raymond the day before, watched nervously to the south as word of Federals coming his way arrived. And he knew a crisis when he saw one, having been captured at Fort Donelson earlier in the war. Having arrived late the afternoon before, Gregg reported that "I found the people in great consternation, being under the impression that the enemy were advancing from Port Gibson." Indeed, indications had been growing of something massive building to the south. The Hinds County *Gazette* reported that "we infer a panic exists south of us. Droves of negroes, mules, etc., are passing through our village—stamped[ed]—appears to have seized some of our citizens who have already started with their property. . . . Village alive with exciting rumors."[3]

Gregg had been sent to Raymond to operate on what the Confederate high command presumed would be the flank or rear of the Union army turning to sweep down on the railroad bridge across the Big Black River. But what he did not know was that two full divisions, McPherson's XVII Corps, were pressing toward him. Worse, Gregg had few scouts out front to give warning of such a predicament. He noted that "I found none of Colonel Adams' cavalry except a single sergeant and 4 men." Adams had been confused by convoluted orders from Pemberton, what historian Ed Bearss calls "a masterful piece of ambiguity," to basically go to two places at one time. He chose the one other than Raymond, leaving Gregg partially blind. Only a small company of Mississippi State Troops were in the area to give warning of the Union advance. Nevertheless, the thankful people of Raymond soon began to turn out and cook a victory lunch for the famished Confederates, to be eaten after their great triumph over the oncoming enemy.[4]

Despite the gathering of the armies there, or at least portions of the armies, there was nothing all that militarily important about what one Federal described as "the prettiest town I have seen yet in the south." But during this particularly hot and dry May when one Louisianan commented in his diary that "a dry spell seems to be setting in," one commodity just to the south of town became especially important: the waters of Fourteenmile Creek that flowed westward toward the Big Black River. Raymond was in fact known for a local spring, Cooper's Well, that supposedly had medicinal value, and "the famous Mississippi Springs" was nearby. But just normal everyday drinking water would serve the purpose at this point. It would be these waters of the "at times . . . considerable stream with steep banks—but now with only about 2 ½ feet of water" that the parched soldiers of the XVII Corps would be seeking on this "warm and sultry" May 12. What they would find was something altogether different, staff officer Wilson expecting "[we] will have to fight for the possession of that stream."[5]

On schedule, which was a surprise in and of itself given the many delays in the previous few days, Grant's Army of the Tennessee lurched forward on the morning of May 12 on many fronts, not the least of which was the rear where several wagon trains were moving out from Grand Gulf. In the lead was Colonel George A. Stone's 25th Iowa with the nearly two hundred wagons that had left Grand Gulf late on May 11. The column moved forward slowly along the narrow and dusty roads again with little to eat despite carrying large numbers of provisions that were obviously off-limits. The column made progress, albeit slowly, making some twelve miles throughout the day before stopping to bivouac for the afternoon when it became almost intolerably hot.[6]

Also leaving Grand Gulf on May 12 were Blair's two brigades that had just crossed the river the day before. "I was ordered to escort a large supply train, consisting of 200 wagons, and this, with my own train, delayed my march," Blair explained, the train itself under the care of Condit Smith. Included among the wagons full of hardtack and ammunition, commodities not readily available in the country, was the only pontoon bridge with the army, not wooden boats but inflatable rubber rafts; Captain Henry C. Freeman was ordered to report with it to Grant's headquarters after traveling with the train. But Blair's troops also soon found the intervening area isolated and inhospitable over and above the dusty roads: "The country we are passing through is becoming hilly and the roads are very crooked and dusty," one member of the 57th Ohio noted, but added, "we did see some fine magnolias in full bloom." Another simply wrote, "miserable looking country, high bluffs, deep ravines, & sandy soil."[7]

But the real show was up front. At the head of this massive series of movements on May 12, Grant's forces approached Fourteenmile Creek (only a mere six or eight miles south of the railroad on average) along three axes of advance. On the far left, McClernand's XIII Corps moved up the Telegraph Road to the Whittaker's Ford crossing point on the main road into Edwards Station. Three divisions took position there, with A. J. Smith's farther to the left at Montgomery's Bridge and a detachment at Baldwin's Ferry. At the ferry itself, the two sides conversed with one another across the river and even swapped some coffee for Vicksburg newspapers; one Federal stripped down and swam the river to make the trade. No such ease occurred at Whittaker's Ford. Hovey's troops, General George McGinnis's brigade in the lead, did most of the fighting on the main road, with the 2nd Illinois Cavalry guiding the way and first encountering Gates's Missourians "concealed in the thick woods and underbrush lining the creek." In the lead in the previous days, Osterhaus had ordered Colonel Daniel B. Bush of the cavalry regiment to report to Hovey that morning as he was taking over the van. Hovey wrote that "we had marched from 4 o'clock in the morning over a rugged country, with little or no water, and our only hope was to force the enemy back beyond Fourteen-Mile Creek. A sharp skirmish ensued, and we drove the enemy back and encamped on both sides of the creek for the night. Our men enjoyed both the skirmish and the water." McClernand sent out scouts farther forward toward Edwards Station, with plans to move entire divisions across soon. "After a sharp skirmish, in which a few of our men were wounded (number not yet ascertained), I seized the main crossing of Fourteen-Mile Creek," McClernand informed Grant that day. Fortunately for the troops of the XIII Corps, venturing into newly occupied territory not only allowed them to access the cool waters of the creek but also allowed for more foraging in an area upswept by Federal troops before. After advancing as far as Mount Moriah, the foremost Union troops lay there the rest of the day and night, building bridges to facilitate an easy crossing by the whole command the next day. "Our men built 7 bridges a crost the crick and had them redy to cross on at day light next morning," one Federal explained.[8]

In the center, Sherman's XV Corps divisions under Steele and Tuttle also had a small fight at W. F. Dillon's plantation on the Port Gibson–Raymond Road, what Grant, who was with him, described as "a little skirmishing." The 4th Iowa Cavalry, which had just come up from its crossing at Grand Gulf guarding wagons on the way, led the column and "ran into an ambuscade," as brigade commander Colonel Charles R. Woods reported, the major's horse being shot from under him. The enemy were concealed along the creek, one Iowan terming it "13 Mile Creek." Sherman explained that "the bushes were so dense that nothing could be seen but the puffs of smoke from their guns." He consequently ordered the lead brigade under Woods deployed, five regiments and a battery (and later others) moving up to the creek itself. While the artillery gave "the bushes a few quick rounds of canister," one cannoneer noting that they "had a beautiful range for our pieces," Wirt Adams's Mississippi Cavalry resisted as long as it could, destroying the bridges over the creek. But they could not keep the Federals from the north side. Woods sent the regiments across in line of battle, which quickly pushed Adams's Confederates back, one of the wounded Confederates left behind actually finding "his brother on our side," an Iowan related. The bridge had burned by this point, however, and Sherman set his pioneer company "to work to make a crossing in lieu of the burned bridge." One 13th Illinois soldier explained in his diary, "carried rails to make a bridge." It was done in a few hours, at which point Sherman crossed just in time "to see the enemy's cavalry disappear over the hill." Meanwhile, with more contact and a developing situation, Grant, in the

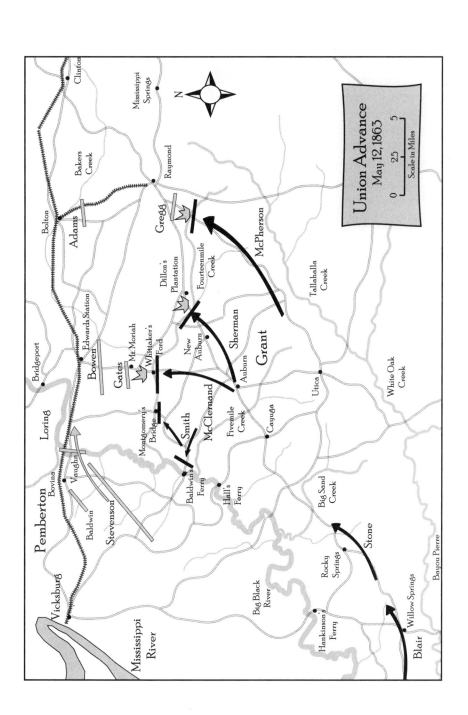

Union Advance
May 12, 1863

Scale in Miles
0   2.5   5

N

Clinton

Mississippi
Springs

Bakers
Creek

Bolton

Adams

Raymond

Gregg

McPherson

Dillon's
Plantation

Fourteenmile
Creek

Edwards Station

Bridgeport

Bowen

Gates

Mt. Moriah

Whittaker's
Ford

New
Auburn

Sherman

Tallahalla
Creek

Loring

Montgomery's
Bridge

Smith

McClernand

Auburn

Grant

Utica

White Oak
Creek

Vaughn

Baldwin's
Ferry

Fivemile
Creek

Cayuga

Pemberton

Bovina

Baldwin

Stevenson

Hall's
Ferry

Big Sand
Creek

Stone

Vicksburg

Big Black
River

Rocky
Springs

Willow Springs

Blair

Mississippi
River

Hankinson's
Ferry

Bayou Pierre

center, cautioned each of his corps commanders to maintain communication with those on their flanks.[9]

Still accompanying Grant was newspaperman Cadwallader, and he told of a pitiful story of the fight at Dillon's. He had come to know a young artillerist in the battery engaged at the Fourteenmile Creek crossing, and the man yelled and saluted as he galloped by on one of the horses leading a limber and gun. Cadwallader happened to look at his watch but sadly noted that after the fight he found the very same man had been one of the few casualties in the fight. His comrades were digging his grave when Cadwallader arrived and found who it was and, looking at his watch again, noted that "only twenty-nine minutes had elapsed between the time of his passing me in robust health, and the march of his comrades away from his newly made grave."[10]

More humorous events occurred as well in the aftermath, including one Illinoisan who shunned orders to never be found without a gun. One of his comrades described how while standing in line in the road at Dillon's he "determined to put down the rebellion by capturing rebel chickens," which he did, four in each hand, right in the yard of the plantation house. Unbeknownst to him, Sherman was inside and the general rushed out "bare-headed, and ordered the man to give him the chickens, which the man did." He added: "The General took the chickens just as the soldier had done, four in each hand, and tugged them out to the road and gave them all to Captain Cole's men who were still standing in line, at the same time sharply rebuking the man for abandoning his gun for foraging."[11]

But while all three of Grant's corps moved forward on May 12, this day would belong to James B. McPherson on the far right. Being in the center, Grant had little thought for McPherson's safety and confidently assumed he would be in Raymond with as little trouble as the other corps had encountered at their own Fourteenmile Creek crossings. In fact, he ordered McPherson to "feel north toward the railroad, and, if possible, destroy it and the telegraph." Grant nonchalantly added that "if the road is opened, I will ride over to see you this evening, but I cannot do so until I know McClernand is secure in his position." Yet the ominous sounds of heavy firing soon coming from the east portended something unexpected. "Rapid and heavy artillery firing has been heard nearly all day in the direction of Raymond," one of Sherman's Federals later noted in his diary.[12]

Grant's concern was to his left, but it should have been to his right.

The nearness of the Federal approach had produced a corresponding, if muted, reaction in the Confederate high command. As long as the enemy moved up the Big Black River watershed, Pemberton had covered the various bridges and ferries along the way. He had known about the massive foraging operations, writing that "[Union] marauders are busily engaged in the immediate rear of the enemy, pressing negroes, horses, mules, and provisions," but he could do little about that. But now with McClernand nearing the railroad at Edwards Station (he likely knew little of the other two corps moving northward farther to the east), simply keeping the enemy army east of the Big Black River would not be enough. He spoke directly of the need "to preserve my communications with the east." If Grant took the rail line, Vicksburg would be cut off and strangled to death. Sitting and waiting would end with only one result, and with Bowen's sensible recommendation the day before, Pemberton began to think of going out and meeting the Federal army in battle. "The enemy is apparently moving in heavy force towards Edwards Depot, Southern Railroad," Pemberton notified both Johnston and Davis. "With my limited force, I will do all I can to meet him. That will be the field of battle if I can carry forward sufficient force."[13]

As Pemberton began to think of going out to meet the enemy, there were many risks involved. He enumerated some of them from his Vicksburg headquarters, including "leaving troops enough to secure the safety of this place." He explained that he had to distribute many of his troops on the ferries to the south of the railroad "lest he cross and take this place." He also felt "compelled to keep a considerable force on either flank of Vicksburg, out of supporting distance of Edwards, to prevent his approach in those directions." As a result, Pemberton asked for more reinforcements: "I urge this as a positive necessity." He especially needed cavalry, still smarting from Johnston removing nearly all his mounted force back in January. Still, the greatest risk, which Pemberton did not mention and may not have even recognized, was leaving not only the defenses of Vicksburg but also even more the shield that was the Big Black River. If he suffered a defeat, he would be hard-pressed to retreat back across such a stumbling block, especially if pressured. And the best defensive aide outside Vicksburg's fortifications was the river itself. Marching out east of the river and its protection was a gamble to be sure, and Edwards, which he noted "will be the field of battle," was east of the river. Yet Pemberton was still primarily focused on the Union movement toward Edwards Station and the railroad bridge, little realizing that McPherson and Sherman were far to the east and could just as easily break the rail line there.[14]

Pemberton began the concentration anyway, first at Big Black River bridge just west of Edwards Station, with the idea then of possibly moving on eastward. "Left camps ordered towards Jackson," one Alabamian wrote; "Yanks down that way." As of now, early on May 12, about all Pemberton had at

Edwards was a detachment of Bowen's division under Colonel Elijah Gates of the 1st Missouri Cavalry dismounted. Gates's scouts had detected the Union movement northward toward Fourteenmile Creek the day before and resisted as best they could with such small numbers. But as the morning of May 12 developed and Gates and his men held the creek south of Edwards, he became more and more convinced that "their whole force was there." Gates reported, and Bowen sent the news on up the chain of command to Pemberton, that "he has been fighting them all morning." Gates's return orders were to hold if he could, but if not to burn the stores at Edwards and fall back to the enclave at the railroad bridge; Bowen reminded him "it is not intended to reinforce you; fall back to road entrenchments when too heavy pressed. You are acting merely as picket." Obviously, Pemberton at this point was still thinking of the defense at the shield of the Big Black River, at least until he could get his divisions assembled together.[15]

All the while, the other Confederate divisions began to slide toward the railroad bridge and then Edwards, leaving less and less force at the river crossings to the south. Fortunately, scouts indicated that many areas along the river were "an impenetrable jungle, intersected with sloughs and ponds." That would limit enemy movement if there was an idea of forcing a crossing of the Big Black. Accordingly, Bowen's entire division in "position in the ditches at Big Black" soon pushed on forward to reinforce Gates; by nightfall, both brigades were on site south of Edwards Station, ready to contest the enemy movement northward. At the same time, Loring was concentrating his three brigades, although spread out in different directions: "Move with two brigades of your division immediately to the support of General Bowen," his orders read. Loring was working hard, he informed Pemberton, to "get them to Bowen as rapidly as possible," but the two lead brigades were at Bovina only by 7:30 p.m. Eventually, two of the three also took position on Bowen's line, extending up and down the valley of Fourteenmile Creek, while the third, Lloyd Tilghman's that had been guarding the ferries to the south, also marched to rejoin the division. Most problematic was getting Carter Stevenson's four brigades up to the Big Black River and beyond. "It appears evident the enemy are advancing in force on Edwards Depot and Big Black Bridge," Pemberton informed Stevenson, adding, "you must take your whole division and move rapidly to the support of Loring and Bowen." The brigades arrived piecemeal but pushed on as well eastward, while Pemberton sent John C. Vaughn's brigade of East Tennesseans to the fortifications at the river itself as a reserve and guard for the bridge and if needed even for support of other areas such as the Yazoo River. In perhaps the most stunning development,

Pemberton himself, worried about Federals from every direction, left Vicksburg as well that evening, moving eastward to Bovina for the night "to be nearer the scene of active operations." And, evidently, he was thinking more and more of battle, writing Stevenson, "it may be necessary for the whole army to cross the river, as the battle may be fought on that side."[16]

But even as three divisions of the Confederate army concentrated near Edwards Station, Pemberton received more bad news. In Richmond, Davis basically wrote that he had sent all the reinforcements he could, that he had called on Governor Pettus to aid him whenever he could, and gave some really unneeded advice that "in your situation, much depends on the good-will and support of the people. To secure this, it is necessary to add conciliation to the discharge of duty. Patience in listening to suggestions which may not promise much, is sometimes rewarded by gaining useful information." Certainly Davis was preaching what he himself did not practice, and he added that Pemberton was basically on his own: "We look anxiously and hopefully for the next intelligence of your campaign."[17]

More tangible trouble came from closer by. Pemberton had ordered John Gregg to hit the enemy flank and rear when he saw they were moving north or west to Edwards. Apparently something was developing out toward Jackson, although he did not know what as yet. But he did get word that a new factor had emerged there, in the presence of Joe Johnston himself. Ordered westward on May 9, Johnston reluctantly took the first train out of Middle Tennessee on the morning of May 10. Pemberton received news on May 12 that Johnston was already at Meridian and that he was "expected here tomorrow." How having his departmental commander, with whom he had never really seen eye to eye, on site would affect his defense was not known.[18]

Pemberton would have to let the generals in Jackson, including possibly Johnston, worry about that flank, however; he had plenty to see to on his own side when he reached Bovina that night. And Loring at least was pushing him to come on out to Edwards: "If you do not come down this evening, please telegraph if you think it best to go out and secure position, with view to attack enemy in morning. Do not know their numbers."[19]

But something was about to happen either way, and Pemberton sent out a circular to his army that day advising that "the hour of trial has come!" He wrote that "the enemy who has so long threatened Vicksburg in front, has, at last, effected a landing in this Department; and his march into the interior of Mississippi has been marked by the devastation of one of the fairest portions of the State." He called on all to do their duty: "Soldiers! Be vigilant, brave and active; let there be no cowards or laggards, nor stragglers from the ranks—and the God of battles will certainly crown our efforts with success."[20]

Perhaps Pemberton would take his own advice about being vigilant and active.

Ulysses S. Grant's concern was obviously misplaced; it should have been on his right instead of his left. On the extreme right of the army, moving up the Utica Road toward Raymond, little concern existed in the lead division under John A. Logan. But as the Federals crept closer and closer to Raymond itself and, perhaps more important, the water in Fourteenmile Creek (one Federal labeled it "Snake Creek," a tributary of Fourteenmile Creek) just to its south on this hot and dusty day, they began to encounter Confederate skirmishers in increasing numbers. "Hello, somebody is shooting squirrels," one Ohioan quipped after two shots rang out up ahead. When three more came in quick succession, the reply was, "the squirrels are shooting back." One Federal wrote in his diary, "we got up in a hurry."[21]

McPherson had put his men on the road early that day because of the heat, Logan's three brigades breaking camp at Roach's Plantation and marching at 3:30 a.m. A brooding Marcellus Crocker's troops followed a half-hour later. But Confederates appeared shortly thereafter, not an uncommon occurrence and not in any concerning numbers. But as they grew throughout the early dawn hours, McPherson began to show more concern. As the hours passed, McPherson noted, "the enemy's vedettes showed themselves frequently, making increased vigilance on our part necessary." McPherson pushed on several miles toward Raymond, but he soon decided to take no chances. The lead brigade was Elias Dennis's, and McPherson ordered Logan to deploy two regiments of the brigade to push forward, one on each side of the road. Skirmishers replaced Captain John S. Foster's cavalry up ahead, which moved to protect the flanks, and the remainder of the brigade, division, and corps followed on the road in rear in column. In such manner the division proceeded another mile and a half, pushing the growing Confederate resistance northward.[22]

The two Union regiments up front pushed forward and by midmorning reached the creek valley some two miles south of Raymond. Logan ordered the division stopped while he looked around a bit. Both Logan's own and McPherson's escorts made up of a company of cavalry each proceeded forward to reconnoiter while the lead regiments broke ranks and began to eat. Soon the cavalrymen found what they wanted to know: Confederates were in heavy force to the front in the valley. By 11:00 a.m., in fact, enough

Confederates and artillery appeared to convince McPherson that "the fight for Raymond was to take place at this point." Enemy infantry was up ahead "judiciously posted," and several hundred yards behind them were what McPherson decided were two Confederate batteries firing from high ground, "so placed as to sweep the road and a bridge over which it was necessary to pass." McPherson ordered the leading infantry to deploy on the right of the road, the 20th Ohio moving all the way forward past a fence to the creek bed itself where the men used "the farther bank as a breastworks," Colonel Force related. McPherson also sent word back to get the trains off the road so that following brigades could move forward quickly. In the rear of Logan's division, brigade commander John D. Stevenson reported that "I received orders to move forward with all possible dispatch, as the enemy were in force in our immediate front."[23]

Meeting such a heavy Confederate force sent Logan and his troops into a frenzy, and after stabilizing the 20th Ohio, which showed some signs of running (the 68th Ohio nearby apparently did flee), Logan galloped back to the crest of the hill to the south where McPherson and his staff sat on their horses by the road. One Illinoisan on pioneer duty related that it was obvious Logan was irritated that McPherson had sent him on into the valley without support. "Gen. Logan came riding up the hill at full speed," Francis Baker recorded in his diary, "his face aflame, covered with perspiration and dust, and his horse bleeding from a wound." The wide-eyed Illinoisan heard Logan shout, "Damn it, general, I told you how it would be." McPherson calmy replied, "Never mind, General, it will come out all right."[24]

The following brigades began to arrive soon thereafter, "coming up to the crest of a hill in full view of the field." Logan deployed them in line of battle as they arrived while Dennis's troops still straddled the road itself and pressed onward slowly, heavy skirmishers in front. But it looked like the main Confederate force was east of the road. Logan therefore sent John E. Smith's brigade to Dennis's right, and then when Stevenson's brigade arrived and went into double lines as a reserve, most of it also moved to the right to take position on the right of Smith's troops to try to outflank the enemy. Arriving artillery also took its positions, first on a ridge farther back but then down in the valley on the left side of the road fronting the bridge itself. Captain Samuel De Golyer's 8th Michigan Battery took a position opposite the Confederate artillery, "on rising ground about 800 yards distant," Logan reported, while the infantry deployed and the two sides prepared for battle.[25]

Slight corrections in the line, including a short move by Smith's troops forward into "a piece of timber" and then all the way to a fence line along the southern edge of Fourteenmile Creek, stirred up the matter sufficiently,

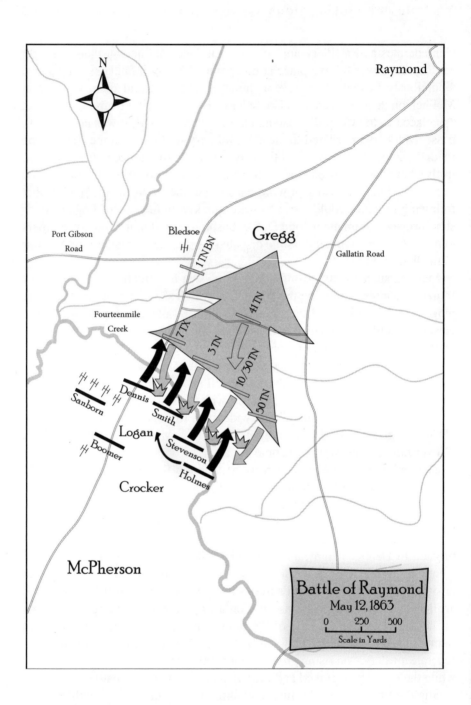

N

Raymond

Port Gibson
Road

Bledsoe

Gregg

1 TN BN

Gallatin Road

Fourteenmile
Creek

41 TN

7 TX

3 TN

10/30 TN

Sanborn

Dennis

50 TN

Smith

Logan

Stevenson

Boomer

Holmes

Crocker

McPherson

Battle of Raymond
May 12, 1863

0   250   500

Scale in Yards

and the Confederate skirmishers arrayed in the "excellent cover" of the creek bed opened up "with great fury." One Illinoisan declared "we met a shower, a terrific shower of bullets." Smith's Federal line nevertheless advanced, aiming to take cover behind the rail fence near the creek. "We formed our lines and advanced across a cotton field about eighty rods and all the time we were crossing that field we were not allowed to fire as our Generals wanted to get to a rail fence at the edge of this field," an Illinoisan explained. "But the Johnies were giving it to us all the time," he added. One 20th Illinois soldier, Jim Lord, refused to get behind the fence cover even after his captain told him he would be shot if not. "O' I guess not," he replied, just before he took a bullet right in the forehead "and almost fell on me as he was standing just behind where I was kneeling," one of his comrades wrote. Logan meanwhile received word from his forward skirmishers sent out to "ascertain the position of the enemy" that they had driven the Confederate skirmishers north of the creek but that they were in line there. "I was soon satisfied that the enemy were formed in line of battle along the margin of the creek, under cover of the bank, awaiting our attack," Logan noted.[26]

Most of the Federals remained at the fence line south of the creek, "quite near the enemy," Logan explained, but at least a few pushed on forward. Colonel Force indicated that his Ohioans "quickly formed in line, advanced to a deep gully, and took position there." The 23rd Indiana actually pushed on forward and crossed the creek, Lieutenant Colonel William P. Davis explaining that "I reached a creek, which was almost impassable, the banks being nearly perpendicular, and covered with dense undergrowth. With much difficulty the regiment crossed it and moved forward a short distance." The Indianans were far out in front, so much so that, within fifty yards or so of the ridge in front, Davis could not see any of the other regiments of Smith's brigade north of the creek. "Not seeing the balance of the line upon my left," Davis wisely noted, "I immediately sent to ascertain its position."[27]

Unfortunately, Davis was not the only one confused and bewildered. Logan and McPherson themselves had little better idea what was going on, but all realized the resistance up ahead was stouter than anyone had expected. And it was only about to get worse.

If McPherson was surprised to locate Confederates in force south of Raymond, the Confederate commander of that force, Brigadier General John Gregg, was just as surprised. Pemberton had sent him orders to work on the Union flank if Grant went after Edwards but followed that up with caution: "Do not attack the enemy until he is engaged at Edwards or Big Black Bridge.

Be ready to fall on his rear or flank at any moment. Do not allow yourself to be flanked or taken in the rear. Be careful that you do not lose your command." But Gregg had stumbled into a fight, although he likewise had no idea how large a force he faced. His scouts sent out the night before notified him early on May 12 that Federals were "advancing rapidly by the road from Utica." Unfortunately, the small size of the militia cavalry command that had arrived (only about forty troopers and "these mostly youths from the neighborhood") limited how much information Gregg could get about these mysterious Federals approaching from the south. Pemberton had told him that the expected advance would be to the west toward the railroad at Edwards, and so Gregg assumed this was a mere "brigade on a marauding excursion." He certainly did not want to fall back if it was such a small command and therefore decided to wait, even eventually pushing his force southward into the valley of Fourteenmile Creek. In fact at one point he decided he would dispatch this wayward brigade quickly: "Believing from the evidence I had that his force was a single brigade, I made my dispositions to capture it."[28]

Little did Gregg know that, instead of merely a brigade, he was about to tangle with two full divisions—the entire present component of McPherson's XVII Corps. But he soon began to suspect there was more to it than he thought. First, Federal cavalry appeared in the field across the valley of Fourteenmile Creek, and Colonel Hiram B. Granbury of the 7th Texas sent several "picked men," mostly with Enfield rifles under Captain Thomas B. Camp of Company B, to the bridge across the creek on the Utica Road to drive away the cavalry. A small fight erupted there, with Camp reporting "3 unhorsed," but soon the Federals brought up artillery as well to the south. That was much more concerning, as about 10:00 a.m. Federal artillery began firing from the creek area. Then heavy forces of infantry began to arrive. It was evidently more than a brigade, and suddenly Gregg, who watched much of this develop from the cupola of the courthouse in Raymond itself, began to become increasingly concerned.[29]

Gregg's force was already spread thin. He kept the 7th Texas at the high ground at the junction of the Port Gibson and Utica Roads, where eventually three guns of Captain Hiram Bledsoe's Missouri Battery took position and began to shell the massing Federals across Fourteenmile Creek. Gregg could already tell the main enemy force was on the Utica Road, but he could not take any chances and had to cover all three byways leading from the south. To cover the Gallatin Road to the east he sent the 50th Tennessee, although the regiment was down three of its largest companies that were on picket duty elsewhere; he later sent the consolidated 10/30th Tennessee under former Nashville mayor and Harvard graduate Colonel Randal MacGavock out the same road. Since it seemed the main force was in the center on the road from Utica, Gregg also sent the 3rd Tennessee from its position near the "grave-yard" out to take a line between the Utica and Gallatin Roads in "a single field, dotted with spots of timber." In compiling a quick plan, Gregg wanted to hold with his right and roll up the enemy with his left. The entire brigade consequently moved forward tired from the long day before and depressed to face the battle in such condition, but they were cheered by "some beautiful girls waving the 'Bonnie Blue Flag'" on the porch of a house they passed.[30]

By this time De Golyer's Michigan guns had opened up and were pelting the Confederates. Gregg realized he could not fall back but instead needed to move farther forward to the better cover around the creek itself. After getting the Missouri guns situated at the road junction and bringing up the small 1st Tennessee Battalion to cover them, Gregg pushed the others forward. On his left he advanced the 50th and 10/30th Tennessee in hopes of turning the enemy position and getting in rear of the guns; Gregg himself rode in that direction to send Lieutenant Colonel Thomas W. Beaumont and his 50th Tennessee to attack the battery "unless I should find it too strongly protected." Supporting would be the consolidated regiment. The Tennesseans were to advance when they heard a corresponding attack on the right of the line. Toward the right, Gregg likewise advanced the 3rd Tennessee between the roads and the 7th Texas from the artillery position, both all the way toward the creek bottom amid some skirmishing that was already picking up, although the heavy un-derbrush was the major complaint at this point: "The undergrowth and briars were so thick we could scarcely make our way through." Finally, Gregg also brought forward his last unit, the 41st Tennessee that had formed in the square in town, to take position where the 3rd Tennessee had previously stood at the town cemetery. This regiment would be the reserve. And they might well be needed, as this perceived single enemy brigade just kept growing; "the enemy continued to re-enforce with fresh troops," Gregg dolefully reported.[31]

But Gregg stuck to the plan, ordering his four frontline regiments forward into the valley of Fourteenmile Creek. Hopefully, his left regiments, the con-solidated 10/30th and 50th Tennessee, could sweep around the flank of the enemy line and get in behind the Union artillery and gobble it up and the in-fantry too as they forced the Federals back onto the following 3rd Tennessee and 7th Texas. But there were more Federals out there than Gregg realized, and as a result the plan began to implode immediately. Yet the advance put fear into the waiting Federals, Colonel Force in the creek itself writing that "all at once, the woods rang with the shrill rebel yell and a deafening din of musketry."[32]

In the initial holding effort to the east, the 3rd Tennessee and 7th Texas

quickly advanced to the assault on the right of the brigade. The Texans moved
up from their artillery duty, crossing the Utica Road and entering the woods
and fields east of it. That put them in line with the Tennesseans to their left,
while Captain Camp's company continued to hold the bridge across the creek
to the right, a small force to be what Granbury described as protection for
"my right flank." Texas skirmishers probed ahead, with the main body of the
regiment a hundred paces to the rear, and both regiments advanced through
scattered woods over a small ridge toward the creek itself. In doing so, they
came across some of the Federals who had crossed the creek in advance of
the majority of Smith's brigade, namely the 23rd Indiana. The two regiments
stopped and prepared for the assault. Colonel Calvin H. Walker of the 3rd
Tennessee addressed his nervous men before he sent them forward: "We will
soon be engaged in a battle and before we begin I wish to say that I do not
command you to go, but to follow this old bald head of mine." Doffing his
cap, he gave the command to move forward, one Tennessean remembering
that "in the twinkling of an eye sadness and despair vanished and in its place
appeared a determination to conquer or die." Walker ordered the charge,
which he explained "was made in the most gallant manner under a galling
fire, driving the enemy before us." The Texans and Tennesseans slammed into
the Federal regiment and began to drive it rearward, back across the creek in
fact. Heavy fighting ensued as the Texans and Tennesseans surged forward
across the difficult passage of the creek bed and toward the open fields to the
south.[33]

Colonel Granbury detailed his Texans' efforts. The regiment moved across
the slight ridge and located the Indianans at the base of the hill near the creek.
Once under fire, Granbury ordered the double-quick, and the Texans "obeyed
with alacrity, and, when in view of the enemy, rushed forward with a shout."
The Texans piled into the 23rd Indiana north of the creek, Granbury writing
that "so near were the enemy and so impetuous the charge, that my regiment
could have blooded a hundred bayonets had the men been supplied with that
weapon." The Indianans did the best they could to resist, one watching Illinoisan admitting that they "fought like tigers," getting off one ragged volley.
Lieutenant Colonel Davis related that "our skirmishers were advanced but a
short distance before the enemy was upon them, advancing rapidly down the
hill in our front." Brigade commander Smith noted that "the Twenty-third
Indiana, being in advance of the line, were suddenly attacked by the unseen
foe."[34]

The Indianans were caught out in front, on the opposite side of the creek
from the rest of the brigade, and consequently paid heavily. "Upon our first
discovery of them," Davis reported, "we opened fire and continued until they

were within bayonet reach." He added, "not having time to fix our bayonets, we attempted to beat them back with our muskets, but, being overpowered by numbers, we were obliged to fall back." But the same obstacle that confronted them moving forward now loomed in the rear, and Davis admitted that "here the same difficulty occurred as before in crossing." Several prisoners fell into Confederate hands, including one of the 23rd Indiana's captains, Alonzo Tubbs, who "struck at Major [K. M.] Vanzandt with his sword, and was disarmed by Sergeant [J. M. C.] Duncan, of Company K." The Federals cobbled together a line for about ten minutes in the creek bed itself but soon had to flee into the field south of the creek, where the Indianans formed next to the 20th Illinois, one of whom described how "the rebels gave a yell and made a charge upon us." He added, "we were ordered not to fire until [they] got up close enough that we could see the whites of their eyes." The Texans jumped into the natural fortification of the creek bed and continued for what seemed like hours to pour a heavy fire into the re-forming Federals in the field. "The firing was uninterrupted and terrific," Granbury added.[35]

The Texans' surge did not move as far forward on Dennis's front to the west, where the 20th Ohio held the creek bed itself. The Ohioans had begun to rest earlier, some even taking their shoes off to soak in the waters of Fourteen-mile Creek; they had to fight barefooted when the Confederates appeared. While Confederates moved to and across the creek to their right on Smith's front, they were stopped at Dennis's position. Colonel Force described how the enemy came to the edge of the creek: "At one time the enemy in our front advanced to the border of the creek, and rifles of opposing lines crossed while firing. Men who were shot were burned by the powder of the rifles that sped the balls." One low-level Ohioan added that "they too gave us volley after volley, always working up toward us breathing our fire until they had come within twenty or even fifteen paces. In one part of the line some of them came nearer than that and had to be poked back with the bayonet."[36]

While the Texans advanced, Colonel Walker similarly detailed the experience of his Tennesseans to the left. He described how the Indianans attempted "to rally behind a deep ravine, with almost perpendicular banks, but our advance was so rapid (the men jumping into the ravine and climbing up the opposite side) that the enemy again gave way and fled out of the woods into the open field." The ravine Walker described was actually the creek bed, and his Tennesseans drove the Federals across the creek and into the field immediately south of it. There was a temporary attempt to make a stand; the Federal color-bearer "planted their colors in the ground," but the surge continued and drove the Federals even farther back into the field. "A sharp volley from our side speedily dispersed them," Walker explained.[37]

The surprised and shattered 23rd Indiana troops managed to get back to their main line, where they went into position on the right of the 20th Illinois. Also in the brigade line were the 45th Illinois, Smith's old regiment, as well as the 124th Illinois, and the fighting ranged all the way westward to the right regiment of Dennis's brigade, the 20th Ohio in the creek bed. These regiments presented a solid line that the charging Texans and Tennesseans, having also to negotiate the creek crossing, found too stout to push back, but the Confederates on Smith's front were able to reach the creek itself to the east of Force's 20th Ohio, fostering an odd situation in which the two sides occupied the opposite banks of the creek next to one another. Still, good field command came into play in the defense; even Colonel Jasper A. Maltby of the 45th Illinois, being in the rear sick and riding in an ambulance, "mounted his horse and assumed command of his regiment."[38]

But then it was Walker and his Tennesseans' turn to be dealt a horrific blow. Just as the stalled Tennesseans emerged into the field on one attempt at advancing, "I received a heavy volley into the rear of my left flank." Walker could not see any troops from that direction but correctly surmised that it was the enemy; in fact, it was Colonel Edward S. McCook's 31st Illinois, which had worked its way around the 3rd Tennessee's left and into the gap between that regiment and the 50th and 10/30th Tennessee farther east. The success came at the loss of McCook himself, wounded in the foot and taken to the rear. Walker seethed with anger as his troops took the blow from the flank, Gregg himself having promised that the 50th and 10/30th Tennessee would cover his right. But the others were nowhere to be seen, an aggravated Walker writing that "supposing that the Tenth and Thirtieth Tennessee were there for my support, as General Gregg assured me would be the case, I did not order a change of position, but directed the whole line to be held firm." But to make sure, Walker tramped to the left to see for himself. "I went to the left and became satisfied that the enemy was in the rear, and at the same time a new column made its appearance in front." Lieutenant Colonel Calvin J. Clack of the Tennessee regiment rushed over to the Texans to inform Granbury of the terrible development, and several nervous minutes passed as the two hard driving regiments wondered what their fate would be, stuck out so far in front of the rest of the Confederates who apparently had not advanced.[39]

Their fate was not long in coming. The Tennesseans could not resist the fire in the flank and even rear at some points, Federal brigade commander Smith explaining that the 31st Illinois "opened fire upon them with such effect that they were driven from the right." Without any aid on their left, Walker's Tennesseans had gone as far as they could, and now had to flee back to the cover of the creek bed.[40]

After the initial Confederate surge across and then back to the creek, however, the fighting settled for a while to one of musketry from the Confederate
position at the creek and the Union line mainly in the field along the fence;
one 124th Illinois soldier wrote of the enemy fire "fair[ly] raking the whole
Regt." But even then, the fighting was hard for a while, the 20th Illinois commander, Lieutenant Colonel Evan Richards, going down in the fight, "struck
down at the head of his men while nobly cheering them on to victory." Logan himself lamented that he "was killed by a musket-shot through the left
breast." In fact, the 20th Illinoisans fought so hard that they lost a third of
their number and were soon nearly out of ammunition. Fortunately, reserve
units of the division were just arriving, including the 8th Illinois of Stevenson's brigade, and Logan immediately sent it to support the 20th Illinois. The
Illinoisans had originally been sent to the extreme right, but "we were not
sufficiently useful here," one of them recalled, and were moved back to the
left; the 8th Illinois actually replaced its comrades in the front line. Brigade
commander Smith noted that the 8th Illinois "proved themselves worthy suc-
cessors of the Twentieth Illinois," and he went on to explain that "the line
from the Twentieth Ohio, on the right of the Second Brigade, to my right,
now the Thirty-first Illinois, sustained the attack of the whole of the enemy
forces." But they had contained the advance, yet neither side moved forward
and more than likely would not unless there was some fulcrum that changed
the dynamics of the fight.[41]

But that new influence did not materialize, as Gregg's left never fulfilled
its part of the overall plan to turn the Union right. Indeed, there was no corresponding assault on the left of the brigade, where the 50th Tennessee and
the consolidated 10/30th Tennessee maneuvered but quickly found that they
faced far too many Federals to achieve Gregg's goal. The advance hinged on
the 50th Tennessee, and when it did not advance, the 10/30th did not either,
Lieutenant Colonel James J. Turner writing that "as they made no attack we
waited for further orders." But Beaumont and the 50th Tennessee were not
idle. He moved forward into a patch of woods, where he was warned that
the Federals were so near that their commands could be easily heard. He
could also perceive the enemy moving to the left toward the Gallatin Road.
Beaumont merely moved forward toward the creek, skirmishers ahead, until
the entire regiment methodically crossed over. But it was not easy. "The skirmishers had to pass over a running stream of water, with steep, abrupt banks,
up which they pulled themselves by the roots or trees and bushes, preserving
their line and marching all the while in admirable order," Beaumont bragged.
The regiment followed behind, likewise crossing the creek, until the skirmishers ran into a force of cavalry obviously on the enemy's flanks. Firing

broke out, and the Tennesseans forced the troopers to disperse, "many of the horses without riders, and many of the riders without horses."[42]

Once across the creek, Beaumont and his Tennesseans pressed on slowly and carefully, "observing the general's precaution to maintain perfect silence." Up in front, Beaumont found that a battery was well supported with infantry "as far as I could see" to the right, with more infantry of undeterminable number to the left. "I was satisfied that an attack would be uninviting," Beaumont admitted. Consequently, he ordered his Tennesseans back to the rear across the creek and to move to the left to counter the effect of the continually unfolding Federal right. Beaumont sent a messenger to Gregg, but he returned saying he could not find the general.[43]

In the confusion, Beaumont drifted to the left, "endeavoring to keep even pace with them." In doing so, he passed Colonel MacGavock's 10/30th Tennessee, which had also been marching around in circles on the Confederate left. With the sounds of the Federals continually moving to the left of the Tennesseans, the 10/30th Tennessee moved to the left to try to correspond to the enemy shift, although not moving to the attack. Those troops moved some six hundred yards at the double-quick, but after sending out skirmishers to locate the enemy again, the racket of the fight back to the west with the 3rd Tennessee and 7th Texas became fearsome and the Tennesseans moved back to the right. Now on the 10/30th Tennessee's left again, Beaumont offered to put his 50th Tennessee under MacGavock, since they were separated from the others. MacGavock worked out a plan of attack, saying those were Gregg's last orders to him, but once all was in place MacGavock informed Beaumont that "he would await orders." Eventually, the other Tennesseans marched off to the right, leaving Beaumont and his regiment isolated: "Our regiment was thus left entirely alone." And worse, action was picking up to the right again.[44]

Beaumont sent word to Gregg that there was no way they could advance, Gregg explaining that "I learned from Colonel Beaumont that no attack was made by the Fiftieth because of the immense force which extended back in the woods as far as he could see, and because the enemy were advancing a large force on his left flank." It was the regiments of Stevenson's brigade that were extending the line to the east, far overlapping Gregg's left. The general had no choice but to bring up his reserve 41st Tennessee and secure the flank, which it soon did, at least temporarily. Colonel Robert Farquharson noted that he could hear the sounds of the fight raging toward the left and could tell the flank was "seriously menaced." He took his position and sent out skirmishers, which stopped the enemy advance for the time being but at the cost of the officer commanding the skirmishers, Captain Abner S. Boone.[45]

But the noise to the right was telling, and finally the 10/30th Tennessee joined the fight. Although being within hearing distance of the Federal line some four hundred yards to the front, the Federal officers' commands being easily discernable, MacGavock moved forward despite a mysterious order arriving that left "it discretionary whether to attack the enemy or not." Then came more firm orders to move back to the right another five hundred or so yards, which brought the consolidated regiment back into the vicinity of the 3rd Tennessee even then fighting at and across the creek. The Tennesseans deployed hurriedly and rushed forward, crossing the small ridge. Then Colonel MacGavock shouted orders to charge. The Tennesseans did so, the men advancing "with alacrity . . . [they] charged forward gallantly, cheering and firing as they went." The Federal defenders fell back, but the gap between the two Tennessee regiments was significant and some of the enemy managed to fire into the flank, slowing and finally stopping the 10/30th Tennessee, just as had happened with the Tennessee and Texas regiments farther to the right.[46]

Making the situation worse, the advance of the 3rd Tennessee and 7th Texas and the comparatively lesser movement of the 50th and 10/30th Tennessee caused a split in the two Confederate wings, opening up the left flank of the 3rd Tennessee to more Federal fire and a potential turning movement. The 7th Texas faced less danger because the bulk of the enemy force was east of the road rather than along or to the west of it, but the Tennesseans were in real trouble; Gregg had to act fast to secure the regiment's flank. He had only one source of reserves aside from the small battalion supporting the artillery in the rear, so he ordered up Colonel Farquharson's 41st Tennessee from its flank duty to support and hold the 3rd Tennessee's left flank. The colonel "moved up in good order and took position promptly," Gregg wrote, but the Confederate advance had been stymied, and by the looks of things a Federal counterattack was building, although it took time. Gregg himself explained that "the firing of musketry was rapid and continuous for more than two hours." But in that time, more and more Federals continually arrived.[47]

James B. McPherson has sometimes been ridiculed for his fight at Raymond and even for his slowness during the entire campaign. Perhaps some of that is justified; a later-arriving artilleryman noted that "it seem[s] that they, our troops, were attacked rather unawares," while another added that "they took us rather by surprise." One of Crocker's following Indianans even wrote home a few days later that Logan "came very near getting whipped." Another explained that "we were marching along not thinking of a battle when all of a sudden we heard firing in the front of the column." In overall command,

McPherson did seem somewhat timid and surprised, although mitigating circumstances were present including odd terrain, the heat and dryness, and his own lack of experience. For the latter, blame could also be placed on Grant himself for not accompanying his most inexperienced corps commander, although neither he nor McPherson thought there would be a battle this day on the right flank. Instead of staying with Sherman in the center, which was also logical due to positioning and communications with each wing, Grant could also have accompanied McPherson or perhaps even McClernand on the most dangerous left flank. Second-guessing is not profitable in history, but it is clear that the young McPherson was caught a little off-guard, and it took a while to gather his equilibrium. He wrote Grant, in fact, at 2:30 p.m. displaying some of his wobbliness: "We have met and engaged the enemy at this point 1000 strong. Thus far we have apparently the advantage, though the battle is not yet ended—Woods, ravines prevent the effective use of our Artillery."[48]

But growing numbers certainly helped McPherson steady his corps. The first reinforcing Federals were of Logan's own division. Without a lot of resistance on the far right, Logan began to peel away regiments from Stevenson's flank attack to contain the Confederate bulge in the left center. The majority of the Confederate thrust had occurred at the right of Dennis's brigade and Smith's (the 20th Ohio of Dennis's unit and the 20th Illinois and 31st Illinois of Smith's brigade). In a near panic, Logan ordered Stevenson to send help, and the 81st Illinois, Stevenson's left regiment, soon moved westward and took a position in support of Smith's troops, firing over the heads of the 45th Illinois flat on the ground, perhaps giving rise to some of the reports of friendly fire. Then, orders arrived for more help, and Stevenson ordered up his fourth regiment that had been far behind as the "rear guard," the just-arriving 8th Illinois, to head to the extreme left; there, it took over for the fought-out 20th Illinois. Ultimately, the 7th Missouri likewise shifted to the left and took a position on the right of the 81st Illinois. That left only the 32nd Ohio on the far right, the only remnants of the powerful flanking movement that was considerably weakened by this point. In fact, most all of the punch was gone from Stevenson's potential flank attack, and he, with only the Ohioans, settled for merely holding the position against the confused movements of the 50th and 10/30th Tennessee over near the Gallatin Road. There was no mention at this point of a forward movement or a continuation of the flanking attack that had promised great results earlier. But their mere presence so befuddled the Confederate attack that it netted nearly the same result.[49]

But even more Federals were soon on the way. Marcellus Crocker's division was marching forward, Colonel John B. Sanborn writing that "after noon heavy cannonading in front announced that the advance had fallen upon the enemy." These rearward Federal troops soon stacked up in rear as Crocker's division topped the ridge to the south and ventured northward into the valley of Fourteenmile Creek. Crocker had three brigades under Colonels John B. Sanborn, George B. Boomer, and Samuel H. Holmes. In consultation with McPherson and Logan, Crocker quickly began to dole out the various brigades to support Logan's hard-fighting troops; a portion of Holmes's brigade moved to the far right to support Stevenson while Sanborn moved his troops forward on the left to support Smith and De Golyer's Battery, which had shifted from its position astride the road to a new location west of the road in the field south of the creek. Colonel Boomer held his rearward troops in reserve to go where needed, but they were not required for the moment, as those ahead seemed now to have the situation in hand. And why not: the two divisions outnumbered the lone Confederate brigade significantly. In fact, Crocker's entire division would sustain a mere two killed and two wounded at Raymond.[50]

Additional artillery likewise came to the front and deployed. Captain Henry A. Rogers's Battery D, 1st Illinois Artillery deployed its heavy 24-pound howitzers and "did some splendid execution," Logan verified; a section of the battery even wound up on the far right and fired down the Gallatin Road. Likewise, Captain William S. Williams's 3rd Ohio Battery also deployed on the far left flank of the Federal line in the big field south of the creek and west of the road. There, eventually as many as twenty-two guns held the critical flank but were only slightly engaged, as the Confederates congregated mainly east of the road. The limited movement of the 1st Tennessee Battalion supporting Bledsoe's Battery farther northward was not enough to cause concern on this far-left flank.[51]

Although more Federals arrived, the truth was that they were not necessarily needed. Logan already had more than enough troops to handle the admittedly large Confederate brigade fronting him, but the surprise contact, lay of the land, and scattered Confederate line wherein Southern regiments kept popping up all over the place caused a delay in the advance and a timidity that the numbers did not necessarily warrant. Colonel Manning Force displayed some of the abruptness of the fight when he mentioned "the suddenness of the attack, the severity of the fire, and the necessity of maneuvering to form line."[52]

Still, the Federal force, having been knocked off its equilibrium temporarily, soon began to recover and take control. "The line was ordered forward and charged," John E. Smith explained, "which they did handsomely, completely routing the enemy, who fled precipitously." Just east of the road, the right regiment of Dennis's brigade, the 20th Ohio, and the whole of Smith's brigade, with the 8th Illinois of Stevenson's brigade also added in, battled the 7th Texas and 3rd Tennessee, stopping their surge south of Fourteenmile Creek and then methodically beginning to advance. "We made a *charge* as grand as has been made during this war," one 8th Illinoisan explained, and "set up a yell as if all the fiends of Hell had broke loose." Logan himself described how his troops "pressed the enemy back under a most galling fire, and crossed the creek over which we had been fighting by wading it." An Illinoisan described the creek itself in his diary that day as "some 10 to 15 feet in width and Bank 10 ft deep some 2 ft of water." He added that "the stream was crimson with blood." At one point in the action, Logan himself led an assault, Surgeon Silas Trowbridge writing that "this was the only bayonet charge I witnessed during the rebellion. That dash of General Logan across the field was one of those gallant acts which would be best described by an artist capable of drawing a dashing officer at full speed."[53]

"Soon the whole line advanced," brigade commander Stevenson wrote, "and the enemy was driven from the position." All across the board, the Federal regiments moved forward to and across the creek. On the left, Colonel Force explained how his 20th Ohio moved out of the creek, across the first ridge and the next creek toward Raymond. The Ohioans "advanced out of the gully across an almost impenetrable tangle of logs and brush, a run waist-deep in some places, and a plowed field, up the hill where the enemy's guns had been placed." Among them was Corporal William H. Borum of Company B, who his colonel noted "insisted upon remaining in the ranks with a ball lodged in his throat." Another unnamed private returned from the hospital that he had been taken to in order to carry water for his comrades. Toward the center, the re-formed 23rd Indiana charged, "the enemy hastily leaving the field." Nearby, the 8th Illinois, having relieved one of Smith's regiments, "at the point of the bayonet dislodged them from a strong position from which they had poured a most destructive fire upon our lines." It cost them Captain Frank Leeper, who fell "in the front of his command in their gallant and successful charge." On the right, the 81st Illinois of Stevenson's brigade also advanced, the men behaving well and driving the Confederates from the valley. Logan himself was amid them "where bullets flew the thickest," according to Illinoisan Edmund Newsome, ordering, "turn back, go to the right FLANK them." Newsome added, "we did so." The Illinoisans' commander noted one problem, however—"objectionable conduct" by Captain Samuel Pyle, who was later "permitted to resign."[54]

The heavy Federal advance drove away the Confederates all along the line. The Texans and Tennesseans on the right gave ground grudgingly, but they had no chance of holding their position without support. Colonel Walker of the 3rd Tennessee explained that "I withdrew the regiment in as good order as the nature of the ground and thick undergrowth would admit, but not soon enough to prevent the capture of many of the men, who were in the most advanced positions." Walker waded among his Tennesseans and "reproached many men for not halting and firing as they retired," but he soon learned that "they had no cartridges, having fired the last one in their boxes before they were ordered from the front." The Tennesseans fled northeastward and re-formed temporarily before shifting to the left upon word that the enemy was still moving around their flank. Their final position was along the Gallatin Road, where they encountered the enemy cavalry guarding the flank. Colonel Granbury's Texans held out a little longer, although a dead courier caused a miscommunication that resulted in part of the regiment withdrawing and part staying put a little while. Granbury himself held the majority of the regiment in position "on the bluff of the creek until the men had exhausted their own ammunition and emptied the cartridge-boxes of the dead of the enemy and of our own killed and wounded." But once that ran out, and soon after the 3rd Tennessee to the left withdrew, Granbury reported that the Federals "doubled round my left flank and were pouring a murderous enfilading fire along my already shattered ranks." He added simply, "I then ordered a retreat." The Texans fell back across the creek onto the hills beyond, leaving many dead, wounded, and particularly missing. Numerous Texans were in the creek itself and were not able to get out. "Captain [E. T.] Broughton, Company C, was among the last to leave the creek," Granbury explained, "having animated his men throughout the affair with his presence and bearing. He is among the missing." Four other Texas captains were down wounded and some were missing as well.[55]

To the east where Stevenson's and Holmes's Federals trudged through fields and spotty timber to continually extend the right, likewise crossing the creek farther up, the 50th and 10/30th Tennessee withdrew in the area north of the creek bed. On the far left, Lieutenant Colonel Beaumont of the 50th Tennessee fell back "in tolerable order" and managed to reach the Gallatin Road before the withdrawing 41st Tennessee emerged, heading to this same road and flank. Unfortunately, Colonel Beaumont took a shot; he "was stricken on the head by a rifle-ball, and for a time disabled while in the midst of the action." Beaumont himself related that "I received a slight wound in the head, which bled profusely, but did not disable me." But he still managed to bark at the men who were not performing exactly as he wished: "Some of the new recruits became confused in some of the maneuvers, and a few of them fired badly, but most of them . . . fought bravely." Similarly, in the heavy fighting,

Colonel Randal W. MacGavock, colonel of the 10th Tennessee but now commanding the consolidated regiment, ordered the Tennesseans to re-form at the
top of the ridge to the rear, Lieutenant Colonel Turner actually posting the
men "immediately in rear of the crest of the hill." In the fighting, Gregg sadly
reported, Colonel MacGavock fell dead "while gallantly urging his command
to the conflict," and at least five commissioned officers of the regiment went
down as well. The lieutenant colonel of the 30th Tennessee, James J. Turner,
took command of the combined unit.[56]

The only real trouble for the Federals came on the right, where a portion
of Stevenson's brigade advanced across the creek and into fierce Confederate
fire. Lieutenant Colonel Turner soon realized, as did everyone else, that the
left flank was the problem spot and shifted his combined unit that direction,
where he met Stevenson's regiments. A gap had opened between his men and
the 50th Tennessee, whose commander was down with his head wound, so
Turner acted on his own and ordered the Tennesseans to advance. He gave
the command to "cheer and haloo and charge the enemy at a double-quick."
They did so, Turner reporting that "at them they went, yelling like savages."
With so much chaos in the neighboring 50th Tennessee, that regiment did
not assault but rather maneuvered forward slightly amid skirmishing, actually crossing behind and moving to a position on the right of the 10/30th
Tennessee.[57]

A similar gap had opened in Stevenson's Union brigade, between the
81st Illinois on the left, which charged ahead "with signal valor," Stevenson
reported, and the 7th Missouri. The Missourians moved through a "dense
thicket" and into a field at the bottom of the ridge on which the Tennesseans
regrouped. Once the Confederates advanced, the Missourians could manage
only a ragged volley before they were upon them. It was, ironically, Irish
regiment versus Irish regiment, both the Tennesseans and Missourians carrying emerald-green flags adorned with gold trim. In the act of moving up the
hill "whilst under a most terrific fire," Major Edwin Wakefield ordered the
Missouri regiment to withdraw, and Stevenson was horrified when the Missourians "retired in great disorder and with heavy loss." The Tennesseans'
commander Turner echoed Stevenson, writing that they "broke in utter confusion, and attempted but once to rally on their colors, but we came up within
30 steps of them and killed their color bearer, and the route was complete."
It was also temporary. Stevenson immediately rode to the Missourians and
re-formed them. Fortunately, more Federals arrived to shore up the nervous
flank, including a pioneer detachment under Captain L. M. Rose and Captain
Greenberry F. Wiles who wanted "to share the work and dangers of the field."
They went into the gap between the 7th Missouri and 81st Illinois; the 80th

Ohio and 10th Missouri of Colonel Samuel Holmes's brigade of Crocker's division arrived as well, the 17th Iowa of that brigade remaining in reserve. With his line re-formed and reinforced, Stevenson renewed the advance and pushed the Tennesseans rearward. Spying the re-formed Union line and the reinforcements all around, Turner thought it best to withdraw his Tennesseans and did so back to the ridge north of the creek, where he ordered them to lie down. The 50th Tennessee remained forward but soon ascertained that everybody but them had withdrawn yet again, Beaumont explaining that "their falling back left me too much exposed." Stevenson followed, but mere skirmishing took place thereafter.[58]

Most of Gregg's Confederates made a slight stand on this same ridge north of Fourteenmile Creek, actually holding for several minutes while the Federals re-formed and pushed on timidly. But it was not to be held indefinitely, as more and more enemy regiments came on line and began to advance. Sanborn sent two regiments to support the center and actually offered to relive the frontline units, but Logan's hard-fighting Federals in this area "declined the offer." And the news grew only worse for Gregg as the afternoon passed. The fighting in the creek valley and hills to the north became so alarming, in fact, that Gregg had to deploy his artillery support up front; he sent the small 1st Tennessee Battalion forward to hold the extreme right flank, probably in response to the growing Federal host in that direction, namely Sanborn's brigade of Crocker's arriving division. Major Stephen H. Colms explained that "I was ordered to check a flank movement of the enemy on their extreme left." The growing Union presence there along the road could easily turn the brigade on the right and perhaps cut off Gregg from the town, so something drastic had to be done, although Gregg had limited options at this point for drastic responses. Nevertheless, Major Colms led his Tennesseans forward and immediately became engaged as well, particularly taking fire from the Federal artillery and sharpshooters. But just the mere presence of the battalion, according to Colms, startled the Federals, who were "in the act of making a flank movement." Sanborn's men withdrew into the woods. If Colms's sudden appearance did in fact startle a potential Federal flank attack, and Sanborn's troops were likely there only to hold and observe rather than to advance, it was a good thing, because the major firepower on that flank was also dwindling. One of the three guns of Bledsoe's Battery, the Whitworth, had burst upon firing, taking down the Confederate artillery capacity by a third. Still, artillery shot ranged all around, one Minnesotan describing a "cannon ball going the length of our line."[59]

Even more troubling for Gregg, a message arrived from cavalry commander Wirt Adams that "the enemy had a large supporting force advancing,"

probably a reference to Crocker but possibly also to the larger context of the
XV and XIII Corps moving forward to the west. That news satisfied Gregg
that he had done just about all he could do at Raymond. He soon ordered a
withdrawal, and fortunately in the process he met several mounted companies
of the 3rd Kentucky arriving from Jackson. He placed the Kentuckians in a
new position with Bledsoe's two remaining guns to hold a rear line while the
various infantry regiments marched off the battlefield.[60]

Colonel Walker of the 3rd Tennessee reported orders to "retire slowly toward town, concealing my movements as much as possible." His tired troops
did so, and the other regiments did as well, although one Tennessean admitted
that as the Federals "had 4 to our one we was obliged to retreat." The rear
guard soon left the field as well. Lieutenant Colonel Turner reported that it
was a welcome order, writing that "at the time we were ordered to retire a
large number were without ammunition, and had we remained much longer
we must have been captured." It was obviously not what Gregg had wanted,
he thinking he would capture the supposed enemy brigade, but he nevertheless declared that the retreat was "effected in admirable order."[61]

T he fierce little battle ended almost as quickly as it began. Casualties were
high, especially for the small Confederate brigade. Gregg's hard-fighting
regiments lost 514 men in total, the vast majority in the 7th Texas and 3rd
Tennessee, which Gregg explained "were in the most trying part of the engagement." Federal losses were 442, all but four in Logan's division, and in
that unit the vast majority (235) came in Smith's brigade. But the numbers
told, and an amazed Gregg, upon getting reports from those captured, soon
realized he had tangled with almost the entire XVII Corps. Perhaps in an
effort to buy time, Gregg "sent in a verbal request, under a flag of truce, for
permission to carry off his wounded." It was denied. After taking part in the
fight itself, the Union pioneer soldiers buried the dead.[62]

"By overwhelming majority we was compelled to leave the place," one
Confederate admitted. Gregg withdrew from Raymond about five miles and
went into camp, his numbers augmented by the arrival of about a thousand
men under Brigadier General William H. T. Walker. Gregg sent Pemberton
a quick note apprising him of the battle and his withdrawal "after fighting
the enemy all day," but Pemberton had already gained such knowledge from
Colonel Elijah Gates at Edwards, who forwarded the news on that evening.
Governor Pettus also reported that Gregg had fought all day and sent him a
message "to see me instantly on arrival at Jackson." Meanwhile, the Federals

moved on into Raymond, Crocker noting that "we proceeded without interruption to Raymond, where we encamped." But the people were not very
welcoming, one of Sanborn's Minnesotans declaring that the residents were
"not verry cordial excepted only by the Blacks." And it would get no better
for the inhabitants as wave after wave of Federals would follow through the
town in the ensuing days.[63]

The somewhat startled Federals managed to follow, McPherson noting
that "pursuit was immediately commenced, and the town of Raymond was
entered by our troops at 5 p. m., the enemy having passed through without
stopping." One Illinoisan explained that "we marched through the town in
line of battle." A Missourian noted the same thing on the outskirts of town,
where they stopped by a small house with a garden of onions. "There was a
little colored girl in the yard," Joel Strong related, and one soldier asked her,
"pull me an onion." She responded, "I'll ask Missus." The lady came out and
cheerfully allowed the soldier the onion, but "her mood soon changed as her
bed of onions seemed likely to disappear when everyone in the company, it
seemed, made similar requests!" Logan nevertheless pushed on and entered
Raymond about twenty minutes after the Confederates passed through, indicating something less than a quick pursuit. Likewise, Lieutenant Colonel
Beaumont of the 50th Tennessee reported that he moved slowly to the rear,
"securing our knapsacks and haversacks, which had been left on the roadside
as we went out to the field." And having fought all day and with nightfall
coming, the Federal commanders were soon content and ordered the regiments into camp for the night around Raymond, some following as much as
a mile north of town before bivouacking for the night. Only Captain Foster's
cavalry moved ahead farther, some three miles before dark, capturing several
prisoners in the pursuit. To hold the town itself, the guns of the 6th Wisconsin Battery "were posted on the entrance of the Jackson road in the public
square, and stood picket." Later-arriving orders to move campsites played
havoc with the Federals preparing food, however, Colonel Force describing
one such order for the 20th Ohio and how "every man picked up his smoking
cup, and stick which bore his sizzling bit of pork, and we incensed the town
with savory odor as we marched through."[64]

Several viewed the battlefield, small but full of carnage nevertheless; an
Illinoisan described the fighting being "as warm as almost any other battle
of war." Colonel Force of the 20th Ohio told of twenty-three dead Texans on
his front, and he saw seven of them behind one log "which was pierced by
seventy-two balls." He also told of "one tree in front of my line [that] was
stripped and hacked near the root by balls, though not a mark was found more

than 2 feet above the ground." The wounded were cared for in the surrounding houses and town, the Federals breaking open cotton bales to make beds and erecting brush arbors to keep them out of the sun.[65]

McPherson put the best possible spin on the fight, this time informing Grant that evening that he had met six thousand Confederates who were "fully prepared to receive us." He explained that the "rough and impracticable nature of the country, filled with ravines and dense undergrowth, prevented anything like an effective use of artillery or a very rapid pursuit." And he limited the casualties: "250 will cover the total killed, wounded and missing."[66]

But when word got out, this little battle had large implications. Grant made his headquarters at Dillon's that evening, where one Federal noted that Dillon "is not smart. We had some fun with him. I asked him how much 4 times 7 were, he said after long calculation, 35. He says he is a Union [man], smart fool indeed. Post and I amused ourselves at the poor fellow's expense." But the decisions made here at the old man's house were no laughing matter. Grant had all the while intended to move northward on his present front, on the three basic axes of advance to the railroad. In fact, that evening he issued orders for just such a movement the next day. Sherman was to move northward and "strike the railroad between Bolton and Edwards Station." Even though Grant knew McPherson was in Raymond "and has had, from the amount of firing heard, a hard fight," he was still ordered to move on to the railroad toward Bolton. The order brought an uncharacteristically negative response from McPherson, at least according to engineer Wilson, who delivered it; if true, perhaps it illustrated the tension that had built up during the dangerous campaign east of the river as well as perhaps McPherson's mental and physical exhaustion from the day's battle. At the same time, McClernand would hold where he was, Grant explaining that "Edwards Station is evidently the point on the railroad the enemy has most prepared for receiving us," and "I therefore want to keep up appearances of moving upon that place, but want to get possession of less guarded points first." He accordingly ordered McClernand to "keep up this appearance, a short distance only from where you are now, with the three advanced divisions, leaving the Fourth, or Smith's in about its present position." In effect, the Army of the Tennessee would pivot to the left on McClernand's corps, gaining the railroad in the process.[67]

Then Grant changed his mind. By 9:15 that evening he sent out revised orders for the next day. Instead of pivoting to the left, he would pivot in the opposite direction, the right. The Confederates who fought McPherson in Raymond this day were obviously a force to be reckoned with, it not being destroyed, and who knew how many others there were in back of this lone, hard-fighting brigade. "I have determined to move on the latter place [Jackson] by way of Clinton and take the capital of the State," Grant informed his commanders, "and work from there westward." The campaign now hinged, literally, on Raymond, and Grant informed his commanders they would be moving east instead of merely north and west to the railroad, ultimately to Jackson itself. In fact, Raymond seemed to become the focal point of the Union movements, as every single Union division of all three corps would at some point funnel through the town, something Port Gibson, Clinton, or even Jackson and Edwards could not say during the campaign; only Rocky Springs had a similar importance.[68]

It was more of the adaptation Grant had almost perfected by this point. Some sources mention him imbibing at times during these tension-filled days, although never to the point of drunkenness. If so, it certainly did not affect his boldness or adaptability. But such a drastic change entailed a huge risk, placing his force as he was between two of the enemy's bodies of unknown strength. But it was a gamble Grant had to make to keep the enemy separated and to meet each contingent on fairer terms.[69]

11

"There Has Been a Slight Change of Plan Since Yesterday"

May 13

"Have you heard of the railroad accident[?]," editorialized the Jackson *Daily Southern Crisis*, to which another responded, "No—where was it?" The reply: "The Western Train left Meridian and arrived at Jackson in schedule time." The other declared he "has heard of no such accident on that route." The deplorable state of the Southern Railroad of Mississippi had by 1863 become the butt of jokes in newspapers and around the area, but the truth was even worse. Famed English traveler Arthur Fremantle later described the railroad as "in a most dangerous state, and enjoys the reputation of being the very worst of all the bad railroads in the South. It was completely worn out and could not be repaired. Accidents are of almost daily occurrence, and a nasty one had happened the day before." The delays, much less the accidents, affected large swaths of people who depended on the rail line, and by May 1863 there was no larger dependent on it than the Confederate army at Vicksburg.[1]

Despite its shortcomings, the Southern Railroad of Mississippi was the main east-west rail line in the state, and as such it acted as one of the chief transportation routes in the western Confederacy. Other major lines ran north and south, such as the Mobile and Ohio and Mississippi Central, which connected at Canton with the New Orleans, Jackson, and Great Northern. Each of those lines began outside the state down on the Gulf of Mexico and ran entirely through Mississippi and into Tennessee and even beyond. The Memphis and Charleston ran east-west, but most of its line lay in Tennessee and Alabama, with only a path through the corner of the state in the northeast.

Conversely, the Southern Railroad of Mississippi ran across the entirety of the state at its midpoint.[2]

While the others were certainly major trunk lines that became very important before and during the war, there was by May 1863 perhaps no more essential rail line in Mississippi than the Southern. Damaged and used though it was, the major reason for its importance was its connection, literally, to Vicksburg. Chartered in 1857, the line first emerged between Vicksburg and Jackson and then extended on eastward to Meridian and then beyond. Crossing the New Orleans, Jackson, and Great Northern at Jackson and the Mobile and Ohio at Meridian, the Southern originally offered vast connections to the wider Confederacy, but by 1863 the options for shipping goods to Vicksburg were much slimmer. Obviously, river transport was out of the question by May, with Federal vessels controlling all but a few miles along Vicksburg's waterfront. Likewise, the rail lines that fed the Southern at Jackson were not as advantageous as they had once been. Moving north out of the capital eventually on the Mississippi Central once led to Tennessee and the wide connection of rail lines there, including the Memphis and Charleston and others. Going south, the New Orleans, Jackson, and Great Northern had led straight to New Orleans and the Gulf itself. But by mid- to late 1862, each of those lines had been lopped off so that traffic could go only to the Grenada area northward and barely into Louisiana southward, and that part was later terribly damaged in Grierson's Raid. That meant that the area of supply served by these lines was significantly restricted, but more important the connections to the larger rail network were also severed.[3]

That left the single line Southern Railroad running through Jackson as the chief supplier of Vicksburg, but it fortunately still connected with the greater Confederacy somewhat, mainly through its junction with the Mobile and Ohio Railroad at Meridian. But going north from Meridian was problematic throughout the war, and by the spring of 1862 the farthest north someone could travel was below Corinth, and sometimes farther south than that also because of Grierson's Raid. But going southward, the line was still in Confederate hands all the way to Mobile, where, although not connected physically with other rail lines, the Mobile and Ohio could ship goods brought across the bay from other lines or from the vast agricultural country that lay nearby. Even in mid-May 1863, there was still a tenuous line for Vicksburg to the outside Confederacy.[4]

That is why the Southern Railroad loomed so large in Federal commanders' plans. The famed Grierson's Raid back in April had planned to break the line between Meridian and Jackson to halt the supply of goods and troops from the east. The strike was successful for a short time, but not permanently. And even with the line broken temporarily at Newton Station, goods could still be brought in from the local areas still serviceable by the rail lines that crossed the Southern at Jackson.[5]

As a result, the place to completely sever Vicksburg from the outside world was to strike the Southern Railroad between Vicksburg and Jackson. That would negate all the connections for the Confederates, leaving Vicksburg isolated. And the best place to do that was perhaps at the Big Black River bridge, which if destroyed would effectively halt traffic to Vicksburg almost indefinitely. Certainly, the Confederates feared as much, establishing elaborate defensive works actually east of the river in April to defend against sabotage efforts by Grierson's raiders. If the idea was to defend the river crossing, then fortifications would best be placed on the higher ground west of the river. But if defending the bridge from a cavalry raid operating to the east, then earthworks on the east side were a necessity. And since then, even more elaborate fortifications had appeared as well.[6]

Ulysses S. Grant certainly knew as much, and almost from the start he opted to make his way northward east of the Big Black River to the railroad instead of diving off into the dangerous triangle south of Vicksburg. The goal of course was the rail line, and it really did not matter where Grant broke it between Jackson and Vicksburg, just as long as he broke it west of Jackson, where the first connections came. That said, taking the Big Black bridge would make the break as permanent as it could be at the time, and at some point Grant would have to cross the river either at the railroad bridge site or elsewhere to get across this last major impediment to reach Vicksburg. And that crossing could very well come down to be the chief area of struggle if the Confederates were not content to defend Vicksburg at its defensive works themselves; their next-best option would be to defend at the major stumbling block that was the Big Black River, although Pemberton was already beginning to waffle even on that and head out eastward from the protective shield of the river.[7]

Even with the change of plan to go to Jackson first, one Federal admitting that "Vicksburg seems to be ignored just now," this major step of breaking the rail line nevertheless came as May 13 dawned. The entire Army of the Tennessee had moved past the impediment of Fourteenmile Creek the day before at three different places, at the cost of a small battle at Raymond and skirmishing elsewhere. But now the army, arrayed in a line east to west, lay poised to pounce on the rail line just six or eight miles to the north. Taking that line and cutting that connection would be a decisive stroke in this already decisive campaign, and one Federal explained that "we are still marching and driving the Rebs before us." But what was up ahead was anybody's guess, Grant and company merely raking in all the intelligence they could from scouts, slaves, and any other source. Indications were that the forces ahead at Clinton and Jackson were small, but no one knew for sure. Even Confederates were not much more knowledgeable. Still, one Louisianan commented in his diary how matters were quickly getting more serious: "The crisis of our fate is now upon us in a few days a drama of blood will come off here. All things point to an immediate great battle."[8]

The revised Union orders for the move to the railroad on May 13 actually went out late the evening before, upon the pivot in plans Grant decided on at Dillon's Plantation. It resulted in a complete shift of priority, from the railroad between Edwards and Bolton to the city of Jackson, but the rail line still played the central part. The railroad could just as well be broken to the east as farther west, and taking Jackson would net two successes at the same time. But the actual initial break would come around Clinton. In fact, as McPherson's XVII Corps was on the point of this new move eastward, being farthest east at the time, he would be the one to actually break the line.[9]

Grant's three corps finished the day on May 12 camped roughly along a straight line north of Fourteenmile Creek. McPherson on the right, having taken the crossing by force south of Raymond, camped around the town that evening. Sherman's two XV Corps divisions bivouacked to McPherson's left about seven miles to the west at Dillon's Plantation and Turkey Creek, he having taken the Port Gibson Road crossing of that creek on May 12 amid minor skirmishing. McClernand's XIII Corps divisions were farther to the west, three at Whittaker's Ford just five miles farther west and only that many south of Edwards Station and the railroad, with one other division two and a half miles farther at Montgomery's Bridge.[10]

With McPherson taking the point, he led the march on May 13 according to Grant's 9:15 p.m. orders of the night before, moving at daylight almost due northward to Clinton. It was only an eight-mile march, but McPherson was entering the enemy's core area and proceeded cautiously. The cavalry battalion under Captain Foster and other mounted units led the divisions, Foster relating that his force proceeded in "scouting the country in every direction, and skirmishing all day with the enemy's cavalry." In fact, McPherson had warned Grant after he received his orders that "it is rumored, but with how much truth I have not been able to ascertain, that heavy re-enforcements are coming to the enemy from Jackson to-night, and that we may expect a battle here in the morning." McPherson added that "I shall try and be prepared for them if they come," and he did alert his commanders to do so, having them "turn out under arms at 3.30 a.m. . . . [and] cautioning the men to be on the alert against any surprise." There was no Confederate offensive planned, of course, but McPherson's caution was evident in his orders and later in his march northward.[11]

Still, McPherson made headway after his 6:00 a.m. start time, Crocker's division leading the way; Logan's troops followed just in rear, one Illinoisans simply describing the day: "No rations—no fighting today." Another who had been issued only flour told of finding an old shovel and cleaning it to cook his dough made of the flour. McPherson described his march as "moved cautiously toward Clinton, my cavalry being ordered to keep well out on my left flank." At times when it looked like Confederate resistance would become strong, Crocker deployed entire brigades, such as when he sent Boomer's troops off on a road that led to the left "to clear the road." Colonel Holden Putnam of the 93rd Illinois noted that he "found nothing but a line of the enemy's skirmishers, who fled after delivering their fire." Crocker soon ordered the brigade back to the main road and continued northward.[12]

There was certainly a fight expected at Clinton, Edward Wood of the 48th Indiana explaining that "we expected to meet the enemy before reaching the R.Rd. which we did not think they would surrender without a severe struggle." The Confederates did not fight for the railroad, however, but a new factor the Federals had not seen lately did enter the picture in the form of a major storm system moving into the area that afternoon, prompting one Iowan to declare that "when it rains in this state, it rains as if its heart would break." It had not rained since the night of May 4, but one Missourian noted that "in spite of that we marched, and got wet to the skin." Brigade commander Stevenson noted that the march was done "in a continuous and heavy rain . . . , making a moist, toilsome march through rain and mud." As such, Crocker did not enter the "very poor little town" of Clinton until around 2:00 p.m. But he was there then, astride the railroad itself, which his engineers began immediately to break up. McPherson ordered his corps engineer, Captain Andrew Hickenlooper, to take a regiment of infantry and begin the work at Clinton and progress westward "as far . . as possible that night." The next day, as McPherson's columns pushed eastward toward Jackson, Hickenlooper was to follow along and continued to break the line in that direction. McPherson described the breaking process as "burning the ties, bending the iron, destroying bridges, culverts, &c." And, in another critical blow, McPherson's men also broke the telegraph, Pemberton's only direct connection to the outside world.[13]

Perhaps helping McPherson's shaky nerves was promise of support from Sherman's two XV Corps divisions, which Grant assured his inexperienced

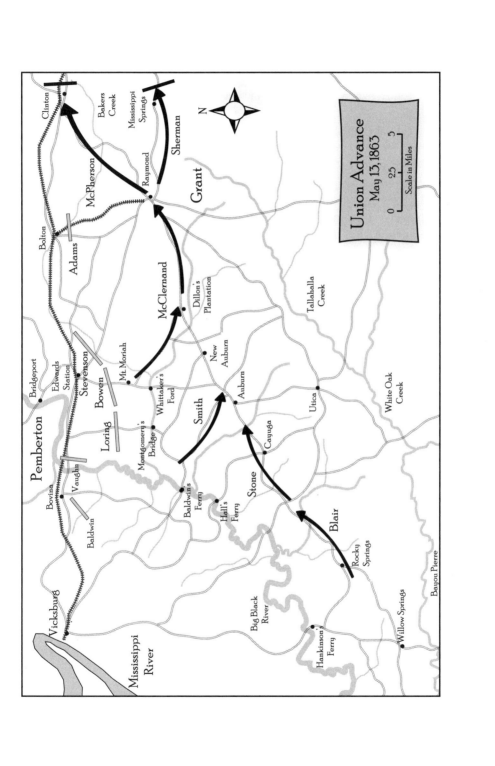

Union Advance
May 13, 1863

Scale in Miles
0 2.5 5

N

Pemberton

Grant

Sherman

McPherson

McClernand

Smith

Blair

Stone

Vicksburg

Mississippi
River

Clinton

Bakers
Creek

Mississippi
Springs

Raymond

Bolton

Adams

Stevenson

Bowen

Loring

Vaughn

Baldwin

Bovina

Edwards
Station

Bridgeport

Mt. Moriah

Whittaker's
Ford

Montgomery's
Bridge

Baldwins
Ferry

Hall's
Ferry

Dillon's
Plantation

New
Auburn

Auburn

Cayuga

Utica

Tallahalla
Creek

White Oak
Creek

Rocky
Springs

Willow Springs

Hankinson's
Ferry

Big Black
River

Bayou Pierre

corps commander would "follow and support you." According to orders, Sherman left Dillon's at 4:00 a.m. and marched along the Port Gibson Road to Raymond, where he arrived by that evening. But there was a slight mix-up in routes when Sherman's van arrived in Raymond before the tail end of McPherson's corps left the place. Grant changed the program slightly by ordering Sherman to move on through Raymond eastward to Mississippi Springs, from which he would "take the direct road to Jackson." Sherman left McPherson's wake and pushed eastward to Mississippi Springs, his men carrying what little provisions they had found in the thoroughly worked-over town of Raymond. Still, one 13th Illinois soldier related that they moved "with many of the men bearing aloft on their bayonets hams and bacon which Mrs. Bush, a kind rebel lady, had generously donated by compulsion to the Union cause." One affected Mississippi woman whose husband was in the army in Tennessee wrote him that, despite losing almost everything, "I bore the whole affair, as a Soldier[']s wife should." Sherman's corps was not in town long, but it was long enough to see, one Missourian wrote, "the extreme astonishment and disgust possessed by southern *ladies* for the Yankee army. Poor beings." At Mississippi Springs, what little contact Sherman had with any enemy occurred: "We surprised a cavalry picket, capturing them."[14]

While McPherson and Sherman positioned themselves closer to Jackson, McClernand's task was a bit trickier. His revised orders the previous evening informed him of McPherson's fight at Raymond and the enemy retreat toward Jackson. "I have determined to follow," Grant wrote, "and take first the capital of the State." Informing him of McPherson's and Sherman's moves east and northward, Grant gave his specific orders from Dillon's: "You will start with three of your divisions as soon as possible, by the road north of Fourteen-Mile Creek, to this place, and on to Raymond. The road is plain, and cannot be mistaken." McClernand's fourth division was to move south to Old Auburn to await the arrival of the two supply trains then on the way from Grand Gulf.[15]

McClernand could not believe what was happening, but he immediately informed Grant it would be "promptly executed." He added, however, that "in moving by the road north of Fourteen-Mile Creek to Dillon's, my flank and rear may be exposed to attack from the enemy's line between Edwards Station and Bolton; nevertheless, I will try and protect myself to the best advantage." One wonders if Grant was beginning to get tired of his corps commanders responding that they will try this or that, as now both McPherson and McClernand had written. "I shall try and be prepared" and "I will try and protect myself" were not ringing endorsements.[16]

McClernand gave the necessary orders nevertheless, telling Hovey, Osterhaus, and Carr that "the general commanding the department has changed the direction of the general movement from Edwards Station to Jackson." One Iowan noted in his diary, "there has been a slight change of plan since yesterday." McClernand ordered that Hovey guard the way at 6:00 a.m. by moving northward toward Edwards to a satisfactory position past Mount Moriah, where he would deploy and "cover the other divisions, while they file in his rear to the right." With Hovey covering the new rear, Osterhaus and Carr would march eastward with Hovey following and the corps' cavalry acting as the rear guard for all. It would be dangerous, McClernand warning his division commanders that "the execution of this movement will pass the flank and rear of our force in the face of the enemy (close by) between Edwards Station and Bolton, and will require great vigilance and promptitude."[17]

Less dangerous would be A. J. Smith's task. His division would not follow the others but instead moved south of Fourteenmile Creek to Old Auburn, where he would await the wagon trains from Grand Gulf. Along with him would be the division trains of the force making the tedious movement north of Fourteenmile Creek. Smith would then be governed by new orders from Grant as to what to do with the trains, although McClernand assumed Blair's division escorting the second one would also soon be on hand. In fact, McClernand was still a little puzzled as to the need for Smith to escort the trains at all, he telling Smith, "I suppose Blair's division will, together with your division, form the escort from Old Auburn forward." To Grant himself McClernand had written, "I infer that General Blair's division will also escort the supply train[?]" But Grant was extremely concerned about the en route supplies, writing directly to Blair, "do not on any account leave the Wagon train behind you until it reaches Raymond." Then he added, in answer to McClernand's questions although not addressed directly to him, "fearing that a single Division would not be sufficient guard between Auburn and Raymond I sent Gen. Smith back with his Division to strengthen you." Perhaps Grant would have been wise to advise McClernand of his reasoning as well.[18]

In fact, McClernand was confused on a number of issues, including what to do with the guards that had been left at the various Big Black River crossings below now that he was marching eastward away from the river. McClernand even admitted to Smith that "the general is inexplicit as to the detachments guarding Baldwin's Ferry, but I cannot believe that he instructs that they should be left behind and exposed to danger of capture or dispersion." Still, McClernand counseled swiftness, writing that Smith should "hasten" to the rear to guard the trains of the division and those from Grand Gulf when they arrived, but he clearly saw the movement north of Fourteenmile Creek as the more serious in scope. He even asked Smith to perform "any movements you can safely make and not delay you, which would impart the design of a

movement against Edwards Station, [which] might assist the delicate movement to be made by the other divisions of the corps."[19]

Still, the mix-up at the least showed Grant's concern for the wagon trains
even then on the way northward to the army across the dangerous intervening
space of land between the well-protected cul-de-sac around Grand Gulf and
the army up ahead. All the while, Colonel Stone plied ahead on May 13 with
his nearly two hundred wagons, with Blair right behind him and catching up.
In fact, Blair itched to be in the fight when it came and actually pulled rank
on Stone, ordering him to the side so that Blair's troops and wagons could
take the lead. Stone had little choice but to do so, but he then reconsidered
that Grant's orders to him to hurry forward outranked Blair's to halt, so Stone
pushed on ahead through Cayuga ("all deserted," John Bell of the 25th Iowa
noted), making some twelve more miles that day despite enemy pickets detected in the area nearer to the Big Black River. "The heat today has been
almost intolerable and the dust awful," Bell scribbled in his diary. "My lungs
are filled with the fine dust." George Rogers added that he left camp "without
breakfast" and there was "no water for either man or beast." Later in the day it
became better as the column reached a creek, and then he noted that the regiment camped that night "on the ground occupied by General Jackson 1812."
The famished men foraged and got what they could, one Illinoisan relating
that "we killed some sheep and chickens for supper, but where they came
from only the Lord and some of our boys knew."[20]

It was also on May 13, as Stone and Blair jockeyed for position up front,
that more troops left Grand Gulf under Thomas Ransom's and John Mc-
Arthur's protection, although McArthur moved on ahead to the army. The brigade had crossed the river the day before and found the same troubles all the
other units had, including hilly terrain and dusty roads at least part of the day
on May 13. Joseph Stockton of the 72nd Illinois related that his regiment was
in the rear as "a large train of supplies and ammunition going out to the armies
in advance." He added, "roads terribly dusty and weather exceedingly hot."
With only one brigade of the division east of the Mississippi River, the Scots-
man John McArthur was itching for a fight and accompanied the lone brigade
of his division east of the river while Colonel William Hall's remained near
Grand Gulf and the third would stay in Louisiana near Milliken's Bend for
the remainder of the campaign.[21]

As with all the columns moving forward, as well as the main army itself,
a great horde of slaves and contrabands met Ransom's troops moving northeastward. Stockton related that the column "met hundreds of 'contrabands'
going into Grand Gulf. No one can imagine the picturesque and comic appearance of the negroes, all ages, shapes and sizes. All seemed happy at the

idea of being free, but what is to become of them—the men can be made soldiers, but women and children must suffer." Once at Grand Gulf, where black regiments were organized, they competed for attention from the hospitals and supply efforts also ongoing at the now thriving but thinly stretched supply base. One wounded soldier in fact wrote that "it is pretty warm here and we are poorly cared for."[22]

Despite the concerns to the rear, McClernand had his divisions on the move by 6:00 a.m. on May 13, all mostly going according to plan. Part of the route was along a newly built military road, just put in service that morning by the pioneers. "Now we are on the way after the Rebels," one of Carr's Iowans joyfully noted. Hovey took his position on time, McClernand agreeing with the "effect to throw the enemy upon his defense against apprehended attack." There was some delay as Osterhaus and Carr branched off to the right while Hovey held the front as near as two and a half miles from Edwards Station itself. The main impediment for Osterhaus and Carr was Bakers Creek, which was a large watershed that flowed into Fourteenmile Creek from the north after making a sweeping curve all the way up toward the railroad. The bridge over Bakers Creek had been destroyed, and it took some time as McClernand's scouts looked around and the engineers improved a ford. The last thing McClernand needed was to become strung up on both sides of Bakers Creek, but he had not exactly had much warning of the need for a bridge there. Finally, the crossing was secured and Osterhaus and Carr moved on, whence they stopped to await Hovey. That rear division disengaged and "followed in successive detachments, under cover of woods." Nevertheless, the two divisions moved onward, and Hovey's troops soon took up the march over what one Federal described as "very dusty [roads]. Never saw so much." The watching Confederates, not knowing what was happening, followed and skirmished lightly with the rear cavalry but did not pursue or attack. Taking no chances, however, Hovey ordered brigade commander James Slack to deploy the 47th Indiana, 28th Iowa, and 56th Ohio to make it a sure thing, and he did. McClernand joyfully noted that "the movement was discovered by the enemy too late to allow him to prevent or embarrass it. His attack upon the rear guard was hesitating and feeble, and was promptly and completely repulsed." Staff officer Henry Warmoth noted that the fight "did not amount to anything." Still, McClernand's relief was evident when he added, "all were now safe beyond Baker's Creek."[23]

The lead division under Osterhaus moved through Dillon's around 3:00 p.m. and pushed on toward Raymond; the rear brigades under Hovey passed through by 4:30 p.m. McClernand himself made his headquarters at Dillon's, staff officer Warmoth noting that "this old man Dillon is a brother to Dillon who lives near Rolla [Missouri]." But before entering the town, Osterhaus in the lead found Frederick Steele's division train blocking the road. Sherman's corps had not fully moved through the town as yet, waiting as it had to for Crocker's train to vacate, and the path was blocked. Tuttle himself was blocked at times even by ambulances from Logan's division caring for wounded and burying the dead from the fight the day before, but McClernand had nevertheless managed to get his corps up to the rear of Sherman's troops, although not exactly to Raymond per se. Still, he was within supporting distance and would simply move on into Raymond early the next morning, providing the guards and skirmishers necessary as the other two corps marched onward. McClernand was also to provide a regiment as provost guard to make sure "soldiers . . . conduct themselves in an orderly manner, and [are] prevented from entering and pillaging houses," Grant ordered; he did so with details from Osterhaus's division. The other divisions followed to their ordered places, and Smith's division made its way to Auburn, where it united with the wagon trains that were coming up from Grand Gulf; the division conducted the train to "Oakland Race Course." Colonel Theodore E. Buehler of the 67th Indiana noted that "meeting the train of our division, we for the first time prided ourselves in the prospect of a change of linen since we left Smith's plantation, La., on April 24."[24]

Once near Raymond, McClernand informed Grant that he was mostly in position: "I am happy to be able to report that this movement has been safely effected without loss, although the rear guard was attacked, and we had to skirmish with the enemy, whom we dispersed." McClernand again alerted Grant to the danger, however, reminding him that "on withdrawing the division from its position, I had anticipated trouble in effecting so delicate a movement with my flank and rear both exposed to attack." Even later in his report he would again add that at the beginning "my corps rested within 4 miles of Edwards Station, with an outpost only 3 and a picket only 2 miles from that place. The outpost of the enemy had been driven back from the creek, and he was fully advised of the fact and of our proximity. The movement ordered was a delicate and hazardous one, but was calculated to deceive the enemy as to our design." Certainly, Grant was grateful, but he did not need the continual reminder. He knew exactly how dangerous it had been and was relieved it had come off without a problem. Now, his full attention could be given to the next day's capture of the capital of the state of Mississippi.[25]

Federal troops at Clinton meant one major thing for the Confederate defenders of Vicksburg: the city was now cut off from the outside world. Once Grant reached the rail line, it became inoperable and would not play a major role in the campaign again. Worse for the Confederates, Grant's move also split the defenders, those around Vicksburg with Pemberton now having no direct rail connection and—probably more important—no telegraphic communication with the other major force near Jackson. Grant had intended to do this very thing all along, and even with the change in plan to go to Jackson first he still managed to cut the rail line on May 13. It was a decisive development in the Vicksburg Campaign.

On the west side of the break Grant created for the Confederate command and army, John Pemberton continued to reel under the pressure of fast-moving events on a small campaign canvas. He knew the desperate situation he was in, even confiding to Davis on May 13 (before the telegraph line was cut) that "my forces are very inadequate. Port Hudson is again threatened, and I have been forced to draw largely from there. Enemy continues to re-enforce heavily." Worse was the news not coming in because of Grant's movements, his commanders near Jackson such as John Adams giving little detail about the fight the day before: "Nothing definite from General Gregg as to who made attack."[26]

Yet even in the fog of war, Pemberton continued his blunder of probing forward with little to gain. Davis's order to hold Vicksburg that conflicted with Johnston's orders to get out continued to divide his thoughts, but the middle-of-the-road approach of proceeding part way out brought danger upon danger. Still, by May 13 the head of the Confederate force moving slowly eastward to deal with Grant reached Edwards Station under William Loring, who advised of what he knew from that place. But all Loring could find out was the same basic news from Adams in Jackson: that the Federals were at Raymond and Mississippi Springs with two corps. Eventually, Gregg himself informed Pemberton what had happened the day before: "I fought Major General Logan's division yesterday from 10 a.m. until 3.30 p.m. My troops fell back in perfect order. . . . Our engagement of yesterday was very severe and loss considerable." At the time of the writing he was watching for the next Federal move, which had not begun, but a subsequent note informed Pemberton that the enemy was "advancing from Raymond in force. I shall retire before them until further re-enforcements or other orders."[27]

With word from Gregg and still retaining telegraphic communication at that point before the Federals reached Clinton, Pemberton gave what orders he could for the force in Jackson. "You must not attack the enemy in superior force, but fall back, if necessary, to Jackson, and occupy entrenchments. All the force now there and arriving will be kept for defense of that place for the present. If enemy fall back, you will advance on his flank and rear, taking care not to get into a position to be cut off." But that was Pemberton's last orders to the force in Jackson, as McPherson soon reached Clinton and cut the lines. From here on, Gregg and whoever was with him in Jackson were on their own.[28]

If he could not oversee the Jackson forces any longer, Pemberton could superintend his army west of the wedge Grant placed in between his forces. Seeing the obvious seriousness of the situation, he had even come out himself to Bovina on May 13, where he pushed his troops on forward to coalesce under Loring at Edwards Station. Remaining at the bridge to man the works there was John C. Vaughn's Tennessee brigade, conscripts from East Tennessee and circumspect at best in loyalty; Pemberton accordingly kept his worst troops in the rear at the least problematic point. Farther out at Edwards Station was Loring's mass of divisions, with Wirt Adams's cavalry even farther along the rail line at Bolton and skirmishing with the advancing Federals. Adams had fallen back northward from Raymond after that battle "to protect the railroad." Of course, McPherson approached the line to the east at Clinton rather than Bolton, so Adams was not successful. Obviously, he could not have saved the line even had he defended Clinton with his few hundred men against two full divisions.[29]

As the Confederate army coalesced near Edwards Station on May 13, it consisted of three of the five divisions Pemberton had. Eventually, Loring's, Stevenson's, and Bowen's troops all gathered near the Big Black River crossing and Edwards, leaving two divisions under Martin L. Smith and John H. Forney to cover Vicksburg itself and the extent of the line north and south, "extending from Snyder's Mill to Warrenton," Pemberton noted. To the north, Forney's troops, mainly Louis Hébert's brigade, still held the positions all the way up to Snyder's and Haynes' Bluffs, while below the city John C. Moore's brigade watched the Warrenton area as well as the fords and crossings of the Big Black River south of the railroad. Martin L. Smith's brigades manned Vicksburg itself, with one, William Baldwin's, also out watching the ferries below the railroad bridge; it had gained some rest after its earlier May escapades marching to and from Port Gibson, one Mississippian commenting that "we had marched about 150 miles in less than five days besides the fighting; and this was no trivial performance for troops unused to long marches." But ominous signs still developed when Moore reported that "wagon trains continue to pass back and forth" from Grand Gulf to Grant's army. Not knowing what was to come, Pemberton simply ordered Forney to "arrange to be able to concentrate all your troops, if necessary, within the defenses of Vicksburg, and that without the loss of any artillery."[30]

Pemberton's major concern, however, was to his front; indeed, the

Missourians out south of Edwards reported being close enough to hear Federal drums. He continued to press the rear parts of his force forward across the Big Black River, one Alabamian describing the fright of crossing the river "on rail road bridge walked Tressel works over 100 feet high." Pemberton soon informed Johnston that he was "in position with eight brigades near Edwards Depot," but he was unable to command the forces at Jackson or Port Hudson, from which he had drawn troops and which needed reinforcements. He also worried about the capital, writing that "I have no major general to command brigades arriving in Jackson."[31]

Throughout the day, Loring had manned the road southward from Edwards Station across Fourteenmile Creek with Bowen's two brigades and two of his own on each flank, Featherston's to the left and Buford's to the right; Tilghman's troops still manned an area southward along the Big Black River. Carter Stevenson's four brigades were shuttling eastward as well, to take a position east of Featherston, but they were making slow progress as they filtered through the railroad bridge area where Vaughn's Tennesseans manned the rear. Despite urging haste, Stevenson's brigades were slow in arriving, but Loring soon described how his line was in "a very strong position . . . about 1 mile south of Edwards Depot, our left resting on the railroad and the right not far from Baker's Creek." Part of the reason for delay was the rain that moved in that afternoon, one Missourian admitting that "most of the time it was raining and consequently it was very disagreeable."[32]

At Edwards Station throughout the day awaiting reinforcements, Loring wondered at the Federal presence along Fourteenmile Creek. "The Enimy was 3 miles of us in line of Batle," one Mississippian scribbled in his diary. Colonel Thomas P. Dockery of Bowen's division related that his troops advanced to Edwards Depot early on May 13 and pushed skirmishers to Fourteenmile Creek but that "all attempts to draw him out from the creek proved fruitless." They located the enemy nonetheless. Loring reported "a force of 10,000 just this side of Fourteen-Mile Creek. Another force is at Montgomery's Bridge, though I do not think it is so large as the other." He was able to pinpoint part of it as being of Osterhaus's division of the XIII Corps, adding that "General Osterhaus' negro, horse, and dinner were captured. . . . The negro says the general told him to cook his dinner and bring it on to Edwards Depot, and he was doing so when captured."[33]

Still at Bovina at this point, Pemberton ordered Loring to find out who was where: "Make a reconnaissance of such a character as you may deem proper, to find out where the main force of the enemy is, and in what direction moving." Pemberton's aide J. C. Taylor wrote Loring that if the enemy were moving on Jackson "he thinks his move will be to fall on their rear and cut their communication, but he must have accurate information from you that he can rely on before making this move, which would leave Vicksburg, by way of Big Black Bridge and the ferries, in so critical a position. It is necessary that the lieutenant general should be informed not only what force has moved on, but the strength of that which is left, and where."[34]

Loring did so and quickly detected McClernand's shift to the east. "Two heavy columns of the enemy moving down the valley on our left in direction of Raymond road," Loring informed Pemberton at 1:30 that afternoon. He sent forces forward to "ascertain the fact," which developed into the slight skirmishing in McClernand's rear. By all indications, Loring reported later that afternoon, "the enemy have moved off from front, and have gone toward Raymond road." An area slave who came into Confederate lines verified the move: "Did not know how many, but counted twenty flags." By 8:00 p.m., Loring was able to inform Pemberton that "from every source, to black and white, I learn that the enemy are marching on Jackson. I think there can be no doubt of this." But in the process, the Confederates missed another opportunity to hit an isolated corps of the enemy, in large part because of the overall lack of direction from a commanding general who would not come to the front and take charge.[35]

But the intelligence of a Federal move eastward was correct, which brought the Jackson forces back into play. The other side of the break that Grant caused on May 13 coalesced at the same time around Jackson under Joseph E. Johnston. Reinforcements were on the way to aid the buildup on this wing, including those ordered from Jefferson Davis himself, such as exchanged prisoners being sent to Mississippi. Others from Pemberton's purging of Port Hudson also approached, a brigade under Brigadier General Samuel Maxey reaching Brookhaven south of Jackson early on May 12 but finding so few rail cars and locomotives as to delay the trip on in to Jackson. Plus, the break where Grierson destroyed the line was critical: "There are but ten cars below the break in the railroad for Maxey to move with," Adams advised from Jackson.[36]

Yet the major arrival Davis hoped would change the dynamics in Mississippi was Johnston himself. He arrived in Jackson late on May 13, having passed Brigadier General States Rights Gist's brigade during that day. He had traveled four straight days "from a sick-room," all the while trying to keep up with the growing crisis. From Meridian, where Johnston encountered the lack of rolling stock on the Southern Railroad, he penned quick notes to both the president and the superintendent of the Mobile and Ohio, asking for rolling stock for the Southern. "The Southern Railroad has not sufficient stock to transport troops from this point to Vicksburg as fast as they arrive here," he wrote. Johnston asked for a loan that "will only be required for a short time," appealing "to you as a patriot."[37]

Johnston arrived in Jackson by late evening and gathered what information he could, much of it erroneous from John Gregg. He managed to fire off a note to Pemberton at 8:40 p.m., however, though by that time the wires were down at Clinton and Pemberton only received the message the next morning. "I have lately arrived," Johnston wrote, "and learn that Major General Sherman is between us, with four divisions, at Clinton." While wrong in number and commander, the sentiment was correct. He continued: "It is important to re-establish communications, that you may be re-enforced. If practicable, come up on his rear at once. To beat such a detachment, would be of immense value. The troops here could co-operate. All the strength you can quickly assemble should be brought. Time is all important." To make sure the message arrived, Johnston sent three different couriers with copies.[38]

Desiring little more than to go to bed, Johnston set up headquarters at the Bowman House hotel just north of the statehouse. There, staff officers and even generals continually came to report, including the senior commanders at that point such as Gregg. But Johnston's bold face toward Pemberton and perhaps others did not represent his actual thoughts. At the same time, he reported to Secretary of War James A. Seddon in Richmond: "I arrived this evening, finding the enemy's force between this place and General Pemberton, cutting off the communication. I am too late."[39]

"We had been making a feint on Edwards Station on the 12th and 13th," wrote Lieutenant Joseph G. Strong of the 28th Iowa, "so as to give General McPherson a better chance to enter Jackson." As part of Hovey's division that was the bait on the morning of May 13, Strong knew all too well just how much of a feint his corps' action was, but also plainly evident was the effect on the rest of the army. Not only did Grant have the railroad broken by the end of the day on May 13; he also was in position to do exactly as Strong suggested: take Jackson. With McPherson's troops positioned at Clinton a mere nine miles west northwest of Jackson and Sherman nearly ten miles west southwest of the city, both were poised for easy marches to the state capital, or at the least to the entrenchments circling the western part of the city. Whether they would meet any defense before that was unknown, but Sherman himself wrote that evening in his orders that "the enemy will not probably stand till near Jackson." Still, his troops bivouacked in line of battle that night.[40]

Grant issued his orders on the evening of May 13, from his headquarters

just north of Raymond at Waverly, home of Major John Peyton. He had visited the wounded in the town, one Confederate testifying that he heard him
say to one surgeon, "give the wounded men every attention which it is possible and make no distinction between Federals and Confederates." From
Raymond, Grant wrote McPherson to "move at early dawn upon Jackson."
It was a simple order, but it also contained information that Sherman would
be moving "at the same hour" on his right flank, directly from Raymond to
Jackson while McClernand would be covering the rear. Similar orders went to
Sherman, who issued his own detailed instructions, including leaving "punc-
tually at 5 a.m." He alerted his commanders that McPherson would be "on
our left and abreast of us," so cavalry scouts would need to be furnished for
the front and right flank. He reminded the men of the forthcoming struggle,
but not just with the Confederates: "Thirst and fatigue are to be expected, but
the safety and success of all will make all good soldiers bear cheerfully the
deprivation of rest and water." He continued with a warning: "Straggling now
is as much a crime as rebellion, and will justify extreme and summary punishment, and officers and rear guards will be justified in inflicting immediate
punishment on men avoiding their full share of duty. Our corps must be first
in the breach, but must be compact and strong."[41]

Sherman also assured Grant that he would keep open communication with
McPherson but, in his usual pessimism, noted that it might be a tough fight
for the state capital. "I have no doubt we will find rifle pits and redoubts,"
he wrote late that evening, also asking because he was still fairly devoid of
rifled artillery that McClernand send forward some of his big guns, 20-pound
Parrotts and "also if possible a couple or more of the 30s." Still, he added that
"we must . . . fight the sooner the better." Orders went out to the commands
to "go into camp early as there would be some work to do the next day and
the men had need of some rest."[42]

Being in the rear, McClernand's task was again more complicated. Grant
initially viewed McClernand's force as a support for both prongs of the advance on Jackson. His orders to McClernand, in addition to explaining what
McPherson and Sherman would be doing, were to array his corps in a line
centered on Raymond and stretching east and west to "the point of diver-
gence of the two advance corps." Two divisions would remain in Raymond,
and one would be down around, if not physically at, Dillon's Plantation. In
all Grant's correspondence about the matter, he indicated that McClernand
would mainly be in support of Sherman and McPherson if needed. In writing
to Sherman, for instance, Grant added that "two of McClernand's divisions
will be thrown forward, one by the Clinton Road, and one by the road where
you are." Similarly, to McPherson he wrote that McClernand "will be brought

up to this point with his rear, and his advance thrown on the two Jackson roads."[43]

Then Grant thought better of this plan, for a couple different reasons. Surely, four divisions of two corps could handle whatever was in Jackson. More important, with the Confederates still lurking to the west, Grant wanted something of a rear guard to block any movement from that direction. Accordingly, he revised McClernand's orders, and while still covering the two major roads that McPherson and Sherman were moving on, he also positioned divisions of the XIII Corps behind each of the other corps with duties not so much tied to Jackson's capture but as a rear guard as well as the beginning movements for the move back westward after Jackson fell. For example, he told McClernand to "move one division of your corps through this place to Clinton, charging it with destroying the railroad." Another was to move to the Mississippi Springs area, and another to Raymond, "ready to support either of the others." With divisions at the rear of each of the other corps, McClernand could either support the advance on Jackson or hold the rear, ready to become the advance when the army pivoted westward. But more important, the new orders aligned the XIII Corps in a north-south stance stretching from the railroad at Clinton southward to Raymond. To make sure he was in position, McClernand was to move at 4:00 a.m.[44]

What Grant was doing, of course, was to place a buffer between the Confederates to the west and his advancing corps moving eastward, with their rears wide open. And it gave McClernand, in addition to McPherson, hold of the railroad, splitting the Confederate forces solidly in two. Certainly, Sherman realized what Grant had done as he prepared to advance to perform his part of the plan: "We must strike before the enemy can concentrate, after we have cut his line in two."[45]

12

"COLORS PLANTED ON THE CAPITOL OF JACKSON"

May 14

"[Jackson] was one of those delightful villages, calling themselves cities," one observer wrote, "of which the sunny South by no means enjoys a monopoly—where everybody knows everybody's business, and where, upon the advent of a stranger, the entire community resolves itself into a Committee of the Whole to learn who he is, where he came from, and what he wants." That was certainly the case on the "rainy and raw" morning of May 14 when thousands of Federals began to bore down on Mississippi's capital city, creating an almost ludicrous scene of panic, fear, confusion, and chaos, all amid a pouring thunderstorm no less. "The peals of thunder seemed to crack just over our heads," admitted a Missourian, "sounding so much like artillery that [we] tried to spot the cannon!" Accordingly, it would be one of the most significant days in the capital city's history.[1]

For all its importance, Jackson was a relatively new place. Established only recently amid the taking of land from the native Choctaw, Jackson first appeared on the bluff overlooking the Pearl River, known locally as Lafleur's Bluff, and the city itself emerged in 1821. Along that major waterway as well as the old native throughfare known in time as the Natchez Trace, the city would eventually come to house other forms of transportation, most importantly the railroads that crossed there. The east-west Southern Railroad of Mississippi, the lifeline to Vicksburg, crossed the north-south New Orleans, Jackson, and Great Northern Railroad in town just up on the bluffs overlooking the Pearl River bottoms to the east. By 1860, the population stood at 3,199. Although overshadowed in population by Natchez, Vicksburg, and Columbus, and certainly by other Southern cities and capitals such as Nashville, New Orleans, and Charleston, Jackson became the economic, political, and cultural center of the state.[2]

While Vicksburg rivaled if not surpassed Jackson in economics and Natchez in society, Jackson was the undisputed political center of the state. It was there that the stately capitol building rose in the eastern part of downtown, right on the river bottom bluffs, and certain other political buildings did as well, some state and some county and city. The governor's mansion sat just down Capitol Street to the west, while both Hinds County and the city of Jackson had elaborate buildings to house their governments. With so much political activity, various establishments—hotels, restaurants, and bars— soon appeared, the most famous being the Bowman Hotel just north of the statehouse. Newspapers, churches, and other businesses also thrived in Jackson. One rising Mississippi politician described the scene there in the 1850s, writing of one party as "a most bilious affair, as they say here." He went on that "there are a great many gentlemen and fine looking ladies in attendance," but he was not overawed in the least: "I find the great men down here are not so very great after all. . . . They grow small as you approach them."[3]

The statehouse, the second one in Jackson and which opened in 1839, sat in "a shaded square," with one observer in 1861 describing it as a "faded, sober edifice, of the style in vogue years ago." It was a three-story structure with "an Iconic portico in front, and an immense dome upon the top," where there was "a miniature dome, like an infinitesimal parasol upon a gigantic umbrella." He went on that "the whole is crowned by a small gilded pinnacle, which has relapsed from its original perpendicular to an angle of 45°, and looks like a little yellow jockey cap, cocked jauntily upon the head of a plethoric Quaker, imparting a rowdyish air, quite at variance with the general gravity." He also described the front and sides made of "faded, cracked freestone, the front and ends walls of stucco, and the rear of brick."[4]

The most famous political activity that occurred there, amid many others such as namesake Andrew Jackson's speech to the legislature and the biannual meetings of that body through the years, was the Mississippi Secession Convention in January 1861. There, under the leadership of fire-eating Governor John J. Pettus, who called on the state to "go down into Egypt while Herod reigns in Judea," a biblical analogy referencing Jesus's escape from Herod by fleeing southward, a hundred delegates overwhelmingly voted to leave the Union and join the Confederacy. Throughout the early part of the war, the legislature met frequently in normal and special called meetings to fund and oversee the war, but there was no more significant meeting than its normal session in December 1862, when the president of the Confederacy himself, Jefferson Davis, arrived in town and addressed the body on the day after Christmas. It was significant that on that very day Federal troops were landing just forty miles away at Chickasaw Bayou in some of the earliest stages of the campaign that was now seeing Union troops bear down on the capital itself.[5]

In fact, Grant informed Halleck that morning of May 14: "I will attack the State capital to-day." Given that Grant had cut his formal line of communication with Grand Gulf and now with only wagon trains guarded by troops moving northward, the courier had to travel back to the Mississippi River "through an unprotected country." But the results were obvious to all, even one Louisianan contextualizing that "the enemy are gradually flanking and Surrounding us."[6]

The defender-in-chief of Jackson was Joseph E. Johnston, who had just arrived the evening before and determined quickly there was no defending the place. He had written Pemberton a quick note describing the enemy between them and ordering Pemberton to attack from his side, assuring his subordinate that he would cooperate from the east. But that would be hard to do while evacuating to the north, which would be done the next day, hopefully before the Federals arrived. If they did, Johnston would keep a rear guard to delay as long as possible so that the stores could be evacuated. Johnston himself left the city about noon on May 14, and one Confederate noted they were "expecting to have a hard fight. But to our surprise the first thing that we know we was [ordered to] retreat and it still raining and had ben all the morning we had to stay in it all the day long. And the mud was verry bad."[7]

Johnston's note had larger ramifications than just at Jackson, however. Still at Bovina, Pemberton was in a quandary, and Johnston's attack message of May 13 that arrived early on May 14 only made matters worse. "Such a movement will be suicidal," Pemberton bellowed to his staff. Called to march eastward to join Johnston in a fight against the Federals near Clinton, Pemberton nevertheless agreed despite replying "the men have been marching several days, are much fatigued, and, I fear, will straggle very much. In directing this move, I do not think you fully comprehend the position that Vicksburg will be left in, but I comply at once with your order." While still at Bovina, Pemberton issued orders to Loring commanding the army up ahead to "have the whole army put in readiness to move forward at a moment's notice." But then thinking better of it on the ride to Edwards Station and labeling Johnston's plan "extremely hazardous," Johnston going so far as to quip that "in the ride of ten or twelve miles to his camp at Edwards Depot he determined to disobey my order," Pemberton at the least decided to seek other opinions. Obviously not trusting himself fully, once at Edwards Station he called a council of war as was his custom to determine the logic of his officers. There, Pemberton spoke "at great length," according to staff officer Jacob Thompson, and also "with great force," that his chief duty was "to defend Vicksburg." The president, after all, had admonished him to do so. Pemberton recited the position of the enemy, his small force, and the potential bad results of a battle so far outside Vicksburg as his main reasons for wishing to withdraw back at the least behind the Big Black River and possibly all the way into the city. He admitted that he analyzed the order "in every view in which it appeared to me, [and] asked their opinions respectively."[8]

As Pemberton took a canvass of the general officers, Loring related that "there was great diversity of opinion," and Alfred Cumming described it as a "division of sentiment." Although accounts differ as to who supported what, staff officer Thompson reported "there was not a voice in favor of moving on Clinton," although most favored cooperating with Johnston in some way. Perhaps Pemberton was relieved, but then another option developed, mainly from the fertile brain of William Loring. He advised a move on the Raymond Road to Dillon's Plantation. He called it "wise and expedient" to cut Grant's supply line since the Union army was near Jackson and only a division or so was between there and Grand Gulf. This would "effectually break up the enemy's communications." Another canvass showed that if not all the officers favored this idea, Stevenson did, thinking Grant was too far away at Jackson to derail the plan. Making the advice more forceful, Loring and Stevenson were the two senior division commanders.[9]

At that point Pemberton lost control of his army. His division commanders, especially Loring and Stevenson, had been increasingly recommending plans for action to Pemberton, and it continued here at the council and even in the days ahead. Lockett wrote that the eventual decision was "a sort of compromise or compound of all these attempts." Pemberton himself wrote that "my own views were strongly expressed as unfavorable to any advance which would separate me farther from Vicksburg, which was my base. I did not, however, see fit to put my own judgment and opinions so far in opposition as to prevent a movement altogether, but believing the only possibility of success to be in the plan of cutting the enemy's communications, it was adopted." Others saw it the same way. "You gave in to the views of the officers with reluctance," staff officer Thompson later wrote Pemberton in summary, "and expressed yourself as doing so against your convictions." But Thompson admitted that "I did not see how you could have done otherwise with any expectation of retaining your hold upon the army." Rumor was that Pemberton was afraid of a fight, and all the officers had decided it was time to do so. As a result, Pemberton, against his own desires, issued orders for the army to march southeastward the next day to cut a supply line that did not formally exist; he termed the move "the lesser of two evils." Pemberton accordingly notified Johnston that morning, "I shall move as early to-morrow morning as practicable with a column of 17,000 men to Dillon's, situated on the main road leading from Raymond to Port Gibson. . . . The object is to cut enemy's communications and force him to attack me, as I do not consider my force sufficient to justify an attack on enemy in position or to attempt to cut my way to Jackson."[10]

With that, Pemberton finalized his plans; "the army is expected to move to-morrow morning in the direction of Dillon's," staff officer Thompson wrote from Edwards. A dumbfounded Lieutenant William Drennan noted to his wife that, as the enemy would not attack at the Big Black River, "the programme was changed and we were to be the attacking party." In preparation, Pemberton informed those in Vicksburg that "this army is about to move forward." Forney was to remain in his defensive mode all along the Vicksburg perimeter but prepare to fall back within the Vicksburg fortifications if Pemberton met defeat. He positioned various troops around his perimeter, including the vacated ferries down along the Big Black River, while Loring's and Stevenson's divisions still finished up their concentration; Pemberton even detailed the limited number of operable locomotives to bring the lagging brigades forward. Leaving the Big Black River enclave, Pemberton and others repeatedly cautioned John Vaughn at the bridge to "keep a sharp look out" and "be on the alert." He also ordered Vaughn to send a force up to the next crossing point upstream, Bridgeport. Finally, Pemberton also ordered tens of thousands of rations eastward by train to Edwards Station.[11]

At the same time, Johnston's determination not to fight for Jackson also had its effect there, of course. "It being evident that the Federal forces advancing upon Jackson were very large," Gregg explained, "General [Joseph E.] Johnston instructed me that the city would be evacuated." Johnston left heading north, leaving a rear guard to fight as long as needed to get as many of the stores out as possible, certainly the wagon train. All the while, he continued to pepper Pemberton with theoretical questions and plans: "Can he supply himself from the Mississippi? Can you not cut him off from it, and, above all, should he be compelled to fall back for want of supplies, beat him?" He positioned "half" of Grant's force at Jackson, adding, "it would decide the campaign to beat it, which can be done only by concentrating." Johnston also worried over what to do about the arriving reinforcements from the south and east; they certainly did not need to get caught up in the evacuation of Jackson.[12]

But with Johnston's decision to evacuate the capital city, made even the night before and beginning to be implemented in the early hours of May 14, the Confederate defenses on Grant's eastern flank faded significantly. Johnston himself left by noon, leaving Brigadier General John Gregg in command of the evacuation. By this time more troops had arrived, including the brigade from South Carolina under William H. T. Walker as well as another under Colonel Peyton H. Colquitt. Gregg placed his own brigade that had fought at Raymond two days before under the senior colonel, Robert Farquharson, and took over basically a division command. But more troops would do little good headed as they were north and away from Pemberton; historian Michael Ballard has surmised that "Grant's task would be easier because he was facing two generals with poor senses of direction."[13]

The evacuation hinged on getting the wagon train and as many supplies as possible out of the city heading north toward Canton. That duty fell to Brigadier General John Adams and his brigade, who "set out upon our line of retreat—the Canton Road." To buy time for Adams to get his train on the road, Gregg issued his defense orders around three o'clock that morning. As indications were that the main enemy force was moving directly eastward from Clinton, Gregg himself led Colquitt and his men westward out the Clinton Road about three miles, well past the city's fortifications, where he posted them along a fairly significant ridge between two creeks. To support him, Gregg ordered Walker to move his newly arrived brigade that direction as well, "to within easy supporting distance." To further solidify the area, he also sent Farquharson and his old Tennessee brigade to the same area with instructions to range around to the north and try to at least demonstrate on the flank of the approaching enemy: "Whenever within sight of the enemy make such a demonstration as might impress him with the idea that it was our intention to fall upon his left flank." Yet by far the most destructive force was Captain James A. Hoskins's Mississippi Battery (Brookhaven Light Artillery), posted on the main Clinton Road at the ridge between Lynch and Town Creeks on which Oliver P. Wright's house sat. Around the guns deployed Colquitt's brigade consisting of a battalion of the 46th Georgia, the 24th South Carolina, and a battalion of the 14th Mississippi.[14]

But then more trouble came. As dawn arrived and skirmishing picked up, reports of Federals approaching from the southwest also arrived. Another large body of troops was coming in from Mississippi Springs, and to hold his position Gregg had to send troops there as well. All attention heretofore had been on the Clinton Road, where Johnston and company thought Sherman's troops were located. But Sherman had vanished and suddenly popped out southwest of town, McPherson being on the Clinton Road. Gregg had only the mounted troopers of the 3rd Kentucky under Colonel Albert P. Thompson available, so he sent them, a battalion of sharpshooters under Major A. Shaaf, and a large conglomeration of artillery under Captain Robert Martin (state guns and his own Georgia's Battery) down the Terry Road to meet and delay the enemy in that direction. Thompson moved forward of the intrenchments as well, locating much of his artillery there before pushing on forward to a high ridge just north of Lynch Creek. But the spires and domes of Jackson could still be seen in the distance, making this defense a very close-run thing.[15]

But it did not need to be an all-out defense. Gregg needed only to delay until Adams could get out of town, following their overall commander Johnston. Gregg hoped he could hinder the Federal movement for a time, but he knew full well that the ultimate result would be the loss of Mississippi's capital city.

William T. Sherman and James B. McPherson were up early preparing for the eventful day ahead on May 14; "we communicated during the night," Sherman explained, "so as to arrive at Jackson about the same hour." Capturing an enemy's capital city was significant, and despite being only a state capital, Jackson still held high importance. Only Nashville and Baton Rouge had fallen at this point in the war, so it was still a novel event. Plus, Jackson held armories, factories, and transportation crossings that made it a significant military objective. It was well worth the effort to take, and Grant pointed his troops eastward that morning to do it.[16]

Nervousness accompanied the marching troops. Obviously, it was expected that the enemy would defend such an important place, and no one quite knew the extent of the Confederate defenders in the city. If the small ruckus at Raymond two days before was any indication, even a small force would fight hard. Plus, there was the rumor that Joseph E. Johnston himself was present, no slouch by reputation at least at the time. McPherson, for instance, notified Grant around 5:30 a.m. that Crocker's division was already on the march and Logan's "is just stretching out on the road." But he also sent word that "General Joe Johnston is in Jackson, and it is reported they have 20,000 men." He added that "I do not think there is that many, though they have collected considerable of a force. They have fortified on the different roads on this side of town, and are forming abatis."[17]

But what troubled the Federals the most, both mentally and physically, was the massive storm front that was moving through the area during the night and into the next morning, producing what Grant described as "roads at first slippery and then miry." It brought heavy rain, Sherman writing that "during the day it rained in torrents, and the roads, which had been very dusty, became equally muddy." McClernand, holding back in the rear and shifting divisions all around, likewise reported that "the tremendous rain storms of last evening and today have made the march laborious and less expeditious than it would have been under more favorable circumstances." In fact, he later termed the day's operations as "the most fatiguing and exhausting day's march that had been made." Division commander Hovey described how "the roads in places having to be drained by the labor of my pioneers before our wagons could pass." The parched Federals who had been on this side of the Mississippi River for fourteen days now mostly without rain needed the cooling effect as well as the water that filled creeks and streams, but not all at once. It came so quickly that it nearly overwhelmed them.[18]

"But we pushed on," Sherman reported, he and his staff riding past the marching troops headed to the front of the column. McPherson similarly moved closer and closer, his troops marching from Clinton due eastward along the rail line and Jackson Road toward the Confederate defenders west of the capital, "that long talked of city towards which we had been going since the evacuation of Corinth." His columns left Clinton about 5:00 a.m., Crocker's division in the lead and followed by Logan's, one of whose officers explained that "my command marched in this position for several miles through mud and rain and almost impenetrable thickets until we came to the town of Jackson." The leading elements of Crocker's division, Captain John S. Foster's cavalry battalion and the 10th Missouri of Colonel Samuel Holmes's brigade, almost immediately met Confederate resistance and skirmished for several miles. By the time the lead division reached a series of ridges some two and a half miles out of Jackson, a major enemy line of battle developed, "crossing the road at nearly right angles," brigade commander Sanborn explained. The Federals stopped to ponder their next moves. McPherson deployed Lieutenant Junius W. MacMurray's Battery M, 1st Missouri Artillery at the W. T. Mann House to take the enemy under fire while the infantry deployed; the main target was the Confederate artillery firing briskly from a distant ridge. Amid the fighting, McPherson's Federals began to realize these were "South Carolina and Georgia regiments, which had only arrived the evening before, and had been immediately marched out and placed in position at the point where the battle took place." Logan soon rode up and remarked on the guns he likewise heard to the south: "What cannon are those over on the right," he queried McPherson. "That must be Sherman pounding away!" McPherson shot back: "I don't know what that is over there, but I do know that this thing just ahead is a rebel line of battle. Form your command on the left and we will go for them."[19]

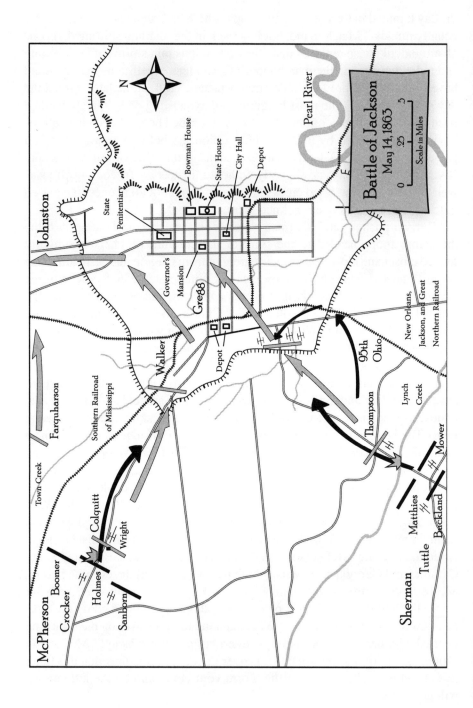

Battle of Jackson
May 14, 1863

Scale in Miles
0   .25   .5

Then came delays. The rain that had been falling on and off became a deluge as the front moved through, drenching everyone thoroughly and filling the roads with running water like creeks. One Indianan in Sanborn's brigade described it as "one of the most drenching thunder storms I ever saw," and an annoyed Ohioan complained that "generals with their aids and orderlies splashed mud and water in every direction in passing." McPherson himself explained that "a very heavy shower set in, which delayed the attack for an hour and a half, the rain coming down in such torrents that there was great danger of the ammunition being spoiled if the men opened their cartridge boxes." One of his Illinoisans similarly explained that "it was '*nip* and *tuck*' between Heaven's artillery and ours, ours finally got ahead." But McPherson used the delay to his advantage. He went on: "The time, however, was well employed in putting the troops in position and bringing up Logan's division as a reserve." Consequently, Crocker formed his lead brigade under Colonel Holmes astride the road, while pushing Boomer's troops to the left into a skirt of woods and Sanborn's to the right, both being nearly in line with Holmes but a little to the rear in both cases. John Logan's division soon arrived as well, and he deployed the three brigades in similar fashion but more so on the left, John E. Smith's on the left in rear of Boomer's troops and John Stevenson's farther to the left across a ravine to search for a road to outflank the enemy line. Elias Dennis's brigade remained as the general reserve in rear, one soldier quipping that "if my own regiment has not had a chance to-day to cover itself with glory it has with mud."[20]

At the same time, Sherman's troops moved by the Mississippi Springs Road slightly northeastward toward the southwestern stretches of the city's defenses. Leaving at daylight, Sherman's force marched as best they could amid the slop, one artilleryman explaining that "the men soon began to get warmed up, and notwithstanding the bad road, made splendid time." But Confederate skirmishers similarly appeared to delay and distract almost immediately, within a mile of leaving Mississippi Springs. They did their job well and skirmished with the lead elements of Sherman's XV Corps all the way nearly to Jackson, at times the fighting reaching skirmish proportions amid the falling rain. Still, with McPherson's guns soon heard to the north, one Illinoisan admitted, "we began to think we should have nothing to do but walk into town—we were within three miles of it."[21]

Sherman pressed on, the "pop popping ahead" getting everyone's attention quickly. He soon pushed forward his leading division under Brigadier General James M. Tuttle. Brigadier General Joseph A. "Fighting Joe" Mower led the division this morning, at the expense of Brigadier General Ralph Buckland, who complained that "according to the regular programme of the march, my brigade was entitled to the lead, but, by order of General Sherman, General

Mower took the advance." Following were Major General Frederick Steele's three brigades in his division, constituting the present portion of the entire XV Corps at the time. Frank Blair's division was at this point still to the rear, bringing up supplies from Grand Gulf, where Lauman's division from Memphis was slated to arrive soon if not already there. Grant issued orders for Lauman's lead brigade under Colonel Isaac Pugh to garrison Grand Gulf itself, and he began preparing for even more wagons trains to move toward the army with those arriving brigades accompanying them. Yet it was a hard march in between the two sites, Colonel De Witt C. Thomas of the 93rd Indiana relating that by the time Blair's column neared Raymond his men were "very much fatigued (it having rained all day incessantly)."[22]

That was certainly the case up front in Mower's brigade. Colonel Lucius F. Hubbard's 5th Minnesota led the march, he writing that the enemy skirmishers appeared immediately after setting out. "A considerable body of the enemy had bivouacked the preceding night within one-half mile of my line of pickets, which retired as we moved forward." Consequently, the march was slow and tedious. "Owing to the broken and wooded nature of the country," Hubbard reported, "and the known proximity of the enemy, we were required to move slowly and with extreme caution." The rain did not help either, Hubbard adding that "it . . . rained furiously all day. The men were very weary and thoroughly wet, having been not only exposed to the storm but required to wade streams and penetrate dense thickets through almost impassable swamps while skirmishing." A lack of food for the past twenty-four hours added to the misery. For miles Hubbard had to maintain three companies of skirmishers out front, "which frequently encountered and exchanged volleys with the skirmishers of the enemy." Still the Minnesotans moved on until within a couple of miles of the city where "a determined stand was made, and a hot fire opened upon us from a full battery of artillery, supported by a strong line of infantry."[23]

As Sherman neared the Lynch Creek crossing point well out in front of the city's fortifications, he began to hear volleys of musketry and artillery to his left. It was McPherson's troops, already engaging the Confederates up on the Clinton Road. About the same time, Sherman moved toward the valley of Lynch Creek, where his cavalry likewise found the enemy posted, at least the battery that began to take them under fire. The Confederate artillery sat on a ridge just across from "a small bridge at the foot of the ridge, along which the road we traveled led." With all the rain, the creek was flooded and thus presented a major impediment.[24]

The Confederate artillery across Lynch Creek was firing rapidly, and Sherman had little time to react. "Hastily reconnoitering the position," he said, he ordered his lead division commander James Tuttle to deploy his brigades. The Minnesotans in the lead remained in skirmish formation while the brigades deployed, after which they took their rightful position in Mower's line. Tuttle pushed his leading brigade under Mower—Illinois, Minnesota, Missouri, and Wisconsin troops including "Old Abe," the famed eagle of the 8th Wisconsin —to the right of the road and positioned Colonel Charles Matthies's Iowa brigade on the left side. In reserve in the rear was Ralph Buckland's Illinois, Indiana, and Ohio brigade, one of the Ohio regiments being the same one he held the Shiloh Church line with over a year ago. One of Buckland's Ohioans related that they "found the enemy in position and ready to receive us. Here I learned of our whereabouts and judge of my surprise when I learned that we were within 100 rods of the fortifications of Jackson." He continued: "The reason of our total ignorance of our locality was 2 or 3 days back we had been told that we were going to guard a bridge on the Big Black River and as the whites had nearly all left the country and the soldiers not allowed much intercourse with the blacks, and our officers not being allowed to be over communitive at that time, made no pretensions of knowing anything about our destination."[25]

An impatient Grant, himself under fire with Sherman as they took refuge in a nearby house and even wading into the Federal forces when a slight withdrawal occurred, wanted matters to progress faster than they were. As the batteries deployed, he penned a quick note to McPherson right after noon, informing him of Sherman's progress and initial meeting with the enemy and asking for a report of matters on the left. Then he added, in obvious nervousness but also impatience: "We must get Jackson or as near it as possible to-night."[26]

"The rain-storm which had been falling during the morning now increased in violence," Major Francis C. Deimling of the 10th Missouri explained amid Crocker's force on the Clinton Road. "We laid down in the mud and dodged cannonballs," an Indianan added. And the rain continued to pour as Crocker deployed his brigades and slogged forward slowly, the leading cavalry moving to secure the flanks and make contact with Sherman farther to the south. "The whole line advanced in a heavy rain," brigade commander Holmes explained, "and under a severe fire of artillery and skirmishers to within 500 yards of the enemy's main line." Major Deimling described the advance as "over two ridges, and formed under the crest of a third ridge." There, Crocker halted and re-formed his lines behind the last ridge "preparatory to the final charge," Sanborn's regiments particularly taking a heavy fire south of the road while deployed in the "newly ploughed cornfields heavy with recent rains." Sanborn in fact wrote that "the troops were more exposed to the enemy's artillery fire than was at first apprehended," and he had to rearrange his deployment slightly to get under cover of the ridge before they pushed forward across the top "in perfect line at a run." Meanwhile the artillery deployed in rear at the Mann House ridge, near a cotton gin. With the Confederate skirmishers in the last ravine pushing the Federals back slightly, orders soon went out to fix bayonets. The time for the attack had arrived.[27]

McPherson wrote that "the rain having partially ceased, at 11 o'clock the advance was ordered." Heavy skirmishers fanned out in front of the deployed Union line, and Crocker pushed his brigades forward toward the main Confederate line up on the ridge on which the Wright House sat. It was, according to Surgeon Silas Trowbridge, "the prettiest display of military maneuvers I ever beheld." One Indianan described the "Hoosier yell" that attended the advance "as our boys came out in full view of the enemy with colors proudly flying." But up ahead was the main Confederate line, McPherson describing it as "stretching across the main road, his right holding a piece of woods, and his center and left commanding rolling ground in his front, over which it would be necessary to pass to attack him." The center on the road was at the farmhouse. He added, "two batteries were in position, one covering the road and the other near his left, having a good range across the open field." The Confederate infantry was a little farther down the slope of the ridge in the ravine in front.[28]

The main attack began around 11:00 a.m., but Gregg reported the enemy advance as "very cautious and slow," he describing the reason as the fire of Captain James A. Hoskins's Mississippi Battery and Colquitt's troops as well as Farquharson's show to the north. McPherson conversely laid the blame on the series of ridges his men had to cross, one "filled with willows." The skirmishers pushed on nevertheless even amid the still "pelting rain," until they could not advance any more, when they were recalled to their regiments and a general order to assault went out. "It was responded to with cheers and determination," McPherson reported; "not a man faltered." The Federals advanced through the last ravine, driving the Confederates out, and began to ascend the ridge itself on which the main Confederate battle line and guns stood: "Drove the enemy out of the ravine at the point of the bayonet, and charged gallantly up the hill." Brigade commander Sanborn boasted that "this charge was one of the most splendid battle scenes that could ever be witnessed."[29]

The fighting was hard in some areas, particularly along the road itself where Holmes's brigade took the vast majority of the casualties that day. McPherson himself was there with a staff officer under heavy fire, a cannonball going right between them. "How he escaped death is beyond my comprehension," another staffer admitted, but McPherson remained at the top of the ridge looking through his field glasses despite several artillery shells landing far too close for comfort. Division commander Crocker reported the enemy let loose "the most galling fire," and Holmes's three regiments, the 17th Iowa on the left of the road and the 80th Ohio and then 10th Missouri on the right, moved forward against Colquitt's Confederates. Colonel David B. Hillis of the 17th Iowa on the left of the road confronted the 24th South Carolina in the ravine to the west of the Wright House, he describing the "heavy underbrush." South Carolina Lieutenant Colonel Ellison Capers had a horse shot from under him and then himself was wounded during the confrontation. Hillis described the "bayonet charge at a double-quick, breaking the enemy's line and pressing him up and over the crest of the next hill." He added that "the principal loss sustained was while charging the enemy down the ravine, where my left wing, being unsupported, was exposed to a severe cross-fire from the right of the enemy's line." In the midst of the fighting, Captain Littleton W. Huston of the 17th Iowa, though terribly wounded in the forearm, took a gun from a Confederate and captured three of the enemy, marching them back with him to the hospital.[30]

Similarly, in the 10th Missouri to the right, Major Deimling noted that "the troops moved forward at double-quick, cheering wildly, driving in first the enemy's skirmishers and then their main line, passing over about 500 yards, under a terrific fire of shell, canister, and musketry, to the house of O. P. Wright, in and behind which, and the hedges, fences, and trees surrounding it, the rebels were hidden and protected." At the head was Color Sergeant Calvin R. Lingle, who, "though weakened by disease, displayed undaunted courage," his commander reported. He added that "here ensued an almost hand-to-hand conflict with the Twenty-fourth Regiment South Carolina Volunteers, the Tenth Missouri suffering severely from the streams of fire which issued from behind every object which could furnish a protection to the enemy."[31]

Over in Sanborn's brigade farther to the right, the 59th Indiana on the extreme right flank watched carefully for any enemy flanking movement, but it participated in the attack when nothing emerged on the flank. "The whole line," Sanborn reported, "with banners unfurled went forward at double-quick and with more regularity than at an ordinary battalion drill." To the Indianans' left was the 48th Indiana and then the 18th Wisconsin and 4th Minnesota, one of whom related that they "had a number of Bayonet charges driving the Rebels straight along." A portion of this line fronted a cotton gin, and Sanborn watched the enemy "throwing out white handkerchiefs at every window and over every cotton bale." It was, he said, "a scene that can never be effaced from the mind of any who witnessed it, and can never be properly represented on paper."[32]

Enduring the least amount of fighting and casualties was George Boomer's brigade on the left of the division. He formed his men in two lines, the 5th Iowa on the front right and 93rd Illinois on the left. In the second line, the 10th Iowa and 26th Missouri supported the front line units. Colonel Holden Putnam explained that he and his 93rd Illinois "moved forward as ordered, receiving a scattering volley from the enemy, who were immediately routed by our skirmishers and fled in confusion." One Illinoisan noted they "drove them like chaff in the wind." One of the members told a different story; the first shot they received was a cannonball that made the entire regiment dodge "like a lot of ducks, very much to the amusement of the old regiments who had seen such before." Still, one Federal summed up that the Confederates "can't stand cold steel."[33]

McPherson related that "the enemy did not wait to receive the full force of the charge, but broke and fled precipitately, followed by our troops." An Indianan added that "the dismayed rebels were fleeing in every direction." Crocker rushed forward MacMurray's guns as well as the following 6th Wisconsin Battery under Captain Henry Dillon. As the Confederates made a stand at their entrenchment line farther back, the two batteries "were wheeled into the first advantageous position, and opened a well-directed and effective fire upon the retreating enemy." The infantry was also corralled and re-formed, having "become somewhat broken marching over the rough ground."[34]

By about 3:00 p.m., while the infantry re-formed, skirmishers moved ahead to locate and reconnoiter the new Confederate line at the entrenchments. The two batteries followed, pouring into the fleeing Confederates "an effective and destructive fire." But Confederate artillery was also firing from the entrenchments, the Federals stopping at "the brow of a hill in front of the earthworks on the outskirts of Jackson." Crocker related that "it was supposed that he would make a stand in his works before Jackson," but then to everyone's surprise the skirmishers came back and reported that the enemy fortifications were empty. McPherson immediately ordered Stevenson's brigade of Logan's division to proceed quickly cross-country to take and sever the road north out of Jackson, hoping to bottle up the withdrawing Confederates, while the remainder of the troops pushed on into the capital itself. Stevenson was unable to do so, and Logan later admitted that "my command was not engaged that day," although the 45th Illinois deployed in a farmyard with numerous beehives that some bullets struck, causing several of the companies to withdraw: "Men can stand up and be shot at, all day, with the deadly musket, but when a swarm of bees pounces upon a company of men in concert," one of the Illinoisans admitted, "it's beyond human nature to stand it, and so two or three companies retired from the field." Conversely, Crocker's brigades triumphantly strode toward Jackson, the 5th Iowa of Boomer's brigade soon approaching the railroad depot. The whole captured some of the Confederate artillery left behind "in great confusion," managing to put out the fires that threatened to engulf the precious ammunition in the limbers and claiming "the honor of having first entered the works and taken possession of the guns." He explained that the troops "advanced into their works and into town without further resistance." Some fortunate ones who entered Jackson found the Confederates' "untasted dinner . . . standing ready cooked, and was very unceremoniously disposed of by men . . . as they came over the works in line of battle and rushed through the camp." Others found that cotton bales made fine beds, "their uniforms next morning bearing evidence that they had 'been in the cotton.'"[35]

After the fighting, Crocker's soldiers took stock of their victory. One Indianan claimed the glory of capturing the enemy artillery for the 59th and 48th Indiana but agreed that "the charge was a most brilliant affair and those who saw it in the distance describe it as grand in the extreme. I only know it was glorious to be in it—every other sense and feeling was absorbed in the excitement of the onset & the glory of the result." One jubilant Missourian even asked an Irish member of his regiment what he thought of the fight. He responded without pause: "I've seen worse difficulties than that in the Old Country with sticks and bricks, but not so many got kilted!"[36]

With the fresh sounds of battle to the left, Sherman also began to press forward on his front. The coordination came as a result of the sounds as well as the cessation of the rain. But the men were tired, brigade commander Matthies relating that "the most drenching rain, which poured down on our men and flooded the roads, made this . . . march very fatiguing." Still, the thought of battle and the sounds of the guns to the left enlivened the troops, and Matthies added that "the men felt cheerful."[37]

To counter the enemy artillery firepower, the division's two batteries also took position "on commanding ground," Captain Allen C. Waterhouse's Battery E, 1st Illinois Artillery on the left with Matthies's men and Lieutenant Joseph R. Reed's 2nd Iowa Battery guns soon giving the Confederates all they could stand from the right side of the road despite shells landing in and among them, taking off tree limbs all around. Indeed, reserve brigade commander Ralph Buckland explained that the enemy's batteries were "served with admirable precision," and one Illinois cannoneer admitted that the enemy "made some splendid shots but we returned their fire with compound interest." Lieu-tenant Reed explained that "I succeeded in getting a commanding position, and engaged the enemy briskly for twenty minutes." Several casualties oc-curred amid the Federal regiments and batteries at this point, Colonel Thomas of the 93rd Indiana describing how his men "suffered considerably from the shells. . . . They were exploding incessantly for over an hour." It was the first hostile fire the Indianans had ever endured.[38]

With the heavy artillery fire from the south and the Federals approaching Lynch Creek, at times moving even at the double-quick to take advantage of some timber, Martin's Confederate artillerymen packed up and withdrew after only about thirty minutes, giving Sherman the crossing without much of a fight. But that still did not make the creek-crossing much easier, Sher-man writing that "the stream, owing to its precipitous banks, could only be passed on the bridge, which the enemy did not attempt to destroy." As soon as the Confederate artillery fell back toward the city fortifications, holding at first an intermediate position in a patch of woods just in front of them but then moving into them fully a little later, the infantry began to cross in the slow and methodical passage at the bridge bottleneck. Buckland reported the "ravine . . . proved to be deeper than was supposed." Still, soon both front-line brigades were across; Mower deployed his men on the left of the road and Matthies on the right. Buckland and the two artillery batteries likewise moved up to new positions despite being under fire while the Confederates in the city's entrenchments poured into the advancing Federal force. By now, quite a conglomeration of Confederate artillery manned the fortifications, a total of fourteen guns, although only four were regular Confederate pieces of Martin's Georgia Battery. The others were hodgepodge Mississippi State Troops.[39]

With his men covered by the same woods the Confederates had inhabited just before, Sherman took stock of the developing situation. The Confeder-ates made "another stand, and obstinately disputed our farther progress," one of Mower's colonels reported. The fight here lasted around an hour, although it was mostly artillery fire. The Confederate artillery was still producing "a pretty brisk fire" from the line of fortifications, but as Sherman gazed to the flanks he could not see any activity. "As we emerged from the woods, to our front and as far to the left as we could see, appeared a line of entrenchments," he explained. Wanting to know how strongly they were manned, Sherman called forward his engineer, Captain Julius Pitzman, and told him to take a regiment of Buckland's reserve brigade and move to the right to see if the fortifications were defended to the east. Pitzman took the 95th Ohio and moved out, while more and more troops arrived in rear, namely Steele's entire division. Sherman had plenty of troops gathering but wanted to know more of what he faced before utilizing them. The Ohioans accordingly moved "on a detour to the right to see what was there."[40]

Sherman soon had his answer. The Ohioans under Colonel William L. McMillen deployed a company as skirmishers and moved forward. McMillen explained that "we advanced to the right of our line until we struck the New Orleans Railroad, and then along that road toward the city, taking possession of a rebel camp and a long line of rifle-pits, both of which we found deserted." McMillen added, "here I formed in line, and planted my colors in full view of the city." He also learned "from a negro who came to me" that the Confederates had evacuated the city, all except those still firing on Tuttle to the west.[41]

Captain Pitzman returned to Sherman about 1:00 p.m. and reported that he had entered the city's defenses at the railroad, and there were no Confederates to be seen. Apparently, the only resistance was on Sherman's front itself. Pitzman had left the Ohioans at the point where the railroad crossed the entrenchments and returned to report, and Sherman sent the entirety of Steele's arriving division "into Jackson by that route." One of his Iowans quipped that "we went in to Jackson and the Rebs went out at the other side."[42]

By this point in the afternoon most of the Confederates had withdrawn, and the artillery on the lower road was left as sacrificial lambs for the others; Grant assumed that they were "instructed to do so, with the expectation of being captured in the end." And they fulfilled their duty, remaining long enough to delay Tuttle but falling to the wide-turning Ohioans who beat Steele to the glory. Guided by the slave, the 95th Ohio moved on and shifted westward, where they came in rear of the Confederate artillery. "I moved my regiment rapidly through a street in the suburbs and gained its rear," Colonel McMillen explained. The regiment formed a line and advanced in rear of the battery. Their brigade commander Buckland, left back as a reserve, was able to crow at last that the Ohioans "found the enemy's rifle-pits unoccupied, and thereupon marched into the city and to the rear of the enemy's batteries, taking them by surprise." The regiment captured a captain, five lieutenants, and about a hundred and fifty men, not to mention nine or ten guns. Even better, Buckland bragged that "the Ninety-fifth Ohio had the honor of being the first to enter the capital of Mississippi."[43]

The men of Tuttle's division could hear the roar of cheering to the east, and Sherman likewise sent them forward, only to find that the Ohioans of Buckland's brigade had already done in the Confederate position. But there was still some nervousness and confusion, as Henry Seaman explained: "Here was a mystery, within thirty rods of the enmeys rifle pits and he don't open upon us with either musketry or artillery. Could it be possible that the enemy had evacuated those extensive works so admirably adapted to defense?" Lieutenant Reed's Iowa battery even threw a few shells into the earthworks but was soon stopped by Tuttle himself. Colonel Hubbard of the 5th Minnesota explained that "all supposing we were about to assault the enemy's works in our front, with bayonets fixed and with exultant shouts the line moved forward at a run." He added: "It was soon discovered, however, that the enemy had evacuated, and that the charge would be a bloodless one." Skirmishers of the 8th Iowa of Matthies brigade soon met the 95th Ohio up ahead. The rest of Tuttle troops and Steele's followed but were too late to do anything besides enter the fortifications with great cheers: "Shouts and yells were sent up—along our entire lines as we advanced." One 8th Wisconsin soldier in Mower's brigade noted that "it was rush between our . . . troops to see which would get over the enemys works first, although we had been marching all morning through mud six inches deep."[44]

The Confederates had indeed evaporated after what Gregg described as a defense in a "spirited manner." Still, quite a few prisoners and several guns fell to the men of the XV Corps. Nevertheless, as the troops entered, "we sent up such a shout that woke up the old town, and gave notice to Gen. Grant that we were in the Capital City of Mississippi."[45]

Colonel Gabriel Bouck of the 18th Wisconsin was short and concise in his report of Jackson: "Gave them battle and whipped them." Others elaborated on the effect, Major Luther Cowan of the 45th Illinois describing the adulation upon entering town: "The victory was ours. The rebels licked, running as usual or captured. This with us was a time when we must win. A defeat would have been most ruinous." An Indianan related that "I guess Genl Joe Johnston concluded that he hadn't got us yet exactly where he wanted to." In an ironic twist, rumors flew fast and rapid on this and in the ensuing days that Richmond itself had fallen to the Federals in Virginia. Obviously false, it was nevertheless true that one of the Confederacy's state capitals, that of the Confederate president no less, had indeed fallen.[46]

Yet the reason there was such an easy entry into the Jackson defensive fortifications was because the bulk of the Confederate force had already left. Around 2:00 p.m., Gregg received the hoped-for news that Adams had the wagon train "already on their way." He could now withdraw his force from the Federals and evacuate as well, and he sent word to his commanders to break contact and withdraw. Colonel Colquitt related that "at 2 p.m., in conformity with orders, I withdrew the brigade," although insisting that "not a man having receded an inch, and having resisted successfully the column of the enemy." Gregg similarly later wrote of his troops "not having permitted the enemy to press them back at any point until the order was given," which was not totally true, but he nevertheless gave the orders for the infantry commands to move out. He reported the different brigades "behaved with the most determined coolness and courage" while Colquitt's and Walker's troops "moved through the streets of Jackson and came into their proper places from the different roads without interference with the movements of each other." That said, Walker was livid that no more attempt had been made to fight: "I know I couldn't hold the place, but I did want to kill a few more of the rascals." To the north across Town Creek, Farquharson moved cross-country to the Canton Road and joined the column, and Thompson's command from the southern defense brought up the rear. It was all done in "excellent order," Gregg added, although one Tennessean admitted that he looked back and "saw a column of black smoke rising over the city, caused by the burning of the ordnance stores. I couldn't help a feeling of pity for the helpless women and children, though the citizens had shown us very little sympathy on a previous visit." Left behind, of course, was Martin's artillery conglomeration to take Federal attention down on the southern lengths of the line, and most of those guns were soon sacrificed to the enemy to allow the rest to escape. Gregg gave Martin credit, however, writing that the guns were "well served."[47]

Despite the evacuation, it was done in a successful way; even Union staff officer James H. Wilson admitted that "the evacuation of the town by Rebels [was] handsomely done." But it left the citizens defenseless, one Tennessean describing their excitement amid the Union arrival as well as the convicts at the penitentiary being set loose. He even mentioned how "as we marched out by the lunatic asylum, the inmates were scattered about the premises in a confused manner." Federal troops accordingly flooded into the city, one relating that they "took possession with great cheering." Fearing that their city would be destroyed, Jackson citizens "came out with the white flag offering to surrender the place." With the way open into Jackson, there was a free-for-all among those who wanted to get to the statehouse first and raise the Union flag over the capitol. Several groups raced for the distinction, including Sylvanus Cadwallader and Fred Grant, who surged ahead intent on gaining the honor. Fred later explained that "the Confederate troops passed me in their retreat," but he was so mud-covered that no one paid him any attention. But the dissatisfaction was real when they arrived too late: "To say that our disappointment was extreme but mildly expresses the state of our feelings." Fred nevertheless looked around the capitol building, wandering into the governor's office and finding a nice pipe, which he "confiscated . . . , primarily and ostensibly for the National service, but secondarily and actually, for my own private and individual use." He added that "it had the advantage of being still loaded and lighted."[48]

The first Federals into the city were actually by order of McPherson himself, who told Colonel Sanborn to send a flag to the capitol building and raise it. Crocker sent his staff officer Captain Cornelius Cadle and Sanborn's assistant adjutant general Captain Lucien B. Martin to do the job, and Martin rode up to the 59th Indiana "and asked for the colors." Colonel Jesse I. Alexander explained: "I ordered them given to him, when he placed our colors on the dome of the capitol, where they remained in charge of my color-guard, whom I had ordered to guard them till next morning." He added: "They were the first and only colors planted on the capitol of Jackson." Cadle and Martin had ridden far ahead of the skirmishers to do so, and one Wisconsin soldier noted that "I wish you could have heard the shouts as the flag went up"; even the 8th Wisconsin's eagle "Old Abe" was enthused: "Our eagle, flopped his wings and looked as if he would like to say 'Bully for us.'" Others performed similar though less dramatic feats. Sanborn aide Lieutenant James H. Donaldson rode to the penitentiary and "seized there a Confederate flag, made of double silk, that a cavalry company had apparently abandoned in its flight." It bore the name "Claiborne Rangers," and was emblazoned "Our Rights" on the other side. Another place seized was not as joyous: "We [also] captured a smallpox hospital and its inmates. We didn't want it, you may be sure, for everybody kept at a respectful distance from it."[49]

"We then marched into the town without further opposition," division commander Tuttle explained, and brigade commander Sanborn added that they entered "unmolested by a shot." "Each individual man seemed to feel it to be the proudest day of his life," Colonel Hubbard of the 5th Minnesota related, "as the old flag of our regiment was unfurled to the breeze in the capital city of the rebel President's own State." He explained further that "even the tattered and faded emblem itself seemed to feel inspired by the occasion, and shook its folds more grandly than ever as a response to the scornful glances of the conquered traitors of this rebellious capital." The Minnesotans and the rest of Mower's brigade took the job of provost guard for the city, camping at the "Capitol Square" and some even within the building itself (the officers took the various state offices for themselves), while the other troops fanned out in good camping spots but soon received orders to man the enemy works for their own defense. Brigade commander Buckland explained how his men were just beginning to dry their clothes, they "having marched most of the day in a drenching rain," and that "this was pretty hard for men who had marched all day in the rain, with very little to eat, the rain still continuing at intervals." He added that "the order was obeyed and submitted to with less complaint than might have been expected under the circumstances." The other troops ranged around the city as well, some camping near the "Deaf and Dumb Asylum." One Iowan described how "by washing my shoes, socks, & pants, and drying myself by a big fire, I managed to get my clothing in a *tolerable* condition by bedtime."[50]

Yet bedlam began almost immediately, despite the provost guards. The 31st Iowa camped in the senate chamber of the statehouse and held a mock session of the legislature in the same house chamber where Mississippi's delegates had passed the ordinance of secession and where Jefferson Davis himself had spoken to the legislature just five months prior. The soldiers passed mock legislation. Other government entities were also affected, including the Institute for the Blind that was "greatly injured by the shot and shell during the investment and bombardment of the city, and [was] entirely destitute of furniture, or movables of any kind"; the Lunatic Asylum was likewise damaged. Individual families also began to suffer, including a "subject of Victoria Queen of Great Britain and Ireland" despite his stated "strict neutrality." A French family also described how "they had been much ill-treated, notwithstanding their French nationality. They showed me their broken furniture, and they assured me that they had been robbed of everything of value." English traveler Arthur Fremantle later described the city as "a miserable wreck" and having "a deplorable aspect."[51]

Part of the confusion and chaos within the Federal ranks also came as a result of the growing problems with supplies and the chance to acquire them here in Jackson. Colonel David B. Hillis of the 17th Iowa wrote that, after encamping in the "suburbs of the city for the night," he "procured a supply of meal and bacon for my boys, who had been for some days on short rations." Major Deimling of the 10th Missouri similarly wrote that "such rations as could be procured were issued to the men." Brigade commander Sanborn explained that "I supplied my command with three days' rations of sugar, bacon, and meal, and some other articles, most of which my quartermaster obtained from the penitentiary." Colonel Holden Putnam of the 93rd Illinois admitted that "the command, being entirely out of provisions, was ordered to forage in the town, and procure three days' subsistence that night." But not all got their fill, one officer relating that his servant "got lost so we had no chance for supper and went to bed with a bite of cracker and coffee begged from the men." And it was not just a lack of food. An Illinoisan explained that "out of rations, many of the men bare-footed, nearly all destitute of blankets, lost them in the last two battles or thrown them away in the hard marches. This is the 20th day of the incessant marching and the fourth fight within this time." Added to the misery were the still-wet clothes from the soaking all had endured the day before and this day. One Illinoisan simply noted in his diary: "We were then very tired wet and hungary." Yet good spirits still prevailed, he adding that "the history of no war in any country presents a case where men have behaved better or shown spirit than has been shown by Grant's army on this occasion throughout. . . . The courage and spirits of the men were not dampened at all. They had marched too far and suffered too much to falter when the enemy was in sight—and the only wish expressed is to be led into the fight."[52]

Despite the issues, Ulysses S. Grant was ecstatic. Mississippi's capital had fallen at a cost of an even three hundred total casualties—the vast majority in Crocker's division and in that unit 215 coming from Holmes's brigade alone. By comparison, the Confederates lost around two hundred. Grant traveled with Sherman and actually came under fire a portion of the time the Confederate battery was in action. He and Sherman had taken refuge from the rain in a "small cottage" in rear of Matthies's brigade, and several shells came uncomfortably close. When it was all over, Grant moved into Jackson as soon as his columns secured the place. In fact, Grant went straight downtown to the statehouse and Bowman Hotel, where he signed the register and was told he would have the same room Johnston had occupied the night before. His headquarters were at the capitol itself, which produced rumors that Governor Pettus had been captured; he had not but had fled eastward. There at the hotel, despite local civilians who almost immediately began to appear to request a guard be placed over their houses, Grant met with McPherson and Sherman and worked out plans for the occupation and destruction of Jackson. He wanted men placed in the Confederate trenches for defense, especially to the west and north where Pemberton and Johnston lurked, and also made plans to destroy the military capacity of the city the next day.[53]

It was at Jackson this afternoon that Grant also received an army-altering message from Washington. Dated May 5, which was obviously too early for a response to his May 3 note that he was not sending troops to Banks, it was a message from Secretary of War Stanton himself to the spook Charles Dana in response to Dana's repeated complaints about John A. McClernand. In fact, the May 5 message had been written the exact same day as one of Dana's messages from Hankinson's Ferry that again mentioned "the exceeding incompetency of General McClernand." Stanton's message (dated May 5 and arrived May 14) stated in full: "General Grant has full and absolute authority to enforce his own commands, and to remove any person who, by ignorance, inaction, or any cause, interferes with or delays his operations. He has the full confidence of the Government, is expected to enforce his authority, and will be firmly and heartily supported; but he will be responsible for any failure to exert his powers. You may communicate this to him." In the midst of an active campaign, Grant obviously did not want to make such a drastic command change as that of the XIII Corps, but he stuck the note in his pocket figuratively if not literally for use in the future if needed.[54]

Grant's ever-working mind was also at full speed on other issues regarding the future. From his headquarters at the Bowman Hotel and statehouse, where Mower's brigade of Tuttle's XV Corps division camped as provost guard (the eagle "Old Abe" perched right in front of the steps to the building), Grant began to realize the larger implications of Jackson's fall. With the Confederates withdrawing to the north and reports of large numbers of Confederates to the west and moving eastward, both of which were true, Grant surmised that the two would seek to join together. McClernand had informed him during the day that "reports are fully ripe that the enemy are in strong force at Edwards Depot; yet, if so, it is surprising that he did not attack my rear yesterday more vigorously than he did." It was a logical assumption, one that many commanders would have made. But this was Pemberton and Johnston he was dealing with, not Robert E. Lee and Stonewall Jackson, and with Davis thrown in for good measure complicating matters as much as he eased them, who knew what exactly would happen? But Grant had to move on the most logical assumptions and with Jackson now in his hands he began to make the shift, even on the evening of May 14, back to the west toward Vicksburg: "Face their troops toward Bolton," Grant ordered.[55]

Confirmation of what he should do came with the arrival of a Confederate courier who purposefully brought Johnston's May 13 attack message to McPherson's headquarters. Johnston had sent three different couriers with the same message westward to Pemberton to assure that at least one got to him, but it also increased the possibility of one falling into enemy hands. One of the riders was a Union spy that Hurlbut had earlier publicly banished from Memphis on false pretenses, and he chose this opportunity to make his break. Grant then knew Johnston wanted Pemberton to attack from the west, and Fred related that the news "caused some activity at headquarters."[56]

"It is evidently the design of the enemy to get north of us and cross the Black River and beat us into Vicksburg," Grant wrote McClernand late on May 14 while informing him of Jackson's capture and the enemy withdrawal to the north. "We must not allow them to do this." Accordingly, he ordered McClernand to "frustrate the design": "Turn all your forces toward Bolton Station, and make all dispatch in getting there. Move troops by the most direct road from wherever they may be on the receipt of this order." He also assured him that McPherson and Sherman would be along to support him, and McPherson ordered his cavalry, the 6th Missouri under Colonel Clark

Wright, to explore to the north of the railroad: "Learn of their movements on your front and right flanks, and report. Be prompt and earnest."[57]

McClernand's troops were by this point concentrated around Raymond, where the locals were none too eager to deal with this most recent wave of Federals. The soldiers even took over the town newspaper and printed the latest edition, presumably with news favorable to them. One staff officer wrote of trying to buy goods from one lady in town, but "she turned on her heel in a very austere manner and left, would not take my money. I took the goods and more, too, anyhow." And it was happening all across the board, even down where Stone's and Blair's troops were leading the wagon trains northward. An Ohioan related that he happened up on a house near Cayuga and found soldiers in the process of taking nearly everything one woman had. He apparently did nothing to stop the looting but remarked to his sister that "she was the first white woman I had spoken to for over four months and only 2 in 7 months[.] What do you think of that, Sallie!" He added, "don't you think we will be very rough and uncouth in the presence of the gentler sex if we ever get home." An Iowan elaborated that "we have little more respect for property on this march than on former ones. Still we forage all we want and some soldiers take many things that are useless to them."[58]

McClernand consequently became the van of the army immediately, moving troops westward toward hopefully the climactic battle of the campaign. Hovey at Clinton, tasked with breaking the rail line and dealing with reports of Wirt Adams's cavalry at Bolton ("if you can pounce upon him and catch him, do so"), was to move westward to Bolton. The other divisions were to move in that direction as well, Grant initially thinking of a one-avenue advance along the Jackson Road and railroad toward Edwards Station. Osterhaus, who reached Raymond in the night, was to proceed northward to join Hovey, as was Carr, who had moved eastward in support of Sherman all the way to Mississippi Springs and beyond at Forest Hill Church. One of his soldiers admitted that the march "today will ever be memorable as one of the most disagreeable in my soldier life," and another mentioned bodies of Confederate dead still on the field at Raymond two days later. A. J. Smith to the south at Dillon's was to move toward Edwards if possible, otherwise to Bolton as well, cooperating with the other divisions and still covering the rear where the supply trains were approaching. McClernand, in the van and headed evidently for a fight, appeared well pleased: "Everything seems to be going on well," he advised Grant.[59]

Those concerning supply trains were indeed coming on, but slowly. The dusty roads that had plagued them initially now turned to mud, a different type of encumbrance. Both met awful roads in their marches, one Illinoisan on the route initially explaining in his diary that "the dust & heat are unendurable it is the hotest day I ever saw." But then another of the 25th Iowa with the lead train, John N. Bell, described how they faced "a very heavy shower of rain and then had to stand long intervals in the rain. The mud became almost impossible to get through and rained all day. . . . Got completely wet through twice today."[60]

And the jockeying for position did not help. Still outranked, Colonel Stone finally had to yield to Blair's train and troops, getting a late start on May 14 while Blair rushed ahead; one 57th Ohio soldier noted "Gen Blair and staff passing." But then more orders arrived from Grant himself telling Stone to "hurry up with the provisions," so Stone moved ahead as well and actually passed Blair's train once more, taking the lead again. The entire leapfrogging column made several more miles that day, passing Dillon's and gaining the cover of Smith's division nearby. Also oncoming were Ransom's troops, a day behind the others but making up time without the baggage of a wagon train to slow them down. They even took a different route to get by the slow-moving trains on the Port Gibson to Raymond road, following McPherson's path through Utica, although that route was just as muddy now with the heavy rains as any of the others. One Illinoisan noted that the rain "made roads very muddy and deep," but some fun was at least had; while passing through Cayuga, another Illinoisan added that "boys got into a secret society lodge, and decorated them-selves in gay style."[61]

Still, Grant seemed to be pulling off a near miracle, operating in the enemy's country, between two enemy forces, and with a very delicate supply line, if even that. But he was glad that at least some supplies were nearing, staff officer Wilson remarking in his diary the relief on May 14 when "report from Blair and wagon-train favorable." Others thought so as well. While not complete by any stretch of the imagination, and still seeking the determining battle of the campaign for Vicksburg, many thought their work heretofore was well done. James McPherson even issued a congratulatory order for the XVII Corps from Jackson on May 14: "Soldiers of the Seventeenth Army Corps! Your general congratulates you on your noble endurance and heroic bravery. . . . Your general is proud of you. Your country honors you, and will remember you and your deeds with gratitude and exultation." But he also reminded them that the task was not yet quite accomplished: "The enemy is still active, though defeated. Let us press him and crush him, till one nationality is ours, and one flag alone, the flag of our fathers, floats over American soil and protects American people."[62]

13

"Gen'l Pemberton Looked as If He Was Confused"

May 15

Major Luther Cowan was in a reflective mood in the wee hours of the morning of May 15. He was awake, sitting by the campfire watching his men sleep around him. He scribbled in his diary his feelings: "I am so full of conflicting thoughts, emotions and cares to sleep, anxious for the future, grateful for the past. Thankful that so many of us are able to stand the hardships of our hard marches and so favored as to escape wounds of death on the battlefield. So I sit here alone trying to think, hardly knowing whether I do or not." He went on: "Hardly know whether it is Lute Cowan 'as went to war' or if it is some new being in some other world. But from my fidgety anxiety and multitude of cares, I guess it is the same old Lute."[1]

If Cowan was not changed much, certainly the context he was in had been changing quite a bit recently. On the most basic level, the rain from the previous two days worked wonders in breaking the oppressive heat: "The heavy rain of night before last and yesterday tended to cool the atmosphere to such a degree, that it is delightful in the extreme," wrote Henry Seaman in his diary on May 15. But in a larger context, warfare itself was also changing. Certainly, the campaign itself was ever-adapting, but warfare itself was also mutating in the largest context of all. Even at the midpoint of 1863, the Civil War had not yet turned primeval, certainly not like it would later in 1864 with the true advent of "total war." At this point in the war's progression, damage and destruction were no doubt seen, sometimes on large scales. This very summer would see the destruction of privately owned entities in the North in the Gettysburg Campaign, as had been seen in Virginia for a couple of years. Even here in the Vicksburg Campaign, ravaging of private dwellings had been common at specific times and with specific commanders, such as on the initial marches of the Mississippi Central Campaign in October and November 1862 and even in Louisiana during the long, wet winter of 1863. Yet there was a distinct change beginning to take place, even here in May 1863 in Mississippi, that would be much more akin to the "hard war" policies of the 1864 Meridian Campaign or the March to the Sea than to the earlier destruction that was mostly individual, isolated, and unauthorized.[2]

Much of the destruction earlier in the war had been at the hands of individuals who took it upon themselves to torch a building or rob a family. Certainly, plenty of examples existed, even in this current campaign when civilians had fled to Vicksburg or elsewhere, one woman declaring ironically: "Ah! Vicksburg, our city of refuge." But the official Union military position was to treat all civilians with grace and to limit the destruction to military targets. And even that was sporadically utilized even while punishment for the private acts of pillage mostly went unpunished, although a few examples of such penalties do exist. But it is clear that, apart from a little railroad-wrecking, the Union authorities did little earlier in the war to destroy whole areas even of military targets. In fact, few if any towns' military assets were wholesale destroyed, much less entire towns themselves. Corinth certainly had not been destroyed, and the towns and cities along the Mississippi Central Railroad during the early stages of the Vicksburg Campaign had not been either. Grand Junction, La Grange, Holly Springs, Oxford, and others dodged the fate of Union torches early in the war if not later on, and when towns were damaged, it was normally by Confederates such as Van Dorn at Holly Springs or Nathan Bedford Forrest on his raid into West Tennessee.[3]

Even into April and May 1863 a certain reserve was maintained here in Mississippi, although Grierson's Raid did manage to destroy military targets such as the railroads of the state and various depots, most famously Newton Station. But there were strict orders, and some punishment, if private dwellings or resources were damaged, Benjamin Grierson himself manning the buckets in an attempt to douse fires that spread to privately owned dwellings or buildings. And Grant himself would have none of the famed Yankee destruction on his march northward from Bruinsburg. Port Gibson residents liked to argue that Grant said their little town was too beautiful to burn, but the truth was that Grant burned none of the towns he marched through, including Rocky Springs, Cayuga, Utica, Raymond, Clinton, and Bolton. Grant simply did not find anything of major military value in them to warrant destruction.[4]

But that changed when he took Jackson on May 14. "Long gone were the old days when Grant sternly forbade his men to trespass on civilian property or to take civilian goods," reflected historian Bruce Catton. One Ohioan who marveled at the local civilians who in turn marveled at the number of Federals and called them all Yankees ("of course they do not know the meaning of the term, but apply it to all Union soldiers") simply noted that "the South must suffer, but out of that suffering will come wisdom." There were obviously militarily viable targets in Mississippi's capital, and Grant wanted them destroyed. And he ordered them torched, for many reasons. But in doing so he still wanted the destruction limited to military targets, and Jackson would indeed see much more destruction later in the "total war" phase of the conflict. Unfortunately for residents there, the city had four more times to be captured and punished during the remainder of the war when it gained its sobriquet "Chimneyville." But the city started to earn that nickname in May 1863.[5]

"Commence immediately the effectual destruction of the river railroad bridge and the road as far east as practicable, as well as north and south," Grant's orders to Sherman read on the evening of May 14. The destruction of the state capital, in terms of military assets, was to begin at first light, and Sherman prepared well. It would be up to him how to do it, Grant's orders only furthermore mentioning a brigade detailed to act as provost to guard the city and the 4th Iowa Cavalry and an infantry brigade sent east of the Pearl River to damage the rail line as far as possible.[6]

The overseer of the destruction would be Joe Mower, brigade commander in Tuttle's division, who would designate a provost and see to the work. The nerve center would be at the statehouse, upon which grounds Mower's brigade camped. Actually performing the destruction were the men of the two XV Corps divisions, Sherman detailing Steele's troops to be responsible for the rail lines to the east and south, the New Orleans, Jackson, and Great Northern line to the south and the Southern Railroad moving across the Pearl River and eastward toward Meridian. Tuttle's troops took the Southern Railroad running westward and the Great Northern line to the north as their target. "The destruction of the roads will be extended out as far as possible, and must be complete," Sherman added. "The rails and ties will be taken up and placed in stacks, and the ties set on fire, in order to warp the rails and so render them unfit for use." He added, "dispatch is of the utmost importance."[7]

"On May 15 began the work of destruction," one Federal wrote in his diary. "All railroads for miles were torn up. All bridges, factories, in short everything that belonged to the Confederacy was wrecked." The work began at daylight on May 15 and continued all day. "The boys went for everything in the town," one Missourian explained, "and destroyed almost all the public buildings and tore up the railroads and bent the iron, and burnt all the bridges." For the most part it went smoothly, although Sherman had to jump in and rectify a few complaints that filtered in. "It is represented to me that the provost marshal is giving license to soldiers to take the contents of stores," Sherman wrote Mower, "taking things not necessary or useful." He added: "This, if true, is wrong. Only such articles should be taken as are necessary to the subsistence of troops, and the private rights of citizens should be respected." In concluding he wrote to "please give the matter your attention. The feeling of pillage and booty will injure the morals of the troops, and bring disgrace on our cause."[8]

Meanwhile, the troops worked on the rail lines, Tuttle's two brigades (Mower's on provost duty in Jackson itself) working on the west and north: Ralph Buckland's troops on the Southern Railroad westward, and Charles Matthies's on the New Orleans, Jackson, and Great Northern to the north. Matthies reported that "I moved with my brigade 5 miles on the railroad leading north out of Jackson, and destroyed 3 miles of that road so thoroughly that every tie was burned and every rail bent, so it will require new material to put that part of the road in operation again." Buckland noted that "we had not a tool of any description, and could procure none from the provost-marshal." He borrowed four axes from a nearby artillery battery and later stumbled on an abandoned Confederate camp where he found "five or six axes and as many picks, and with these we commenced the work of destruction."[9]

The 12th Iowa managed to find something good to eat as well. Working near "the splendid residence of the late Brigadier General [Richard] Griffith, C.S.A.," the Iowans spotted several "grayback geese belonging to the forces of the said General Griffith." The men had a trial; "their uniforms proved them enemies, and they were condemned to be executed." David Reed noted that one company report read "full rations of goose and enough left over for tomorrow."[10]

At the same time, Steele's brigades concentrated on the lines east and south of town. Colonel Charles Woods explained that he crossed the Pearl River and destroyed the line to the east "by tearing up the track and burning the iron on piles of ties. Some 5 miles of track were destroyed, including the large bridge across Pearl River, twenty barrels of tar being placed upon it and fired." Several other major bridges and trestle work were also hit. In all, Sherman estimated the rail line destruction extended "4 miles east of Jackson, 3 south, 3 north, and 10 west." One of John Thayer's Iowans noted that the work never stopped: "We have had a pretty tough time since we left Milliken's Bend."[11]

Sherman also wanted the military capacity in the city destroyed, and several mentioned various places damaged or ruined. Woods described "a cotton factory, two foundries, and an extensive work shop, used by the rebels in the manufacture of caissons and gun carriages, together with twelve new caissons, and a large amount of Confederate cotton." Questions arose concerning what to do with the cotton, whether to save it or not. Sherman added to the list an arsenal building as well as "stable, carpenter, and paint shops." But he bemoaned the fact that the state penitentiary also burned, "I think, by some convicts who had been set free by the Confederate authorities." One of the prisoners was a German who went along with the 8th Illinois: "He *cried* with *joy* at our coming." Newspaperman Cadwallader described how the "lurid flames added to the holocaust elsewhere prevailing."[12]

Also burned was the famous cotton factory that Grant described in his memoirs. He left the Bowman Hotel that morning, his staff paying the owner in Confederate money. The proprietor, who had expected to be paid in greenbacks, balked that the charge would be higher if paying with Confederate scrip, as it was much less valuable—the sum was subsequently raised from sixty to ninety dollars. Moving through Jackson, Grant witnessed the destruction, and while doing so he and Sherman soon stumbled on the Green brothers' cotton factory. The brothers Green "made strong appeals," Sherman noted, but Grant and Sherman would not give in, Sherman noting that the machinery would easily be used for "hostile uses." When the argument that the workers' families would be destitute also emerged, Sherman offered for them to "come to the river, where we would feed them till they could find employment or seek refuge in some more peaceful land." Fred related that soon "a column of flame arose that seemed a hundred yards high."[13]

But not all the destruction was ordered: "At Jackson we had a fine old time," an Iowan admitted, and "the soldiers was allowed to take whatever they wanted." Sherman wrote that "other buildings were destroyed in Jackson by some mischievous soldiers (who could not be detected) which was not justified by the rules or war, including the Catholic church and Confederate Hotel—the former resulting from accidental circumstances and the latter from malice." The episode of the Confederate Hotel was especially unique, Sherman writing that "a very fat man came to see me, to inquire if his hotel, a large frame-building near the depot, were doomed to be burned." He argued that he was "a law-abiding Union man," which brought out Sherman's playful side, he pointing out that it was certainly "manifest from the sign of his hotel, which was the 'Confederate Hotel'; the sign 'United States' being faintly painted out, and 'Confederate' painted over it!" The hotel had been used as a meal station on the railroad line, and Union Shiloh prisoners had been rudely denied service there back in 1862. These exchanged prisoners were now back with a conquering army and "quietly and stealthily applied the fire underneath the hotel just as we were leaving the town." Sherman later admitted that, even though Mower patrolled the streets with his brigade and two companies of cavalry and "maintained as much order as he could among the mass of soldiers and camp-followers that thronged the place during our short stay there[,] yet many acts of pillage occurred that I regret, arising from the effect of some bad rum found concealed in the stores of the town." Other entities that could evacuated, such as the Memphis *Appeal* that had been printed in Jackson since the fall of the namesake city. Now, the paper moved out again, its last issue on May 14 entertaining the now-occupying Federals. The Union soldiers also had a lively time with the last issue of the Jackson *Daily Mississippian*, which told its readers that Johnston had arrived the night before and assured them that "he will immediately make such disposition of the troops at his command as to foil all attempts of the Yankees to capture our state capitol."[14]

Common soldiers told a more vivid tale. "Repeated raids were made by the soldiers upon dry goods stores and public buildings—for clothing and other necessary articles of which they stood in need," explained Henry Seaman. "Some of the house breakers chief object was to accumulate plunder and all articles of real value, while others smashed open the doors of dry goods and commissary store houses to see the poor people of the town 'go in and carry off.'" One Missourian admitted that "all stores were plundered, so the niggers and workers had a rich harvest and booty." An Iowan similarly related that the soldiers "gutted the stores notwithstanding the provost marshall and guards." He added that "the citizens look sour or sad. Oh how I wish they would submit to proper authority and end the war." One Illinoisan marveled that "the guards made very feeble effort to prevent [it]," but finally, by eleven o'clock that night, the 4th Iowa Cavalry was ordered to end the looting. "They at once proceeded to do so and with good success, charging up and down with drawn sabres."[15]

But more destruction came as the evening moved on, one Missourian declaring "all is confusion and tumult. The confiscated whiskey is suffering severely and three fourths of the men are drunk." He added, "deliver me from another such place as this." One Wisconsin soldier noted in his diary that "some one started a fire just at dark, and the City is burning, and although every effort is being made to put out the fire it is spreading, and it looks as though the whole City will be destroyed." An Ohioan described burning a large cache of sugar and that "melted sugar or rather burnt taffy ran out knee deep." Another noted that "the Div. is overloaded with trophies from Jackson. Fine clothes of every kind, tobacco, sugar, cigars, horses, buggies, fine coaches, in fact everything imaginable and the quantity destroyed is beyond calculation." One Illinoisan even described the plundering of the Mississippi State Library, many taking volumes they wanted. "I secured a few small volumes such as I could carry conveniently," admitted the soldier, "but saw a good many expensive works that I would have liked, could I have obtained transportation."[16]

Individual families bore the brunt of the destruction, one artilleryman writing in his diary that "the soldiers are ransacking the town to their hearts content. . . . The towns wasted generally." An Illinoisan described the very pro-Confederate Freeman family, whose house was looted. One young lady staying with them was especially vicious, admitting that "it is getting to be a pretty state of things, when a few miserable Black Republicans can come and take the capitol of the State," but assuring her enemies that "we wouldn't be here long: that the terrible General Joseph Johnston would soon be back, and then—not one of us would get out of Mississippi alive." The Illinoisan felt some sorrow for the personal suffering but concluded that "the misfortunes of war could not have fallen where there would be less reason to regret them than in this case."[17]

But it was not just Federal soldiers looting. Henry Seaman continued that

the streets were thronged with the poor class of the town, of both sexes of different ages—the majority however, were females employee's of a large factory which was or had been running for the benefit of the southern army. These women would go into stores after our soldiers had smashed in the doors and load themselves with as much as they could carry away, of calico, shoes, hoop skirts, large bolts of factory cloth, thread and everything imaginable that they usually keep in a dry goods store. They was not content with one load but came again and again. They were the poor class of the town and were unable to procure those goods at the exorbitant prices for which they had been selling. Flour appeared to be a great treat to them all and many among the crowd said they had not tasted wheat flour in over a year. That rich and poore might fare alike the provision stores were thrown open and large quantities of flour taken therefrom and rolled into the street, and such a rush I never before witnessed as made for the flour. Women, children and the free colored population of the town—went home loaded and covered from head to foot with flour.

An Iowan added: "What we did not take with us or give to the poorer class of Mississippians was burnt."[18]

At times, even Mower himself stepped in to stop the pillaging. J. W. Greenman described how "this evening some of the Boys got into the Lodge of the Masons, and soon were decorated with aprons and sashes and Collars, and then started to go out on the street for a parade." The Masonic Hall was in the upper level of Jackson's City Hall, and the Mississippi Secession Convention had actually met there temporarily in January 1861 when it conflicted with the meeting of the legislature in the statehouse. Mower was not in a jovial mood when he heard what happened: "Col. Mower heard of the business and met the Boys just as they came down the stairs from the Lodge room. He ordered the Boys to take everything back and then get out, which was quickly done."[19]

Nevertheless, in preparing an exit strategy, Sherman informed Mower of his goal to leave the next morning by 10:00 a.m. "We will march for Bolton, via Mississippi Springs, to-morrow at noon," he informed Mower, cautioning him to "push the work of destruction, especially of types, presses, sugar, and everything public not needed by us. The work should be all done by 10 a.m. to-morrow." Sherman even reaffirmed that "you must work at night, if necessary, to destroy what might be useful to an enemy" and added that, once Mower brought up the rear the next afternoon, "you may release all prisoners (citizens) whom we don't want to carry along."[20]

Sherman consequently gave his final orders, working out the exit plan after the destruction was "prosecuted with the utmost energy." Work parties were to be in by 11:00 a.m. the next morning, with Steele's division marching out at noon toward Mississippi Springs, Tuttle's brigades following at 1:00 p.m. Mower's brigade would be the rear of the column, departing from the statehouse itself and leaving the state capital a smoking ruin in terms of military effect. Particularly worried about the soldiers burning private entities on their way out, Sherman also advised Mower to "take every possible precaution against fires at the time of our leaving to-morrow." Still, one Illinoisan noted that they "left Jackson Miss in ashes." Of course, McClernand and McPherson would be already moving westward, and Sherman's divisions, now with his third also nearing—Blair's (except Hugh Ewing's brigade that would cross the Mississippi River on May 15 and join the division on May 18) somewhere to the west operating with McClernand for the time being—would take their rightful place within the army's structure hopefully for the climactic battle of the campaign.[21]

By the end of the day on May 15 Sherman was able to say that "this work of destruction was well accomplished, and Jackson, as a railroad center or Government depot of stores and military factories, can be of little use to the enemy for six months." Grant was well satisfied, writing that "this was accomplished in the most effectual manner." One of his soldiers agreed, writing of even throwing artillery into the Pearl River: "Nothing was left which could in the least aid the rebels." But the destruction continued through the night, one Missourian relating that "the night from the 15th to the 16th the beautiful city of Jackson was in bright flames. The sight was terrible." Another added in his diary the next day that "their was considerable burning of 'Confederate' property last night."[22]

By the morning of May 15, matters were spiraling out of control for the Confederates. With the break in the telegraph line, Pemberton and Johnston had no way to quickly and effectively communicate; in fact, messages would run back and forth but would get out of order and cause even more confusion. Communications lagged with the greater Confederacy as well, the news of the defeat at Raymond arriving two days later in Richmond, where one clerk spoke for many that "this is a dark cloud over the hopes of patriots, for Vicksburg is seriously endangered. Its fall would be the worst blow we have yet received." News of the fall of Jackson came quicker, just a day later, prompting the same clerk to acknowledge that Vicksburg "may be doomed to fall at last." If Grant intended anything out of his move to the railroad and breaking communication with Vicksburg, it succeeded, because the Confederate right hand literally did not know what the left was doing during these critical days of mid-May.[23]

That said, there was no shortage of talk, especially from Johnston, who assumed he was in ultimate command and that Pemberton would obey his orders. He had ordered Pemberton earlier to join him and concentrate against the enemy, but unknown to him until now Pemberton had opted not to do so—certainly something very dangerous in military operations. But Johnston continued his barrage of messages. In fact, he wrote from a point about nine or ten miles north of Jackson on the Canton Road at 8:30 a.m. this morning, he dictating to a staff officer in response to Pemberton's explanation of moving against Grant's supply lines: "Your dispatch just received. Our being compelled to evacuate Jackson renders your plan impracticable. Therefore, move in the direction of Clinton, and communicate with me, that I may unite with you with about 6,000 troops." Due to the delay in transit, the message would not arrive at Pemberton's mobile headquarters until early on May 16. In fact, it would arrive prior to his message of the afternoon before.[24]

By this point, however, Pemberton was not planning to meet up with Johnston. His council of war the day before had resulted in a plan that even he himself was not interested in, but he saw it as the lesser of two evils. His heart was still in Vicksburg, but he allowed himself to be talked into the movement against the enemy supply line. As a result, orders went out the evening before for the march southeastward, Wirt Adams's cavalry leading the way, followed by Loring's, Bowen's, and Stevenson's divisions totaling nine brigades. Then would come the army's wagon train and more cavalry in the rear. Pemberton added that "straggling, always disgraceful in an army, is particularly forbidden. Stringent orders will be issued by the division commanders to prevent this evil. The rear guard is especially instructed to permit no one to fall to the rear under any circumstances."[25]

The orders called for a movement on the morning of May 15, but it was early afternoon before it began, some indicating as late as 2:00 p.m. It was "with the view of cutting the enemy's line of communication with his depot of supplies and forcing him to give battle on our own ground," Carter Stevenson explained. But it was not the start that was needed, delayed as it was several hours in even getting on the road. Much of the culprit was shuffling supplies, mainly ammunition, to the army. One Missourian in fact described his time in line of battle at Edwards Station as "without tents and on short rations." Forney in Vicksburg was sending the supplies posthaste by rail, but Pemberton also needed wagons to get them to the army. He took twenty from Vaughn at the Big Black River, to be replaced by those coming out of Vicksburg, and ordered them to Edwards Depot to "take on ammunition here." Pemberton counseled haste, writing Forney that "this army is about to move. . . . This is all-important." But in the chaos Pemberton evidently forgot to mention how many men he needed rations for, prompting Forney to have to ask: "Please let me know for how many men." Pemberton also drew on Vaughn for troops to man Edwards while the main army was away: "The troops are about to move from this depot, and you will send up one regiment to act as an advance guard at Edwards Depot," his orders read.[26]

Due to the odd planning and late start, many Confederates had less confidence than was needed. William Drennan wrote his wife how "I had a fine view of the troops as they passed." He described how "an army in motion is a grand sight, with its long lines of bayonets glistening and flashing in the sun—the rumbling of the artillery and the noise of the trains—all conspire to throw over one a feeling of the greatness and magnificence of war." But he still felt an odd sensation of dread, confiding as well: "Everything being considered, we had nothing to look for but victory—yet I felt gloomy on the event of our starting—and although I could assign no reasonable ground for my fears—yet I had them—and they weighed heavily. That superstition had something to do with my fears, I am candid enough to admit—yet even when I would shake off that feeling—and leave myself free to reason I had an innate feeling that all was not going to turn out well."[27]

Then another major problem developed. As the Confederate army began to lurch out of Edwards Station on the main road to Raymond, leaving sick and stragglers behind, the van of the army suddenly found the bridge over Bakers Creek was out and the creek itself a raging torrent, one Georgian scribbling in his diary: "Heavy rain, creek non-passable." The thunderstorms that plastered the troops at Jackson on the night of May 13 and morning of May 14 had also flooded Bakers Creek, over which passed the Raymond Road Pemberton intended to travel. The bridge on the main road had washed out back in April, Pemberton describing how "the country bridge had been washed away by previous freshets," but now the creek was so high that the adjacent ford could not be used; Jacob Thompson explained that the creek could not be crossed "without swimming." The trouble was that the floodwaters had to recede to be able to repair the bridge or find a new ford, and consequently "the march was delayed for several hours," Pemberton seethed.[28]

It was a classic example of poor planning, scouting, and staff work; one staffer merely mentioned "Bakers Creek reported swimming on the Raymond Road." The Confederate army had been situated around Edwards just a mere mile or two from this very bridge since early on May 13 (and certainly since the orders for the march had gone out on May 14). There was no doubt that very ford would be needed, and there was likewise no missing the heavy rains that pelted this portion of the Confederate army just like it did those in Jackson. But apparently no one thought to check the crossing.[29]

Loring, who seemed to be the only one with staffers out scouting, soon realized there was another crossing farther north on the Jackson Road, and if the army detoured to the north "there was a fair road leading into the road it was intended to take." That would put the army back on track. Pemberton described some of the route as "along a neighborhood road," but it was the only choice Pemberton had other than sitting and waiting.[30]

The route led from the washed-out bridge site on the Raymond Road northward to the next crossing upstream, where the bridge on the Jackson Road still stood despite the torrent. A march eastward on that main thoroughfare would lead to a crossroads near the Roberts family house. A left turn at the crossroads would keep the Jackson Road, which moved up and over a hill on the Champion Plantation and thence on to Bolton, Clinton, and Jackson. But that was not where Pemberton wanted to go, and so a right turn at the crossroads would lead on that "neighborhood road" southward back into the Raymond Road near the Coker family residence. To get from the washed-out bridge site to the Raymond Road where the neighborhood road joined it east of the creek, a mere two miles by the Raymond Road, it took a detour of more than six and a half miles. It was a winding and lengthy detour, but it was about the only option Pemberton had if he was going to get his army moving immediately.[31]

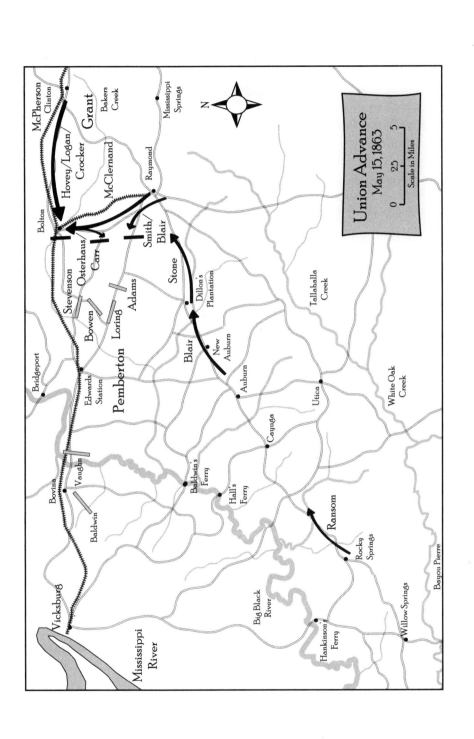

Union Advance
May 15, 1863

Scale in Miles
0   2.5   5

N

McPherson
Clinton
Grant
Bakers Creek
Mississippi Springs

Hovey/Logan/Crocker
Bolton
McClernand
Raymond

Stevenson
Osterhaus/
Carr
Smith/
Blair

Bowen
Loring
Adams
Stone

Pemberton
Dillon's Plantation

Bridgeport
Blair
New Auburn

Edwards Station
Auburn

Tallahalla Creek

Cayuga
Utica
White Oak Creek

Vaughn
Bovina

Baldwin
Baldwin's Ferry

Hall's Ferry

Ransom
Rocky Springs

Vicksburg

Mississippi River

Big Black River

Hankinson's Ferry
Willow Springs

Bayou Pierre

Pemberton gave the order, and Loring, led in advance by Adams's cavalry, moved northward to the Jackson Road and thence eastward to the crossroads and then south past the Roberts' house toward the Raymond Road. The head of the division reached the Raymond Road late in the evening and turned left, moving on the main road across Jackson Creek. At the Sarah Ellison Plantation, Pemberton called a halt to rest his troops around midnight, he making his headquarters at the Ellison House itself, where Loring also made his headquarters, though complaining of "a great scarcity of water." The other divisions stacked up behind Loring, his three brigades all on the Raymond Road but Bowen's division not reaching that far and bivouacking on the neighborhood road itself. Stevenson's division in the rear, still marching early into the morning of May 16 trying to keep pace with the van, was strung out farther to the north up near the crossroads and beyond. The wagon train was even farther behind, even back still on the Jackson Road.[32]

Confusion reigned. "March much confused by bad road and darkness of night," one of Pemberton's staff officers noted in his diary. Lieutenant Drennan's superstitious fears grew worse as the army plodded along that day. "From all that I could gather, those in power knew very little of the movements of the Enemy. I saw no evidences of an organized system of information—no couriers passing to and fro from H'dquarters, no signal corps in operation—nothing that led me to believe that Gen'l Pemberton knew either the number, intentions either real or probable of the Enemy and more than that—not even his exact whereabouts." Drennan was willing to give Pemberton the benefit of the doubt because of the near unwinnable situation he was in, but not all were. "Many were the curses loud and deep that men in all positions poured on Lt. Gen'l Pemberton's devoted head," he added, admitting at the same time that "Gen'l Pemberton looked as if he was confused—and he gave orders in that uncertain manner that implied to me that he had no *matured* plans for the coming battle."[33]

It was a disaster in the making as the exhausted Confederate army lurched to a stop in the wee hours of the night. Pemberton knew as much and issued orders that because the men, "having been on the march until past midnight, and the men considerably fatigued—desiring also to receive reports of reconnaissances made in my front before proceeding farther—I did not issue orders to continue the movement at an early hour the following morning." Pemberton would let his exhausted and on-edge army rest a little before moving on.[34]

But he did take precautions. He sent for Wirt Adams and ordered him to picket "all approaches in my front, and directed him to send out scouting parties to discover the enemy's whereabouts." Pemberton also tried "strenuous efforts" to gather as much information from the local citizens as possible, "but without success," he admitted. Loring had better luck with the civilians, even gleaning information from Mr. Montgomery, who lived near Montgomery's Bridge across Fourteenmile Creek. The man had been confined by the Federals when they took position there a couple days prior but had since been released. Nevertheless, Pemberton amazingly lay down confident that night, later reporting that all seemed well: "Nothing unusual occurred during the night."[35]

"The army is absolutely nomadic," newspaperman Cadwallader wrote home to his wife; "we march and fight alternately." Others picked up on the feeling of wandering and isolation, Charles Dana remarking that the "march toward Jackson proved to be no easy affair," adding that "so complete was our isolation that it was ten days after we left Rocky Springs, on May 11, before I was able to get another dispatch to Mr. Stanton." Still, it all seemed to be part of a larger plan, one Iowan noting on May 15, "we turned our course toward Vicksburg." Another declared the watchword was "On to Vicksburg." Confederates joked that it was the beginning of "Grant's retreat on Vicksburg."[36]

A large part of that nomadic clan consisted of the two wagon trains moving northward. Colonel Stone retook the lead on May 15 and, despite hunger amid plenty (John Bell of the 25th Iowa relating to his diary that "we are now living on 2 crackers per day with a fair prospect of a less quantity soon"), moved on toward Raymond. But the threat of the Confederate surge southeastward, easily detected by McClernand's forces up ahead, caused a delay, and the Iowans even went into line of battle to protect the wagons. "We loaded and waited for reinforcements which came from Blair's Div.," Bell explained. The news of the fall of Jackson arrived about the same time, the men cheering despite their ticklish circumstances. Bell admitted that they "almost desired a Rebel attack to show their willingness to assist in the glorious work." The concern soon lessened, however, and the column moved on to Raymond, passing the battlefield where "our men were yet taking off the Rebel wounded and burying their dead."[37]

The arrival at Raymond was a right of passage that made all feel much safer. There was, after all, two regiments left behind to garrison the town (54th Indiana and 120th Ohio) and to care for the wounded and prisoners. Bell described the arrival at Raymond and how all the buildings, including the courthouse and hotel, were filled with wounded. "Raymond is a tolerably large place of about 600 inhabitants," he explained, and "has a fine Court House." But the column did not remain in town, pushing on that evening to Clinton, where it was to meet Steele's division. Bell noted that "there were plenty of fine looking young females in the town who came out of doors to witness our departure, whereat the Col. called for '3 cheers for the girls we leave behind us' which were given with a will." He also added that "our Major (Taylor) diverted the boys by running a race with some woman who is with us, said to be a hospital attendant, both on horseback. The Major was beat. 'Bully for the gal.'" One 54th Indiana soldier who remained to garrison the town also described interacting with the local people: "Dinner with a dashing secesh lady drunk a glass of fine native wine with her she said she hoped to convert me over to her cause."[38]

Stone's wagon train continued on in the afternoon to Clinton, where it went into camp awaiting the arrival of its parent division from Jackson. At the same time, Blair's column of troops and trains also arrived late that afternoon at Raymond after "making good time on half rations," and Ransom was still on the way in the rear, his men also on half-rations. McArthur himself remained in contact with Grant about the progress. Yet these arriving supplies were a seeming drop in the bucket of what was needed; even those several hundred wagons' worth of goods were not that telling. Much of it was ammunition, which did nothing to alleviate the growing hunger that even the captured supplies in Jackson and Raymond could not quench. Only a limited amount of hardtack and other items were available, only enough in fact that "two crackers were issued to each man." It was not much at all, but it was enough that "for once the much despised 'Hard tack' received a hearty welcome."[39]

Still, those additional supplies were very helpful as Grant worked to get his army arrayed for another fight to the west even as Sherman was destroying Jackson to the east. The Army of the Tennessee was, after all, lodged between two Confederate forces. Back to the west, which by now had become the front of the Army of the Tennessee, McClernand was moving toward Edwards and the reported position of the Confederate army. Osterhaus, in fact, had left the two regiments at Raymond as garrison troops and "seized" Bolton first on the morning of May 15 from the south. Hovey's division marched in shortly thereafter from Clinton to the east. The Federals had word that the enemy was moving toward them, and staff officer Henry Warmoth admitted that there were some uneasy times with only Osterhaus present before Hovey came up for support: "Soon Hovey came up and we felt a little easier but not much." The troops spread out foraging, leading to a confrontation not with Confederates but with a local French woman who had a bulldog who attacked one Federal as he argued with the woman, whom he could not understand. "I ran my bayonet through the dog's ribs," he admitted, adding, "this made the old lady jump up and down and swear like a trooper."[40]

Carr was still moving from Mississippi Springs, and Smith up from

Dillon's at the same time, but the farther west McClernand pushed his forces the more he found out. Much more had been realized about the road network between Bolton and Edwards Station, for instance, prompting McClernand to make changes in the original plan of all divisions except perhaps A. J. Smith's moving along the Jackson Road from Bolton. McClernand quickly figured out that there were actually three roads leading toward Edwards Station. The Jackson Road along the rail line, on which Osterhaus and Hovey sat already, was farthest north, and then there was the Raymond-to-Edwards road to the south, although not the one that McClernand had utilized on May 13 in his move from Whittaker's Ford to Raymond; it was still farther south, and McClernand never reached this far north in his previous move through this general area. And then there was yet another, smaller road in the middle, aptly termed "the Middle Road."[41]

Making this road network more concerning were reports of Confederates on each, and especially on the Raymond Road. McClernand had scouts and skirmishers out all day on May 15, some under his cavalry chief, Colonel John J. Mudd, locating these roads and Confederate activity on each. "Reports were rife," he informed Grant, "that the enemy were moving in strong force upon me by the Edwards Station and Bolton Road [Jackson Road], and particularly by the Edwards Station and Raymond road." McClernand added that he "pushed forward reconnaissances in every direction toward Edwards Station and Brownsville." His scouts began to skirmish throughout the day, but McClernand knew he had to cover all the byways, especially the lower Raymond Road. For his part, Grant moved westward himself to Clinton that afternoon in such plain dress that local civilians thought they were being fooled when told it was him.[42]

To cover all three roads, McClernand ordered Hovey to remain on the main Jackson Road and Osterhaus to retrace his steps southward to the entrance of the Middle Road, "marching back on the Raymond road about 3 miles," Osterhaus explained amid some skirmishing with forward Confederates. Carr's division arriving from Mississippi Springs would join Osterhaus and support him. Farther south, Blair's XV Corps division was nearly to Raymond by the evening of May 15 and would cover that road, with A. J. Smith's troops moving up from Dillon's to support Blair. That would put two divisions on both the Raymond and Middle Roads, with only Hovey on the Jackson Road. To support him, McClernand requested Grant and McPherson move up on the Jackson Road area not only to support Hovey but also perhaps to outflank the Confederates from the north. "Hovey having the right, and resting his right near the railroad, Osterhaus and Carr center, and Blair and Smith the left," McClernand informed Grant.[43]

McPherson did move, early that morning in fact, Logan's division starting at 5:00 a.m. for Bolton and Crocker's not far behind with a 7:00 a.m.
departure; the troops, some without rations, soon passed over the battlefield
of the day before, where they saw "our men burying the dead 40 in number."
Samuel Holmes's brigade of Crocker's division remained behind at Clinton
for the time being, where one of McPherson's Federals explained that "the
women at Clinton would not believe that we had been to Jackson, but supposed that Gen. Johnston had driven us back." The troops marched all day,
Logan's division camping on Wolf Creek that evening. As McPherson arrived
at Jones Plantation near Hovey's camp at Bolton late in the day he sent a message forward: "Genl. McPherson's compliments to Genl. Hovey & wishes to
know if there is any important news from the front." Hovey scribbled back on
the bottom of the message: "No news from the front since last evening about
sun down. Our pickets at that time were driven by the enemy."[44]

With the positions set, "night found Generals Hovey's, Osterhaus', and
Carr's divisions, in the order stated, at the entrance to these several roads,"
McClernand reported. One Iowan noted that "[we] hat our forses scattered
over consieterable spase of country." McClernand then gave his orders for the
next day, May 16. All divisions would push forward on their respective roads
at 6:00 a.m., except Blair an hour earlier. "The starting of different divisions
at different hours was in consequence of the difference in the distances they
had to march," McClernand explained, "and was designed to secure a parallel
advance of the different columns." His own four division commanders were
so informed, but he also sent word to Blair to act under his orders, per Grant's
instructions. So there would be no debate or confusion, McClernand even
sent Blair Grant's original order. In it, Grant had cautioned McClernand and
by extension Blair to push forward, "marching so as to feel the force of the
enemy, should you encounter him, and without bringing on an engagement,
unless you feel entirely able to contend with him." McClernand wrote that
he intended "to feel the enemy and to engage him if it be found expedient
to do so." He added, "let each division keep up communication with that or
those next to it, and all move on parallel with each other as near as may be."
To Blair specifically, he added, "keep up communication with Osterhaus and
Carr, on your right," and to "communicate with me often."[45]

McClernand went to sleep that night confident in his plans, but they still
had to be executed the next morning in the face of the enemy. He sent Grant
news that a captured letter from Vicksburg rated the Confederate force at
forty thousand and the estimation of the Federals at seventy thousand. He was
very concerned about his right, again bringing up the need for McPherson
to move on Hovey's rear. Nevertheless, he informed Grant he was moving

forward at 6:00 a.m. the next morning to "at least feel the enemy." As a result, his orders were methodical, defensive, and timid. He added that "the purpose is first to feel the enemy, and then engage him, if we find it can be done with success."[46]

Back in Jackson where the Federals were having their way with the city without any opposition, a different conclusion took form. "I don't think we will have any more fighting to do to take Vicksburg than we had at this place," one of Sherman's soldiers confided. The stage set back to the west between Bolton and Edwards Depot certainly told a different tale.[47]

The night of May 15 could not have demonstrated more the differences in Grant and Pemberton as commanders. While most of Grant's troops were well secured in their bivouacs early that evening in the perfect jump-off positions to move on all three major axes of advance the next morning, Pemberton's troops were still marching late into the night, well after midnight even at the front of the column and nearer to dawn in the rear of it. That was no way to prepare an army for the climactic showdown that was coming the next morning, although only one of the commanders knew it. That in and of itself spoke volumes about these generals.[48]

But there were some in the Confederate army who were not so blind. Despite Pemberton's adamance that nothing unusual occurred that night, several reported odd happenings that would only make sense the next day. For instance, Colonel Edward Goodwin of the 35th Alabama in Loring's division noted that "during the night an occasional gun was fired by the cavalry pickets of each army." That certainly indicated that at least some enemy presence was nearby, even if unknown in what force. Most telling, Colonel Francis Cockrell, commanding one of Bowen's brigades, related that he could see "a number of lights, which I supposed to be the camp fires of the enemy." One of his Missourians added that "we could see the light of their fires and hear them moving into line of battle all night."[49]

These were foreboding sights and sounds, but what was even worse were the thoughts of what such clues would mean the next morning.

14

"THE HILL OF DEATH"
May 16 Morning

Matilda Champion was in a fix. She and her husband, Sidney, owned a plantation squarely amid the armies converging on May 16: "The reputed property of a citizen by the name of Champion," John McClernand explained. In fact, the "two-story white frame on the left of the road where it turned up the hill" sat just on the east side of the Jackson Road after its great turn to the south, where it continued on past the house and up the slope of the knoll that would forever carry the name Champion Hill. Some 140 feet high, "the hill was bald," James B. McPherson wrote, "giving the enemy a commanding point for his artillery, and was really the key of the position." The Jackson Road of course just to the east was already bulging with three divisions of the XIII and XVII Corps, marching toward this very spot. And just to the south atop the high hill that bore the family name lay a Confederate line of battle studded with artillery. A fight was assured; one Louisianan in fact wrote in his diary: "[A] general engagement is expected to-day or tomorrow."[1]

Matilda had bigger issues than just the converging armies, which was big enough, as destruction normally attended wherever they clashed. Indeed, the "mansion house," as one Iowan termed it, itself would be used as a hospital amid the upcoming fight, amputations being performed even on her dining table, on which bloodstains still exist today. And as might be expected, the Champion House would not survive the campaign, being burned down in the months after the battle.[2]

The biggest problem for Mrs. Champion at the moment, however, was that she was in the midst of the chaos without her husband Sid. Although over the military age limit at thirty-eight, he had joined the Confederate army in 1862, becoming a member of the 28th Mississippi Cavalry. Champion had been operating with his unit all around the Vicksburg events and was actually on this day just to the west of his property near Edwards Station. Worse, thirty-five-year-old Matilda had four small children as well and had to see to their safety by herself. She departed at some point for her parents' plantation in Madison County north of Jackson, probably even just the day before when she would have had to travel against the current of the westward marching Federals. She did manage to take with her the most valuable items she could carry, but on top of all the concern for herself, her husband, and children was the similar worry over the land and home she loved so much.[3]

And there was indeed need to worry, as a seeming hurricane was sweeping down on the Champion Plantation that would forever alter not only the path of the Champion family but also the course of the Vicksburg Campaign and indeed the war itself. "Everything betokens an early collision with the enemy," one Federal correctly surmised that morning.[4]

The "clear and unclouded" morning of May 16 conversely brought confusion and then confrontation. Confusion reigned in the Confederate army as the long, snakelike column that stretched from Ellison's Plantation back up the Raymond Road to the Ratliff Road, thence to the Crossroads, and then westward along the Jackson Road to the upper crossing of Bakers Creek continued to slither forward in the rear areas. While the head of the column had halted during the night, the tail end kept moving to catch up. Next to last in line was Stephen D. Lee's brigade, and he explained that "the army marched during the greater part of the night, halting a short time before daylight." It was even worse in the rear, consisting of Stevenson's last brigade under Colonel Alexander W. Reynolds, along with the wagon train. It was still on the move as dawn approached, Reynolds reporting that he finally stopped "about daylight." These Tennesseans could only hope that it would take a while for the column to get going again at the head, and the rubber-band effect would allow them time for a rest before they had to take to the road again.[5]

But the hopes of the rear brigade and teamsters, as well as the Confederate high command, were dashed as two major events occurred. The first confirmed grave danger in such a delicate position, and it came in the form of contact with the enemy. The 35th Alabama and 22nd Mississippi, who acted as the skirmishers and pickets in front of Loring's lead brigade, made contact with the enemy around daylight, before the column headed eastward again, and that changed the calculus entirely. It was the van of the Federal divisions marching on the Raymond Road. "Moving rapidly upon my pickets," Loring explained, "he opened a brisk cannonade," and Loring "suggested to General Pemberton that the sooner he formed a line of battle the better, as the enemy would very soon be upon us." Obviously limited as to the choices of continuing forward, Loring and soon Pemberton realized the middle-choice option of hitting Grant's supply line was unrealistic. In actuality, it had been unrealistic long before this, but the presence of Federals in any size on the Raymond Road indicated more enemy behind them. There would be no more forward movement.[6]

The second event was a courier who arrived early that morning from Johnston. It was his "makes your plan impracticable" message, and the note ordered Pemberton to move to a junction north of the railroad, somewhere around Brownsville, for a combined fight against Grant. The indecisive Pemberton, who was perhaps looking for a way out of this option that he had not been in favor of to begin with and who was now in contact with the enemy, immediately called another council of war with his generals and laid the message before them, stating that "I no longer felt at liberty to deviate from General Johnston's positive orders." Carter Stevenson, for instance, wrote that "at sunrise I was summoned to appear at headquarters." All agreed the army had to turn around and move back toward Edwards Station to link up with Johnston, Loring writing that "this necessitated a movement toward Edwards Depot." At the least, Pemberton had to get back behind Bakers Creek, which ran in the course of a semicircle, with his army currently on the same side of it as the enemy. "The order of countermarch has been issued," Pemberton quickly notified Johnston, and he described how "I immediately directed a countermarch, or rather a retrograde movement, by reversing the column as it then stood." One exasperated surgeon in the army confided in his diary: "Indecision, Indecision, Indecision."[7]

But with the movements that brought the entire army out not only from behind the protective shield that was the Big Black River but also Bakers Creek, Pemberton was now extremely vulnerable. "We were soon made aware when morning broke of the proximity of that army, and of the perilous position in which our own found itself," brigade commander Alfred Cumming wrote. "Not knowing whether this was an attack in force or simply an armed reconnaissance," Pemberton admitted, the danger was especially so if other Federals existed on the other roads that led into the flanks of his long, marching column. Both the Middle and Jackson Roads led into the center of the column at the all-important Crossroads. If Federals were on those roads as well—and given the location of the Union army on May 13 it was a good bet that they were—an attack could sweep in and sever the Confederate column in two. Worse, if anything occurred along this route that the army now lay upon, it would immediately make the two crossings of Bakers Creek extremely important, as they would be the only ways westward to safety. And unfortunately, one of them, the lower crossing, was still underwater.[8]

That simple scenario made it exceedingly important that Pemberton, having first decided against joining with Johnston as well as now being thwarted from marching on Grant's line of supply, get his army back behind Bakers Creek at the least. He was far out of position, with his army strung up on a long, single, winding route that was further complicated by limited crossings of high water. He had wanted to stay in Vicksburg all along and defend it per Jefferson Davis's orders and had become known as "adverse to a fight"; now he decided, for once, to head westward for either a defense of Vicksburg or a union with Johnston. But for either, he had to turn around and get out of what with each passing minute was likely becoming a dangerous trap. An officer later admitted that "I am quite confident Pemberton was not expecting to fight here for it was evident from his movements he had no plan for battle."[9]

Nerves were certainly fraying as the high command decided on the change of plan. One staff officer in attendance, Lieutenant William Drennan, wrote his wife what he saw:

Pemberton said something which I did not catch, and Loring replied as I thought rather testily—"Gen'l Pemberton you did not tell me this last night" to which Pemberton said "Yes, Loring, you know I did." Their manner was warm—and no good feeling was evinced by either party. There was ill-will and that too displayed in a manner that was to the credit of neither party. That there was no harmony— no unity of action, no clear understanding of the aims and designs of our army was clearly apparent—and instead of there existing mutual confidence on the part of the Commanding general and his subordinates—there was just the opposite— and it amounted to what in an ordinary matter would have been called distrust.

In fact, Drennan admitted that he later "listened to General Loring, Tilghman and Featherston engage in quite an animated conversation the principal topic being General Pemberton—and the affairs of the Country generally. They all said harsh, ill-natured things, made ill-turned jests in regard to Gen. Pemberton and when an order came from him, the courier who brought it was not out of hearing, before they would make light of it and ridicule the plans he proposed."[10]

Nevertheless, Pemberton ordered his army to about-face and march westward out of danger; Cumming described how "[it was] no longer a question of this or the other strategic plan. Our only hope *to get away*." Stephen D. Lee explained that "soon after daylight on the 16th, the army commenced a retrograde movement over the same route it had taken on the preceding night." There would be no countermarching of Lew Wallace fame as at Shiloh to get the best troops in the most needed positions. The column simply turned and withdrew the same way it had marched out, and that meant the exhausted rear brigade of Stevenson's division as well as the wagon train were now the head of the marching column. That was beneficial in some ways, as it would put the all-important wagon train first across Bakers Creek to safety, but it also meant that the units that had just stopped the march would get no rest whatsoever. They had to turn and march while the new tail end of the column, which got at least a little rest the night before, had to wait until the entire army advanced to begin their trek. The head that was the first to stop was now the last to leave and so inherited a double-rest, taking that of the poor new head's place. Accordingly, Pemberton told Stevenson to move the wagon train across Bakers Creek "as rapidly as possible" and then stop it, "arranged to the right and left of the road in such a manner as would afford uninterrupted passage to the infantry and artillery." Reynolds, the brigade commander in charge of the train, was told that "I would alone be held responsible for its safety."[11]

So began the retrograde to get out the same way they had come in, Stevenson writing that "I immediately caused the trains to be turned." Pemberton staff officer Jacob Thompson explained that the train "now became, under the new order, the advance guard." But before it could hardly even begin, the Federals appeared on all roads leading to Edwards Station. Loring's lead, now rear, brigade under Brigadier General Lloyd Tilghman suddenly came under pressure from the advance Union elements on the Raymond Road and withdrew incrementally to the Jackson Creek watershed, where it went into line in the big fields and among the tall ridges to the west. Loring's entire division thus deployed under Pemberton's watchful eye astride the Raymond Road to not only hold that thoroughfare but more importantly to hold the rear of the army, brigade commander Abraham Buford declaring the line "quite defensible." With the lower crossing still inoperable, there was nowhere else to go anyway until the divisions ahead of them cleared the Crossroads and upper creek crossing point. Loring consequently deployed his three brigades first along the high ridge just west of Jackson Creek but then shifted rearward about 11:00 a.m. for a better position on the ridge on which sat the Coker House. The division deployed in order of its march, with Abraham Buford north of the road, Winfield S. Featherston astride the road itself, and Tilghman's brigade manning the far right. Artillery unlimbered and skirmishers kept to the front, delaying the approaching enemy, but indications were that this was a heavy force forthcoming and there was nowhere else as yet to go.[12]

Likewise, John Bowen's two-brigade division moved only slightly northward before it too began to deploy due to fear of Federals' arrival in the vicinity and also not having any other place to go; the road to the Crossroads and upper crossing was still clogged with Stevenson's division. Bowen accordingly deployed his brigades along the Ratliff Road that connected the Crossroads with the Raymond Road, Francis Cockrell's Missouri brigade up closer to the Crossroads and Martin Green's farther southward along the road and connecting with Loring's left. Ahead of the division were large rolling fields on the right and dense woods on the left, but no major roads led into their position; thus few Federals would probably wander into its area except purposefully to attack. But over the course of the morning as the Confederates on the left shifted northward and westward to counter Union moves in that area, Bowen, as well as Loring, continually shifted northward to keep the line closed up. Loring explained that "soon a series of orders came, specifically and with great particularity, for two of my brigades to move to the left, closing the line as often as Bowen moved, and we in this manner followed him." Buford related that Bowen asked him to move northward to stay connected with him "as he had moved to the left to join General Stevenson's right."[13]

Matters were more difficult for Carter Stevenson's four brigades that now assumed the lead of the marching army. Colonel Reynolds's tired troops soon had the wagon train across Bakers Creek and situated on the sides of the road by 9:30 a.m., but the other three brigades had to also deploy, although they continually shifted to the left as events developed. Two roads on which Federals could approach led into their area of concern, the Middle Road from the east and the Jackson Road from the north. As Stevenson's brigades halted and waited, smaller-unit commanders had the foresight to send out skirmishers and reconnoiter ahead, especially on the roads. Some consequently moved eastward along the Middle Road and eventually made contact with the two approaching Federal divisions there. But the major development came as skirmishers from Stephen D. Lee's brigade moved up the Jackson Road all the way to the highest position they could find: Champion Hill. From there, Lieutenant Colonel Edmund W. Pettus could see into the valley of Bakers Creek below (it made a sweeping curve to the east around the high ground at Champion Hill) and could plainly see a huge array of Federals gathering and marching southward toward the Crossroads. Lee shouted the word quickly, and Stevenson's three brigades still east of the creek had to deploy as well, Alfred Cumming's Georgians eventually around the Crossroads and Champion Hill itself, although there was too much distance and not enough troops for a continuous line. Stevenson opted to cover the transportation routes instead. Up at Champion Hill itself, Lee first manned the hill line but shifted westward as more and more Federal troops appeared and headed that direction, forcing

Cumming to shift as well, widening the gap. Worse, Lee had to make an angle in his line at the hill itself, which Cumming had to keep as he shifted to Lee's old position. It was first "an angle more or less obtuse," but then it became "nearly a right angle . . . what may be termed the second front of the square." It was such a dangerous salient that Cumming himself remained very near the turn during much of the initial fighting: "I stationed myself within a few paces of that point to superintend in person its more rapid clearance."[14]

Division commander Stevenson was also on hand to oversee and approve the moves: "The enemy, in columns of divisions," Stevenson explained, "moved steadily around our left, forcing it to change direction to correspond, and their movement was so rapid as to keep my line (a single one) in constant motion by the left flank." Ultimately, to rectify the open left flank and to cover the critical upper Bakers Creek crossing, Stevenson moved the entirety of Seth Barton's Georgia brigade from the Crossroads area to Lee's left "by the rear." Barton moved a mile and a half at the double-quick and went into the fight "as rapidly as the nature of the ground would admit." Also along were the guns of both the Cherokee Georgia Artillery and Captain Samuel Ridley's 1st Mississippi Light Artillery, first deployed at Pemberton's headquarters at the Isaac Roberts House but then moving to the left. Stevenson's line stretched down the ridge that emanated from the hill itself and ran westward, but he knew it was problematic: "The position was not a good one; the country much broken and covered in most part with dense woods." And Barton's removal left an even larger gap between the now two regiments left at the Crossroads and the hill itself, but it was the best Stevenson could do: "This separation was necessary to protect the right and rear of the new line."[15]

"As early as 10 o'clock in the morning," Lee explained, "it became evident that the enemy was in heavy force and determined on battle, as his skirmishers were bold and aggressive, and several divisions of his troops were visible in front of our left." Pemberton had wanted to get his army out of the closing noose east of Bakers Creek, but now it did not look like he would be able to do so without a fight. And he had never led an army in one of those. Stevenson quickly notified him that "the enemy had massed a large force on the left, which would doubtless be the main point of attack." Of course, Bowen and Loring to the south likewise thought that their areas were the focal points as well. The brigades consequently deployed and prepared, hoping to hold long enough to extricate themselves perhaps even at the lower crossing, if enough time could be bought for the creek's water level to fall throughout the day. But the army fortunately covered all three major roads leading into its column, engineer Lockett describing how the army "was formed on a commanding ridge, and so disposed as to cover all approaches from the front." Pemberton himself described how "the line of battle was quickly formed, without any interference on the part of the enemy. The position selected was naturally a strong one, and all approaches from the front well covered." And the Confederate army also had the benefit of interior lines of communication, with which they could shuffle troops if need be along the web of roads they held.[16]

But it was still anybody's guess where the main attack would fall—if not on all three roads. One of Pemberton's staff officers testified that "the skirmishing was equally severe on the right and left, and no definite conclusion could be formed as to which was the advance of the bulk of the enemy's force." But if the entire army had to depend on the one upper crossing, when the vast majority of the force was strung out far to its south, it was not going to turn out well. Pemberton had been out of position for several days now, but no more so than when contact occurred all along the line at Champion Hill on the morning of May 16. Carter Stevenson had mentioned cutting the enemy line of supply and "forcing him to give battle on our own ground." This was certainly not that. Instead, Cumming explained that "the attack broke upon us with great impetuosity and vehemence, in over whelming force, and in a manner wholly unexpected and unlooked for."[17]

That contact came from a total of seven Federal divisions sweeping down on the hastily formed Confederate line, from three different directions no less. Unlike Pemberton, who had all his troops on one single axis of advance and marched deep into the night, some of them until dawn, McClernand had positioned nearly equal amounts of divisions on each of the three roads leading to what would become the battlefield. Even better, each had made short marches the day before and had gone into camp early so that plenty of rest could be had. There were consequently enormous contrasts between the Army of the Tennessee that awoke to fight on May 16 and its Confederate counterpart. But it was an increasingly hungry Union army that awoke that morning, one Iowan explaining of the order to cook breakfasts: "That was an easy undertaking, considering how scanty the raw material. The 5th Iowa Infantry had absolutely nothing but some poor wet flour at this time. Of this we made little dough balls, and cooked them at the ends of our ramrods over the few bivouac fires we were permitted to kindle." Another soldier on the march toward Vicksburg told of "spying a piece of bacon rind at the road side, which some more fortunate soldier had thrown away, and grabbing it as a great treasure I removed the dirt and ate it with a ravenous appetite."[18]

Yet for all the planning, the Federal trap did not spring quite like it was supposed to. Grant seemed to be in a particularly cautious mode, perhaps a result of not knowing the ground or the positioning of the lead elements. An odd arrival of two railroaders (William Hennessey and Peter McCardle) who said they had come to Edwards Station by train and then on foot through Pemberton's army the night before and told of some eighty Confederate regiments may also have made him think twice, especially wondering if the news was true or planted to deceive him; word of moving locomotives sounded odd, but there were additional reports of trains operating in the local area even on May 15 and 16. McPherson sent the news to Grant, the courier awakening him and Fred as they slept at Clinton. Grant consequently cautioned McClernand, writing of "requiring the utmost celerity in the march towards Edwards Depot." He similarly wrote Blair that "precautions in approaching Baker's Creek are necessary. Before doing so, know where friend and enemy both are." That caution seemed to filter down to the corps and division commanders as well, but there is no doubt that, if each of the three wings had attacked in force, there was no way Pemberton could have withstood determined assaults from all three different directions. But because of several factors, only one of the three springs sprung, allowing the Confederates to shift troops from less threatened areas to the main fight. Grant had no need to do so. He had plenty of troops on each route and would have crushed the Confederates had each launched a determined assault.[19]

Consequently, little occurred in terms of heavy fighting down on the Raymond Road, Colonel Arthur E. Reynolds of the 26th Mississippi relating that "up to about 12 m., nothing of importance occurred." Blair's division had led the march out of the Raymond area around 5:00 a.m., but McClernand finagled a way to get his own XIII Corps division under A. J. Smith in the lead. "If you are prompt in your movement, at 4 a.m. you will take the lead in the left wing, General Blair having orders to move at 5 a.m.," McClernand wrote Smith early on May 16. Smith did so and was now in front, where he deployed his lead brigade to confront Loring's entire division. Stephen G. Burbridge pushed his regiments into line to confront first the skirmishers of the Confederate division and then the division itself on the Coker House ridge. Behind was William Landram's brigade, and behind that were two more brigades of Frank Blair's arriving division of the XV Corps. Sherman of course was back nearer to Jackson, having destroyed the military means of the place the day before and heading westward this day. But he had acted with only Tuttle's and Steele's divisions, his third, Blair's, having arrived only the night before from Grand Gulf ferrying the large wagon train that the army desperately needed. Blair arrived at the southernmost portion of the army and joined the proceedings there rather than continuing on up to rejoin his parent corps, which would have added several more miles to the march. Plus, he was needed in the fight emerging on May 16.[20]

But it turned out that Blair was not really utilized on the Raymond Road, as A. J. Smith never advanced with any degree of determination: "We are feeling the enemy cautiously," Blair informed Grant that morning. Smith merely skirmished during the forenoon ("nothing but heavy skirmishing," one of his soldiers admitted), while the full content of Loring's division remained intact, highly outnumbering the one deployed brigade. The commander of that brigade, Stephen Burbridge, explained that "we skirmished along gradually, driving the enemy before us, while our main force followed along the road." Burbridge consequently pushed across Jackson Creek, where the bridge had been destroyed by the withdrawing Confederates, and pushed on up the high ridge beyond. "Finding the enemy was in retreat but a short distance ahead," Burbridge continued, "and apprehending they might avail themselves of some prominent hills, from which they could sweep the plain we were in, I pushed my brigade rapidly until the skirmishers began to find it a hot contest." Burbridge's troops nevertheless took the first ridge and found he had "abundant reason to congratulate myself upon my speed," but there he met the main Confederate line on the next ridge arrayed around the Coker House. And there matters would stand as the fight began to rage to the north and even as some of these very units, certainly Bowen's and two-thirds of Loring's divisions, shifted northward "to keep the interval closed between himself and General Stevenson." But Smith and Blair never pressed firmly, despite Burbridge's "repeated application" for reinforcements, certainly not in the morning while the full compliment of Confederates manned that Coker House ridge. In fact, Colonel Theodore E. Buehler of the 67th Indiana related that "for about three hours four pieces of artillery belched forth their iron messengers of death with the utmost rapidity, while my skirmishers reported them supported by about eleven regiments of infantry." All the while, the forces on the Raymond Road could hear "the roar of heavy volleys of musketry" to their right.[21]

Similarly, there were more than enough Union troops on the Middle Road to effectively break through the Confederate defense there, especially after Barton's Georgia brigade shifted to the extreme left of the Confederate line near Bakers Creek itself. But as the lead division of the two on this road moved westward "with all those safeguards in front and flank which the enemy's vicinity rendered indispensable," division commander Peter Osterhaus explained, he developed the same kind of funk that strangled Smith down on the Raymond Road. There was stiff Confederate resistance; cavalry commander Captain John L. Campbell of the 3rd Illinois Cavalry out front explained

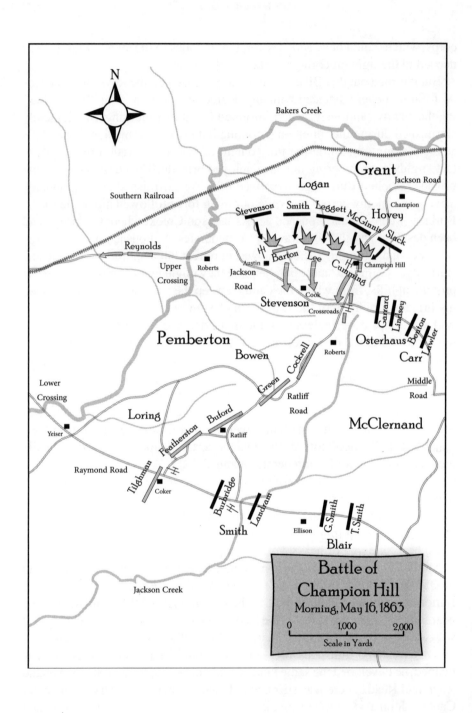

N

Bakers Creek

Grant

Jackson Road

Logan

Southern Railroad

Stevenson Smith Leggett McGinnis Hovey

Champion

Slack

Reynolds

Upper
Crossing

Roberts

Austin Barton Lee Cumming Champion Hill

Jackson

Road

Cook

Stevenson

Crossroads

Garrard

Lindsey

Pemberton

Bowen

Cockrell

Roberts

Osterhaus

Benton

Lawler

Carr

Lower
Crossing

Middle
Road

Loring

Green

Ratliff
Road

Buford

Ratliff

McClernand

Yeiser

Raymond Road

Featherston

Tilghman

Coker

Burbridge

Landram

Smith

Ellison

G. Smith

T. Smith

Blair

**Battle of
Champion Hill**
Morning, May 16, 1863

0   1,000   2,000

Scale in Yards

that "the road was enfiladed by deep canyons, heavily timbered. The enemy yielded their ground with great reluctance, contesting every inch of it." And there were times when the Federals even fell back; at one point troops driving the Confederate skirmishers backward were "ordered by General [Theophilus T.] Garrard to fall back." Colonel John G. Fonda of the 118th Illinois related that, during one of the timid forward movements, "my regiment was thrown into a very unfavorable position, and received a heavy fire from the enemy." Osterhaus's other brigade commander, Daniel Lindsey, similarly reported that he ordered some of his regiments backward as well, "the enemy having brought up a battery to rake the woods, with a much stronger infantry force than my own to support it." He added: "I regarded my advance as an important one, and regret exceedingly my inability to maintain it."[22]

The rugged terrain obviously did not help, Osterhaus describing it as "a very broken section of timbered land," although it was nowhere near the scope of that at Port Gibson. Still, he elaborated that it was "one of the most difficult terrains (grounds) for the passage of troops which can be imagined. A chaos of ravines and narrow hills, sloping very abruptly into sink-hole-like valleys, diverge in all directions." He also described how "all is covered densely by trees and brush, except the public road, which winds its track in bizarre curves, and follows the hills and valleys, without permitting at any point an open view of more than 50 or 100 yards." As a result, Osterhaus slowly pushed westward and met Confederates out in front of the main line at the Crossroads, where he seemingly stalled as well, even though his two brigades under Garrard and Lindsey deployed and pressed forward cautiously. And behind Osterhaus was Eugene Carr's division of two brigades, with William Benton and Michael Lawler's regiments stacking up in the rear. It was a force of two divisions of four brigades that at one point faced no more than two Georgia regiments and four guns at the Crossroads. Oddly enough, John McClernand himself traveled with Osterhaus and Carr on this route, and the aggressive McClernand could normally be counted on to push on to a fight. But not today, when a determined attack here likewise could have proved fatal to the withdrawing Confederate army. In his defense, his skirmishers had already captured prisoners who reported the Confederate force at "50,000 to 60,000 strong," and he had received several orders advising caution from Grant already.[23]

It was consequently only up on the Jackson Road that any semblance of a major attack occurred. McClernand had continued lobbying for McPherson to support Hovey, even riding to Bolton that morning and getting to McPherson's headquarters "before he had risen," McClernand noted; he later sent an additional message that "I am, as I advised you this morning, convinced that if you will move on the far side of the railroad and fall on the enemy's flank and rear, it would be decisive; besides, Hovey may need support by a co-operative movement by you." McClernand received "assurances altogether satisfactory," and indeed McPherson was moving forward from Bolton on the Jackson Road according to Grant's orders of 5:45 that morning: "I have just received information that the enemy have crossed Big Black with the entire Vicksburg force. He was at Edwards Depot last night, and still advancing. You will, therefore, pass all trains, and move forward to join McClernand." Eventually, three divisions of the XIII and XVII Corps congregated on the Jackson Road, the eight total brigades marching in one road with cavalry on the flanks, Captain Foster's battalion even "visiting the plantation of Jefferson Davis, capturing his overseer."[24]

The massing of so many brigades quickly produced a slow and methodical deployment as brigade after brigade arrived and had to take its place in line. In fact, the last of the eight brigades would not arrive and deploy until later in the afternoon, although behind them were two more divisions of Sherman's XV Corps, still too far out to make a difference this day. Grant would have to fight with whatever he had on the Jackson Road already. But Grant himself also soon moved out on that avenue as well, one Illinoisan describing how the general "with a few mounted attendants went through Clinton at a rapid pace." Similarly, brigade commander John Sanborn noted that Grant and staff "passed me and the head of my column at a very rapid rate, he announcing to me as he passed that 'to-day we shall fight the battle for Vicksburg.'" He eventually arrived around the Champion House and found Hovey's division "at a halt . . . bringing his troops into line ready for battle, and could have brought on an engagement at any moment."[25]

But Grant took no chances, in case this fight lasted more than today. Digesting the news from the two railroaders, he sent quick word to Sherman at 5:30 a.m. to "start one of your divisions on the road at once, with their ammunition wagons, and direct the general commanding the division to move with all possible speed until he comes up with our rear beyond Bolton." He emphasized speed of movement: "It is important that the greatest celerity should be shown in carrying out this movement, as I have evidence that the entire force of the enemy was at Edwards Depot at 7 p.m. last night, and was still advancing. The fight may, therefore, be brought on at any moment. We should have every man in the field." Sherman had to change his original orders and rush the troops out, Steele moving first around 10:00 a.m. and then Tuttle following a couple hours later, not through Mississippi Springs as originally planned but through Clinton and Bolton. One of Sherman's men admitted that "we set fire to the city and started for Vicksburg," and another added that "we completely demolished the city of Jackson before we left burning nearly all the houses and stores." Confederate cavalry reentered the smoldering city "just as the enemy was leaving it," capturing some Federal stragglers and actually killing the colonel of the 47th Illinois, John N. Cromwell, who went back after a few stragglers. The Bowman Hotel owner cared for the wounded colonel (where he died) despite the outrage of the citizens, likely producing the arson that destroyed his hotel just weeks later. Johnston began work almost immediately to repair the damage, Governor Pettus putting a price on it at around five to ten million dollars. But it would be a long time coming.[26]

Although on the way, Sherman was still miles out and would be of no help this day. But what Grant had on the Jackson Road was likewise enough, and McClernand was querying, "Shall I hold, or bring on an engagement?" Having sent staff officer James H. Wilson ahead to confer with McClernand and then moving westward himself, Grant of course was soon on the field, making his headquarters at the Champion House. He quickly determined to attack, spurred forward by the thought of McClernand fighting the battle himself. McPherson, too, was concerned, having written Grant earlier that morning, "I think it advisable for you to come forward to the front as soon as you can." But Grant was of the same opinion as McClernand, sending the Federals on the Jackson Road to the assault almost immediately when he arrived. He quickly sent word to McClernand down on the Middle Road ordering that, "as soon as your command is all in hand, throw forward skirmishers and feel the enemy, and attack him in force if an opportunity occurs." He added, "I am with Hovey and McPherson, and will see that they fully co-operate." But the distances involved in couriers going back to the common-denominator road connecting all three of the axes of advance delayed the riders, as the Union army was operating on exterior lines of communication; a situation soon emerged in which Hovey, who had Grant with him, was asking permission to advance from McClernand, who had to ask Grant, who was with Hovey. McClernand informed Hovey: "I have referred the question of bringing on an engagement to General Grant, who is said to be close by. . . . So soon as I am advised by General Grant, I will communicate with you. Meantime, take any advantage you can, without bringing on a general engagement. Watch your left as well as right. Communicate often." The unneeded caution that prevailed was coming to play a large role.[27]

Leading the advance on the Jackson Road was Alvin Hovey's XIII Corps division of two brigades under George McGinnis and James Slack, the latter of which had been up since two o'clock that morning writing his wife. The division left its Bolton encampment around 7:00 a.m., under orders to "advance rapidly and cautiously." More orders came from McClernand to move "cautiously but promptly." That of course made the lead divisions on all three roads XIII Corps divisions, which McClernand himself had orchestrated the day before; in fact, McClernand had written McPherson early that morning (6:00 a.m.) that Pemberton was found and that his troops "were already in motion to meet him." Close behind Hovey, however, was the lead division of McPherson's XVII Corps under "our much beloved Genl [John] Logan," one Illinoisan explained, and Logan was in a fit of rage at being detained by Hovey's troops up ahead. "I rarely ever witnessed such an exhibition of rage, profanity and disappointment as Logan then gave," newspaperman Cadwallader explained, adding that "the air was just blue with oaths, till speech was exhausted." He added, "McPherson's arrival a few minutes after was the signal for another outburst." Logan's division contained three brigades, Mortimer Leggett's, John E. Smith's, and John D. Stevenson's, and was close enough to act in tandem with Hovey despite the delay. The other present division of the XVII Corps under Marcellus Crocker was farther out and would not arrive in time for the initial attack, but it would appear later. Like Sherman, McPherson was missing his third division under John McArthur, and in fact only one of its brigades was currently on the way to the army and would arrive that night. Another of McArthur's brigades would join in the days ahead, although the third one never did and would remain in Louisiana for the duration.[28]

Hovey's brigades deployed astride the Jackson Road after it took a sharp turn from a westward direction to a southerly line; it only headed back westward after passing over Champion Hill itself and then reaching the Crossroads. But between the Champion House at the sharp turn and the Crossroads to the south was the Confederate battle line, Cumming, Lee, and Barton from east to west, Cumming's right turning at a ninety-degree angle around Champion Hill itself but not reaching all the way down to the Crossroads, where two of Cumming's regiments were detached. Hovey's own escort under Lieutenant James L. Carey of the 1st Indiana Cavalry, along with companies of the 24th and 46th Indiana of McGinnis's brigade, had ranged ahead as skirmishers and the "advance guard" and had located the Confederates first near "the Champion buildings" but then in force "posted on the crest of the hill, with a battery of four guns in the woods near the road, and on the highest point for many miles around." Hovey himself spurred his horse forward and verified the report, writing that "Pemberton has a most formidable position on the crest of a wooded hill," all the while ordering his brigades to deploy in the process.[29]

Fortunately for Hovey, the van of McPherson's XVII Corps soon also arrived, in the form of Logan's division. McClernand had sent yet another note to Grant advising that "McPherson, I think, should move up to the support of Hovey, who thinks his right flank will encounter severe resistance." But in moving westward himself, Grant had run upon McPherson's troops stalled in the road behind a wagon train. He immediately ordered "all quartermasters and wagon masters to draw their teams to one side and make room for the passage of troops." Now free to march, Logan's soon-arriving division also deployed, on Hovey's right, with brigades under Leggett, Smith, and then Stevenson filling out the line to the right toward Bakers Creek. The artillery, including De Golyer's 8th Michigan Battery, deployed in rear and began to pound the enemy lines. One deploying Federal asked Logan himself if they had better not unsling knapsacks, to which the stern Logan shot back: "No, . . . damn them, you can whip them with your knapsacks on." The movement continually westward "rendered a corresponding movement necessary on our part," Pemberton's engineer Samuel Lockett explained. The result was that "this ground was not reconnoitered with a view of taking up a position for battle until we were on the move facing the enemy," Carter Stevenson complained.[30]

In hindsight, it would have been most productive to make the major Union attack along the Middle Road, where only two Georgia regiments stood in defense, rather than along the Jackson Road, where three brigades faced Hovey and Logan. But Grant himself was on the Jackson Road, along with McPherson and two division commanders with another arriving soon. With all those stars on the shoulders it was logical that the attack would be pressed here, but in reality the only stars that mattered were those on Grant's shoulders, and he ordered the divisions on the Jackson Road forward around 10:00 a.m. There was no corresponding assault by the Federals on the Middle and Raymond Roads, however, which was also a byproduct of Grant's action and his physically being on the Jackson Road; in fact, he wrote McClernand at 10:15, still in a careful mode, that "from all information gathered from citizens and prisoners, the mass of the enemy are south of Hovey's division. . . . . Close up all your forces as expeditiously as possible, but cautiously. The enemy must not be allowed to get in our rear." He had earlier cautioned McClernand to wait until ordered to assault, admitting that "I would not permit an attack to be commenced by our troops until I could hear from McClernand." By the time these orders traveled around the lengthy road network it was well on in the afternoon before word finally reached McClernand on the Middle Road to attack, and then it took even longer for word to travel on down to the Raymond Road. Couriers could have attempted to move cross-country, but it was so rugged and confusing that even regular troop movements were not forthcoming; the area between the Jackson and Middle Roads was, one general noted, "utterly impracticable for any military movements," and Hovey himself explained that "I attempted to communicate with Brigadier General Osterhaus, but my messengers, not knowing the country nor his exact locality, were unable to find his division." Rather, the lead division commander on the Middle Road, Osterhaus, seemed to be more interested in securing his own flanks and girding for an attack than giving one; he frequently mentioned concern for his flanks in his report and prepared a rallying point "in case my advancing infantry had to fall back." That was not the stuff of aggressiveness, and in fact Osterhaus seems to have lost some of his forcefulness even as early as Port Gibson and perhaps during the river crossing. Yet McClernand vouched for the bad terrain, "a seeming chaos of abrupt hills and yawning ravines." In the meantime, the majority of the fighting occurred up on the Jackson Road, mainly in the areas approaching Champion Hill itself and leading down to the Crossroads.[31]

With the command to assault the Confederate line, Grant's troops on the Jackson Road lurched forward around 10:30 a.m. in the opening attack at Champion Hill. On the Jackson Road itself, Alvin Hovey's two brigades straddled the byway, advancing, he said, "to within sight of the enemy's battery." On the east side, James Slack's four regiments deployed initially "in the field of one Champion," Lieutenant Colonel John A. McLaughlin of the 47th Indiana explaining that his regiment went into position "in rear of the houses" but then "advanced beyond the houses about 100 yards." The brigade then moved forward in two lines, the 47th Indiana and 28th Iowa in front supported by the 56th Ohio and 24th Iowa. On the west side, George McGinnis's five regiments also plodded forward over the rough terrain, three regiments (the 24th Indiana, 29th Wisconsin, and 11th Indiana) in front, supported by the 34th Indiana and 46th Indiana in the rear line.[32]

Both brigades charged forward through the low ground still in the Bakers Creek plain but then began to ascend the ridges on which the Confederate line stood. On the left, brigade commander Slack reported that "the thick growth of underbrush and vines, ravines, and hills made it very difficult to advance, but it was accomplished with little disorder." Hovey's other brigade commander, George McGinnis, was unsure of the exact location of the enemy and ranged forward himself with a cavalry scout "to satisfy myself by personal observation." Sure enough, he found "a point from which could be distinctly seen one section of artillery." Pressing forward, both brigades (plus Logan's division, for that matter) began to adapt to the terrain: "Its line conformed to the shape and became crescent-like, with the concave toward the hill," Hovey related. The Jackson Road followed a spur of the hill to the north, but the terrain fell off on either side where Slack and McGinnis advanced. Accordingly, the ground was filled with gullies and ravines as the slope gradually rose toward the hill itself.[33]

Worse was the Confederate fire emanating from the line. Atop the hill itself were four pieces of artillery, the two remaining ones from the Botetourt (Virginia) Artillery hit so heavily at Port Gibson earlier and two from Waddell's Alabama Battery. Alfred Cumming's Georgians, although because of skirmishers and detached duty there were only six companies per regiment, also lined the slope of the hill, the three Georgia regiments bending around the curve of the eminence, the 36th, 34th, and 39th Georgia from right to left manning the eastern and northern faces of the slope while the artillery sat atop it. The other two regiments of the brigade, the 56th and 57th Georgia, were detached a half-mile southward at the Crossroads itself with the rest of Waddell's guns. It was a line on good ground, but as division commander Stevenson noted, it was "single, irregular, divided, and without reserves." Hovey nevertheless reported that "the fire opened briskly along the whole line, from my extreme left to the right of the forces engaged under Major General McPherson." By 11:00 a.m., he added, "the battle opened hotly all along the line."[34]

"We did not fire a shot until we got within about 20 steps of the rebels," one of Hovey's Federals explained; "then we let a volley in to them . . . [and] then went in to them with the Bayonet." Hovey's Federals slammed into Cumming's Georgians in a mismatch of sizes; Carter Stevenson claimed his right was "crushed by overwhelming numbers." Slack's four regiments had nothing on their immediate front east of the road but swiveled to the west to confront the refused Confederate line before continuing on toward the Crossroads itself. McGinnis's five regiments slammed into the northern-facing regiment-and-a-half of Georgians, the wings of the 34th Georgia in the center facing both east and north. One colonel wrote that "by this time the action became general along the whole line, and very severe." It was a total of nine Federal regiments against three Georgia ones—certainly odds not in the Confederates' favor. And the terrain, while so helpful in many situations, could not multiply the defense enough to maintain the line. But the Confederates fought back, McGinnis reporting that "the rebel battery opened upon us with volley after volley of grape and canister."[35]

Worse for Cumming, who was quickly becoming the center of the attack, he had little warning that the main assault was at hand. As he shifted to the left, his skirmishers out ahead did not get the word and as a result remained in their former positions. That covered the gap from the hill to the Crossroads well, but Cumming's line now had no skirmishers out front. "While thus engaged in rectifying the line," he explained, "the battle broke upon us, and without previous intimation received, the skirmishers having been unable for the reasons hitherto given to keep pace with the movement of the line, and being no longer interposed between it and the enemy, though of this I was not informed until afterward." He later admitted that the Federals approached to within fifty yards mostly unseen.[36]

As Hovey's Federals pushed farther up the slope toward the hill and the Confederate fire became heavier, McGinnis used whatever he could to keep the men sheltered. "The whole line moved forward, with bayonets fixed," he wrote, "slowly, cautiously, and in excellent order, and when within about 75 yards of the battery every gun was opened upon us and every man went to the ground." With his troops protected, McGinnis realized it would take time for the enemy to reload and so he quickly ordered the charge. "As soon as the volley of grape and canister had passed over us," he added, "the order was given to charge, when the whole line moved forward as one man, and so suddenly and apparently so unexpected to the rebels was the movement, that, after a desperate conflict of five minutes, in which bayonets and butts of muskets were freely used, the battery of four guns was in our possession, and a whole brigade in support was fleeing before us."[37]

At the same time, Slack's Federals pivoted to the right and hit the eastern face of the square, driving the right of Cumming's brigade back and westward in the rear of the Confederates facing north. Worst hit was the right regiment, the 36th Georgia. In fact, Slack's Federals "penetrated in his rear as far as his colors," Cumming wrote. No wonder the Georgians fell back from the hill that was already becoming covered with blood and the bodies of the killed and wounded. Hovey himself christened it "the hill of death."[38]

Accordingly, Hovey's Federals broke through the Georgians in hand-to-hand combat, sweeping up and over the hill. Cumming himself, "throwing myself at the point at which the break had been made," waded into the melee but was not able to re-form his lines. "For over 600 yards up the hill my division gallantly drove the enemy before them," Hovey noted. Falling amid the Georgians' retreat were the four guns atop Champion Hill, certainly a destructive development, as they provided a lot of the firepower to the outnumbered Georgians. Hovey credited the 11th Indiana and 29th Wisconsin with taking the four guns atop the hill itself "at the point of the bayonet." Nevertheless, the Confederate line cracked and fell back, giving Hovey's troops the hill. But they were not satisfied.[39]

With the Georgians withdrawing southward in chaos, Cumming among them trying in vain to rally the broken regiments, Hovey followed, pushing his brigades onward. "From the edge of the timber we drove the enemy," wrote Colonel William T. Spicely of the 24th Indiana, "step by step, for nearly 800 yards, over deep ravines and abrupt hills." Artillery support soon arrived, mainly in the form of some of the 16th Ohio Battery guns. East of the road, Slack's Federals reached a cornfield that sat in the northeastern quadrant of the Crossroads. West of the road McGinnis continued southward through the revolving ravines and ridges, all the way to the Crossroads as well. But given that the Confederate line here was east of the intersection, it fell to Slack's brigade to deal with it. Slack thus pushed his troops out into the cornfield and approached the Crossroads from the northeast.[40]

Fortunately for Slack, the 56th and 57th Georgia's attention was firmly (and logically) faced toward the two full divisions approaching timidly on the Middle Road. So for that matter were the four guns of Waddell's Battery. But the enemy was not pushing hard on the Middle Road, and suddenly a more imminent threat emerged from the north. On the flank came Slack's Federals, with the lead elements of McGinnis's brigade even farther to the left rear. The Georgians had to turn their line and guns to the north to stop this advance if they hoped to hold the Crossroads, but it was a futile effort. Slack's Federals also ran up and over these Georgians, driving them back from the all-important Crossroads and capturing Waddell's four guns. Cumming wrote that the two regiments "were compelled in succession, by the uncovering of their left and the pressure of the enemy on their front, to fall back." What was left of Cumming's Georgia brigade, all five regiments, retreated hastily to the south toward the Roberts House, where Pemberton himself kept his headquarters. It was a disaster in the making; the critical Crossroads, the key to the Confederate escape, was in enemy hands.[41]

But it soon became even worse. The Confederate line extending down a similar ridge emanating off Champion Hill to the west was also being handled roughly despite the slight cover of a rail fence. Stephen D. Lee commanded the Alabama brigade to Cumming's left, the 23rd, 30th, 46th, 31st, and 20th Alabama from left to right holding the line. Heading toward them was an entire division as well, Logan's of McPherson's corps. While Hovey deployed along the Jackson Road, Logan shifted farther to the Union right and went into position with two brigades, holding the third initially in reserve but then sending it out to the far right to outflank the Confederate line. Mortimer Leggett's and John E. Smith's brigades had formed in the lowlands of the Bakers Creek bottom and prepared to head up the same series of ridges that Hovey's troops were ascending to their left. Union artillery deployed in support, one Ohioan describing how "it seemed as if every shell burst just as it reached the fence and rails and rebs flew into the air together."[42]

Returning early from a leave of absence and relieving Elias Dennis, who had fought the brigade at Raymond and Jackson, Mortimer Leggett formed his brigade on Hovey's right, also in two lines; he had heard of the pending movement and did not want to miss it, arriving with the army after the trek up from Grand Gulf. (Dennis was assigned to a brigade in another division but apparently never took command.) Up front were the 30th Illinois and 20th Ohio, in rear the 68th and 78th Ohio. To his right surged Smith's brigade of five regiments, three in front (the 31st and 20th Illinois and 23rd Indiana), with the 45th and 124th Illinois in rear. Logan himself rode among the troops shouting, "'now boys the hotter the quicker' meaning the harder we fought the sooner it would be over." He particularly addressed his old regiment, the 31st Illinois: "Thirty onesters remember the blood of your mammas." Leggett and Smith soon pushed forward at the same time as Hovey, finding the same rough and steep terrain that ascended up to the ridge that held the Confederate line; one Illinoisan termed it "a right steep hill." There, they met Lee's Alabamians.[43]

Unfortunately for the Confederate defense, Lee could not hold due to the almost two-to-one odds his men faced as well as the breaking of the brigade on his right, "their right flank having become exposed and the enemy having gained their rear." With Cumming's departure from Champion Hill itself as well as the loss of the guns that provided Lee cover, Lee's Alabamians broke and fled from their ridgetop position back across the ravines and gullies to a ridge in rear. Lee tried to rally his men, one Alabamian explaining how "Gen Lee taken our colors just as the Color bearer got kill." Lee would lose three horses that day, his clothes pierced by several bullets and his arm bruised terribly by a spent ball. But he could not stem the tide. In fact, his troops would not stop until they reached the ridge on which the Jackson Road sat after it left the Crossroads going west. A Federal noted they drove the enemy over the hill and beyond, but "then being very tired and fatigued so that we could go no faster than a walk we quit running after them."[44]

Additional fighting also occurred farther to the west as both sides put in more brigades to secure or take the Jackson Road avenue of escape, namely the upper creek crossing. Logan's third brigade under John D. Stevenson pushed on farther to the Union right and deployed three regiments on the extreme right flank, the 7th Missouri being in the rear with the trains; it would arrive only later in the battle. The 8th and 81st Illinois and 32nd Ohio positioned themselves in a flanking manner but soon ran into the Confederate response to the threat to the flank. "We marched through fields and over ditches, fences, through woods, until we met the enemy," explained Lieutenant Colonel Franklin Campbell of the 81st Illinois. Carter Stevenson had sent Barton's

Georgia brigade to the left cross-country behind the original Confederate line, and these regiments went into position near the Jackson Road itself as the defending ridge and the road ridge angled toward one another the farther west they ran and ultimately played out nearer to Bakers Creek. To turn this position, John Stevenson was told to attack and "throw forward his right." That was exactly the area of the critical upper creek crossing, the only route of escape for the Confederate army out of the trap that was Bakers Creek.[45]

Yet as Barton formed his four regiments—the 52nd, 40th, 41st, and 43rd Georgia left to right—Stevenson's Federals were on him quickly. Barton's defense, amid the shock of the breaking lines to the right and his hurried deployment, could hold no better than Lee and Cumming. Barton explained that, as Lee's troops to his right gave way, "my right flank was soon turned and overwhelmed." He added, "the left was in like manner enveloped and a heavy fire poured in from the rear." The Georgians had to fall back, leaving several guns of the Cherokee Georgia Artillery and Ridley's 1st Mississippi Light Artillery, which poured fire into the oncoming Federals until overwhelmed; one 8th Illinois soldier even described how the Confederate artillerymen fired over their heads when within a mere ten feet of the guns. Killed in the fight for the guns were both Ridley and Carter Stevenson's artillery chief, Major Joseph W. Anderson. Barton explained that "the enemy had so nearly surrounded the whole brigade that this movement was necessarily accompanied by some confusion. . . . The brigade had been terribly handled." One Georgian related that in the retreat uphill an older member of his company begged him to stop and give him some water: "I cannot go any further!" He did so but related that "I thought he never would get through drinking." All the while, the Federals were right behind them, one Illinoisan relating that they were "driving them like sheep."[46]

Particularly gratifying was the charge of the 32nd Ohio. Having moved forward and taken some of the guns, the Ohioans seemed jubilant that they had resurrected their honor. The regiment had served initially in the east and had actually surrendered in September 1862 at Harpers Ferry during the Antietam Campaign. Sent west, the Ohioans endured no end of shaming from their new comrades, who called them "Harper's Ferry cowards." They had not had an opportunity to regain their honor at Raymond, being stuck off on the far right flank and hardly in action, but they made up for it now. Upon charging forward on Barton's brigade and the Confederate guns, the Ohioans themselves yelled, "Go in, Harper's Ferry cowards."[47]

As a result, as John Stevenson moved toward Barton's Georgians and broke their line as well, one Illinoisan describing "killing them in great numbers and set[ting] them in flight," Stevenson actually advanced far enough to take the Jackson Road itself, although no one in the Union high command actually knew what they had done; soon McPherson "peremptorily ordered" him to fall back to support the left of the division when it was threatened in the afternoon. It would be highly significant if the Federals took and held the Jackson Road between the Crossroads and the upper crossing of Bakers Creek, because at the time that was the only crossing point available to the entire Confederate army (minus the wagon train and Reynolds's brigade that had already passed). It was a major disaster in the making, but in one of the many fog-of-war stumbles, Stevenson's Union troops ranged back somewhat to re-form their victorious lines with the rest of the division. In doing so, they reopened the Jackson Road to the Confederates temporarily, but Barton knew the significance and sent a hasty note to fellow brigade commander Reynolds to get the wagon train, now in grave danger, headed westward across the Big Black River. Still, in the words of engineer Lockett, "the enemy had succeeded by his vastly superior numbers in completely turning our left."[48]

The Federals were jubilant anyway. "Our boys did nobly but paid dearly for ground gained," one of Hovey's Federals explained. But Logan's troops were indeed on the verge of an especially major breakthrough, one confident veteran arguing that "our division did all the fighting at Raymond and a principal part in every other engagement." Grant seemed to think the division carried its weight, and he would have been even more convinced had Stevenson held the Jackson Road for good. Still, watching from the rear, Grant instructed a staff officer: "Go down to Logan and tell him he is making history to-day."[49]

15

"I AM OF THE OPINION THAT THE BATTLE FOR VICKSBURG HAS BEEN FOUGHT"

May 16 Afternoon

Crisis time was here for John C. Pemberton. His army was perched out across Bakers Creek with only one crossing to utilize, he was being confronted from three directions, and his northern flank had just broken dramatically up on the Jackson Road and at Champion Hill. In fact, the key crossroads that the majority of the army had to funnel through to get to that one usable creek crossing was now in enemy hands, and the crossing itself was terribly vulnerable. It was indeed crisis time; if Pemberton did not ease the situation quickly, he and the vast majority of his army probably would not survive the day as a fighting force and maybe not at all.[1]

As bad as it was, there were still some bright points. On two of the three roads leading to his position, there was little to no Union effort to advance, much less assault. If that lethargy continued on the Raymond and Middle Roads—and there was no guarantee that it would—it would at least allow Pemberton to move some of the troops defending in those quiet areas up to the crisis point to the north. In fact, Pemberton had somehow worked his way into a situation where the vast majority of his army, two full divisions, was confronting a minority of the enemy on the Raymond Road. That ratio, of course, meant that elsewhere a minority of his army confronted the major-ity of Grant's force. The numbers bore that out. Carter Stevenson's division, minus one of his brigades that had already crossed Bakers Creek to safety, confronted ultimately the three Union divisions on the Jackson Road and the two on the Middle Road. Essentially, three Confederate brigades faced a pos-sible twelve Union brigades on the two roads.[2]

It was certainly not Pemberton's finest moment as a commander, but then it was his only moment as a tactical commander. He had never before led in battle, certainly one of this scope, and he was obviously outmatched. Just be-ing out of position east of the Big Black River and especially Bakers Creek told as much, but his tactical deployment and battle handling was not the stuff of genius either. Nevertheless, Pemberton saw an opening with such little movement down on the Raymond Road. If the numerous Confederate brigades holding against a very timid force down there were not needed, he would call them northward and counterattack against the Federal incursion that was pointed, strong, and potentially fatal to his chances. As a result, he sent messages to John Bowen and William Loring to push troops northward to rectify the situation at the Crossroads.[3]

Put simply, if Pemberton did not correct the issues spiraling out of control at the Crossroads, his army was doomed. He did not necessarily have to re-take Champion Hill itself, but he did need the Crossroads and the upper creek crossing to extricate his army—that is, if the lower crossing was still inoper-able. But he was working on that too.

P roblems innumerable developed almost immediately as Pemberton began to deal with his difficult situation. And a lot of them traced back to his own fault. The main issue at this point was that both Bowen and Loring refused to send troops, even after Pemberton repeatedly ordered them to do so. Both responded that there were plenty of Federals on their front, and they could certainly see them in the large fields down along the Raymond Road. Yet the problems went deeper than the potential for Union advance down there, and it all had to do with Pemberton's command system, which was chaotic to start with. Loring related that "during this time I received an order to retire, also one to advance, both of which were countermanded." Then, Bowen and Loring outright disobeyed orders, but it was not the first time command chaos had arisen. Lloyd Tilghman was currently under arrest by Pemberton, and there was quite a feud going on especially between Loring and Pemberton. It did not help that brigade commander Tilghman outranked Bowen, a division commander.[4]

While Loring and Pemberton were not serving their chief very effectively or efficiently (or even honorably, for that matter), Pemberton was not blame-less in the situation. He remained confused, and he even ordered both Loring and Bowen to attack all those Federals that they reported on their fronts, but then he came back to his senses and ordered them once more to the left. But in not moving, they, in fact, were doing nothing more than what they had watched Pemberton do with his own superior, Joseph E. Johnston. The departmental commander had been ordering Pemberton away from Vicksburg for weeks now, and Pemberton had refused, disobeying those orders. That Jefferson Davis had become involved and was ordering the direct opposite made the matter tricker and murkier, but Pemberton's generals nevertheless watched as he disobeyed Johnston's direct orders, and now they were doing the exact same thing. Eventually, when Carter Stevenson informed Pemberton that "unless Loring's division was brought up we could not hold the field," Pemberton responded that "it had been repeatedly ordered to come forward." The commander himself rode southward "to hasten their movement."[5]

Obviously, this was not the time for petty or even deserving quarrels, as the fate of the army and perhaps Vicksburg stood in the balance. Pemberton kept ordering, one of his staff officers explaining that "this important order I heard urgently and repeatedly sent, and two or three of General Loring's staff officers who rode up meantime were sent immediately back with these instructions." He concluded that "there seemed to be great delay in obeying this order." Indeed, both division commanders kept delaying, Loring testifying of the enemy "showing every indication of an attack in force upon my position, both in front and upon the right flank." Pemberton certainly was in no mood for nonsense and soon sent a peremptory order for Bowen to move his entire division and eventually to Loring to move two of his three brigades northward. Bowen finally rode forward to Pemberton, who repeated the order in person to make sure, although Pemberton had even broken the chain of command by this point by sending orders directly to brigade commanders to move; Cockrell reported that "I received an order directly from Lieutenant General Pemberton." He had to have help now and would brook no opposition at this point. The result was more confusion, Loring writing that "General Bowen was summarily ordered in that direction, without warning either to myself or to General Buford, commanding a brigade of my division next to him."[6]

Bowen acquiesced under the peremptory order and soon marched his two brigades northward along the Ratliff Road. But there was more confusion, Cockrell reporting that he first received orders to go to the left of Stevenson's line, but that was countermanded with orders to go to the right. Likewise, Loring later in the afternoon would eventually start Buford's and Featherston's brigades as well, Loring leading the latter in person and riding with Featherston at its head. Pemberton staff officer Jacob Thompson had ridden at the general's request to Loring "at the full speed of my horse" and told Loring the order, to which he responded that the command would not have been given "if General Pemberton knew that the enemy was in great force on his front." Thompson simply repeated the order and added that if he refused "the responsibility was his, not mine." Loring finally moved, although Pemberton complained that "in the transmission of these various messages to and fro, over a distance of more than a mile, much valuable time was necessarily consumed, which the enemy did not fail to take advantage of." But Loring was moving now. "The march was as rapid as possible under the circumstances," Featherston noted; "the troops moved at a double-quick . . . most of the way." Even Tilghman was ordered to be ready to move northward, such was the lack of Union movement on the Raymond Road.[7]

Yet due to Loring's continual delay, at this point the two brigades of Bowen's division were all Pemberton had to stem the tide, but he quickly deployed them south of the Crossroads for the big advance. Francis Cockrell placed his leading brigade of Missourians to the left of the road while Martin Green's trailing brigade of Missourians and Arkansans moved to the right side and went into line, a saber-wielding Cockrell helping form the lines. One Missourian described the process:

> We marched to the scene of action and went into line "on the left by file into line," was the order. If a good drill master had taken the men one at a time and placed them into line, they would not have been more in their respective places than they were, when we were all in line. It put me in mind of taking a rope by one end and holding to one end and making it straighten out in the road before you.

And it was all done under heavy fire, as well as in front of a group of ladies oddly enough singing "Dixie" by the roadside. When all was done, Bowen motioned his hard-hitting division forward to retake the Crossroads. It was about 2:30 p.m.[8]

The trans-Mississippians did so and more, led as they were by their near idol John Bowen. One doting Missourian later wrote that "it appeared to me that there was a halo of glory around his head and face." A Missourian described how they formed in the road between two worm-rail fences and were soon ordered behind the southernmost one, only to be quickly thereafter ordered back to the road. When the order to advance came, the men "took hold of the bottom rail of the fence in front of them and lifted it clear of the ground and threw it twenty or thirty feet, and away we went across a little field and into the edge of the woods." One 5th Missouri soldier explained that "very soon we gave them the Missouri yell . . . and gave them a charge in REBEL style."[9]

"The enemy, being rallied under cover of the woods," Alvin Hovey explained, "poured down the road in great numbers upon the position occupied by my forces." West of the Crossroads, Cockrell led his Missourians against the re-forming and stunned units of George McGinnis's brigade lingering near the intersection and the northwest quadrant of the Jackson Road; he held aloft a sword in one hand and a Magnolia bloom in the other. McGinnis wrote that "being strongly reenforced, they turned upon us and made a most determined stand." He added, "at this point occurred one of the most obstinate and murderous conflicts of the war. For half an hour each side took their turn in driving and being driven." Action quickly became heavy as the Missourians rushed forward, even driving back a section of the 16th Ohio Battery that had moved up to the new line. Proud brigade commander Cockrell described how his troops "in the most gallant, dashing, fearless manner, officers and men with loud cheers threw themselves forward at a run against the enemy's hitherto victorious lines." And then the Missourians began to steadily push McGinnis's Federals back toward Champion Hill itself. McGinnis could only send word to Hovey that he was being pressed back "and asking for assistance."[10]

Hovey had none to give, because east of the road the same thing occurred as Green's brigade pushed forward against Slack's re-forming units near the Crossroads and in the cornfield in the northeastern quadrant. "We routed them and took after them," one Confederate wrote. Colonel Thomas P. Dockery of the 19th Arkansas related that the brigade formed "between our retreating forces and the advancing foe, and charged the enemy. . . . The formation of the country was such that the troops could scarcely advance faster than a walk, and many of the hills were ascended with great difficulty; notwithstanding, the command pushed impetuously forward, driving back in confusion the many fresh lines formed to meet our gallant troops." Slack himself reported that "a new rebel line, which had not been in action, appeared in treble our force, and opened a most murderous fire upon our lines." Then they advanced through the cornfield, Colonel Elijah Gates relating that his Missourians "obeyed as promptly as I ever saw troops in my life," retaking the four Alabama guns that had fallen to Slack's Federals. The brigade then pushed on, all the while with two full Federal divisions sitting on their right flank just down the Middle Road. But the startling counterattack so frightened Osterhaus and company on the Middle Road that the reaction was not to advance and take advantage of the situation but rather to hunker down and

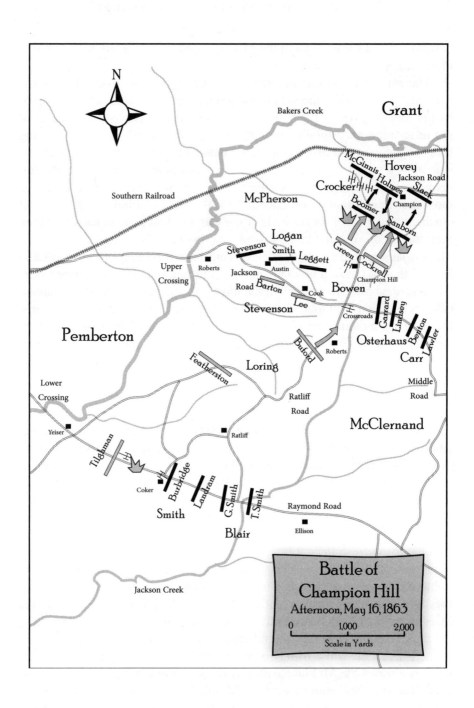

N

Grant

Bakers Creek

Southern Railroad

McPherson

McGinnis   Hovey
Crocker   Holmes   Jackson Road
Champion   Slack

Boomer
Sanborn

Logan
Stevenson   Smith
Leggett
Green   Cockrell

Upper
Crossing   Roberts
Jackson   Austin
Road   Barton
Lee   Cook   Champion Hill
Bowen

Stevenson

Crossroads
Pemberton
Garrard   Lindsey
Buford   Barton   Lawler
Roberts   Osterhaus

Lower
Crossing   Loring   Carr

Featherston   Middle
Road
Ratliff
Road

Yeiser   McClernand
Ratliff

Tilghman
Coker   Burbridge   Smith
Landram   G. Smith   T. Smith
Raymond Road
Smith   Ellison
Blair

Jackson Creek

Battle of
Champion Hill
Afternoon, May 16, 1863

0   1,000   2,000
Scale in Yards

hold what they had. Osterhaus himself described the resistance on the Middle Road as "very fierce," adding that "the enemy made a most desperate attempt to prevent the junction of the divisions. We could see his columns advancing in great numbers, and I considered it prudent to strengthen my line." As a result, Green likewise began to drive Slack's regiments back northward along the Jackson Road, out of the cornfield and up toward the Champion Hill ridge. Pemberton himself noted that the attack "for the time turned the tide of battle in our favor."[11]

Others became engaged as well, including Lee's re-forming brigade farther to the west on the Jackson Road, effectively on Bowen's left. Lee marveled at Bowen's attack, later writing that "the charge of this magnificent division, for dash and gallantry, was not surpassed by any troops on either side." Barton was also re-forming and still holding the area of the upper crossing of Bakers Creek. Parts of both brigades moved forward as well, although less than Bowen's fresh troops who by midafternoon had driven Hovey and some of Logan's troops all the way back to Champion Hill itself, Logan's German artillery chief Major Charles Stolbrand yelling at brigade commander Smith: "Sheneral Schmitt dey are sharging you mitt double column By damn tit dey vant mine guns." Smith calmly retorted, "Let 'em come, we're ready." While some of Logan's troops held, Hovey's continued to fall back. Union brigade commander Slack noted that "I directed the whole command to retire gradually from the field and take position near the crest of the hill where the rebel lines were first formed." Taken at the top of the hill, of course, were the four Virginia and Alabama guns, which Bowen's Confederates soon recaptured. Hovey knew his division was the main target, writing that the Confederates on Logan's front "would not dare advance on the open ground before General McPherson, who had handled them roughly on the right." Amid the re-formed regiments of Hovey's division, one Ohioan noted that he saw Grant and staff, along with the general's son, Fred, right among them.[12]

Nevertheless, Bowen's counterattack did what Pemberton had hoped and more, but it had been "an awfully hard fight," one of the surging Missourians admitted. "Being overwhelmed by numbers," George McGinnis explained, "the First Brigade began to fall back, not in disorder and confusion, but in good order, step by step, contesting every inch of ground." Still, the critical Crossroads were now in Confederate hands once more, as was the summit of Champion Hill itself, and the Confederates were continuing their surge northward along the Jackson Road. Portions of Cumming's and Lee's brigades had joined in, Cumming writing that some of his Georgians "advanced considerably beyond the line on which they had first encountered him in the morning." And they were meeting their old foes of the morning fight and exacting some revenge. "My division in the mean time had been compelled to yield ground before overwhelming numbers," Hovey admitted. "Slowly and stubbornly they fell back, contesting with death every inch of the field they had won." The hill itself was less critical than the Crossroads, but both were in Confederate hands now, and there seemed to be little to no desire on the part of the Federals on the Middle Road to begin actively advancing.[13]

But it came at a high cost to Bowen, certainly in casualties in an already small division. "Our little division advanced unchecked," one Missourian noted. Many men were down, as was Colonel Gates's horse, shot three times; "he lay down and died like a soldier." Yet despite the triumph, there was concern for the division's tactical safety. Bowen's attack had been so successful that it had outranged the rest of the Confederate lines, broken as they were but still somewhat intact. There was little more to defend along the Middle Road than had been there all morning, but Lee's and Barton's troops, with Cumming's also around, were re-forming if not advancing as far as Bowen; Pemberton himself re-formed the 56th and 57th Georgia, telling them he would lead them personally if their officers would not, at which point the officers "petitioned you to let them lead them." Pemberton also sent his staff officers to rally others, all the while casting longing glances down the Ratliff Road and asking: "Where is Loring?" But Bowen had surged perhaps too far, eventually approaching the Champion House itself. An Arkansas colonel related that their orders were to drive the enemy "as long as it were possible to advance the lines, if it had to be done with empty guns." Certainly, he had driven mainly Hovey's two brigades all the way back to their original positions of the morning, but not so Logan's troops or Osterhaus's or Carr's on the Middle Road. In effect, Bowen had bored a hole into the Federal army right along the Jackson Road, retaking the Crossroads. But Federals elsewhere had not withdrawn in response, and the result was Bowen being stuck way out into the Federal army in a bulge while both his flanks were open, and Federals actually dominated the ground in rear of both of those flanks. Samuel Lockett explained that Bowen's division made "one of its grand old charges, in which it bored a hole through the Federal army." One foot soldier added that "we had pierced the enemy center and were far in advance of all the rest of our army." It was ticklish position to be sure, but Pemberton would take it. Perhaps it would have been better to simply retake the Crossroads and solidify a line close by, retaining ammunition and strength for additional fighting rather than spending all the force the division had on going as far as possible and then petering out. But who could tell Bowen's hard-charging trans-Mississippians to stop while they were driving the enemy?[14]

The tide was definitely turning, at least in terms of possession of the Cross-roads. But the larger context still had a badly managed Confederate army in dire straits as it struggled to just get off the field and away. And that became harder to do as more Federals arrived. There were certainly already enough to do the job, if Osterhaus and Carr made a grand assault into the flank and then rear of Bowen's driving brigades. But they stood still, and as had happened throughout the morning, the northern sector along the Jackson Road was destined to continue to be the significant point of conflict. One of Osterhaus's Indianans wrote of being "so anxious and ready but was not ordered up." The brigades merely maneuvered for position, including Colonel Giles A. Smith's brigade of Blair's division down on the Raymond Road moving up to connect Osterhaus and Smith's divisions; Carr was ordered to do the same thing from above. Although wounded soon began to pour through the lines on the Middle Road, the divisions did not fully engage yet; one Iowan in Carr's division merely noted that "our route was through timber brush across deep ravines matted with cane brakes which made it impossible to keep in line making our movement slow." There was also some reports of friendly fire in Carr's lines, which certainly would have added to the confusion, as did conscripts running, which "caused other good men to suffer," one Illinoisan complained.[15]

Fortunately for Grant, he had more troops arriving at the critical area on the Jackson Road, ushered in by the sound of the guns: "Rapid firing of artillery in front again announced the presence of the enemy," one of the commanders explained. But not all were enthused, one Indianan in Sanborn's brigade admitting that "we were not looking for a fight so soon again, but it seemed as tho we were in for it every other day." While Hovey's and Logan's divisions had fought the battle pretty much all morning and into the afternoon, now began to arrive a new division under Marcellus Crocker. Its original commander, Isaac Quinby, had left it prior to crossing the Mississippi River back in April, suffering from the effects of the Yazoo Pass operation, but he crossed to Grand Gulf on May 14 and arrived on site with the army after a sixteen-mile ride the day before, arriving with Blair's division train. But switching division commanders, even to an old and known one, was problematic upon going into battle, so Quinby watched as Crocker fought the brigades that afternoon. "It was deemed inexpedient," Quinby explained, "to [change] the command of the division at the moment it was engaging the enemy." The change occurred later that evening, after the battle.[16]

Newspaperman Cadwallader claimed he had been to the front and notified Grant himself of the breaking of Hovey's troops in front of Bowen and warning that the brigades "would soon come over the brow of the hill, with very little show of military formation." About that time McPherson rode up to Grant, who told him the news, which McPherson had already heard. Others say that one of Hovey's brigade commanders, George McGinnis himself, "came dashing down the road, from the hill, spurring his horse at every jump." Grant pointed and ordered, "then I would move Quinby [Crocker] into line here" and pointed elsewhere, adding, "I would place a battery here; another there." McPherson moved to do so, and Crocker's first two brigades soon entered the fight.[17]

Crocker sent the lead brigades directly into the action once Grant himself became involved and ordered them ahead. Hovey had been begging for help as his broken brigades fell back, but they being from a different corps it was time-consuming to get it done: "I sent to them for support, but being unknown to the officers of that command, considerable delay (not less than half an hour) ensued, and I was compelled to resort to Major General Grant to procure the order for their aid." Finally, Grant himself stepped in and gave direct orders to George Boomer and John Sanborn to enter the fight; Colonel Holden Putnam of the 93rd Illinois in Boomer's brigade noted that one of Grant's staff officers "brought orders from General Grant for us to move instantly to the support of General Hovey's division, then being forced back by a superior force of the enemy." They did so, Hovey's brigade commander McGinnis writing that soon "we were greeted by the shouts of the long-promised re-enforcements, and one brigade, under command of Colonel Boomer, came looming over the hill." All knew it was the critical time, Lieutenant Colonel Ezekiel S. Sampson of the 5th Iowa declaring that "the imminent peril of the moment caused us to be ordered immediately forward upon the enemy."[18]

One of Crocker's common soldiers, Samuel Byres, also knew what it meant: "'My time has probably come now,' I said to myself." But the brigade surged forward anyway, meeting the disorganized bands of Hovey's divisions. One reinforcing officer yelled for Hovey's "stragglers" to join them, to which one of the Federals of Hovey's division yelled back, "these are the men who have fought this battle; there are no stragglers here." The fresh officer "looked at our powdered, blackened faces, took off his hat and said: 'I beg your pardon; true enough, there are no stragglers on this line.'" It helped, of course, that Grant himself was at times right behind the nervous Federals.[19]

Sanborn was Crocker's lead brigade and pushed off to the left of the road after it made the ninety-degree turn north of the Champion House, deploying in two lines of two regiments each. "The men threw their knapsacks and blankets from their shoulders," Lieutenant Colonel John E. Tourtellotte of the 4th Minnesota wrote, "and dashed forward in the direction indicated at the double-quick step up the hill, into the woods, and upon the body of the enemy." But it soon met the surging Confederates, Colonel Jesse I. Alexander of the 59th Indiana explaining that the enemy "made a violent assault on my command." Edward Wood of the 48th Indiana admitted that "it was now just past midday and the heat was extreme—some of our men dropped from sheer exhaustion & more from rebel bullets." George Boomer's following brigade went into similar deployment east of the road, although as they advanced the brigade shifted across the road to the west to try to stall Cockrell's hard-charging Missourians first. But neither was able to stop Bowen entirely, Colonel William T. Spicely of the 24th Indiana in Hovey's division writing that it was "the most desperate and destructive [fighting] of the day." The Missourians and Arkansans swarmed around the flanks of the new Federal brigades, Colonel Sampson of the 5th Iowa writing that "I was informed from three different sources that the enemy was passing completely around our left. . . . I then ordered the regiment to retire to the next ridge." Even worse, the lead elements of the Confederate counterattack ranged all the way near the Champion House itself, within sight of the Federal wagon train parked well to the rear. It would be a disaster if Bowen's troops reached those wagons, partially filled with ammunition.[20]

Crocker's veteran brigades started to stem the Confederate tide but were unable to stop it entirely despite Sanborn arguing that some of his men "stood like a wall of adamant." McGinnis explained that "the rebel advance was momentarily checked, but they came down upon us in such immense numbers that in a short time the whole line, re-enforcements and all, were compelled to give ground." An Indianan admitted that "it soon became evident that the work before us was no holiday employment." Cockrell agreed from his side, writing that "fresh troops of the enemy were rapidly thrown in front of our lines, and were immediately engaged and repulsed." Also obviously coming at the Federal reinforcements were the remnant of Hovey's division, Colonel Putnam adding that as his men were "moving down into the hollow . . . the men of General Hovey's division [were] constantly passing through their ranks."[21]

Despite the Union reinforcements, Bowen's Confederates still trudged down the slope in front of Champion Hill even amid growing casualties and dwindling ammunition. Calls went out for help, but there were no more troops to send or ammunition to distribute. Loring had not made his appearance as yet, and the ammunition wagons had been sent to safety west of the creek. Bowen fought on nevertheless, for a couple of hours in fact, rolling over Boomer and Sanborn as well. "In about three hundred yards we came on another line who were lying down over the hill, they raised on their knees and gave us a fire, we kept crawling on them until we got, in many places, within ten paces of them. They soon gave way in wild disorder. We again gave the Missouri Yell and took after them." In the melee the flag of the 93rd Illinois fell captive but was recovered with twenty-seven holes in it, with four or five more gashes on the staff.[22]

Now it was time for the Federals to face the crisis; McPherson in fact related that "the tide of battle was turning against us," and McClernand directly admitted that "a crisis had come." But just about the time Bowen's attack finally began to slow down, two things occurred. First, Alvin Hovey, always an artilleryman as seen at Port Gibson just days ago, managed to arrange as many as sixteen Federal guns near a knob in the Bakers Creek lowlands, and they began to fire into the already slowing Confederates, stopping further progress. He ordered Captain George W. Schofield's Company A, 1st Missouri Light Artillery and Captain James A. Mitchell's 16th Ohio Battery into position, and they were soon joined by Captain Henry Dillon's 6th Wisconsin Battery. Artillery had been little used thus far because of the terrain and woods, but this was the perfect chance for the long arm to add its strength, and it did so loudly and decisively. "Through the rebel ranks these batteries hurled an incessant shower of shot and shell, entirely enfilading the rebel columns," a satisfied Hovey reported.[23]

The second major event was the arrival of the third and last brigade of Crocker's division under Colonel Samuel Holmes. The brigade had been far in the rear guarding the wagon train and rushed forward upon Grant's order to help, as it was the last body of troops on the Jackson Road that could be utilized except for Sherman's two divisions, which were far too far in the rear to be of help that day. Colonel David B. Hillis of the 17th Iowa reported that his regiment was "double-quicked through dust and a burning sun." Holmes would have to turn the tide if anyone would do so. Crocker threw them into the fight immediately upon arrival, writing that "it was apparent that he [Boomer] sorely needed assistance."[24]

But it was a small brigade, just two present regiments: the 17th Iowa on the right and the 10th Missouri on the left (the 80th Ohio being left behind with the wagon train). The regiments had marched hard, Crocker advising that the brigade, "being informed of the position of affairs, proceeded with the greatest alacrity and enthusiasm to the front." And it was just in time. "I arrived in the vicinity of the hills on which the battle was being fought about 2 p.m.," Colonel Hillis of the 17th Iowa related, "and without having time to rest my men (who had that day marched 12 miles through dust and a burning sun with knapsacks on their backs) was ordered forward at a double-quick." Despite being temporarily relieved of command by McPherson for taking a swig of whiskey at this critical moment, which Grant promptly rescinded,

Holmes formed his two present regiments in line "at a point midway up and on the north side of the hill" and dashed forward to the hill itself that Holmes reported "was in the act of being retaken by the enemy." These two regiments moved up along the Jackson Road "up the hill over ground of the roughest and most broken character," according to Major Francis C. Deimling of the 10th Missouri, and slammed into the Confederates just as they reached their point of overextension, adding just enough force to tip the scales the other way. Leading the Missourians this time, with Color Sergeant Calvin Lingle (who had carried the colors at Jackson) now prostrated by sickness, Corporal Martin C. Carmody carried the flag despite being seriously wounded in the face. McPherson himself termed their attack as "a dashing charge," although it cost the 10th Missouri their lieutenant colonel, Leonidas Horney. One Irish Missourian had run to the brink of a ravine and called his comrades, "come on, here they are!" Horney rode to the ravine but was hit, prompting one to reflect "apparently the little old Irishman was too small game for them."[25]

Meanwhile, the 17th Iowa took the colors of the 31st Alabama in the surge forward. Also retaken were the four artillery pieces atop the hill, Holmes writing that they had been "captured by our forces and again retaken by the enemy . . . [and] recaptured by the Seventeenth Iowa." That seemed to break the Confederate thrust for good. "This caused the enemy to give way," Colonel Hillis continued, "but he soon rallied, and again gave way, and in this way I advanced, driving him slowly, inch by inch, from the ravines and ditches in which he had effected a lodgment, up one declivity and down another, and finally onto the summit of the ridge along which the road runs, and charged him down the slope on the other (south) side."[26]

Holmes's attack stopped Bowen's further progress and added just enough force to start the retrograde; McClernand noted that "the enemy gave way and the fortune of the day in this part of the field was retrieved." As additional regiments of Hovey's division as well as Boomer's and Sanborn's brigades re-formed and reentered the fight in order, they too added to the pressure starting Bowen back southward; the 59th Indiana took the colors of the 46th Alabama in the process. The combined force, Hovey explained, "drove them again over the ground which had been hotly contested for the third time during the day." Confederate brigade commander Alfred Cumming described the withdrawal, writing that "the enemy, flushed with his previous success, and in numbers much superior to ours, drove our men apparently along the whole division front; slowly at first, afterwards more rapidly, till on reaching the road the flight became precipitate." Additional problems were that Logan's troops were behind Bowen on the left, Grant writing that his presence and continued fight "weakened his [Bowen's] front attack wonderfully," and Osterhaus's and Carr's full divisions were behind his right flank. Nearly surrounded and pushed back at the front, Bowen logically started the long retrograde back toward the Crossroads, General Green loudly proclaiming that "he never would have been driven back but for the fact that he had not a cartridge left."[27]

Lockett again explained of Bowen's division: "Finding itself unsupported [it] turned around and bored its way back again." A Missourian elaborated on the ticklish position, writing that "to get out, we had to pass between two lines of the enemy, which were not far apart and receive a fire from both lines, one on either side of us, and one that was now advancing in our front." If Bowen could not hold at Champion Hill, the Crossroads itself absolutely had to be held. He could only hope that more help, in the form of some of Loring's brigades, was on the way to do just that.[28]

Help did arrive for the beleaguered Confederates, but it was far too little and far too late. As Cockrell fought for dear life at the hill and Crossroads, he sent requests for reinforcements but heard from Pemberton himself that "he had not a man until General Loring should arrive." With orders to retreat in hand, Cockrell nevertheless delayed, hoping Loring would soon appear. Then as Bowen's nearly ammunitionless division began to fall back first toward Champion Hill "slowly and reluctantly, although terribly cut to pieces," and then all the way to the Crossroads (Union brigade commander James Slack gloating that "utter annihilation could only be prevented by a precipitate flight"), Abraham Buford's brigade of Loring's division finally made its appearance on the Ratliff Road. His men had heard the ruckus all day, Buford noting that "from the heavy firing in the direction of the left, it was evident that the enemy had massed his forces and was throwing them on the left wing of the army." Featherston's brigade followed but took a different route, finally getting thoroughly turned around; Pemberton called their route "a country road which was considerably longer than the direct route." When one of Pemberton's staff officers located Loring and Featherston at the head of the brigade, he told them they were "on the wrong road and going in the wrong direction." The brigade as a result played little significant part in the fight except at the very end of the day, when it provided some last line defense as the Confederate army withdrew. Featherston described the chaos nonetheless, writing that "we found a large number of stragglers going to the rear in great confusion." But Buford's brigade did engage, lending support at a critical spot.[29]

Buford moved his regiments quickly, explaining that "my command double-quicked the distance (about 2 miles) under a scorching sun, through corn and rye fields, in about half an hour, when I arrived about the rear of the right wing of General Bowen's division, which was falling back in disorder before an overpowering force of the enemy." But moving up the Ratliff Road put the brigade squarely in the path of McClernand's forces on the Middle Road. By this point, later in the afternoon, McClernand had rectified many of the problems on that road. There was a definite feeling of fear and unknown, as the basic mode all along had been one of defense rather than offense. It did not help now that Bowen's troops, almost literary fighting their way back out the way they went in while boring the hole through the Federal army, backed into the right flank of Osterhaus's division as it lay astride the Middle Road. "The direction of the enemy's retreat on that flank," Osterhaus explained, "was such that he fell (rather unexpectedly to both parties) on the left [right] of the First Brigade, which was advancing and fighting on the main road." He added that "the appearance of the enemy on their flank stopped for some time the advance of our troops."[30]

But McClernand had also received Grant's earlier order to advance, delayed because of the length of time it took to get from one wing to another. Despite Grant later castigating him viciously in his memoirs and staff officers complaining at the time ("he has had no serious fighting," one staff officer wrote in his diary at 4:40 p.m.), McClernand began doing so, sending out orders that "Generals Smith and Osterhaus will attack the enemy vigorously, and press for victory." Historian Steve Woodworth has surmised that "if McClernand sincerely thought that Grant's orders not to initiate a battle prohibited him from joining one already in progress less than half a mile away," his competence certainly could be called into question; rather, Woodworth saw something more sinister in the continually eroding Grant–McClernand relationship.[31]

McClernand pushed on nonetheless but soon met a reinforced Confederate Crossroads. Buford's brigade fanned out to the south and west in another ninety-degree line much like Cumming's earlier one at Champion Hill itself. This time, much of the brigade went into line west of the Crossroads on the Jackson Road facing north, where Buford described "our men were hastening in wild disorder and in consternation before a very heavy fire of the enemy," he adding later that "my column was continually broken by men of other brigades, who, driven back, were rushing pell-mell from the scene of action and resisting all attempts made to rally them." Worse, Buford's numbers were "at this critical moment . . . unceremoniously and materially reduced, this being done without my knowledge." Pemberton himself peeled off one of the regiments and Bowen another, both ordered to face eastward on the Ratliff Road where they became heavily engaged. In particular, the 12th Louisiana and 35th Alabama did noble work in stemming McClernand's renewed Union advance on the Middle Road, which again never did amount to much of anything. Colonel Thomas M. Scott of the 12th Louisiana even resorted to "cold steel," launching an advance that drove some of Osterhaus's Federals back for a time. "We charged the entire brigade," a proud Scott explained, although he added, "I did not consider it prudent to pursue the enemy." Still, the heavy divisions on the reestablished Confederate flank were concern enough, Cockrell writing of "the enemy . . . rapidly advancing on the right, in order of battle almost perpendicular to our own."[32]

Worse for the Confederates, the Unions forces on the Raymond Road were by this time also making some headway. With all of Bowen's division and two-thirds of Loring's now gone northward, only one lone Confederate brigade remained to confront the two full "idle" divisions of Smith and Blair on the Raymond Road. The task of holding the line fell to Lloyd Tilghman who, although under arrest, was temporarily allowed to command; he was a fighter, as demonstrated at his defense of Fort Henry earlier in the war. But the crisis was so real on the left that Tilghman too was soon ordered to proceed in that direction, leaving only skirmishers on the Raymond Road, although Pemberton quickly sent a countermanding order and rode there himself to make sure of it. Pemberton actually arrived before the order did, carried as it was by engineer Lockett who rode up to Pemberton and Tilghman as Tilghman was moving back into position. In the process, Tilghman had to pull back from the Coker House ridge to the next one to the west, Cotton Hill, where he placed the artillery and dueled with the still-timid Federals who soon occupied the Coker House ridge. There, the Federals used the ridge to shield the infantry while the artillery in the yard fought the Confederates up ahead; a few shells hit the house itself. Colonel Theodore Buehler of the 67th Indiana explained that as he was moving forward "all at once a battery opened fire on us with grape, canister, and shell while ascending a hill of some eminence." Colonel Friend S. Rutherford of the 97th Illinois interestingly noted that the Confederates "fired ricochet shot." Burbridge halted there despite the reinforcements from William Landram's following brigade that he said was "ready and impatiently awaiting orders," but many realized the opportunity had been missed. "It was my conviction at the time, confirmed by all I have learned since," Burbridge wrote later, "that, properly supported by General Blair's division, we could have captured the whole rebel force opposed to us, and reached Edwards Station before sunset." For his part, one of Landram's soldiers reported being "run . . . from one hill to another until I was pretty near gone up the spout."[33]

Meanwhile, a disgusted Pemberton seethed that "had the movement in support of the left been promptly made when first ordered, it is not improbable that I might have maintained my position, and it is possible the enemy might have been driven back." But now all he could do was manage the disaster. "I was then directed by the lieutenant-general to inform General Tilghman that the position he occupied was one of vast importance in securing our retreat, and that he must hold it at all hazards," Lockett wrote. Pemberton also sent word to maintain the position "at all hazards until sundown." Unfortunately for Tilghman, his defense came to an end when, in the act of personally sighting a cannon, he took a shell in the chest. Taken rearward to the Yieser House near the lower crossing of Bakers Creek, Tilghman's mangled body lay there while the fate of the Confederate army perhaps hung in the balance.[34]

But Tilghman's stand was not in vain, nor was his successor's, namely Colonel Arthur E. Reynolds. And Reynolds was not wrong when he declared "from the time of my assuming command of the brigade until I was ordered off the field, the fire of the enemy was very warm." But Pemberton and almost every other person in the Confederate army who knew the lay of the land and the road network had been hoping all day that the water level in Bakers Creek would fall enough to allow a crossing at the Raymond Road, or lower crossing. That would allow the army an additional escape route, especially now that the Crossroads had been taken and retaken, and the looks of things were that it would soon be re-retaken by the Federals for good. For that matter, the Jackson Road and upper crossing could also fall into Federal hands any minute now as well; Stevenson's brigade had already done so (although not knowing it), and indeed Logan soon severed Barton's brigade "from the rest of the division," Stevenson reported, and Barton crossed the upper bridge. His were the last Confederates to do so before Logan's troops took control for good. Consequently, Bowen sent Loring a message to "hold your position until sundown and save the army."[35]

Pemberton had his chief engineer, Samuel Lockett, working on the lower Bakers Creek crossing all day, and by late afternoon there was some progress. Lockett's orders were to "throw a bridge as soon as possible across Bakers Creek, on the main Raymond Road, where the country bridge had been washed away." The bridge was one thing, and there were doubts about rebuilding it in time to cross the army, but Lockett was also working on a ford just upstream. The main issue would be that the almost vertical banks of the creek would have to be dug down to allow troops and artillery a route into and out of the deep stream bed. But if Lockett could work a near miracle and open up a new route of escape, it would potentially save the army.[36]

The lower crossing consequently became more and more important as the late afternoon dragged on. The combined Federal units that connected at the

Crossroads, some five divisions' worth, were soon pressing southwestward against the conglomeration of Confederates who were trying to hold them back. "Lawler's brigade here cast the trembling balance in our favor," Mc-Clernand explained. Grant himself was there, writing dramatically of how he reached the Crossroads, and "I saw to my left and on the next ridge a column of troops, which proved to be Carr's division, and McClernand with it in person." He soon issued orders for Carr and Osterhaus to press ahead, doing so to Carr personally when he met him on the field. One Indianan explained that "we hallowed at them and they started to run and we let a volley after them." At one point, McClernand's advancing divisions came across "a family or part of a family, three women and young children. They had hidden in a deep ravine while the battle raged over and around them." Another Federal located a woman who said she had "trembled with fright down [in her] cellar" during the battle.[37]

In front of the surging Federals, the Confederates were a jumbled mess of regiments, brigades, and even divisions, tired, bloody, and some ammunitionless; Cockrell reported that the troops "took from the cartridge boxes of their fallen and wounded soldiers, and even stripped the slain and wounded of the enemy, with whom the ground was thickly strewn." A staff officer described the fleeing mass "looking as if they had just escaped from the Lunatic Asylum." Pemberton noted that "a part of Stevenson's division broke badly and fell back in great disorder." Lockett himself described the flight: "Our troops began to break and fall back in considerable disorder toward the main Raymond Road." Loring noted the lack of command when he took position with Featherston's brigade, writing that "I found the whole country, on both sides of the road, covered with the fleeing of our army, in many cases in large squads, and . . . there was no one endeavoring to rally or direct them." Featherston similarly noted that "here we found no one to give us direction or to tell us what to do. General Pemberton was not there, and no one present could tell us where he was. Neither of the major generals who had been conducting the battle was present on this part of the line." Finally, Featherston and Loring met Stephen D. Lee: "Recognizing him [Loring] as the senior officer on the field, and not seeing my division commander (Major General Stevenson), I reported to him for orders." Lee quickly formed his men alongside the Mississippians and tried to hold. In fact, Featherston and Lee provided a stout defense in the rough terrain in the southwestern quadrant of the Crossroads, fighting ridgetop to ridgetop as they continually withdrew toward the only hope of escape by this time: the lower crossing. Colonel Marcus D. L. Stephens explained the predicament, writing that after he took his position "the enemy was on my left, my right and in front." He asked his brigade commander which direction to face, and Featherston barked, "it makes no difference. Face any way and go to fighting!"[38]

But Featherston and Buford were about the only cohesive brigades still in action, Colonel Edward Goodwin of the 35th Alabama explaining that "at this time our friends gave way and came rushing to the rear panic-stricken. I rushed to the front, and ordered them to halt, but they heeded neither my orders nor those of their commanders." He continued: "I brought my regiment to the charge bayonets, but even this could not check them in their flight. The colors of three regiments passed through the Thirty-fifth. Both my officers and my men, undismayed, united with me in trying to cause them to rally. We collared them, begged them, and abused them in vain." The fugitives fled southward toward the only remaining crossing, one writing that "it was evident that the enemy had obtained possession of the bridge across the creek on the upper road." By late in the afternoon, in fact, Benton's brigade of Carr's division managed to take the crossing for good and was even pushing troops southward toward the lower crossing. Benton's artillery was already shelling the area from the upper crossing point as well. Carter Stevenson explained that "the enemy had crossed the bridge above, and were advancing artillery in the direction of the road."[39]

Yet Lockett had worked miracles down at the lower crossing, and by the time the fleeing Confederate brigades reached the creek it was ready, both the ford and a hastily constructed bridge built by Lockett assistant Sergeant S. McD. Vernon. With the bridge built, Pemberton ordered his troops rearward, admitting that "I felt it to be too late to save the day." The orders soon trickled down the chains of command that still existed, but total chaos reigned. Staff officer Drennan described the stampede: it "look[ed] like what I have read of Bull-run and thought of a rapid retreat." Mixed elements of Stevenson's division first crossed and began making their way back toward the Big Black River defenses, given time by a last-minute defense of some of Loring's troops. Buford explained that his fire "effectually checked the ardor of his pursuit, and caused him to follow our immediate rear with great caution." Next came Bowen's thrashed brigades, tired but with plenty of fight left. Orders from Pemberton, who also began his trek westward, were to hold for Loring's division coming along next. For his part, Loring himself posited that Tilghman's stand had "kept open the only line of retreat left to the army. The bold stand of this brigade under the lamented hero saved a large portion of the army." He added that the "brigade wept over the dying hero; alike beautiful as it was touching."[40]

But Loring never arrived while Bowen held out near the bridge. And the Federals were getting uncomfortably close, Featherston writing that "the enemy advanced on our rear, as well as on the right and left flanks, and a brisk skirmish ensued, in which they were held completely in check until the brigade and artillery were withdrawn slowly and in good order." Only a few of Loring's regiments ever appeared at the creek, some even crossing but then heading back east of the waterway to rejoin the division, which was obviously not crossing at this point. Bowen was already taking artillery fire from the left as Benton's Federals lunged closer and closer, and it was a matter of limited time that he could remain in position covering the crossing for Loring. If Loring's rear division was going to cross, at least with Bowen's help, it had to be now.[41]

Pemberton himself was not witness to these final acts of chaos. Contrary to rumors in the Union army that he had been killed, he headed back to the railroad bridge over the Big Black River "to make the necessary arrangement for holding that point during the passage of the river." While riding westward, a courier from Johnston arrived with his May 14 note, written eleven hours previous to the May 15 one that had arrived that morning causing the withdrawal. It advised Pemberton that half of Grant's army was at Jackson and that "it would decide the campaign to beat it." In fact, Johnston recommended in that earlier-written but later-arriving message the very thing Pemberton had set out to do: cut Grant's communication line. Had the messages arrived in order, matters may have turned out differently. Nevertheless, Pemberton scribbled a note of endorsement in disgust: "Original dispatch from General J. E. Johnston delivered at 5.35 p.m., May 16, 1863, on the field, whilst in retreat."[42]

"The Rebels are in a perfect Skedadle of a run leaving everything," one of Blair's Federals gloated. And that was nowhere more true than with Loring's division, which one Federal simply explained "wandered off." Loring was out there but would not cross the creek at the ford Bowen was holding; his stiff rear-guard defense was the last Pemberton's army had seen of him despite messages from Bowen to get out quickly. Confident that he had given Loring ample time to cross, and taking enemy fire from almost all directions with artillery even now "playing upon the crossing," Bowen ordered his men to retreat quickly toward Edwards.[43]

Loring did plan to cross at the bridge, however, determined "to force my way through by the ford" and follow the army toward Vicksburg. But arriving at the creek after Bowen had left, he could see enemy skirmishers advancing, and a distinct line of infantry, he said, "occupied the commanding ridge across the creek, his artillery playing upon the crossing." Loring realized the enemy had boxed him in on three sides. He later muddled something about "we had been sold," an obvious reference to Pemberton. Still intent on rejoining the army, although unable to retreat on the Raymond Road, Loring began to search for other possibilities to escape. Unfortunately, the only open route was south, away from Vicksburg and the army. But there was no time to analyze the decision; Loring had to move quickly. The enemy was already pressing his bottled-up brigades, prompting one private to remember the nervousness that erupted when the line stopped and the column backed up. Taking fire from the trailing enemy, he could only ascribe the soldiers' ability to remain in line to "grit."[44]

With the help of guides from companies raised in the area, Loring immediately sent Buford's brigade in the growing darkness to find a ford south of the Raymond Road. The division first marched southward on the east side of Bakers Creek across plantations, swamps, and marshes, Loring writing that "by a well-concerted movement we eluded the enemy upon three sides." The division marched some distance southward in search of the crossing, but it had to countermarch back nearly to the field of battle to find a substantial road. Marching near the Coker House, many Confederates reported moving within two hundred yards of Federal camps, seeing enemy campfires on both sides of the column. Some even reported hearing the enemy talking. One Confederate remembered, "we marched all night passing by and even through some Federal bivouacs without molestation." A few Union soldiers, probably half-asleep, asked about the regiment, whereupon wily Confederates would answer with "ours," "go to Sheol," or "99th Rhode Island." At other points, Loring and his generals placed staff officers to remind the men not to "speak above a whisper." Anxiety reached a climax when a member of the 31st Mississippi tripped and fell. His gun went off, putting the entire division in even more danger. Silently, however, the division made its way out of the greatest danger, utilizing what one participant described as "neighborhood roads and paths long unused."[45]

As the march continued along, "the night being dark and the trail a blind one," Loring first had to sacrifice his artillery, twelve guns that were spiked in a swamp, and then much of the division's arms, ammunition, and basically anything that would prove a hindrance. One Confederate remembered that the small arms were "safely deposited in the bed of the river." Spying a tremendous fire in the direction of Edwards, Loring rightly concluded Pemberton had passed on through Edwards Station toward the Big Black, which necessitated crossing not only Bakers Creek but also the river. By now down in the area where McClernand had operated on May 12 and 13, Loring could likewise not find a suitable crossing of the river there, even with local civilian guides. One reported the crossings "swimming" with high water and a massive swamp east of the river. There seemed no way the division could succeed in such a march, especially in the pitch blackness of night. Loring called a conference of his officers, and after a "full consultation," one of them recalled, the men determined that to march to Vicksburg would be suicidal. "The entire division would certainly be lost," one of his brigade commanders remembered. With no other option, Loring reluctantly ordered his exhausted and poorly supplied men southeastward toward the New Orleans, Jackson, and Great Northern Railroad. Perhaps he could escape toward Jackson and link up with Joseph E. Johnston.[46]

The division marched all that night on May 16. By 3:00 a.m. on May 17, the troops reached Dillon's, ironically their intended destination on May 15 before the battle at Champion Hill changed the course of the campaign and perhaps the war. Loring pushed his men onward. Later during the night, the general learned from a local citizen that the column was near the town of Utica but that around five hundred Federals held the place. Although Loring had more than 5,000 men, he decided to march away from a confrontation. His men were exhausted and too poorly armed for combat. One officer in the division remembered: "We kept up our weary march all night and all the next day without food or water, for as we approached the good people would remove the buckets, ropes and pumps from their wells or cisterns and no water could be had[—]only from ponds or creeks that we chanced to cross." From Utica, the division marched for Crystal Springs, taking a short pause at dawn on May 17 to take roll. There, it became obvious that the division was melting away, but the brigades stammered on, entering Crystal Springs on the night of May 17. There, the remnants of the division encountered the famous Lieutenant Colonel James A. L. Fremantle of England's Coldstream Guards, who was busily touring the Confederacy and would soon witness the horrors of Gettysburg. Also met along the way was Hugh Ewing's arriving Union brigade of Blair's division, which actually scooped up some of Loring's stragglers as they pushed forward after their May 15 river crossing at Grand Gulf, perhaps being the force mentioned near Utica. After twenty-four hours of marching, Loring's division had made forty miles. Now in relative safety, the division marched more conventionally to Jackson. It crossed the Pearl River to protect its flank and on May 19 arrived near Jackson, where Loring reported to Johnston, although the division was in terrible shape. Loring, in fact, quipped that he "had the best stragglers in the world."[47]

On his way back westward, Pemberton had no idea what had happened to Loring, but he knew he needed to hold at the Big Black River for him to rejoin the army before heading once and for all back to Vicksburg, where his heart had been all along. Stevenson's troops were already started that way, and it fell to Bowen's fought-out division to hold only temporarily at the Big Black for Loring. Pemberton in fact ambled by Bowen's headquarters that night to solidify the plan, Pemberton writing that "I had a personal interview in his tent on the night of the 16th."[48]

But there was growing chaos in the army that night as Loring never showed and never would, many already blaming the commander whose "men had not fired a gun during the day." Some of the rest of the army was likewise scattered, Reynolds and the wagon train taking a different retreat route across the Big Black River at Bridgeport on "a light pontoon bridge" before being confronted by Colonel Wright's 6th Missouri Cavalry. Yet there was ultimately a feeling that Loring's troops were the fortunate ones to get out, especially with what lay ahead for those falling back into Vicksburg. Perhaps the results on the personal level were the most sad, one Missourian noting that, of his six messmates that started together that morning, only he was left. "I felt very lonesome that night I can tell you."[49]

The victorious Federals also faced the growing darkness and confusion, although in much better spirits. "Night alone put an end to the pursuit of the enemy," related brigade commander Stevenson. The vast majority of the Confederates managed to get away to the west, toward Vicksburg, but many never reached the river; the lead elements of Grant's army had pushed forward even that night and gobbled them up. The Federals rounded up equipment and prisoners, Osterhaus reporting that "thousands of the enemy were found scattered everywhere, and fell into our hands as prisoners of war." Division commander Carr explained that the prisoners "were simply ordered back to the rear. I made it a rule, whenever I was in front, to dispose of prisoners in that way, thus saving my own men for more important duties, and being satisfied that some one in the rear would pick up and secure the prisoners." Some of the divisions even reached Edwards Station and put out part of a fire in an ammunition train on the rail line even as the ammunition cooked off; a few of the cars were destroyed, but the Federals captured five intact with more than ninety thousand precious cartridges and artillery ammunition as well. One Iowan admitted the loss of the other cars, adding that "we concluded it would not be healthy to make a too close investigation, if I was without rations." It was a boon for an army that was having supply difficulties and had just fought a major battle. But it was taxing. One of Carr's Federals related that "I was never as tired in all my life before[.] We had been exposed [to] the heat of a burning sun all day doble quacking charging through cane brakes besides this we had nothing to eat for dinner our knapsacks and blankets were left behind."[50]

Fortunately for him, Grant received comparatively fresh troops to take over the advance, Sherman's XV Corps soon arriving. One of his Iowans related that they "marched 13 hours without refreshments," although they did find several Federal wounded from Chickasaw Bayou in a Confederate hospital set up at Bolton. Grant ordered Sherman to move north of the railroad to Bridgeport, upstream from the railroad bridge where all figured the Confederates would make their stand. To get around the Confederate defense, Sherman was to outflank the railroad bridge and force the enemy back hopefully without a battle. To do so, Grant also sent Blair's division, lately under McClernand's orders (even this evening when McClernand ordered Blair to proceed to the railroad bridge), to join his parent corps at Bridgeport. With Blair was the only pontoon bridge in the army, and Sherman could use it to get across and turn the enemy position. Sherman issued his orders from Bolton that night, telling his hard-working soldiers "our destination is now the Big Black River, 13 miles distant, beyond which lies Vicksburg. The commanding general announces that the other corps with which we are acting have to-day signally repulsed the enemy, and our part is to make that repulse a complete defeat." Tuttle likewise addressed his division, in person, telling them he had required a hard march that day and needed another the next day because he had just gotten word of Champion Hill and that the enemy was "endeavoring to escape, and he [Tuttle] was to follow up and cut them off from getting back to Vicksburg." One Illinoisan related that "three cheers were given for the good news, and we lost no time in spreading the blankets and turning in, very badly used up after the long march."[51]

It was accordingly a tired Union army that ended the day on May 16, the effort of the day exhausting most who were already growing weak without adequate provisions. The supply trains Stone and Blair accompanied had provided some sustenance, although not nearly enough to carry the army onward for days. Ransom also arrived at Raymond early on May 16, without a train, but was blocked on the route by Blair's wagons still entering the town; one medical officer with the convoy also noted that they only "advanced as far as they would let the train [go]." Ransom's troops could hear the fight raging to the west and itched to get into it, but it was later in the afternoon before they were able to get on the road toward Champion Hill and thus missed the fight, arriving after it ended. Continual foraging provided some sustenance as well, although some of the areas, especially around Raymond and Clinton, in which the army had been operating for the previous couple days, had already been covered by the army as far back as May 13. And as the army slowed down its movements, the likelihood of still finding food from the countryside dwindled proportionately. One Iowan in McClernand's XIII Corps in fact related that "the troops had left their camp in the morning with nothing to eat except a few cracker-crumbs soaked in coffee, and were on the point of exhaustion from hunger." He added that, after the battle, "the dead Confederate haversacks were even rifled for corn-pone, and many tasty morsels were obtained in this way."[52]

But there was a definite sense that the day had been a very good one for the Federals, despite its hard fighting and large losses. "I cannot think of this bloody hill without sadness and pride," Alvin Hovey lamented. His brigade commander James Slack added that "I thought the battle of Port Gibson was terrific, but it was a mere skirmish in comparison with yesterday's fight." The Union casualties bore out the hard fighting: 410 killed, 1,844 wounded, and 187 missing for a grand total of 2,441. The Confederates reported 381 killed, 1,018 wounded, and 2,441 missing for a total of 3,840. "The ambulances were busy but could not get them away fast enough," one Federal explained, and another described how the surgeons "never worked harder." Medical officer Silas Trowbridge described operating and caring for the wounded all night "by the light of but one candle, and that of the most inferior quality." Then there was the effort to glean as much as possible from the battlefield, the lot falling to Hovey's hard-hit division. Huge amounts of ammunition and ordnance were captured, as well as some food. One Illinoisan noted, "I threw away my dirty shirt and drawers and picked up a clean pair which was in a Secesh Knapsack." Worse, Hovey's troops, who considered themselves the heroes of Champion Hill, also remained to bury the dead.[53]

Grant was especially ecstatic as he and several of his generals rode the battlefield to the thunderous applause of the soldiers. Son Fred wandered far out in front of the army, at one point reaching a Confederate hospital where the inhabitants "were not feeling very friendly toward the Yankees, and they threatened to kill me." Later, he returned to the Union troops; once they realized who it was, they gave "three cheers for young Grant." Fred noted the cheers were "given with a will." Indeed, there was a growing sense that this had been a game-changing day. "This was unquestionably the great battle of the campaign," Union brigade commander John D. Stevenson argued. Captain Charles N. Lee was only partially correct when he wrote that "on that memorable day was fought the bloodiest battle of the war, ending in the most disastrous defeat of the rebel army under General Pemberton." McPherson was more on point when he related that Champion Hill was "by far the hardest fought battle of all since crossing at Bruinsburg, and the most decided victory for us. . . . The blood poured out on Champion's Hill was not spilt in vain." When news arrived at Sherman's camps, "the whole Div. gave three cheers for the result," the general noted. "This may be the battle decisive of the fate of Vicksburg," another Federal added, and "I hope it may be so as to save the further loss of life." Perhaps Grant himself said it best in writing to Sherman that evening from the battlefield: "I am of the opinion that the battle for Vicksburg has been fought."[54]

If there was little debate on how decisive this day had been, there was one other debate that persisted: the naming of the battle that just perhaps decided the fate of Vicksburg. One German in the 118th Illinois described it as "Schemigien Hill," stating "both sides fought like lions." Grant used the name "Baker's Creek" in his dispatches, but newspaperman Cadwallader admitted that the general was too late to claim naming rights. The reporter had already sent back dispatches that would be widely printed all over the nation, and he claimed to have "christened it 'Champion's Hill.'" He further argued that the name would stick because "millions of people would read of it by that name in my dispatches, while his [Grant's] official report naming it Baker's Creek, was growing mouldy in the pigeon-holes of the War Department." Cadwallader claimed that Grant laughed and agreed "but that he thought he ought to have the one small privilege of naming it."[55]

16

"A Victory Could Hardly Have Been More Complete"

May 17

John C. Pemberton was in a no-win situation, literally. He had just been soundly defeated earlier at Champion Hill, and now the traumatized Confederate army was hurriedly withdrawing westward through Edwards toward Vicksburg on the mighty Mississippi River. One lieutenant in command of a train of wagons described the miserable retreat from the Champion Hill battlefield: "It was slow progress from then until we arrived at Big Black—as it was covered with Artillery, the trains of the Army—straggling and wounded men—every conceivable conveyance with women and children fleeing their homes and abandoning them to the Yankees." And if that was not bad enough, as Pemberton and his devastated army sullenly moved onward, the general no doubt also rehearsed in his mind the fact that he was disobeying his departmental commander by falling back into Vicksburg.[1]

But the larger strategic context was not the most difficult decision Pemberton had to make. His army had been devastated and literally broken apart. The best-case scenario was to concentrate the divisions and march to Vicksburg as a cohesive army; the next-best scenario was to man the Big Black River line of defense on the western bank, as he probably should have done all along. Unfortunately, neither was totally possible. Carter Stevenson's division was moving safely toward Vicksburg, but Bowen's was next to arrive at the river; Pemberton ordered him to wait for Loring, everyone thinking he would be only a short distance behind. But Loring never showed, and Pemberton began to fret about what to do. For all he knew, Loring was still marching westward to join the rest of the army, perhaps fighting a rear-guard effort on his way out. "It was necessary to hold the position to enable him [Loring] to cross the river, should the enemy, which was probable, follow him closely up," Pemberton wrote. And even if Loring did not arrive at the railroad bridge, he could still cross somewhere else, which even more necessitated holding the line at the Big Black. Obviously, Pemberton needed all his troops to defend Vicksburg; if all could get across the Big Black River, he would then have his entire army concentrated once again around Vicksburg — stunned, yes, but together and ready to defend the city. It was a gamble he had to take.[2]

"I awaited in vain intelligence of the approach of General Loring," Pemberton later wrote. The result was disastrous. Loring never showed, and Pemberton sadly confessed, "for this purpose [Loring] alone I continued the troops in position until it was too late to withdraw them under cover of night." He later related that he had "determined not to abandon so strong a front while there was yet hope of his arrival." Consequently, instead of Loring arriving the next morning, Sunday, May 17, Grant's blue columns appeared. Obviously, Loring was not coming, at least not on the direct route. But Loring's whereabouts, although he was the reason Pemberton had determined to hold at the Big Black, was now of secondary importance to the Confederate commander. He now once again confronted Grant's victorious army east of the Big Black River, and he could not retreat quickly. His exhausted men would have to fight another battle.[3]

Conversely, U. S. Grant sat in an ideal position. He had defeated the enemy soundly at Champion Hill and could pursue with vigor. He had wounded the Confederate army; now he hoped for the kill. He thus made plans to move his Army of the Tennessee westward toward Vicksburg. Even better, more units steadily arrived during the waning hours of May 16 and the morning of May 17, including the majority of Sherman's XV Corps that had recently been destroying Jackson; moving north of the battlefield at Champion Hill, Sherman had in the process run across one of Jefferson Davis's plantations, where he spied a book on the ground and asked a soldier to hand it to him. It was a copy of the United States Constitution with Davis's signature on the title page. Sherman also located Davis's brother Joseph nearby, "attended by a young and affectionate niece; but they were overwhelmed with grief to see their country overrun and swarming with Federal troops."[4]

Now with his entire army available, Grant could take several routes toward Vicksburg, hoping to mop up the shattered Confederate commands, turn any defensive positions Pemberton might take along the Big Black River, and perhaps bag the whole lot. Leaving the hardest-fighting units to rest on the Champion Hill battlefield itself, Grant shoved Carr's and Osterhaus's divisions farther toward Edwards Station on the Jackson Road even during the night. A. J. Smith moved his division across Bakers Creek and also turned toward Edwards. Meanwhile, Grant sent Sherman's corps northward to Bridgeport, the place the Confederate wagon train had crossed the night before: "Your moving North of the rail-road may enable you to get across at Bridgeport whilst the enemy are engaged at the bridge." In addition to the swelled numbers, spirits were high within the Federal ranks; they had just won a magnificent victory and even reveled in rumors that Pemberton himself had been killed.[5]

With Edwards Station in Federal hands, Grant resumed the pursuit when the sun rose the next morning, he having spent the night on a porch of a local farmhouse that was serving as a hospital for the wounded from Champion Hill. Units of Carr's and Osterhaus's divisions led the way, the bugle sounding at 2:00 a.m.; one of Carr's soldiers explained that "a pint of corn meal and a slice of bacon was issued to each man[.] We made mush of the meal and broiled the meat on forked sticks." The only remaining impediment was the Big Black River. Grant knew that if the Confederates made a stand it would be there. He and his high-spirited Federals accordingly moved onward to locate the enemy. Union soldiers described the dawn of May 17 as bright and beautiful, much like the day before. Unfortunately, this day would also see bloodshed and destruction as the armies continued to grapple with one another.[6]

On the surface, Pemberton's new line at the Big Black River was a strong one. The river made a huge curve exactly where the main Jackson Road as well as the railroad crossed over, Pemberton describing the area as "somewhat in the shape of a horseshoe." The road and railroad entered the open end of the horseshoe on the eastern side and crossed the river on the extreme western edge. The sixty-foot bluffs on the western side of the river were substantially higher than the flood plain on the east bank, thus offering the Confederates an opportunity to cover the crossing points with artillery and infantry. In addition, a line of breastworks had been erected earlier in May across the opening of the horseshoe east of the river, about midway between the opening and the river crossings. This *tête de pont* had gone up in the first two weeks of May as part of a larger Big Black River line of defense intended to protect the Vicksburg approaches from Grant's inland advance. Made of cotton bales covered with dirt, these works provided ample cover for infantrymen and also contained embrasures for artillery along the southern end, where all thought an attack would develop; only one artillery unit took position on the northern end of the line. Confederates manning these defenses running on a north-to-south line had an extremely favorable position in that their flanks were secured on the bending river on the northern end and a small oxbow lake that was once part of the river to the south. Moreover, the field of battle for an attack on this line was constricted, offering a smaller zone to cover and shoving Federal units into a somewhat manageable area of combat. Perhaps most important, there were natural factors that aided the Confederate defense as well, such as wide-open fields along most of the line to the south and center, as well as a large slough some ten to twenty feet wide and two to three feet deep that meandered along the northern and middle part of the line and ran into the river on the north side of the horseshoe. This small bayou was not an end-all deterrent to attacking the line, but it would hopefully slow any advancing enemy column long enough to allow the defenders to rake them with artillery and musketry. Pemberton himself noted that it "opposed a serious obstacle to an assault upon the pits." In addition, an abatis of felled trees existed at points along the line, mainly in the bayou itself, and there was a detached section of works east of the bayou on the extreme northern end of the line, from which the Confederates could enfilade any attack moving toward the bayou and main line. Only on the northern sector along the river would an attacking army have any cover in the form of what one soldier described as "a copse of wood." A stand of cypress trees also stood along the southern portion of the Confederate line, but it was far too small to provide any aid to the Federals in approaching from that direction. Consequently, most any Federals attacking this Confederate line of earthworks would have immediate difficulty in even getting to the enemy position.[7]

As his tired troops reached this new line, Pemberton had a decision to make. Obviously, he would keep his forces at the river crossing to allow Loring a chance to rejoin the army, but how he would post his men and who he would deploy would be critical. Instead of forming his entire line west of the river on the higher ground, which in retrospect would have been the better option, Pemberton decided he needed to man the line of entrenchments east of the river to allow Loring a chance at an uninterrupted crossing, especially if followed closely by the enemy. Loring would have a hard time crossing the river if the Confederate line was on the western side, taking the pursuing enemy under fire. He would also have to cross his men while fighting a rearguard action. Pemberton deemed it best to hold the line of entrenchments east of the river and allow all the divisions to hopefully cross without molestation, maybe during the night. Unfortunately, not all agreed with the commanding general. One Missourian, for instance, later wrote: "The position would have been a strong one, if the fortifications had been on the other side of the stream, and it would certainly have been better to take position there with no

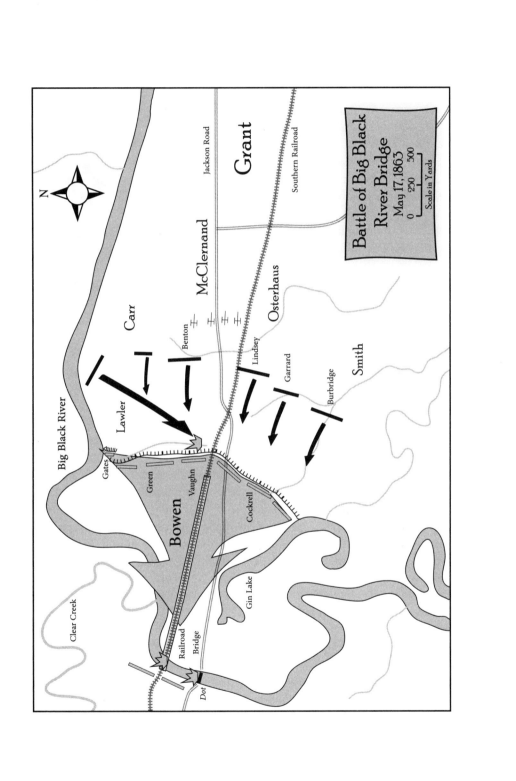

Battle of Big Black
River Bridge
May 17, 1863

0   250   500
Scale in Yards

N

Grant

McClernand

Carr

Jackson Road

Southern Railroad

Osterhaus

Benton

Lindsey

Garrard

Burbridge

Smith

Big Black River

Lawler

Gates

Green

Vaughn

Bowen

Cockrell

Clear Creek

Gin Lake

Railroad

Bridge

Dot

fortifications, than to be in them where we were, with a river at our back to cross in case of accident or disaster."[8]

Still, by the early hours of May 17 Pemberton's hopes rested on crossing all of his army, including Loring, without fighting another battle. The Confederate commander was obviously gun-shy after the whipping he had taken at Champion Hill the day before, and his main goal was to reach the Vicksburg defenses, where additional troops awaited his mobile army and where major fortifications could help the tired foot soldiers fend off a Union attack. In fact, Pemberton had already begun to move in that direction himself, riding to Bovina and leaving Bowen in charge at the river before riding back to the battlefield when the fighting started. In order to make the crossing as easy as possible, Bowen planned to use the railroad bridge as well as a steamboat, the *Dot*; its machinery removed, it had been converted into a bridge by turning it crossways in the river and building approaches onto and off of the vessel. Engineers also planked the railroad bridge to allow wheeled vehicles to move across, and Confederate teamsters soon had the wagons that still accompanied the individual brigades across safely, which was a high priority for Pemberton. In order to place a major obstacle between them and Grant as soon as Loring arrived, engineers also prepared to douse the bridge and boat with turpentine and set them afire.[9]

The decision to hold east of the river made, Pemberton also had a decision to make about who was to man the trenches. Most of Stevenson's division, which was just now concentrating after the debacle at Champion Hill the day before, had already marched on through the area and was moving toward Bovina. With Loring still missing and Pemberton's other two divisions back at Vicksburg and vicinity, that left only Bowen's depleted division to man the works. But that division was not in ideal shape. It had been mauled at Port Gibson sixteen days earlier, then made the dramatic counterattack at Champion Hill the day before, losing nearly a thousand men in the process. When the attack lost its steam, the division had recoiled under the pressure of a Federal counterattack and had retreated during the night to the river and crossed it. Tired as they were, the trans-Mississippians were nevertheless all Pemberton had to man the trenches and hold out for Loring's arrival. Having moved over the river, Bowen's troops crossed back over to the east side of the Big Black River and moved into the trenches.[10]

Bowen's exhausted division consequently had to defend the works, which one Southerner affectionately termed "our ditches." The Missourian placed his best men, Francis Cockrell's brigade, on the right of the line where there was no covering bayou and the line was accordingly more exposed. Bowen put Green's men on the left, with Colonel Elijah Gates's 1st Missouri Cavalry (dismounted) eventually occupying the detached works east of the bayou near the river. In between, along the railroad where Bowen felt sure no attack would come, was the only fresh unit he had at his disposal: a small brigade of Tennesseans commanded by Brigadier General John C. Vaughn of Smith's division. The 60th, 61st, and 62nd Tennessee had manned these works for several days now and, as a result, had seen no fighting as yet, but they were somewhat circumspect in their loyalty. Most of the men had been conscripted from East Tennessee, a region blatant in its Unionism. Fortunately, the 4th Mississippi of William Baldwin's brigade took position amid the Tennesseans to add to their strength and morale. Among the infantry, artillery crews placed some twenty guns at advantageous spots, mostly south of the railroad where all expected the attack would come. Amazingly, the artillery horses were sent to safety to the rear near the river, too far to remove the guns if something went wrong.[11]

Despite the issues, Pemberton was confident that Bowen could hold the line. He stated matter-of-factly: "I knew that the Missouri troops, under their gallant leaders, could be depended upon." He also noted that the four thousand or so men manning the trenches were "as many as could be advantageously employed in defending the line." In fact, Pemberton's only major worry was Grant turning his line. "So strong was the position," Pemberton later wrote, "that my greatest, almost only, apprehension was a flank movement by Bridgeport or Baldwin's Ferry, which would have endangered my communications with Vicksburg."[12]

Not everyone was so convinced, however. Some questioned the length of the line with only four to five thousand troops to defend it; one historian has even surmised there was only about one man to every foot of earthworks. Likewise, Pemberton's chief engineer, Samuel H. Lockett, later wrote that he began preparing to destroy the two bridges in the event of a break because even early that morning as he stood on the railroad bridge he was "seeing signs of unsteadiness among our troops." No doubt the situation made them unsteady. If the men in the fortifications did not hold, there was little hope for the troops. Pemberton himself noted that, "between the works and the bridge, about three-quarters of a mile, the country was open, being either old or cultivated fields, offering no cover should the troops be driven from the trenches." Hemmed in by the curve in the river, which one Federal described as "muddy and turgid at this time of the year," the men would be stranded. Moreover, a bottleneck would undoubtedly occur at the river. The only means of escape was the railroad bridge and the steamer *Dot*. Even in possession of those two means of escape, Bowen's entire division with Vaughn's brigade would not be able to evacuate before the Federals surrounded them. Accordingly, Bowen had to hold—at least until Loring arrived.[13]

John A. McClernand had his Federal XIII Corps up and marching early on May 17, even before daylight. It had been "a very disagreeable night," one Iowan admitted; "I am chilled to the bone and nothing to eat." One member of Carr's division remembered that "the unwelcome sound of the bugle greeted our ears" at 2:00 a.m. Rations were quickly issued, and the soldiers sleepily downed what one Federal described as a "pint of corn meal and a slice of bacon." Another reported, "we made mush of the meal and broiled our meat on forked sticks." By this time, some soldiers had had enough of this almost continuous campaigning. One grumbled, "there is no fun in soldiering neither is there any fun on the battlefield when bullets are whistling around our heads[.] Shells bursting and cannon balls and grape shot tareing up the ground all around us[.] My curiosity is satisfied." Nevertheless, William Benton's men of Carr's division led the way westward at 3:30 a.m. The 33rd Illinois moved forward "as skirmishers and advance guard," frequently running into the enemy that remained along the road. One Federal described how the litter strewn about was "abundant evidence that the rebels had skedaddled most hurriedly." After heavier skirmishing with Confederates in the early hours after sunup, during which locals told the Federals they would have to fight to get across the river to the west, McClernand's XIII Corps arrived near the Big Black. There the troops found the Confederate positions across their path, complete with artillery unlimbered and battle flags flying. Lieutenant Colonel John Lucas of the 7th Kentucky described the area as "an extensive open plain for nearly 1 mile," and Charles Dana described it as Pemberton's "bridgehead."[14]

Carr's division led the advance and ultimately deployed in line along the northern section of the Confederate fortifications, McClernand describing them as "forming the segment of a rude circle." Michael Lawler's brigade, after supporting Benton's forward troops in a second line, formed with its right on the river in response to the Confederate occupation of the extended works east of the bayou, which they deemed as an advance and thus a threat to the right flank. Peter Osterhaus, next in line, formed his division along the middle and southern portions of the enemy position, although two of his regiments of Garrard's brigade went northward to support Carr's men. Daniel Lindsey's brigade formed the right, and the remainder of Garrard's men, although initially in a second line behind Lindsey, took position on the left rear of the division to watch the flank when unidentified Confederate movements in that area also falsely signaled an enemy attack: "Advices from the left informed me that large numbers of the enemy were on that flank," Osterhaus explained even amid yelling "git em out mit de bayonet—I'm mit you." A space still existed south of Garrard's line, but Stephen Burbridge's brigade of A. J. Smith's division soon arrived and filled that expanse. Finally, McClernand's artillery took position near the line, mainly Captain Jacob T. Foster's six guns of the 1st Wisconsin Battery. Eventually, the guns of the 1st Indiana, 7th Michigan, Chicago Mercantile, and Battery A, 2nd Illinois Artillery also deployed and raked the Confederate line as well. One infantryman explained that "as soon as our batteries was in position they commenced the fun."[15]

Soon after the lines formed, a spirited artillery duel ensued. The exhausted soldiers of Bowen's division huddled quietly behind their breastworks during the bombardment, keeping an open eye for Loring and the end of such misery. With the arrival of Federals across the way, however, it looked increasingly less likely that Loring would show up. Thoughts thus turned to getting out of what was becoming a trap, but the officers tried to calm the unsteady soldiers' nerves. Such bravery almost cost General Vaughn his life; a Union cannonball came close enough to cut the reins of his horse. An aide tied the reins together, noting "he seemed unconscious of fear." As bad as the barrage was for the Confederates behind the breastworks, even worse conditions existed for the Federal soldiers. They had no cover and could only lay flat in the dusty fields and hope the Confederate gunners missed their mark. Many did. One Federal infantryman described how "the rebels replied with very heavy artillery[.] The shells flew thick and over our heads bursting in the tops of the trees[.] The rebels over shot us and not a man was touched."[16]

That may have been the case at some points, but there were some casualties elsewhere. A 22nd Iowa soldier on the northern portion of the line, Samuel D. Pryce, reported "broadside after broadside came hurtling through the woods. Havoc was terrific among the big trees. Earth and sky seemed tumbling together. . . . Missiles crashed through the giant elms and tore them to pieces. Great lordly trees were peeled and stripped and looked like splintered bones." Aquilla Standifird of the 23rd Iowa wrote in his diary how the enemy shot and shell was "making it [a] very unsafe place to stop." Illustrating the exposed nature of the Federal line, a Confederate shell hit a Union limber in the Wisconsin battery, causing a tremendous explosion and disabling the gun. In placing the battery, Osterhaus admitted that "my movements must have attracted the attention of the enemy," and before he could place the guns both he and Foster fell wounded from the exploding limber. The blast sent shrapnel flying, some of which hit General Osterhaus in the leg as he conversed with

Captain Foster about where to locate his artillery pieces. While Foster was also hit, a cannoneer was likewise "burned and bruised," and two drivers were thrown from their horses. Osterhaus's wound was severe enough to force him from the field, although he resumed command of the division the next day. Brigadier General Albert Lee temporarily took command of his troops.[17]

Amid the barrage, one Federal commander saw his men's plight and determined to remedy the situation. Grant and McClernand were soon up, Carr later demanding that he had done the deployment himself without McClernand's order. Cadwallader claimed that Grant himself even came under fire for a short time while approaching the Confederate lines. But even lower down the hierarchy came three-hundred-pound Michael Lawler, the hard-fighting Irishman described by one of the soldiers that day as "rushing around in his shirt sleeves." Cadwallader described him as "a large and excessively fat man—a fine type of the generous, rollicking, fighting Irishman." He reported that his men faced large open areas, a deep bayou with felled trees in it, and formidable earthworks to the front. Lawler admitted the Confederate position was "really formidable and difficult of approach." He nevertheless formed his brigade with the 11th Wisconsin on the left of a line and the 21st Iowa on the right. The 23rd Iowa took position in a second line a hundred yards behind the Wisconsin regiment, and the last regiment of the brigade, the 22nd Iowa, remained in rear as a reserve and as support for the section of the Illinois artillery battery engaging the enemy even then. As Lawler's men moved through the woods and into the open fields fronting the enemy line only about four hundred yards away, they could see their work would be difficult if called upon to attack. And because of the wooded area through which they had moved, only two guns of Battery A, 2nd Illinois Artillery were able to deploy. One of the soldiers wrote his brother that they "engaged them with their muskets but the rebels were so well protected that our firing did but little execution and it seemed as nothing but a bayonet charge would drive them from behind their strong position."[18]

But then came good news. Lawler received word from McClernand's chief of cavalry, Colonel John J. Mudd, that a covered opening existed near the bank of the river toward a small grove of trees. With the Confederates' attention diverted because of the artillery exchange as well as other arriving units such as A. J. Smith's division, Lawler led the three frontline regiments of his brigade into cover on the extreme right of the Union line where a small copse of woods and the lay of the land offered protection. One Iowan described the move: "We was soon ordered to the right through some timber to the river. We was ordered to move down the river and to get as near the enemy's intrenchments as possible which we did." Ultimately, Lawler reached the riverbank and deployed the men in a line behind the bluff, the 11th Wisconsin, 21st Iowa, and 23rd Iowa left-to-right. A soldier described the place as "a growth of small timber between the bank and water which gave us good protection." The 22nd Iowa was not as fortunate and remained farther to the left in the field for a time before moving to the bank as well and deploying near the 11th Wisconsin.[19]

By the time his men had gained cover, despite the continuous blistering fire from Confederate artillery and small arms, Lawler saw that he was surprisingly close enough to assault the Confederate works. In fact, Colonel William H. Kinsman of the 23rd Iowa, closest to the enemy line, came to Lawler and told him of the situation and asked permission to advance. Knowing better than to send only one regiment, Lawler ordered his entire brigade to fix bayonets. One officer in the 21st Iowa remembered how "the command was quietly passed along the line to fix bayonets, and as quietly obeyed." Cadwallader further added that Lawler was "precisely the kind of officer to make an assault, and ask permission to do so afterwards." In that sense, this was Grant's kind of officer—as the commanding general was doing the exact same thing in the larger context.[20]

In what Grant described as a "brilliant and daring movement," Lawler's brigade then burst from the lowland in columns of fours with a yell that took the Confederates by surprise. Closest to the assault, Colonel Gates described how "they brought their men out by the right flank in column of fours about 140 yards in front of my regiment at a double-quick." An Iowan described the brigade "yelling like the furies." One Confederate also described the Union yell: "It is much more regular than ours and is clearly distinguishable from it." The screaming 23rd Iowa, closest to the Confederates, "sprang forward to the works," Lawler remembered, followed closely by the 21st Iowa on the left. The 23rd Iowa's Colonel Kinsman had worked out a plan by which his left wing would start first by moving into the open field, whereupon the right would follow when the left moved as far as the colors. One member of the regiment remembered in his diary that all planning went awry once the attack began, however: "When we leaped up over the bank a perfect storm of lead was hurled at us but did not check those that was not hit." A member of the 21st Iowa agreed, later writing that the regiment "began to toil up the steep bank, but as the head of the column appeared above the bank it was met by a storm of shot. The movement in that order would have been impossible, and Colonel [Samuel] Merrill, seeing the difficulty, immediately shouted the order: 'By the left flank, CHARGE!'" He added, "and the silent river overflowed its banks and poured a flood of living men upon the plain—living, yelling, screaming madmen."[21]

The 11th Wisconsin followed closely behind the 23rd Iowa as the two front-line units angled southwesterly toward the Confederate line. "We went on the run the boys falling all the way across," an Iowan remembered. Meanwhile, the 22nd Iowa moved out into the field behind the 21st Iowa and toward the Confederate line as well, while Lawler also got Garrard's two regiments, the 49th and 69th Indiana, going forward farther to the left. But in the main attack, the Iowans and Wisconsin troops swept forward across Green's front toward Vaughan's Tennesseans near the railroad. Lieutenant Colonel Cornelius W. Dunlap of the 21st Iowa reported that his men moved forward some eight hundred yards: "The bullets came in showers from the flanks, and, combined with those coming from the horde of rebels in the rifle-pits in front, made an awful hail storm, through which it seemed a miracle that a single man passed uninjured." Many did not, in fact. One Iowan told of passing a fellow soldier lying wounded, yelling to his comrades "go in boys, . . . they have fixed me." Another member of the regiment described how "regimental and company organizations immediately broke . . . up, the fastest runners ahead."[22]

Several high-ranking Federals went down as the charge moved onward. Colonel Kinsman, closest to the Confederate line, was hit as his Iowans raced ahead. He went down but somehow managed to get to his feet and push his men onward. "He staggered a few paces to the front," Lawler reported, "and fell again, this time to rise no more, pierced through by a second ball." He was shot in the "Bowels and Lungs." Colonel Merrill of the 21st Iowa also went down in the assault, shot through both thighs. Even the 23rd Iowa's sutler fell; Lawler described him as "a brave old man, who took a gun at the commencement of the battle, went into the ranks, fought nobly, and fell, mortally wounded." Scores more Iowa and Wisconsin troops fell as well. But other officers soon raced forward to take the positions of wounded leaders, Lieutenant Colonel Samuel L. Glasgow taking command of the 23rd Iowa and, because Lieutenant Colonel Dunlap of the 21st Iowa was out, having been wounded at Port Gibson earlier in the month, Major Salue G. Van Anda took over the 21st Iowa while Dunlap watched from the rear with pride.[23]

As the Union regiments neared the bayou, they stopped only to deliver a volley into the Confederate line. One Federal remembered, "the rebels poured in a dreadful volley of musketry into the ranks of our brave boys but on they went yelling. . . . The rebs stood firm until our boys got within a few yards of their breastworks." Lawler reported the men then "dashed forward through the bayou, filled with water, fallen timber, and brush, on to the rebel works with the shout of victors, driving the enemy in with confusion from their breastworks and rifle-pits, and entering in triumph the rebel stronghold."

Another Iowan reported "leaping from tree to tree, from branch to branch, through mud and water, none knew how, but the bayou was passed."[24]

Despite the wounding of several important officers, the Federal attack accomplished its goal of shattering the Confederate line where the unnerved 61st Tennessee stood. Colonel Gates, who was in the trenches himself since his horse "received a very bad wound in the face," later admitted that the Federals had massed "on the river in the timber where we could not see them." Moving southward along and somewhat parallel to the Confederate defenses and the bayou, Lawler's Iowans were on top of the Southern line in no time, literally before the Confederates could react. One remembered that "our troops were completely surprised and were really surrounded before they knew it." The stunned Missourians and Arkansans let loose a wild volley as the Union regiments passed but watched them, no doubt in relief, move on to their right. There, Lawler's men, after stopping and delivering the massive volley, hit Vaughn's brigade. The Tennesseans, although some of the freshest men in the entire Confederate army, simply could not hold their positions, prompting one Missourian to cajole: "Here a Tennessee Brigade on the left disgraced themselves by running in wild disorder, which caused a great many of the Missourians to get captured." As Lawler's men poured over the "deep, miry slough," as McClernand described it, and scaled the accompanying earthworks, Vaughn's Tennesseans melted away. A Federal reported to his brother that "some of them ran but the majority of them threw down their arms." The veteran 4th Mississippi could not stem the tide either, with so many around them giving way. The Mississippians' honor was tinged in the debacle, one Missourian calling them the "flying Mississippians."[25]

Panic ran like an electric shock through the remainder of the Confederate army. Although the Southerners continued firing, Bowen's men could not hold on. Green's brigade, not hearing much fighting from the right, soon saw the Federals pouring through the line and took to the rear. Colonel Gates alarmingly noted, "I discovered that they had crossed the ditches and were between me and the bridge." He ordered his men to swim the river. Likewise, those of Cockrell's Missouri brigade on the right who braved to climb the railroad embankment saw the Federals making their way down the north side of the railroad toward the river crossings. The disgust can be heard in Cockrell's voice as he later wrote, "I saw the line between the railroad and the first skirt of timber north of the railroad beginning to give way, and then running in disorder." Soon, it dawned on Cockrell that their retreat would have a marked effect on his men. "I watched this disorderly falling back a few minutes, when I saw that the enemy had possession of the trenches . . . and were rapidly advancing toward the bridge," Cockrell reported in disbelief. "The enemy [was] now . . . nearer this crossing than my line," he added. Accordingly, Cockrell ordered his brigade to the rear to escape, and one Missourian admitted that the men "soon showed that they were as fleet-footed and expert in running as they were obstinate, stubborn and courageous in the fight." Another described the "long, hard run of a mile from our position." Due to increasing artillery covering fire from the west bank, many of the Missourians got across, as did Cockrell and Green, but some had to take to the river to get away. Still, in only about three minutes, Lawler had shattered the Confederate line and driven away an entire division and another brigade.[26]

Almost in disbelief, the other Union regiments retained their composure and followed Lawler's example, launching attacks on their own fronts. Lawler managed to ride over toward the 49th and 69th Indiana of Garrard's brigade, which were supporting him, and ordered the Indianans to charge at the same time his Iowans did. They did so, on Lawler's left. Colonel James Keigwin remembered that his men charged over "a heavy abatis" toward the Confederate line. As the Indianans reached the bayou and entered it, they began to see the Confederates "putting cotton on their ramrods and showing a willingness to surrender." Keigwin later noted that his unit, despite being in reserve, was the "second in the works, although they had farther to charge and deeper water to wade through than three others that started in advance of us." Despite being in the forefront of the charge, the 49th Indiana lost only one man wounded. "It was the poorest fight I ever saw the rebels make," Keigwin admitted. Lawler also sent his reserve regiment, the 22nd Iowa, far to the right to dislodge a pocket of Confederates near the river. They did so, and one of the other regiments quickly took them prisoner.[27]

The farther south along the Confederate line, the easier the Union assault was. Several commanders in the lower sectors reported taking the enemy works "without opposition." One of Osterhaus's brigade commanders, Daniel W. Lindsey, went so far as to report that "we had no trouble in possessing the works in our immediate front." Portions of Benton's (the 33rd and 99th Illinois) and Lindsey's troops cut off a significant number of Confederates and drove them "to the left and down the river" for other waiting Federals to gobble up. Brigade commander Stephen Burbridge, on the far left flank, noted that as his men approached the Confederate line "a white handkerchief was displayed on their intrenchments." Evidently, for all the Confederates cared, Loring could fend for himself.[28]

Colonel Theodore E. Buehler of the 67th Indiana of Burbridge's brigade of Smith's division left a vivid account of the advance on this southern sector of the Confederate line. Although his men were tired and had not had anything to eat since the previous night, he remembered that "all fatigue was forgotten." "We advanced by the right oblique through brush and bayous," he recalled, "over fences and hedges, at a rapid rate." He continued: "With a shout unequalled, forward we went on the double-quick, over plowed fields and across bayous, to receive the surrender of the Sixtieth Tennessee (rebel) Regiment." As a testament to just how shocked the Confederates fronting him were by Lawler's advance, the 67th Indiana, as well as the vast majority of the rest of the army, suffered few casualties, and Buehler declared that "the flag of the Sixty-seventh was the first on the breast-works."[29]

Relatively few Confederate casualties occurred in the charge itself. Pemberton reported a loss of a mere twenty killed and wounded, although the number was surely higher. The loss in artillery was quite severe, however, due to that fact that someone (and none of the Confederate officers would ever admit to such a thing) had ordered all the artillery horses away. Eighteen guns, along with limbers and caissons, were thus stranded with no way to move them, prompting one Illinoisan to quip that "at this rate Pemberton will be apt to get short of light guns before long." The Federals took advantage and turned at least one of the guns on the retreating Confederates, one Iowan declaring that Federal General John Logan was on the scene and barking orders to turn the guns around. Conversely, the main Confederate loss in men occurred when the retreat began; Bowen here suffered more than seventeen hundred taken prisoner, prompting one Iowan to remark that the "rebels were hemmed in like rats in a trap." With only two small avenues over which to cross the river, the feared bottleneck quickly developed. One lowly Confederate termed the region between the river and defenses as the "Jeff Davis Slaughter pen," and Pemberton himself wrote that "it very soon became a matter of *save qui peut*," or every man for himself. Indeed, as Bowen's division and Vaughn's brigade tried to cross the river, hundreds fell captive to the pursuing Federals, Lawler marveling that "more men were captured by my brigade than I had men in the charge." Many Confederates tried to swim the river, and some made their way to safety. Others sadly drowned or were shot trying to escape. Most simply threw down their weapons rather than try to run the gauntlet of Union fire. One elated member of the 23rd Wisconsin of Burbridge's brigade wrote home, "our Brigade captured the 60th Tenn. Reg. every single one, the Colonel and all." One of Burbridge's staff officers actually received the regiment's colors.[30]

The Confederate crisis was apparent, but many tried to stem the tide. Pemberton staff officer Brigadier General Thomas H. Taylor related that the men "were crossing in great confusion." He attempted to rally the troops, "but in vain." About all he could do was to rally a few on the western side of the river "to get them formed in some order on the bluff." But even that was difficult in the extreme. "It is supposed they are gone back to Vicksburg," one Iowan declared, and another wrote that the Confederates ran "like frightened sheep." A fleeing Missourian could only relate that "the race was both exciting and dangerous." Those who knew they were doomed prepared for prison, Major Joseph J. Gee of the 4th Mississippi cutting off his bars so that he could go with his men to an enlisted prison camp; he was outed by a lieutenant in the regiment. Despite a lack of rations in the Union army, many of the Confederate wounded and prisoners were provided with food.[31]

But it was not without cost to the Federals. One Union soldier described the fields in front of the breastworks: "The dead and wounded lay thick on the field we were compelled to charge over." Another wrote how he saw "wounded and dead laying in all directions dead horses broken guns and gun carriages." An Iowan even described one soldier who had been hit thirteen times; he was taken to a hospital and left until last because no one thought he would live anyway. Miraculously, he survived, recovered, and later rejoined his unit. That was all in the future, however, and now details were made to gather the wounded and bury the dead. Lawler reported he lost 14 killed and 185 wounded in three minutes. Total Union casualties in the attack amounted to 39 killed, 237 wounded, and three missing. Obviously, the Southerners were even more devastated. One Federal wrote of the results of the chaotic retreat at the river: "Bodies could be seen floating in the brush and dead-wood for two or three hundred yards. . . . The banks were covered with guns, hats, and clothing of almost every conceivable description. It is impossible to imagine a wilder scramble." Confederate casualty totals were not fully reported, but killed and wounded were slight, although Federals reported for months thereafter that a faithful dog would come at night and howl on his owner's grave on the bluff overlooking the railroad bridge. Obviously, the main Confederate loss came in the number captured, which totaled some seventeen hundred. Even among the carnage, however, most realized that Big Black River was nothing like the battle of the day before. One Federal, in fact, wrote "the engagement was not so severe. They were anxious to get across the river and burn the bridge."[32]

General Lawler himself was in a historic mood after the battle. Perusing the field, he stopped Aquilla Standifird of the 23rd Iowa and asked him to show him exactly where the regiment had begun its attack from behind the riverbank. Standifird said the general wanted to know how far the brigade had charged. When Standifird showed him the place, Lawler was amazed, remarking that it was nearly a quarter of a mile to the Confederate works.

Later, Grant himself came around and offered Lawler's entire brigade his personal thanks.[33]

Despite the losses, Federals of all ranks were ecstatic. A lower-level soldier wrote that "a more gallant charge was never made," and one Illinoisan declared in his diary, "we expect to be in Vicksburg in a few days." John McClernand later described the feat as "eminently brilliant" and wrote that "a victory could hardly have been more complete." Division commander Carr, perhaps with Hovey's touting of his own division at Port Gibson, declared fully that "this battle was fought and won by my division." William F. Jones of the 42nd Ohio wrote his cousin that "in half a day we whipped them and took 3000 prisoners." Of course, rumors had by that time begun to swell the numbers, one Federal even reporting that they "captured 25000 more prisoners[—]have seen about that many myself." The Federals mopping up the field felt the same surge of enthusiasm, one captain remarking that they had routed "the flower of the rebel army." And as the victorious Federals confronted the beaten Confederates behind the surging lines, several struck up conversations. One Northerner marveled at the sight of the Southern soldiers. "None of them have uniforms," he said in disbelief. "They have all kinds of clothing[—]they are hard looking critters." The same soldier asked a disheartened Confederate what he thought of the Federals: "He thought they could go where they pleased."[34]

"Again defeated," one Confederate wrote in his diary. And the results of that defeat were disastrous, especially for the Confederate soldiers who managed to get away and start the long trek back to Vicksburg, not to mention what all lay in their future there. For those captured, their very different odyssey was also just beginning, although prisoners of the 4th Mississippi were overjoyed when they learned that the regiment guarding them back at Edwards Station was the 54th Indiana. "To our great surprise," one Mississippian noted, "they proved to be our old acquaintances of the 54th Indiana who guarded us at Camp Morton and whom we had captured at Chickasaw Bayou. Quite an attachment had grown up between us."[35]

The commander of those hard-luck Confederate soldiers fleeing back toward Vicksburg was feeling no better. John Pemberton later wrote in his report, "a strong position, with an ample force of infantry and artillery to hold it, was shamefully abandoned almost without resistance." But with the loss of the Big Black River defenses and nearly two thousand prisoners, Pemberton knew his effort to connect with Loring had gone awry. For all he knew, the Federals had captured or destroyed Loring's entire division. As a result, Loring now had to fend for himself; Pemberton had to extricate the remaining parts of his army. He sadly admitted, "under these circumstances nothing remained but to retire the army within the defenses of Vicksburg." But the army was falling apart fast, one officer describing it as "shockingly demoralized." Pemberton noted his first duty was to "endeavor as speedily as possible to reorganize the depressed and discomfited troops."[36]

Indeed, many soldiers had already begun their retreat into the city. One artilleryman reported to his diary, "the retreat of our army may be properly denominated a *rout*." A wagon master described "the indiscriminate flight . . . wagons at the gallop—men rushing madly along with citizens half crazy and women frantic, asking for assistance, all rendered it as confused a scene as you well could imagine." Despite so many straggling, Pemberton officially ordered Bowen's whipped command to retreat. The army marched westward led by Pemberton, who made his way to the city to prepare its defense. He knew the hard-hitting Grant would not let up.[37]

As Pemberton made his way toward Vicksburg, he fully realized the terrible situation he was in. He had lost two battles and nearly half his mobile army in two days. Furthermore, he now faced the prospects of becoming trapped in Vicksburg, with no way to escape. Perhaps he best summed up the situation when he calmly confided to an accompanying officer: "Just thirty years ago I began my military career by receiving my appointment to a cadetship at the U.S. Military Academy, and to-day—the same date—that career is ended in disaster and disgrace." Rumors that Pemberton had "sold Vicksburg" were rife, one surgeon adding, "and many believe it."[38]

While Pemberton was slipping toward depression, however, portions of his army at the bridge were still holding on. As soon as all who could passed over, Major Lockett ordered the soldiers to destroy the bridge and the *Dot*, thereby halting Grant long enough for Pemberton to make sense of his disorganized situation. Lockett had earlier placed rails and cotton "at intervals," he said, and had a barrel of turpentine ready to ignite the *Dot*; he also kept an officer at each crossing ready to apply fire. As Lockett watched the retreat in disgust, "I gave a signal to apply the torch" to the bridges when satisfied that all who could had made it out. Lockett himself was on the *Dot*, and "I touched a match to the barrel of turpentine, and with the aid of one of my lieutenants tipped it over." Fortunately for the Confederates, when lit the bridges burned beyond further use and soon collapsed, although one Missourian noted that "a great many ran over under the fire in the upper deck of the boat." One Mississippian explained that getting across the burning bridges was "a very perilous act, but we did it." "In a few moments," Lockett remembered, "both bridges were in flames, and were quickly and thoroughly burned."[39]

Meanwhile, two Confederate brigades, Stephen D. Lee's and William Baldwin's, arrived on the west bank to annoy the Federals and delay any bridge-building activity. So did artillery, which shelled the enemy across the river, they being amazed as the "bright flames leaped into the air." One irritated Federal even noted that "we got the railroad bridge but the buggers put fire to it and burned it after they got across." They tried to put the fires out, but the bridge being forty feet high and nearly two miles long (bridge and trestles) and because of the intensity of the flames as well as the Confederate fire from the other side of the river, they were unable to do so; some six hundred yards of trestle was ultimately burned. In fact, Cockrell explained that some of the artillery west of the river fired on the Federals even as the Southerners withdrew: "Did valuable service in checking the enemy until we crossed." Federal artillery responded while the infantrymen made, according to one Iowan, "Herculean efforts" to extinguish the fires, but they were unsuccessful. Union sharpshooters of Lindsey's Federal brigade of Osterhaus's division soon peppered the Confederates, but few casualties resulted despite a mix-up in orders that left the 23rd Alabama in line well after everyone else had departed. The Alabamians barely made their getaway late in the evening.[40]

Confederate sharpshooters on the high bluffs west of the river in particular helped blunt the Federal advance. Division commander A. J. Smith moved to the bank and spied the enemy through his glasses, but "they seen him and made the dirt fly around him but did not strike him," one Indianan explained. But he added, "he soon came down and chatted with us boys behind the levee." The advance to the river also inexplicably included Grant's son, Fred. The young boy very much enjoyed himself as he pursued the retreating Confederates to the river and even watched some swim to the west bank. Fred's enthusiasm was quickly dampened when a Confederate sharpshooter hit him in the leg. Thinking he was dead, Fred called to a nearby staff officer, "I am killed." The officer, probably chagrined at his babysitting role in the first place, told the boy to "move your toes," whereupon both learned the wound "was slight but very painful." On realizing the boy would live, the officer "recommended our hasty retreat," the younger Grant remembered years later. "This we accomplished in good order," he added.[41]

Meanwhile, slowly but surely, the defeated Confederate army stumbled toward Vicksburg; "army shockingly demoralized," one staff officer admitted. The residents of Vicksburg had heard the heavy firing on the morning of May 17 and wondered about its outcome. Soon, they found out. Solemn looks and dejected countenances marked the army's entrance. Stories of defeat and rumors of treachery abounded as many began to lay blame for the debacle. One member of Pemberton's staff described to his diary how "our troops shamefully abandoned the trenches." A member of Cockrell's brigade wrote in his diary, "the troops in line there [on the left] ingloriously gave way, on which account the troops on the right were necessitated to fall back." Several soldiers retold rumors of Pemberton selling Vicksburg, one said for $100,000. As a result, many offered mournful recollections in diaries and letters. One Confederate remembered the army being "all dejected." Another prophesied, "if an attack is made tomorrow, we are lost." He continued to grumble, "I have never been low spirited, but things look too dark for even me to be hopeful."[42]

Pemberton's arrival with the army clearly horrified the citizens. One related that Champion Hill even that far away had the "sound of a vast cane brake on fire" and that it shattered windows miles away. The two unengaged divisions, Smith's and Forney's, presented an effective appearance as they entered the city, but then came the veterans of Champion Hill and Big Black River Bridge. Emma Balfour remembered her anguish as the troops passed: "I hope never to witness again such a scene as the return of our routed army. From twelve o'clock until late in the night the streets and roads were *jammed* with wagons, cannons, horses, men, mules, stock, sheep, everything you can imagine that appertains to an army—being brought hurriedly within the intrenchment. Nothing like order prevailed, of course, as divisions, brigades, and regiments were broken and separated." Emile McKinley similarly noted: "Oh! my heart ached, ached, as I hope it never will again." Despite their shock, the people of Vicksburg turned out in full force to aid the troops. Many opened their pantries, and others carried water to the street corners for the exhausted men. Emma Balfour could only look on with desperation, however. "Poor fellows," she wailed, "it made my heart ache to see them." No doubt many soldiers agreed with the desperation. Pemberton even recommended all noncombatants leave the city, but with the railroad blocked few had anywhere to go. One simply termed May 17 as "one long day."[43]

Obviously, the exact opposite feeling prevailed in the Union ranks. Grant had reaped huge benefits from his pursuit and attack at the Big Black River, so much so that he could in good faith disregard, according to Grant's memory, an order carried by Brigadier General William Dwight of Banks's staff, who had passed through Grand Gulf on May 16. Grant recalled it being from Washington telling him again to support Major General Nathaniel P. Banks's efforts at Port Hudson, Louisiana, but it was more likely a message from Banks himself. At any rate, the small-statured brigadier even stood on his toes to deliver what he assumed was a very important message. But Grant had routed the enemy army, captured more than seventeen hundred prisoners, and driven Pemberton headlong into Vicksburg for total casualties of only 279 in a battle that really did not have to take place anyway. And Grant had no mind to stop now. He had Vicksburg within his grasp and would not let go. He thus ordered his three corps across the Big Black River toward his ultimate objective: Vicksburg.[44]

And confident Grant was, mainly because "the enemy have been so terribly beaten yesterday and today." One Iowan even declared the river fight as "the most decisive battle of the campaign." Informing Sherman that McClernand defeated the enemy at the railroad bridge, Grant added that, "if the information you [Sherman] gain after crossing warrants you in believing you can go immediately into the city, do so." Sherman was just as confident, asking in his own message after getting across the Big Black at Bridgeport: "Shall I push on into the city, or secure a point on the ridge?"[45]

But there were still concerns, especially with Johnston somewhere in the rear. While Jackson had been negated as a center to build up a force to the east, Johnston's presence still concerned Grant and he sent Colonel Amory K. Johnson's cavalry back that direction "to ascertain if he can the position and intentions of Jo Johnson." Supplies were also still an issue, especially in Sherman's XV Corps, which seemingly was always in rear of the other two and therefore devoid of goods that could be acquired from the country. Grant especially ordered twenty additional teams to supply the corps already devoid of adequate transportation.[46]

But despite the remaining concerns, Sherman was making good headway. Blair had moved forward with the pontoon train, ordered by McClernand initially to the railroad bridge. At Edwards Station, however, Grant countermanded the order and sent Blair northward to Bridgeport to meet Sherman's other two divisions, which had arrived at the river at noon on May 17. Once at the river, a small exchange of cannon fire with Confederates on the opposite bank convinced the enemy that they could not hold the critical crossing. "The enemy displayed a white flag and surrendered themselves," Blair explained, and some of the prisoners even offered to help lay the pontoon bridge. His engineers soon had the inflatable India rubber pontoons laid, and by nightfall Blair was crossing troops.[47]

Ransom's brigade also arrived during this period, it having moved forward to Grand Gulf on the west side of the Mississippi River, "cleaning up the whole *debris* of the army in advance of me." Once across, Ransom had moved out of Grand Gulf on May 13, reaching Raymond early on May 16 but being blocked by Blair's still-present division, which "occupied the road

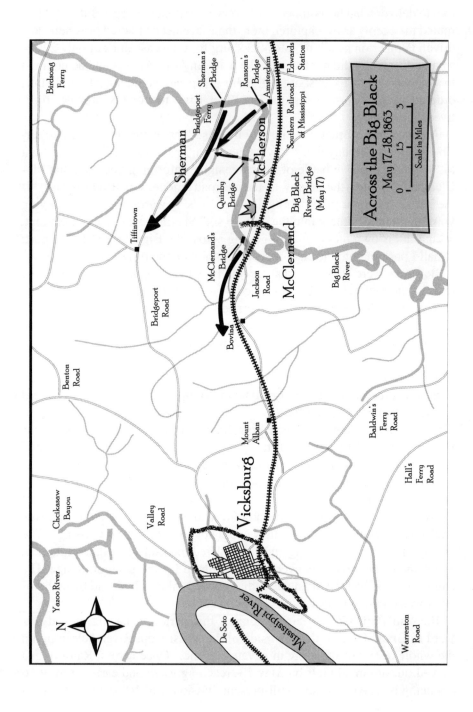

Across the Big Black
May 17–18, 1863

Scale in Miles

0   1½   3

north of me." Ransom's troops could hear the fight raging to the west all day on May 16 ("we know they are having it hot and heavy up there," one Illinoisan scribbled in his diary), and McClernand ordered the brigade forward even during the day, but Ransom did not reach the field until after the fighting ended. But he was present now.[48]

Sherman was not the only one making good progress toward Vicksburg, however. Although Sherman was partially across the Big Black River by the end of the day, three other bridges were also in the process of being constructed farther south along the river. Grant soon had a total of four crossing points to leap the now undefended Big Black River, the last geographical impediment to reaching Vicksburg and, perhaps more important at this particular point, the last impediment of any kind to reaching the Yazoo River, Grant's new source of supplies. And that was critical; his famished and exhausted army was reaching its limit of endurance and more than likely running mostly on adrenaline at this point. But even adrenaline would run out eventually, especially as a new and perhaps even harder phase of the campaign now began as the Federals approached the very ramparts of Vicksburg itself.[49]

Epilogue

"We Have Performed the Greatest Campaign of the War"

———

"I have seen stirring times since the first day of May," one Federal wrote home, encapsulating a flood of sentiments from both sides about what had just happened the prior two and a half weeks. Alvin Hovey wrote his wife that "I have been in almost constant battle since the 1st of May." He stated inaccurately that "the battles of Port Gibson and Champion Hills were fought principally by my Division," before boasting how "my division alone has done more hard fighting than the balance of the army." Those from other divisions had their equal say, however, XV Corps brigade commander T. Kilby Smith waxing eloquent while writing his mother: "We have driven the enemy to his stronghold. We have desolated his towns and villages, and of pleasant places have made a wilderness. He has fled before us like chaff before the wind." More common soldiers explained simply that "we have whipped them in every fight that we have had" and "we have been on the march for over a month and a half and fighting all the way."[1]

Many marveled at the campaign itself, Sherman explaining to his wife that "we made a full circuit." Another wrote that "I marched all through from wheir we Crossed the River out to Jackson and back to this place, fighting at Intervals." And another described "marching through Dust, Mud, rain and intolerable heat," fighting several battles "besides skirmishing nearly all the way." Indeed, wounded and prisoners dotted the route, not to mention hundreds if not thousands of freshly dug graves. Conversely, some were so busy on the march that they left diary entries blank and did not write home because of such heavy activity.[2]

But even amid the larger movement there was a growing conclusion that Champion Hill had been the "key to the whole of that brilliant campaign." Grant and Sherman certainly expressed those sentiments at the time, and others did so as well, although perhaps Sid Champion himself had more of a stake in what had happened there than anyone. "The fight was at Cooks Robert Ratliffs & Cokers also at Mrs. Ellison," he wrote Matilda just two days later as he struggled to find out what had happened and if he still had a house; "I am fearful our home is nearly destroyed—probably the house burned as I saw a large fire in that direction—but I have no regrets on that score—I have ceased to regret about property." One Federal put it in more homespun terms: Pemberton "got whacked over the cocanut at Champion Hills."[3]

But even with the decisive Union victory on May 16 and the follow-up the day after, all realized there was still more fighting to do as the armies approached one another at Vicksburg itself. "Now for the great prize," one Federal exclaimed, another terming the city as "our Vicksburg pen." Many understood the significance, Ohioan Isaac Williams writing in simple fashion what many were thinking: "Our regiment (30th Ohio Infantry) has been marched and conveyed on steamboats a great many miles backwards and forwards until at last here we are besieging the city of Vicksburg Miss the vaunted stronghold of the rebel army. General U.S. Grant our commander has been trying for a long time to occupy the position we now hold."[4]

Indianan Edward Wood perhaps summed it up best: "We have penetrated 100 miles into the enemy's country, leaving our rear and communication with the river unguarded, have subsisted for three weeks entirely upon the country, have made forced marches on short & on no rations, in five days from the 12th to the 16th inclusive we fought three pitched battles marching fifty miles capturing Jackson the State Capital more than fifty pieces of artillery and over five thousand prisoners." He added: "I know that in the light of history these achievements will be regarded as only preliminary to the grand struggle for the capture of Vicksburg, but to the actors they have been real victories in themselves."[5]

There was accordingly a tangible feeling that one part of the campaign had ended and another was beginning. Sherman himself realized as much even as he and Grant made their way to the very Yazoo River bluffs he had tried to take back in December at Chickasaw Bayou. With total and open access to the Yazoo River above Vicksburg, and now that the defending Confederates there had scampered back into Vicksburg itself, Sherman realized that everything had been worth it and that he and all the others who had not believed fully in Grant's plan were wrong and that Grant had been right; his commanding general had in fact pulled off the nearly unthinkable. Now with complete access to any and all supplies that would shortly start being unloaded, a new phase of the Vicksburg Campaign was beginning: taking possession of the city itself. All the efforts up to now had been just to get to a position to take Vicksburg — and now that could begin.[6]

Sherman very incisively admitted as much to Grant as they viewed the Yazoo River bottom from the high ground, knowing full well supplies would be flowing very soon: "He turned to me," Grant later remembered, "saying that up to this minute he had felt no positive assurance of success. This, however, he said was the end of one of the greatest campaigns in history and I ought to make a report of it at once. Vicksburg was not yet captured, and there was no telling what might happen before it was taken; but whether captured or not, this was a complete and successful campaign."[7]

$\mathbf{B}$ad news filtered constantly into Richmond as the torrid events in Mississippi continued unabated. First news of the defeat at Champion Hill came on May 19, the very day Grant was beginning his assaults on Vicksburg itself, although clerk John B. Jones noted "Pemberton was *forced back*. This is all we know yet." Jones imagined the effect the news had on the president, sick as he was and unable even to go to his office, writing, "no doubt he is also worried at the dark aspects in his own State—Mississippi." Confirmation came the next day of Pemberton withdrawing west of the Big Black River, prompting Jones to surmise that "something decisive must occur before Vicksburg in a few days." Although that "something decisive" had already taken place on May 16, news continued to filter in, with the news of Big Black River arriving on May 22, the very day Grant assaulted the city with his entire army. Noting that Vicksburg was "closely invested," clerk Jones added that "there is much gloom and despondency in the city among those who credit these unofficial reports." In time, it was found that those unofficial reports were completely accurate.[8]

Almost all saw the disaster that was unfolding. Now back in Jackson, Joe Johnston wrote Pemberton advising what Grant and Sherman already knew: "If Haynes' Bluff is untenable, Vicksburg is of no value, and cannot be held. If, therefore, you are invested in Vicksburg, you must ultimately surrender. Under such circumstances, instead of losing the troops and place, we must, if possible, save the troops. If it is not too late, evacuate Vicksburg and its dependencies, and march to the northeast." But Pemberton, under President Davis's orders to hold the city, would not budge at this point and even called in all his outlying troops into the city. "I knew and appreciated the earnest desire of the Government and of the people that it should be held," Pemberton explained. Orders had accordingly gone out to evacuate Snyder's and Haynes' Bluffs, saving all the supplies and guns that the troops could before marching into Vicksburg. The men at those outlying points had been subject to "innumerable conflicting rumors," although the sounds coming from the south were pretty plain on both May 16 and the morning of May 17. Stragglers alerted everyone that the "Yankees are coming." Civilians were in a panic, one writing later that "I shall never forget this awful night, no one undressed or went to bed." Moore's brigade down toward Warrenton also marched in from the south.[9]

It was simply too late to evacuate, and Pemberton informed Johnston that his line at Big Black River had melted "owing to the demoralization consequent upon the retreat of yesterday." He added that "the army has fallen back to the line of intrenchments around Vicksburg," abandoning all outlying fortifications. Then he added a final thought, second-guessing himself at moving out from behind the shield of the Big Black River. "I deemed the movement very hazardous, preferring to remain in position behind the Big Black and near to Vicksburg," Pemberton wrote. He added, "I greatly regret that I felt compelled to make the advance beyond Big Black, which has proved so disastrous in its results."[10]

Pemberton later explained that he did not want to "abandon the line of the Big Black, . . . (although I had crossed when I learned that the main body of General Grant's army was approaching the Southern Railroad, to protect my communications with the east and more easily to avail myself of the assistance of my re-enforcements, which were daily arriving)." But communication with an out-of-touch superior who was moving the opposite direction from him would not be worth anything anyway, although from Richmond's vantage point even the attempt to concentrate had not been made. Davis simply endorsed a message from Johnston on May 16: I "do not perceive why a junction was not attempted, which would have made our force nearly equal in number to the estimated strength of the enemy."[11]

Pemberton would spend the rest of his life trying to rationalize his actions, although he oftentimes indicted himself in the process. In his report he wrote that "I think it due to myself, in bringing this portion of my report to a conclusion, to state emphatically that the advance movement of the army from Edwards Depot on the afternoon of May 15 was made against my judgement, in opposition to my previously expressed intentions, and to the subversion of my matured plans." He concluded: "The safety of Vicksburg was of paramount importance; under no circumstances could I abandon my communications with it." Pemberton obviously had not wanted to leave Vicksburg and certainly not the Big Black River, later describing how "I had resisted the popular clamor for an advance, which began from the moment the enemy set his polluting foot upon the eastern bank of the Mississippi River. I had resisted the universal sentiment, I believe of the army—I know of my general officers—in its favor, and yielded only to the orders of my superior. I was not invited by General Johnston to submit my plans to him for his consideration."[12]

But Pemberton, not Johnston, became the scapegoat for the disaster in the making. Many considered him a traitor, brigade commander Martin Green supposedly telling a civilian that "he hoped the Yankees would catch General Pemberton, because he had sold the army." Others gave him the benefit of the doubt as to loyalty to the Confederacy, although most realized his competence was a fair question: "That there was great mismanagement is evident—if not serious blunders." One admitted that "he meant well—but lacked the capacity to control so large a Dept." Lieutenant Drennan wrote home that with what he saw on May 16: "I feel convinced of his incapacity." Even Stephen D. Lee admitted that "Grant's movements were more rapid and decisive than those of the Confederate generals." In fact, he went so far as to claim that "Gen. Pemberton never fully comprehended Gen. Grant's campaign, till Bowen was defeated at Port Gibson." Perhaps most clear in his assessment, Lee surmised that Grant "outwitted his antagonist." Pemberton biographer Michael Ballard has surmised that by this point Pemberton "had lost control of himself and the campaign."[13]

But Johnston was not free from blame, one Federal writing that "there was manifestly both a lack of good judgment and great generalship, not only on the part of Pemberton, but of Johnston as well." A historian has written of Johnston's "characteristically imprecise and wishful orders," and Jefferson Davis biographer William C. Davis opined that Johnston "was being almost no help at all." But in hindsight Johnston was ultimately right about not losing the army in eventually losing the place. What one common Confederate soldier later described as the point where "Pemberton made the great mistake of his life" was when he retreated into Vicksburg instead of marching away to safety.[14]

There was the exact opposite feeling in the Union ranks as this most dangerous portion of the campaign drew to a close. One Federal wrote on May 18, once across the Big Black River, that "this is truly a solemn day to me and no doubt to many others who properly meditate on the Scenes of yesterday and the day before." Many referred to the last eighteen days as "that matchless campaign" or some variation of it. Luther Cowan wrote in the midst of it how

"they may say what they please about the big things of war, this our last campaign has been one of the biggest things of the season; we, this part of Grant's
army, have performed the hardest march, and the best one that had been done
in the war, here since we left Milliken's Bend." He complained: "We have
marched about ninety miles in eight days, through rain, mud, dust, the hottest
kind of weather, without tents to lie in and on short rations, foraging and subsisting the men in great measure on the country." Another noted that "Vicksburg has been long talked of and I presume almost despaired of. . . . We have
performed the greatest campaign of the war."[15]

Many had a good view of history and where this campaign fit in. One Federal simply stated that "history will record it as one of the noblest movemen[ts]
that our army ever made." Newspaperman Cadwallader described the movements as "splendid beyond description—almost beyond conception—are
scarcely equaled in history—and may be profitably studied for all time. They
are certain to be handed down to posterity as military classics, for the imita-
tion of future generations." Given the danger of operating between two forces
of the enemy and on short and suspect supply lines, one Federal even went so
far as to declare: "Challenge this statement who may, we believe God Himself
commanded the Federal army from the 14th to the 17th of May, 1863." Indeed, the campaign had many of the attributes of current warfare, especially
supply issues, and is studied by the modern military for its conception and
conduct.[16]

Obviously, the author and finisher of that campaign received just acclaim,
many references to Napoleonic comparisons being made. One Federal declared the Army of the Tennessee as great: "Napoleon never had a superior
one." Another explained that "Gen Grant has managed this campaign admirably displaying Great Generalship. . . . I am satisfied that Grant is one of the
great military men of the present age." And so it went: "Grant has nodoubt-
edly done more toward putting down this cursed rebellion than any other
man," argued another. "True Napoleonic style" exclaimed someone else.[17]

Higher-level officers who presumably knew more about the art of warfare
agreed. Brigade commander George Boomer wrote home in the midst of the
campaign that "since General Grant commenced to move his columns he has
displayed great tact and skill, together with immense energy and nerve. The
passage of this army over the Mississippi River and up to this point is one
of the most masterly movements known in the history of any warfare, and it
is a success." Even Sherman admitted to his senator brother later that month
that the plan had "appeared to me too risky at the time, and General Grant is
entitled to all the merit of its conception and execution." Most surprising was
Henry Halleck's confirmation that "in boldness of plan, rapidity of execution,

and brilliancy of results, these operations will compare most favorably with those of Napoleon about Ulm."[18]

But perhaps the opinion that most mattered was President Lincoln's, and he was thrilled. He watched closely but said nothing even when he thought Grant was making a mistake by moving up the east side of the Big Black River. That of course proved the right decision, as Lincoln later acknowledged ("you were right, and I was wrong"). Closer to the campaign itself, Lincoln also wrote on May 26 that "whether Gen. Grant shall or shall not consummate the capture of Vicksburg, his campaign from the beginning of this month up to the twenty second day of it, is one of the most brilliant in the world."[19]

But it was not a foregone conclusion that the campaign to reach Vicksburg would turn out the way that it did. In fact, while there was not any real concern that the Confederates would defeat Grant on the battlefield per se, Grant outnumbering the enemy at each battle (which in and of itself was a testament to his operational control and genius), success and failure was a much closer run thing in terms of supplies. If the Confederates had any real chance to defeat or stop Grant's Inland Campaign, it would have been on the logistical level when Grant's army was being supplied less and less to the point that by the May 15–18 time frame the situation was becoming critical. In fact, Grant's force had nearly reached, if not actually already arrived at, Clausewitz's "culminating point." Obviously, through hindsight we know that Pemberton made drastic mistakes, but we do not know whether different actions would have garnered any more success. Chances are, operating differently would not have brought any worse disaster for Pemberton, but there is at least the possibility that it could have fostered more positive results. Essentially, had Pemberton remained behind the Big Black River and defended the various crossings from Bridgeport southward to Baldwin's Ferry, but most especially at the railroad bridge, victory may not have resulted in battle but Pemberton possibly could have delayed Grant long enough for the adrenaline his army was operating on to subside and Grant's supply issues to become acute. Pemberton did not have to win a battle at the Big Black River; he just needed to hold the line for a few days in the May 15–18 time frame, depriving Grant of the linkup with his new outlet of supplies on the Yazoo River. Obviously, whether or not such a strategy would have worked is not known, but it likely would not have produced any worse results and could potentially have forced Grant to fight in a disadvantageous position at the Big Black River.[20]

While what would have happened is conjecture, we do know for certain that Grant's army was getting in bad shape logistically by mid-May, even with the arrival of the various wagon trains with supplies that took several days to sort out and distribute. Ammunition was not the critical issue, because Grant had enough to fight even on May 19 as he ordered the first assault on Vicksburg. But in terms of food, even the arriving supplies when spread out over the entire army were insufficient to fully supply it. The existing record bears this out conclusively.[21]

According to the soldiers themselves and the officers commanding them, supplies were very critical by the time Grant reached the Big Black River. One of Ransom's Illinoisans related on May 17 that "by this time we were out of rations almost entirely, having coffee, and a hard tack or so left." One Iowan in McClernand's corps explained that he and his comrades tore through Confederate haversacks at Big Black River bridge, finding cornbread, which they "ate . . . with relish." He continued: "All I had eaten that day was a piece of beef I had cooked in the blaze of the fire, just the juice of that had sustained me, until one of the boys gave me two of these delicious pones." One Federal explained that even foraging was not an option once the armies came in close contact with one another and the movement slowed down on May 12. Foraging was much more dangerous and often stopped, and besides, there was only so much to go around, and a concentrated and slow-moving army devoured what was available very quickly. One veteran recalled in his regimental history that by the morning of May 17 Grant's troops were even "on the verge of famine."[22]

In the XIII Corps, it is interesting that, for all of McClernand's complaining about supplies and favoritism given to other corps, few if any of his officers in their reports expressed protests; the vast majority of any complaints came from the XV and XVII Corps. McClernand simply noted in his report that "during these thirteen days my command subsisted on six days' rations and what scanty supply the country in the immediate vicinity of the route afforded."[23]

But some of McClernand's lower-level officers did comment on the supply situation. One of A. J. Smith's soldiers declared that they were "given five days rations of hard-tack and sow belly" when they crossed the Mississippi River "and we did not get anything more for twenty days." He later described how "our rations were running low and we stripped the bark from slippery elm trees eating it as we marched along. The day before I managed to steal an ear of corn from the horses." After Champion Hill, he added, "the Lord was good to us that night. Just before dark a bunch of hogs ran through our

Company and we got one for Company A so we had something to eat. This was the 16th day on five days rations and we were beginning to feel a little bit slim."[24]

More evidence came from the XVII Corps. William E. Strong on McPherson's staff related that by the time the XVII Corps crossed the Big Black River "our supply trains were empty, and the haversacks of the men had but little in them for twenty-four hours." Brigade commander Sanborn noted that, during the move northward from Hankinson's Ferry, "my command was entirely out of rations at this time, except what could be gathered from the country, and so remained until the evening of the 17th, at which time the regimental teams came up from Grand Gulf." Colonel David B. Hillis of the 17th Iowa of Holmes's brigade noted that "during the marches from Milliken's Bend the regiment received less than an average of one-third rations, but, notwithstanding this, it is worthy of note that during the whole of this trying but brilliant campaign not a murmur was heard in the ranks."[25]

Colonel John E. Tourtellotte of the 4th Minnesota gave more detail of the brigade's issues. He wrote:

> The only Government transportation of any kind with the regiment was 2 ambulances, 1 medicine wagon, and 1 six-mule team. The men carried their knapsacks, blankets, rations, and 60 rounds of ammunition. The six-mule team carried a few boxes of ammunition, the blankets and provisions of officers, and such supplies for the men as the regimental quartermaster was able to secure along our route. On said march we have drawn rations from Government as follows: We took with us five days' rations from Milliken's Bend. On or about May 1 we drew four days' rations of hard bread alone. May 4 we drew three-fifth rations of hard bread, sugar and tea for five days, beyond which time, up to May 17, all rations used by the regiment, and all forage used by regimental horses and mules, were secured by the regimental quartermaster in the country through which we passed. The rations procured by the quartermaster for the regiment consisted chiefly of sugar, molasses, salt, corn meal, and bacon. On May 17, the five regimental teams left behind overtook us, bringing five days' part rations of hard bread, flour, sugar, and coffee.

He added: "May 23, we drew full rations for the first time since leaving Milliken's Bend."[26]

Brigade commander John E. Smith noted larger issues than food, writing that the delay at Hankinson's Ferry was welcomed,

> giving the men ample time to rest and clean themselves, which they needed very much after the severe marches in the heat and dust, which at times was suffocat-

ing. Nearly one-third of the command at this time had no shoes, having worn them out on the march, and in consequence were very foot-sore. This, together with their want of supplies, which at times were very short, were subjects of pleasantries with the men, who consoled themselves with the prospect of a fight every other day to make amends for their privations.[27]

Sherman's XV Corps was in the rear for much of the Inland Campaign and therefore suffered the most, as much of the plenty the countryside afforded had already been swooped up by the XIII and XVII Corps up ahead. Colonel De Witt C. Thomas of the 93rd Indiana in Buckland's brigade noted that he left Grand Gulf on May 8 "without transportation or rations. On the third day after leaving Grand Gulf, I received three-fifths rations of crackers for my men (having been four days without bread). From that time until I arrived at Clinton, on our return from Jackson, I did not receive any rations from the Government, but had to rely upon the country for provisions." Similarly, Charles Matthies noted only "drawing three days' rations" on May 8.[28]

Ralph Buckland gave a running report of his brigade's supply odyssey. He actually crossed the Mississippi River on May 7 but was "not able to cross our teams, which contained all the rations we had." It only became worse:

> During the night word was sent to me that the commissary was prepared to issue rations of hard bread, &c., but when applied for early in the morning all the hard bread had been issued to the other brigades, reserving none for mine. Notwithstanding this unjustifiable conduct of the commissary, when the command "forward" was given, every man was in his place, and my brigade moved promptly forward, without transportation and with empty haversacks, not knowing where the next meal was to come from. Other troops having gone before us, it was difficult to procure provisions on the road. Every effort was made to supply the deficiency, but many of the officers and men suffered extreme hunger. We encamped that night at Willow Springs, where we remained until 4 p. m. the next day. A plenty of fresh meat was procured, but very little meal, not enough for one-tenth part of the command. Having no cooking utensils, the soldiers cooked their meat on sticks and as best they could. We reached Rocky Springs some time after dark on the evening of the 9th, where we remained until the morning of the 11th. Here the commissary brought up some rations of hard bread and meat, and issued three-fifth rations for three days. This scanty supply of hard bread was a great relief and a great luxury for the soldiers, who renewed their march on the morning of the 11th, refreshed and in fine spirits.

Thereafter, the brigade took part in Jackson's capture "with very little to eat" yet foraged even while destroying the rail lines, and they "collected an abundance of cattle and sheep; but we had no bread." Buckland added: "At Clinton the regimental teams joined the brigade with ammunition and a very small supply of hard bread."[29]

The lack of provisions became dire as the campaign entered the critical phase after May 15. "We are all out of rations," one of McClernand's Federals wrote as early as May 14. One Iowan admitted by May 18 that "living on less than half rations has almost used me up." An artilleryman on May 17 noted that after crossing the Big Black River "we retired soon after without supper." One of Ransom's Illinoisans related on May 17 that "we are quite short of provisions. Have to live on what we can get-corn meal, etc." One Illinoisan told of May 16 when "in some instances they paid fifty cents apiece for crackers." A pioneer in Logan's division tasked with burying the dead at Champion Hill reported on May 17 how he "camped at midnight, no dinner and no supper." An Ohioan described breakfast on the morning of May 16 with only flour and salt and the result was pancakes "which lie on a man's stomach like cakes of lead." One Iowan simply noted the supply situation brought Grant to "the crisis of his career."[30]

The overwhelming evidence is that, despite the arrival of the two wagon trains, Grant's troops were as a whole borderline famished by the time they reached and crossed the Big Black River. And it continued for a couple more days, even after Haynes' and Snyder's Bluffs came into Union possession. Obviously, it took a while for the flow of supplies to begin, and one Ohioan wrote on May 19 in his diary, "most of the boys entirely out of rations and suffering much from lack of food." Another noted that he offered a soldier five dollars for a piece of cornbread, but it was not accepted, the man responding that "bread was worth more to him than money." Captain John L. Woods, quartermaster for Tuttle's division of the XV Corps, reported simply that supplies eventually started flowing from the Yazoo River and that they "were much needed."[31]

Iowan Calvin Ainsworth elaborated on his hunger on May 18, writing in his diary: "For three days we have had nothing to eat. I have seen the boys offer a dollar for a hard tack, but no one had any to sell. I have had nothing myself for three days, still I am not so very hungry. I picked a few blackberries once or twice when there was a halt." One Ohioan was excited that he "captured a goose skinned and roasted it for supper." Yet another explained how "our men then marched or rather fought & starved their way up." And it was not confined to the lower ranks. Osborn Oldroyd told how "General Leggett walked into our camp, and in his usual happy way inquired, 'Well, boys, have you had your supper?'" The troops responded with, "No, General, we have not had any," to which Leggett shot back: "Well, boys, I have not had any either, and we shall probably have to fight for our breakfast." That satisfied the men: "Very well, General; guess we can stand it as well as you."[32]

As a result, there were opportunities for the Confederates to capitalize on the Union logistical issues. Pemberton saw one clearly: "With a moderate cavalry force at my disposal, I am firmly convinced that the Federal Army under General Grant would have been unable to maintain its communications with the Mississippi River, and that the attempt to reach Jackson and Vicksburg from that base would have been as signally defeated in May, 1863, as a like attempt from another base had by the employment of cavalry been defeated in December, 1862." Similarly, staff officer Jacob Thompson wrote Pemberton a couple of months later that "the almost total want of cavalry not only kept you in ignorance of his movements, but deprived you of all means of annoying or retarding him in his movements." But Johnston had removed much of the department's cavalry in January 1863.[33]

Likewise, Pemberton remaining behind the Big Black River could potentially have provided the delay for Grant's supply crisis to become acute. One Federal even picked up on the potential for trouble as the army reached and then began crossing the Big Black River: "The rebs may be drawing us into a trap, but as yet we have not a moment's fear of the result, for when Grant tells us go over a thing we go, and feel safe in going."[34]

Other actions or developments could also have helped a Confederate delaying defense. Grant was fortunate to have mostly good dry weather, which could have delayed his progress and multiplied the supply issues if forced to deal with muddy and boggy roads to bring up what supplies he ultimately did. Likewise, if timing was a key feature in bogging down the Federals east of the Big Black River and counterattacking at their Clausewitzian culminating point, then Johnston's defenseless withdrawal from Jackson was too early and too easy. With more troops scheduled to arrive even that day on May 14, he could certainly have at the very least delayed longer than what he did, and even one more day at this critical point could have been decisive for the half-starved Federal army. But alas Joe Johnston struck yet again! Most significant, if Pemberton could have delayed long enough to turn the whirlwind Federal process of taking command of and crossing the Big Black River into a multiday effort, he potentially could have caused Grant to make drastic choices and decisions that might have altered the campaign.[35]

But Grant managed to thread the needle, moving just fast enough and with just enough supplies to reach the critical Yazoo River in time for his army to once again receive the needed supplies. But the entire operation has been heavily misunderstood, many asserting that there was no supply line at all. Making the issue more confusing were Grant's statements in his memoirs. At

the point of discussing his trip to Grand Gulf itself and notifying Halleck that
he was moving on to Vicksburg and not cooperating with Banks, he wrote that
"Grand Gulf was accordingly given up as a base and the authorities at Washington were notified." He obviously did no such thing on May 3, and it was
not until the major moves forward on May 9 or 10 that he left the protective
cul-de-sac that had allowed for safe travel of wagons back and forth without
guard. Even then, however, he kept wagon trains moving forward, guarded
by larger troop units. It was not until the last of these left Grand Gulf on
May 12 that he actually cut loose from his base, as he stated later in his
memoirs. In describing the movement to Jackson he noted that "I uncovered
my own communication. So I finally decided to have none—to cut loose altogether from my base and move my whole force eastward. I then had no fears
for my communications." But even in that statement Grant was not totally
accurate, as he did have enormous fears for his communications, even sending Smith's entire division back to Dillon's to help defend the wagon trains
then rolling northward.[36]

Still, Grant managed to squeak by, with the help of an army that would
follow him wherever he went even with as few rations as possible. "We have
had hard times since we commenced this campaign," one of his Federals
wrote, "but as long as we can drive the scoundrels as we have been I am willing to endure harder times." And indeed there would be more fighting ahead,
but these battles would be fought by an Army of the Tennessee largely with
full supplies. "Vicksburg is now completely invested," Grant informed Halleck. "I have possession of Haynes' Bluff and the Yazoo; consequently have
supplies."[37]

Obviously, the May 1–17 march and battles loomed large in the greater
Vicksburg Campaign, with Champion Hill tagged as the "decisive battle for
Vicksburg." And after Grant acquired his new base of supplies on the Yazoo
River there could be little speculation as to how it would end. Of course, no
one knew the eventual outcome and would not be comfortable making bold
claims. But these operations in May 1863 in Mississippi would persist into
the future; as the days and months passed, and certainly the years, recollections of the pangs of hunger and sore muscles subsided. Only the positive
moments remained engrained in the victorious Federals' minds. That said,
the pains of defeat and destruction never quite left those affected on the Confederate side. For instance, Grant later noted that Green, the proprietor of the
cloth factory in Jackson that Grant had ordered burned, later petitioned for
reimbursement when Grant was president. "I declined," he simply wrote.[38]

Many others recalled events together. One member of the Union 11th Indiana who had cared for a wounded soldier of the Confederate 36th Georgia on Champion Hill later moved to Arkansas, where the former Confederate did as well. Their conversations, first jibing each other about the war, later turned serious when the details of their service and previous acquaintance became known. The Union man was a Methodist preacher, and the Confederate was his parishioner. On another occasion, a wounded Confederate recalled the gentle care he had received at Raymond and decades later sent letters to the postmaster there inquiring into the names of young ladies he remembered. One of the girls, now a grown woman, responded, and a wonderful correspondence emerged; the lady's daughter, "a beautiful young lady of nineteen, [even] paid myself and family a visit several years ago," the thankful Confederate explained.[39]

Perhaps most pitiful, John Pemberton in later years also realized just how outmatched he had been. Once the Adam Badeau biography of Grant came out in the late 1860s, Pemberton perused it and probably learned a lot about what had happened to him back in May 1863. He was especially taken aback by the news that one of Johnston's three couriers on the evening of May 13 had purposefully delivered the order for Pemberton to attack from the west directly to McPherson. That was news to Pemberton, who promptly wrote Grant to see if it was true. Obviously, by that time their different roles had been solidified. Pemberton was persona non grata in the Confederacy and certainly at Vicksburg, and he was then living in Philadelphia. Of course Grant was in Washington, living in the White House no less and serving as president of the United States. No two reputations could have been on more divergent paths than these two. And the obviousness of their positions was reinforced when Grant himself did not personally respond to Pemberton; instead an aide replied to the former Confederate commander. The aide, Levi P. Luckey, wrote to confirm that indeed McPherson had gained a copy of Johnston's note divulging what Pemberton should do. That of course explained to Pemberton a lot, and he wanted to go public with the news with Grant's approval. Luckey again wrote back agreeing, saying the news was already public in Badeau's book. But Pemberton wanted to use it as just a little more evidence of why he was nearly running in circles in May 1863—and why it seemed Grant was always a step or two ahead the entire time.[40]

Appendix A

Union Orders of Battle
May 1–17, 1863

Battle of Port Gibson
May 1, 1863

ARMY OF THE TENNESSEE
  Major General Ulysses S. Grant

THIRTEENTH ARMY CORPS
  Major General John A. McClernand

NINTH DIVISION
  Brigadier General Peter J. Osterhaus

First Brigade
  Brigadier General Theophilus T. Garrard
    118th Illinois
    49th Indiana
    69th Indiana
    7th Kentucky
    120th Ohio

Second Brigade
  Colonel Lionel A. Sheldon
    54th Indiana
    22nd Kentucky
    16th Ohio
    42nd Ohio
    114th Ohio

Artillery
>   7th Battery Michigan Light Artillery
>   1st Battery Wisconsin Light Artillery

TENTH DIVISION
>   Brigadier General Andrew J. Smith

First Brigade
>   Brigadier General Stephen G. Burbridge
>   16th Indiana
>   67th Indiana
>   83rd Ohio
>   23rd Wisconsin

Second Brigade
>   Colonel William J. Landram
>   77th Illinois
>   97th Illinois
>   108th Illinois
>   130th Illinois
>   19th Kentucky
>   48th Ohio

Artillery
>   17th Battery Ohio Light Artillery

TWELFTH DIVISION
>   Brigadier General Alvin P. Hovey

First Brigade
>   Brigadier General George F. McGinnis
>   11th Indiana
>   24th Indiana
>   34th Indiana
>   46th Indiana
>   29th Wisconsin

Second Brigade
>   Colonel James L. Slack
>   47th Indiana
>   24th Iowa
>   28th Iowa
>   56th Ohio

Artillery
> 2nd Illinois Light Artillery, Battery A
> 1st Missouri Light Artillery, Battery A
> 2nd Battery Ohio Light Artillery
> 16th Battery Ohio Light Artillery

FOURTEENTH DIVISION
Brigadier General Eugene A. Carr

First Brigade
Brigadier General William P. Benton
> 33rd Illinois
> 99th Illinois
> 8th Indiana
> 18th Indiana

Second Brigade
Colonel William M. Stone
> 21st Iowa
> 22nd Iowa
> 23rd Iowa
> 11th Wisconsin

Artillery
> 1st Battery Indiana Light Artillery
> 1st Battery Iowa Light Artillery

SEVENTEENTH ARMY CORPS
Major General James B. McPherson

THIRD DIVISION
Major General John A. Logan

First Brigade
Brigadier General John E. Smith
> 20th Illinois
> 31st Illinois
> 45th Illinois
> 124th Illinois
> 23rd Indiana

Second Brigade
Brigadier General Elias S. Dennis
30th Illinois
68th Ohio
78th Ohio

Third Brigade
Brigadier General John D. Stevenson
8th Illinois
81st Illinois
7th Missouri
32nd Ohio

Artillery
8th Battery Michigan Light Artillery

Cavalry
2nd Illinois Cavalry, Company A

Battle of Raymond
May 12, 1863

SEVENTEENTH ARMY CORPS
Major General James B. McPherson

THIRD DIVISION
Major General John A. Logan

First Brigade
Brigadier General John E. Smith
20th Illinois
31st Illinois
45th Illinois
124th Illinois
23rd Indiana

Second Brigade
Brigadier General Elias S. Dennis
30th Illinois
20th Ohio

68th Ohio
78th Ohio

Third Brigade
Brigadier General John D. Stevenson
    8th Illinois
    81st Illinois
    7th Missouri
    32nd Ohio

Artillery
    1st Illinois Light Artillery, Battery D,
    8th Battery Michigan Light Artillery
    3rd Battery Ohio Light Artillery

SEVENTH DIVISION
Brigadier General Marcellus M. Crocker

First Brigade
Colonel John B. Sanborn
    48th Indiana
    59th Indiana
    4th Minnesota

Second Brigade
Colonel Samuel A. Holmes
    17th Iowa
    10th Missouri
    80th Ohio

Third Brigade
Colonel George B. Boomer
    93rd Illinois
    5th Iowa
    10th Iowa
    26th Missouri

Artillery
    11th Battery Ohio Light Artillery

Battle of Jackson
May 14, 1863

ARMY OF THE TENNESSEE
   Major General Ulysses S. Grant

FIFTEENTH ARMY CORPS
   Major General William T. Sherman

THIRD DIVISION
   Brigadier General James M. Tuttle

First Brigade
   Brigadier General Ralph P. Buckland
      114th Illinois
      93rd Indiana
      72nd Ohio
      95th Ohio

Second Brigade
   Brigadier General Joseph A. Mower
      47th Illinois
      5th Minnesota
      11th Missouri
      8th Wisconsin

Third Brigade
   Brigadier General Charles L. Matthies
      8th Iowa
      12th Iowa
      35th Iowa

Artillery
   Captain Nelson T. Spoor
      1st Illinois Light Artillery, Battery E
      2nd Battery Iowa Light Artillery

SEVENTEENTH ARMY CORPS
   Major General James B. McPherson

SEVENTH DIVISION
   Brigadier General Marcellus M. Crocker

First Brigade
Colonel John B. Sanborn
48th Indiana
59th Indiana
4th Minnesota
18th Wisconsin

Second Brigade
Colonel Samuel A. Holmes
17th Iowa
10th Missouri
24th Missouri
80th Ohio

Third Brigade
Colonel George B. Boomer
93rd Illinois
5th Iowa
10th Iowa
26th Missouri

Artillery
1st Missouri Light Artillery, Battery M
6th Battery Wisconsin Light Artillery

Battle of Champion Hill
May 16, 1863

ARMY OF THE TENNESSEE
Major General Ulysses S. Grant

THIRTEENTH ARMY CORPS
Major General John A. McClernand

NINTH DIVISION
Brigadier General Peter J. Osterhaus

First Brigade
Brigadier General Theophilus T. Garrard
118th Illinois
49th Indiana

69th Indiana
7th Kentucky

Second Brigade
Colonel Daniel W. Lindsey
22nd Kentucky
16th Ohio
42nd Ohio
114th Ohio

Artillery
7th Battery Michigan Light Artillery
1st Battery Wisconsin Light Artillery

TENTH DIVISION
Brigadier General Andrew J. Smith

First Brigade
Brigadier General Stephen G. Burbridge
16th Indiana
67th Indiana
83rd Ohio
23rd Wisconsin

Second Brigade
Colonel William J. Landram
77th Illinois
97th Illinois
108th Illinois
130th Illinois
19th Kentucky
48th Ohio

Artillery
Chicago Mercantile Battery
17th Battery Ohio Light Artillery

TWELFTH DIVISION
Brigadier General Alvin P. Hovey

First Brigade
Brigadier General George F. McGinnis
11th Indiana

24th Indiana
34th Indiana
46th Indiana
29th Wisconsin

Second Brigade
Colonel James L. Slack
47th Indiana
24th Iowa
28th Iowa
56th Ohio

Artillery
1st Missouri Light Artillery, Battery A
2nd Battery Ohio Light Artillery
16th Battery Ohio Light Artillery

FOURTEENTH DIVISION
Brigadier General Eugene A. Carr

First Brigade
Brigadier General William P. Benton
33rd Illinois
99th Illinois
8th Indiana
18th Indiana

Second Brigade
Brigadier General Michael K. Lawler
21st Iowa
22nd Iowa
23rd Iowa
11th Wisconsin

Artillery
2nd Illinois Light Artillery, Battery A
1st Battery Indiana Light Artillery

FIFTEENTH ARMY CORPS
Major General William T. Sherman

SECOND DIVISION
Major General Frank P. Blair, Jr.

First Brigade
    Colonel Giles A. Smith
        113th Illinois
        116th Illinois
        6th Missouri
        8th Missouri
        13th United States, 1st Battalion

Second Brigade
    Colonel Thomas Kilby Smith
        55th Illinois
        127th Illinois
        83rd Indiana
        54th Ohio
        57th Ohio

Artillery
        1st Illinois Light Artillery, Battery A
        1st Illinois Light Artillery, Battery B

SEVENTEENTH ARMY CORPS
    Major General James B. McPherson

THIRD DIVISION
    Major General John A. Logan

First Brigade
    Brigadier General John E. Smith
        20th Illinois
        31st Illinois
        45th Illinois
        124th Illinois
        23rd Indiana

Second Brigade
    Brigadier General Mortimer D. Leggett
        30th Illinois
        20th Ohio
        68th Ohio
        78th Ohio

Third Brigade
Brigadier General John D. Stevenson
8th Illinois
81st Illinois
7th Missouri
32nd Ohio

Artillery
1st Illinois Light Artillery, Battery D,
2nd Illinois Light Artillery, Battery L
8th Battery Michigan Light Artillery
3rd Battery Ohio Light Artillery

SEVENTH DIVISION
Brigadier General Marcellus M. Crocker

First Brigade
Colonel John B. Sanborn
48th Indiana
59th Indiana
4th Minnesota
18th Wisconsin

Second Brigade
Colonel Samuel A. Holmes
17th Iowa
10th Missouri
24th Missouri, Company E

Third Brigade
Colonel George B. Boomer
93rd Illinois
5th Iowa
10th Iowa
26th Missouri

Artillery
1st Missouri Light Artillery, Battery M
11th Battery Ohio Light Artillery
6th Battery Wisconsin Light Artillery
12th Battery Wisconsin Light Artillery

Battle of Big Black River Bridge
May 17, 1863

ARMY OF THE TENNESSEE
Major General Ulysses S. Grant

THIRTEENTH ARMY CORPS
Major General John A. McClernand

NINTH DIVISION
Brigadier General Peter J. Osterhaus (w)
Brigadier General Albert L. Lee

First Brigade
Brigadier General Theophilus T. Garrard
118th Illinois
49th Indiana
69th Indiana
7th Kentucky

Second Brigade
Colonel Daniel W. Lindsey
22nd Kentucky
16th Ohio
42nd Ohio
114th Ohio

Artillery
7th Battery Michigan Light Artillery
1st Battery Wisconsin Light Artillery

TENTH DIVISION
Brigadier General Andrew J. Smith

First Brigade
Brigadier General Stephen G. Burbridge
16th Indiana
67th Indiana
83rd Ohio
23rd Wisconsin

Artillery
Chicago Mercantile Battery

FOURTEENTH DIVISION
Brigadier General Eugene A. Carr

First Brigade
Brigadier General William P. Benton
33rd Illinois
99th Illinois
8th Indiana
18th Indiana

Second Brigade
Brigadier General Michael K. Lawler
21st Iowa
22nd Iowa
23rd Iowa
11th Wisconsin

Artillery
2nd Illinois Light Artillery, Battery A
1st Battery Indiana Light Artillery

Appendix B

CONFEDERATE ORDERS OF BATTLE
MAY 1–17, 1863

Battle of Port Gibson
May 1, 1863

CONFEDERATE FORCES
Brigadier General John S. Bowen

BOWEN'S DIVISION
Brigadier General John S. Bowen

First Brigade
Colonel Francis M. Cockrell
3rd Missouri
5th Missouri
6th Missouri
Guibor's (Missouri) Battery
Landis's (Missouri) Battery

Second Brigade
Brigadier General Martin E. Green
15th Arkansas
21st Arkansas
12th Arkansas Battalion (Sharpshooters)
6th Mississippi
Pettus (Mississippi) Flying Artillery

Baldwin's Brigade
Brigadier General W. E. Baldwin
17th Louisiana

31st Louisiana
4th Mississippi
46th Mississippi

Third Brigade
Brigadier General Edward D. Tracy (k)
Colonel Isham W. Garrott
20th Alabama
23rd Alabama
30th Alabama
31st Alabama
46th Alabama
Botetourt (Virginia) Artillery

Battle of Raymond
May 12, 1863

Gregg's Brigade
Brigadier General John Gregg
3rd Tennessee
10/30th Tennessee
41st Tennessee
50th Tennessee
1st Tennessee Battalion
7th Texas
Bledsoe's (Missouri) Battery

Battle of Jackson
May 14, 1863

Confederate Forces
Brigadier General John Gregg

Gregg's Brigade
Colonel Robert Farquharson
3rd Tennessee
10/30th Tennessee
41st Tennessee
50th Tennessee

1st Tennessee Battalion
7th Texas
Bledsoe's (Missouri) Battery

Gist's Brigade
Colonel Peyton H. Colquitt
46th Georgia
14th Mississippi
24th South Carolina
Brookhaven (Mississippi) Light Artillery

Walker's Brigade
Brigadier General William H. T. Walker
30th Georgia
1st Georgia Battalion Sharpshooters
4th Louisiana Battalion
Martin's (Georgia) Battery

Miscellaneous
3rd Kentucky Mounted Infantry

Battle of Champion Hill
May 16, 1863

ARMY OF VICKSBURG
Lieutenant General John C. Pemberton

STEVENSON'S DIVISION
Major General Carter L. Stevenson

First Brigade
Brigadier General Seth M. Barton
40th Georgia
41st Georgia
42nd Georgia
43rd Georgia
52nd Georgia
Cherokee (Georgia) Artillery

Second Brigade
    Brigadier General Stephen D. Lee
        20th Alabama
        23rd Alabama
        30th Alabama
        31st Alabama
        46th Alabama
        Waddell's (Alabama) Battery

Third Brigade
    Brigadier General Alfred Cumming
        34th Georgia
        36th Georgia
        39th Georgia
        56th Georgia
        57th Georgia

Fourth Brigade
    Colonel Alexander W. Reynolds
        3rd Tennessee (Provisional Army)
        31st Tennessee
        43rd Tennessee
        59th Tennessee
        3rd Maryland Battery

BOWEN'S DIVISION
    Brigadier General John S. Bowen

First Brigade
    Colonel Francis M. Cockrell
        1st Missouri
        2nd Missouri
        3rd Missouri
        5th Missouri
        6th Missouri
        Guibor's (Missouri) Battery
        Landis's (Missouri) Battery
        Wade's (Missouri) Battery

Second Brigade
    Brigadier General Martin E. Green
        15th Arkansas
        19th Arkansas

20th Arkansas
21st Arkansas
1st Arkansas Cavalry Battalion (dismounted)
12th Arkansas Battalion (Sharpshooters)
1st Missouri Cavalry (dismounted)
3rd Missouri Cavalry (dismounted)
3rd Missouri Battery
Lowe's (Missouri) Battery

LORING'S DIVISION
Major General William W. Loring

First Brigade
Brigadier General Lloyd Tilghman (k)
Colonel Arthur E. Reynolds
 1st Confederate Battalion
 6th Mississippi
 23rd Mississippi
 26th Mississippi
 Culberson's (Mississippi) Battery
 Cowan's (Mississippi) Battery

Second Brigade
Brigadier General Winfield S. Featherston
 3rd Mississippi
 22nd Mississippi
 31st Mississippi
 33rd Mississippi
 1st Mississippi Sharpshooter Battalion
 Wofford's (Mississippi) Battery

Third Brigade
Brigadier General Abraham Buford
 27th Alabama
 35th Alabama
 54th Alabama
 55th Alabama
 9th Arkansas
 3rd Kentucky
 7th Kentucky
 8th Kentucky
 12th Louisiana
 Pointe Coupee (Louisiana) Artillery, Company A and C

Artillery
    Botetourt (Virginia) Artillery
    Ridley's (Mississippi) Battery

Cavalry
    Wirt Adams's Mississippi Cavalry
    20th Mississippi Mounted Infantry

Battle of Big Black River Bridge
May 17, 1863

BOWEN'S DIVISION
    Brigadier General John S. Bowen

First Brigade
    Colonel Francis M. Cockrell
        1st Missouri
        2nd Missouri
        3rd Missouri
        5th Missouri
        6th Missouri
        Guibor's (Missouri) Battery
        Landis's (Missouri) Battery
        Wade's (Missouri) Battery

Second Brigade
    Brigadier General Martin E. Green
    Colonel T. P. Dockery
        15th Arkansas
        19th Arkansas
        20th Arkansas
        21st Arkansas
        1st Arkansas Cavalry Battalion (dismounted)
        12th Arkansan Battalion (Sharpshooters)
        1st Missouri Cavalry (dismounted)
        3rd Missouri Cavalry (dismounted)
        3rd Missouri Battery
        Lowe's (Missouri) Battery

Vaughn's Brigade
    Brigadier General John C. Vaughn
        60th Tennessee
        61st Tennessee
        62nd Tennessee

Attached
        4th Mississippi
        Hooker's (Mississippi) Battery

NOTES

Abraham Lincoln Presidential Library	ALPL
Alabama Department of Archives and History	ADAH
Archives of Michigan	AM
Auburn University	AU
Augustana College	AC
Chicago History Museum	CHM
Cincinnati Historical Society	CHS
Civil War Documents Collection	CWD
Civil War Times Illustrated Collection	CWTI
Cornell University	CU
Duke University	DU
Emory University	EU
Filson Historical Society	FHS
Georgia Department of Archives and History	GDAH
Gettysburg College	GC
Harrisburg Civil War Roundtable Collection	HCWRT
Harvard University	HU
Huntington Library	HL
Indiana Historical Society	IHS
Indiana State Library	ISL
Indiana State University	ISU
Indiana University	INU
Iowa State University	ISU
Library of Congress	LC
Louisiana State University	LSU
Minnesota Historical Society	MNHS
Mississippi Department of Archives and History	MDAH
Missouri Historical Society	MHS
National Archives and Records Administration	NARA

Newberry Library	NL
Old Courthouse Museum	OCM
Ohio Historical Society	OHS
War of the Rebellion: A Compilation of the Official Records of the Union and Confederate Armies	OR
The Official Records of the Union and Confederate Navies	ORN
Papers of Ulysses S. Grant	PUSG
Southern Illinois University	SIU
Stanford University	SU
State Historical Society of Iowa, Iowa City	SHSIIC
State Historical Society of Missouri, Columbia	SHSMC
State Historical Society of Missouri, Rolla	SHSMR
State Historical Society of Missouri, St. Louis	SHSMS
State Historical Society of Wisconsin	SHSW
Supplement to the Official Records	SOR
Tennessee State Library and Archives	TSLA
Tulane University	TU
United States Army History and Education Center	USAHEC
University of Alabama	UA
University of Arkansas	UAR
University of Chicago	UCH
University of Colorado–Boulder	UCB
University of Georgia	UGA
University of Illinois	UIL
University of Iowa	UIA
University of Memphis	UMEM
University of Michigan Bentley Library	UMB
University of Michigan Clements Library	UMC
University of Mississippi	UM
University of Missouri	UMO
University of North Carolina	UNC
University of Notre Dame	ND
University of South Carolina	USC
University of Southern Mississippi	USM
University of Tennessee	UTK
University of Texas at Austin	UTA
Vicksburg National Military Park	VICK
Virginia Tech University	VT
Western Kentucky University	WKU
Wisconsin Historical Society	WHS

Preface

1. Timothy B. Smith, *The Golden Age of Battlefield Preservation: The Decade of the 1890s and the Establishment of America's First Five Military Parks* (Knoxville: University of Tennessee Press, 2008), 179–209.

2. John F. Marszalek, David F. Nolen, and Louie P. Gallo, eds., *The Personal Memoirs of Ulysses S. Grant: The Complete Annotated Edition* (Cambridge, MA: Harvard University Press, 2017), 342, 348, 355.

3. William B. Feis, "'Developed by Circumstances': Grant, Intelligence, and the Vicksburg Campaign," in Steven E. Woodworth and Charles D. Grear, eds., *The Vicksburg Campaign: March 29–May 18, 1863* (Carbondale: Southern Illinois University Press, 2013), 169; Terrence J. Winschel, "Fighting Politician: John A. McClernand," in *Grant's Lieutenants: From Cairo to* Vicksburg, Steven E. Woodworth, ed. (Lawrence: University Press of Kansas, 2001), 138; Phillip Thomas Tucker, *The Forgotten "Stonewall of the West": Major General John Stevens Bowen* (Macon, GA: Mercer University Press, 1997), 291; James C. Mahan, *Memoirs of James Curtis Mahan* (Lincoln, NE: The Franklin Press, 1919), 114; William L. Shea and Terrence J. Winschel, *Vicksburg Is the Key: The Struggle for the Mississippi River* (Lincoln: University of Nebraska Press, 2003), 120; Terrence J. Winschel, *Triumph and Defeat: The Vicksburg Campaign, Volume 2* (New York: Savas Beatie, 2006), 15; Herman Hattaway and Archer Jones, *How the North Won: A Military History of the Civil War* (Urbana: University of Illinois Press, 1983), 391.

4. Terrence J. Winschel, "The Vicksburg Campaign," in *The Cambridge History of the American Civil* War, 3 vols., Aaron Sheehan-Dean, ed. (Cambridge: Cambridge University Press, 2019), 1:258; Terrence J. Winschel, "Applicability in the Modern Age: Ulysses S. Grant's Vicksburg Campaign," *Journal of Mississippi History* 80, nos. 1 and 2 (Spring/Summer 2018): 35–47; *Field Manual 100-5: Operations* (Washington, DC: Department of the Army, 1986), 91–94; *War of the Rebellion: A Compilation of the Official Records of the Union and Confederate Armies* (Washington, DC: Government Printing Office, 1880–1901), Series 1, Volume 24 (Part 1): 63, hereafter cited as *OR*, with all references to Series 1 unless otherwise noted, followed by volume and part number.

5. Edwin C. Bearss, *The Vicksburg Campaign*, 3 vols. (Dayton, OH: Morningside, 1985); Timothy B. Smith, *Champion Hill: Decisive Battle for Vicksburg* (New York: Savas Beatie, 2004); Chris Mackowski, *The Battle of Jackson, Mississippi, May 14, 1863* (El Dorado Hills, CA: Savas Beatie, 2022).

6. Timothy B. Smith, *The Decision Was Always My Own: Ulysses S. Grant and the Vicksburg Campaign* (Carbondale: Southern Illinois University Press, 2018); Timothy B. Smith, *The Real Horse Soldiers: Benjamin Grierson's Epic 1863 Civil War Raid Through Mississippi* (El Dorado Hills, CA: Savas Beatie, 2018).

PROLOGUE: "AN ARMY MARCHES ON ITS STOMACH"

1. Warren E. Grabau, *Ninety-Eight Days: A Geographer's View of the Vicksburg Campaign* (Knoxville: University of Tennessee Press, 2000), xvii; *Congressional Record*, 76th Congress, 3rd Session, 86(1):987. For more on logistics in war, see Martin van Creveld, *Supplying War: Logistics from Wallenstein to Patton*, 2nd ed. (Cambridge: Cambridge University Press, 2004).

2. J. F. C. Fuller, *The Generalship of Ulysses S. Grant* (Bloomington: Indiana University Press, 1958), 140–141. There is a small collection of writing about logistical issues in the Vicksburg Campaign. Most of it is cursory, relying mainly on the *Official Records* and Grant's published papers and rarely if ever delving into the manuscript sources. See George M. Stephenson, "Logistics of the Vicksburg Campaign," *Army Logistician: The Official Magazine of United States Army Logistics* 15, no. 4 (July–August 1983): 26–29; W. B. Droke, "Grant—the Logistician," *Army Logistician: Professional Bulletin of United States Army Logistics* PB 700-90-3 (May–June 1990): 28–31; Edwin L. Buffington, "Logistics During Grant's Vicksburg Campaign," (MA thesis, US Army War College, 1992); Mark S. Hurley, "Union Logistics in the Vicksburg Campaign," (MA thesis, US Army Command and General Staff College, 1992); Earl J. Hess, *Civil War Supply and Strategy: Feeding Men and Moving Armies* (Baton Rouge: Louisiana State University Press, 2020), 56–102. By far, the most incisive treatment is Phillip R. Kemmerly, "Logistics of U.S. Grant's 1863 Mississippi Campaign: From the Amphibious Landing at Bruinsburg to the Siege of Vicksburg," *Journal of Military History* 86 (July 2022): 573–611.

3. *OR*, 24(3):809.

4. *OR*, 24(1):296–318; Hess, *Civil War Supply and Strategy*, 84–102.

5. *OR*, 24(1):296–318; *OR*, 24(3):867–869.

6. Sallie B. McCrae Diary, April 26, 1862, Ray Fulton Collection, UM, copy in the Sallie B. McCrae Diary, MSU; Ben Wynne, *Mississippi's Civil War: A Narrative History* (Macon, GA: Mercer University Press, 2006), 90–91; John K. Bettersworth, ed., *Mississippi in the Confederacy: As They Saw It* (Baton Rouge: Louisiana State University Press, 1961), 263; Luther S. Baechtel Diary, May 7, 1863, MDAH. For more on railroad accidents, see Bettersworth, ed., *Mississippi in the Confederacy*, 261–263. For the Southern Railroad, see the Southern Railroad Records, AU.

7. *OR*, 24(3):867. For a study of the Yazoo River's shipping, see Harry P. Owens, *Steamboats and the Cotton Economy: River Trade in the Yazoo-Mississippi Delta* (Jackson: University Press of Mississippi, 1990).

8. For Grierson's Raid, see Smith, *The Real Horse Soldiers*.

9. *OR*, 24(1):71.

10. *OR*, 24(3):867.

11. Provisions Issues in Memphis and Young's Point, April and May, 1863, RG 192, E 36, NARA, 49, 56, 97, 116; Hess, *Civil War Supply and Strategy*, 56–83. For the route in Louisiana, see Timothy B. Smith, *Bayou Battles for Vicksburg: The Swamp and River Expeditions, January 1–April 30, 1863* (Lawrence: University Press of Kansas, 2023).

12. Paul L. Schmelzer, "Politics, Policy, and General Grant: Clausewitz on the

Operational Art as Practiced in the Vicksburg Campaign," in *The Vicksburg Campaign: March 29–May 18, 1863*, Steven E. Woodworth and Charles D. Grear, eds. (Carbondale: Southern Illinois University Press, 2013), 222; Donald Stoker, *The Grand Design: Strategy and the U.S. Civil War* (New York: Oxford University Press, 2010), 265; Carl Von Clausewitz, *On War*, Michael Howard and Peter Paret, eds. (New York: Knopf, 1993), 403. For Jomini, see Henri de Jomini, *Summary of the Art of War, or, A New Analytical Compend of the Principal Combinations of Strategy, of Grand Tactics and of Military Policy* (New York: G. P. Putnam & Co., 1854), and *The Art of War* (Philadelphia: J. B. Lippincott & Co., 1862).

13. Smith, *Bayou Battles for Vicksburg*, 336–388.

14. John Y. Simon and John F. Marszalek, eds., *The Papers of Ulysses S. Grant*, 32 vols. (Carbondale: Southern Illinois University Press, 1967–2014), 8:4, 12, hereafter cited as *PUSG*.

15. Simon and Marszalek, *PUSG*, 7:463; Samuel P. Harrington Diary, April 30, 1863, Haerle Collection, USAHEC.

16. Marszalek, Nolen, and Gallo, eds., *The Personal Memoirs of Ulysses S. Grant*, 301.

17. John G. Moore, "Mobility and Strategy in the Civil War," *Military Affairs* 24, no. 2 (Summer 1960): 69; Joseph C. G. Kennedy, *Population of the United States in 1860: Compiled from the Original Returns of the Eighth Census Under the Direction of the Secretary of the Interior* (Washington, DC: Government Printing Office, 1864), xiix.

18. Kennedy, *Population of the United States in 1860*, iv, xvi.

19. Kennedy, *Population of the United States in 1860*, iv, 72–73, 516, 518.

20. Kennedy, *Population of the United States in 1860*, 270.

21. Grabau, *Ninety-Eight Days*, 209; Ronald C. White, *American Ulysses: A Life of Ulysses S. Grant* (New York: Random House, 2016), 272; Henry Ward Beecher, *Patriotic Addresses in America and England, from 1850 to 1885, on Slavery, the Civil War, and the Development of Civil Liberty in the United States* (New York: Fords, Howard, & Hulbert, 1891), 851.

22. Clausewitz, *On War*, 443, 453, 633, 639, 684–693; Kemmerly, "Logistics of U.S. Grant's 1863 Mississippi Campaign," 599–601; Smith, *The Decision Was Always My Own*, 130; Bruce Catton, *U.S. Grant and the American Military Tradition* (Boston: Little, Brown and Co., 1954), 101.

CHAPTER 1. "I HAVE TO OVERCOME OBSTACLES TO REACH HIM"

1. *OR*, 24(1):48; Robert V. Remini, *Andrew Jackson and the Course of American Empire, 1767–1821* (New York: Harper & Row, 1977), 55, 62; Milton Lomask, *Aaron Burr: The Conspiracy and Years of Exile, 1805–1836* (New York: Farrar, Straus & Giroux, 1982), 208–216; "Vinegar Bend," Natchez *Times*, September 30, 1953, copy in Bruinsburg Subject File, MDAH; "Beginning of the End," Jackson *Daily News*, December 21, 1979, copy in Bruinsburg Subject File, MDAH; "So Much History Unfolded at

Bruinsburg, So Little Remains," Vicksburg *Evening Post*, March 23, 1986, copy in Bruinsburg Subject File, MDAH; Marszalek, Nolen, and Gallo, eds., *Memoirs*, 332–333; Isaac H. Elliott, *History of the Thirty-third Regiment Illinois Veteran Volunteer Infantry in the Civil War, 22nd August 1861, to 7th December, 1865* (Gibson City, IL: The Association, 1902), 236–237; Simon and Marszalek, eds., *PUSG*, 8:113–114; M. A. Sweetman, "From Milliken's Bend to Vicksburg," August 22, 1895, *National Tribune*; S. C. Beck, "A True Sketch of His Army Life," 1902, VICK, 6, copy in OCM; Fred Grant Memoir, undated, USGPL, 11; for a condensed and published version of Fred Grant's memoir, see Frederick D. Grant, "A Boy's Experience at Vicksburg," in *Personal Recollections of the War of the Rebellion: Addresses Delivered before the Commandery of the State of New York, Military Order of the Loyal Legion of the United States*, A. Noel Blakeman, ed. (New York: G. P. Putnam's Sons, 1907), 86–100.

2. *OR*, 24(1):48; "Champion's Hill," *National Tribune*, October 3, 1901; Elliott, *History of the Thirty-third Regiment Illinois Veteran Volunteer Infantry*, 236–237; Simon and Marszalek, eds., *PUSG*, 8:113–114; Marszalek, Nolen, and Gallo, eds., *Memoirs*, 332–333; S. C. Beck, "A True Sketch of His Army Life," 1902, VICK; Sweetman, "From Milliken's Bend to Vicksburg," August 22, 1895, *National Tribune*.

3. *Supplement to the Official Records of the Union and Confederate Armies*, 100 vols. (Wilmington, NC: Broadfoot Publishing Company, 1994), 3:369, hereafter cited as *SOR*; Edwin C. Bearss with J. Parker Hills, *Receding Tide: Vicksburg and Gettysburg, The Campaigns that Changed the Civil War* (Washington, DC: National Geographic, 2010), 105; "Burning of the Daniell Residence," Port Gibson *Southern Reveille*, February 21, 1890, copy in Windsor Subject File, MDAH; "Windsor's Grandeur Lives on in Ruins," Jackson *Clarion Ledger*, July 18, 1965, copy in Windsor Subject File, MDAH; Bearss, *The Vicksburg Campaign*, 2:345; Shea and Winschel, *Vicksburg Is the Key*, 108; C. H. Twining to Kate, June 9, 1863, Moody Family Papers, MHS; R. L. Howard, *History of the 124th Regiment Illinois Infantry Volunteers, Otherwise Known as the "Hundred and Two Dozen," From August, 1862, to August, 1865* (Springfield, IL: H. W. Rokker, 1880), 76; Paul H. Hass, ed., "The Vicksburg Diary of Henry Clay Warmoth: Part II (April 28 1863—May 26, 1863)," *Journal of Mississippi History* 32, no. 1 (February 1970): 64; Carlos W. Colby, "Memoirs of Military Service," undated, Carlos W. Colby Papers, Bilby Collection, USAHEC, 1–2, 4; William Murray Diary, April 30, 1863, VICK; John Sherriff Diary, April 30, 1863, John Sherriff Family Papers, ALPL; F. H. Mason, *The Forty-second Ohio Infantry: A History of the Organization and Services of That Regiment in the War of the Rebellion; With Biographical Sketches of Its Field Officers and a Full Roster of the Regiment* (Cleveland: Cobb, Andrews and Co., Publishers, 1876), 190; William A. Shunk, "The Vicksburg Campaign," in *War Papers Read Before the Commandery of the State of Wisconsin, Military Order of the Loyal Legion of the United States*, 4 vols. (Milwaukee: Burdick & Allen, 1914), 4:151; Manning F. Force, "Personal Recollections of the Vicksburg Campaign," in *Sketches of War History, 1861–1865: Papers Read Before the Ohio Commandery of the Military Order of the Loyal Legion of the United States 1883–1886, Volume 1* (Cincinnati: Robert Clarke & Co., 1888), 296; "Military History of Captain Thomas Sewell," 1889, DU. For a drawing of Windsor, see Henry Otis Dwight Papers, OHS.

4. Simon and Marszalek, eds., *PUSG*, 7:479–480.

5. For the earlier attempts, see Timothy B. Smith, *Early Struggles for Vicksburg: The Mississippi Central Campaign and Chickasaw Bayou, October 25–December 31, 1862* (Lawrence: University Press of Kansas, 2022), and Smith, *Bayou Battles for Vicksburg*.

6. Marszalek, Nolen, and Gallo, eds., *Memoirs*, 334; John Hipple Memoir, undated, OCM.

7. David Dixon Porter, *Incidents and Anecdotes of the Civil War* (New York: D. Appleton and Company, 1885), 96. For the history of the Mississippi River, see Stephen E. Ambrose and Douglas Brinkley, *The Mississippi and the Making of a Nation: From the Louisiana Purchase to Today* (Washington, DC: National Geographic, 2002).

8. *OR*, 1, 7:161. For early Tennessee operations, see Timothy B. Smith, *Grant Invades Tennessee: The 1862 Battles for Forts Henry and Donelson* (Lawrence: University Press of Kansas, 2016).

9. William Preston Johnston, *The Life of Gen. Albert Sidney Johnston: His Service in the Armies of the United States, The Republic of Texas, and the Confederate States* (New York: D. Appleton and Co., 1879), 568–571, 583–584, 613. For Johnston's reaction, see Timothy B. Smith, *The Iron Dice of Battle: Albert Sidney Johnston and the Civil War in the West* (Baton Rouge: Louisiana State University Press, 2023).

10. Johnston, *The Life of Gen. Albert Sidney Johnston*, 584; *OR* 10(2):403. For operations around Shiloh and Corinth, see Timothy B. Smith, *Shiloh: Conquer or Perish* (Lawrence: University Press of Kansas, 2014), and Timothy B. Smith, *Corinth 1862: Siege, Battle, Occupation* (Lawrence: University Press of Kansas, 2012).

11. *OR*, 15:6. For New Orleans, see Chester G. Hearn, *The Capture of New Orleans 1862* (Baton Rouge: Louisiana State University Press, 1995).

12. *The Official Records of the Union and Confederate Navies in the War of the Rebellion*, 30 vols. (Washington, DC: Government Printing Office, 1894–1922), Series 1, Volume 18:492, 610, hereafter cited as *ORN*, with all references to Series 1; *OR*, 15:13. For this first action around Vicksburg, see Edwin C. Bearss, *Rebel Victory at Vicksburg* (Vicksburg: Vicksburg Centennial Commission, 1963).

13. *OR*, 10(1):671. For Halleck, see John F. Marszalek, *Commander of All Lincoln's Armies: A Life of General Henry W. Halleck* (Cambridge: Harvard University Press, 2004).

14. For Perryville and the Kentucky Campaign, see Kenneth W. Noe, *Perryville: This Grand Havoc of Battle* (Lexington: University Press of Kentucky, 2001).

15. For the fall battles around Corinth, see Smith, *Corinth 1862*.

16. *OR*, 17(2):728, 732; Arthur B. Carter, *The Tarnished Cavalier: Major General Earl Van Dorn, C.S.A.* (Knoxville: University of Tennessee Press, 1999), 115; Michael B. Ballard, *Pemberton: The General Who Lost Vicksburg* (Jackson: University Press of Mississippi, 1991), 116; John Pemberton to Samuel Cooper, November 1 and 2, 1862, RG 109, Chapter 2, Volume 57, NARA, 63, 67.

17. Marszalek, Nolen, and Gallo, eds., *Memoirs*, 289.

18. *OR*, 17(2):296; Henry W. Halleck, *Elements of Military Art and Science: Or, Course of Instruction in Strategy, Fortification, Tactics of Battles, &c.; Embracing the Duties of Staff, Infantry, Cavalry, Artillery, and Engineers. Adapted to the Use of Volunteers and Militia* (New York: D. Appleton and Company, 1846).

19. *OR*, 17(2):445; Simon and Marszalek, eds., *PUSG*, 7:81.

20. *OR*, 17(1):608, 613.

21. Marszalek, Nolen, and Gallo, eds., *Memoirs*, 294.

22. Smith, *Bayou Battles for Vicksburg*, 83–265.

23. *OR*, 24(3):38, 40, 51–52.

24. Milt Shaw to Alf, March 10, 1863, Milton W. Shaw Letter, USM; Timothy B. Smith, "Victory at Any Cost: The Yazoo Pass Expedition," *Journal of Mississippi History* 67, no. 2 (Summer 2007): 147–166.

25. *OR*, 24(1):28, *OR*, 24(3):112, 119, 134–135.

26. Henry G. Hicks, "The Campaign and Capture of Vicksburg," in *Glimpses of the Nation's Struggle: Military Order of the Loyal Legion*, 6 vols. (St. Paul, MN: Davis, 1909), 6:93; Smith, *Bayou Battles for Vicksburg*, 83–265.

27. *OR*, 24(3):168.

28. Catton, *U. S. Grant and the American Military Tradition*, 98; *OR*, 24(1):31; Simon and Marszalek, eds., *PUSG*, 7:480, 491; Simon and Marszalek, eds., *PUSG*, 8:132.

29. Marszalek, Nolen, and Gallo, eds., *Memoirs*, 319; John Russell Young, *Around the World with General Grant: A Narrative of the Visit of General U.S. Grant, Ex-President of the United States, to Various Countries in Europe, Asia, and Africa, in 1877, 1878, 1879. To which are Added Certain Conversations with General Grant on Questions Connected with American Politics and History* (New York: American News Company 1879), 2: 615.

30. *OR*, 24(3):152; *ORN*, 24:479; Gary D. Joiner, "Running the Gauntlet: The Effectiveness of Combined Forces in the Vicksburg Campaign," in Steven E. Woodworth and Charles D. Grear, eds., *The Vicksburg Campaign: March 29–May 18, 1863* (Carbondale: Southern Illinois University Press, 2013), 8–23; William Daniel to wife, March 31, 1863, William T. Daniel Letters, GDAH.

31. *ORN*, 24:552–553, 555–556, 682; M. N. Twiss Statement, July 9, 1863, Joseph Forrest Papers, ALPL; Porter, *Incidents and Anecdotes*, 176; R. W. Memminger, "The Surrender of Vicksburg—A Defense of General Pemberton," *Southern Historical Society Papers* 12, nos. 7–9 (July–September 1884): 354; James Worthington to Lizzie, April 23, 1863, James K. Worthington Letters, CWTI, USAHEC; William Gaster Report, December 23, 1863, RG 92, E 1127, NARA, 2:713–716.

32. Luther Cowan to Mollie, May 5, 1863, Luther H. Cowan Papers, TSLA; Smith, *Bayou Battles for Vicksburg*, 266–335; Charles Calvin Enslow Diary, April 17, 1863, LC; George Hildt to parents, April 28, 1863, George H. Hildt Correspondence, OHS.

33. *ORN*, 24:608, 610–611; *OR*, 24(1):48, 82.

34. *OR*, 24(1):34, 48; "The First Troops to Land at Bruinsburg," *National Tribune*, October 16, 1884; Larry J. Daniel, "Bruinsburg: Missed Opportunity or Postwar Rhetoric?," *Civil War History* 32, no. 3 (September 1986): 259; Carlos W. Colby, "Memoirs of Military Service," undated, Carlos W. Colby Papers, Bilby Collection, USAHEC, 4; Andrew Hickenlooper Reminiscences, undated, Hickenlooper Collection, CHS; Reuben H. Falconer Diary, April 30, 1863, OHS. For Grierson's Raid, see Smith, *The Real Horse Soldiers*.

35. Edward Wood to wife, May 8, 1863, Edward J. Wood Papers, IHS; James Harrison

Wilson, "A Staff Officer's Journal of the Vicksburg Campaign, April 30 to July 4, 1863," *Journal of the Military Service Institution of the United States* 43, no. 154 (July–August 1908): 93.

36. *OR*, 24(3):188, 190; Simon and Marszalek, eds., *PUSG*, 8:19; Samuel Lougheed to wife, April 30, 1863, Samuel D. Lougheed Papers, UW.

37. A. Achen to unknown, April 25, 1863, A. Achen Papers, CHM; Smith, *Bayou Battles for Vicksburg*, 364–388.

38. Smith, *Early Struggles for Vicksburg*, 426; Smith, *Bayou Battles for Vicksburg*, 83–265.

39. Smith, *Bayou Battles for Vicksburg*, 83–265.

40. *OR*, 24(3):687, 692–693; M. R. Banner to Addie, April 29, 1863, Banner Family Papers, OCM, 96; John Wilson to Lizzie, May 2, 1863, John A. Wilson Letters, MDAH; Smith, *Bayou Battles for Vicksburg*, 336–388; G. H. Burns to wife, April 29, 1863, George H. Burns Letters, VICK; John Douthit to Companion, May 6, 1863, John M. Douthit Letters, VICK; Thomas White to mother, May 11, 1863, Thomas K. White Papers, OHS.

41. *OR*, 24(3):730; Smith, *The Real Horse Soldiers*, 300–301.

42. *OR*, 24(3):782–785, 787, 790–791, 805; *OR*, 24(1):253.

43. *OR*, 24(1):257, 296–318, 328–329, 660; Smith, *The Real Horse Soldiers*, 232; S. H. Lockett, "The Defense of Vicksburg," in *Battles and Leaders of the Civil War*, 4 vols. (New York: Century Company, 1884–1887), 3:486; Marszalek, Nolen, and Gallo, eds., *Memoirs*, 335.

44. *OR*, 24(1):658, 675, 678.

45. *OR*, 24(3):809; Lemuel Cline to Lizzie, May 2, 1863, Lemuel Cline Letter, VICK.

CHAPTER 2. "I AM PUSHING FORWARD"

1. Kennedy, *Population of the United States in 1860*, 271.

2. Dunbar Rowland, *Mississippi; Comprising Sketches of Counties, Towns, Events, Institutions and Persons, Arranged in Cyclopedic Form*, 3 vols. (Atlanta: Southern Historical Printing Association, 1907), 2:456; Isaac Vanderwarker Diary, May 3, 1863, CWD, USAHEC.

3. Bearss and Hills, *Receding Tide*, 127; William P. Chambers, "My Journal," in *Publications of the Mississippi Historical Society, Centenary Series*, 5 vols. (Jackson: Mississippi Historical Society, 1925), 5:263. For Van Dorn, see Carter, *The Tarnished Cavalier* and Robert G. Hartje, *Van Dorn: The Life and Times of a Confederate General* (Nashville, TN: Vanderbilt University Press, 1967).

4. Bearss and Hills, *Receding Tide*, 127.

5. *OR*, 24(3):248.

6. Chambers, "My Journal," 263.

7. *OR*, 24(1):186; Marszalek, Nolen, and Gallo, eds., *The Personal Memoirs of Ulysses S. Grant*, 334; Richard L. Howard, "The Vicksburg Campaign," in *War Papers*

Read Before the Commandery of the State of Maine, Military Order of the Loyal Legion of the United States, Volume 2 (Portland, ME: Lefavor-Tower Company, 1902), 2:32; Thomas Morrow to sister, May 4, 1863, Elliot Morrow Papers, OHS.

8. *OR*, 24(1):624, 628; George Crooke, *The Twenty-first Regiment of Iowa Volunteer Infantry: A Narrative of Its Experience in Active Service, Including a Military Record of Each Officer, Non-Commissioned Officer, and Private Soldier of the Organization* (Milwaukee: King, Fowle & Co., 1891), 55; Hass, ed., "The Vicksburg Diary of Henry Clay Warmoth," 63; Ezra J. Warner, *Generals in Blue: Lives of the Union Commanders* (Baton Rouge: Louisiana State University Press, 1964), 70; Augustus G. Sinks Memoir, undated, ISL, 33; Daniel Roberts to family, May 6, 1863, Daniel Roberts Correspondence, ISL.

9. *OR*, 24(1):615, 620; *OR*, 24(2):204; T. B. Marshall, *History of the Eighty-third Ohio Volunteer Infantry, The Greyhound Regiment* (Cincinnati: N.p., 1912), 74; Francis A. Dawes Diary, April 30, 1863, CWTI, USAHEC; Isaac Jackson to Sallie, May 27, 1863, Isaac Jackson Papers, James S. Schoff Civil War Collection, UMC.

10. Marszalek, Nolen, and Gallo, eds., *The Personal Memoirs of Ulysses S. Grant*, 340; Walter Scates to Captain, April 29, 1863, and Special Orders 120, April 30, 1863, John A. McClernand Papers, ALPL; Edwin Loosley to wife, May 6, 1863, Edwin A. Loosley Papers, SIU.

11. *OR*, 24(1):628; C. H. Twining to Kate, June 9, 1863, Moody Family Papers, MHS.

12. *OR*, 24(1):628, 631; Samuel D. Pryce, *Vanishing Footprints: The Twenty-Second Iowa Volunteer Infantry in the Civil War*, Jeffry C. Burden, ed. (Iowa City, IA: Camp Pope Bookshop, 2008), 93; Crooke, *The Twenty-first Regiment of Iowa Volunteer Infantry*, 57–58; Gilbert Gulbrandsen to unknown, May 3, 1863, Gilbert Gulbrandsen Papers, HCWRTC, USAHEC.

13. *OR*, 24(1):582–583, 601; C. H. Twining to Kate, June 9, 1863, Moody Family Papers, MHS.

14. *OR*, 24(1):593, 599; *OR*, 24(2):31, 36, 235; Florison D. Pitts Diary, May 1, 1863, CHM, published as Leo M. Kaiser, ed., "The Civil War Diary of Florison D. Pitts," *Mid America: An Historical Review* 40, no. 1 (January 1958): 37.

15. Jenkin L. Jones Diary, May 1, 1863, UCH, copy in WHS and published as Jenkin Lloyd Jones, "An Artilleryman's Diary," *Wisconsin History Commission: Original Papers, No. 8* (February 1914): 1–368; James S. McHenry Diary, May 1, 1863, ALPL; Samuel Churchill Memoir, undated, OCM; USS *Pittsburg* Logbook, May 1, 1863, RG 24, E 118, NARA.

16. *OR*, 24(1):599, 631; S. C. Jones, *Reminiscences of the Twenty-second Iowa Volunteer Infantry, Giving Its Organization, Marches, Skirmishes, Battles, and Sieges, as Taken from the Diary of Lieutenant S. C. Jones of Company A* (Iowa City, IA: N.p., 1907), 30; Pryce, *Vanishing Footprints*, 94; Gilbert Gulbrandsen to unknown, May 3, 1863, Gilbert Gulbrandsen Papers, HCWRTC, USAHEC.

17. *OR*, 24(1):33, 663; Allen J. Ottens, *General John A. Rawlins: No Ordinary Man* (Bloomington: Indiana University Press, 2021), 269.

18. Smith, *The Real Horse Soldiers*, 232.

19. George B. Davis, Leslie J. Perry, and Joseph W. Kirkley, *Atlas to Accompany the Official Records of the Union and Confederate Armies* (Washington, DC: Government Printing Office, 1891–1895), Plate XXXVI.

20. *OR*, 24(1):661, 663; Samuel Fowler Diary, May 13, 1863, SU, 159.

21. *OR*, 24(1):661, 663, 672; Tucker, *The Forgotten "Stonewall of the West,"* 236, 265.

22. *OR*, 24(1):663; Tucker, *The Forgotten "Stonewall of the West,"* 236, 265; Samuel P. Harrington Diary, May 1, 1863, Haerle Collection, USAHEC; William L. Roberts Diary, April 30, 1863, ADAH.

23. *OR*, 24(1):663, 678; William L. Roberts Diary, April 29, 1863, ADAH.

24. *OR*, 24(1):678.

25. *OR*, 24(1):675; Chambers, "My Journal," 262.

26. *OR*, 24(1):672.

27. Bearss and Hills, *Receding Tide*, 108; Mary Bobbitt Townsend, *Yankee Warhorse: A Biography of Major General Peter Osterhaus* (Columbia: University of Missouri Press, 2010), 89, 92.

28. *OR*, 24(1):143; Bearss and Hills, *Receding Tide*, 112; Terrence J. Winschel, *Triumph and Defeat: The Vicksburg Campaign* (Mason City, IA: Savas Publishing Company, 1999), 63; Pryce, *Vanishing Footprints*, 94; George W. Gordon Diary, May 1, 1863, USAHEC.

29. *OR*, 24(1):143; Bearss, *The Vicksburg Campaign*, 2:355; Michael B. Ballard, *Vicksburg: The Campaign that Opened the Mississippi* (Chapel Hill: University of North Carolina Press, 2004), 228; Pryce, *Vanishing Footprints*, 94; "Port Gibson," *National Tribune*, December 4, 1884; Crooke, *The Twenty-first Regiment of Iowa Volunteer Infantry*, 57–58; George W. Gordon Diary, May 1, 1863, USAHEC.

30. *OR*, 24(1):615, 620, 628, 631, 661, 664, 672; Crooke, *The Twenty-first Regiment of Iowa Volunteer Infantry*, 57–58; Gilbert Gulbrandsen to unknown, May 3, 1863, Gilbert Gulbrandsen Papers, HCWRTC, USAHEC.

31. *OR*, 24(1):625, 628–629, 632; Henry Steele Commager, ed., *The Blue and the Gray*, 2 vols. (New York: Meridian, 1994), 2:67; Pryce, *Vanishing Footprints*, 94.

32. *OR*, 24(1):631–632, 673; Gilbert Gulbrandsen to unknown, May 3, 1863, Gilbert Gulbrandsen Papers, HCWRTC, USAHEC.

33. *OR*, 24(1):625, 629; Pryce, *Vanishing Footprints*, 95.

34. *OR*, 24(1):615, 620, 629, 664, 673; Bearss, *The Vicksburg Campaign*, 2:356.

35. *OR*, 24(1):143, 629, 632.

36. *OR*, 24(1):599, 601, 614, 726, 774; Kaiser, ed., "The Civil War Diary of Florison D. Pitts," 37; John B. Sanborn, "The Campaign Against Vicksburg," in *Glimpses of the Nation's Struggle, Second Series: A Series of Papers Read Before the Minnesota Commandery of the Military Order of the Loyal Legion of the United States, 1887–1899*, 6 vols. (St. Paul, MN: St. Paul Book and Stationery Company, 1890), 2:126; Martin N. Bertera, *De Golyer's 8th Michigan Black Horse Light Battery* (Wyandotte, MI: TillieAnn Press, 2015), 98.

37. *OR*, 24(1):614, 625.

38. *OR*, 24(1):615, 625, 678; Commager, ed., *The Blue and the Gray*, 2:67; Hass, ed., "The Vicksburg Diary of Henry Clay Warmoth," 64.

39. *OR*, 24(1):625; Hass, ed., "The Vicksburg Diary of Henry Clay Warmoth," 64; Mason, *The Forty-second Ohio Infantry*, 191.

40. Townsend, *Yankee Warhorse*, 89; John Pemberton to James George, May 3, 1863, RG 109, Chapter 2, Volume 60, NARA; Sanborn, "The Campaign Against Vicksburg," 129; Stephens Croom Diary, April 30, 1863, VICK; James Ferguson to wife, May 1, 1863, James Ferguson Letters, OCM; J. H. Jones Memoir, undated, J. F. H. Claiborne Papers, UNC, 2; Curtis P. Lacey Diary, May 1, 1863, NL.

41. Claudius W. Sears Diary, April 30, 1863, MDAH.

42. Jason M. Frawley, "'In the Enemy's Country': Port Gibson and the Turning Point of the Vicksburg Campaign," in Steven E. Woodworth and Charles D. Grear, eds., *The Vicksburg Campaign: March 29–May 18, 1863* (Carbondale: Southern Illinois University Press, 2013), 43–64.

Chapter 3. "A Good Day for a Fight"

1. Marszalek, Nolen, and Gallo, eds., *The Personal Memoirs of Ulysses S. Grant*, 336; *OR*, 24(1):34, 48.

2. Daniel Roush to wife, undated, Daniel L. Roush Letters, 99th Illinois File, VNMPR; John G. Jones to parents, May 6, 1863, John G. Jones Papers, LC; M. Ellis to W. W. Thomas, June 2, 1863, Hubbard T. Thomas Papers, IHS.

3. Grabau, *Ninety-Eight Days*, 545.

4. *OR*, 24(1):663.

5. Grabau, *Ninety-Eight Days*, 545.

6. Grabau, *Ninety-Eight Days*, 545.

7. William F. Hollingsworth Diary, May 1, 1863, OCM; John Bowen to John Pemberton, May 1, 1863, RG 109, E 97, NARA.

8. Mason, *The Forty-second Ohio Infantry*, 192; Luther Cowan to Mollie, May 5, 1863, Luther H. Cowan Papers, TSLA.

9. *OR*, 24(1):143; Francis A. Dawes Diary, May 1, 1863, CWTI, USAHEC.

10. *OR*, 24(1):143; *SOR*, 4:370; Reuben H. Falconer Diary, May 1, 1863, OHS. Osterhaus's original report not printed in the *Official Records* is in the James W. Thompson Papers, FHS.

11. *SOR*, 4:370; Townsend, *Yankee Warhorse*, 93; Bearss, *The Vicksburg Campaign*, 2:358.

12. *OR*, 24(1):678; Bearss and Hills, *Receding Tide*, 116.

13. *OR*, 24(1):679–680; John Francis to Cassia Roberts, May 9, 1863, Luke R. Roberts Papers, HCWRTC, USAHEC; John M. Gould, "History of Company E," undated, 20th Alabama Papers, ADAH; William L. Roberts Diary, May 1, 1863, ADAH.

14. *OR*, 24(1):585–589, 591–592; *SOR*, 4:370; "Troops in the Battle of Port Gibson," *Confederate Veteran* 23, no. 5 (May 1915): 205; Townsend, *Yankee Warhorse*, 89, 92–93;

R. B. Scott, *The History of the 67th Regiment Indiana Infantry Volunteers, War of the Rebellion* (Bedford, IN: Herald Book and Job Print, 1892), 28–29; "Dedication of a Bronze Tablet in Honor of Botetourt Battery," *Southern Historical Society Papers* 35 (1907): 39–41; Alexander Sholl Diary, May 1, 1863, VICK; Samuel Gordon to wife, May 6, 1863, and "Battle of Thompson's Hill," Samuel Gordon Papers, ALPL; W. L. Rand to parents, May 6, 1863, Rand Family Papers, ALPL.

15. *OR*, 24(1):679; *SOR*, 4:370–371; John Francis to Cassia Roberts, May 9, 1863, Luke R. Roberts Papers, HCWRTC, USAHEC.

16. *SOR*, 4:371.

17. *OR*, 24(1):586, 588, 590; *SOR*, 4:370–372; Alexander Sholl Diary, May 1, 1863, VICK; Samuel Gordon to wife, May 6, 1863, Samuel Gordon Papers, ALPL; Frederick A. Henry, *Captain Henry of Geauga: A Family Chronicle* (Cleveland: Gates Press, 1942), 156–157; Mason, *The Forty-second Ohio Infantry*, 191–198; M. Ellis to uncle, June 2, 1863, Hubbard T. Thomas Letters, IHS; Reuben H. Falconer Diary, May 1, 1863, OHS; Asa Sample Diary, May 1, 1863, ISL, copy in IHS; W. L. Rand to parents, May 6, 1863, Rand Family Papers, ALPL.

18. *OR*, 24(1):679; John Francis to Cassia Roberts, May 9, 1863, Luke R. Roberts Papers, HCWRTC, USAHEC.

19. *OR*, 24(1):588–589.

20. *OR*, 24(1):590; Carolyn S. Bridge, ed., *These Men Were Heroes Once: The Sixty-ninth Indiana Volunteer Infantry* (West Lafayette, IN: Twin Publications, 2005), 119–127; Mason, *The Forty-second Ohio Infantry*, 191–198; Peter J. Perrine Diary, May 1, 1863, OHS; Reuben H. Falconer Diary, May 1, 1863, OHS.

21. *OR*, 24(1):680–681; John M. Gould, "History of Company E," undated, 20th Alabama Papers, ADAH; William L. Roberts Diary, May 1, 1863, ADAH.

22. *OR*, 24(1):680–681; John Francis to Cassia Roberts, May 9, 1863, Luke R. Roberts Papers, HCWRTC, USAHEC.

23. *OR*, 24(1):679; Winschel, *Triumph and Defeat*, 69; John M. Gould, "History of Company E," undated, 20th Alabama Papers, ADAH.

24. *OR*, 24(1):679–680.

25. *OR*, 24(1):679.

26. *OR*, 24(1):144; George W. Gordon Diary, May 1, 1863, USAHEC.

27. *OR*, 24(1):144.

28. *OR*, 24(1):144; Commager, ed., *The Blue and the Gray*, 2:67; C. H. Twining to Kate, June 9, 1863, Moody Family Papers, MHS.

29. *OR*, 24(1):672–673; H. Grady Howell, Jr., *Going to Meet the Yankees: A History of the "Bloody Sixth" Mississippi Infantry, C.S.A.* (Jackson: Chickasaw Bayou Press, 1981), 155.

30. *OR*, 24(1):144, 615, 623, 625, 629; C. H. Twining to Kate, June 9, 1863, Moody Family Papers, MHS; Commager, ed., *The Blue and the Gray*, 2:67; Jones, *Reminiscences of the Twenty-second Iowa Volunteer Infantry*, 31; Judson Gill to Sophie, May 6, 1863, C. Judson Gill Letters, VICK; Pryce, *Vanishing Footprints*, 96; Williamson Murray Diary, May 1, 1863, VICK; Louis K. Knobe Reminiscences, undated, ISL, 28–30; Daniel

Roberts to family, May 6, 1863, Daniel Roberts Correspondence, ISL; James F. Elliott Diary, May 1, 1863, IHS; Samuel P. Harrington Diary, May 1, 1863, Haerle Collection, USAHEC.

31. *OR*, 24(1):144, 615, 623, 625, 629; C. H. Twining to Kate, June 9, 1863, Moody Family Papers, MHS; Commager, ed., *The Blue and the Gray*, 2:67; Jones, *Reminiscences of the Twenty-second Iowa Volunteer Infantry*, 31; Judson Gill to Sophie, May 6, 1863, C. Judson Gill Letters, VICK; Pryce, *Vanishing Footprints*, 96; Williamson Murray Diary, May 1, 1863, VICK; Louis K. Knobe Reminiscences, undated, ISL, 28–30; Daniel Roberts to family, May 6, 1863, Daniel Roberts Correspondence, ISL; James F. Elliott Diary, May 1, 1863, IHS; Samuel P. Harrington Diary, May 1, 1863, Haerle Collection, USAHEC.

32. *OR*, 24(1):661, 664, 673; Tucker, *The Forgotten "Stonewall of the West,"* 239, 255; "Dedication of a Bronze Tablet in Honor of Botetourt Battery," 39–41; Marszalek, Nolen, and Gallo, eds., *The Personal Memoirs of Ulysses S. Grant*, 336.

33. *OR*, 24(1):144–145, 601–602.

34. *OR*, 24(1):144, 602, 606–607; Richard J. Fulfer, *A History of the Trials and Hardships of the Twenty-Fourth Indiana Volunteer Infantry* (Indianapolis: Indianapolis Printing Company, 1913), 56–57; Hovey Manuscript, undated, Alvin Hovey Papers, IU, 48. The Hovey Manuscript was not written by Hovey but is virtually identical to the Harry Watts Reminiscences, undated, ISL. Citations hereafter will be the Hovey Manuscript from IU.

35. *OR*, 24(1):144, 602, 611; Shelby Harriel, *Behind the Rifle: Women Soldiers in Civil War Mississippi* (Jackson: University Press of Mississippi, 2019), 110; Crooke, *The Twenty-first Regiment of Iowa Volunteer Infantry*, 57–58; James Slack to wife, May 8, 1863, James R. Slack Letters, ISL; William T. Rigby Diary, May 1, 1863, UIA.

36. *OR*, 24(1):144, 625–626; C. H. Twining to Kate, June 9, 1863, Moody Family Papers, MHS; Daniel Roberts to family, May 6, 1863, Daniel Roberts Correspondence, ISL; James K. Bigelow, *Abridged History of the Eighth Indiana Volunteer Infantry, from Its Organization, April 21st, 1861, to the Date of Re-enlistment as Veterans, January 1, 1864* (Indianapolis: Ellis Barnes Book and Job Printer, 1864), 18; Williamson Murray Diary, May 1, 1863, VICK; Judson Gill to Sophie, May 6, 1863, C. Judson Gill Letters, VICK; Louis K. Knobe Reminiscences, undated, ISL, 28–30; Samuel P. Harrington Diary, May 1, 1863, Haerle Collection, USAHEC.

37. *OR*, 24(1):664, 673; Bearss and Hills, *Receding Tide*, 111.

38. *OR*, 24(1):144, 602, 626; James Slack to wife, May 8, 1863, James R. Slack Letters, ISL; Augustus G. Sinks Memoir, undated, ISL, 33–34.

39. *OR*, 24(1):144, 626, 629; Gilbert Gulbrandsen to unknown, May 3, 1863, Gilbert Gulbrandsen Papers, HCWRTC, USAHEC.

40. *OR*, 24(1):664, 674; Winschel, *Triumph and Defeat*, 70; Howell, *Going to Meet the Yankees*, 155–157; Tucker, *The Forgotten "Stonewall of the West,"* 239.

41. *OR*, 24(1):144, 602, 611, 615, 624, 626; James Slack to wife, May 8, 1863, James R. Slack Letters, ISL; Unknown Diary, May 1, 1863, Howard County Documents, IHS.

42. *OR*, 24(1):602–603, 607, 611, 626; Bearss, *The Vicksburg Campaign*, 2:380;

History of the Forty-sixth Regiment Indiana Volunteer Infantry, September, 1861–September, 1865 (Logansport, IN: Press of Wilson, Humphreys and Co., 1888), 57–58; Jeffrey L. Patrick, ed., *Three Years With Wallace's Zouaves: The Civil War Memoirs of Thomas Wise Durham* (Macon, GA: Mercer University Press, 2003), 115–119; Louis K. Knobe Reminiscences, undated, ISL, 28–30; Hovey Manuscript, undated, Alvin Hovey Papers, IU, 49; Israel Piper Diary, May 1, 1863, VICK, copy in OCM; Augustus G. Sinks Memoir, undated, ISL, 33–34; Unknown Diary, May 1, 1863, Howard County Documents, IHS.

43. *OR*, 24(1):144, 603, 615, 624; Hass, ed., "The Vicksburg Diary of Henry Clay Warmoth," 65.

44. *OR*, 24(1):673; Pryce, *Vanishing Footprints*, 97; "Dedication of a Bronze Tablet in Honor of Botetourt Battery," 41.

45. *OR*, 24(1):603, 607, 609, 611, 621, 624, 629; Israel Piper Diary, May 1, 1863, VICK; Augustus G. Sinks Memoir, undated, ISL, 33–34; *History of the Forty-sixth Regiment Indiana Volunteer Infantry*, 57–58; Patrick, ed., *Three Years With Wallace's Zouaves*, 115–119; Louis K. Knobe Reminiscences, undated, ISL, 28–30; Hovey Manuscript, undated, Alvin Hovey Papers, IU, 49; Unknown Diary, May 1, 1863, Howard County Documents, IHS.

46. *OR*, 24(1):144, 603, 621, 623, 626.

47. *OR*, 24(1):144–145, 603; Richard L. Kiper, *Major General John A. McClernand: Politician in Uniform* (Kent, OH: Kent State University Press, 1999), 225, 228; Marszalek, Nolen, and Gallo, eds., *The Personal Memoirs of Ulysses S. Grant*, 336; Winschel, *Triumph and Defeat*, 73; Brooks D. Simpson, *Ulysses S. Grant: Triumph Over Adversity, 1822–1865* (Boston: Houghton Mifflin Company, 2000), 191; Smith, *The Decision Was Always My Own*, 103; John M. Adair, *Historical Sketch of the Forty-fifth Illinois Regiment, With a Complete List of the Officers and Privates and an Individual Record of Each Man in the Regiment* (Lanark, IL: Carroll County Gazette Print, 1869), 10; Pryce, *Vanishing Footprints*, 96; John G. Jones to parents, May 6, 1863, John G. Jones Papers, LC.

48. *OR*, 24(1):661, 664.

49. *OR*, 24(1):626–627, 629.

CHAPTER 4. "BOWEN IS HARD PRESSED"

1. *OR*, 24(3):807; *OR*, 24(1):257, 659; Winschel, *Triumph and Defeat*, 63; John Pemberton to Jefferson Davis, May 1, 1863, RG 109, E 97, NARA; John Bowen to John Pemberton, May 1, 1863, RG 109, E 97, NARA.

2. *OR*, 24(1):659; John Bowen to John Pemberton, May 1, 1863, RG 109, E 97, NARA.

3. *OR*, 24(3):809.

4. *OR*, 24(3):807–808, 814; John L. Power Diary, May 1, 1863, MDAH.

5. *OR*, 24(3):808–810, 812; John Adams to John Pemberton, May 1, 1863, RG 109, E 97, NARA.

6. *OR*, 24(3):811–813; *OR*, 24(1):655.

7. *OR*, 24(3):248.

8. *OR*, 24(1):49, 592, 726; Hass, ed., "The Vicksburg Diary of Henry Clay Warmoth," 65.

9. *OR*, 24(1):661–662, 664, 668; Chambers, "My Journal," 264; Claudius W. Sears Diary, April 30, 1863, MDAH.

10. *OR*, 24(1):661–662, 664, 668; Chambers, "My Journal," 264.

11. *OR*, 24(1):661, 664; Chambers, "My Journal," 264.

12. *OR*, 24(1):586–588, 670, 673, 681; John M. Gould, "History of Company E," undated, 20th Alabama Papers, ADAH; William L. Roberts Diary, May 1, 1863, ADAH.

13. *OR*, 24(1):586–589; *SOR*, 4:372–373; Bridge, ed., *These Men Were Heroes Once*, 119–127; Mason, *The Forty-second Ohio Infantry*, 191–198; Samuel Gordon to wife, May 6, 1863, Samuel Gordon Papers, ALPL; Alexander Sholl Diary, May 1, 1863, VICK; W. L. Rand to parents, May 6, 1863, Rand Family Papers, ALPL; Asa Sample Diary, May 1, 1863, ISL; Reuben H. Falconer Diary, May 1, 1863, OHS.

14. *SOR*, 4:37373–374; Bridge, ed., *These Men Were Heroes Once*, 124; Mason, *The Forty-second Ohio Infantry*, 191–198; Peter J. Perrine Diary, May 1, 1863, OHS.

15. *OR*, 24(1):671, 673; "Dedication of a Bronze Tablet in Honor of Botetourt Battery," 41; Bearss and Hills, *Receding Tide*, 119.

16. *OR*, 24(1):587, 670–671; R. S. Bevier, *History of the First and Second Missouri Confederate Brigades 1861–1865 and From Wakaruse to Appomattox, A Military Anagraph* (St. Louis: Bryan, Brand and Company, 1879), 180.

17. *OR*, 24(1):587, 670–671.

18. *OR*, 24(1):32, 143, 635, 643, 673; S. C. Beck, "A True Sketch of His Army Life," 1902, VICK, 6; Luther Cowan to Mollie, May 5, 1863, Luther H. Cowan Papers, TSLA; Howard, *History of the 124th Regiment Illinois Infantry Volunteers*, 77–79; W. S. Morris, *History, 31st Regiment Illinois Volunteers: Organized by John A. Logan* (Herrin, IL: Crossfire Press, 1991), 57; Job H. Yaggy Diary, May 1, 1863, ALPL; John Sheriff Diary, May 1, 1863, John Sheriff Family Papers, ALPL; James B. Owen to Sally, May 5, 1863 and James B. Owen to father, May 6, 1863, James B. Owen Letters, TSLA; Edward McGlynn to unknown, May 22, 1863, Edward McGlynn Letters, UIL.

19. *SOR*, 4:374–375; S. C. Beck, "A True Sketch of His Army Life," 1902, VICK, 6; Cyrus Randall to mother, May 25, 1863, Cyrus W. Randall Papers, ALPL. See also John E. Smith's report, May 5, 1863, in J. W. Miller Papers, ALPL.

20. *OR*, 24(1):144, 635, 643; Luther Cowan to Mollie, May 5, 1863, Luther H. Cowan Papers, TSLA; Job H. Yaggy Diary, May 1, 1863, ALPL; Henry Oman to wife, May 1, 1863, Henry Oman Papers, UNC.

21. *SOR*, 4:375–376; Earl J. Hess, "Grant's Ethnic General: Peter J. Osterhaus," in *Grant's Lieutenants: From Cairo to Vicksburg*, Steven E. Woodworth, ed. (Lawrence: University Press of Kansas, 2001), 208; "History of the Corps," *National Tribune*, February 16, 1893.

22. *OR*, 24(1):144, 662, 673–674; "Dedication of a Bronze Tablet in Honor of Botetourt Battery," 41.

23. *OR*, 24(1):662, 664.

24. *OR*, 24(1):670, 675–676; Bearss and Hills, *Receding Tide*, 120; Abner J. Wilkes Memoir, undated, OCM, 5; Chambers, "My Journal," 264; Claudius W. Sears Diary, April 30, 1863, MDAH; Joseph W. Westbrook Memoir, 1903, CWD, USAHEC, 4.

25. *OR*, 24(1):145, 629–630; Bearss, *The Vicksburg Campaign*, 2:388; Steven E. Woodworth, *Nothing but Victory: The Army of the Tennessee, 1861–1865* (New York: Knopf, 2005), 344.

26. *OR*, 24(1):603, 607, 615–616, 621, 626–627, 630; James Slack to wife, May 8, 1863, James R. Slack Letters, ISL; Hovey Manuscript, undated, Alvin Hovey Papers, IU, 49; Pryce, *Vanishing Footprints*, 99; Samuel P. Harrington Diary, May 16, 1863, Haerle Collection, USAHEC.

27. *OR*, 24(1):611, 652.

28. *OR*, 24(1):145, 593–594599–600; *OR*, 24(2):31; Marshall, *History of the Eighty-third Ohio Volunteer Infantry*, 75; Scott, *The History of the 67th Regiment Indiana Infantry Volunteers*, 28–29; John A. Bering and Thomas Montgomery, *History of the Forty-Eighth Ohio Vet. Vol. Inf.* (Hillsboro, OH: Highland News Office, 1880), 79–80; W. R. Eddington Memoir, undated, ALPL, 8; George Chittenden to wife, May 4, 1863, Chittenden Family Papers, ISL; John G. Jones to parents, May 6, 1863, John G. Jones Papers, LC.

29. *OR*, 24(1):634–635, 643; Lyman M. Baker Memoir, undated, ALPL, 8; John W. Griffith Diary, May 1, 1863, OHS.

30. *OR*, 24(1):643–644, 655; Martin N. Bertera, *A Soldier at Dawn: A Remarkable and Heroic Exodus* (N.p.: N.p., n.d.), 58; Thomas Morrow to sister, May 4, 1863, Elliot Morrow Papers, OHS; John W. Griffith Diary, May 1, 1863, OHS; Gould D. Molineaux Diary, May 1, 1863, AC.

31. *OR*, 24(1):603, 607–608, 611, 613, 627; Samuel P. Harrington Diary, May 16, 1863, Haerle Collection, USAHEC; James Slack to wife, May 8, 1863, James R. Slack Letters, ISL; William T. Rigby Diary, May 1, 1863, UIA.

32. *OR*, 24(1):662, 664, 669; Bearss, *The Vicksburg Campaign*, 2:391; Tucker, *The Forgotten "Stonewall of the West,"* 250; Phillip Thomas Tucker, *Westerners in Gray: The Men of and Missions of the Elite Fifth Missouri Infantry Regiment* (Jefferson, NC: McFarland & Company, 1995), 121–160; James Woodard to family, May 8, 1863, James W. Woodard Letters, OCM; I. V. Smith Memoir, 1902, SHSMC, 27.

33. *OR*, 24(1):603–605, 607–608; Bevier, *History of the First and Second Missouri Confederate Brigades*, 176–181; Unknown Diary, May 1, 1863, Howard County Documents, IHS; Augustus G. Sinks Memoir, undated, ISL, 33–34.

34. *OR*, 24(1):611; Ballard, *Vicksburg*, 239; Unknown Diary, May 1, 1863, Howard County Documents, IHS; James Slack to wife, May 8, 1863, James R. Slack Letters, ISL.

35. *OR*, 24(1):603, 607–608; Fulfer, *A History of the Trials and Hardships of the Twenty-Fourth Indiana Volunteer Infantry*, 56–57; Hovey Manuscript, undated, Alvin Hovey Papers, IU, 50; James Slack to wife, May 8, 1863, James R. Slack Letters, ISL.

36. *OR*, 24(1):612–613; Bevier, *History of the First and Second Missouri Confederate Brigades*, 180; I. V. Smith Memoir, 1902, SHSMC, 27; James Slack to wife, May 8 and June 11, 1863, James R. Slack Papers, ISL.

37. *OR*, 24(1):604, 607, 627; Bigelow, *Abridged History of the Eighth Indiana Volunteer Infantry*, 18; Samuel P. Harrington Diary, May 16, 1863, Haerle Collection, USAHEC; Louis K. Knobe Reminiscences, undated, ISL, 28–30; Daniel Roberts to family, May 6, 1863, Daniel Roberts Correspondence, ISL.

38. *OR*, 24(1):662, 676.

39. *OR*, 24(1):676; Chambers, "My Journal," 264; Claudius W. Sears Diary, April 30, 1863, MDAH; Joseph W. Westbrook Memoir, 1903, CWD, USAHEC, 4; Abner J. Wilkes Memoir, undated, OCM, 5; Louis K. Knobe Reminiscences, undated, ISL, 28–30.

40. *OR*, 24(1):604, 608, 627; Unknown Diary, May 1, 1863, Howard County Documents, IHS; Israel Piper Diary, May 1, 1863, VICK; Ernest A. Warden Diary, May 1, 1863, OHS; Samuel P. Harrington Diary, May 16, 1863, Haerle Collection, USAHEC.

41. *OR*, 24(1):643–644.

42. *OR*, 24(1):145, 662, 666, 677, 682; Magnus Brucker to wife, May 5, 1863, Magnus Brucker Letters, IHS; I. V. Smith Memoir, 1902, SHSMC, 28.

43. Chambers, "My Journal," 265.

44. *OR*, 24(1):659–661; John Bowen to John Pemberton, May 1, 1863, RG 109, E 97, NARA.

45. *OR*, 24(2):31; *OR*, 24(1):610, 644, 677; *OR*, 24(3):260; Winschel, "The Vicksburg Campaign," 257; Commager, ed., *The Blue and the Gray*, 2:68; Pryce, *Vanishing Footprints*, 97; Gould D. Molineaux Diary, May 1, 1863, AC; Leonard Loomis to Elizabeth, May 24, 1863, Leonard G. Loomis Letters, Dwight B. Yntema Collection, AM; C. H. Twining to Kate, June 9, 1863, Moody Family Papers, MHS; William L. Roberts Diary, May 1, 1863, ADAH.

46. *OR*, 24(1):32, 143, 145, 589, 604; Samuel Styre to parents, May 28, 1863, Samuel Styre Papers, DU; William A. Sypher Diary, May 1, 1863, CHM; Townsend, *Yankee Warhorse*, 96; Judson Gill to Sophie, May 6, 1863, C. Judson Gill Letters, VICK; Commager, ed., *The Blue and the Gray*, 2:68; John W. Griffith Diary, May 2, 1863, OHS; Job H. Yaggy Diary, May 1, 1863, ALPL.

47. *OR*, 24(1):32, 143, 145, 589, 604; Judson Gill to Sophie, May 6, 1863, C. Judson Gill Letters, VICK; Commager, ed., *The Blue and the Gray*, 2:68; William A. Sypher Diary, May 1, 1863, CHM; John W. Griffith Diary, May 2, 1863, OHS; Samuel Styre to parents, May 28, 1863, Samuel Styre Papers, DU.

48. *OR*, 24(1):145, 258, 582–585, 667; Jenkin L. Jones Diary, May 2, 1863, UCH; Silas T. Trowbridge, *Autobiography of S. T. Trowbridge, M.D.* (N.p.: N.p., 1872), 119–121, later reissued as Silas T. Trowbridge, *Autobiography of Silas Thompson Trowbridge, M.D.* (Carbondale: Southern Illinois University Press, 2004); George W. Gordon Diary, May 1, 1863, USAHEC.

49. *OR*, 24(1):32; *OR*, 24(3):260; Marszalek, Nolen, and Gallo, eds., *The Personal Memoirs of Ulysses S. Grant*, 335; Williamson Murray Diary, May 2, 1863, VICK.

CHAPTER 5. "I SUPPOSE GRANT KNOWS WHERE HE IS TAKING US"

1. *OR*, 24(1):630.

2. *OR*, 24(1):631.

3. Simon and Marszalek, eds., *PUSG*, 8:189.

4. E. B. Long, *The Civil War Day by Day: An Almanac, 1861–1865* (New York: Doubleday, 1971), 346–347.

5. For Chancellorsville, see Ernest B. Ferguson, *Chancellorsville 1863: The Souls of the Brave* (New York: Knopf, 1993), and Stephen W. Sears, *Chancellorsville* (Boston: Houghton Mifflin, 1996).

6. Emory M. Thomas, *Robert E. Lee: A Biography* (New York: W. W. Norton & Company, 1995), 287. For Jackson, see James I. Robertson, *Stonewall Jackson: The Man, The Soldier, The Legend* (New York: Macmillan, 1997).

7. Hass, ed., "The Vicksburg Diary of Henry Clay Warmoth," 68. For comparative coverage of Chancellorsville and the Vicksburg Campaign, see J. B. Jones, *A Rebel War Clerk's Diary: At the Confederate States Capital, Volume 1: April 1861–July 1863*, 2 vols., James I. Robertson, Jr., ed. (Lawrence: University Press of Kansas, 2015), 1:270–277.

8. *OR*, 24(1):635; Osborn H. Oldroyd, *A Soldier's Story of the Siege of Vicksburg From the Diary of Osborn H. Oldroyd* (Springfield, IL: Self-published, 1885), 6; Job H. Yaggy Diary, May 2, 1863, ALPL; Kaiser, ed., "The Civil War Diary of Florison D. Pitts," 38; James C. Sinclair Diary, May 1, 1863, CHM.

9. *OR*, 24(1):145, 594–595, 635; *OR*, 24(2):31, 38, 234; Scott, *The History of the 67th Regiment Indiana Infantry Volunteers*, 30; "A Lady Mayor," *National Tribune*, September 25, 1884; Mason, *The Forty-second Ohio Infantry*, 200; Kaiser, ed., "The Civil War Diary of Florison D. Pitts," 38; Simon and Marszalek, eds., *PUSG*, 8:142, 189; John G. Jones to parents, May 6, 1863, John G. Jones Papers, LC.

10. Hass, ed., "The Vicksburg Diary of Henry Clay Warmoth," 66; Kiper, *Major General John A. McClernand*, 228–229.

11. *OR*, 24(1):145, 594–595, 635; *OR*, 24(2):31, 38, 234; Ron Chernow, *Grant* (New York: Penguin Press, 2017), 260; White, *American Ulysses*, 269; John Sheriff Diary, May 2, 1863, John Sheriff Family Papers, ALPL; William T. Rigby Diary, May 3, 1863, UIA; Hass, ed., "The Vicksburg Diary of Henry Clay Warmoth," 66; Charles A. Hobbs, "War News," Alexandria *Gazette*, May 18, 1863; William F. Hollingsworth Diary, May 2, 1863, OCM; Kaiser, ed., "The Civil War Diary of Florison D. Pitts," 38; Oldroyd, *A Soldier's Story*, 5; Myron E. Knight Diary, May 2, 1863, OCM; Ernest A. Warden Diary, May 2, 1863, OHS; Simon and Marszalek, eds., *PUSG*, 8:142, 189; Luther Cowan to Mollie, May 5, 1863, Luther H. Cowan Papers, TSLA.

12. *OR*, 24(1):145, 594–595, 635; *OR*, 24(2):31, 38, 234; Hass, ed., "The Vicksburg Diary of Henry Clay Warmoth," 66; Simon and Marszalek, eds., *PUSG*, 8:142, 189; Hovey Manuscript, undated, Alvin Hovey Papers, IU, 50, 52; Job H. Yaggy Diary, May 2, 1863, ALPL.

13. *OR*, 24(1):33, 129, 146, 635; *OR*, 24(2):31, 204; Marshall, *History of the Eighty-third Ohio Volunteer Infantry*, 76; *Harper's Weekly*, June 13, 1863; Winschel, *Triumph and Defeat: The Vicksburg Campaign, Volume 2*, 3; S. H. M. Byers, *With Fire and Sword* (New York: The Neale Publishing Company, 1911), 65–66; Marszalek, Nolen, and Gallo, eds., *The Personal Memoirs of Ulysses S. Grant*, 338; Hicks, "The Campaign and Capture of Vicksburg," 96; Jenkin L. Jones Diary, May 2, 1863, UCH.

14. *OR*, 24(3):262–263; *OR*, 24(1):722, 727; Marszalek, Nolen, and Gallo, eds., *The Personal Memoirs of Ulysses S. Grant*, 347; *Sanborn Family in the United States and Brief Sketch of Life of John B. Sanborn* (St. Paul, MN: H. M. Smyth Printing Co., 1887),

56; Olynthus B. Clark, ed., *Downing's Civil War Diary* (Des Moines: The Historical Department of Iowa, 1916), 112; Alonzo L. Brown, *History of the Fourth Regiment of Minnesota Infantry Volunteers During the Great Rebellion 1861–1865* (St. Paul, MN: The Pioneer Press Company, 1892), 187; Sanborn, "The Campaign Against Vicksburg," 127–128; Edward Wood to wife, May 4, 1863, Edward J. Wood Papers, IHS; Michael Lawler to John, May 11, 1863, Michael K. Lawler Papers, SIU.

15. Brown, *History of the Fourth Regiment of Minnesota Infantry*, 187.

16. Marszalek, Nolen, and Gallo, eds., *The Personal Memoirs of Ulysses S. Grant*, 339–340; Albert D. Richardson, *A Personal History of Ulysses S. Grant* (Hartford, CT: American Publishing Company, 1868), 305; Sylvanus Cadwallader, *Three Years with Grant*, Benjamin P. Thomas, ed. (Lincoln: University of Nebraska Press, 1996), 63; Charles A. Dana, *Recollections of the Civil War* (New York: D. Appleton and Co., 1898), 45–46; Fred Grant Memoir, undated, USGPL, 11–14.

17. *OR*, 24(3):262–263; Dana, *Recollections of the Civil War*, 47; Wilson, "A Staff Officer's Journal," 95.

18. *OR*, 24(1):33, 128, 146, 616, 635, 653, 706; *OR*, 24(3):266; Bearss and Hills, *Receding Tide*, 128; Ballard, *Vicksburg*, 242; Force, "Personal Recollections of the Vicksburg Campaign," 297; Oldroyd, *A Soldier's Story*, 6; Simon and Marszalek, eds., *PUSG*, 8:207; S. C. Beck, "A True Sketch of His Army Life," 1902, VICK, 7; Job H. Yaggy Diary, May 2, 1863, ALPL; William F. Hollingsworth Diary, May 3, 1863, OCM; Luther Cowan to Mollie, May 5, 1863, Luther H. Cowan Papers, TSLA.

19. *OR*, 24(3):266; *OR*, 24(1):33, 128, 146, 616, 635, 653; Bearss and Hills, *Receding Tide*, 128; Fred Grant Memoir, undated, USGPL, 15; John W. Griffith Diary, May 2–3, 1863, OHS; Gould D. Molineaux Diary, May 2, 1863, AC; Ulysses Grant to John McClernand, May 3, 1863, RG 393, E 4709, NARA.

20. *OR*, 24(3):265; *OR*, 24(1):129, 595, 635, 651, 683, 734; Kaiser, ed., "The Civil War Diary of Florison D. Pitts," 38.

21. *OR*, 24(3):814–815; John C. Pemberton to Richard C. Memminger, May 2 and 3, 1863, RG 109, E97, NARA.

22. *OR*, 24(3):814.

23. *OR*, 24(3):808–812, 818; Maurice K. Simons Diary, May 1, 1863, OCM; John Douthit to Companion, May 6, 1863, John M. Douthit Letters, VICK.

24. *OR*, 24(3):814–815; William T. Mumford Diary, May 2, 1863, OCM.

25. *OR*, 24(3):808–812, 815, 818; *OR*, 24(1):258, 656; Bearss, *The Vicksburg Campaign*, 2:422–423; William T. Mumford Diary, May 2, 1863, OCM.

26. *OR*, 24(3):815; H. N. Faulkinbury Diary, May 3, 1863, MDAH; Samuel Lockett to wife, May 3, 1863, Samuel H. Lockett Papers, UNC.

27. *OR*, 24(3):815; "History of Company B," 1902, Chickasaw Bayou File, OCM, 32, printed as *History of Company B (Originally Pickens Planters) 40th Alabama Regiment Confederate States Army 1862–1865* (Anniston, AL: Norwood, 1902), 32; Martin Van Kees Diary, May 3, 1863, OCM.

28. *OR*, 24(3):808–812, 815, 817–818, 822–824; Wilson, "A Staff Officer's Journal," 97; John Pemberton to William Loring, May 5, 1863, RG 109, Chapter II, Volume 60, NARA.

29. *OR*, 24(3):815–816.

30. *OR*, 24(3):816, 824; *OR*, 24(1):655, 657, 666; Winschel, *Triumph and Defeat: The Vicksburg Campaign, Volume 2*, 6; William L. Roberts Diary, May 2, 1863, ADAH; John Bowen to John Pemberton, May 2–3, 1863, RG 109, Chapter II, Volume 274, NARA.

31. *OR*, 24(3):265; *OR*, 24(1):666; Bearss and Hills, *Receding Tide*, 135; Ephraim McD. Anderson, *Memoirs: Historical and Personal Including the Campaigns of the First Missouri Confederate Brigade* (St. Louis: Times Publishing Co., 1868), 297–300; I. V. Smith Memoir, 1902, SHSMC, 28; Samuel Fowler Diary, May 13, 1863, SU, 168; J. V. Boucher to Polly, May 6, 1863, Boucher Family Papers, CWD, USAHEC; William A. Ruyle, May 2, 1863, HCWRTC, USAHEC; John N. Bell Diary, May 4, 1863, OHS.

32. *OR*, 24(3):818, 820; Herman Hattaway, *General Stephen D. Lee* (Jackson: University Press of Mississippi, 1988), 85; William A. Sypher Diary, April 30, 1863, CHM.

33. *OR*, 24(1):656–657, 666, 669; Bearss and Hills, *Receding Tide*, 136–137; Grabau, *Ninety-Eight Days*, 177–178; J. Parker Hills, *Vicksburg Campaign Driving Tour Guide* (N.p.: Friends of the Vicksburg Campaign and Historic Trail, Inc., 2008), 94–96; Anderson, *Memoirs*, 301–305; Chambers, "My Journal," 266; Samuel Fowler Diary, May 3, 1863, SU, 168; William L. Roberts Diary, May 3, 1863, ADAH.

34. *OR*, 24(1):656–657, 666, 669; Grabau, *Ninety-Eight Days*, 177–178; Bearss and Hills, *Receding Tide*, 136–137; Hills, *Vicksburg Campaign Driving Tour Guide*, 94–96; I. V. Smith Memoir, 1902, SHSMC, 28; Chambers, "My Journal," 266; Samuel Fowler Diary, May 3, 1863, SU, 168; Anderson, *Memoirs*, 301–305; William L. Roberts Diary, May 3, 1863, ADAH.

35. *OR*, 24(3):819–821, 824–825.

36. *OR*, 24(3):821–823, 826.

37. Samuel Lockett to wife, May 3, 1863, Samuel H. Lockett Papers, UNC; Maurice K. Simons Diary, May 2, 1863, OCM.

38. *OR*, 24(1):129, 727; *OR*, 24(2):198, 204; Peter J. Perrine Diary, May 3, 1863, OHS.

39. *OR*, 24(3):263; Tucker, *The Forgotten "Stonewall of the West*," 264–265; Simon and Marszalek, eds., *PUSG*, 8:141; John Francis to Cassia Roberts, May 9, 1863, Luke R. Roberts Papers, HCWRTC, USAHEC; Joseph R. Winslow Diary, May 3 and 4, 1863, VICK; John G. Jones to parents, May 6, 1863, John G. Jones Papers, LC.

40. *OR*, 24(1):635; Edward E. Schweitzer Diary, May 1, 1863, CWTI, USAHEC.

41. *OR*, 24(3):260–261; Thomas White to mother, May 11, 1863, Thomas K. White Papers, OHS; Curtis P. Lacey Diary, May 4, 1863, NL.

42. *OR*, 24(3):262–263; Henry J. Seaman Diary, May 1, 1863, CWTI, USAHEC, copy in VICK.

43. *OR*, 24(1):49.

44. *OR*, 24(1):49.

45. *OR*, 24(3):264.

46. *OR*, 24(3):268, 264; *OR*, 24(2):187; William L. B. Jenney, "With Sherman and Grant from Memphis to Chattanooga: A Reminisce," in *Military Essays and Recollections: Papers Read Before the Commandery of the State of Illinois, Military Order of the Loyal Legion of the United States*, 5 vols. (Chicago: Cozzens and Beaton Company, 1907), 4:203; Henry Franks to family, May 10, 1863, Henry W. Franks Letters, OHS;

Arnold Rickard Diary, May 1–17, 1863, CHM; Simon and Marszalek, eds., *PUSG*, 8:215; Richard Owen to John A. Rawlins, May 9, 1863, RG 393, E 4720, NARA; John A. Mc-Clernand to U. S. Grant, May 14, 1863, RG 393, E 4720, NARA.

47. J. D. Bingham Report, October 7, 1863, RG 92, E 1127, NARA, 1:291–295; "Military History of Brevet Brigadier General Judson D. Bingham, Assistant Quartermaster General, U.S.A.," undated, RG 94, E 297, NARA; "Report of Officers Doing Duty in the Subsistence Department, in the Army of the Tenn., During the Month of September 1863," October 10, 1863, RG 192, E 82A, NARA; Robert Macfeely Service History, October 22, 1872, RG 94, E 297, NARA; Stephen C. Lyford Military History, 1861–1864, RG156, E 176, NARA, 2:88; Simon and Marszalek, eds., *PUSG*, 8:84, 136, 186; Dana, *Recollections of the Civil War*, 73.

48. *OR*, 24(3):265; I. V. Smith Memoir, 1902, SHSMC, 28.

CHAPTER 6. "THE ROAD TO VICKSBURG IS OPEN"

1. David G. Chandler, *The Campaigns of Napoleon: The Mind and Method of History's Greatest Soldier* (New York: Scribner, 1966), 390–402; *Field Manual 3-0: Operations* (Washington, DC: Department of the Army, 1993), 2–5, 2–10.

2. Timothy B. Smith, "Ulysses S. Grant and the Art of War," in *Grant at 200: Reconsidering the Life and Legacy of Ulysses S. Grant*, Chris Mackowski and Frank J. Scaturro, eds. (El Dorado Hills, CA: Savas Beatie, 2023), 37–46.

3. For details, see Smith, *Early Struggles for Vicksburg* and Smith, *Bayou Battles for Vicksburg*.

4. Hicks, "The Campaign and Capture of Vicksburg," 97.

5. Hicks, "The Campaign and Capture of Vicksburg," 97.

6. *OR*, 24(3):265; *OR*, 24(1):707; Pryce, *Vanishing Footprints*, 100; Howard, *History of the 124th Regiment Illinois Infantry Volunteers*, 82.

7. *OR*, 24(1):635–636; *OR*, 24(1):644; Kiper, *Major General John A. McClernand*, 229; Wilson, "A Staff Officer's Journal," 95; Peter J. Perrine Diary, May 3, 1863, OHS; Edward Wood to wife, May 4, 1863, Edward J. Wood Papers, IHS; Jenkin L. Jones Diary, May 3, 1863, UCH.

8. *OR*, 24(1):49, 84, 636, 645, 656–657, 666, 669, 722–723, 727, 735, 781; *OR*, 24(3):268–269; *OR*, 24(2):198, 204–205; Bearss and Hills, *Receding Tide*, 136–137; Grabau, *Ninety-Eight Days*, 177–178; Hills, *Vicksburg Campaign Driving Tour Guide*, 94–96; Bearss, *The Vicksburg Campaign*, 2:424; I. V. Smith Memoir, 1902, SHSMC, 28; Chambers, "My Journal," 266; Samuel Fowler Diary, May 3, 1863, SU, 168; James A. Woodson Diary, May 3, 1863, ALPL; John Sheriff Diary, May 3, 1863, John Sheriff Family Papers, ALPL; Marszalek, Nolen, and Gallo, eds., *The Personal Memoirs of Ulysses S. Grant*, 341; Anderson, *Memoirs*, 301–305; William L. Roberts Diary, May 3, 1863, ADAH; Edward Wood to wife, May 4, 1863, Edward J. Wood Papers, IHS; Magnus Brucker to wife, May 5, 1863, Magnus Brucker Letters, IHS; Hass, ed., "The Vicksburg Diary of Henry Clay Warmoth," 67; William H. Kinkade Diary, May 3, 1863, ALPL.

9. *OR*, 24(1):49, 84, 636, 645, 656–657, 666, 669, 683, 723, 727, 735, 774, 781; *OR*, 24(3):268–269; *OR*, 24(2):198, 204–205; Bearss, *The Vicksburg Campaign*, 2:424; Bearss and Hills, *Receding Tide*, 136–137; Grabau, *Ninety-Eight Days*, 177–178; Hills, *Vicksburg Campaign Driving Tour Guide*, 94–96; I. V. Smith Memoir, 1902, SHSMC, 28; Chambers, "My Journal," 266; Samuel Fowler Diary, May 3, 1863, SU, 168; Anderson, *Memoirs*, 301–305; William L. Roberts Diary, May 3, 1863, ADAH; Magnus Brucker to wife, May 5, 1863, Magnus Brucker Letters, IHS; James A. Woodson Diary, May 3, 1863, ALPL; John Sheriff Diary, May 3, 1863, John Sheriff Family Papers, ALPL; Marszalek, Nolen, and Gallo, eds., *The Personal Memoirs of Ulysses S. Grant*, 341; Hass, ed., "The Vicksburg Diary of Henry Clay Warmoth," 67; William H. Kinkade Diary, May 3, 1863, ALPL; Edward Wood to wife, May 4, 1863, Edward J. Wood Papers, IHS.

10. *OR*, 24(1):49, 84, 636, 645, 656–657, 666, 669, 683, 723, 727, 735, 774, 781; *OR*, 24(3):268–269; *OR*, 24(2):198, 204–205; Bearss, *The Vicksburg Campaign*, 2:424; Bearss and Hills, *Receding Tide*, 136–137; Grabau, *Ninety-Eight Days*, 177–178; Hills, *Vicksburg Campaign Driving Tour Guide*, 94–96; I. V. Smith Memoir, 1902, SHSMC, 28; Chambers, "My Journal," 266; Samuel Fowler Diary, May 3, 1863, SU, 168; Anderson, *Memoirs*, 301–305; William L. Roberts Diary, May 3, 1863, ADAH; Magnus Brucker to wife, May 5, 1863, Magnus Brucker Letters, IHS; James A. Woodson Diary, May 3, 1863, ALPL; John Sheriff Diary, May 3, 1863, John Sheriff Family Papers, ALPL; Marszalek, Nolen, and Gallo, eds., *The Personal Memoirs of Ulysses S. Grant*, 341; Hass, ed., "The Vicksburg Diary of Henry Clay Warmoth," 67; William H. Kinkade Diary, May 3, 1863, ALPL; Edward Wood to wife, May 4, 1863, Edward J. Wood Papers, IHS.

11. *OR*, 24(3):268–269; *OR*, 24(1):84, 636, 645, 723, 727, 735, 781; *OR*, 24(2):198, 204–205; Tucker, *The Forgotten "Stonewall of the West,"* 268; Force, "Personal Recollections of the Vicksburg Campaign," 297–298; Brown, *History of the Fourth Regiment of Minnesota Infantry*, 189; George W. Modil Diary, May 4, 1863, MDAH, copy in OCM; John Logan to wife, May 4, 1863, John A. Logan Papers, LC.

12. *OR*, 24(3):267; *OR*, 24(1):146; *OR*, 24(2):133; Williamson Murray Diary, May 5, 1863, VICK; Samuel P. Harrington Diary, May 2, 1863, Haerle Collection, USAHEC.

13. Kaiser, ed., "The Civil War Diary of Florison D. Pitts," 38; Sweetman, "From Milliken's Bend to Vicksburg," *National Tribune*, August 22, 1895; Edward Wood to wife, May 8, 1863, Edward J. Wood Papers, IHS.

14. Hass, ed., "The Vicksburg Diary of Henry Clay Warmoth," 67; Bearss and Hills, *Receding Tide*, 136; George G. Meade to M. W. Stokes, November 5, 1867, George G. Meade Letter, LSU; W. Maury Darst, ed., "The Vicksburg Diary of Mrs. Alfred Ingraham: May 2–June 13, 1863," *Journal of Mississippi History* 44, no. 2 (May 1982): 148, 155, 166; H. S. Fulkerson, *A Civilian's Recollections of the War Between the States*, P. L. Rainwater, ed. (Baton Rouge, LA: Otto Claitor, 1939), 156–158.

15. *OR*, 24(3):266.

16. *OR*, 24(3):267–268; Commager, ed., *The Blue and the Gray*, 2:68–69, Kaiser, ed., "The Civil War Diary of Florison D. Pitts," 38.

17. *OR*, 24(3):267–268; Commager, ed., *The Blue and the Gray*, 2:68–69, Kaiser, ed., "The Civil War Diary of Florison D. Pitts," 38.

18. *OR*, 24(3):266; Kaiser, ed., "The Civil War Diary of Florison D. Pitts," 38.

19. *ORN*, 24:626–627; Samuel Fowler Diary, May 13, 1863, SU, 163; Gilbert Gulbrandsen to unknown, May 3, 1863, Gilbert Gulbrandsen Papers, HCWRTC, USA-HEC; Chester G. Hearn, *Admiral David Dixon Porter: The Civil War Years* (Annapolis, MD: Naval Institute Press, 1996), 226–227; Simon and Marszalek, eds., *PUSG*, 8:138, 142; Charles E. Affeld Diary, May 11, 1863, VICK; USS *Pittsburg* Logbook, May 2, 1863, RG 24, E 118, NARA.

20. *OR*, 24(3):266; *OR*, 24(1):33, 735; James Harrison Wilson, *Under the Old Flag: Recollections of Military Operations in the War for the Union, the Spanish War the Boxer Rebellion, Etc.,* 2 vols. (New York: D. Appleton and Co., 1912), 1:194–196; Dana, *Recollections of the Civil War,* 47; Fred Grant Memoir, undated, USGPL, 16; J. W. Greenman Diary, May 13, 1863, MDAH.

21. *OR*, 24(1):33–34, 49; Simon and Marszalek, eds., *PUSG*, 8:144; Marszalek, Nolen, and Gallo, eds., *The Personal Memoirs of Ulysses S. Grant,* 340; J. Parker Hills, "Roads to Raymond," in Steven E. Woodworth and Charles D. Grear, eds., *The Vicksburg Campaign: March 29–May 18, 1863* (Carbondale: Southern Illinois University Press, 2013), 68; W. A. C. Michael, "How the Mississippi Was Opened," in *Civil War Sketches and Incidents: Papers Read by Companions of the Commandery of the State of Nebraska, Military Order of the Loyal Legion of the United States.* Omaha: The Commandery, 1902), 50; Dana, *Recollections of the Civil War,* 47–48; Wilson, "A Staff Officer's Journal," 93.

22. William Hillyer to wife, May 23, 1863, William S. Hillyer Papers, UVA; Simon and Marszalek, eds., *PUSG*, 8:137, 175, 219, 550; Smith, *The Decision Was Always My Own,* 102; William Hillyer to wife, April 2 and May 3, 1863, William S. Hillyer Subject File, USGPL.

23. John Y. Simon, ed., *The Personal Memoirs of Julia Dent Grant [Mrs. Ulysses S. Grant]* (New York: G. P. Putnam's Sons, 1975), 113; Hills, "Roads to Raymond," 68; Simon and Marszalek, eds., *PUSG*, 8:155; James B. Logan Diary, May 2, 1863, ALPL.

24. Marszalek, Nolen, and Gallo, eds., *The Personal Memoirs of Ulysses S. Grant,* 341–342; Unidentified Soldier Memoir, undated, 35th Iowa Infantry File, OCM.

25. *OR*, 24(1):6, 33, 36, 49; Marszalek, Nolen, and Gallo, eds., *The Personal Memoirs of Ulysses S. Grant,* 341–343; Marszalek, *Commander of All Lincoln's Armies,* 177.

26. *OR*, 24(3):225, 265, 281, 288–289, 298; Simon, *PUSG*, 8:196.

27. *OR*, 24(1):84; Gilbert Gulbrandsen to unknown, May 3, 1863, Gilbert Gulbrandsen Papers, HCWRTC, USAHEC; Charles Dana to Edwin Stanton, May 4, 1863, Edwin M. Stanton Papers, LC.

28. Marszalek, Nolen, and Gallo, eds., *The Personal Memoirs of Ulysses S. Grant,* 342; Young, *Around the World with General Grant,* 2:621.

29. *OR*, 24(3):268; *OR*, 24(1):33; Simon and Marszalek, eds., *PUSG*, 8:139.

30. Simon and Marszalek, eds., *PUSG*, 8:138, 162; Marszalek, Nolen, and Gallo, eds., *The Personal Memoirs of Ulysses S. Grant,* 340.

31. Simon and Marszalek, eds., *PUSG*, 8:137; Carlos W. Colby, "Memoirs of Military Service," undated, Carlos W. Colby Papers, Bilby Collection, USAHEC, 4; Henry J. Seaman Diary, May 8, 1863, CWTI, USAHEC.

32. *OR*, 24(1):687; William T. Mumford Diary, May 4, 1863, OCM; Frank Blair to General, May 4, 1863, RG 393, E 5928, NARA.

33. *OR*, 24(1):688; Bruce Catton, *Grant Moves South* (Boston: Little, Brown and Company, 1960), 430; Joseph A. Saunier, *A History of the Forty-seventh Regiment Ohio Veteran Volunteer Infantry, Second Brigade, Second Division, Fifteenth Army Corps, Army of the Tennessee* (Hillsboro, OH: The Lyle Printing Company, 1903), 134–139; John N. Bell Diary, May 5, 1863, OHS.

34. *OR*, 24(1):125; Simon and Marszalek, eds., *PUSG*, 8:155; J. D. Bingham to U. S. Grant, May 12, 1863, RG 393, E 4720, NARA.

35. Edward Wood to wife, May 8, 1863, Edward J. Wood Papers, IHS.

36. *OR*, 24(3):269; Simon and Marszalek, eds., *PUSG*, 8:156, 158; Hills, "Roads to Raymond," 70; Marszalek, Nolen, and Gallo, eds., *The Personal Memoirs of Ulysses S. Grant*, 342; Dana, *Recollections of the Civil War*, 48; Isaac Vanderwarker Diary, May 4, 1863, CWD, USAHEC.

37. *OR*, 24(3):818.

38. *OR*, 24(3):818, 821, 824.

39. *OR*, 24(3):818, 823.

40. *OR*, 24(3):822–825; John C. Taylor Diary, May 3, 1863, Taylor Family Papers, UVA.

41. *OR*, 24(2):69; Larry J. Daniel, *Engineering in the Confederate Heartland* (Baton Rouge: Louisiana State University Press, 2022), 84–87.

42. *OR*, 24(3):822–825; *OR*, 24(1):662; James B. Owen to Sally, May 5, 1863, James B. Owen Letters, TSLA.

43. *OR*, 24(3):821, 824.

CHAPTER 7. "RATIONS NOW ARE THE ONLY DELAY"

1. Kennedy, *Population of the United States in 1860*, 272; John Ritter to Margarett, May 27, 1863, John Ritter Papers, NC.

2. "Auburn . . . Now A Ghost Town," October 23, 1987, Hinds County *Gazette*, copy in Auburn Subject File, MDAH; "Cayuga," undated, Cayuga Subject File, MDAH; "Utica Stands at Crossroads of History," March 13, 1941, Utica Subject File, MDAH; Will H. Price, "Know Utica," January 9, 1942, Utica *Advertiser*, copy in Utica Subject File, MDAH; Keith A. Baca, *Native American Place Names in Mississippi* (Jackson: University Press of Mississippi, 2007), 20; H. G. Hawkins, "History of Port Gibson, Mississippi," in *Publications of the Mississippi Historical Society*, 13 vols. (Oxford: Mississippi Historical Society, 1909), 10:290.

3. Cadwallader, *Three Years with Grant*, 64–66.

4. Sarah Fitch Poates Diary, July 7 and December 24, 1863 and March 4, April 7, and May 9, 1865, Asa Fitch Papers, CU; May Agnes Marston, "The Lady of the Diary or The Little Yankee Goes South," Asa Fitch Papers, CU; Introduction to Sarah Fitch Poates Diary, Asa Fitch Papers, CU.

5. James Slack to wife, May 11, 1863, James R. Slack Letters, ISL; Pryce, *Vanishing Footprints*, 100–101; J. V. Boucher to Polly, May 6, 1863, Boucher Family Papers, CWD, USAHEC.

6. James McPherson to mother, May 4, 1863, Wilfred S. Foerster Collection, Rutherford B. Hayes Presidential Center.

7. Luther Cowan to Mollie, May 6, 1863, Luther H. Cowan Papers, TSLA; Dana, *Recollections of the Civil War*, 48; Pryce, *Vanishing Footprints*, 102; Marshall, *History of the Eighty-third Ohio Volunteer Infantry*, 77; W. H. Bentley, *History of the 77th Illinois Volunteer Infantry, Sept. 2, 1862 — July 10, 1865* (Peoria, IL: Edward Hine, Printer, 1883), 138–139; Asa Sample Diary, May 6, 1863, ISL; Hovey Manuscript, undated, Alvin Hovey Papers, IU, 53; Isaac Vanderwarker Diary, May 5, 1863, CWD, USAHEC; Israel Piper Diary, May 6, 1863, VICK; John W. Griffith Diary, May 4, 1863, OHS; J. V. Boucher to Polly, May 6, 1863, Boucher Family Papers, CWD, USAHEC; James Thomas to friend, May 26, 1863, Robert T. Jones Letters, UT.

8. Cadwallader, *Three Years with Grant*, 66; Henry Oman to wife, May 4, 1863, Henry Oman Papers, UNC.

9. *OR*, 24(1):84, 645; Bertera, *De Golyer's 8th Michigan Black Horse Light Battery*, 101; Ernest A. Warden Diary, May 4–6, 1863, OHS; James S. McHenry Diary, May 5, 1863, ALPL; John F. Lester Diary, May 3, 1863, IHS; John W. Griffith Diary, May 6, 1863, OHS; George W. Modil Diary, May 4, 1863, MDAH.

10. James McPherson to mother, May 4, 1863, Wilfred S. Foerster Collection, Rutherford B. Hayes Presidential Center; Oldroyd, *A Soldier's Story*, 7–9; James Slack to wife, May 11, 1863, James R. Slack Letters, ISL; *History of the Forty-sixth Regiment Indiana Volunteer Infantry*, 59.

11. William H. Kinkade Diary, May 6, 1863, ALPL; Marszalek, Nolen, and Gallo, eds., *The Personal Memoirs of Ulysses S. Grant*, 343; John W. Griffith Diary, May 5–6, 1863, OHS; Hovey Manuscript, undated, Alvin Hovey Papers, IU, 53–54; Thomas N. McCluer Diary, May 3, 1863, OCM; Asa Sample Diary, May 5 and 6, 1863, ISL; Job H. Yaggy Diary, May 4, 1863, ALPL; Kenneth W. Noe, *Through the Howling Storm: Weather, Climate, and the American Civil War* (Baton Rouge: Louisiana State University Press, 2020), 303; Bridge, ed., *These Men Were Heroes Once*, 129–131; Thomas Watson to parents, May 6, 1863, Thomas Watson Papers, ALPL; William L. Rand Diary, May 4, 1863, Rand Family Papers, ALPL.

12. William H. Kinkade Diary, May 6, 1863, ALPL; Marszalek, Nolen, and Gallo, eds., *The Personal Memoirs of Ulysses S. Grant*, 343; John W. Griffith Diary, May 5–6, 1863, OHS; Hovey Manuscript, undated, Alvin Hovey Papers, IU, 53–54; Thomas N. McCluer Diary, May 3, 1863, OCM; Asa Sample Diary, May 5 and 6, 1863, ISL; Job H. Yaggy Diary, May 4, 1863, ALPL; Bridge, ed., *These Men Were Heroes Once*, 129–131; Thomas Watson to parents, May 6, 1863, Thomas Watson Papers, ALPL; William L. Rand Diary, May 4, 1863, Rand Family Papers, ALPL.

13. Hovey Manuscript, undated, Alvin Hovey Papers, IU, 53–54; Marszalek, Nolen, and Gallo, eds., *The Personal Memoirs of Ulysses S. Grant*, 343; William T. Rigby Diary, May 11, 1863, UIA; John W. Griffith Diary, May 5–6, 1863, OHS; Thomas N. McCluer

Diary, May 3, 1863, OCM; Asa Sample Diary, May 5 and 6, 1863, ISL; William H. Kinkade Diary, May 5, 1863, ALPL.

14. Steven Nathaniel Dossman, "The 'Stealing Tour': Soldiers and Civilians in Grant's March to Vicksburg," in Steven E. Woodworth and Charles D. Grear, eds., *The Vicksburg Campaign: March 29–May 18, 1863* (Carbondale: Southern Illinois University Press, 2013), 199; Cadwallader, *Three Years with Grant*, 72; Job H. Yaggy Diary, May 8, 1863, ALPL; William A. Sypher Diary, May 3–6, 1863, CHM; James C. Sinclair Diary, May 8 and 10, 1863, CHM; "Amount of Stock and Property Consumed and Taken Off by Gen. U. S. Grant's Army 1863," Confederate Collection, Series 608, Box 398, MDAH; Fonsylvania Plantation Diary, May 23, 25, and 31, 1863, MDAH; "A List of Names and Ages of Negroes Belonging to Howell Hobbs of Hinds County & Made Free by Acts of the Government of the States and Their Cash Valuation at the Time They were Made Free," undated, Hobbs Family Papers, MSU; "Claim Against US Government," undated, Calhoun-Kincannon-Orr Family Papers, MSU; Claim of Josiah M. Stephenson, September 7, 1871, Josiah M. Stephenson Collection, UM; E. E. Holman to J. W. Denver, April 25, 1871, E. E. Holman Letter, UM. There is a wealth of material concerning damages to Mississippians in the files of the Southern Claims Commission. See *Consolidated Index of Claims Reported by the Commissioners of Claims to the House of Representatives from 1871 to 1880* (Washington, DC: Government Printing Office, 1892), and the thousands of pages of testimony and affidavits are in "Records of Committees Relating to Claims," RG 233, "Records of the United States House of Representatives," NARA, and "Records of the Land, Files, and Miscellaneous Division," RG 217, "Records of the Accounting Officers of the Department of the Treasury," NARA. There is also a wealth of information in "Union Provost Marshal's File of Papers Relating to Individual Civilians," "Union Provost Marshal's File of Papers Relating to Two or More Civilians," and "Confederate Papers Relating to Citizens or Business Firms," all in "War Department Collection of Confederate Records," RG 109, NARA. For the Southern Claims Commission, see Frank L. Klingberg, *The Southern Claims Commission* (Berkely: University of California Press, 1955), 89, 117, 157, 168–169.

15. *Military History and Reminiscences of the Thirteenth Regiment of Illinois Volunteer Infantry in the Civil War in the United States 1861–1865* (Chicago: Women's Temperance Publishing Association, 1892), 314; Cyrus Willford, "Reminiscences of the Civil War," 1899, OHS, 240; Fulfer, *A History of the Trials and Hardships of the Twenty-Fourth Indiana Volunteer Infantry*, 60.

16. William Clemans Memoir, undated, UIL, 8; General Orders No. 17, May 9, 1863, Frank W. Tupper Papers, ALPL; Luther Cowan to Mollie, May 6, 1863, Luther H. Cowan Papers, TSLA; General Orders No. 6, May 5, 1863, RG 393, E 3230, NARA; Brown, *History of the Fourth Regiment of Minnesota Infantry*, 190; General Orders No. 68, May 7, 1863, RG 393, E 5541, NARA; General Orders, May 5, 1863, John A. McClernand Papers, ALPL; General Orders No. 31, May 5, 1863, Ulysses S. Grant Collection, Unpublished Correspondence, USGPL; General Orders No. 15, May 6, 1863, RG 393, E 6305, NARA; General Orders No. 16, May 9, 1863, RG 393, E 6305, NARA; General Orders No. 17, May 9, 1863, RG 393, E 6305, NARA.

17. *OR*, 24(3):269; *OR*, 24(1):131, 735; Feis, "'Developed by Circumstances,'" 165; Fred Grant Memoir, undated, USGPL, 18–19.

18. *OR*, 24(3):269; *OR*, 24(1):131, 735; Feis, "'Developed by Circumstances,'" 165.

19. *OR*, 24(3):270; Reuben H. Falconer Diary, May 4–6, 1863, OHS.

20. *OR*, 24(3):277; *OR*, 24(2):12; Peter Osterhaus to John McClernand, May 5 and 6, 1863, RG 393, E 3221, NARA; C. B. Haddon Memoir, 1922, OCM, 10; J. M. Love Diary, May 4, 1863, UM.

21. *OR*, 24(3):272; *OR*, 24(1):684.

22. *OR*, 24(3):274; James A. Woodson Diary, May 6, 1863, ALPL.

23. *OR*, 24(1):84; *OR*, 24(2):198; Bearss, *The Vicksburg Campaign*, 2:446; Jenkin L. Jones Diary, May 5, 1863, UCH; Maurice K. Simons Diary, May 5, 1863, OCM; George Boomer to General, May 5, 1863, RG 393, E 4720, NARA.

24. *OR*, 24(1):723; Simon and Marszalek, eds., *PUSG*, 8:159.

25. John C. Taylor Diary, May 4, 1863, Taylor Family Papers, UVA; Operators to John Pemberton, May 5, 1863, RG 109, E 97, NARA.

26. *OR*, 1, 24, 3: 821, 845, 864; "The Fight at Grand Gulf Yesterday," May 2, 1863, Jackson *Daily Mississippian*; "Grierson's Raid," May 1, 1863, Jackson *Daily Mississippian*; "Letter from Snyder's Bluff," May 1, 1863, Jackson *Daily Mississippian*; "Fighting at Grand Gulf Last Night," May 1, 1863, Jackson *Daily Mississippian*; "The Grierson Raid," May 5, 1863, Jackson *Daily Mississippian*; "Yankees in Jackson," May 7, 1863, Jackson *Daily Mississippian*; Junius H. Browne, *Four Years in Secessia: Adventures within and Beyond the Union Lines* (Hartford: O. D. Case and Company, 1865), 248–249; "Proceedings of the Board of Mayor and Aldermen," May 2, 1863, Jackson *Daily Mississippian*; "The Capture of Jackson, Mississippi," May 20, 1863, New York *Herald*; John J. Pettus Order, May 3 and 5, 1863, Executive Journals, 1817–1887, John J. Pettus, Series 758, MDAH; Special Order 135, May 5, 1863, Mississippi Governor, John J. Pettus, Military Orders, 1862–1863, Series 769, Box 951, MDAH; Richard Memminger to John Pemberton May 5, 1863, RG 109, Chapter II, Volume 60, NARA; Jones Hamilton to John Pettus, May 9, 1863, Mississippi Governor, John J. Pettus, Incoming Telegrams, 1862–1863, Series 762, MDAH.

27. *OR*, 1, 24, 3: 821, 845, 864; John Ray Skates, *Mississippi's Old Capitol: Biography of a Building* (Jackson: Mississippi Department of Archives and History, 1990), 68; "Proclamation," May 5, 1863, Jackson *Daily Mississippian*; "Proceedings of the Board of Mayor and Aldermen," May 2, 1863, Jackson *Daily Mississippian*; "The Capture of Jackson, Mississippi," May 20, 1863, New York *Herald*; John J. Pettus Order, May 3 and 5, 1863, Executive Journals, 1817–1887, John J. Pettus, Series 758, MDAH; Special Order 135, May 5, 1863, Mississippi Governor, John J. Pettus, Military Orders, 1862–1863, Series 769, Box 951, MDAH; Richard Memminger to John Pemberton May 5, 1863, RG 109, Chapter II, Volume 60, NARA.

28. *OR*, 1, 24, 3: 821, 845, 864; Jarret Ruminski, *The Limits of Loyalty: Ordinary People in Civil War Mississippi* (Jackson: University Press of Mississippi, 2017), 111; "The Darkest Hour Just Before Day," May 5, 1863, Jackson *Daily Mississippian*; Bettersworth, ed., *Mississippi in the Confederacy*, 116; *Journal of the House of Representatives*

of the State of Mississippi: December Session of 1862, and November Session of 1863 (Jackson: Cooper and Kimball, 1864), 89; Luther S. Baechtel Diary, May 2 and 7, 1863, MDAH; A. M. West to Carrie, May 5, 1863, Absolem West Collection, UM.

29. William Vannerson to John J. Pettus, May 26, 1863, Mississippi Governor, John J. Pettus, Correspondence and Papers, 1859–1863, Series 757, MDAH; Harold S. Wilson, *Confederate Industry: Manufactures and Quartermasters in the Civil War* (Jackson: University Press of Mississippi, 2002), 192; Nannie M. Tilley, ed., "Letter of Judge Alexander M. Clayton Relative to Confederate Courts in Mississippi," *Journal of Southern History* 6 (1940): 392–401; *Journal of the House of Representatives of the State of Mississippi: December Session of 1862, and November Session of 1863*, 89–92, appendix, 103, 108, 132, 181; Jones Hamilton to John Pettus, May 12, 1863, and John Shorter to John Pettus, May 3, 1863, Mississippi Governor, John J. Pettus, Incoming Telegrams, 1862–1863, Series 762, MDAH.

30. *OR*, 24(3):837, 840.

31. *OR*, 24(3):839.

32. *OR*, 24(3):827, 833, 835, 838; John Wilson to Lizzie, May 6, 1863, John A. Wilson Letters, MDAH.

33. *OR*, 24(3):828, 835, 839–840; John Pemberton to Major Mims, May 4, 1863, RG 109, Chapter II, Volume 60, NARA.

34. *OR*, 24(3):828, 830–831, 836–838; J. V. Harris Telegram, May 7, 1863, UM; Edward J. Dunn Memoir, undated, OCM, 6; "List of Negroes working on the fortifications at Fort Pemberton," May 6, 1863, John G. Devereux Papers, UNC.

35. *OR*, 24(3):838–839; Jefferson Davis to John Pemberton, May 1, 1863, RG 109, E 97, NARA.

36. *OR*, 24(3):838.

37. *OR*, 24(3):827; *OR*, 24(1):662; William Foster to Mildred, June 20, 1863, William L. Foster Letter, UA, copy in MDAH; Samuel Fowler Diary, May 4, 1863, SU, 171; Claudius W. Sears Diary, May 3, 1863, MDAH.

38. *OR*, 24(3):827; Catton, *Grant Moves South*, 430.

39. *OR*, 24(3):827.

40. *OR*, 24(3):828; James Jermyn Diary, May 6, 1863, OCM; Elbert D. Willett Diary, May 9, 1863, ADAH.

41. *OR*, 24(3):828–829.

42. *OR*, 24(3):829.

43. *OR*, 24(3):829, 835–836.

44. *OR*, 24(3):830, 833; Maurice K. Simons Diary, May 7, 1863, OCM; John Douthit to Companion, May 6, 1863, John M. Douthit Letters, VICK.

45. *OR*, 24(3):829, 835, 836; *OR*, 52(2):466; John C. Taylor Diary, May 4, 1863, Taylor Family Papers, UVA; "History of Company B," 1902, Chickasaw Bayou File, OCM, 32.

46. *OR*, 24(3):834; William A. Ruyle, May 7, 1863, HCWRTC, USAHEC.

47. *OR*, 24(3):836, 840–841; John C. Taylor Diary, May 5, 1863, Taylor Family Papers, UVA; C. Irvin Hutto to Thomas M. Owen, May 22, 1909, 23rd Alabama Papers,

ADAH; Edmund Pettus to John Pettus, May 6, 1863, Mississippi Governor, John J. Pettus, Incoming Telegrams, 1862–1863, Series 762, MDAH.

48. *OR*, 24(3):841.

49. *OR*, 24(3):830; William Drennan to wife, May 30, 1863, William Drennan Papers, MDAH, copy in VICK.

50. Douglas Maynard, ed., "Vicksburg Diary: The Journal of Gabriel M. Killgore," *Civil War History* 10, no 1 (March 1964): 46.

51. *OR*, 24(3):269; Kiper, *Major General John A. McClernand*, 233; John Smith to Aimee, May 5, 1863, John E. Smith Letters, Kirby Smith Collection.

52. *OR*, 24(3):270.

53. *OR*, 24(3):277; Bearss, *The Vicksburg Campaign*, 2:428.

54. William T. Rigby Diary, May 5–6, 1863, UIA; Peter Osterhaus to John McClernand, May 6, 1863, RG 393, E 3221, NARA; General Orders No. 5, May 4, 1863, RG 393, E 3230, NARA; John T. Allen Report, September 9, 1863, RG 92, E 1127, NARA, 1:33–40; J. Dunlap Report, January 8, 1864, RG 92, E 1127, NARA, 2:245–266; M. C. Garber Report, September 19, 1863, RG 92, E 1127, NARA, 2:653–664.

55. *OR*, 24(3):271–272.

56. *OR*, 24(3):271; Seth Hall to wife, May 8, 1863, Seth E. Hall Letters, OCM.

57. *OR*, 24(3):271; John F. Marszalek, *Sherman: A Soldier's Passion for Order* (New York: Free Press, 1993), 221; John F. Marszalek, "'A Full Share of All the Credit': Sherman and Grant to the Fall of Vicksburg," in *Grant's Lieutenants: From Cairo to Vicksburg* (Lawrence: University Press of Kansas, 2001), 19.

58. *OR*, 24(3):271–273; William T. Sherman, *Memoirs of General William T. Sherman: Written by Himself*, 2 vols. (New York: D. Appleton and Co., 1875), 1:320; John McClernand to commanders, May 2, 1863, RG 393, E5524, NARA.

59. *OR*, 24(3):273–274; John N. Bell Diary, May 5, 1863, OHS; Frank Tupper to parents, May 6, 1863, Frank W. Tupper Papers, ALPL; *Military History and Reminiscences*, 308; Isaac Mylar to Libbie, May 7, 1863, Isaac S. Mylar Papers, ALPL; Andrew Sproul Statement, May 10, 1863, Andrew J. Sproul Papers, UNC; John Merrilees Diary, May 6, 1863, CHM; Henry J. Seaman Diary, May 4, 1863, CWTI, USAHEC; John McClernand to Eugene Carr, May 6, 1863, RG 393, E 5524, NARA; Frederick Steele to Ulysses Grant, May 4, 1863, Ulysses S. Grant Collection, Unpublished Correspondence, USGPL.

60. *OR*, 24(3):273; Adoniram Withrow to Lib, May 13, 1863, Adoniram J. Withrow Papers, UNC.

61. *OR*, 24(3):277–278.

62. *OR*, 24(3):274; *OR*, 24(1):759; Marszalek, Nolen, and Gallo, eds., *The Personal Memoirs of Ulysses S. Grant*, 334; Sherman, *Memoirs*, 1:321; *Military History and Reminiscences*, 309; Charles Miller Memoirs, undated, VICK, 42, later published as Stewart Bennett and Barbara Tillery, eds., *The Struggle for the Life of the Republic: A Civil War Narrative by Brevet Major Charles Dana Miller, 76th Ohio Volunteer Infantry* (Kent, OH: Kent State University Press, 2004); David W. Reed, *Campaigns and Battles of the Twelfth Regiment Iowa Veteran Volunteer Infantry from Its Organization, September, 1861, to Muster Out, January*

20, 1866 (N.p.: N.p., 1903), 115; John Merrilees Diary, May 7–8, 1863, CHM; George Ditto Diary, May 10, 1863, ALPL; John N. Bell Diary, May 5–10, 1863, OHS; Henry J. Seaman Diary, May 7, 1863, CWTI, USAHEC; N. W. Wood Diary, May 7, 1863, UCB.

63. John Merrilees Diary, May 8, 1863, CHM; Augustus G. Sinks Memoir, undated, ISL, 35; Reed, *Campaigns and Battles of the Twelfth Regiment Iowa*, 115–116; Job H. Yaggy Diary, May 5, 1863, ALPL; N. W. Wood Diary, May 8, 1863, UCB.

64. *OR*, 24(3):272; *OR*, 52(1):61–62; Simon and Marszalek, eds., *PUSG*, 8:150, 156; Henry Walke, *Naval Scenes and Reminiscences of the Civil War in the United States, on the Southern and Western Waters During the Years 1861, 1862 and 1863* (New York: F. R. Reed, 1877), 394; James Vanderbilt to mother, May 25 and 26, 1863, James C. Vanderbilt Papers, ISL; Abram J. Vanauken Diary, May 8–9, 1863, ALPL; Seth R. Wells Diary, May 8–9, 1863, OCM; John A. McClernand to U. S. Grant, May 6, 1863, RG 393, E 4720, NARA.

65. *OR*, 24(3):274–275, 288, 291; Jeffrey N. Lash, *A Politician Turned General: The Civil War Career of Stephen Augustus Hurlbut* (Kent, OH: Kent State University Press, 2003), 128; Simon and Marszalek, eds., *PUSG*, 8:168; Payson Shumway to wife, May 12, 1863, Z. Payson Shumway Papers, ALPL; W. A. Montgomery to sister, May 18, 1863, Ann Sturtivant Collection, CWD, USAHEC.

66. *OR*, 24(3):275; George O. Smith, "Brief History of the 17th Regiment of the Illinois Volunteer Infantry, U.S.A.," undated, ALPL, 5; Green B. Raum, "With the Western Army," *National Tribune*, December 19, 1901; George Ditto Diary, May 10, 1863, ALPL.

67. *OR*, 24(3):275; Simon and Marszalek, eds., *PUSG*, 8:162.

68. *OR*, 24(3):279; *OR*, 24(1):35, 85; Simon and Marszalek, eds., *PUSG*, 8:165; William Gaster Report, December 23, 1863, RG 92, E 1127, NARA, 2:713–716.

69. *OR*, 24(3):279.

70. *OR*, 24(3):278–279; Simon and Marszalek, eds., *PUSG*, 8:158.

71. Lockett, "The Defense of Vicksburg," 486; Wilson, "A Staff Officer's Journal," 99.

72. *OR*, 24(1):50, 83; Marszalek, Nolen, and Gallo, eds., *The Personal Memoirs of Ulysses S. Grant*, 343–345; Joseph R. Winslow Diary, May 6, 1863, VICK; Henry O. Dwight, "A Soldier's Story," New York *Daily Tribune*, November 21, 1886, copy in "A Soldier's Story," 1886, OHS.

73. *OR*, 24(3):273, 290; *OR*, 24(1):50, 84; Bearss, *The Vicksburg Campaign*, 2:480; A. S. Abrams, *A Full and Detailed History of the Siege of Vicksburg* (Atlanta: Intelligencer Steam Power Presses, 1863), 24; Wilson, *Under the Old Flag*, 1:197; J. V. Boucher to Polly, May 6, 1863, Boucher Family Papers, CWD, USAHEC; Isaac Vanderwarker Diary, May 7, 1863, CWD, USAHEC; George Chittenden to wife, May 4, 1863, Chittenden Family Papers, ISL; Gilbert Gulbrandsen to unknown, May 3, 1863, Gilbert Gulbrandsen Papers, HCWRTC, USAHEC.

74. William F. Hollingsworth Diary, May 6, 1863, OCM; John Hancox to brother, May 5, 1863, John B. Hancox Letter, VICK; J. V. Boucher to Polly, May 6, 1863, Boucher Family Papers, CWD, USAHEC; Henry Oman to wife, May 4, 1863, Henry Oman Papers, UNC.

CHAPTER 8. "I THINK HE KNOWS WHAT HE IS DOING"

1. Maynard, ed., "Vicksburg Diary," 46.
2. Samuel Lockett to wife, May 8, 1863, Samuel H. Lockett Papers, UNC.
3. J. V. Boucher to Polly, May 6, 1863, Boucher Family Papers, CWD, USAHEC.
4. Almon Phillips to family, May 7, 1863, George T. Fowler Papers, GDAH.
5. Grabau, *Ninety-Eight Days*, 210.
6. Kemmerly, "Logistics of U.S. Grant's 1863 Mississippi Campaign," 593–597.
7. Bearss and Hills, *Receding Tide*, 160–161; Kemmerly, "Logistics of U.S. Grant's 1863 Mississippi Campaign," 593–597.
8. Kemmerly, "Logistics of U.S. Grant's 1863 Mississippi Campaign," 593–597.
9. Jean Powers Soman and Frank L. Byrne, eds., *A Jewish Colonel in the Civil War: Marcus M. Spiegel of the Ohio Volunteers* (Kent, OH: Kent State University Press, 1985), 275; A. S. Abrams Diary, May 1863, VICK.
10. Andrew McCornack to family, May 7, 1863, Andrew McCornack Papers, Sword Collection, USAHEC.
11. *OR*, 24(1):35; General Orders, May 7, 1863, William S. Hillyer Papers, UVA.
12. John W. Griffith Diary, May 6, 1863, OHS; Will Jolly to family, May 7, 1863, William H. Jolly Letters, Keen Family Papers, SHSIIC, copy in VICK.
13. *OR*, 24(1):728, 781; Charles E. Affeld Diary, May 13, 1863, VICK; John W. Griffith Diary, May 7, 1863, OHS; Luther Cowan Diary, May 7, 1863, Luther H. Cowan Papers, TSLA; J. H. Wickizer Report, September 22, 1863, RG 92, E 1127, NARA, 5:761–764.
14. *OR*, 24(3):279; Peter J. Perrine Diary, May 6, 1863, OHS; John A. McClernand to U. S. Grant, May 7, 1863, RG 393, E 4720, NARA; Samuel P. Harrington Diary, May 11, 1863, Haerle Collection, USAHEC.
15. *OR*, 24(3):279–280; *OR*, 24(1):35; Brown, *History of the Fourth Regiment of Minnesota Infantry*, 187; Simon, *PUSG*, 8:155; Dana, *Recollections of the Civil War*, 49; Grant, "A Boy's Experience at Vicksburg," 91; Young, *Around the World with General Grant*, 2:99; Adam Badeau, *Military History of Ulysses S. Grant, From April, 1861, to April, 1865*, 2 vols. (New York: D. Appleton & Co., 1881), 1:226; Simon and Marszalek, eds., *PUSG*, 8:174; Fred Grant Memoir, undated, USGPL, 15, 17–18; Asa Sample Diary, May 7, 1863, ISL.
16. *OR*, 24(3):279–280; *OR*, 24(1):35; Simon, *PUSG*, 8:155; Dana, *Recollections of the Civil War*, 49; Young, *Around the World with General Grant*, 2:99; Badeau, *Military History of Ulysses S. Grant*, 1:226; Simon and Marszalek, eds., *PUSG*, 8:174; Asa Sample Diary, May 7, 1863, ISL.
17. *OR*, 24(3):279; John McClernand to William Hillyer, May 8, 1863, William S. Hillyer Papers, UVA.
18. *OR*, 24(3):279–280; N. W. Wood Diary, May 9, 1863, UCB; Simon and Marszalek, eds., *PUSG*, 8:155, 166, 186; J. D. Bighman to U. S. Grant, May 8, 1863, RG 393, E 4720, NARA.
19. *OR*, 24(3):280; John McClernand to William Hillyer, May 8, 1863; William S.

Hillyer Papers, UVA; Simon and Marszalek, eds., *PUSG*, 8:178; Israel Piper Diary, May 7, 1863, VICK; Asa Sample Diary, May 7, 1863, ISL.

20. Ulysses Grant to William Sherman, May 8, 1863, Ulysses S. Grant Collection, Unpublished Correspondence, USGPL; Simon and Marszalek, eds., *PUSG*, 8:179–181, 186; William Caldwell to parents, May 8, 1863, William C. Caldwell Correspondence, UMB.

21. *OR*, 24(3):280; Soman and Byrne, eds., *A Jewish Colonel in the Civil War*, 274.

22. *OR*, 24(3):280–281.

23. Simon and Marszalek, eds., *PUSG*, 8:174; Bearss and Hills, *Receding Tide*, 163; Michael B. Ballard, "Grant, McClernand, and Vicksburg: A Clash of Personalities and Backgrounds," in Steven E. Woodworth and Charles D. Grear, eds., *The Vicksburg Campaign: March 29–May 18, 1863* (Carbondale: Southern Illinois University Press, 2013), 145.

24. *OR*, 24(3):282; Simon and Marszalek, eds., *PUSG*, 8:176–177; John A. McClernand to U. S. Grant, May 8, 1863, RG 393, E 4720, NARA.

25. *OR*, 24(3):282–283; *OR*, 24(1):85; Simon and Marszalek, eds., *PUSG*, 8:176; Luther Cowan Diary, May 7 and 8, 1863, Luther H. Cowan Papers, TSLA.

26. *OR*, 24(3):283–284; Flavius J. Thackara Diary, May 8, 1863, OHS; Soman and Byrne, eds., *A Jewish Colonel in the Civil War*, 274; General Orders No. 5, May 4, 1863, RG 393, E 3230, NARA.

27. *OR*, 24(3):283–284; Soman and Byrne, eds., *A Jewish Colonel in the Civil War*, 274; General Orders No. 5, May 4, 1863, RG 393, E 3230, NARA; Flavius J. Thackara Diary, May 8, 1863, OHS.

28. *OR*, 24(3):281–282.

29. *OR*, 24(3):285; Simon and Marszalek, eds., *PUSG*, 8:174–175.

30. *OR*, 24(3):282; Simon and Marszalek, eds., *PUSG*, 8:175, 187; John W. Griffith Diary, May 8, 1863, OHS; John G. Jones to parents, May 10, 1863, John G. Jones Papers, LC.

31. Simon and Marszalek, eds., *PUSG*, 8:175; Edward Tittman to William S. Hillyer, May 7, 1863, RG 393, E 4720, NARA.

32. Reuben H. Falconer Diary, May 8–9, 1863, OHS; Bennet Grigsby to family, May 18, 1863, Bennet Grigsby Letters, IHS.

33. *OR*, 24(3):283; *OR*, 24(1):779.

34. *OR*, 24(3):842; Clausewitz, *On War*, 443–444.

35. *OR*, 24(3):843, 846.

36. *OR*, 24(3):844–845; *OR*, 24(1):215; Joseph E. Johnston, "Jefferson Davis and the Mississippi Campaign," in *Battles and Leaders of the Civil War*, 4 vols. (New York: Century Company, 1884–1887), 3:478.

37. *OR*, 24(3):843, 845, 850; John Pemberton to Theo Johnston, May 9, 1863, RG 109, Chapter II, Volume 60, NARA.

38. *OR*, 24(3):842, 845; Craig L. Symonds, *Joseph E. Johnston: A Civil War Biography* (New York: Norton, 1992), 207.

39. *OR*, 24(3):846; Ballard, *Pemberton*, 142; Lockett, "The Defense of Vicksburg," 487; Archer Jones, "Tennessee and Mississippi, Joe Johnston's Strategic Problem," in

Confederate Generals in the Western Theater: Essays on America's Civil War, 4 vols., Lawrence Lee Hewitt and Arthur W. Bergeron Jr., eds. (Knoxville: University of Tennessee Press, 2010), 1:98.

40. *OR*, 24(3):842, 846–847, 849–850; *OR*, 24(1):215; John C. Taylor Diary, May 6, 1863, Taylor Family Papers, UVA; William Royal Oake, *On the Skirmish Line Behind a Friendly Tree: The Civil War Memoirs of William Royal Oake, 26th Iowa Volunteers*, Stacy D. Allen, ed. (Helena, MT: Farcountry Press, 2006), 116; Lockett, "The Defense of Vicksburg," 487.

41. *OR*, 24(3):842; Arthur W. Bergeron, Jr., "Martin Luther Smith and the Defense of the Lower Mississippi River Valley, 1861–1863," in *Confederate Generals in the Western Theater: Essays on America's Civil War*, 4 vols., Lawrence Lee Hewitt and Arthur W. Bergeron Jr., eds. (Knoxville: University of Tennessee Press, 2011), 3:75; "History of Company B," 1902, Chickasaw Bayou File, OCM, 33; Maurice K. Simons Diary, May 11, 1863, OCM; Elbert D. Willett Diary, May 9, 1863, ADAH; Louis Hebert Autobiography, 1894, UNC, 12, copy in LSU.

42. *OR*, 24(3):843, 846–848; Abrams, *A Full and Detailed History of the Siege of Vicksburg*, 25; William A. Ruyle, May 12, 1863, HCWRTC, USAHEC; Lockett, "The Defense of Vicksburg," 487; John Pemberton to John Adams, May 7, 1863, RG 109, E 97, NARA.

43. Claudius W. Sears Diary, May 3–14, 1863, MDAH.

44. *OR*, 24(3):849; Ballard, *Pemberton*, 148; James W. Raab, *W. W. Loring: Florida's Forgotten General* (Manhattan, KS: Sunflower University Press, 1996), 108; J. S. Wheeler Diary, May and June 1863, OCM; A. S. Abrams Diary, May 1863, VICK; William A. Ruyle, May 12, 1863, HCWRTC, USAHEC.

45. *OR*, 24(3):850.

46. *OR*, 24(3):284; *OR*, 24(2):12; Hass, ed., "The Vicksburg Diary of Henry Clay Warmoth," 68; Reuben H. Falconer Diary, May 8, 1863, OHS; Winchester Hall, *The Story of the 26th Louisiana Infantry, In the Service of the Confederate States* (N.p.: N.p., 1890), 38; Alexander Ewing to parents, May 18, 1863, Alexander K. Ewing Papers, ALPL; William F. Hollingsworth Diary, May 8, 1863, OCM; Asa Sample Diary, May 9, 1863, ISL; Hovey Manuscript, undated, Alvin Hovey Papers, IU, 54; William L. Rand Diary, May 8–9, 1863, Rand Family Papers, ALPL; Williamson Murray Diary, May 8, 1863, VICK; Joseph R. Winslow Diary, May 8, 1863, VICK; Soman and Byrne, eds., *A Jewish Colonel in the Civil War*, 276; John A. McClernand to U. S. Grant, May 9, 1863, RG 393, E 4720, NARA.

47. John Smith to Aimee, May 5, 1863, John E. Smith Letters, Kirby Smith Collection; Luther Cowan Diary, May 8, 1863, Luther H. Cowan Papers, TSLA; William A. Sypher Diary, May 10, 1863, CHM; Hass, ed., "The Vicksburg Diary of Henry Clay Warmoth," 68; Soman and Byrne, eds., *A Jewish Colonel in the Civil War*, 275; John A. McClernand to U. S. Grant, May 9, 1863, RG 393, E 4720, NARA.

48. *OR*, 24(3):287; Scott, *The History of the 67th Regiment Indiana Infantry Volunteers*, 31; Peter J. Perrine Diary, May 11, 1863, OHS; Augustus G. Sinks Memoir, undated, ISL, 35; John McArthur to "Officer in Charge of Transportation Grand Gulf," May 8, William S. Hillyer Papers, UVA.

49. *OR*, 24(3):287–288; *OR*, 24(1):636, 779; Bearss and Hills, *Receding Tide*, 159; Luther Cowan Diary, May 9, 1863, Luther H. Cowan Papers, TSLA; James B. McPherson to U. S. Grant, May 9, 1863, RG 393, E 4720, NARA; John W. Griffith Diary, May 9, 1863, OHS; George W. Modil Diary, May 9–10, 1863, MDAH.

50. *OR*, 24(3):283; *OR*, 24(1):759; Henry J. Seaman Diary, May 8, 1863, CWTI, USAHEC; Lewis F. Phillips Memoir, 1911, CWTI, USAHEC, 33.

51. John Merrilees Diary, May 9, 1863, CHM; Townsend, *Yankee Warhorse*, 98; James B. McPherson, *Battle Cry of Freedom: The Civil War Era* (New York: Oxford University Press, 1988), 629; Catton, *Grant Moves South*, 438.

52. *OR*, 24(3):284–285; *The Story of the Fifty-fifth Regiment Illinois Volunteer Infantry in the Civil War, 1861–1865* (Clinton, MA: W. J. Coulter, 1887), 229; James H. St. John Diary, May 7–10, 1863, ISL; Curtis P. Lacey Diary, May 7, 1863, NL; General Orders No. 31, May 9, 1863, Benjamin J. Spooner Letters, ISL; John L. Woods Report, September 30, 1863, RG 92, E 1127, NARA, 5:911–918.

53. *OR*, 24(3):284–285; *The Story of the Fifty-fifth Regiment Illinois Volunteer Infantry*, 229; William E. Parrish, *Frank Blair: Lincoln's Conservative* (Columbia: University of Missouri Press, 1998), 166; James H. St. John Diary, May 7–10, 1863, ISL; Curtis P. Lacey Diary, May 7, 1863, NL; General Orders No. 31, May 9, 1863, Benjamin J. Spooner Letters, ISL.

54. *OR*, 24(3):285; Charles Bracelen Flood, *Grant and Sherman: The Friendship That Won the Civil War* (New York: Farrar, Straus and Giroux, 2005), 162; William A. Sypher Diary, May 9, 1863, CHM; Joseph R. Winslow Diary, May 7, 1863, VICK.

55. *OR*, 24(3):285; Hovey Manuscript, undated, Alvin Hovey Papers, IU, 54; Job H. Yaggy Diary, May 9, 1863, ALPL; John McClernand to General, May 11, 1863, John A. McClernand Papers, ALPL.

56. *OR*, 24(3):285–286; Ulysses Grant to William Sherman, May 9, 1863, Rocky Springs Letter, ALPL.

57. *OR*, 24(3):285–286.

58. *OR*, 24(3):286; Thomas White to mother, May 11, 1863, Thomas K. White Papers, OHS; Hugh Ewing to wife, May 3, 1863, Hugh Ewing Papers, OHS. For Ewing, see Kenneth J. Heinman, *Civil War Dynasty: The Ewing Family of Ohio* (New York: New York University Press, 2012).

59. *OR*, 24(3):284; General Orders No. 32, May 9, 1863, Benjamin J. Spooner Letters, ISL.

60. Trowbridge, *Autobiography*, 122.

61. Edward Wood to wife, May 8, 1863, Edward J. Wood Papers, IHS; Simon and Marszalek, eds., *PUSG*, 8:189; Williamson Murray Diary, May 9, 1863, VICK.

CHAPTER 9. "MISSISSIPPI IS MORE SERIOUSLY THREATENED THAN EVER BEFORE"

1. William F. Willey Diary, May 10, 1863, OHS. For Hooker, see Walter H. Hebert, *Fighting Joe Hooker* (Lincoln: University of Nebraska Press, 1999).

2. Robertson, *Stonewall Jackson*, 748–749.

3. Robertson, *Stonewall Jackson*, 754–755; Maurice K. Simons Diary, May 11, 1863, OCM.

4. Robertson, *Stonewall Jackson*, 756–762; Jones, *A Rebel War Clerk's Diary*, 1:283, 285.

5. Hass, ed., "The Vicksburg Diary of Henry Clay Warmoth," 68–69; Maynard, ed., "Vicksburg Diary," 46; Mortimer D. Leggett to Morilla, May 10, 1863, Mortimer D. Leggett Papers, Lincoln Memorial Shrine, copy in VICK.

6. *OR*, 24(3):288–289; *OR*, 24(1):36; Grabau, *Ninety-Eight Days*, 200.

7. *OR*, 24(3):284; Wilson, "A Staff Officer's Journal," 96.

8. *OR*, 24(3):289.

9. Ulysses Grant to Michael Lawler, May 9, 1863, RG 393, E 4709, NARA; Wilson, *Under the Old Flag*, 182–183, 198.

10. *OR*, 24(3):286, 290; *OR*, 24(1):636; *OR*, 24(2):250; Bearss and Hills, *Receding Tide*, 160; Winschel, *Triumph and Defeat: The Vicksburg Campaign, Volume 2*, 15; Isaac Vanderwarker Diary, May 10, 1863, CWD, USAHEC; John W. Griffith Diary, May 10, 1863, OHS; George M. Shearer Diary, May 11, 1863, UIA; Luther Cowan Diary, May 10, 1863, Luther H. Cowan Papers, TSLA; George W. Modil Diary, May 10, 1863, MDAH; Job H. Yaggy Diary, May 10, 1863, ALPL; Jenkin L. Jones Diary, May 10, 1863, UCH; Mark Grimsley and Todd D. Miller, eds., *The Union Must Stand: The Civil War Diary of John Quincy Adams Campbell, Fifth Iowa Volunteer Infantry* (Knoxville: University of Tennessee Press, 2000), 93; Simon and Marszalek, eds., *PUSG*, 8:183; James B. McPherson to U. S. Grant, May 10, 1863, RG 393, E 4720, NARA.

11. *OR*, 24(3):289–290; S. H. M. Byers, "How Men Feel in Battle; Recollections of a Private at Champion Hills," *Annals of Iowa* 2, no. 6 (July 1896): 438; Flavius J. Thackara Diary, May 10, 1863, OHS; Samuel P. Harrington Diary, May 8, 1863, Haerle Collection, USAHEC.

12. *OR*, 24(3):289–290; Byers, "How Men Feel in Battle," 438; Samuel P. Harrington Diary, May 8, 1863, Haerle Collection, USAHEC; Flavius J. Thackara Diary, May 10, 1863, OHS.

13. John Sheriff Diary, May 10, 1863, John Sheriff Family Papers, ALPL; George M. Lucas Diary, May 10, 1863, ALPL; John G. Jones to parents, May 10, 1863, John G. Jones Papers, LC.

14. Oldroyd, *A Soldier's Story*, 11–12.

15. *OR*, 24(3):290; *OR*, 24(1):735.

16. *OR*, 24(3):289; John B. Fletcher Diary, May 11, 1863, ALPL.

17. *OR*, 52(2):464, 467–468; Samuel Fowler Diary, May 12, 1863, SU, 172.

18. *OR*, 52(2):467–469; Jones, *A Rebel War Clerk's Diary*, 1:288; Chambers, "My Journal," 267; "Enemy Approaches Edwards Depot," May 6, 1863, Jackson *Daily Mississippian*; "Grierson's Raid," May 7, 1863, Jackson *Daily Mississippian*; "The Grierson Raid," May 9, 1863, Jackson *Daily Mississippian*; "Position of Grant," May 12, 1863, Jackson *Daily Mississippian*.

19. *OR*, 52(2):469.

20. *OR*, 24(3):855–857; W. A. Rorer to cousin, June 13, 1863, DU, copies in Baxter Collection, CWTI, USAHEC and MDAH; Sid H. Griffin to Colonel, May 12, 1863, RG 109, E 97, NARA.

21. *OR*, 24(3):854, 856–857.

22. *OR*, 24(3):851.

23. *OR*, 24(3):852, 856–858; Bearss, *The Vicksburg Campaign*, 2:476; Ballard, *Pemberton*, 150; H. N. Faulkinbury Diary, May 10, 1863, MDAH.

24. *OR*, 24(3):850–851, 853, 858; *OR*, 24(1):736; Emma G. Cobbs, "The Battle of Raymond, Miss.," *Confederate Veteran* 9, no. 9 (September 1901): 406; Edwin L. Drake, ed., *The Annals of the Army of Tennessee and Early Western History* (Nashville, TN: A. D. Haynes, 1878), 167.

25. *OR*, 24(3):851.

26. *OR*, 24(3):854–855.

27. *OR*, 24(3):854.

28. *OR*, 24(3):855.

29. *OR*, 24(3):855.

30. *OR*, 24(3):858.

31. *OR*, 24(1):327.

32. *OR*, 24(3):292–294, 296; *OR*, 24(1):762; Grabau, *Ninety-Eight Days*, 202; Luther Cowan Diary, May 11, 1863, Luther H. Cowan Papers, TSLA; Hass, ed., "The Vicksburg Diary of Henry Clay Warmoth," 68; George Remley to Howard, May 25, 1863, Remley Family Papers, NC; Jordan Harriss to Velery, May 11, 1863, Jordan C. Harriss Papers, NC; J. Brumback to U. S. Grant, May 12, 1863, RG 393, E 4720, NARA; John A. McClernand to U. S. Grant, May 11, 1863, RG 393, E 4720, NARA.

33. *OR*, 24(3):292–294, 296; *OR*, 24(1):762; Grabau, *Ninety-Eight Days*, 202; Luther Cowan Diary, May 11, 1863, Luther H. Cowan Papers, TSLA; Hass, ed., "The Vicksburg Diary of Henry Clay Warmoth," 68; George Remley to Howard, May 25, 1863, Remley Family Papers, NC; Jordan Harriss to Velery, May 11, 1863, Jordan C. Harriss Papers, NC; J. Brumback to U. S. Grant, May 12, 1863, RG 393, E 4720, NARA; John A. McClernand to U. S. Grant, May 11, 1863, RG 393, E 4720, NARA.

34. *OR*, 24(3):292–293; *OR*, 24(2):12; John A. McClernand to U. S. Grant, May 11, 1863, RG 393, E 4720, NARA; Peter Osterhaus to Colonel, May 10, 1863, RG 393, E 3221, NARA; Peter Osterhaus to General, May 10, 1863, RG 393, E 3221, NARA; Peter Osterhaus to Captain, May 10, 1863, RG 393, E 3221, NARA.

35. *OR*, 24(3):295–296, 854; *OR*, 24(1):636; Bearss and Hills, *Receding Tide*, 162; Simon and Marszalek, eds., *PUSG*, 8:199; Job H. Yaggy Diary, May 11, 1863, ALPL; Townsend, *Yankee Warhorse*, 99; Military *History and Reminiscences*, 312; Bering and Montgomery, *History of the Forty-Eighth Ohio Vet. Vol. Inf.*, 82; John W. Griffith Diary, May 11, 1863, OHS; Joseph Child Diary, May 11, 1863, UIA; George M. Lucas Diary, May 11, 1863, ALPL; Frederick Steele to Colonel, May 11, 1863, RG 393, E 4720, NARA; John A. McClernand to U. S. Grant, May 11, 1863, RG 393, E 4720, NARA.

36. *OR*, 24(3):295–296, 854; *OR*, 24(1):636; Frederick Steele to Colonel, May 11, 1863, RG 393, E 4720, NARA; John A. McClernand to U. S. Grant, May 11, 1863, RG 393, E 4720, NARA; Bearss and Hills, *Receding Tide*, 162; Simon and Marszalek, eds., *PUSG*, 8:199; Job H. Yaggy Diary, May 11, 1863, ALPL; Townsend, *Yankee Warhorse*, 99; Military *History and Reminiscences*, 312; Bering and Montgomery, *History of the*

Forty-Eighth Ohio Vet. Vol. Inf., 82; John W. Griffith Diary, May 11, 1863, OHS; Joseph Child Diary, May 11, 1863, UIA; George M. Lucas Diary, May 11, 1863, ALPL.

37. *OR*, 24(3):295–296, 854; *OR*, 24(1):636; Simon and Marszalek, eds., *PUSG*, 8:199; George M. Lucas Diary, May 11, 1863, ALPL; John W. Griffith Diary, May 11, 1863, OHS; Frederick Steele to Colonel, May 11, 1863, RG 393, E 4720, NARA; John A. McClernand to U. S. Grant, May 11, 1863, RG 393, E 4720, NARA.

38. *OR*, 24(1):701.

39. *OR*, 24(3):296; *OR*, 24(1):35.

40. *OR*, 24(3):295–296; General Orders No. 116, May 11, 1863, RG 393, E 3230, NARA.

41. *OR*, 24(3):292, 296.

42. *OR*, 24(3):297; Tamara A. Smith, "A Matter of Trust: Grant and James B. McPherson," in *Grant's Lieutenants: From Cairo to Vicksburg*, Steven E. Woodworth, ed. (Lawrence: University Press of Kansas, 2001), 157; Reuben H. Falconer Diary, May 11, 1863, OHS.

43. Green Raum Orders, May 11, 1863, William S. Hillyer Papers, UVA; N. W. Wood Diary, May 10, 1863, UCB; Simon and Marszalek, eds., *PUSG*, 8:201; James B. McPherson to U. S. Grant, May 11, 1863, RG 393, E 4720, NARA.

44. *OR*, 24(3):297.

45. *OR*, 24(3):284.

46. *OR*, 24(3):286; Chernow, *Grant*, 262; David Grier to Anna, May 14, 1863, Grier Family Papers, MHS; John Merrilees Diary, May 11, 1863, CHM; Henry J. Seaman Diary, May 10, 1863, CWTI, USAHEC.

47. *OR*, 24(3):296–297; *OR*, 24(1):36; *OR*, 24(2):279; George D. Carrington Diary, May 11, 1863, CHM; Henry J. Seaman Diary, May 5, 1863, CWTI, USAHEC; George Russell to friend, May 11, 1863, George W. Russell Papers, ALPL; John Merrilees Diary, May 3, 1863, CHM; Curtis P. Lacey Diary, May 7 and 10, 1863, NL.

48. *OR*, 24(3):296–297; *OR*, 24(1):36; *OR*, 24(2):279.

49. *OR*, 24(3):, 245, 285, 296–297, 300; *OR*, 24(2):255, 276, 279, 297; Simon and Marszalek, *PUSG*, 8:184; George D. Carrington Diary, May 12–13, 1863, CHM; Judson Bingham to William Hillyer, May 10, 1863, William S. Hillyer Papers, UVA; Robert J. Van Dorn and Daniel A. Masters, eds., *The 57th Ohio Veteran Volunteer Infantry* (Perrysburg, OH: Columbian Arsenal Press, 2021), 158; J. Grecian, *History of the Eighty-third Regiment, Indiana Volunteer Infantry. For Three Years With Sherman* (Cincinnati: John F. Uhlhorn, Printer, 1865), 30; Special Orders No. 129, May 9, 1863, Ulysses S. Grant Collection, Unpublished Correspondence, USGPL; Special Orders No. 80, May 9, 1863, RG 393, E 6254, NARA; Special Orders No. 8, April 25, 1863, RG 393, E 5924, NARA; Special Orders No. 29, May 7, 1863, RG 393, E 5925, NARA.

50. *OR*, 24(3):, 245, 285, 296–297, 300; *OR*, 24(2):255, 276, 279, 297; Simon and Marszalek, *PUSG*, 8:184; George D. Carrington Diary, May 12–13, 1863, CHM; Judson Bingham to William Hillyer, May 10, 1863, William S. Hillyer Papers, UVA; Van Dorn and Masters, eds., *The 57th Ohio Veteran Volunteer Infantry*, 158; Grecian, *History of the Eighty-third Regiment, Indiana Volunteer Infantry*, 30; Special Orders No. 129, May 9, 1863, Ulysses S. Grant Collection, Unpublished Correspondence, USGPL; Special Orders No. 80, May 9, 1863, RG 393, E 6254, NARA; Special Orders No. 8, April 25,

1863, RG 393, E 5924, NARA; Special Orders No. 29, May 7, 1863, RG 393, E 5925, NARA.

51. *SOR*, 2, 20:521; John N. Bell Diary, May 10–11, 1863, OHS; James Howell to parents, May 8, 1863, White Family Papers, UIA; Calvin Ainsworth Diary, May 11, 1863, UMB, copy in VICK.

52. *OR*, 24(3):296–297, 300; *OR*, 24(2):255, 276, 279; M. A. DeWolfe Howe, ed., *Home Letters of General Sherman* (New York: Charles Scribner's Sons, 1909), 260, originals in William T. Sherman Papers, LC; George D. Carrington Diary, May 12–13, 1863, CHM; Van Dorn and Masters, eds., *The 57th Ohio Veteran Volunteer Infantry*, 158; Delos Van Deusen to Hennie, May 10, 1863, Delos Van Deusen Correspondence, HL.

53. W. L. Duff to Thomas Mather, May 9, 1863, Ulysses S. Grant Collection, Unpublished Correspondence, USGPL.

CHAPTER 10. "THE FIGHT FOR RAYMOND WAS TO TAKE PLACE AT THIS POINT"

1. John W. Griffith Diary, May 13, 1863, OHS; Henry J. Seaman Diary, May 12, 1863, CWTI, USAHEC; Rowland, *Mississippi*, 1:869; Rowland, *Mississippi*, 2:519.

2. Kennedy, *Population of the United States in 1860*, 271; Rowland, *Mississippi*, 2:519; Hills, "Roads to Raymond," 82; Bearss, *The Vicksburg Campaign*, 2:484; Bearss and Hills, *Receding Tide*, 164; Winschel, *Triumph and Defeat: The Vicksburg Campaign, Volume 2*, 21–22; Estelle T. Oltrogge, "Raymond, Miss., in War Times," *Confederate Veteran* 19, no. 8 (August 1911): 370–371; Oldroyd, *A Soldier's Story*, 18; Wilson, "A Staff Officer's Journal," 97; George Remley to Howard, May 25, 1863, Remley Family Papers, NC; Charles E. Affeld Diary, May 15, 1863, VICK; Isaac Vanderwarker Diary, May 13, 1863, CWD, USAHEC.

3. Oldroyd, *A Soldier's Story*, 18; Oltrogge, "Raymond, Miss., in War Times," 370–371; Wilson, "A Staff Officer's Journal," 97; George Remley to Howard, May 25, 1863, Remley Family Papers, NC; Charles E. Affeld Diary, May 15, 1863, VICK; Isaac Vanderwarker Diary, May 13, 1863, CWD, USAHEC.

4. Hills, "Roads to Raymond," 82; Oldroyd, *A Soldier's Story*, 18; Bearss, *The Vicksburg Campaign*, 2:484; Bearss and Hills, *Receding Tide*, 164; Winschel, *Triumph and Defeat: The Vicksburg Campaign, Volume 2*, 21–22; Oltrogge, "Raymond, Miss., in War Times," 370–371; Wilson, "A Staff Officer's Journal," 97; George Remley to Howard, May 25, 1863, Remley Family Papers, NC; Charles E. Affeld Diary, May 15, 1863, VICK; Isaac Vanderwarker Diary, May 13, 1863, CWD, USAHEC.

5. *OR*, 24(1):708, 736; Rowland, *Mississippi*, 2:519; Calvin Ainsworth Diary, May 15, 1863, UMB; George Remley to Howard, May 25, 1863, Remley Family Papers, NC; Wilson, "A Staff Officer's Journal," 100; Maynard, ed., "Vicksburg Diary," 46; Luther Cowan Diary, May 12, 1863, Luther H. Cowan Papers, TSLA.

6. John N. Bell Diary, May 12, 1863, OHS.

7. *OR*, 24(3):296–297, 300; *OR*, 24(2):255, 276, 279; Winschel, *Triumph and Defeat: The Vicksburg Campaign, Volume 2*, 33; Parrish, *Frank Blair*, 167; George D. Carrington

Diary, May 12–13, 1863, CHM; Van Dorn and Masters, eds., *The 57th Ohio Veteran Volunteer Infantry*, 158; *History of the 37th Regiment, O.V.V.I., Furnished by Comrades at the Ninth Reunion Held at St. Mary's, Ohio, Tuesday and Wednesday, September 10 and 11, 1889* (Toledo, OH: Montgomery and Vrooman, 1890), 20; Charles E. Affeld Diary, May 12, 1863, VICK; John N. Bell Diary, May 12–13, 1863, OHS; George M. Rogers Diary, May 12, 1863, ISL; Special Orders No. 122, May 2, 1863, Ulysses S. Grant Collection, Unpublished Correspondence, USGPL.

8. *OR*, 24(3):293, 299; *OR*, 24(2):40–41; *OR*, 24(1):146–147; Bearss, *The Vicksburg Campaign*, 2:472; Grabau, *Ninety-Eight Days*, 215; Bearss and Hills, *Receding Tide*, 166; William Rigby to brother, May 15, 1863, Rigby Family Papers, UIA; James Slack to wife, May 12, 1863, James R. Slack Letters, ISL; Augustus G. Sinks Memoir, undated, ISL, 35; Alexander Ewing to parents, May 18, 1863, Alexander K. Ewing Papers, ALPL; W. R. Eddington Memoir, undated, ALPL, 8; William T. Rigby Diary, May 12, 1863, UIA; Hovey Manuscript, undated, Alvin Hovey Papers, IU, 55; Peter Hains to General, May 12, 1863, John A. McClernand Papers, ALPL; William F. Hollingsworth Diary, May 12, 1863, OCM; Peter Osterhaus to Colonel, May 11, 1863, RG 393, E 3221, NARA; Walter Scates to Peter Osterhaus, May 12, 1863, RG 393, E 5545, NARA.

9. *OR*, 24(3):300–301, 860; *OR*, 24(2):250; *OR*, 24(1):753; Winschel, *Triumph and Defeat: The Vicksburg Campaign, Volume 2*, 25; Henry J. Seaman Diary, May 12, 1863, CWTI, USAHEC; Paul Dorweiler Diary, May 12, 1863, CWTI, USAHEC; James F. Mallinckrodt Diary, May 12, 1863, OCM; Timothy C. Young Diary, May 12, 1863, VICK; Charles Miller Memoirs, undated, VICK, 43; Uley Burk to family, June 8, 1863, 30th Iowa File, VICK; Simon and Marszalek, eds., *PUSG*, 8:188; Unknown 13th Illinois Diary, May 12, 1863, GC; N. W. Wood Diary, May 12, 1863, UCB.

10. Cadwallader, *Three Years with Grant*, 68; Ephraim Shay Diary, May 12, 1863, UMB.

11. *Military History and Reminiscences*, 313.

12. *OR*, 24(3):300–301; Henry J. Seaman Diary, May 12, 1863, CWTI, USAHEC.

13. *OR*, 24(3):859, 863; *OR*, 24(1):260; John Pemberton to Jefferson Davis, May 12, 1863, RG 109, E 97, NARA.

14. *OR*, 24(3):859.

15. *OR*, 24(2):118; *OR*, 24(3):861; Wilson, "A Staff Officer's Journal," 104; John T. Appler Diary, May 12, 1863, MHS; William L. Roberts Diary, May 12, 1863, ADAH.

16. *OR*, 24(2):115, 124–125; *OR*, 24(3):860–866; *OR*, 24(1):261; Theodore D. Fisher Diary, May 12, 1863, Civil War Collection, MHS, copy in VICK.

17. *OR*, 24(3):859.

18. *OR*, 24(3):859–861; Johnston, "Jefferson Davis and the Mississippi Campaign," 478.

19. *OR*, 24(3):864.

20. Bearss, *The Vicksburg Campaign*, 2:482.

21. *OR*, 24(1):714; Henry O. Dwight, "A Soldier's Story," New York *Daily Tribune*, November 21, 1886; Oldroyd, *A Soldier's Story*, 15; "The Battle of Raymond," *National Tribune*, October 12, 1905; Thomas H. Barton, *Autobiography of Dr. Thomas H. Barton, The Self-made Physician of Syracuse, Ohio* (Charleston: West Virginia Printing Co.,

1890), 117; Joseph C. Gordon Diary, May 12, 1863, OCM; Thomas N. McLuer Diary, May 12, 1863, OCM; Henry O. Dwight, "A Soldier's Story," 1886, CWD, USAHEC; John W. Griffith Diary, May 12, 1863, OHS.

22. *OR*, 24(1):637, 735; Smith, "A Matter of Trust: Grant and James B. McPherson," 157.

23. *OR*, 24(1):637, 645, 714, 716; Henry O. Dwight, "A Soldier's Story," New York *Daily Tribune*, November 21, 1886; Oldroyd, *A Soldier's Story*, 16; D. W. Wood, *History of the 20th O. V. V. I. Regiment, and Proceedings of the First Reunion at Mt. Vernon, Ohio, April 6, 1876* (Columbus, OH: Paul and Thrall, Book and Job Printers, 1876), 21; Force, "Personal Recollections of the Vicksburg Campaign," 299; John W. Griffith Diary, May 12, 1863, OHS.

24. Bearss, *The Vicksburg Campaign*, 2:495; Smith, "A Matter of Trust: Grant and James B. McPherson," 157; Francis R. Baker Diary, May 12, 1863, ALPL.

25. *OR*, 24(1):637, 645–646, 716, 721; Bertera, *A Soldier at Dawn*, 59; John W. Griffith Diary, May 12, 1863, OHS.

26. *OR*, 24(1):637, 645, 708, 714; William Clemans Memoir, undated, UIL, 8; John Sheriff Diary, May 12, 1863, John Sheriff Family Papers, ALPL.

27. *OR*, 24(1):637, 645, 708, 711, 714; Force, "Personal Recollections of the Vicksburg Campaign," 299.

28. *OR*, 24(1):737; *OR*, 24(3):862; John Gregg to John Pemberton, May 12, 1863, RG 109, E 97, NARA.

29. *OR*, 24(1):737, 747; Dan Donnell, "After the Battle of Raymond, Miss.," *Confederate Veteran* 20, no. 2 (February 1912): 87–88.

30. *OR*, 24(1):737, 739, 741, 743, 746; Bearss, *The Vicksburg Campaign*, 2:494; Bearss and Hills, *Receding Tide*, 177; Mamie Yeary, *Reminiscences of the Boys in Gray, 1861–1865* (Dallas: Wilkinson Printing Company, 1912), 329.

31. *OR*, 24(1):737, 743, 746; Flavel C. Barber Diary, May 12, 1863, IU, later published as Robert H. Ferrell, ed., *Holding The Line: The Third Tennessee Regiment, 1861–1864* (Kent, OH: Kent State University Press, 1994); Bertera, *A Soldier at Dawn*, 59; Drake, ed., *The Annals of the Army of Tennessee*, 167; H. K. Nelson, "Battles of Raymond and Jackson," *Confederate Veteran* 12, no. 1 (January 1904): 12.

32. *OR*, 24(1):737, 743–744; Noe, *Through the Howling Storm*, 303; Force, "Personal Recollections of the Vicksburg Campaign," 299.

33. *OR*, 24(1):738, 747; Morris, *History*, 60–61; Yeary, *Reminiscences of the Boys in Gray, 1861–1865*, 329; Flavel C. Barber Diary, May 12, 1863, IU.

34. *OR*, 24(1):708, 747; Luther Cowan Diary, May 12, 1863, Luther H. Cowan Papers, TSLA.

35. *OR*, 24(1):708, 712, 747; William Clemans Memoir, undated, UIL, 8.

36. Henry O. Dwight, "A Soldier's Story," New York *Daily Tribune*, November 21, 1886; Force, "Personal Recollections of the Vicksburg Campaign," 299; Wood, *History of the 20th O. V. V. I. Regiment*, 21.

37. *OR*, 24(1):740.

38. *OR*, 24(1):637, 646, 708; Cyrus Randall to mother, May 25, 1863, Cyrus W.

Randall Papers, ALPL; Howard, *History of the 124th Regiment Illinois Infantry Volunteers*, 87–90; William H. Kinkade Diary, May 12, 1863, ALPL; Force, "Personal Recollections of the Vicksburg Campaign," 299; Job H. Yaggy Diary, May 12, 1863, ALPL; Luther Cowan Diary, May 12, 1863, Luther H. Cowan Papers, TSLA; Gould D. Molineaux Diary, May 12, 1863, AC; George W. Modil Diary, May 12, 1863, MDAH; George Durfee to uncle, May 21, 1863, George S. Durfee Papers, UIL.

39. *OR*, 24(1):646, 708, 740, 747; Ira A. Payne Diary, May 12, 1863, ALPL; Flavel C. Barber Diary, May 12, 1863, IU.

40. *OR*, 24(1):708.

41. *OR*, 24(1):637, 646, 708; Gould D. Molineaux Diary, May 12, 1863, AC; George W. Modil Diary, May 12, 1863, MDAH; Cyrus Randall to mother, May 25, 1863, Cyrus W. Randall Papers, ALPL; George Durfee to uncle, May 21, 1863, George S. Durfee Papers, UIL; Howard, *History of the 124th Regiment Illinois Infantry Volunteers*, 87–90; William H. Kinkade Diary, May 12, 1863, ALPL; Force, "Personal Recollections of the Vicksburg Campaign," 299; Job H. Yaggy Diary, May 12, 1863, ALPL; Luther Cowan Diary, May 12, 1863, Luther H. Cowan Papers, TSLA.

42. *OR*, 24(1):738, 741, 744.

43. *OR*, 24(1):744.

44. *OR*, 24(1):738, 744.

45. *OR*, 24(1):738, 743; Drake, ed., *The Annals of the Army of Tennessee*, 168.

46. *OR*, 24(1):738, 741.

47. *OR*, 24(1):738; Drake, ed., *The Annals of the Army of Tennessee*, 168.

48. Winschel, "Fighting Politician: John A. McClernand," 139; Simon and Marszalek, eds., *PUSG*, 8:206; Wilson, *Under the Old Flag*, 1:199; Elizabeth J. Whaley, *Forgotten Hero: General James B. McPherson* (New York: Exposition Press, 1955), 129; William Clemans Memoir, undated, UIL, 8; Charles E. Affeld Diary, May 15, 1863, VICK; Timothy C. Young Diary, May 13, 1863, VICK; Edward Stanfield to father, May 26, 1863, Edward P. Stanfield Letters, IHS.

49. *OR*, 24(1):716; William H. Kinkade Diary, May 12, 1863, ALPL; Edmund Newsome Diary, May 12, 1863, MDAH, copy in OCM; Luther Cowan Diary, May 12, 1863, Luther H. Cowan Papers, TSLA; George Durfee to uncle, May 21, 1863, George S. Durfee Papers, UIL; John W. Griffith Diary, May 12, 1863, OHS.

50. *OR*, 24(1):646, 706, 723–724, 728, 772; *OR*, 24(1):65; Bertera, *A Soldier at Dawn*, 59; John F. Lester Diary, May 12, 1863, IHS; James A. Woodson Diary, May 3, 1863, ALPL; Edward Wood to wife, May 25, 1863, Edward J. Wood Papers, IHS.

51. *OR*, 24(1):646, 712; Bearss and Hills, *Receding Tide*, 178.

52. *OR*, 24(1):715.

53. *OR*, 24(1):646, 708, 738; James Pickett Jones, *Black Jack: John A. Logan and Southern Illinois in the Civil War Era* (Carbondale: Southern Illinois University Press, 1967), 162; Oldroyd, *A Soldier's Story*, 17; Trowbridge, *Autobiography*, 128; Force, "Personal Recollections of the Vicksburg Campaign," 299; George W. Modil Diary, May 12, 1863, MDAH; Gould D. Molineaux Diary, May 12, 1863, AC.

54. *OR*, 24(1):712, 714–717, 721; George W. Modil Diary, May 12, 1863, MDAH; Edmund Newsome Diary, May 12, 1863, MDAH.

55. *OR*, 24(1):740, 748; Flavel C. Barber Diary, May 12, 1863, IU.

56. *OR*, 24(1):646, 708, 738, 741, 743–746, 748; Drake, ed., *The Annals of the Army of Tennessee*, 168; John W. Griffith Diary, May 12, 1863, OHS.

57. *OR*, 24(1):716–717, 741, 745; John W. Griffith Diary, May 12, 1863, OHS.

58. *OR*, 24(1):134, 716–717, 741–742, 745, 775, 779, 782; *OR*, 24(1):205; Bearss and Hills, *Receding Tide*, 177; John W. Griffith Diary, May 12, 1863, OHS; Edmund Newsome Diary, May 12, 1863, MDAH.

59. *OR*, 24(1):721, 728, 738, 746; *OR*, 24(1):61; Bearss, *The Vicksburg Campaign*, 2:501; Isaac Vanderwarker Diary, May 12, 1863, CWD, USAHEC.

60. *OR*, 24(1):738.

61. *OR*, 24(1):738, 740, 742; C. J. Orr Memoir, undated, TSLA, 1.

62. *OR*, 24(1):637, 705–706, 708, 738–739; *OR*, 24(1):205; Flavel C. Barber Diary, May 12, 1863, IU.

63. *OR*, 24(1):723, 739; *OR*, 24(3):862, 864; L. J. Sanders Diary, May 12, 1863, WKU; William Rigby to brother, May 15, 1863, Rigby Family Papers, UIA; Isaac Vanderwarker Diary, May 13, 1863, CWD, USAHEC; Elijah Gates to John Pemberton, May 12, 1863, RG 109, E 97, NARA; John Gregg to John Pemberton, May 12, 1863, RG 109, E 97, NARA.

64. *OR*, 24(1):637, 646, 729, 735, 745; Force, "Personal Recollections of the Vicksburg Campaign," 300; Edmund Newsome Diary, May 12, 1863, MDAH; Joel Strong Reminiscences, 1910, MHS, 11, copy in OCM; Jenkin L. Jones Diary, May 12, 1863, UCH.

65. *OR*, 24(1):715; Donnell, "After the Battle of Raymond, Miss.," 87–88; Luther Cowan Diary, May 12, 1863, Luther H. Cowan Papers, TSLA; Letitia Dabney Miller Recollections, 1926, UM, 11.

66. *OR*, 24(1):704–705; James McPherson to General, May 12, 1863, RG 393, E 6294, NARA.

67. *OR*, 24(3):299–300; Hass, ed., "The Vicksburg Diary of Henry Clay Warmoth," 69; Wilson, *Under the Old Flag*, 1:198–199.

68. *OR*, 24(3):300; *OR*, 24(1):50; Kenneth P. Williams, *Grant Rises in the West: From Iuka to Vicksburg, 1862–1863* (Lincoln: University of Nebraska Press, 1997), 370; Kiper, *Major General John A. McClernand*, 239.

69. Young, *Around the World with General Grant*, 2:619; Ottens, *General John A. Rawlins*, 275–276; James Lee McDonough, *William Tecumseh Sherman: In the Service of My Country: A Life* (New York: Norton, 2016), 408.

CHAPTER 11. "THERE HAS BEEN A SLIGHT CHANGE OF PLAN
SINCE YESTERDAY"

1. Arthur J. L. Fremantle, *Three Months in the Southern States: April–June, 1863* (Edinburgh: W. Blackwood and Sons, 1863), 127; Wynne, *Mississippi's Civil War*, 90–91; John K. Bettersworth, *Confederate Mississippi: The People and Policies of a Cotton State in Wartime* (Baton Rouge: Louisiana State University Press, 1943), 142; Bettersworth,

ed., *Mississippi in the Confederacy*, 263; Luther S. Baechtel Diary, May 7, 1863, MDAH. For more on railroad accidents, see Bettersworth, ed., *Mississippi in the Confederacy*, 261–263; John Bannon Diary, May 12, 1863, USC.

2. N. G. Bryson to A. J. McConnico, April 10, 1861, Southern Railroad Company Papers, USM. For railroad script, see "Southern Railroad Company 25 Cents," 1861, Baker Library, HU.

3. "The Legislature," Mississippi *Free Trader*, January 22, 1861; "Damage to the Southern Road," Vicksburg *Evening Citizen*, January 17, 1861; Smith, *Mississippi in the Civil War*, 36. For more on the Southern Railroad and it rebuilding after the war, see Southern Railroad Records, AU.

4. Davis, Perry, and Kirkley, *Atlas to Accompany the Official Records of the Union and Confederate Armies*, Plate 155.

5. Smith, *The Real Horse Soldiers*, 299.

6. *OR*, 24(1):266.

7. *OR*, 24(1):50.

8. Wilson, "A Staff Officer's Journal," 404; Joseph Lesslie to wife, May 13, 1863, Joseph Lesslie Letters, VICK; Maynard, ed., "Vicksburg Diary," 46; Williamson Murray Diary, May 13, 1863, VICK.

9. *OR*, 24(3):300.

10. *OR*, 24(1):146–147.

11. *OR*, 24(3):301; *OR*, 24(1):735; J. P. Lesslie to wife, May 13, 1863, 4th Indiana Cavalry File, VNMPR.

12. *OR*, 24(1):50, 638, 717; *OR*, 24(2):65; John Merrilees Diary, May 16, 1863, CHM; Pryce, *Vanishing Footprints*, 102; Lyman M. Baker Memoir, undated, ALPL, 8; John T. Buegel Diary, May 13, 1863, SHSMC, 28, published as William G. Bek, ed., "The Civil War Diary of John T. Buegel, Union Soldier," *Missouri Historical Review* 40, no. 4 (July 1946): 503–530; Edward Wood to wife, May 25, 1863, Edward J. Wood Papers, IHS; Luther Cowan Diary, May 13, 1863, Luther H. Cowan Papers, TSLA.

13. *OR*, 24(1):50, 638, 717; *OR*, 24(2):65; John Merrilees Diary, May 16, 1863, CHM; Pryce, *Vanishing Footprints*, 102; Luther Cowan Diary, May 13, 1863, Luther H. Cowan Papers, TSLA; Lyman M. Baker Memoir, undated, ALPL, 8; John T. Buegel Diary, May 13, 1863, SHSMC, 28; Edward Wood to wife, May 25, 1863, Edward J. Wood Papers, IHS.

14. *OR*, 24(3):300–301; *OR*, 24(1):638, 753; Allen C. Ashcraft, ed., "Mrs. Russell and the Battle of Raymond, Mississippi," *Journal of Mississippi History* 25, no. 1 (January 1963): 38–40; *Military History and Reminiscences*, 314; George M. Lucas Diary, May 13, 1863, ALPL.

15. *OR*, 24(3):300.

16. *OR*, 24(3):301, 307; John A. McClernand to U. S. Grant, undated, RG 393, E 4720, NARA.

17. *OR*, 24(3):306; Reuben H. Falconer Diary, May 13, 1863, OHS; William T. Rigby Diary, May 13, 1863, UIA.

18. *OR*, 24(3):306–307; Simon and Marszalek, eds., *PUSG*, 8:214.

19. *OR*, 24(3):306–307.

20. John N. Bell Diary, May 13, 1863, OHS; Bjorn Skaptason, "The Chicago Light Artillery at Vicksburg," *Journal of the Illinois State Historical Society* 106, no. 3–4 (Fall/Winter 2013): 439; Henry R. Brinkerhoff, *History of the Thirtieth Regiment Ohio Volunteer Infantry, From Its Organization, To the Fall of Vicksburg, Miss.* (Columbus, OH: James W. Osgood, Printer, 1863), 66–67; George M. Rogers Diary, May 13, 1863, ISL; John J. Kellogg Memoirs, undated, VICK, 23; James P. Boyd Diary, May 13, 1863, ALPL; Calvin Ainsworth Diary, May 13, 1863, UMB.

21. *OR*, 24(2):297; *SOR*, 2, 13:637; Bearss and Hills, *Receding Tide*, 182; Shea and Winschel, *Vicksburg Is the Key*, 119; Wilson, "A Staff Officer's Journal," 106; Clark, ed., *Downing's Civil War Diary*, 112–115; Robert Ridge Diary, May 13, 1863, ALPL; Anson Hemingway Diary, May 13, 1863, VICK; Wales W. Wood, *A History of the Ninety-fifth Regiment Illinois Infantry Volunteers, From its Organization in the Fall of 1862, Until Its Final Discharge from the United States Service, in 1865* (Chicago: Tribune Company's Book and Job Printing Office, 1865), 73; William Christie to brother, May 26, 1863, James C. Christie and Family Papers, MNHS; Joseph Stockton Diary, May 13, 1863, ALPL, copy in VICK and Coco Collection, HCWRT, USAHEC.

22. Letitia Dabney Miller Recollections, 1926, UM, 10; Joseph Stockton Diary, May 13, 1863, ALPL; Lan to parents, May 14, 1863, Thomas Marshall Letters, IHS; William J. Pittenger Diary, May 13–17, 1863, VT.

23. *OR*, 24(3):305; *OR*, 24(1):147; *OR*, 24(2):41; Alexander Ewing to parents, May 18, 1863, Alexander K. Ewing Papers, ALPL; Hovey Manuscript, undated, Alvin Hovey Papers, IU, 56; William L. Rand Diary, May 13, 1863, Rand Family Papers, ALPL; Hass, ed., "The Vicksburg Diary of Henry Clay Warmoth," 69; Gilbert Gulbrandsen to family, May 11, 1863, Gilbert Gulbrandsen Papers, HCWRTC, USAHEC; James Slack to wife, May 12, 1863, James R. Slack Letters, ISL.

24. *OR*, 24(3):305; *OR*, 24(1):147, 595; Ernest A. Warden Diary, May 13, 1863, OHS; James C. Sinclair Diary, May 13, 1863, CHM; Hass, ed., "The Vicksburg Diary of Henry Clay Warmoth," 69; Albert C. Boals Diary, May 13, 1863, ALPL; Simon and Marszalek, eds., *PUSG*, 8:209; John A. McClernand to U. S. Grant, May 12, 1863, RG 393, E 4720, NARA; John A. McClernand to U. S. Grant, May 13, 1863, RG 393, E 4720, NARA; Francis R. Baker Diary, May 13, 1863, ALPL; William Rigby to brother, May 15, 1863, Rigby Family Papers, UIA; John Merrilees Diary, May 13, 1863, CHM; Peter Osterhaus to John McClernand, May 13, 1863, RG 393, E 3221, NARA.

25. *OR*, 24(3):305; *OR*, 24(1):147.

26. *OR*, 24(3):870.

27. *OR*, 24(3):870, 873; Symonds, *Joseph E. Johnston*, 209–210; Stephen D. Lee, "The Campaign of Vicksburg, Mississippi, in 1863—From April 15 to and Including the Battle of Champion Hills, or Baker's Creek, May 16, 1863," in *Publications of the Mississippi Historical Society*, 13 vols. (Oxford: Mississippi Historical Society, 1900), 3:31.

28. *OR*, 24(3):873.

29. *OR*, 24(3):871; Charles Swift Northern, III, ed., *All Right Let Them Come: The Civil War Diary of an East Tennessee Confederate* (Knoxville: University of Tennessee Press, 2003), 93; John T. Appler Diary, May 13, 1863, MHS; Samuel W. Ferguson Memoir, undated, LSU, 35, copy in VICK.

30. *OR*, 24(3):871–872, 874, 877; *OR*, 24(1):261; Chambers, "My Journal," 266; Samuel Fowler Diary, May 12, 1863, SU, 173; John A. Leavy Diary, May 15, 1863, VICK, copy in OCM.

31. *OR*, 24(3):872; William L. Roberts Diary, May 13, 1863, ADAH; S. M. Thornton to his wife, May 15, 1863, Gardner Collection, MSU.

32. *OR*, 24(3):873–874; *OR*, 24(2):74; William A. Ruyle, May 12, 1863, HCWRTC, USAHEC; Theodore D. Fisher Diary, May 13, 1863, Civil War Collection, MHS; Samuel Fowler Diary, May 12, 1863, SU, 173; M. D .L. Stephens Memoir, undated, MDAH, 17.

33. *OR*, 24(2):116, 125; *OR*, 24(3):875; Samuel Fowler Diary, May 12, 1863, SU, 173; H. N. Faulkinbury Diary, May 13, 1863, MDAH.

34. *OR*, 24(3):873.

35. *OR*, 24(3):874–875; Bearss, *The Vicksburg Campaign*, 2:561.

36. *OR*, 24(3):864, 869, 871; Winschel, *Triumph and Defeat: The Vicksburg Campaign, Volume 2*, 121.

37. *OR*, 24(3):875.

38. *OR*, 24(3):870; John R. Lundberg, "'I Am Too Late': Joseph E. Johnston and the Vicksburg Campaign," in Steven E. Woodworth and Charles D. Grear, eds., *The Vicksburg Campaign: March 29–May 18, 1863* (Carbondale: Southern Illinois University Press, 2013), 122; Joseph Johnston to John Pemberton, May 14, 1863, RG 109, E 97, NARA.

39. *OR*, 24(1):215; Johnston, "Jefferson Davis and the Mississippi Campaign," 478–479; Steven E. Woodworth, "The First Capture and Occupation of Jackson, Mississippi," in Steven E. Woodworth and Charles D. Grear, eds., *The Vicksburg Campaign: March 29–May 18, 1863* (Carbondale: Southern Illinois University Press, 2013), 100; Richard M. McMurry, *The Civil Wars of General Joseph E. Johnston, Confederate States Army: Volume 1: Virginia and Mississippi, 1861–1863* (El Dorado Hills, CA: Savas Beatie, 2023), 239–240.

40. *OR*, 24(2):58; *OR*, 24(3):308; Robert S. Martin Diary, May 13, 1863, SIU.

41. *OR*, 24(3):307–308; Bearss and Hills, *Receding Tide*, 182; Yeary, *Reminiscences of the Boys in Gray, 1861–1865*, 331.

42. Carlos Forbes to Mary, June 6, 1863, Carlos Forbes Papers, OHS; Simon and Marszalek, eds., *PUSG*, 8:212; W. T. Sherman to U. S. Grant, May 13, 1863, RG 393, E 4720, NARA.

43. *OR*, 24(3):305, 307–308, 312.

44. *OR*, 24(3):305–306; Winschel, "Fighting Politician: John A. McClernand," 139; Marszalek, Nolen, and Gallo, eds., *The Personal Memoirs of Ulysses S. Grant*, 350; General Orders No. 117, May 13, 1863, RG 393, E 3230, NARA.

45. *OR*, 24(3):308.

CHAPTER 12. "COLORS PLANTED ON THE CAPITOL OF JACKSON"

1. John Merrilees Diary, May 14, 1863, CHM; Richardson, *The Secret Service*, 79; Joel Strong Reminiscences, 1910, MHS, 11; Unidentified Soldier of the 31st Iowa Infantry Diary, May 14, 1863, MHS.

2. Kennedy, *Population of the United States in 1860*, 271.

3. J. Z. George to Bettie, January 19, 1855 and January 1 and 10 and February 1, 1856, and January 2, 1858, James Z. George Papers, MDAH; Rowland, *Mississippi*, 1: 353–356, 950; Isaac O. Shelby Diary, May 16, 1863, UNC.

4. Rowland, *Mississippi*, 1: 353–356; "The Pro-Slavery Rebellion," March 30, 1861, Secession Subject File, MDAH.

5. *Journal of the Senate of the State of Mississippi: Called Session* (Jackson: E. Barksdale, State Printer, 1860), 11; *Journal of the House of Representatives of the State of Mississippi: December Session of 1862, and November Session of 1863*, 5, 26, 39; Lynda Laswell Crist, et al., eds., *The Papers of Jefferson Davis, 14 vols. (Baton Rouge: Louisiana State University Press, 1971–2015)*, 8:565–84; *OR*, 24(1):36.

6. *OR*, 24(1):36; Marszalek, Nolen, and Gallo, eds., *The Personal Memoirs of Ulysses S. Grant*, 350; Maynard, ed., "Vicksburg Diary," 46.

7. *OR*, 24(1):221; Simon and Marszalek, eds., *PUSG*, 8:214; Dempsey Ashford Diary, May 14, 1863, VICK; L. J. Sanders Diary, May 14, 1863, WKU; Joseph Johnston to Samuel Cooper, November 1, 1863, Louis T. Wigfall Papers, LC.

8. *OR*, 24(2):125; *OR*, 24(3):877, 879; *OR*, 24(1):261, 269; Johnston, "Jefferson Davis and the Mississippi Campaign," 479; John C. Taylor Diary, May 13, 1863, Taylor Family Papers, UVA.

9. *OR*, 24(2):74, 125; *OR*, 24(1):261; Ballard, *Pemberton*, 155–156; Steven E. Woodworth, *Jefferson Davis and His Generals: The Failure of Confederate Command in the West* (Lawrence: University Press of Kansas, 1990), 206; John C. Taylor Diary, May 13, 1863, Taylor Family Papers, UVA; Alfred Cumming to Stephen Lee, November 3, 1899, Letters and Papers Covering Organizations: Miscellaneous—Georgia, Massachusetts, New Hampshire, and Rhode Island, MDAH; Winfield Featherston Report, November 10, 1867, Winfield S. Featherston Collection, UM.

10. *OR*, 24(2):125; *OR*, 24(3):876; *OR*, 24(1):217, 261–262, 328; Lockett, "The Defense of Vicksburg," 487; William Loring to John Pemberton, May 14 and 15, 1863, RG 109, E 97, NARA; Carter Stevenson to John Pemberton, May 17, 1863, RG 109, E 97, NARA; John Pemberton to Joseph Johnston, May 14, 1863, RG 109, Chapter II, Volume 60, NARA.

11. *OR*, 24(3):878–881, 885; William Drennan to wife, May 30, 1863, William Drennan Papers, MDAH.

12. *OR*, 24(1):785; *OR*, 24(3):877–878, 881, 883; McMurry, *The Civil Wars of General Joseph E. Johnston*, 241–243.

13. Terrence J. Winschel, "The Absence of Will: Joseph E. Johnston and the Fall of Vicksburg," in *Confederate Generals in the Western Theater: Essays on America's Civil War*, 4 vols. Lawrence Lee Hewitt and Arthur W. Bergeron Jr., eds. (Knoxville: University of Tennessee Press, 2010), 2:82; Ballard, *Pemberton*, 157.

14. *OR*, 24(1):785–787; Bearss and Hills, *Receding Tide*, 186; Russell K. Brown, *To the Manner Born: The Life of William H. T. Walker* (Athens: University of Georgia Press, 1994), 151.

15. *OR*, 24(1):786; Bearss, *The Vicksburg Campaign*, 2:527, 529; J. V. Greif, "The Battle of Raymond, Miss.," *Confederate Veteran* 12, no. 3 (March 1904): 112.

16. *OR*, 24(1):753.

17. *OR*, 24(1):753; *OR*, 24(3):309.

18. *OR*, 24(1):50, 147, 753; *OR*, 24(3):311; *OR*, 24(2):41; Hovey Manuscript, un-dated, Alvin Hovey Papers, IU, 56; Special Orders No. 460, May 14, 1863, RG 393, E 5545, NARA.

19. *OR*, 24(1):638, 721, 729, 735, 753, 759, 775, 777; James B. Logan Diary, May 14, 1863, ALPL; Mackowski, *The Battle of Jackson, Mississippi, May 14, 1863*, 66; Joel Strong Reminiscences, 1910, MHS, 11; Edward Stanfield to father, May 26, 1863, Ed-ward P. Stanfield Letters, IHS; Brown, *History of the Fourth Regiment of Minnesota Infantry*, 193; Edward Wood to wife, May 25, 1863, Edward J. Wood Papers, IHS; John Merrilees Diary, May 14, 1863, CHM.

20. *OR*, 24(1):638, 723; Oldroyd, *A Soldier's Story*, 20–21; John W. Griffith Diary, May 14, 1863, OHS; John Wickiser to Judge, May 24, 1863, John H. Wickiser Papers, ALPL; Howard, *History of the 124th Regiment Illinois Infantry Volunteers*, 92–94; San-born, "The Campaign Against Vicksburg," 130; Job H. Yaggy Diary, May 14, 1863, ALPL; Cyrus Randall to mother, May 25, 1863, Cyrus W. Randall Papers, ALPL; Gould D. Molineaux Diary, May 14, 1863, AC; George W. Modil Diary, May 14, 1863, MDAH; Edward Wood to wife, May 25, 1863, Edward J. Wood Papers, IHS.

21. *OR*, 24(1):638, 753, 759; John Merrilees Diary, May 14, 1863, CHM.

22. *OR*, 24(1):762, 765; Simon and Marszalek, eds., *PUSG*, 8:218; John Merrilees Diary, May 14, 1863, CHM; Edward H. Reynolds Diary, May 13–17, 1863, CWTI, USA-HEC; William M. Reid Diary, May 16, 1863, ALPL; Abiel M. Barker Diary, May 12–17, 1863, OCM; Mortimer Rice Diary, May 13–17, 1863, ALPL; Wilfred B. McDonald Di-ary, May 17, 1863, IHS; Unnamed Soldier's Diary, May 13–17, 1863, UMEM; Albert Chipman to unknown, May 16, 1863, Albert Chipman Papers, ALPL; Balzar Grebe Mem-oir, undated, ALPL, 18; Frederick Pell Diary, May 13–17, 1863, CWTI, USAHEC; An-thony Burton Diary, May 16–17, 1863, VICK; Charles S. Howell to father, May 5, 1863, Howell–Taylor Family Papers, USAHEC; George Thomas to Minerva, May 18, 1863, Thomas Family Correspondence, ND. See also the Van Bennett and H. H. Bennett diaries, May 13–17, 1863, WHS; Ulysses Grant to Cyrus Hall, May 16, 1863, Ulysses S. Grant Collection, Unpublished Correspondence, USGPL.

23. *OR*, 24(1):767–768; John Merrilees Diary, May 14, 1863, CHM.

24. *OR*, 24(1):753; Bearss and Hills, *Receding Tide*, 187; John Merrilees Diary, May 14, 1863, CHM.

25. *OR*, 24(1):753, 759, 762, 765; *OR*, 24(2):284; John Merrilees Diary, May 14, 1863, CHM; Lewis F. Phillips Memoir, 1911, CWTI, USAHEC, 33–34; Mackowski, *The Battle of Jackson*, 84; Stanley D. Buckles, *Not Afraid to Go Any Whare: A History of the 114th Regiment Illinois Volunteer Infantry* (Bend, OR: Maverick Publications, 2019), 37–38; Timothy C. Young Diary, May 14, 1863, VICK; Carlos Forbes to Mary, June 6, 1863, Carlos Forbes Papers, OHS; Leroy Crockett Report, June 9, 1863, Hugh Ewing Papers, OHS.

26. Simon and Marszalek, eds., *PUSG*, 8:217; Fred Grant Memoir, undated, USGPL, 20.

27. *OR*, 24(1):729, 735, 775, 782; *OR*, 24(2):61; Edward Stanfield to father, May

26, 1863, Edward P. Stanfield Letters, IHS; Joel Strong Reminiscences, 1910, MHS, 11; Edward Wood to wife, May 25, 1863, Edward J. Wood Papers, IHS.

28. *OR*, 24(1):638, 772, 775; Mackowski, *The Battle of Jackson*, 69; Trowbridge, *Autobiography*, 131; Edward Wood to wife, May 25, 1863, Edward J. Wood Papers, IHS.

29. *OR*, 24(1):638–639, 729, 779, 786; Sanborn, "The Campaign Against Vicksburg," 130.

30. *OR*, 24(1):777–778, 783; *OR*, 24(1):785; Mackowski, *The Battle of Jackson*, 73; Joel Strong Reminiscences, 1910, MHS, 11; William Strong Memoir, undated, William E. Strong Papers, ALPL, 133–135.

31. *OR*, 24(1):777–778, 783; *OR*, 24(1):785; Joel Strong Reminiscences, 1910, MHS, 11; Mackowski, *The Battle of Jackson*, 73; William Strong Memoir, undated, William E. Strong Papers, ALPL, 133–135.

32. *OR*, 24(1):729; Brown, *History of the Fourth Regiment of Minnesota Infantry*, 192–193; John F. Lester Diary, May 14, 1863, IHS; Isaac Vanderwarker Diary, May 14, 1863, CWD, USAHEC; Edward Wood to wife, May 25, 1863, Edward J. Wood Papers, IHS.

33. *OR*, 24(2):65; Aaron Dunbar and Harvey M. Trimble, *History of the Ninety-third Regiment Volunteer Infantry from Organization to Muster Out* (Chicago: The Blakely Printing Co., 1898), 25–26; Byers, *With Fire and Sword*, 69; Grimsley and Miller, eds., *The Union Must Stand*, 95; James S. McHenry Diary, May 14, 1863, ALPL; Ira A. Payne Diary, May 14, 1863, ALPL; Lyman M. Baker Memoir, undated, ALPL, 8.

34. *OR*, 24(1):639; Edward Wood to wife, May 25, 1863, Edward J. Wood Papers, IHS; Jenkin L. Jones Diary, May 14, 1863, UCH.

35. *OR*, 24(1):639, 646, 723, 778, 783; *OR*, 24(2):314–315; Wilbur F. Crummer, *With Grant at Fort Donelson, Shiloh and Vicksburg, and An Appreciation of General U.S. Grant* (Oak Park, IL: E. C. Crummer and Co., 1915), 100–101; Trowbridge, *Autobiography*, 133; Reed, *Campaigns and Battles of the Twelfth Regiment Iowa*, 118–119; John W. Griffith Diary, May 14, 1863, OHS; Gould D. Molineaux Diary, May 14, 1863, AC.

36. Edward Wood to wife, May 25, 1863, Edward J. Wood Papers, IHS; Joel Strong Reminiscences, 1910, MHS, 11; Edward Wood to wife, May 25, 1863, Edward J. Wood Papers, IHS.

37. *OR*, 24(1):769; Woodworth, "The First Capture and Occupation of Jackson, Mississippi," 102.

38. *OR*, 24(1):753, 759, 762, 765; *OR*, 24(2):284; John Merrilees Diary, May 14, 1863, CHM; Lewis F. Phillips Memoir, 1911, CWTI, USAHEC, 33–34; Mackowski, *The Battle of Jackson*, 84; Leroy Crockett Report, June 9, 1863, Hugh Ewing Papers, OHS; Buckles, *Not Afraid to Go Any Whare*, 37–38; Timothy C. Young Diary, May 14, 1863, VICK; Carlos Forbes to Mary, June 6, 1863, Carlos Forbes Papers, OHS.

39. *OR*, 24(1):753, 759, 762, 767; Bearss and Hills, *Receding Tide*, 191; Cloyd Bryner, *Bugle Echoes: The Story of the Illinois 47th* (Springfield, IL: Phillips Bros. Printers, 1905), 79; Carlos Forbes to Mary, June 6, 1863, Carlos Forbes Papers, OHS; John Merrilees Diary, May 14, 1863, CHM.

40. *OR*, 24(1):753–754, 767; Charles A. Willison, *Reminiscences of a Boy's Service*

with the 76th Ohio, In the Fifteenth Army Corps, Under General Sherman, During the Civil War, By That "Boy" at Three Score (Menasha, WI: The George Banta Publishing Company, 1908), 53; Flavius J. Thackara Diary, May 14, 1863, OHS; John Merrilees Diary, May 14, 1863, CHM; Henry J. Seaman Diary, May 14, 1863, CWTI, USAHEC.

41. *OR*, 24(1):766.

42. *OR*, 24(1):754; James A. Fowler and Miles M. Miller, *History of the Thirtieth Iowa Infantry Volunteers. Giving a Complete Record of the Movements of the Regiment from Its Organization Until Muster Out* (Mediapolis, IA: T. A. Merrill, Printer, 1908), 16–27; Uley Burk to family, June 8, 1863, 30th Iowa File, VICK; Charles Miller Memoirs, undated, VICK, 44. See also the hand drawn maps of the Jackson area in the Frederik Steele Papers, SU.

43. *OR*, 24(1):51, 753–754, 759, 762, 766; Flavius J. Thackara Diary, May 14, 1863, OHS; John Merrilees Diary, May 14, 1863, CHM.

44. *OR*, 24(1):754, 768, 770, 786; *OR*, 24(2):284–285; "Capture of Jackson," *National Tribune*, July 27, 1893; Timothy C. Young Diary, May 14, 1863, VICK; Flavius J. Thackara Diary, May 14, 1863, OHS; Henry J. Seaman Diary, May 14, 1863, CWTI, USAHEC.

45. *OR*, 24(1):754, 768, 770, 786; *OR*, 24(2):284–285; J. W. Greenman Diary, May 14, 1863, MDAH.

46. *OR*, 24(1):773, 786–787; Sergeant Dykes to Mr. Dykes, May 10, 1863, Dykes Family Letters, OHS; Luther Cowan Diary, May 14, 1863, Luther H. Cowan Papers, TSLA; Edward Stanfield to father, May 26, 1863, Edward P. Stanfield Letters, IHS; John N. Bell Diary, May 14, 1863, OHS; John W. Griffith Diary, May 15, 1863, OHS; Flavius J. Thackara Diary, May 17, 1863, OHS; Daniel Hughes Diary, May 10, 1863, IHS, copy in ISL; Joseph Young to wife, May 11, 1863, Joseph W. Young Letters, IHS.

47. *OR*, 24(1):773, 786–787; Drake, ed., *The Annals of the Army of Tennessee*, 169; Brown, *To the Manner Born*, 151.

48. Wilson, "A Staff Officer's Journal," 106; Nelson, "Battles of Raymond and Jackson," 12; Richard Burt to wife, May 23, 1863, Richard W. Burt Papers, SHSMC; Cadwallader, *Three Years with Grant*, 74; Fred Grant Memoir, undated, USGPL, 21–22; Edward Wood to wife, May 25, 1863, Edward J. Wood Papers, IHS.

49. *OR*, 24(1):639, 723–724, 730, 772; Mahan, *Memoirs*, 114; Crummer, *With Grant*, 101; W. B. Britton to editors, May 15, 1863, William B. Britton Letters, OCM; Edward Wood to wife, May 25, 1863, Edward J. Wood Papers, IHS; Isaac Vanderwarker Diary, May 14, 1863, CWD, USAHEC.

50. *OR*, 24(1):639, 712, 730, 759, 762, 768, 770; "Capture of Jackson," *National Tribune*, August 3, 1893; Grimsley and Miller, eds., *The Union Must Stand*, 95; George M. Lucas Diary, May 15, 1863, ALPL; W. B. Britton to editors, May 15, 1863, William B. Britton Letters, OCM; John P. Davis Diary, May 15, 1863, ALPL: Sewall Farwell to unknown, May 15, 1863, Sewall S. Farwell Papers, SHSIIC.

51. John P. Davis Diary, May 15, 1863, John P. Davis Papers, ALPL; S. S. Farwell Letter, May 15, 1863, Sewall S. Farwell Papers, SHSIIC; *OR*, 1, 24, 1: 312, 754; *OR*, 1, 24, 3: 845; *Journal of the House of Representatives of the State of Mississippi: December*

Session of 1862, and November Session of 1863, 90–91, 103, 108, 132, 181, appendix; Fremantle, *Three Months in the Southern States*, 105, 109–110; S. M. Lathan to sister, August 4, 1863, Lucas-Ashley Papers, DU; James Meagher Affidavit, March 30, 1866, James Meagher Papers, DU; Tilley, ed., "Letter of Judge Alexander M. Clayton Relative to Confederate Courts in Mississippi," 392–401.

52. *OR*, 24(1):730, 779; *OR*, 24(2):65; John Merrilees Diary, May 14, 1863, CHM; Luther Cowan Diary, May 14, 1863, Luther H. Cowan Papers, TSLA; Job H. Yaggy Diary, May 14, 1863, ALPL; N. W. Wood Diary, May 14, 1863, UCB.

53. *OR*, 24(1):6, 59, 724, 751, 754, 759, 770, 786–787; Symonds, *Joseph E. Johnston*, 208; Simon and Marszalek, eds., *PUSG*, 8:189; Marszalek, Nolen, and Gallo, eds., *The Personal Memoirs of Ulysses S. Grant*, 352; John J. Pettus Order, June 11, 1863, Executive Journals, 1817–1887, John J. Pettus, Series 758, MDAH; John J. Pettus to Jefferson Davis, July 9, 1863, Mississippi Governor, John J. Pettus, Correspondence and Papers, 1859–1863, Series 757, MDAH; Various military orders dated May 1–July 16, Mississippi Governor, John J. Pettus, Military Orders, 1862–1863, Series 769, Box 951, MDAH; Cadwallader, *Three Years with Grant*, 74; Sherman, *Memoirs*, 1:321; Fred Grant Memoir, undated, USGPL, 22; Bennet Grigsby to family, May 18, 1863, Bennet Grigsby Letters, IHS.

54. *OR*, 24(1):84.

55. *OR*, 24(3):311; *OR*, 24(1):51; F. A. F., *Old Abe, The Eighth Wisconsin War Eagle. A Full Account of His Capture and Enlistment, Exploits in War and Honorable As Well As Useful Career in Peace* (Madison, WI: Curran and Bowen, 1885), 39; John Melvin Williams, *"The Eagle Regiment," 8th Wis. Inf'ty Vols.: A Sketch of Its Marches, Battles and Campaigns from 1861–1865 with Complete Regimental and Company Roster, and a Few Portraits and Sketches of Its Officers and Commanders* (Belleville, WI: Recorder Print, 1890), 17; Robert S. Martin Diary, May 14, 1863, SIU.

56. Simon and Marszalek, eds., *PUSG*, 8:214; Marszalek, Nolen, and Gallo, eds., *The Personal Memoirs of Ulysses S. Grant*, 353; Fred Grant Memoir, undated, USGPL, 23.

57. *OR*, 24(3):310, 312; *OR*, 24(1):148.

58. Hass, ed., "The Vicksburg Diary of Henry Clay Warmoth," 69–70; Isaac Jackson to Sallie, May 27, 1863, Isaac Jackson Papers, James S. Schoff Civil War Collection, UMC; John Merrilees Diary, May 13, 1863, CHM; N. W. Wood Diary, May 11, 1863, UCB.

59. *OR*, 24(3):310–311, 878; *OR*, 24(1):147; John N. Bell Diary, May 14, 1863, OHS; Curtis P. Lacey Diary, May 12, 1863, NL; Williamson Murray Diary, May 14, 1863, VICK; Aquilla Standifird Diary, May 14, 1863, SHSMR; Hass, ed., "The Vicksburg Diary of Henry Clay Warmoth," 69–70; General Orders No. 119, May 14, 1863, RG 393, E 3230, NARA.

60. *OR*, 24(3):310–311, 878; *OR*, 24(1):147; John N. Bell Diary, May 14, 1863, OHS; Curtis P. Lacey Diary, May 12, 1863, NL; Hass, ed., "The Vicksburg Diary of Henry Clay Warmoth," 69–70; General Orders No. 119, May 14, 1863, RG 393, E 3230, NARA.

61. *OR*, 24(2):297; *SOR*, 2, 13:637; William Hillyer to wife, May 3, 1863, William S. Hillyer Subject File, USGPL George M. Rogers Diary, May 14, 1863, ISL; John N. Bell

Diary, May 14, 1863, OHS; Abram J. Vanauken Diary, May 8–9, 1863, ALPL; Anson Hemingway Diary, May 14, 1863, VICK; James P. Boyd Diary, May 14, 1863, ALPL; George R. Lee Diary, May 13–15, 1863, ALPL; Calvin Ainsworth Diary, May 14, 1863, UMB.

62. *OR*, 24(3):312–313; Wilson, "A Staff Officer's Journal," 105; General Orders No. 18, May 14, 1863, RG 393, E 6305, NARA.

Chapter 13. "Gen'l Pemberton Looked as If He Was Confused"

1. Luther Cowan Diary, May 15, 1863, Luther H. Cowan Papers, TSLA.

2. Henry J. Seaman Diary, May 15, 1863, CWTI, USAHEC. For the developing harshness, see Mark Grimsley, *The Hard Hand of War: Union Military Policy Toward Southern Civilians, 1861–1865* (Cambridge: Cambridge University Press, 1995).

3. Mary Ann Loughborough, *My Cave Life in Vicksburg: With Letters of Trial and Travel* (New York: D. Appleton and Company, 1864), 29.

4. Smith, *The Real Horse Soldiers*, 221, 248.

5. Catton, *U. S. Grant and the American Military Tradition*, 102; Winschel, *Triumph and Defeat: The Vicksburg Campaign, Volume 2*, 46; Oldroyd, *A Soldier's Story*, 10; John P. Worthing to mother, June 28, 1863, John P. Worthing Letters, USM; Edward M. Main, *The Story of the Marches, Battles and Incidents of the Third United States Cavalry: A Fighting Regiment in the War of the Rebellion, 1861–5. With Official Orders and Reports Relating Thereto, Compiled From the Rebellion Records* (Louisville: The Globe Printing Company, 1908), 176, 295; "Proclamation," May 20, 1865, Mississippi Governor's Papers, Charles Clark, Correspondence and Papers, 1863- 1865, Series 767, Box 953, MDAH; Charles Clark Address to Legislature, May 1865, Executive Journals, 1817–1887, Charles Clark, Series 758, MDAH; "A Bill to be entitled 'An Act to provide for a Convention of the people of the State of Mississippi,'" May 20, 1865, Mississippi Governor's Papers, Charles Clark, Correspondence and Papers, 1863- 1865, Series 767, Box 953, MDAH; James Wilford Garner, *Reconstruction in Mississippi* (New York: MacMillan Company, 1902), 40, 57, 59–60; Rowland, *Mississippi*, 1: 443; *OR*, 1, 49, 2: 879; James L. Power, "The Black and Tan Convention," *Publications of the Mississippi Historical Society* (Oxford: Mississippi Historical Society, 1900), 3: 74; "From the Southwest," New York *Times*, May 18, 1865; Special Order 58, May 11, 1865, Mississippi Governor, Charles Clark, Order Book, 1863–1865, Series 770, Box 952, MDAH. In addition to the "siege" of Jackson in July 1863 and the Meridian Campaign in February 1864, Federals also took the city in July 1864 and May 1865. For the title of Chimneyville, see H. Grady Howell, Jr., *Chimneyville: "Likenesses" of Early Days in Jackson, Mississippi* (Jackson: Chickasaw Bayou Press, 2007).

6. *OR*, 24(3):312.

7. *OR*, 24(3):312; J. W. Greenman Diary, May 14, 1863, MDAH.

8. *OR*, 24(3):315; John T. Buegel Diary, May 15, 1863, SHSMC, 28; Richard Burt to wife, May 23, 1863, Richard W. Burt Papers, SHSMC.

9. *OR*, 24(1):759, 763, 770; Leroy Crockett Report, June 9, 1863, Hugh Ewing Papers, OHS.

10. Reed, *Campaigns and Battles of the Twelfth Regiment Iowa*, 119; Francis A. Dawes Diary, May 15, 1863, CWTI, USAHEC.

11. *OR*, 24(2):251; *OR*, 24(1):754; Charles Miller Memoirs, undated, VICK, 44; Jim Giauque to family, May 15, 1863, Giauque Family Papers, UIA; Paul Dorweiler Diary, May 15, 1863, CWTI, USAHEC; Joseph Child Diary, May 15, 1863, UIA.

12. *OR*, 24(2):251; *OR*, 24(1):754; Cadwallader, *Three Years with Grant*, 75; Gould D. Molineaux Diary, May 15, 1863, AC; T. H. Yeatman to James McPherson, May 15, 1863, James B. McPherson Papers, LC.

13. *OR*, 24(1):754; Marszalek, Nolen, and Gallo, eds., *The Personal Memoirs of Ulysses S. Grant*, 353; Wilson, *Under the Old Flag*, 1:203; Cadwallader, *Three Years with Grant*, 75; Fred Grant Memoir, undated, USGPL, 22.

14. *OR*, 24(1):754; Sherman, *Memoirs*, 1:322; Edward Stanfield to father, May 26, 1863, Edward P. Stanfield Letters, IHS; W. B. Britton to editors, May 15, 1863, William B. Britton Letters, OCM; Bruce to cousin, May 29, 1863, Robert B. Hoadley Papers, DU.

15. Henry J. Seaman Diary, May 15, 1863, CWTI, USAHEC; John T. Buegel Diary, May 15, 1863, SHSMC, 28; John Merrilees Diary, May 15, 1863, CHM; N. W. Wood Diary, May 15, 1863, UCB.

16. George M. Lucas Diary, May 10, 1863, ALPL; John Bowman to friends, May 27, 1863, John A. Bowman Letters, OCM; J. W. Greenman Diary, May 15, 1863, MDAH; John N. Bell Diary, May 16, 1863, OHS; Charles Miller Memoirs, undated, VICK, 44; James Patterson Diary, May 16, 1863, SHSIIC.

17. Timothy C. Young Diary, May 15, 1863, VICK; John Merrilees Diary, May 16, 1863, CHM.

18. Henry J. Seaman Diary, May 15, 1863, CWTI, USAHEC; Bruce to cousin, May 29, 1863, Robert B. Hoadley Papers, DU.

19. J. W. Greenman Diary, May 14, 1863, MDAH.

20. *OR*, 24(3):314–315; Joseph Child Diary, May 15, 1863, UIA.

21. *OR*, 24(3):315; *OR*, 24(2):281; Bearss, *The Vicksburg Campaign*, 2:662; James B. Owen to Sally, May 26, 1863, James B. Owen Letters, TSLA; Clarkson Fogg to father, May 10, 1863, Clarkson Fogg Letters, VICK; Edward E. Schweitzer Diary, May 15, 1863, CWTI, USAHEC.

22. *OR*, 24(1):51, 754; Daniel A. Masters, ed., *Sherman's Praetorian Guard: Civil War Letters of John McIntyre Lemmon, 72nd Ohio Volunteer Infantry* (Perrysburg, OH: Columbian Arsenal Press, 2017), 116; John Merrilees Diary, May 15, 1863, CHM; John T. Buegel Diary, May 15, 1863, SHSMC, 28; Enoch P. Williams Diary, May 16, 1863, VICK.

23. Jones, *A Rebel War Clerk's Diary*, 1:287–288; Lundberg, "'I Am Too Late,'" 116.

24. *OR*, 24(3):876–877, 882; *OR*, 24(1):270.

25. *OR*, 24(1):262; Alfred Cumming to Stephen Lee, November 3, 1899, Letters and Papers Covering Organizations: Miscellaneous—Georgia, Massachusetts, New Hampshire, and Rhode Island, MDAH.

26. *OR*, 24(2):93, 116; *OR*, 24(3):882–883; Theodore D. Fisher Diary, May 15, 1863,

Civil War Collection, MHS; I. V. Smith Memoir, 1902, SHSMC, 28; John Forney to John Pemberton, May 15, 1863, RG 109, E 97, NARA.

27. William Drennan to wife, May 30, 1863, William Drennan Papers, MDAH.

28. *OR*, 24(2):125; *OR*, 24(1):262; Grabau, *Ninety-Eight Days*, 270; William Kelly, "A History of the Thirtieth Alabama Volunteer (Infantry) C.S.A.," 30th Alabama Papers, ADAH, 25; James McCulloch Diary, May 15, 1863, UGA.

29. John C. Taylor Diary, May 14, 1863, Taylor Family Papers, UVA; Michael B. Ballard, "Misused Merit: The Tragedy of John C. Pemberton," in *Confederate Generals in the Western Theater*, 4 vols., Lawrence Lee Hewitt and Arthur W. Bergeron Jr., eds. (Knoxville: University of Tennessee Press, 2010), 1:116, originally printed as Michael B. Ballard, "Misused Merit: The Tragedy of John C. Pemberton," in *Civil War Generals in Defeat*, Steven E. Woodworth, ed. (Lawrence: University Press of Kansas, 1999), 141–160.

30. *OR*, 24(2):125; M. D. L. Stephens Memoir, undated, MDAH, 17.

31. *OR*, 24(1):262.

32. *OR*, 24(1):262; *OR*, 24(3):882–883; *OR*, 24(2):75; Shea and Winschel, *Vicksburg Is the Key*, 130; John C. Taylor Diary, May 15, 1863, Taylor Family Papers, UVA.

33. John C. Taylor Diary, May 15, 1863, Taylor Family Papers, UVA; William Drennan to wife, May 30, 1863, William Drennan Papers, MDAH.

34. *OR*, 24(1):262–263.

35. *OR*, 24(1):263; *OR*, 24(3):883.

36. E. Z. Hays, *History of the Thirty-second Regiment Ohio Veteran Volunteer Infantry* (Columbus, OH: Cott & Evans Printers, 1896), 42; Dana, *Recollections of the Civil War*, 50; Cadwallader, *Three Years with Grant*, 80; Francis A. Dawes Diary, May 15, 1863, CWTI, USAHEC; Carlos Forbes to Mary, June 6, 1863, Carlos Forbes Papers, OHS.

37. James H. St. John Diary, May 12–15, 1863, ISL; John N. Bell Diary, May 15, 1863, OHS; John W. Griffith Diary, May 15, 1863, OHS; Ulysses Grant to Samuel Holmes, May 15, 1863, Ulysses S. Grant Collection, Unpublished Correspondence, USGPL.

38. Asa Sample Diary, May 14, 1863, ISL; John N. Bell Diary, May 15, 1863, OHS; Adnan Eaton Diary, May 16, 1863, NC; Asa Sample Diary, May 16, 1863, ISL.

39. *OR*, 24(2):255; Reed, *Campaigns and Battles of the Twelfth Regiment Iowa*, 120; John N. Bell Diary, May 15, 1863, OHS; Andrew McCormack to family, May 24, 1863, Andrew McCormack Letters, NC; Wilson, "A Staff Officer's Journal," 106; Anson Hemingway Diary, May 15, 1863, VICK; Thomas Hawley to parents, May 18, 1863, Thomas S. Hawley Papers, MHS.

40. *OR*, 24(3):313; *OR*, 24(2):12; Hass, ed., "The Vicksburg Diary of Henry Clay Warmoth," 70; Fulfer, *A History of the Trials and Hardships of the Twenty-Fourth Indiana Volunteer Infantry*, 63; Hovey Manuscript, undated, Alvin Hovey Papers, IU, 56; John A. McClernand to U. S. Grant, May 15, 1863, RG 393, E 4720, NARA.

41. "Heavy Losses in Battle," *National Tribune*, February 22, 1906; Reuben H. Falconer Diary, May 15, 1863, OHS.

42. *OR*, 24(3):313; *OR*, 24(1):51, 148; Brown, *History of the Fourth Regiment of Minnesota Infantry*, 198.

43. *OR*, 24(3):313; *OR*, 24(1):639; *OR*, 24(2):13, 255; Peter J. Perrine Diary, May 15, 1863, OHS; Edmund Newsome Diary, May 15, 1863, MDAH; Isaac Vanderwarker Diary, May 15, 1863, CWD, USAHEC; George W. Modil Diary, May 15, 1863, MDAH; James B. McPherson to Alvin P. Hovey, May 15, 1863, RG 393, E 4720, NARA; James B. McPherson to U. S. Grant, May 15, 1863, RG 393, E 4720, NARA.

44. *OR*, 24(3):313; *OR*, 24(1):639; *OR*, 24(2):13, 255; Isaac Vanderwarker Diary, May 15, 1863, CWD, USAHEC; George W. Modil Diary, May 15, 1863, MDAH; Peter J. Perrine Diary, May 15, 1863, OHS; Edmund Newsome Diary, May 15, 1863, MDAH; James B. McPherson to Alvin P. Hovey, May 15, 1863, RG 393, E 4720, NARA; James B. McPherson to U. S. Grant, May 15, 1863, RG 393, E 4720, NARA.

45. *OR*, 24(3):313–314; *OR*, 24(1):148; John Myers, "'Dear and Mutch Loved One'—An Iowan's Vicksburg Letters," Edward G. Longacre, ed. *Annals of Iowa* 43, no. 1 (Summer 1975): 53; Reuben H. Falconer Diary, May 15, 1863, OHS.

46. *OR*, 24(3):313–314.

47. Charles Shedd to unknown, May 15, 1863, Shedd Family Papers, SHSIIC.

48. Lee, "The Campaign of Vicksburg," 35–36; Bearss, *The Vicksburg Campaign*, 2:576–577; Bearss and Hills, *Receding Tide*, 197; Winschel, *Triumph and Defeat*, 98; Rebecca Blackwell Drake and Margie Riddle Bearss, eds., *My Dear Wife: Letters to Matilda: The Civil War Letters of Sid and Matilda Champion of Champion Hill* (N.p.: N.p., 2005), 96.

49. *OR*, 24(2):87, 114; James T. Kidd Memoir, undated, OCM, 12; I. V. Smith Memoir, 1902, SHSMC, 28.

CHAPTER 14. "THE HILL OF DEATH"

1. *OR*, 24(2):44; *OR*, 24(1):150, 639; Marshall, *History of the Eighty-third Ohio Volunteer Infantry*, 81–82; Maynard, ed., "Vicksburg Diary," 46; Brown, *History of the Fourth Regiment of Minnesota Infantry*, 206; Smith, *Champion Hill*, 129.

2. Smith, *Champion Hill*, 178, 477; Drake and Bearss, eds., *My Dear Wife*, 96, 107–108; William T. Rigby Diary, May 16, 1863, UIA.

3. Drake and Bearss, eds., *My Dear Wife*, 15, 57–59, 97; Donald L. Miller, *Vicksburg: Grant's Campaign that Broke the Confederacy* (New York: Simon and Schuster, 2019), 395, 399.

4. Owen Johnston Hopkins, *Under the Flag of the Nation: Diaries and Letters of a Yankee Volunteer in the Civil War*, Otto F. Bond, ed. (Columbus: Ohio State University Press, 1961), 60; Thomas O. Hall, "The Key to Vicksburg," *The Southern Bivouac* 2, no. 9 (May 1884): 393–396; Frank Johnston, "The Vicksburg Campaign," in *Publications of the Mississippi Historical Society* (Oxford: Mississippi Historical Society, 1909), 10:63–90.

5. *OR*, 24(2):101, 107; Samuel Fowler Diary, May 16, 1863, SU, 179.

6. *OR*, 24(2):75, 82, 87; J. P. Cannon, "History of the 27th Reg. Alabama Volunteer Infantry, C.S.A.," undated, 27th Alabama Papers, ADAH.

7. *OR*, 24(2):75, 93; *OR*, 24(3):884; *OR*, 24(1):263, 269; David M. Smith, ed., *Compelled to Appear in Print: The Vicksburg Manuscript of General John C. Pemberton* (Cincinnati: Ironclad Publishing, 1999), 117–118, 125; John A. Leavy Diary, May 16, 1863, VICK; John Pemberton to Carter Stevenson, May 16, 1863, RG 109, E 97, NARA.

8. *OR*, 24(1):263; Alfred Cumming to Stephen Lee, November 3, 1899, Letters and Papers Covering Organizations: Miscellaneous—Georgia, Massachusetts, New Hampshire, and Rhode Island, MDAH.

9. *OR*, 24(2):125; James R. Binford Memoir, undated, Patrick Henry Papers, MDAH.

10. William Drennan to wife, May 30, 1863, William Drennan Papers, MDAH.

11. *OR*, 24(2):75, 94, 101, 103, 108; Alfred Cumming to Stephen Lee, November 3, 1899, Letters and Papers Covering Organizations: Miscellaneous—Georgia, Massachusetts, New Hampshire, and Rhode Island, MDAH.

12. *OR*, 24(2):75, 82, 91, 94, 126; M. D. L. Stephens Memoir, undated, MDAH, 18; Carter Stevenson to John Pemberton, May 16, 1863, RG 109, E 97, NARA.

13. *OR*, 24(2):75, 83.

14. *OR*, 24(2):94, 100, 104; William L. Roberts Diary, May 16, 1863, ADAH; Alfred Cumming to Stephen Lee, November 3, 1899, Letters and Papers Covering Organizations: Miscellaneous—Georgia, Massachusetts, New Hampshire, and Rhode Island, MDAH; William Terry Moore Reminiscences, undated, UM.

15. *OR*, 24(2):94, 100, 104; Ballard, *Pemberton*, 161; William L. Roberts Diary, May 16, 1863, ADAH; W. O. Connor to William Rigby, February 24, 1904, Cherokee Georgia Artillery File, VNMPR; Alfred Cumming to Stephen Lee, November 3, 1899, Letters and Papers Covering Organizations: Miscellaneous—Georgia, Massachusetts, New Hampshire, and Rhode Island, MDAH; William Terry Moore Reminiscences, undated, UM.

16. *OR*, 24(2):70, 93–94, 101, 122; *OR*, 24(1):263; Townsend, *Yankee Warhorse*, 101; Ballard, "Misused Merit," 1:116; Alfred Cumming to Stephen Lee, November 3, 1899, Letters and Papers Covering Organizations: Miscellaneous—Georgia, Massachusetts, New Hampshire, and Rhode Island, MDAH.

17. *OR*, 24(2):70, 93–94, 101, 122; *OR*, 24(1):263; Ballard, "Misused Merit," 1:116; Townsend, *Yankee Warhorse*, 101; Alfred Cumming to Stephen Lee, November 3, 1899, Letters and Papers Covering Organizations: Miscellaneous—Georgia, Massachusetts, New Hampshire, and Rhode Island, MDAH.

18. *OR*, 24(1):52; *OR*, 24(3):314; Byers, "How Men Feel in Battle," 439; Charles L. Longley, "Champion's Hill," in *War Sketches and Incidents* (Des Moines, IA: Press of P. C. Kenyon, 1893), 1:210; Crummer, *With Grant*, 107.

19. *OR*, 24(3):319; *OR*, 24(1):51–52; Kiper, *Major General John A. McClernand*, 244; Wilson, "A Staff Officer's Journal," 106–107; Simon and Marszalek, eds., *PUSG*, 8:224, 227; Fred Grant Memoir, undated, USGPL, 23; James B. McPherson to U. S. Grant, May 15, 1863, RG 393, E 4720, NARA; J. C. Taylor to Conductor, May 14, 1863, RG 109, Chapter II, Volume 60, NARA.

20. *OR*, 24(2):79, 91; *OR*, 24(3):317; Bering and Montgomery, *History of the Forty-Eighth Ohio Vet. Vol. Inf.*, 82–83; David Grier to Anna, May 24, 1863, Grier Family Papers, MHS; Charles E. Affeld Diary, May 16, 1863, VICK; George M. Rogers Diary, May 16, 1863, ISL; John A. McClernand to U. S. Grant, May 16, 1863, RG 393, E 4720, NARA.

21. *OR*, 24(2):32, 70, 263; *OR*, 24(1):596; *OR*, 24(3):319; John Carr Diary, May 16, 1863, HCWRTC, USAHEC; John E. Wilkins Reminiscences, 1911, IHS, 2; Scott, *The History of the 67th Regiment Indiana Infantry Volunteers*, 32–33; *The Story of the Fifty-fifth Regiment Illinois Volunteer Infantry*, 232–233; John M. Roberts Diary, May 16, 1863, IHS, 36; Isaac Jackson to Sallie, May 27, 1863, Isaac Jackson Papers, James S. Schoff Civil War Collection, UMC.

22. *OR*, 24(2):13–14, 24, 26, 28–29, 95, 233; W. L. Rand to parents, May 25, 1863, Rand Family Papers, ALPL; Samuel Gordon to wife, May 25, 1863, Samuel Gordon Papers, ALPL; Don Pardee to unknown, May 24, 1863, Don A. Pardee Papers, TU; Henry, *Captain Henry of Geauga*, 159–160; George B. Marshall Reminiscences, 1912, ISL, 43; James Leeper to Mary, May 23, 1863, James Leeper Papers, IHS; William A. Sypher Diary, May 16, 1863, CHM.

23. *OR*, 24(2):13–14, 24; *OR*, 24(3):316; Crooke, *The Twenty-first Regiment of Iowa Volunteer Infantry*, 63–66; Louis K. Knobe Reminiscences, undated, ISL, 31–32; Reuben H. Falconer Diary, May 16, 1863, OHS; Peter J. Perrine Diary, May 16, 1863, OHS; James F. Elliott Diary, May 16, 1863, IHS; Samuel P. Harrington Diary, May 16, 1863, Haerle Collection, USAHEC.

24. *OR*, 24(1):52, 148, 184, 736; *OR*, 24(3):316, 320; John J. Kellogg Memoirs, undated, VICK, 24.

25. *OR*, 24(1):52, 148, 184, 736; *OR*, 24(3):316, 320; Sanborn, "The Campaign Against Vicksburg," 131; Sherman, *Memoirs*, 1:323; John J. Kellogg Memoirs, undated, VICK, 24.

26. *OR*, 24(3):319, 884, 889; *OR*, 24(1):52, 755; John Pettus Telegram, May 16, 1863, Mississippi Governor, John J. Pettus, Outgoing Telegrams, 1861–1862, Series 763, MDAH; Woodworth, "The First Capture and Occupation of Jackson, Mississippi," 111–112; H. W. Allen to "My Dear Hunter," June 13, 1863, Henry Watkins Allen Letter, LSU; Robert W. Dubay, *John Jones Pettus: Mississippi Fire Eater, His Life and Times 1813–1867* (Jackson: University Press of Mississippi, 1975), 174–175; Robert J. Burdette, *The Drums of the 47th* (Indianapolis: The Bobbs-Merrill Company, 1914), 158; Dossman, "The 'Stealing Tour,'" 207; Bryner, *Bugle Echoes*, 81–82; Charles Willison to Ellie, May 26, 1863, 76th Ohio Volunteer Regiment Correspondence, OHS; Timothy C. Young Diary, May 16, 1863, VICK; J. W. Greenman Diary, May 20, 1863, MDAH; Robert S. Martin Diary, May 16, 1863, SIU.

27. *OR*, 24(3):317–318, 320; *OR*, 24(1):52; Bearss, *The Vicksburg Campaign*, 2:594; Townsend, *Yankee Warhorse*, 101; John A. McClernand to Alvin P. Hovey, May 16, 1863, RG 393, E 4720, NARA; John A. McClernand to U. S. Grant, May 16, 1863, RG 393, E 4720, NARA.

28. *OR*, 24(2):48, 55; *OR*, 24(1):639; *OR*, 24(3):316; "Champion's Hill," *National*

Tribune, September 11, 1884; Cadwallader, *Three Years with Grant*, 77; John W. Griffith Diary, May 16, 1863, OHS; James Slack to wife, May 12, 1863, James R. Slack Letters, ISL; Gould D. Molineaux Diary, May 16, 1863, AC; Thomas Morrow to sister, May 4, 1863, Elliot Morrow Papers, OHS.

29. *OR*, 24(2):41, 47–48, 58, 70, 95; *History of the Forty-sixth Regiment Indiana Volunteer Infantry*, 60–63; August Leich Speech, May 6, 1899, August Leich Collection, ISL; Augustus G. Sinks Memoir, undated, ISL, 36; Alexander Ewing to parents, May 18, 1863, Alexander K. Ewing Papers, ALPL; Hovey Manuscript, undated, Alvin Hovey Papers, IU, 57; Joshua W. Underhill Diary, May 16, 1863, IHS.

30. *OR*, 24(2):41, 47–48, 58, 70, 95; *OR*, 24(3):316–317; *OR*, 24(1):52; Bertera, *De Golyer's 8th Michigan Black Horse Light Battery*, 124; Oldroyd, *A Soldier's Story*, 25; John W. Griffith Diary, May 16, 1863, OHS.

31. *OR*, 24(2):14, 41–42; *OR*, 24(3):317–318; *OR*, 24(1):52, 149.

32. *OR*, 24(2):41, 55, 57; *History of the Forty-sixth Regiment Indiana Volunteer Infantry*, 60–63; James Slack to wife, May 12, 1863, James R. Slack Letters, ISL; Hovey Manuscript, undated, Alvin Hovey Papers, IU, 57; Samuel Ransom Diary, May 1863, SHSIIC; Alexander Ewing to parents, May 18, 1863, Alexander K. Ewing Papers, ALPL; William T. Rigby Diary, May 16, 1863, UIA; Joshua W. Underhill Diary, May 16, 1863, IHS; Francis A. Dawes Diary, May 16, 1863, CWTI, USAHEC.

33. *OR*, 24(2):42, 49, 55; Terrence J. Winschel, "The Guns at Champion Hill (Part II)," *Journal of Confederate History* 6 (1990): 94–105; Alexander Ewing to parents, May 18, 1863, Alexander K. Ewing Papers, ALPL; James Slack to wife, May 12, 1863, James R. Slack Letters, ISL; Joshua W. Underhill Diary, May 16, 1863, IHS.

34. *OR*, 24(2):42, 95, 104; James McCulloch Diary, May 16, 1863, UGA; Francis Obenchain to John Johnston, January 8, 1903, Botetourt Virginia Artillery File, VNMPR; "Dedication of a Bronze Tablet in Honor of Botetourt Battery," 43; Francis Obenchain to William Rigby, June 27, 1903, Letters and Papers Covering Organizations: Virginia (Botetourt Artillery), MDAH. See also Waddell's Battery File, ADAH.

35. *OR*, 24(2):49, 53, 95; William F. Hollingsworth Diary, May 16, 1863, OCM; Alexander Ewing to parents, May 18, 1863, Alexander K. Ewing Papers, ALPL; Joshua W. Underhill Diary, May 16, 1863, IHS; James Slack to wife, May 12, 1863, James R. Slack Letters, ISL.

36. *OR*, 24(2):105; Alfred Cumming to Stephen Lee, November 3, 1899, Letters and Papers Covering Organizations: Miscellaneous—Georgia, Massachusetts, New Hampshire, and Rhode Island, MDAH.

37. *OR*, 24(2):49; Hovey Manuscript, undated, Alvin Hovey Papers, IU, 57; Joshua W. Underhill Diary, May 16, 1863, IHS; Alexander Ewing to parents, May 18, 1863, Alexander K. Ewing Papers, ALPL.

38. *OR*, 24(2):44, 105; James McCulloch Diary, May 16, 1863, UGA.

39. *OR*, 24(2):42, 105; Patrick, ed., *Three Years with Wallace's Zouaves*, 129–136; Aurelius L. Voorhis Diary, May 16, 1863, IHS; James McCulloch Diary, May 16, 1863, UGA.

40. *OR*, 24(2):42, 53; Alexander Ewing to parents, May 18, 1863, Alexander K.

Ewing Papers, ALPL; Fulfer, *A History of the Trials and Hardships of the Twenty-Fourth Indiana Volunteer Infantry*, 64–67; "At Champion's Hill," *National Tribune*, August 30, 1883; Alfred Cumming to Stephen Lee, November 3, 1899, Letters and Papers Covering Organizations: Miscellaneous—Georgia, Massachusetts, New Hampshire, and Rhode Island, MDAH; James Slack to wife, May 12, 1863, James R. Slack Letters, ISL; Joshua W. Underhill Diary, May 16, 1863, IHS.

41. *OR*, 24(2):105; Alexander Ewing to parents, May 18, 1863, Alexander K. Ewing Papers, ALPL; Joshua W. Underhill Diary, May 16, 1863, IHS; James Slack to wife, May 12, 1863, James R. Slack Letters, ISL.

42. *OR*, 24(1):647; Oldroyd, *A Soldier's Story*, 23; William L. Roberts Diary, May 16, 1863, ADAH; Lewis T. Hickok Journal, May 16, 1863, James S. Schoff Civil War Collection, UMC.

43. *OR*, 24(1):647; Oldroyd, *A Soldier's Story*, 22–25; Howard, *History of the 124th Regiment Illinois Infantry Volunteers*, 95–99; Morris, *History*, 63–66; Ira Blanchard, *I Marched With Sherman: Civil War Memoirs of the 20th Illinois Volunteer Infantry*, Nancy Ann Mattingly, ed. (New York: toExcel, 1992), 83–86; Wood, *History of the 20th O. V. V. I. Regiment*, 22; Force, "Personal Recollections of the Vicksburg Campaign," 301; Manning Force to Mrs. Perkins, May 21, 1863, Manning F. Force Papers, UWA, copies in LC; Cyrus Randall to mother, May 25, 1863, Cyrus W. Randall Papers, ALPL; S. C. Beck, "A True Sketch of His Army Life," 1902, VICK, 8; George W. Modil Diary, May 16, 1863, MDAH; Job H. Yaggy Diary, May 16, 1863, ALPL; Special Orders No. 86, May 15, 1863, RG 393, E 6254, NARA.

44. *OR*, 24(2):102; Hattaway, *General Stephen D. Lee*, 87; Blanchard, *I Marched With Sherman*, 83–85; Job H. Yaggy Diary, May 16, 1863, ALPL; William L. Roberts Diary, May 16, 1863, ADAH.

45. *OR*, 24(1):640; *OR*, 24(1):717–718, 721; Hays, *History of the Thirty-second Regiment Ohio Veteran Volunteer Infantry*, 42–45; John W. Griffith Diary, May 16, 1863, OHS; George Durfee to uncle, May 21, 1863, George S. Durfee Papers, UIL; Gould D. Molineaux Diary, May 16, 1863, AC.

46. *OR*, 24(2):70, 100, 108; *OR*, 24(1):640, 718, 721; Smith, *Champion Hill*, 228; John W. Griffith Diary, May 16, 1863, OHS; Joseph Bogle Memoir, undated, GDAH, copy in OCM, 9; W. O. Connor to William Rigby, February 24, 1904, Cherokee Georgia Artillery File, VNMPR; George Durfee to uncle, May 21, 1863, George S. Durfee Papers, UIL; Ira Batterton to sister, May 27, 1863, Ira A. Batterton Papers, ALPL; Thomas Morrow to sister, May 25, 1863, Elliot Morrow Papers, OHS; Arthur P. McCullough Diary, May 16, 1863, ALPL; Manning Force to Mrs. Perkins, May 21, 1863, Manning F. Force Papers, UWA.

47. Hays, *History of the Thirty-second Regiment Ohio Veteran Volunteer Infantry*, 43.

48. *OR*, 24(2):70, 100, 108; *OR*, 24(1):640, 718, 721; Joseph Bogle Memoir, undated, OCM, 9; John W. Griffith Diary, May 16, 1863, OHS; Hicks, "The Campaign and Capture of Vicksburg," 100; Thomas Morrow to sister, May 25, 1863, Elliot Morrow Papers, OHS; Gould D. Molineaux Diary, May 16, 1863, AC; John Logan Report, May 26, 1863, RG 393, E 6225, NARA.

49. Israel M. Ritter Diary, May 16, 1863, CWD, USAHEC; Smith, *The Decision Was Always My Own*, 133; Logan Roots to Sir, July 24, 1863, Edwin C. Hewett Correspondence, UIL; James S. McHenry Diary, May 16, 1863, ALPL.

CHAPTER 15. "I AM OF THE OPINION THAT THE BATTLE FOR
VICKSBURG HAS BEEN FOUGHT"

1. *OR*, 24(1):264.
2. *OR*, 24(1):264.
3. *OR*, 24(1):264.
4. *OR*, 24(2):75, 121; Tucker, *The Forgotten "Stonewall of the West*," 276; Raab, *W. W. Loring*, 111; Lloyd Tilghman to Richard Memminger and Lloyd Tilghman to Jacob Thompson, May 15, 1863, John C. Pemberton Papers, RG 109, E 131, NARA; Ezra J. Warner, *Generals in Gray: The Lives of the Confederate Commanders* (Baton Rouge: Louisiana State University Press, 1959), 30, 306.
5. *OR*, 24(2):96, 121–122.
6. *OR*, 24(2):75–76, 110, 122–123.
7. *OR*, 24(2):76, 79, 91, 95, 110, 118, 126; *OR*, 24(1):264; Anderson, *Memoirs*, 309–315; M. D. L. Stephens Memoir, undated, MDAH, 17–18.
8. *OR*, 24(2):76, 79, 91, 95, 110, 118, 126; *OR*, 24(1):264; Tucker, *The Forgotten "Stonewall of the West*," 278–280; Theodore D. Fisher Diary, May 16, 1863, Civil War Collection, MHS; Anderson, *Memoirs*, 312; Bevier, *History of the First and Second Missouri Confederate Brigades*, 183–193; I. V. Smith Memoir, 1902, SHSMC, 28.
9. *OR*, 24(2):42, 49–50, 111; Hovey Manuscript, undated, Alvin Hovey Papers, IU, 57; Joshua W. Underhill Diary, May 16, 1863, IHS; Anderson, *Memoirs*, 312; Tucker, *Westerners in Gray*, 161–204; L. B. Claiborne Memoirs, CWTI, USAHEC, 14; Alexander Ewing to parents, May 18, 1863, Alexander K. Ewing Papers, ALPL; Theodore D. Fisher Diary, May 16, 1863, Civil War Collection, MHS; Augustus G. Sinks Memoir, undated, ISL, 36–37; George Bradley Memoir, undated, OCM, 8; I. V. Smith Memoir, 1902, SHSMC, 28; William A. Ruyle Diary, May 16, 1863, HCWRTC, USAHEC.
10. *OR*, 24(2):42, 49–50, 111; Hovey Manuscript, undated, Alvin Hovey Papers, IU, 57; Joshua W. Underhill Diary, May 16, 1863, IHS; Anderson, *Memoirs*, 312; Tucker, *Westerners in Gray*, 161–204; Theodore D. Fisher Diary, May 16, 1863, Civil War Collection, MHS; I. V. Smith Memoir, 1902, SHSMC, 28; William A. Ruyle Diary, May 16, 1863, HCWRTC, USAHEC; Augustus G. Sinks Memoir, undated, ISL, 36–37; L. B. Claiborne Memoirs, CWTI, USAHEC, 14; Alexander Ewing to parents, May 18, 1863, Alexander K. Ewing Papers, ALPL; George Bradley Memoir, undated, OCM, 8.
11. *OR*, 24(2):15, 55, 116, 119; *OR*, 24(1):264; A. H. Reynolds, "Vivid Experiences at Champion Hill, Miss," *Confederate Veteran* 18, no. 1 (January 1910): 21–22; Mason, *The Forty-second Ohio Infantry*, 207–211; William A. Ruyle Diary, May 16, 1863, HCWRTC, USAHEC; James Slack to wife, May 12, 1863, James R. Slack Letters, ISL.
12. *OR*, 24(2):42, 55–56; T. J. Williams, "The Battle of Champion's Hill," *Sketches of*

War History, 1861–1865 (Cincinnati: The Robert Clarke Company, 1903), 5:210; Jones, *Black Jack*, 166; Lee, "The Campaign of Vicksburg," 47; Joseph Bogle Memoir, undated, OCM, 9; Francis Obenchain to John Johnston, November 27, 1903, Letters and Papers Covering Organizations: Virginia (Botetourt Artillery), MDAH.

13. *OR*, 24(2):44, 50, 106; Alexander Ewing to parents, May 18, 1863, Alexander K. Ewing Papers, ALPL; I. V. Smith Memoir, 1902, SHSMC, 29; Augustus G. Sinks Memoir, undated, ISL, 37; Hovey Manuscript, undated, Alvin Hovey Papers, IU, 57; Joshua W. Underhill Diary, May 16, 1863, IHS.

14. *OR*, 24(2):116, 119–120, 123, 126; *OR*, 24(1):264; Lockett, "The Defense of Vicksburg," 487; Samuel Fowler Diary, May 16, 1863, SU, 186–187.

15. *OR*, 24(2):263; *OR*, 24(3):317–318; Samuel P. Harrington Diary, May 16, 1863, Haerle Collection, USAHEC; G. H. Fifer to unknown, May 30, 1863, Joseph W. Fifer Papers, ALPL; U. G. McAlexander, *History of the Thirteenth Regiment United States Infantry, Compiled from Regimental Records and Other Sources* (N.p.: Regimental Press, Thirteenth Infantry, 1905), 36; John Dinsmore to wife, June 8, 1863, John C. Dinsmore Papers, ALPL; John Carr Diary, May 16, 1863, HCWRTC, USAHEC; Aquilla Standifird Diary, May 16, 1863, SHSMR.

16. *OR*, 24(2):60; *OR*, 24(1):730; *OR*, 24(3):320; Henry Cole Quinby, *Genealogical History of the Quinby (Quimby) Family In England and America* (Rutland, VT: The Tuttle Company, 1915), 429; George Ditto Diary, May 14, 1863, ALPL; Edward Wood to wife, May 25, 1863, Edward J. Wood Papers, IHS; William Cotton to unknown, May 27, 1863, William L. Cotton Letters, SHSIIC.

17. Cadwallader, *Three Years with Grant*, 79; Dunbar and Trimble, *History of the Ninety-third Regiment*, 30; Richardson, *A Personal History of Ulysses S. Grant*, 318.

18. *OR*, 24(2):42–44, 50, 66, 111, 315; *OR*, 24(1):731; Hicks, "The Campaign and Capture of Vicksburg," 100; Thomas Watson to parents, May 24, 1863, Thomas Watson Papers, ALPL; Alexander Ewing to parents, May 18, 1863, Alexander K. Ewing Papers, ALPL; Hovey Manuscript, undated, Alvin Hovey Papers, IU, 57; Joshua W. Underhill Diary, May 16, 1863, IHS; Ira A. Payne Diary, May 16, 1863, ALPL; Augustus G. Sinks Memoir, undated, ISL, 37; Edward Wood to wife, May 25, 1863, Edward J. Wood Papers, IHS.

19. Byers, "How Men Feel in Battle," 442; Williams, "The Battle of Champion's Hill," 210; Byers, *With Fire and Sword*, 74.

20. *OR*, 24(2):53, 62, 111, 117, 315; *OR*, 24(1):772; Smith, *Champion Hill*, 270; Edward Wood to wife, May 25, 1863, Edward J. Wood Papers, IHS; Byers, *With Fire and Sword*, 70–80; James A. Woodson Diary, May 16, 1863, ALPL; Grimsley and Miller, eds., *The Union Must Stand*, 95–98; Hicks, "The Campaign and Capture of Vicksburg," 99–101; Brown, *History of the Fourth Regiment of Minnesota Infantry*, 198–203; I. V. Smith Memoir, 1902, SHSMC, 29; S. E. Sneier to Sir, June 21, 1863, Samuel E. Sneier Letter, IHS; John F. Lester Diary, May 16, 1863, IHS; Isaac Vanderwarker Diary, May 16, 1863, CWD, USAHEC; John Whitten Diary, May 16, 1863, LC.

21. *OR*, 24(2):42–44, 50, 66, 111, 315; *OR*, 24(1):731; Hicks, "The Campaign and Capture of Vicksburg," 100; Thomas Watson to parents, May 24, 1863, Thomas Watson Papers, ALPL; Alexander Ewing to parents, May 18, 1863, Alexander K. Ewing Papers,

ALPL; John B. Sanborn, "Battles and Campaigns of September, 1862," in *Glimpses of the Nation's Struggle: Military Order of the Loyal Legion*, 6 vols. (St. Paul, MN: Review Publishing Company, 1908), 5:233–244; Hovey Manuscript, undated, Alvin Hovey Papers, IU, 57; Joshua W. Underhill Diary, May 16, 1863, IHS; Ira A. Payne Diary, May 16, 1863, ALPL; Byers, "How Men Feel in Battle," 442; Augustus G. Sinks Memoir, undated, ISL, 37; Edward Wood to wife, May 25, 1863, Edward J. Wood Papers, IHS.

22. Dunbar and Trimble, *History of the Ninety-third Regiment*, 27–32; William A. Ruyle Diary, May 16, 1863, HCWRTC, USAHEC; Nicholas Buswell to Richard Yates, undated, Nicholas C. Buswell Papers, ALPL.

23. *OR*, 24(2):44; *OR*, 24(1):150, 640; Jenkin L. Jones Diary, May 16, 1863, UCH.

24. *OR*, 24(1):724; *OR*, 24(1):779; Mary Amelia (Boomer) Stone, *Memoir of George Boardman Boomer* (Boston: Press of Geo. C. Rand & Avery, 1864), 252–253; John N. Bell Diary, May 16, 1863, OHS; Ulysses Grant to Samuel Holmes, May 16, 1863, Ulysses S. Grant Collection, Unpublished Correspondence, USGPL.

25. *OR*, 24(2):44, 63; *OR*, 24(1):640, 724, 776, 783, 785; Smith, *Champion Hill*, 279–280; Joel Strong Reminiscences, 1910, MHS, 11–12.

26. *OR*, 24(2):44, 63; *OR*, 24(1):640, 724, 776, 783, 785; Joel Strong Reminiscences, 1910, MHS, 11–12.

27. *OR*, 24(2):44, 63, 76, 106; *OR*, 24(1):53, 150, 731, 772; Mahan, *Memoirs*, 115–120; Lockett, "The Defense of Vicksburg," 487; John F. Lester Diary, May 16, 1863, IHS; Edward Wood to wife, May 25, 1863, Edward J. Wood Papers, IHS; Isaac Vanderwarker Diary, May 16, 1863, CWD, USAHEC.

28. *OR*, 24(2):44, 63, 76, 106; *OR*, 24(1):53, 150, 731, 772; I. V. Smith Memoir, 1902, SHSMC, 29; Lockett, "The Defense of Vicksburg," 487.

29. *OR*, 24(2):56, 76, 83, 91, 111, 117, 121; *OR*, 24(1):265; M. D. L. Stephens Memoir, undated, MDAH, 17–18.

30. *OR*, 24(2):15, 83; J. V. Greif, "Baker's Creek and Champion Hill," *Confederate Veteran* 4, no. 10 (October 1896): 350–352; Shunk, "The Vicksburg Campaign," 158.

31. *OR*, 24(2):83, 88–89; *OR*, 24(3):318; Charles A. Hobbs, "Vanquishing Vicksburg," *National Tribune*, January 28, 1892; Woodworth, *Nothing but Victory*, 387; Kiper, *Major General John A. McClernand*, 247; Townsend, *Yankee Warhorse*, 104; Wilson, "A Staff Officer's Journal," 108; Marszalek, Nolen, and Gallo, eds., *The Personal Memoirs of Ulysses S. Grant*, 357, 360; Howard, "The Vicksburg Campaign," 33; Reuben H. Falconer Diary, May 16, 1863, OHS.

32. *OR*, 24(2):32, 40, 80, 83, 88–89, 112; *OR*, 24(1):595; *OR*, 24(3):318; Hobbs, "Vanquishing Vicksburg," *National Tribune*, January 28, 1892; Kiper, *Major General John A. McClernand*, 247; Townsend, *Yankee Warhorse*, 104; Wilson, "A Staff Officer's Journal," 108; Marszalek, Nolen, and Gallo, eds., *The Personal Memoirs of Ulysses S. Grant*, 357, 360; Howard, "The Vicksburg Campaign," 33; Reuben H. Falconer Diary, May 16, 1863, OHS.

33. *OR*, 24(2):32, 40, 80, 112; *OR*, 24(1):595; Skaptason, "The Chicago Light Artillery at Vicksburg," 440; James C. Sinclair Diary, May 16, 1863, CHM; Howell, *Going to Meet the Yankees*, 172–173; Marshall, *History of the Eighty-third Ohio Volunteer*

Infantry, 80; Kaiser, ed., "The Civil War Diary of Florison D. Pitts," 39; John E. Wilkins Reminiscences, 1911, IHS, 8; Marshall, *History of the Eighty-third Ohio Volunteer Infantry*, 78–80; Merrick J. Wald Diary, May 16, 1863, OCM; Isaac Jackson to Sallie, May 27, 1863, Isaac Jackson Papers, James S. Schoff Civil War Collection, UMC.

34. *OR*, 24(2):70, 80; *OR*, 24(1):265; D. M. Matthews, "A Reminisce of Champion Hill," *Confederate Veteran* 21, no. 5 (May 1913): 208; Bryan S. Bush, *Lloyd Tilghman: Confederate General in the Western Theater* (Morley, MO: Acclaim Press, 2006), 190–193; "Gen. Lloyd Tilghman," *Confederate Veteran* 18, no. 7 (July 1910): 318–319; T. C. Ryan, "Experiences of a Soldier in the Civil War," undated, T. C. Ryan File, OCM; Thomas Gore Memoir, undated, Gore Civil War Collection, USM, 77–79; Francis Baxter to Ret, May 23, 1863, Francis Marion Baxter Papers, MDAH; William Drennan to wife, May 30, 1863, William Drennan Papers, MDAH.

35. *OR*, 24(2):77, 80, 95–96; *OR*, 24(1):53.

36. *OR*, 24(2):70, 127; *OR*, 24(1):265.

37. *OR*, 24(2):70, 76, 85, 88, 91, 96, 102, 111; *OR*, 24(1):53, 151, 264; Samuel P. Harrington Diary, May 16, 1863, Haerle Collection, USAHEC; Jenney, "With Sherman and Grant from Memphis to Chattanooga: A Reminisce," 204; William L. B. Jenney, "Personal Recollections of Vicksburg," in *Military Essays and Recollections: Papers Read before the Commandery of the State of Illinois, Military Order of the Loyal Legion of the United States*, 5 vols. (Chicago: The Dial Press, 1899), 3:260; Aquilla Standifird Diary, May 16, 1863, SHSMR; Marszalek, Nolen, and Gallo, eds., *The Personal Memoirs of Ulysses S. Grant*, 359; Reuben H. Falconer Diary, May 16, 1863, OHS; Louis K. Knobe Reminiscences, undated, ISL, 31–32.

38. *OR*, 24(2):70, 76, 85, 88, 91, 96, 102, 111; *OR*, 24(1):53, 151, 264; M. D. L. Stephens Recollections, undated, MDAH, 18; Reuben H. Falconer Diary, May 16, 1863, OHS; William Drennan to wife, May 30, 1863, William Drennan Papers, MDAH; Marszalek, Nolen, and Gallo, eds., *The Personal Memoirs of Ulysses S. Grant*, 359; Louis K. Knobe Reminiscences, undated, ISL, 31–32.

39. *OR*, 24(2):70, 76, 85, 88, 91, 96, 102, 111; *OR*, 24(1):53, 151, 264; Marszalek, Nolen, and Gallo, eds., *The Personal Memoirs of Ulysses S. Grant*, 359; Reuben H. Falconer Diary, May 16, 1863, OHS; Louis K. Knobe Reminiscences, undated, ISL, 31–32.

40. *OR*, 24(2):70, 77, 85, 92; *OR*, 24(1):265; William Drennan to wife, May 30, 1863, William Drennan Papers, MDAH; George Forney to Ma, May 27, 1863, George H. Forney Papers, DU.

41. *OR*, 24(2):77, 81, 88, 92; Louis K. Knobe Reminiscences, undated, ISL, 31–32; John C. Swift Diary, May 16, 1863, IHS.

42. *OR*, 24(3):878; *OR*, 24(1):265, 270; Wilson, "A Staff Officer's Journal," 108; George E. Brewer, "Reminiscences in the Life of George E. Brewer," undated, 46th Alabama Papers, ADAH.

43. *OR*, 24(2):77, 84, 96–97, 112; Howard, "The Vicksburg Campaign," 33; Curtis P. Lacey Diary, May 16, 1863, NL; William A. Drennan to his wife, May 30, 1863, William A. Drennan Papers, MDAH; L. B. Claiborne Memoirs, CWTI, USAHEC, 13; James R. Arnold, *Grant Wins the War: Decision at Vicksburg* (New York: John Wiley & Sons,

1997), 194. Much of the following appeared in longer form as Timothy B. Smith, "Mississippi Nightmare," *Civil War Times* 48, no. 4 (August 2009): 54–58.

44. *OR*, 24(2):77, 85, 90; J. W. Harmon Memoirs, TSLA, 30; J. W. Harmon, "A Recollection From an Old Confederate," 35th Alabama Papers, ADAH, 17; T. A. Manahan, "Letters From Veterans," *Confederate Veteran* 2, no. 8 (August 1894): 227; George Forney to his mother, May 27, 1863, George H. Forney Papers, DU; L. B. Claiborne Memoirs, CWTI, USAMHI, 13; Winfield S. Featherston Report, November 10, 1867, Featherston Collection, UM; John W. Taylor to his father, May 20, 1863, Taylor Family Letters, Clyde Hughes Collection, UNC; L. B. Northrop, "A Hill of Death," *Civil War Times Illustrated* 30, no. 2 (May/June 1991): 62–63; J. P. Cannon, "History of the 27th Reg. Alabama Volunteer Infantry C.S.A.," 27th Alabama Papers, ADAH, 41.

45. *OR*, 24(2):77–78, 85–86, 90, 92; Clay Sharkey, H. Clay Sharkey Memoir, undated, H. Clay Sharkey Papers, MDAH, 4; M. D. L. Stephens Recollections, undated, MDAH, 19; "The War Between the States," Isaac E. Hirsh Papers, MSU, 32; Binford, "Recollections," Patrick Henry Papers, MDAH, 42; J. P. Cannon, "History of the 27th Reg. Alabama Volunteer Infantry C.S.A.," 27th Alabama Papers, ADAH, 41- 42.

46. *OR*, 24(2):32, 73–74, 78, 81, 85–86, 92–93; M. D. L. Stephens Recollections, undated, MDAH, 19; "The War Between the States," Isaac E. Hirsh Papers, MSU, 32–33; George Forney to his mother, May 27, 1863, George H. Forney Papers, DU; Greif, "Baker's Creek and Champion Hill," 352; Winfield S. Featherston Report, November 10, 1867, Featherston Collection, UM, copy in CWD, USAHEC.

47. *OR*, 24(2):78, 81, 86, 281; Jenney, "With Sherman and Grant from Memphis to Chattanooga: A Reminisce," 203; Thomas White to mother, May 11, 1863, Thomas K. White Papers, OHS; Henry Schmidt to wife, May 24, 1863, Schmidt Family Papers, FHS; M. D. L. Stephens Recollections, undated, MDAH, 19–20; "The War Between the States," Isaac E. Hirsh Papers, MSU, 33; Binford, "Recollections," Patrick Henry Papers, MDAH, 42; Thomas M. Gore, History of Company D, 15th Mississippi Infantry, Gore Civil War History Collection, USM, 79; James Arthur Lyon Fremantle, *The Fremantle Diary: Being the Journal of Lieutenant Colonel James Arthur Lyon Fremantle, Coldstream Guards, on His Three Months in the Southern States*, ed. Walter Lord (Boston: Little, Brown and Company, 1954), 83; J. P. Cannon, "History of the 27th Reg. Alabama Volunteer Infantry C.S.A.," 27th Alabama Papers, ADAH, 42; Alfred Theodore Goodloe, *Confederate Echoes: A Voice From the South in the Days of Secession and of the Southern Confederacy* (Nashville, TN: Publishing House of the M.E. Church, 1907), 279; Greif, "Baker's Creek and Champion Hill," 352; John W. Taylor to his father, May 20, 1863, Taylor Family Letters, Clyde Hughes Collection, UNC; Binford, "Recollections," Patrick Henry Papers, MDAH, 42; Raab, *W. W. Loring*, 120; Joseph N. Thompson, "History of the Thirty-Fifth Alabama Infantry Regiment Confederate States of America," 35th Alabama Papers, ADAH, 11.

48. *OR*, 24(1):267.

49. *OR*, 24(2):108, 143; I. V. Smith Memoir, 1902, SHSMC, 29; James to Kate, December 22, 1863, Israel L. Adams Family Papers, LSU; Henry George, *History of the 3d, 7th, 8th and 12th Kentucky C.S.A.* (Louisville, KY: C. T. Dearing Printing Co., 1911), 62.

50. *OR*, 24(2):16; *OR*, 24(1):616, 718; *OR*, 24(3):885; William A. Sypher Diary, May 16, 1863, CHM; Hass, ed., "The Vicksburg Diary of Henry Clay Warmoth," 71; Aquilla Standifird Diary, May 16, 1863, SHSMR; Lyman T. Shaw Diary, May 16, 1863, 99th Illinois File, VNMPR; Robert S. Shuey to brother, May 18, 1863, John C. Pemberton Papers, RG 109, E 131, NARA.

51. *OR*, 24(3):318, 320; John Merrilees Diary, May 16, 1863, CHM; Henry J. Seaman Diary, May 16, 1863, CWTI, USAHEC; N. W. Wood Diary, May 16, 1863, UCB.

52. *OR*, 24(2):297; Pryce, *Vanishing Footprints*, 104.

53. *OR*, 24(2):10, 44, 52, 99, 418; Thomas Hawley to parents, May 18, 1863, Thomas S. Hawley Papers, MHS; James Slack to wife, May 12, 1863, James R. Slack Letters, ISL; David Shockley to family, June 3, 1863, David Shockley Letters, IHS; James D. Heath Diary, May 16, 1863, OCM; "A Post Camp-Fire," *National Tribune*, October 18, 1883; Sarah Bigelow to Mrs. Woodson, June 16, 1863, Samuel B. Hamacker Letters, SHSMC; Job H. Yaggy Diary, May 16, 1863, ALPL; William Brotherton to Levy Brotherton, May 18, 1863, William Brotherton Papers, EU; Adam Showers to Thomas Fogle, May 18, 1863, James S. Fogle Papers, ISL; Eugene B. Harrison Diary, May 16, 1863, CWD, USAHEC; Marcus Frost to sister, June 5, 1863, Marcus O. Frost Letters, CWTI, USAHEC; Bearss, *The Vicksburg Campaign*, 2:645; "Champion's Hill," *National Tribune*, May 17, 1888; Trowbridge, *Autobiography*, 139; "Champion's Hill," *National Tribune*, April 5, 1894.

54. *OR*, 24(1):640, 718; *OR*, 24(2):243–244; Oldroyd, *A Soldier's Story*, 23; Fred Grant Memoir, undated, USGPL, 26; Thomas C. Skinner to Hannah, May 20, 1863, Ulysses S. Grant Papers, LC; John N. Bell Diary, May 16, 1863, OHS; Simon and Marszalek, eds., *PUSG*, 8:228.

55. *OR*, 24(2):103; Andrew Flick Diary, May 16, 1863, ALPL; Cadwallader, *Three Years with Grant*, 81.

CHAPTER 16. "A VICTORY COULD HARDLY HAVE BEEN
MORE COMPLETE"

1. William Drennan to wife, May 30, 1863, William A. Drennan Papers, MDAH; Hall, "The Key to Vicksburg," 395.

2. *OR*, 24(1):266; Bearss, *The Vicksburg Campaign*, 2: 654; Grabau, *Ninety-Eight Days*, 332.

3. *OR*, 24(1):266; Smith, "Mississippi Nightmare," 54–58.

4. James H. Wilson Journal, May 16, 1863, James H. Wilson Papers, LC; *OR*, 24(1):53; Simon and Marszalek, eds., *PUSG*, 8:229; Sherman, *Memoirs*, 1:323; Reed, *Campaigns and Battles of the Twelfth Regiment Iowa*, 121.

5. James H. Wilson Journal, May 16, 1863, James H. Wilson Papers, LC; *OR*, 24(1):53; Reed, *Campaigns and Battles of the Twelfth Regiment Iowa*, 121; Simon and Marszalek, eds., *PUSG*, 8:229.

6. Robert S. Shuey to brother, May 18, 1863, John C. Pemberton Papers, RG 109,

E 131, NARA; William Clemans Memoirs, UIL, 9; Jenney, "Personal Recollections of Vicksburg," 260; Marszalek, Nolen, and Gallo, eds., *The Personal Memoirs of Ulysses S. Grant*, 361.

7. *OR*, 24(1):54, 86, 266–267; Crooke, *The Twenty-first Regiment of Iowa Volunteer Infantry*, 69; Bearss, *The Vicksburg Campaign*, 2:454, 655–657; Lockett, "The Defense of Vicksburg," 487; J. H. Jones, "The Rank and File at Vicksburg," in *Publications of the Mississippi Historical Society*, Franklin L. Riley, ed. (Oxford: Mississippi Historical Society, 1903), 7:19; J. W. Harmon Memoirs, undated, TSLA.

8. Anderson, *Memoirs*, 317.

9. *OR*, 24(1):266; Bearss, *The Vicksburg Campaign*, 2:678; John B. Bannon Diary, May 17, 1863, USC; William Drennan to wife, May 30, 1863, Drennan Papers, MDAH.

10. *OR*, 24(2):119. Tucker, *The Forgotten "Stonewall of the West,"* 286–290.

11. *OR*, 24(1):266; Joseph W. Westbrook Memoir, 1903, CWD, USAHEC, 5; Edmond W. Pettus, "Colonel Franklin K. Beck — A Sketch," Edmond W. Pettus Papers, ADAH, 1; Francis V. Greene, *The Mississippi* (New York: Charles Scribner's Sons, 1882), 162; George R. Elliott Diaries, May 17, 1863, TSLA; *OR*, 24(1):113, 119, 266–267; Bearss, *The Vicksburg Campaign*, 2:665; Tucker, *Westerners in Gray*, 206. For Vaughn and his brigade, see Larry Gordon, *The Last Confederate General: John C. Vaughn and His East Tennessee Cavalry* (Minneapolis: Zenith Press, 2009), 57–62.

12. *OR*, 24(1):267.

13. *OR*, 24(1):266–267; *OR*, 24(2):73; Pryce, *Vanishing Footprints*, 106; Grabau, *Ninety-Eight Days*, 331; Lockett, "The Defense of Vicksburg," 488.

14. Robert S. Shuey to brother, May 18, 1863, John C. Pemberton Papers, RG 109, E 131, NARA; William Drennan to wife, May 30, 1863, Drennan Papers, MDAH; Bearss, *The Vicksburg Campaign*, 2:665, 667, 671; Elliott, *History of the Thirty-third Regiment Illinois Veteran Volunteer Infantry*, 40–41; Aquilla Standifird Diary, May 17, 1863, SHSMR; *OR*, 24(1):53–54, 152, 616; *OR*, 24(2):16, 24, 32, 132, 135–136; C. H. Twining to Kate, June 9, 1863, Moody Family Papers, MHS; George Nester to William Rigby, January 29, 1902, 1st Battery Indiana Light Artillery File, VNMPR; Charles F. Smith Diary, May 17, 1863, NC; A. G. Fraser to sisters, November 14, 1863, A. G. Fraser Papers, MDAH; Charles Dana to Edwin Stanton, May 23, 1863, Charles A. Dana Papers, LC.

15. Peter J. Perrine Diary, May 17, 1863, OHS; Reuben H. Falconer Diary, May 17, 1863, OHS; Samuel P. Harrington Diary, May 17, 1863, Haerle Collection, USAHEC; Townsend, *Yankee Warhorse*, 106; Bentley, *History of the 77th Illinois Volunteer Infantry*, 141–142; James F. Elliott Diary, May 17, 1863, IHS; James C. Sinclair Diary, May 17, 1863, CHM; Bearss, *The Vicksburg Campaign*, 2:665, 667, 671; *OR*, 24(1):53–54, 152, 616; *OR*, 24(2):16, 132, 135–136; Richard Blackstone Diary, May 17, 1863, LMU.

16. Aquilla Standifird Diary, May 17, 1863, SHSMR; Robert S. Shuey to brother, May 18, 1863, John C. Pemberton Papers, RG 109, E 131, NARA; Pryce, *Vanishing Footprints,* 105–106; Gordon, *The Last Confederate General*, 60; *OR*, 24(2):16, 26, 29–30, 132, 136; *OR*, 24(1):152; Israel Piper Diary, May 17, 1863, VICK; DeBenneville Randolph Keim Diary, May 15, 1863, UMEM; Bearss, *The Vicksburg Campaign*, 2:666; General Orders No. 46, May 18, 1863, RG 393, E 3230, NARA.

17. Israel Piper Diary, May 17, 1863, VICK; DeBenneville Randolph Keim Diary, May 15, 1863, UMEM; Bearss, *The Vicksburg Campaign*, 2:666; Robert S. Shuey to brother, May 18, 1863, John C. Pemberton Papers, RG 109, E 131, NARA; Pryce, *Vanishing Footprints*, 105–106; Gordon, *The Last Confederate General*, 60; Aquilla Standifird Diary, May 17, 1863, SHSMR; *OR*, 24(2):16, 26, 29–30, 132, 136; *OR*, 24(1):152; General Orders No. 46, May 18, 1863, RG 393, E 3230, NARA.

18. *OR*, 24(1):624; Jack D. Welsh, *Medical Histories of Union Generals* (Kent, OH: Kent State University Press, 1996), 200; *OR*, 24(2):136; Robert S. Shuey to brother, May 18, 1863, John C. Pemberton Papers, RG 109, E 131, NARA; Bearss, *The Vicksburg Campaign*, 2:671; Crummer, *With Grant*, 107; Cadwallader, *Three Years with Grant*, 83.

19. *OR*, 24(2):135–137; *OR*, 24(1):152; Charles Boarman Cleveland, "With the Third Missouri Regiment," *Confederate Veteran* 31, no. 1 (January 1923): 19; "Black River Bridge," *National Tribune*, November 5, 1891; Aquilla Standifird Diary, May 17, 1863, SHSMR; Woodworth, *Nothing but Victory*, 393; Edwin C. Bearss, *Fields of Honor: Pivotal Battles of the Civil War* (Washington, DC: National Geographic, 2006), 231.

20. *OR*, 24(2):136–137; Crooke, *The Twenty-first Regiment of Iowa Volunteer Infantry*, 73; Cadwallader, *Three Years with Grant*, 83–84.

21. Michael Lawler to John, May 11, 1863, Michael K. Lawler Papers, SIU; George W. Gordon Diary, May 24, 1863, HCWRT, USAHEC; Aquilla Standifird Diary, May 17, 1863, SHSMR; Pryce, *Vanishing Footprints*, 106; Robert S. Shuey to brother, May 18, 1863, John C. Pemberton Papers, RG 109, E 131, NARA; Crooke, *The Twenty-first Regiment of Iowa Volunteer Infantry*, 73; *OR*, 24(2):119, 137, 142; William Drennan to wife, May 30, 1863, Drennan Papers, MDAH; Bearss, *The Vicksburg Campaign*, 2:673; Jones, *Reminiscences of the Twenty-second Iowa Volunteer Infantry*, 34–35; Robert S. Shuey to brother, May 18, 1863, John C. Pemberton Papers, RG 109, E 131, NARA.

22. Jones, *Reminiscences of the Twenty-second Iowa Volunteer Infantry*, 34–35; Michael Lawler to John, May 11, 1863, Michael K. Lawler Papers, SIU; George W. Gordon Diary, May 24, 1863, USAHEC; William Drennan to wife, May 30, 1863, Drennan Papers, MDAH; Bearss, *The Vicksburg Campaign*, 2:673; Aquilla Standifird Diary, May 17, 1863, SHSMR; Pryce, *Vanishing Footprints*, 106; Robert S. Shuey to brother, May 18, 1863, John C. Pemberton Papers, RG 109, E 131, NARA; Crooke, *The Twenty-first Regiment of Iowa Volunteer Infantry*, 73; *OR*, 24(2):119, 137, 142; Robert S. Shuey to brother, May 18, 1863, John C. Pemberton Papers, RG 109, E 131, NARA.

23. Crooke, *The Twenty-first Regiment of Iowa Volunteer Infantry*, 70; *OR*, 24(2):137, 139; Hass, ed., "The Vicksburg Diary of Henry Clay Warmoth," 71–72; George W. Gordon Diary, May 24, 1863, HCWRT, USAHEC.

24. Crooke, *The Twenty-first Regiment of Iowa Volunteer Infantry*, 73; *OR*, 24(2):137, 142; Aquilla Standifird Diary, May 17, 1863, SHSMR; Pryce, *Vanishing Footprints*, 106; Robert S. Shuey to brother, May 18, 1863, John C. Pemberton Papers, RG 109, E 131, NARA.

25. W. L. Foster to his wife, June 20, 1863, Civil War Papers, MDAH; *OR*, 24(2):119, 128–143; Northern, III, ed., *All Right Let Them Come*, 94; Gordon, *The Last Confederate General*, 60; *OR*, 24(1):54, 152, 267; Joseph W. Westbrook Memoir, 1903, CWD,

USAHEC, 5; Ben Bounds Memoir, undated, MDAH, copy in OCM, 14; Robert S. Shuey to brother, May 18, 1863, John C. Pemberton Papers, RG 109, E 131, NARA; Bevier, *History of the First and Second Missouri Confederate Brigades*, 194; William A. Ruyle, May 17, 1863, HCWRTC, USAHEC.

26. George W. Gordon Diary, May 24, 1863, George W. Gordon Papers, USAHEC; Anderson, *Memoirs*, 319; Theodore D. Fisher Diary, May 17, 1863, Civil War Collection, MHS; *OR*, 24(1):267–268; George Bradley Memoir, undated, OCM, 9; Bearss, *The Vicksburg Campaign*, 2:675; *OR*, 24(2):113–114, 119–120; Tucker, *The Confederacy's Forgotten Stonewall of the West*, 286; Tucker, *Westerners in Gray*, 205–214; Bevier, *History of the First and Second Missouri Confederate Brigades*, 195; Samuel Fowler Diary, May 17, 1863, SU, 193.

27. *OR*, 24(2):23, 137.

28. *OR*, 24(2):24, 26, 32; *OR*, 24(1):152; Charles A. Hobbs, "Vanquishing Vicksburg," *National Tribune*, February 4, 1892; Reuben H. Falconer Diary, May 17, 1863, OHS; Samuel P. Harrington Diary, May 17, 1863, Haerle Collection, USAHEC; Mason, *The Forty-second Ohio Infantry*, 212–216; Williamson Murray Diary, May 17, 1863, VICK; Louis K. Knobe Reminiscences, undated, ISL, 31–32; James Leeper to Mary, May 23, 1863, James Leeper Correspondence, IHS.

29. *OR*, 24(1):596, 617; Marshall, *History of the Eighty-third Ohio Volunteer Infantry*, 82.

30. John Griffin Jones to his parents, May 29, 1863, John Griffin Jones Papers, LC; Pryce, *Vanishing Footprints*, 108; *OR*, 24(1):267–268; *OR*, 24(2):32, 39, 113, 131, 138; Anderson, *Memoirs*, 319; Carlos W. Colby, "Bulletts, Hardtack and Mud: A Soldier's View of the Vicksburg Campaign," edited by John S. Painter, *Journal of the West* 4, no. 2 (April 1965): 151; Robert L. Bachman Memoir, undated, OCM, 19; Winschel, "The Guns at Champion Hill (Part II)," 105; John Merrilees Diary, May 17, 1863, CHM; Robert S. Shuey to brother, May 18, 1863, John C. Pemberton Papers, RG 109, E 131, NARA.

31. *OR*, 24(2):124; George Remley to Howard, May 25, 1863, Remley Family Papers, NC; Samuel Fowler Diary, May 17, 1863, SU, 194; Ben Bounds Memoir, undated, OCM, 15; Charles F. Vogel Diary, May 17, 1863, MDAH; Robert S. Shuey to brother, May 18, 1863, John C. Pemberton Papers, RG 109, E 131, NARA.

32. Robert S. Shuey to brother, May 18, 1863, John C. Pemberton Papers, RG 109, E 131, NARA; Thomas S. Hawley to parents, May 18, 1863, Thomas S. Hawley Papers, MHS; Pryce, *Vanishing Footprints*, 106; Aquilla Standifird Diary, May 17, 1863, SHSMR; Jones, *Reminiscences of the Twenty-second Iowa Volunteer Infantry*, 35; *OR*, 24(2):138; William Clemans Memoir, undated, Clemans Papers, UIL, 9; Crooke, *The Twenty-first Regiment of Iowa Volunteer Infantry*, 73; Ballard, *Vicksburg*, 318; "A Faithful Dog," *National Tribune*, July 5, 1888.

33. Aquilla Standifird Diary, May 17, 1863, SHSMR; Pryce, *Vanishing Footprints*, 106.

34. Williamson Murray Diary, May 17, 1863, VICK; Robert S. Shuey to his brother, May 18, 1863, John C. Pemberton Papers, RG 109, E 131, NARA; *OR*, 24(1):152, 267, 624; *OR*, 24(2):244; Thomas S. Hawley to parents, May 18, 1863, Thomas S. Hawley

Papers, MHS; William F. Jones to cousin, June 13, 1863, William F. Jones Papers, SHSMC.

35. George H. Hynds Diary, May 17, 1863, VICK; Ben Bounds Memoir, undated, OCM, 15; Price F. Kellogg Diary, May 17, 1863, ALPL; Albert C. Boals Diary, May 17, 1863, ALPL; James Horn to family, June 6, 1863, James R. Horn Letters, GDAH.

36. George H. Hynds Diary, May 17, 1863, VICK; John C. Taylor Diary, May 17, 1863, Taylor Family Papers, UVA; *OR*, 24(1):152, 267–269; *OR*, 24(2):244.

37. Leonard B. Plummer, ed., "Excerpts from the Hander Diary," *Journal of Mississippi History* 26, no. 2 (May 1964): 142; John Power Logan Diary, May 17, 1863, MDAH; *OR*, 24(1):268–269; William Drennan to wife, May 30, 1863, Drennan Papers, MDAH.

38. Lockett, "The Defense of Vicksburg," 488; J. T. Hogane, "Reminiscences of the Siege of Vicksburg," *Southern Historical Society Papers* 2, no. 4–5 (April–May 1883): 223; Joseph D. Alison Diary, May 17, 1863, UNC, copy in MDAH and OCM.

39. *OR*, 24(2):73, 114, 124, 132, 229, 350, 352; *OR*, 24(1):268; Jasper N. Whiphers Diary, May 17, 1863, Alexander Roberts Papers, ALPL; William Clemans Memoir, undated, Clemans Papers, UIL, 9; John Fiske, *The Mississippi Valley in the Civil War* (New York: Houghton, Mifflin and Company, 1900), 240; Pryce, *Vanishing Footprints*, 108; I. V. Smith Memoir, 1902, SHSMC, 29; Joseph W. Westbrook Memoir, 1903, CWD, USAHEC, 5; John Ritter to Margaret, June 8, 1863, John Ritter Papers, NC; Samuel H. Lockett, "How We Defended Vicksburg Against Farragut and Grant," Washington, DC *Sunday Star*, November 26, 1911; Lockett, "The Defense of Vicksburg," 488; Claudius W. Sears Diary, May 17, 1863, MDAH; James Palmer Diary, May 17, 1863, MDAH, 9; Samuel Styre to parents, May 28, 1863, Samuel Styre Papers, DU.

40. *OR*, 24(2):73, 114, 124, 132, 229, 350, 352; *OR*, 24(1):268; Jasper N. Whiphers Diary, May 17, 1863, Alexander Roberts Papers, ALPL; William Clemans Memoir, undated, Clemans Papers, UIL, 9; Fiske, *The Mississippi Valley in the Civil War*, 240; Pryce, *Vanishing Footprints*, 108; I. V. Smith Memoir, 1902, SHSMC, 29; Joseph W. Westbrook Memoir, 1903, CWD, USAHEC, 5; John Ritter to Margaret, June 8, 1863, John Ritter Papers, NC; Samuel H. Lockett, "How We Defended Vicksburg Against Farragut and Grant," Washington, DC *Sunday Star*, November 26, 1911; Lockett, "The Defense of Vicksburg," 488; Claudius W. Sears Diary, May 17, 1863, MDAH; James Palmer Diary, May 17, 1863, MDAH, 9; Samuel Styre to parents, May 28, 1863, Samuel Styre Papers, DU.

41. Grant, "A Boy's Experience at Vicksburg," 94–95; Fred Grant Memoir, undated, USGPL, 28–29; Ottens, *General John A. Rawlins*, 279; Samuel P. Harrington Diary, May 17, 1863, Haerle Collection, USAHEC.

42. John C. Taylor Diary, May 17, 1863, Taylor Family Papers, UVA; Emma Balfour Diary, May 17, 1863, MDAH; J. M. Love Diary, May 16, 1863, UM; Joseph Dill Alison Diary, May 17, 1863, UNC; Theodore D. Fisher Diary, May 17, 1863, Civil War Collection, MHS; James E. Payne, "General Pemberton and Vicksburg," *Confederate Veteran* 36, no. 7 (July 1928): 247.

43. Emma Balfour Diary, May 17, 1863, MDAH; Emile R. McKinley Diary, May 18,

1863, MHS; Thomas C. Skinner to "Hannah," May 20, 1863, U. S. Grant Papers, LC; Loughborough, *My Cave Life in Vicksburg*, 33; Mrs. W. W. Lord Diary, May 1863, LC; "A Recollection of Thirty Years Ago," undated, Annie Laurie Harris Broidrick Collection, UNC, 15, 17; J. M. Love Diary, May 17, 1863, UM.

44. George Ditto Diary, May 16, 1863, ALPL; Woodworth, *Nothing but Victory*, 395; Charles A. Dana to Edwin M. Stanton, May 23, 1863, Charles A. Dana Papers, LC; Marszalek, Nolen, and Gallo, eds., *The Personal Memoirs of Ulysses S. Grant*, 363; Young, *Around the World with General Grant*, 2:623.

45. *OR*, 24(2):244; *OR*, 24(3):321–322.

46. Simon and Marszalek, eds., *PUSG*, 8:233–235.

47. *OR*, 24(2):256; *OR*, 24(3):322; *OR*, 52(1):358; *OR*, 24(1):125, 130, 755; Skaptason, "The Chicago Light Artillery at Vicksburg," 440–441; John N. Bell Diary, May 17, 1863, OHS; J. W. Egleston Diary, May 18, 1863, IHS; Charles E. Affeld Diary, May 17, 1863, VICK; Sherman, *Memoirs*, 1:323; Henry J. Seaman Diary, May 17, 1863, CWTI, USAHEC.

48. *OR*, 24(1):641; *OR*, 24(2):297; Benjamin Underwood to Mary, May 25, 1863, Benjamin W. Underwood Letters, OCM; J. H. Rowell Diary, May 13–17, 1863, Eureka College; Simon and Marszalek, eds., *PUSG*, 8:225–226; George D. Carrington Diary, May 16, 1863, CHM.

49. George Remley to Howard, May 23, 1863, Remley Family Papers, NC; Timothy B. Smith, *The Union Assaults at Vicksburg: Grant Attacks Pemberton, May 17–22, 1863* (Lawrence: University Press of Kansas, 2020), 58–64.

Epilogue: "We Have Performed the Greatest Campaign of the War"

1. William Jones to cousin, June 134, 1863, William F. Jones Papers, SHSMC; Alvin Hovey to Mary, May 23, 1863, Alvin Hovey Papers, IU; Walter George Smith, *Life and Letters of Thomas Kilby Smith, Brevet Major-General United States Volunteers, 1820–1877* (New York: G. P. Putnam's Sons, 1898), 296–297; James B. Owen to Sally, May 26, 1863, James B. Owen Letters, TSLA; Samuel Styre to parents, May 28, 1863, Samuel Styre Papers, DU.

2. Howe, ed., *Home Letters of General Sherman*, 261; David Turnbull to friend, May 29, 1863, David C. Turnbull Papers, ISL; William Lewis to Margaret, June 11, 1863, William E. Lewis Letters, SHSMC; "History of J. D. Brownley," undated, John D. Brownley Papers, Anders Collection, USAHEC; John Smith to Aimee, May 31, 1863, John E. Smith Letters, Kirby Smith Collection; John Higgins to Nancy, May 28, 1863, John A. Higgins Papers, ALPL; Solomon Lynn to father, May 24, 1863, Lynn Family Papers, FHS; A. R. Dyson to Louisa, June 8, 1863, Dyson-Bell-Sans Souci Papers, SHSMS; Edwin May Diary, May 2–20, 1863, ALPL; David Grier to Anna, May 14, 1863, Grier Family Papers, MHS.

3. "Strategic Significance of the Battle of Champion Hill," undated, Alvin Hovey

Papers, IU; Sid Champion to wife, May 18, 1863, Sidney S. Champion Papers, DU; Enos Pierson, *Proceedings of Eleven Reunions Held by the 16th Regiment, O. V. I., Including Roll of Honor, Roster of the Survivors of the Regiment, Statistics, &c., &c.* (Millersburg, OH: Republican Steam Press, 1887), 30.

4. John Merrilees Diary, May 17, 1863, CHM; Joseph Skipworth to Ann, May 28, 1863, Joseph Skipworth Papers, SIU; Cyrus Dickey to sister, May 29, 1863, Wallace-Dickey Family Papers, ALPL; Isaac Williams to brother, June 18, 1863, Isaac Williams Papers, Brookes Collection, USAHEC.

5. Edward Wood to wife, May 25, 1863, Edward J. Wood Papers, IHS.

6. Marszalek, Nolen, and Gallo, eds., *The Personal Memoirs of Ulysses S. Grant*, 365.

7. Marszalek, Nolen, and Gallo, eds., *The Personal Memoirs of Ulysses S. Grant*, 365.

8. Jones, *A Rebel War Clerk's Diary*, 1:291–292; Edward Ingraham to aunt, May 21, 1863, E. H. and D. G. Ingraham Papers, ALPL; John L. Power Diary, May 17, 1863, MDAH; Joseph D. Alison Diary, May 17, 1863, UNC; Jared Young Sanders Diary, May 17, 1863, VICK, copy in OCM; Rowland Chambers Diary, May 17, 1863, LSU; Christian W. Hander Diary, May 17, 1863, UTA.

9. *OR*, 24(3):888–889; *OR*, 24(1):272; W. H. Tunnard, *A Southern Record: The History of the Third Regiment Louisiana Infantry* (Baton Rouge, LA: N.p., 1866), 231, 235; Hogane, "Reminiscences of the Siege of Vicksburg," 226; George Powell Clarke, *Reminiscence and Anecdotes of the War for Southern Independence* (N.p.: N.p., n.d.), 99; James Carlisle Diary, May 17, 1863, VICK; Hall, *The Story of the 26th Louisiana Infantry*, 62; "History of Company B," 1902, Chickasaw Bayou File, OCM, 33; Eli W. Thornhill Memoir, undated, OCM, 9; Allen C. Richard, Jr. and Mary Margaret Higginbotham Richard, *The Defense of Vicksburg: A Louisiana Chronicle* (College Station: Texas A&M University Press, 2004), 145; Louisa R. Conner Memoir, undated, MDAH, 11; Thomas Smith Manuscript, undated, MDAH, 5, copy in T. T. Smith Memoir, undated, Columbus Sykes Papers, CWD, USAHEC; W. R. McCrary Diary, May 17, 1863, VICK; Henry J. Reynolds Memoir, undated, CWTI, USAHEC, 4; Louis Hebert Autobiography, 1894, UNC, 12.

10. *OR*, 24(1):217; *OR*, 24(3):887; John Pemberton to Joseph Johnston, May 17, 1863, RG 109, Chapter II, Volume 60, NARA.

11. *OR*, 24(1):216, 327.

12. *OR*, 24(1):269–270.

13. Wilson, "A Staff Officer's Journal," 109; A. S. Abrams Diary, May 1863, VICK; John A. Leavy Diary, May 16, 1863, VICK; A. L. Slack Diary, April 1863, VICK; Joseph D. Alison Diary, May 17, 1863, UNC; William Drennan to wife, May 30, 1863, William Drennan Papers, MDAH; Sid Champion to wife, May 18, 1863, Sidney S. Champion Papers, DU; "The Defenders of Vicksburg." *Southern Historical Society Papers* 21 (1893): 196; Lee, "The Campaign of Vicksburg," 30, 51; Ballard, "Misused Merit," 1:115; Unknown to L. P. Taylor, May 20, 1863, Taylor Family Letters, UNC.

14. Jacob B. Wilkin, "Vicksburg," in *Military Essays and Recollections: Papers Read Before the Commandery of the State of Illinois, Military Order of the Loyal Legion of the United States, Volume 4* (Chicago: Cozzens and Beaton Company, 1907), 226; Robert

K. Krick, "'Snarl and Sneer and Quarrel': General Joseph E. Johnston and an Obsession with Rank," in *Leaders of the Lost Cause: New Perspectives on the Confederate High Command*, Gary W. Gallagher and Joseph T. Glatthaar, eds. (Mechanicsburg, PA: Stackpole Books, 2004), 188; William C. Davis, *Jefferson Davis: The Man and His Hour: A Biography* (New York: HarperCollins, 1991), 501; Clarke, *Reminiscence and Anecdotes of the War for Southern Independence*, 99.

15. Robert S. Shuey to brother, May 18, 1863, John C. Pemberton Papers, RG 109, E 131, NARA; E. B. Reese Memoir, 1930s, Mayfield and Sanders Family Materials, IHS, 10; David Poak to Sadie, June 12, 1863, David W. Poak Papers, ALPL; Luther Cowan to Mollie, May 5, 1863, Luther H. Cowan Papers, TSLA; John Jones to wife, May 27, 1863, John P. Jones Papers, FHS.

16. Andrew McCormack to family, May 24, 1863, Andrew McCornack Letters, NC; Cadwallader, *Three Years with Grant*, 84; Lewis F. Phillips Memoir, 1911, CWTI, USA-HEC, 35; Eugene Carr to unknown, June 7, 1863, Eugene A. Carr Papers, USAHEC; Bearss, *The Vicksburg Campaign*, 2:479, 481.

17. John Wickiser to Judge, May 24, 1863, John H. Wickiser Papers, ALPL; John Ritter to Margarett, June 8, 1863, John Ritter Papers, NC; Levi Williams to uncle, May 29, 1863, Richard E. Blair Letters, IHS; George Chittenden to wife, May 4, 1863, Chittenden Family Papers, ISL.

18. Stone, *Memoir of George Boardman Boomer*, 250; Rachel Sherman Thorndike, ed., *The Sherman Letters: Correspondence Between General and Senator Sherman from 1837 to 1891* (New York: Charles Scribner's Sons, 1894), 205–206; Archer Jones, *Civil War Command and Strategy: The Process of Victory and Defeat* (New York: The Free Press, 1992), 161; *OR*, 24(1):63.

19. Roy P. Basler, ed., *Collected Works of Abraham Lincoln*, 9 vols. (New Brunswick, NJ: Rutgers University Press, 1953), 6:230, 326; T. Harry Williams, *Lincoln and His Generals* (New York: Alfred A. Knopf, 1952), 228–229.

20. Clausewitz, *On War*, 443.

21. Special Orders No. 134, May 17, 1863, Ulysses S. Grant Collection, Unpublished Correspondence, USGPL; Smith, *The Union Assaults at Vicksburg*, 76–127.

22. George D. Carrington Diary, May 17, 1863, CHM; Jones, *Reminiscences of the Twenty-second Iowa Volunteer Infantry*, 36; Bering and Montgomery, *History of the Forty-Eighth Ohio Vet. Vol. Inf.*, 84; Mason, *The Forty-second Ohio Infantry*, 212.

23. *OR*, 24(1):146.

24. Terrence J. Winschel, ed., *The Civil War Diary of a Common Soldier: William Wiley of the 77th Illinois Infantry* (Baton Rouge: Louisiana State University Press, 2001), 48; W. R. Eddington Memoir, undated, ALPL, 7–9.

25. *OR*, 24(1):728, 780; William Strong Memoir, undated, William E. Strong Papers, ALPL, 142; William E. Strong, "The Campaign Against Vicksburg," in *Military Essays and Recollections: Papers Read Before the Commandery of the State of Illinois, Military Order of the Loyal Legion of the United States*, 4 vols. Chicago: A. C. McClurg and Company, 1894), 2:330.

26. *OR*, 24(2):61.

27. *OR*, 24(1):707.

28. *OR*, 24(1):764–765, 769; Eric Michael Burke, *Soldiers from Experience: The Fighting of Sherman's Fifteenth Army Corps 1862–1863* (Baton Rouge: Louisiana State University Press, 2023), 150–157.

29. *OR*, 24(1):761–763; Buckles, *Not Afraid to Go Any Whare*, 40.

30. Aquilla Standifird Diary, May 14, 1863, SHSMR; Robert S. Shuey to brother, May 18, 1863, John C. Pemberton Papers, RG 109, E 131, NARA; Charles E. Affeld Diary, May 17, 1863, VICK; Anson Hemingway Diary, May 17, 1863, VICK; Charles Miller Memoirs, undated, VICK, 44–45; Francis R. Baker Diary, May 17, 1863, ALPL; Oldroyd, *A Soldier's Story*, 22; Byers, *With Fire and Sword*, 85.

31. Anthony Burton Diary, May 17–22, 1863, Journals/Letters/Diaries, VICK; Charles F. Smith Diary, May 19, 1863, NC; John L. Woods Report, September 30, 1863, RG 92, E 1127, NARA, 5:916.

32. Calvin Ainsworth Diary, May 18, 1863, UMB; George to sister, June 2, 1863, Safford Family Papers, ALPL; Thomas B. Beggs to aunt, June 19, 1863, Thomas B. Beggs Papers, ALPL; George M. Rogers Diary, May 18 and 20, 1863, ISL; Henry Clay Leeson to father, May 27, 1863, Leeson Family Papers, ISL; Charles Henry Snedeker Diary, May 29, 1863, AU; Oldroyd, *A Soldier's Story*, 27; George Carrington Diary, May 20, 1863, CHM; Jesse M. Lee Diary, May 20, 1863, 59th Indiana File, VICK.

33. *OR*, 24(1):259; *OR*, 24(2):124.

34. Ballard, "Misused Merit," 1:115; Ballard, *Pemberton*, 149; Hattaway and Jones, *How the North Won*, 393; Oldroyd, *A Soldier's Story*, 25.

35. Bearss and Hills, *Receding Tide*, 161; Winschel, "The Absence of Will," 82; Ballard, *Pemberton*, 158.

36. Marszalek, Nolen, and Gallo, eds., *The Personal Memoirs of Ulysses S. Grant*, 342, 348, 355; Hicks, "The Campaign and Capture of Vicksburg," 98; Richardson, *A Personal History of Ulysses S. Grant*, 312; Hicks, "The Campaign and Capture of Vicksburg," 98; Badeau, *Military History of Ulysses S. Grant*, 1:220.

37. Robert S. Shuey to brother, May 18, 1863, John C. Pemberton Papers, RG 109, E 131, NARA; Charles Peck to brother, May 17, 1863, Charles Peck Papers, Haerle Collection, USAHEC; *OR*, 24(1):37.

38. *OR*, 24(1):754; Marszalek, Nolen, and Gallo, eds., *The Personal Memoirs of Ulysses S. Grant*, 353; Wilson, *Under the Old Flag*, 1:203; Cadwallader, *Three Years with Grant*, 75; Fred Grant Memoir, undated, USGPL, 22.

39. James Llewellyn, "Battle of Champion Hill, Miss.," *Confederate Veteran* 14, no. 8 (August 1906): 363; Yeary, *Reminiscences of the Boys in Gray, 1861–1865*, 330.

40. Simon and Marszalek, eds., *PUSG*, 8:214.

BIBLIOGRAPHY

MANUSCRIPTS

Abraham Lincoln Presidential Library, Springfield, Illinois
    Francis R. Baker Memoir
    Lyman M. Baker Memoir
    Ira A. Batterton Papers
    Thomas B. Beggs Papers
    Albert C. Boals Diary
    James P. Boyd Diary
    Nicholas C. Buswell Papers
    Albert Chipman Papers
    John P. Davis Diary
    John C. Dinsmore Papers
    George Ditto Diary
    W. R. Eddington Memoir
    Alexander K. Ewing Papers
    Joseph W. Fifer Papers
    John B. Fletcher Diary
    Andrew Flick Diary
    Joseph Forrest Papers
    Samuel Gordon Papers
    Balzar Grebe Memoir
    John A. Higgins Papers
    E. H. and D. G. Ingraham Letters
    William H. Kinkade Diary
    George R. Lee Diary
    James B. Logan Diary
    George M. Lucas Diary
    John A. McClernand Papers
    Arthur P. McCullough Diary
    James S. McHenry Diary

J. W. Miller Papers
Isaac S. Mylar Papers
Ira A. Payne Papers
David W. Poak Papers
Cyrus W. Randall Papers
Rand Family Papers
William M. Reid Diary
Mortimer Rice Diary
Robert Ridge Diary
Alexander Roberts Papers
Rocky Springs Letter
George W. Russell Papers
Safford Family Papers
John Sherriff Family Papers
Payson Shumway Papers
George O. Smith Papers
William E. Strong Papers
Joseph Stockton Diary
Frank W. Tupper Papers
Abram J. Vanauken Diary
Wallace-Dickey Family Papers
Thomas Watson Papers
John H. Wickiser Papers
James A. Woodson Diary
Job H. Yaggy Diary
Alabama Department of Archives and History, Montgomery, Alabama
20th Alabama Papers
23rd Alabama Papers
27th Alabama Papers
30th Alabama Papers
35th Alabama Papers
46th Alabama Papers
Edmund W. Pettus Papers
William L. Roberts Diary
Waddell's Battery File
Elbert D. Willett Diary
Archives of Michigan, Lansing, Michigan
Douwe B. Yntema Collection
Leonard G. Loomis Letters
Auburn University, Auburn, Alabama
Charles Henry Snedeker Diary
Southern Railroad Records

Augustana College, Rock Island, Illinois
   Gould D. Molineaux Diary
Chicago History Museum, Chicago, Illinois
   A. Achen Papers
   George D. Carrington Diary
   John Merrilees Diary
   Florison D. Pitts Papers
   Arnold Rickard Diary
   James C. Sinclair Diary
   William A. Sypher Diary
Cincinnati Historical Society, Cincinnati, Ohio
   Andrew Hickenlooper Collection
Cornell University, Cornell, New York
   Asa Fitch Papers
      Sarah Fitch Poates Diary
Duke University, Durham, North Carolina
   Sidney S. Champion Papers
   George H. Forney Papers
   Robert B. Hoadley Papers
   Lucas-Ashley Papers
   James Meagher Papers
   "Military History of Captain Thomas Sewell"
   W. A. Rorer Letters
   Samuel Styre Papers
Emory University, Atlanta, Georgia
   William Brotherton Papers
Eureka College, Eureka, Illinois
   J. H. Rowell Diary
Filson Historical Society, Louisville, Kentucky
   John P. Jones Papers
   Lynn Family Papers
   Schmidt Family Papers
   James W. Thompson Papers
Georgia Department of Archives and History, Atlanta, Georgia
   Joseph Bogle Memoir
   William T. Daniel Letters
   George T. Fowler Papers
Gettysburg College, Gettysburg, Pennsylvania
   Unknown 13th Illinois Diary
Harvard University, Cambridge, Massachusetts
   Baker Library
      "Southern Railroad Company 25 Cents"

Huntington Library, San Marino, California
    Delos Van Deusen Correspondence
Indiana Historical Society, Indianapolis, Indiana
    Richard E. Blair Letters
    Magnus Brucker Letters
    J. W. Egleston Diary
    James F. Elliott Diary
    Bennett Grigsby Papers
    Howard County Documents
    Daniel Hughes Diary
    James Leeper Correspondence
    John F. Lester Diary
    Thomas Marshall Letters
    Mayfield and Sanders Family Papers
    Wilfred B. McDonald Diary
    John M. Roberts Diary
    Asa Sample Diary
    David Shockley Letters
    Samuel E. Sneier Letter
    Edward P. Stanfield Letters
    John C. Swift Diary
    Hubbard T. Thomas Papers
    Joshua W. Underhill Diary
    Aurelius L. Voorhis Diary
    John E. Wilkins Reminiscences
    Edward J. Wood Papers
    Joseph W. Young Letters
Indiana State Library, Indianapolis, Indiana
    Chittenden Family Papers
    James S. Fogle Papers
    Daniel Hughes Diary
    Louis K. Knobe Reminiscences
    Leeson Family Papers
    August Leich Collection
    George B. Marshall Reminiscences
    Daniel Roberts Correspondence
    George M. Rogers Diary
    Asa Sample Diary
    Augustus G. Sinks Papers
    James R. Slack Letters
    Benjamin Spooner Letters
    James H. St. John Diary
    David C. Turnbull Papers

James C. Vanderbilt Papers
Harry Watts Reminiscences
Indiana University, Bloomington, Indiana
Flavel C. Barber Diary
Alvin Hovey Papers
Kirby Smith Collection, Barrington, Illinois
John E. Smith Letters
Library of Congress, Washington, DC
Charles A. Dana Papers
Charles Calvin Enslow Papers
Ulysses S. Grant Papers
John G. Jones Papers
John A. Logan Papers
Mrs. W. W. Lord Diary
James B. McPherson Papers
William T. Sherman Papers
Edwin M. Stanton Papers
John Whitten Diary
Louis T. Wigfall Papers
James H. Wilson Papers
Lincoln Memorial Shrine, Redlands, California
Mortimer D. Leggett Papers
Louisiana State University, Baton Rouge, Louisiana
Israel L. Adams Family Papers
Henry Watkins Allen Letter
Rowland Chambers Diary
Samuel W. Ferguson Papers
Autobiography of Louis Hébert
George G. Meade Letter
Loyola Marymount University, Los Angeles, California
Richard Blackstone Diary
Minnesota Historical Society, St. Paul, Minnesota
James C. Christie and Family Papers
Mississippi Department of Archives and History, Jackson, Mississippi
Joseph D. Alison Diary
Luther S. Baechtel Diary
Emma Balfour Diary
Francis M. Baxter Papers
Ben Bounds Memoir
Civil War Papers
Confederate Collection
Louisa Russell Conner Memoir
William A. Drennan Papers

H. N. Faulkinbury Diary
Fonsylvania Plantation Diary
William L. Foster Letter
A. G. Fraser Papers
James Z. George Papers
J. W. Greenman Diary
Patrick Henry Papers
    James R. Binford, "Recollections of the Fifteenth Regiment of Mississippi
        Infantry, C.S.A."
Letters and Papers Covering Organizations: Miscellaneous — Georgia,
    Massachusetts, New Hampshire, and Rhode Island
Letters and Papers Covering Organizations: Virginia (Botetourt Artillery)
John Power Logan Diary
Mississippi Governor, Charles Clark, Order Book, 1863–1865, Series 770
Mississippi Governor, John J. Pettus, Correspondence and Papers, 1859–1863,
    Series 757
Mississippi Governor, John J. Pettus, Executive Journals, 1817–1887, John J. Pettus,
    Series 758
Mississippi Governor, John J. Pettus, Incoming Telegrams, 1861–1862, Series 762
Mississippi Governor, John J. Pettus, Military Orders, 1862–1863, Series 769
Mississippi Governor, John J. Pettus, Outgoing Telegrams, 1861–1862, Series 763
Mississippi Governor's Papers, Charles Clark, Correspondence and Papers,
    1863–1865, Series 767
Mississippi Governor's Papers, Charles Clark, Executive Journals, 1817–1887,
    Charles Clark, Series 758
George W. Modil Diary
Edmund Newsome Diary
James Palmer Diary
John L. Power Diary
W. A. Rorer Letters
Claudius W. Sears Diary
H. Clay Sharkey Papers
Thomas Smith Manuscript
M. D. L. Stephens Recollections
Subject Files
    Auburn Subject File
    Bruinsburg Subject File
    Cayuga Subject File
    Secession Subject File
    Utica Subject File
    Windsor Subject File
Charles F. Vogel Diary
John A. Wilson Letters

Mississippi State University, Starkville, Mississippi
  Calhoun–Kincannon–Orr Family Papers
  Ray Fulton Collection
    Sallie B. McCrae Diary
  Gardner Collection
  Isaac E. Hirsh Papers
  Hobbs Family Papers
Missouri Historical Society, St. Louis, Missouri
  Alphabetical Files
    Joel Strong Reminiscences
  John T. Appler Diary
  Civil War Collection
    Theodore D. Fisher Diary
    Thomas S. Hawley Papers
  Grier Family Papers
  Emile R. McKinley Diary
  Moody Family Papers
  Unidentified Soldier of the 31st Iowa Infantry Diary
National Archives and Records Administration, Washington, DC
  RG 24—Records of the Bureau of Naval Personnel
    E 118—Logbooks of U.S. Navy Ships
      USS *Pittsburgh* Logbook
  RG 92—Records of the Office of the Quartermaster General
    E 1127—Annual Reports of Quartermaster Officers, 1863
  RG 94—Records of the Adjutant General's Office, 1780s–1917
    E 297—Appointment, Commission and Personnel Branch File
  RG 109—War Department Collection of Confederate Records, 1825–1900
    E 97—Army of the Mississippi, Orders and Circulars, 1861–1865
    E 131—John C. Pemberton Papers
    E 180—Confederate Papers Relating to Citizens or Business Firms
    E 465—Union Provost Marshal's File of Papers Relating to Two or More Civilians
    M 345—Union Provost Marshal's File of Papers Relating to Individual Civilians
    Chapter 2, Volume 57—Letters and Telegrams Sent, Department of Mississippi and East Louisiana, 1862–1863
    Chapter 2, Volume 60—Letters and Telegrams Sent, Department of Mississippi and East Louisiana, 1863
    Chapter 2, Volume 274—Letter Book, Brig. Gen. J. S. Bowen's Command, August 1862—November 1863
  RG 156—Records of the Office of the Chief or Ordnance
    E 176—Military Service Histories of Ordnance Officers, 1832–1922
  RG 192—Records of the Office of the Commissary General of Subsistence
    E 36—Provision Book—1863 and 1864

E 82A—Reports of Chief Commissaries on Duty in Military Departments, 1863–1864

RG 217—Records of the Accounting Officers of the Department of the Treasury
E 732—Records of the Land, Files, and Miscellaneous Division

RG 233—Records of the United States House of Representatives
Records of Committees Relating to Claims

RG 393—Records of the United States Army Continental Commands
E 3221—9th Division, XIII Corps, Letters Sent, 1861–1863
E 3230—9th Division, XIII Corps, General and Special Orders Issued, 1863
E 4709—Department of the Tennessee, Letters Sent, 1862–1863
E 4720—Department of the Tennessee, Letters Received, 1863–1867
E 5524—XIII Corps, Letters Sent, 1862–1864
E 5541—XIII Corps, General Orders Issued, 1863–1864
E 5545—XIII Corps, Special Orders Issued, 1863
E 5924—2nd Division, XV Corps, General Orders Issued, 1863–1865
E 5925—2nd Division, XV Corps, Special Orders Issued, 1863–1864
E 5928—2nd Division, XV Corps, Letters and Circulars Sent and a Few Received, 1863–1864
E 6225—3rd Division, XVII Corps, Letters Sent, 1863–1865
E 6254—3rd Division, XVII Corps, Register of Rations Issued, 1863–1864
E 6294—XVII Corps, Letters Sent, 1862–1865
E 6305—XVII Corps, General Orders Issued, 1862–1865

Navarro College, Corsicana, Texas
Jordan C. Harriss Papers
Andrew McCornack Letters
Remley Family Papers
John Ritter Papers
Charles F. Smith Diary

Newberry Library, Chicago, Illinois
Curtis P. Lacey Diary

Ohio Historical Society, Columbus, Ohio
76th Ohio Volunteer Regiment Correspondence
"A Soldier's Story"
John N. Bell Diary
Henry Otis Dwight Papers
Dykes Family Papers
Hugh Ewing Papers
Rueben H. Falconer Diary
Henry W. Franks Letters
Carlos Forbes Papers
John W. Griffith Diary
George H. Hildt Letters
Elliot Morrow Papers

Peter J. Perrine Diary
Flavius J. Thackara Diary
Ernest A. Warden Diary
Thomas K. White Papers
William F. Willey Diary
Cyrus Willford Reminiscences
Old Courthouse Museum, Vicksburg, Mississippi
35th Iowa Infantry Memoir
Joseph D. Alison Diary
Robert L. Bachman Memoir
Banner Family Letters
Abiel M. Barker Diary
S. C. Beck, "A True Sketch of His Army Life"
Joseph Bogle Memoir
Ben Bounds Memoir
John A. Bowman Letters
George Bradley Memoir
William B. Britton Letters
Chickasaw Bayou File
Samuel Churchill Memoir
Edward J. Dunn Memoir
James Ferguson Letters
Joseph C. Gordon Diary
C. B. Haddon Memoir
Seth Hall Letters
James D. Heath Diary
John Hipple Letter
William F. Hollingsworth Diary
James Jermyn Diary
James T. Kidd Memoir
Myron Knight Diary
John A. Leavy Diary
James F. Mallinckrodt Diary
Thomas N. McCluer Diary
George W. Modil Diary
William T. Mumford Diary
Edmund Newsome Diary
Israel M. Piper Diary
T. C. Ryan Memoir
Jared Sanders Letter
Maurice K. Simons Diary
Joel Strong Reminiscences
Eli W. Thornhill Memoir

Benjamin W. Underwood Letters
Martin Van Kees Diary
Merrick J. Wald Diary
Seth Wells Diary
Abner J. Wilkes Memoir
J. S. Wheeler File
James W. Woodard Letters
Rutherford B. Hayes Presidential Center, Fremont, Ohio
Wilfred S. Foerster Collection
Southern Illinois University, Carbondale, Illinois
Michael K. Lawler Papers
Edwin A. Loosley Papers
Robert S. Martin Diary
Joseph Skipworth Papers
Stanford University, Stanford, California
Samuel Fowler Diary
Frederick Steele Papers
State Historical Society of Iowa, Iowa City, Iowa
William L. Cotton Letters
Sewall S. Farwell Papers
Keen Family Papers
William H. Jolly Letters
James Patterson Diary
Samuel Ransom Diary
Shedd Family Papers
State Historical Society of Missouri, Columbia, Missouri
John T. Buegel Diary
Richard W. Burt Papers
Samuel B. Hamacker Letters
William F. Jones Papers
William E. Lewis Letters
I. V. Smith Memoir
State Historical Society of Missouri, Rolla, Missouri
Aquilla Standifird Diary
State Historical Society of Missouri, St. Louis, Missouri
Dyson-Bell-Sans Souci Papers
Tennessee State Library and Archives, Nashville, Tennessee
Luther H. Cowan Papers
George R. Elliott Diaries
J. W. Harmon Memoirs
C. J. Orr Memoir
James B. Owen Letters

Tulane University, New Orleans, Louisiana
    Don A. Pardee Papers
Ulysses S. Grant Presidential Library, Starkville, Mississippi
    Fred Grant Memoir
    Ulysses S. Grant Collection, Unpublished Correspondence
    William S. Hillyer Subject File
United States Army History and Education Center, Carlisle, Pennsylvania
    Anders Collection
        John D. Brownley Memoir
    Bilby Collection
        Carlos Colby Memoir
    Brookes Collection
        Isaac Williams Papers
    Eugene A. Carr Papers
    Civil War Documents Collection
        Boucher Family Papers
        Henry O. Dwight, "A Soldier's Story"
        Winfield S. Featherston Collection
        Eugene B. Harrison Diary
        Israel M. Ritter Diary
        Ann Sturtivant Collection
            William A. Montgomery Letters
        Columbus Sykes Papers
        Isaac Vanderwarker Diary
        Joseph W. Westbrook Memoir
    Civil War Times Illustrated Collection
        Lionel Baxter Collection
            W. A. Rorer Letters
        L. B. Claiborne Memoirs
        Francis A. Dawes Diary
        Paul Dorweiler Diary
        Marcus O. Frost Letters
        Frederick Pell Diary
        Lewis F. Phillips Papers
        Edward H. Reynolds Diary
        Henry J. Reynolds Memoir
        Henry J. Seaman Diary
        Edward E. Schweitzer Diary
        James K. Worthington Letters
    Harrisburg Civil War Roundtable Collection
        John Carr Diary
        Coco Collection
            Joseph Stockton Diary

Gilbert Gulbrandsen Papers
Luke R. Roberts Letters
William A. Ruyle Memoir
George W. Gordon Diary
Rudolph Haerle Collection
Samuel P. Harrington Diary
Charles Peck Papers
Howell–Taylor Family Papers
Wiley Sword Collection
Andrew McCornack Letters
University of Alabama, Tuscaloosa, Alabama
William L. Foster Letter
University of Chicago, Chicago, Illinois
Jenkin L. Jones Diary
University of Colorado Boulder, Boulder, Colorado
Noble W. Wood Diary
University of Georgia, Athens, Georgia
James McCulloch Diary
University of Illinois, Urbana, Illinois
William Clemans Memoir
George S. Durfee Papers
Edwin C. Hewett Correspondence
Edward McGlynn Letters
University of Iowa, Iowa City, Iowa
Joseph Child Diary
Giauque Family Papers
William T. Rigby Papers
University of Memphis, Memphis, Tennessee
Civil War Collection
DeBenneville Randolph Keim Notebook
Unnamed Soldier's Diary
University of Michigan, Ann Arbor, Michigan
Bentley Library
Calvin Ainsworth Diary
William C. Caldwell Correspondence
Ephraim Shay Diary
Clements Library
Schoff Civil War Collection
Lewis T. Hickok Journal
Isaac Jackson Papers
University of Mississippi, Oxford, Mississippi
Winfield S. Featherston Collection

Ray Fulton Collection
    Sallie B. McCrae Diary
J. V. Harris Telegram
E. E. Holman Letter
J. M. Love Diary
Letitia Dabney Miller Recollections
William Terry Moore Reminiscences
Josiah M. Stephenson Collection
Absolem West Collection
University of North Carolina, Chapel Hill, North Carolina
    Joseph D. Alison Diary
    Annie Laurie Harris Broidrick Collection
    J. F. H. Claiborne Papers
    John G. Devereux Papers
        Autobiography of Louis Hébert
    Clyde Hughes Collection
        Taylor Family Letters
    Samuel H. Lockett Papers
    Henry Oman Papers
    Isaac O. Shelby Diary
    Andrew J. Sproul Papers
    Taylor Family Letters
    Adoniram Judson Withrow Papers
University of Notre Dame, South Bend, Indiana
    Thomas Family Correspondence
University of South Carolina, Columbia, South Carolina
    John Bannon Diary
University of Southern Mississippi, Hattiesburg, Mississippi
    Thomas Gore Memoir
    Milton W. Shaw Letter
    Southern Railroad Company Papers
    John P. Worthing Letters
University of Tennessee, Knoxville, Tennessee
    Robert T. Jones Letters
University of Texas at Austin, Austin, Texas
    Christian W. Hander Diary
University of Virginia, Charlottesville, Virginia
    William S. Hillyer Papers
    Taylor Family Papers
University of Washington, Seattle, Washington
    Manning F. Force Papers
    Samuel D. Lougheed Papers

Vicksburg National Military Park, Vicksburg, Mississippi
    Letters/Diaries/Journals
        A. S. Abrams Diary
        Charles E. Affeld Diary
        Calvin Ainsworth Diary
        Dempsey J. Ashford Diary
        S. C. Beck, "A True Sketch of His Army Life"
        George H. Burns Letters
        Anthony Burton Diary
        James N. Carlisle Diary
        Lemuel Cline Letters
        Stephen Croom Diary
        John M. Douthit Letters
        William A. Drennan Letter
        Samuel W. Ferguson Memoir
        Theodore D. Fisher Diary
        Clarkson Fogg Letters
        C. Judson Gill Letters
        John B. Hancox Letter
        Anson Hemingway Diary
        George H. Hynds Diary
        Will H. Jolly Letters
        John J. Kellogg Memoirs
        John A. Leavy Diary
        Mortimer D. Leggett Papers
        Joseph Lesslie Letters
        W. R. McCrary Diary
        Charles Dana Miller Memoir
        William Murray Diary
        Israel M. Piper Diary
        Jared Sanders Letters
        Henry J. Seaman Diary
        Alexander Sholl Diary
        A. L. Slack Diary
        Joseph Stockton Diary
        Enoch P. Williams Diary
        Joseph R. Winslow Diary
        Timothy C. Young Diary
    Regimental Files
        Botetourt Virginia Artillery File
        Cherokee Georgia Artillery File
        Uley Burk Letters, 30th Iowa File
        Jesse M. Lee Diary, 59th Indiana File

J. P. Lesslie Letters, 4th Indiana Cavalry File
George Nester Letter, 1st Battery Indiana Light Artillery File
Daniel L. Roush Letters, 99th Illinois File
Lyman T. Shaw Diary, 99th Illinois File
Virginia Tech University, Blacksburg, Virginia
William J. Pittenger Diary
Western Kentucky University, Bowling Green, Kentucky
L. J. Sanders Diary
Wisconsin Historical Society, Madison, Wisconsin
H. H. Bennett Diary
Van Bennett Diary
Jenkins Lloyd Jones Diary

Newspapers

Alexandria (Virginia) *Gazette*
Harper's Weekly
Hinds County *Gazette*
Jackson *Daily Mississippian*
Jackson *Daily News*
Mississippi *Free Trader*
Natchez *Times*
New York *Daily Tribune*
New York *Herald*
New York *Times*
Port Gibson *Southern Reveille*
Utica *Advertiser*
Vicksburg *Evening Citizen*
Vicksburg *Evening Post*
Washington, DC *Sunday Star*

Published Primary and Secondary Sources

"A Faithful Dog." *National Tribune*, July 5, 1888.
"A Lady Mayor." *National Tribune*, September 25, 1884.
"A Post Camp-Fire." *National Tribune*, October 18, 1883.
Abrams, A. S. *A Full and Detailed History of the Siege of Vicksburg*. Atlanta: Intelli-
    gencer Steam Power Presses, 1863.
Adair, John M. *Historical Sketch of the Forty-fifth Illinois Regiment, With a Complete List
    of the Officers and Privates and an Individual Record of Each Man in the Regiment*.
    Lanark, IL: Carroll County Gazette Print, 1869.

Ambrose, Stephen E., and Douglas Brinkley. *The Mississippi and the Making of a Nation: From the Louisiana Purchase to Today*. Washington, DC: National Geographic, 2002.

Anderson, Ephraim McD. *Memoirs: Historical and Personal Including the Campaigns of the First Missouri Confederate Brigade*. St. Louis: Times Publishing Co., 1868.

Arnold, James R. *Grant Wins the War: Decision at Vicksburg*. New York: John Wiley & Sons, 1997.

Ashcraft, Allen C., ed. "Mrs. Russell and the Battle of Raymond, Mississippi." *Journal of Mississippi History* 25, no. 1 (January 1963): 38–40.

"At Champion's Hill." *National Tribune*, August 30, 1883.

Baca, Keith A. *Native American Place Names in Mississippi*. Jackson: University Press of Mississippi, 2007.

Badeau, Adam. *Military History of Ulysses S. Grant, From April, 1861, to April, 1865*, 2 vols. New York: D. Appleton & Co., 1881.

Ballard, Michael B. "Grant, McClernand, and Vicksburg: A Clash of Personalities and Backgrounds." In *The Vicksburg Campaign: March 29–May 18, 1863*, Steven E. Woodworth and Charles D. Grear, eds. Carbondale: Southern Illinois University Press, 2013, 129–152.

———. "Misused Merit: The Tragedy of John C. Pemberton." In *Confederate Generals in the Western Theater*, 4 vols. Lawrence Lee Hewitt and Arthur W. Bergeron Jr., eds. Knoxville: University of Tennessee Press, 2010, 1:103–121; originally printed as "Misused Merit: The Tragedy of John C. Pemberton," in *Civil War Generals in Defeat*, Steven E. Woodworth, ed. Lawrence: University Press of Kansas, 1999, 141–160.

———. *Pemberton: The General Who Lost Vicksburg*. Jackson: University Press of Mississippi, 1991.

———. *Vicksburg: The Campaign that Opened the* Mississippi. Chapel Hill: University of North Carolina Press, 2004.

Barton, Thomas H. *Autobiography of Dr. Thomas H. Barton, The Self-made Physician of Syracuse, Ohio*. Charleston: West Virginia Printing Co., 1890.

Basler, Roy P., ed. *Collected Works of Abraham Lincoln*, 9 vols. New Brunswick, NJ: Rutgers University Press, 1953.

"The Battle of Raymond." *National Tribune*, October 12, 1905.

Bearss, Edwin C. *Fields of Honor: Pivotal Battles of the Civil War*. Washington, DC: National Geographic, 2006.

———. *Rebel Victory at Vicksburg*. Vicksburg, MS: Vicksburg Centennial Commission, 1963.

———. *The Vicksburg Campaign*, 3 vols. Dayton, OH: Morningside, 1985.

Bearss, Edwin C., with J. Parker Hills. *Receding Tide: Vicksburg and Gettysburg, The Campaigns that Changed the Civil War*. Washington, DC: National Geographic, 2010.

Beecher, Henry Ward. *Patriotic Addresses in America and England, from 1850 to 1885, on Slavery, the Civil War, and the Development of Civil Liberty in the United States*. New York: Fords, Howard, & Hulbert, 1891.

Bek, William G., ed. "The Civil War Diary of John T. Buegel, Union Soldier." *Missouri Historical Review* 40, no. 4 (July 1946): 503–530.

Bennett, Stewart, and Barbara Tillery, eds. *The Struggle for the Life of the Republic: A Civil War Narrative by Brevet Major Charles Dana Miller, 76th Ohio Volunteer Infantry.* Kent, OH: Kent State University Press, 2004.

Bentley, W. H. *History of the 77th Illinois Volunteer Infantry, Sept. 2, 1862–July 10, 1865.* Peoria, IL: Edward Hine, Printer, 1883.

Bergeron, Arthur W., Jr. "Martin Luther Smith and the Defense of the Lower Mississippi River Valley, 1861–1863." In *Confederate Generals in the Western Theater: Essays on America's Civil War*, 4 vols. Lawrence Lee Hewitt and Arthur W. Bergeron Jr., eds. Knoxville: University of Tennessee Press, 2011, 3:61–85.

Bering, John A., and Thomas Montgomery. *History of the Forty-Eighth Ohio Vet. Vol. Inf.* Hillsboro, OH: Highland News Office, 1880.

Bertera, Martin N. *De Golyer's 8th Michigan Black Horse Light Battery.* Wyandotte, MI: TillieAnn Press, 2015.

Bettersworth, John K. *Confederate Mississippi: The People and Policies of a Cotton State in Wartime.* Baton Rouge: Louisiana State University Press, 1943.

Bettersworth, John K., ed. *Mississippi in the Confederacy: As They Saw It.* Baton Rouge: Louisiana State University Press, 1961.

Bevier, R. S. *History of the First and Second Missouri Confederate Brigades 1861–1865 and From Wakaruse to Appomattox, A Military Anagraph.* St. Louis, MO: Bryan, Brand and Company, 1879.

"Black River Bridge." *National Tribune*, November 5, 1891.

Bigelow, James K. *Abridged History of the Eighth Indiana Volunteer Infantry, from Its Organization, April 21st, 1861, to the Date of Re-enlistment as Veterans, January 1, 1864.* Indianapolis: Ellis Barnes Book and Job Printer, 1864.

Blanchard, Ira. *I Marched with Sherman: Civil War Memoirs of the 20th Illinois Volunteer Infantry*, Nancy Ann Mattingly, ed. New York: toExcel, 1992.

Bridge, Carolyn S., ed. *These Men Were Heroes Once: The Sixty-ninth Indiana Volunteer Infantry.* West Lafayette, IN: Twin Publications, 2005.

Brinkerhoff, Henry R. *History of the Thirtieth Regiment Ohio Volunteer Infantry, From Its Organization, To the Fall of Vicksburg, Miss.* Columbus, OH: James W. Osgood, Printer, 1863.

Brown, Alonzo L. *History of the Fourth Regiment of Minnesota Infantry Volunteers during the Great Rebellion 1861–1865.* St. Paul, MN: The Pioneer Press Company, 1892.

Brown, Russell K. *To the Manner Born: The Life of William H. T. Walker.* Athens: University of Georgia Press, 1994.

Browne, Junius H. *Four Years in Secessia: Adventures within and Beyond the Union Lines.* Hartford: O. D. Case and Company, 1865.

Bryner, Cloyd. *Bugle Echoes: The Story of the Illinois 47th.* Springfield, IL: Phillips Bros. Printers, 1905.

Buckles, Stanley D. *Not Afraid to Go Any Whare: A History of the 114th Regiment Illinois Volunteer Infantry.* Bend, OR: Maverick Publications, 2019.

Buffington, Edwin L. "Logistics During Grant's Vicksburg Campaign." MA thesis, US Army War College, 1992.

Burdette, Robert J. *The Drums of the 47th*. Indianapolis: The Bobbs-Merrill Company, 1914.

Burke, Eric Michael. *Soldiers from Experience: The Fighting of Sherman's Fifteenth Army Corps 1862–1863*. Baton Rouge: Louisiana State University Press, 2023.

Bush, Bryan S. *Lloyd Tilghman: Confederate General in the Western Theater*. Morley, MO: Acclaim Press, 2006.

Byers, S. H. M. "How Men Feel in Battle; Recollections of a Private at Champion Hills." *Annals of Iowa* 2, no. 6 (July 1896): 438–449.

———. *With Fire and Sword*. New York: The Neale Publishing Company, 1911.

Cadwallader, Sylvanus. *Three Years with Grant*, Benjamin P. Thomas, ed. Lincoln: University of Nebraska Press, 1996.

"Capture of Jackson." *National Tribune*, July 27, 1893.

Carter, Arthur B. *The Tarnished Cavalier: Major General Earl Can Dorn, C.S.A.* Knoxville: University of Tennessee Press, 1999.

Catton, Bruce. *Grant Moves South*. Boston: Little, Brown, and Company, 1960.

———. *U. S. Grant and the American Military Tradition*. Boston: Little, Brown and Co., 1954.

Chambers, William P. "My Journal." *Publications of the Mississippi Historical Society, Centenary Series*, 5 vols. Jackson: Mississippi Historical Society, 1925, 5:221–386.

"Champion's Hill." *National Tribune*, September 11, 1884.

"Champion's Hill." *National Tribune*, May 17, 1888.

"Champion's Hill." *National Tribune*, April 5, 1894.

"Champion's Hill." *National Tribune*, October 3, 1901.

Chandler, David G. *The Campaigns of Napoleon: The Mind and Method of History's Greatest Soldier*. New York: Scribner, 1966.

Chernow, Ron. *Grant*. New York: Penguin Press, 2017.

Clark, Olynthus B., ed. *Downing's Civil War Diary*. Des Moines: The Historical Department of Iowa, 1916.

Clarke, George Powell *Reminiscence and Anecdotes of the War for Southern Independence*. N.p.: n.p., n.d.

Clausewitz, Carl Von. *On War*. London: N. Trubner and Co., 1873.

———. *On War*. Michael Howard and Peter Paret, eds. New York: Knopf, 1993.

Cleveland, Charles Boarman. "With the Third Missouri Regiment." *Confederate Veteran* 31, no. 1 (January 1923): 19.

Cobbs, Emma G. "The Battle of Raymond, Miss." *Confederate Veteran* 9, no. 9 (September 1901): 406.

Colby, Carlos W. "Bulletts, Hardtack and Mud: A Soldier's View of the Vicksburg Campaign." edited by John S. Painter, *Journal of the West* 4, no. 2 (April 1965): 129–168.

Commager, Henry Steele, ed. *The Blue and the Gray*, 2 vols. New York: Meridian, 1994.

Congressional Record, 76th Congress, 3rd Session.

Consolidated Index of Claims Reported by the Commissioners of Claims to the House of Representatives from 1871 to 1880. Washington, DC: Government Printing Office, 1892.

Crist, Lynda Laswell, et. al., eds. *The Papers of Jefferson Davis*, 14 vols. Baton Rouge: Louisiana State University Press, 1971–2015.

Crooke, George. *The Twenty-first Regiment of Iowa Volunteer Infantry: A Narrative of Its Experience in Active Service, Including a Military Record of Each Officer, Non-Commissioned Officer, and Private Soldier of the Organization*. Milwaukee: King, Fowle & Co., 1891.

Crummer, Wilbur F. *With Grant at Fort Donelson, Shiloh and Vicksburg, and An Appreciation of General U.S. Grant*. Oak Park, IL: E. C. Crummer and Co., 1915.

Dana, Charles A. *Recollections of the Civil War*. New York: D. Appleton and Co., 1898.

Daniel, Larry J. "Bruinsburg: Missed Opportunity or Postwar Rhetoric?" *Civil War History* 32, no. 3 (September 1986): 256–267.

———. *Engineering in the Confederate Heartland*. Baton Rouge: Louisiana State University Press, 2022.

Darst, W. Maury, ed. "The Vicksburg Diary of Mrs. Alfred Ingraham: May 2–June 13, 1863." *Journal of Mississippi History* 44, no. 2 (May 1982): 148–179.

Davis, George B., Leslie J. Perry, and Joseph W. Kirkley. *Atlas to Accompany the Official Records of the Union and Confederate Armies*. Washington, DC: Government Printing Office, 1891–1895.

Davis, William C. *Jefferson Davis: The Man and His Hour: A Biography*. New York: HarperCollins, 1991.

"Dedication of a Bronze Tablet in Honor of Botetourt Battery." *Southern Historical Society Papers* 35 (1907): 29–49.

"The Defenders of Vicksburg." *Southern Historical Society Papers* 21 (1893): 183–206.

Donnell, Dan. "After the Battle of Raymond, Miss." *Confederate Veteran* 20, no. 2 (February 1912): 87–88.

Dossman, Steven Nathaniel. "The 'Stealing Tour': Soldiers and Civilians in Grant's March to Vicksburg." In *The Vicksburg Campaign: March 29–May 18, 1863*, Steven E. Woodworth and Charles D. Grear, eds. Carbondale: Southern Illinois University Press, 2013, 194–213.

Drake, Edwin L., ed. *The Annals of the Army of Tennessee and Early Western History*. Nashville, TN: A. D. Haynes, 1878.

Drake, Rebecca Blackwell, and Margie Riddle Bearss, eds. *My Dear Wife: Letters to Matilda: The Civil War Letters of Sid and Matilda Champion of Champion Hill*. N.p.: n.p., 2005.

Droke, W. B. "Grant—the Logistician." *Army Logistician: Professional Bulletin of United States Army Logistics* PB 700-90-3 (May–June 1990): 28–31.

Dubay, Robert W. *John Jones Pettus, Mississippi Fire-eater: His Life and Times, 1813–1867*. Jackson: University Press of Mississippi, 1975.

Dunbar, Aaron, and Harvey M. Trimble. *History of the Ninety-third Regiment Volunteer Infantry from Organization to Muster Out*. Chicago: The Blakely Printing Co., 1898.

Elliott, Isaac H. *History of the Thirty-third Regiment Illinois Veteran Volunteer Infantry in the Civil War, 22nd August 1861, to 7th December, 1865*. Gibson City, IL: The Association, 1902.

F., F. A. *Old Abe, The Eighth Wisconsin War Eagle. A Full Account of His Capture and Enlistment, Exploits in War and Honorable as Well as Useful Career in Peace*. Madison, WI: Curran and Bowen, 1885.

Feis, William B. "'Developed by Circumstances': Grant, Intelligence, and the Vicksburg Campaign." In *The Vicksburg Campaign: March 29–May 18, 1863*, Steven E. Woodworth and Charles D. Grear, eds. Carbondale: Southern Illinois University Press, 2013, 153–172.

Ferguson, Ernest B. *Chancellorsville 1863: The Souls of the Brave*. New York: Knopf, 1993.

Ferrell, Robert H., ed. *Holding the Line: The Third Tennessee Regiment, 1861–1864*. Kent, OH: Kent State University Press, 1994.

Field Manual 100-5: Operations. Washington, DC: Department of the Army, 1986.

Field Manual 100-5: Operations. Washington, DC: Department of the Army, 1993.

"The First Troops to Land at Bruinsburg." *National Tribune*, October 16, 1884.

Fiske, John. *The Mississippi Valley in the Civil War*. New York: Houghton, Mifflin and Company, 1900.

Flood, Charles Bracelen. *Grant and Sherman: The Friendship That Won the Civil War*. New York: Farrar, Straus and Giroux, 2005.

Force, Manning F. "Personal Recollections of the Vicksburg Campaign." In *Sketches of War History, 1861–1865: Papers Read Before the Ohio Commandery of the Military Order of the Loyal Legion of the United States 1883–1886, Volume 1*. Cincinnati: Robert Clarke & Co., 1888, 293–309.

Fowler, James A., and Miles M. Miller. *History of the Thirtieth Iowa Infantry Volunteers. Giving a Complete Record of the Movements of the Regiment from Its Organization Until Muster Out*. Mediapolis, IA: T. A. Merrill, Printer, 1908.

Frawley, Jason M. "'In the Enemy's Country': Port Gibson and the Turning Point of the Vicksburg Campaign." In *The Vicksburg Campaign: March 29–May 18, 1863*, Steven E. Woodworth and Charles D. Grear, eds. Carbondale: Southern Illinois University Press, 2013, 43–64.

Fremantle, Arthur J. L. *The Fremantle Diary: Being the Journal of Lieutenant Colonel James Arthur Lyon Fremantle, Coldstream Guards, on His Three Months in the Southern States*, ed. Walter Lord. Boston: Little, Brown and Company, 1954.

———. *Three Months in the Southern States: April–June, 1863*. Edinburgh: W. Blackwood and Sons, 1863.

Fulfer, Richard J. *A History of the Trials and Hardships of the Twenty-Fourth Indiana Volunteer Infantry*. Indianapolis: Indianapolis Printing Company, 1913.

Fulkerson, H. S. *A Civilian's Recollections of the War Between the States*. P. L. Rainwater, ed. Baton Rouge, LA: Otto Claitor, 1939.

Fuller, J. F. C. *The Generalship of Ulysses S. Grant*. Bloomington: Indiana University Press, 1958.

Garner, James Wilford. *Reconstruction in Mississippi*. New York: Macmillan Company, 1902.

"Gen. Lloyd Tilghman." *Confederate Veteran* 18, no. 7 (July 1910): 318–319.

George, Henry. *History of the 3d, 7th, 8th and 12th Kentucky C.S.A.* Louisville, KY: C. T. Dearing Printing Co., 1911.

Goodloe, Alfred Theodore. *Confederate Echoes: A Voice from the South in the Days of Secession and of the Southern Confederacy.* Nashville, TN: Publishing House of the M. E. Church, 1907.

Gordon, Larry. *The Last Confederate General: John C. Vaughn and His East Tennessee Cavalry.* Minneapolis: Zenith Press, 2009.

Grabau, Warren E. *Ninety-Eight Days: A Geographer's View of the Vicksburg Campaign.* Knoxville: University of Tennessee Press, 2000.

Grant, Frederick D. "A Boy's Experience at Vicksburg." In *Personal Recollections of the War of the Rebellion: Addresses Delivered before the Commandery of the State of New York, Military Order of the Loyal Legion of the United States*, A. Noel Blakeman, ed. New York: G. P. Putnam's Sons, 1907:86–100.

Grecian, J. *History of the Eighty-third Regiment, Indiana Volunteer Infantry. For Three Years with Sherman.* Cincinnati: John F. Uhlhorn, Printer, 1865.

Greene, Francis V. *The Mississippi.* New York: Charles Scribner's Sons, 1882.

Greif, J. V. "Baker's Creek and Champion Hill." *Confederate Veteran* 4, no. 10 (October 1896): 350–352.

———. "The Battle of Raymond, Miss." *Confederate Veteran* 12, no. 3 (March 1904): 112.

Grimsley, Mark. *The Hard Hand of War: Union Military Policy Toward Southern Civilians, 1861–1865.* Cambridge: Cambridge University Press, 1995.

Grimsley, Mark, and Todd D. Miller, eds. *The Union Must Stand: The Civil War Diary of John Quincy Adams Campbell, Fifth Iowa Volunteer Infantry.* Knoxville: University of Tennessee Press, 2000.

Hall, Thomas O. "The Key to Vicksburg." *The Southern Bivouac* 2, no. 9 (May 1884): 393–396.

Hall, Winchester. *The Story of the 26th Louisiana Infantry, In the Service of the Confederate States.* N.p.: n.p., 1890.

Halleck, Henry W. *Elements of Military Art and Science: Or, Course of Instruction in Strategy, Fortification, Tactics of Battles, &c.; Embracing the Duties of Staff, Infantry, Cavalry, Artillery, and Engineers. Adapted to the Use of Volunteers and Militia.* New York: D. Appleton and Company, 1846.

Harriel, Shelby. *Behind the Rifle: Women Soldiers in Civil War Mississippi.* Jackson: University Press of Mississippi, 2019.

Hartje, Robert G. *Van Dorn: The Life and Times of a Confederate General.* Nashville, TN: Vanderbilt University Press, 1967.

Hass, Paul H., ed. "The Vicksburg Diary of Henry Clay Warmoth: Part II (April 28, 1863–May 26, 1863)." *Journal of Mississippi History* 32, no. 1 (February 1970): 60–74.

Hattaway, Herman. *General Stephen D. Lee.* Jackson: University Press of Mississippi, 1988.

Hattaway, Herman, and Archer Jones. *How the North Won: A Military History of the Civil War.* Urbana: University of Illinois Press, 1983.

Hawkins, H. G. "History of Port Gibson, Mississippi." In *Publications of the Mississippi Historical Society*, 13 vols. Oxford: Mississippi Historical Society, 1909, 10:279–299.

Hays, E. Z. *History of the Thirty-second Regiment Ohio Veteran Volunteer Infantry*. Columbus, OH: Cott & Evans Printers, 1896.

"Heavy Losses in Battle." *National Tribune*, February 22, 1906.

Hebert, Walter H. *Fighting Joe Hooker*. Lincoln: University of Nebraska Press, 1999.

Hearn, Chester G. *Admiral David Dixon Porter: The Civil War Years*. Annapolis, MD: Naval Institute Press, 1996.

———. *The Capture of New Orleans 1862*. Baton Rouge: Louisiana State University Press, 1995.

Heinman, Kenneth J. *Civil War Dynasty: The Ewing Family of Ohio*. New York: New York University Press, 2012.

Henry, Frederick A. *Captain Henry of Geauga: A Family Chronicle*. Cleveland: Gates Press, 1942.

Hess, Earl J. *Civil War Supply and Strategy: Feeding Men and Moving Armies*. Baton Rouge: Louisiana State University Press, 2020.

———. "Grant's Ethnic General: Peter J. Osterhaus." In *Grant's Lieutenants: From Cairo to Vicksburg*, Steven E. Woodworth, ed. Lawrence: University Press of Kansas, 2001, 199–216.

Hicks, Henry G. "The Campaign and Capture of Vicksburg." In *Glimpses of the Nation's Struggle: Military Order of the Loyal Legion*, 6 vols. St. Paul, MN: Davis, 1909, 6:82–107.

Hills, J. Parker. "Roads to Raymond." In *The Vicksburg Campaign: March 29–May 18, 1863*, Steven E. Woodworth and Charles D. Grear, eds. Carbondale: Southern Illinois University Press, 2013, 65–95.

———. *Vicksburg Campaign Driving Tour Guide*. N.p.: Friends of the Vicksburg Campaign and Historic Trail, Inc., 2008.

History of Company B (Originally Pickens Planters) 40th Alabama Regiment Confederate States Army 1862–1865. Anniston, AL: Norwood, 1902.

History of the 37th Regiment, O.V.V.I., Furnished by Comrades at the Ninth Reunion Held at St. Mary's, Ohio, Tuesday and Wednesday, September 10 and 11, 1889. Toledo, OH: Montgomery and Vrooman, 1890.

"History of the Corps." *National Tribune*, February 16, 1893.

History of the Forty-sixth Regiment Indiana Volunteer Infantry, September, 1861–September, 1865. Logansport, IN: Press of Wilson, Humphreys and Co., 1888.

Hobbs, Charles A. "Vanquishing Vicksburg." *National Tribune*, January 28, 1892.

———. "Vanquishing Vicksburg." *National Tribune*, February 4, 1892.

Hogane, J. T. "Reminiscences of the Siege of Vicksburg." *Southern Historical Society Papers* 11, nos. 4–5 (April–May 1883): 223–227.

Hopkins, Owen Johnston. *Under the Flag of the Nation: Diaries and Letters of a Yankee Volunteer in the Civil War*, Otto F. Bond, ed. Columbus: Ohio State University Press, 1961.

"Hovey's Division at Port Gibson." January 8, 1885, *National Tribune*.

Howard, Richard L. "The Vicksburg Campaign." In *War Papers Read Before the Commandery of the State of Maine, Military Order of the Loyal Legion of the United States, Volume 2*. Portland, ME: Lefavor-Tower Company, 1902, 2:28–40.

Howard, R. L. *History of the 124th Regiment Illinois Infantry Volunteers, Otherwise Known as the "Hundred and Two Dozen," From August, 1862, to August, 1865*. Springfield, IL: H. W. Rokker, 1880.

Howe, M. A. DeWolfe, ed. *Home Letters of General Sherman*. New York: Charles Scribner's Sons, 1909.

Howell, H. Grady Jr. *Chimneyville: "Likenesses" of Early Days in Jackson, Mississippi*. Jackson: Chickasaw Bayou Press, 2007.

———. *Going to Meet the Yankees: A History of the "Bloody Sixth" Mississippi Infantry, C.S.A.* Jackson: Chickasaw Bayou Press, 1981.

Hurley, Mark S. "Union Logistics in the Vicksburg Campaign." MA thesis, US Army Command and General Staff College, 1992.

Jenney, William L. B. "Personal Recollections of Vicksburg." In *Military Essays and Recollections: Papers Read before the Commandery of the State of Illinois, Military Order of the Loyal Legion of the United States*, 5 vols. Chicago: The Dial Press, 1899, 3:247–265.

———. "With Sherman and Grant from Memphis to Chattanooga: A Reminisce." In *Military Essays and Recollections: Papers Read Before the Commandery of the State of Illinois, Military Order of the Loyal Legion of the United States*, 5 vols. Chicago: Cozzens and Beaton Company, 1907, 4:193–214.

Johnston, Frank. "The Vicksburg Campaign." In *Publications of the Mississippi Historical Society*. Oxford: Mississippi Historical Society, 1909, 10:63–90.

Johnston, Joseph E. "Jefferson Davis and the Mississippi Campaign." In *Battles and Leaders of the Civil War*, 4 vols. New York: Century Company, 1884–1887, 3:472–482.

Johnston, William P. *The Life of Gen. Albert Sidney Johnston, Embracing His Services in the Armies of the United States, the Republic of Texas, and the Confederate States*. New York: D. Appleton and Co., 1878.

Joiner, Gary D. "Running the Gauntlet: The Effectiveness of Combined Forces in the Vicksburg Campaign." In *The Vicksburg Campaign: March 29–May 18, 1863*, Steven E. Woodworth and Charles D. Grear, eds. Carbondale: Southern Illinois University Press, 2013, 8–23.

Jomini, Henri de. *The Art of War*. Philadelphia: J. B. Lippincott & Co., 1862.

———. *Summary of the Art of War, or, A New Analytical Compend of the Principal Combinations of Strategy, of Grand Tactics and of Military Policy*. New York: G. P. Putnam & Co., 1854.

Jones, Archer. *Civil War Command and Strategy: The Process of Victory and Defeat*. New York: The Free Press, 1992.

———. "Tennessee and Mississippi, Joe Johnston's Strategic Problem." In *Confederate Generals in the Western Theater*, 4 vols. Lawrence Lee Hewitt and Arthur W. Bergeron Jr., eds. Knoxville: University of Tennessee Press, 2010, 1:89–100.

Jones, James Pickett. *Black Jack: John A. Logan and Southern Illinois in the Civil War Era*. Carbondale: Southern Illinois University Press, 1967.

Jones, J. B. *A Rebel War Clerk's Diary: At the Confederate States Capital, Volume 1: April 1861–July 1863*, 2 vols. James I. Robertson, Jr., ed. Lawrence: University Press of Kansas, 2015.

Jones, Jenkins Lloyd. *An Artilleryman's Diary*. Madison: Wisconsin History Commission, 1914.

Jones, J. H. "The Rank and File at Vicksburg." In *Publications of the Mississippi Historical Society*, Franklin L. Riley, ed. Oxford: Mississippi Historical Society, 1903, 7:17–31.

Jones, S. C. *Reminiscences of the Twenty-second Iowa Volunteer Infantry, Giving Its Organization, Marches, Skirmishes, Battles, and Sieges, as Taken from the Diary of Lieutenant S. C. Jones of Company A*. Iowa City, IA: n.p., 1907.

Journal of the House of Representatives of the State of Mississippi: December Session of 1862, and November Session of 1863. Jackson: Cooper and Kimball, 1864.

Journal of the Senate of the State of Mississippi: Called Session. Jackson: E. Barksdale, State Printer, 1860.

Kaiser, Leo M., ed. "The Civil War Diary of Florison D. Pitts." *Mid America: An Historical Review* 40, no. 1 (January 1958): 22–63.

Kennedy, Joseph C. G. *Population of the United States in 1860: Compiled from the Original Returns of the Eighth Census Under the Direction of the Secretary of the Interior*. Washington, DC: Government Printing Office, 1864.

Kemmerly, Phillip R. "Logistics of U.S. Grant's 1863 Mississippi Campaign: From the Amphibious Landing at Bruinsburg to the Siege of Vicksburg." *Journal of Military History* 86 (July 2022): 573–611.

Kiper, Richard L. *Major General John A. McClernand: Politician in Uniform*. Kent, OH: Kent State University Press, 1999.

Klingberg, Frank L. *The Southern Claims Commission*. Berkeley: University of California Press, 1955.

Krick, Robert K. "'Snarl and Sneer and Quarrel': General Joseph E. Johnston and an Obsession with Rank." In *Leaders of the Lost Cause: New Perspectives on the Confederate High Command*, Gary W. Gallagher and Joseph T. Glatthaar, eds. Mechanicsburg, PA: Stackpole Books, 2004, 165–203.

Kountz, John S. *Record of the Organizations Engaged in the Campaign, Siege, and Defense of Vicksburg*. Knoxville: University of Tennessee Press, 2011.

Lash, Jeffrey N. *A Politician Turned General: The Civil War Career of Stephen Augustus Hurlbut*. Kent, OH: Kent State University Press, 2003.

Lee, Stephen D. "The Campaign of Vicksburg, Mississippi, in 1863—From April 15 to and Including the Battle of Champion Hills, or Baker's Creek, May 16, 1863." In *Publications of the Mississippi Historical Society*, 13 vols. Oxford: Mississippi Historical Society, 1900, 3:21–53.

Llewellyn, James. "Battle of Champion Hill, Miss." *Confederate Veteran* 14, no. 8 (August 1906): 363.

Lockett, S. H. "The Defense of Vicksburg." In *Battles and Leaders of the Civil War*, 4 vols. New York: Century Company, 1884–1887, 3:482–492.

Lomask, Milton. *Aaron Burr: The Conspiracy and Years of Exile, 1805–1836*. New York: Farrar, Straus & Giroux, 1982.

Long, E. B. *The Civil War Day by Day: An Almanac, 1861–1865*. New York: Doubleday, 1971.

Longley, Charles L. "Champion's Hill." In *War Sketches and Incidents*. Des Moines: Press of P. C. Kenyon, 1893, 1:208–214

Loughborough, Mary Ann. *My Cave Life in Vicksburg: With Letters of Trial and Travel*. New York: D. Appleton and Company, 1864.

Lundberg, John R. "'I Am Too Late': Joseph E. Johnston and the Vicksburg Campaign." In *The Vicksburg Campaign: March 29–May 18, 1863*, Steven E. Woodworth and Charles D. Grear, eds. Carbondale: Southern Illinois University Press, 2013, 116–128.

Mackowski, Chris. *The Battle of Jackson, Mississippi, May 14, 1863*. El Dorado Hills, CA: Savas Beatie, 2022.

Mahan, James C. *Memoirs of James Curtis Mahan*. Lincoln, NE: The Franklin Press, 1919.

Main, Edward M. *The Story of the Marches, Battles and Incidents of the Third United States Cavalry: A Fighting Regiment in the War of the Rebellion, 1861–5. With Official Orders and Reports Relating Thereto, Compiled from the Rebellion Records*. Louisville, KY: The Globe Printing Company, 1908.

Manahan, T. A. "Letters from Veterans." *Confederate Veteran* 2, no. 8 (August 1894): 227.

Marshall, T. B. *History of the Eighty-third Ohio Volunteer Infantry, The Greyhound Regiment*. Cincinnati: n.p., 1912.

Marszalek, John F. *Commander of All Lincoln's Armies: A Life of General Henry W. Halleck*. Cambridge, MA: Harvard University Press, 2004.

———. "'A Full Share of All the Credit': Sherman and Grant to the Fall of Vicksburg." In *Grant's Lieutenants: From Cairo to Vicksburg*. Lawrence: University Press of Kansas, 2001, 5–20.

———. *Sherman: A Soldier's Passion for Order*. New York: The Free Press, 1993.

Marszalek, John F., David F. Nolen, and Louie P. Gallo, eds. *The Personal Memoirs of Ulysses S. Grant: The Complete Annotated Edition*. Cambridge, MA: Harvard University Press, 2017.

Mason, F. H. *The Forty-second Ohio Infantry: A History of the Organization and Services of That Regiment in the War of the Rebellion; With Biographical Sketches of Its Field Officers and a Full Roster of the Regiment*. Cleveland: Cobb, Andrews and Co., Publishers, 1876.

Masters, Daniel A., ed. *Sherman's Praetorian Guard: Civil War Letters of John McIntyre Lemmon, 72nd Ohio Volunteer Infantry*. Perrysburg, OH: Columbian Arsenal Press, 2017.

Matthews, D. M. "A Reminisce of Champion Hill." *Confederate Veteran* 21, no. 5 (May 1913): 208.

Maynard, Douglas, ed. "Vicksburg Diary: The Journal of Gabriel M. Killgore." *Civil War History* 10, no 1 (March 1964): 33–53.

McAlexander, U. G. *History of the Thirteenth Regiment United States Infantry, Compiled from Regimental Records and Other Sources*. N.p.: Regimental Press, Thirteenth Infantry, 1905.

McDonough, James Lee. *William Tecumseh Sherman: In the Service of My Country: A Life*. New York: Norton, 2016.

McMurry, Richard M. *The Civil Wars of General Joseph E. Johnston, Confederate States Army: Volume 1: Virginia and Mississippi, 1861–1863*. El Dorado Hills, CA: Savas Beatie, 2023.

McPherson, James B. *Battle Cry of Freedom: The Civil War Era*. New York: Oxford University Press, 1988.

Memminger, R. W. "The Surrender of Vicksburg—A Defense of General Pemberton," *Southern Historical Society Papers* 12, nos. 7–9 (July–September 1884): 352–360.

Michael, W. A. C. "How the Mississippi Was Opened." In *Civil War Sketches and Incidents: Papers Read by Companions of the Commandery of the State of Nebraska, Military Order of the Loyal Legion of the United States*. Omaha, NE: The Commandery, 1902, 34–58.

Military History and Reminiscences of the Thirteenth Regiment of Illinois Volunteer Infantry in the Civil War in the United States 1861–1865. Chicago: Women's Temperance Publishing Association, 1892.

Miller, Donald L. *Vicksburg: Grant's Campaign That Broke the Confederacy*. New York: Simon and Shuster, 2019.

Moore, John G. "Mobility and Strategy in the Civil War." *Military Affairs* 24, no. 2 (Summer 1960): 68–77.

Morris, W. S. *History, 31st Regiment Illinois Volunteers: Organized by John A. Logan*. Herrin, IL: Crossfire Press, 1991.

Myers, John. "'Dear and Mutch Loved One'—An Iowan's Vicksburg Letters," Edward G. Longacre, ed. *Annals of Iowa* 43, no. 1 (Summer 1975): 49–61.

Myers, Joseph. "The First to Land at Bruinsburg." May 20, 1886, *National Tribune*.

Nelson, H. K. "Battles of Raymond and Jackson." *Confederate Veteran* 12, no. 1 (January 1904): 12.

Noe, Kenneth W. *Perryville: This Grand Havoc of Battle*. Lexington: University Press of Kentucky, 2001.

———. *Through the Howling Storm: Weather, Climate, and the American Civil War*. Baton Rouge: Louisiana State University Press, 2020.

Northern, Charles Swift, III, ed. *All Right Let Them Come: The Civil War Diary of an Eats Tennessee Confederate*. Knoxville: University of Tennessee Press, 2003.

Northrop, L. B. "A Hill of Death." *Civil War Times Illustrated* 30, no. 2 (May/June 1991): 24–26, 28–33, 62–67.

Oake, William Royal. *On the Skirmish Line Behind a Friendly Tree: The Civil War Memoirs of William Royal Oake, 26th Iowa Volunteers*, Stacy D. Allen, ed. Helena, MT: Farcountry Press, 2006.

The Official Records of the Union and Confederate Navies in the War of the Rebellion, 30 vols. Washington, DC: Government Printing Office, 1894–1922.

Oldroyd, Osborn H. *A Soldier's Story of the Siege of Vicksburg From the Diary of Osborn H. Oldroyd*. Springfield, IL: Self-published, 1885.

Oltrogge, Estelle T. "Raymond, Miss., in War Times." *Confederate Veteran* 19, no. 8 (August 1911): 370–371.

Ottens, Allen J. *General John A. Rawlins: No Ordinary Man.* Bloomington: Indiana University Press, 2021.

Owens, Harry P. *Steamboats and the Cotton Economy: River Trade in the Yazoo-Mississippi Delta.* Jackson: University Press of Mississippi, 1990.

Parrish, William E. *Frank Blair: Lincoln's Conservative.* Columbia: University of Missouri Press, 1998.

Patrick, Jeffrey L., ed. *Three Years with Wallace's Zouaves: The Civil War Memoirs of Thomas Wise Durham.* Macon, GA: Mercer University Press, 2003.

Payne, James E. "General Pemberton and Vicksburg." *Confederate Veteran* 36, no. 7 (July 1928): 247.

Pemberton, John C. *Pemberton: Defender of Vicksburg.* Chapel Hill: University of North Carolina Press, 1942.

Pierson, Enos. *Proceedings of Eleven Reunions Held by the 16th Regiment, O. V. I., Including Roll of Honor, Roster of the Survivors of the Regiment, Statistics, &c., &c.* Millersburg, OH: Republican Steam Press, 1887.

Plummer, Leonard B., ed. "Excerpts from the Hander Diary." *Journal of Mississippi History* 26, no. 2 (May 1964): 141–149.

Porter, David Dixon. *Incidents and Anecdotes of the Civil* War. New York: D. Appleton and Company, 1885.

"Port Gibson." *National Tribune*, December 4, 1884.

Power, James L. "The Black and Tan Convention." In *Publications of the Mississippi Historical Society.* Oxford: Mississippi Historical Society, 1900, 3:73–83.

Pryce, Samuel D. *Vanishing Footprints: The Twenty-Second Iowa Volunteer Infantry in the Civil War*, Jeffry C. Burden, ed. Iowa City, IA: Camp Pope Bookshop, 2008.

Quinby, Henry Cole. *Genealogical History of the Quinby (Quimby) Family in England and America.* Rutland, VT: The Tuttle Company, 1915.

Raab, James W. *W. W. Loring: Florida's Forgotten General.* Manhattan, KS: Sunflower University Press, 1996.

Raum, Green B. "With the Western Army." December 19, 1901, *National Tribune.*

Reed, David W. *Campaigns and Battles of the Twelfth Regiment Iowa Veteran Volunteer Infantry From Its Organization, September, 1861, to Muster Out, January 20, 1866.* N.p.: n.p., 1903.

Remini, Robert V. *Andrew Jackson and the Course of American Empire, 1767–1821.* New York: Harper & Row, 1977.

Reynolds, A. H. "Vivid Experiences at Champion Hill, Miss." *Confederate Veteran* 18, no. 1 (January 1910): 21–22.

Richard, Allen C., Jr., and Mary Margaret Higginbotham Richard. *The Defense of Vicksburg: A Louisiana Chronicle.* College Station: Texas A&M University Press, 2004.

Richardson, Albert D. *A Personal History of Ulysses S. Grant.* Hartford, CT: American Publishing Company, 1868.

Robertson, James I. *Stonewall Jackson: The Man, The Soldier, The Legend.* New York: Macmillan, 1997.

Rowland, Dunbar. *Mississippi; Comprising Sketches of Counties, Towns, Events, Institutions and Persons, Arranged in Cyclopedic Form*, 3 vols. Atlanta: Southern Historical Printing Association, 1907.

Ruminski, Jarret. *The Limits of Loyalty: Ordinary People in Civil War Mississippi*. Jackson: University Press of Mississippi, 2017.

Sanborn, John B. "Battles and Campaigns of September, 1862." In *Glimpses of the Nation's Struggle: Military Order of the Loyal Legion*, 6 vols. St. Paul, MN: Review Publishing Company, 1908, 5:208–273.

———. "The Campaign Against Vicksburg." In *Glimpses of the Nation's Struggle, Second Series: A Series of Papers Read Before the Minnesota Commandery of the Military Order of the Loyal Legion of the United States, 1887–1899*, 6 vols. St. Paul, MN: St. Paul Book and Stationary Company, 1890, 2:114–145.

Sanborn Family in the United States and Brief Sketch of Life of John B. Sanborn. St. Paul, MN: H. M. Smyth Printing Co., 1887.

Saunier, Joseph A. *A History of the Forty-seventh Regiment Ohio Veteran Volunteer Infantry, Second Brigade, Second Division, Fifteenth Army Corps, Army of the Tennessee*. Hillsboro, OH: The Lyle Printing Company, 1903.

Schmelzer, Paul L. "Politics, Policy, and General Grant: Clausewitz on the Operational Art as Practiced in the Vicksburg Campaign." In *The Vicksburg Campaign: March 29–May 18, 1863*, Steven E. Woodworth and Charles D. Grear, eds. Carbondale: Southern Illinois University Press, 2013:214–228.

Scott, R. B. *The History of the 67th Regiment Indiana Infantry Volunteers, War of the Rebellion*. Bedford, IN: Herald Book and Job Print, 1892.

Sears, Stephen W. *Chancellorsville*. Boston: Houghton Mifflin, 1996.

Shea, William L., and Terrence J. Winschel. *Vicksburg Is the Key: The Struggle for the Mississippi River*. Lincoln: University of Nebraska Press, 2003.

Sherman, William T. *Memoirs of General William T. Sherman: Written by Himself*, 2 vols. New York: D. Appleton and Co., 1875.

Shunk, William A. "The Vicksburg Campaign." In *War Papers Read Before the Commandery of the State of Wisconsin, Military Order of the Loyal Legion of the United States*, 4 vols. Milwaukee: Burdick & Allen, 1914, 4:141–159.

Simon, John Y., ed. *The Personal Memoirs of Julia Dent Grant [Mrs. Ulysses S. Grant]*. New York: G. P. Putnam's Sons, 1975.

Simon, John Y., and John F. Marszalek, eds. *The Papers of Ulysses S. Grant*. 32 vols. Carbondale: Southern Illinois University Press, 1967–2014.

Simpson, Brooks D. *Ulysses S. Grant: Triumph Over Adversity, 1822–1865*. Boston: Houghton Mifflin Company, 2000.

Skaptason, Bjorn. "The Chicago Light Artillery at Vicksburg." *Journal of the Illinois State Historical Society* 106, no. 3–4 (Fall/Winter 2013): 422–462.

Skates, John Ray. *Mississippi's Old Capitol: Biography of a Building*. Jackson: Mississippi Department of Archives and History, 1990.

Smith, David M., ed. *Compelled to Appear in Print: The Vicksburg Manuscript of General John C. Pemberton*. Cincinnati: Ironclad Publishing, 1999.

Smith, Tamara A. "A Matter of Trust: Grant and James B. McPherson." In *Grant's Lieu-tenants: From Cairo to Vicksburg*, Steven E. Woodworth, ed. Lawrence: University Press of Kansas, 2001, 151–167.

Smith, Timothy B. *Bayou Battles for Vicksburg: The Swamp and River Expeditions, January 1–April 30, 1863*. Lawrence: University Press of Kansas, 2023.

———. *Champion Hill: Decisive Battle for Vicksburg*. New York: Savas Beatie, 2004.

———. *Corinth 1862: Siege, Battle, Occupation*. Lawrence: University Press of Kansas, 2012.

———. *The Decision Was Always My Own: Ulysses S. Grant and the Vicksburg Campaign*. Carbondale: Southern Illinois University Press, 2018.

———. *Early Struggles for Vicksburg: The Mississippi Central Campaign and Chickasaw Bayou, October 25–December 31, 1862*. Lawrence: University Press of Kansas, 2022.

———. *The Golden Age of Battlefield Preservation: The Decade of the 1890s and the Establishment of America's First Five Military Parks*. Knoxville: University of Tennessee Press, 2008.

———. *Grant Invades Tennessee: The 1862 Battles for Forts Henry and Donelson*. Lawrence: University Press of Kansas, 2016.

———. *The Iron Dice of Battle: Albert Sidney Johnston and the Civil War in the West*. Baton Rouge: Louisiana State University Press, 2023.

———. *James Z. George: Mississippi's Great Commoner*. Jackson: University Press of Mississippi, 2012.

———. *Mississippi in the Civil War: The Home Front*. Jackson: University Press of Mississippi, 2010.

———. "Mississippi Nightmare." *Civil War Times* 48, no. 4 (August 2009): 54–58.

———. *The Real Horse Soldiers: Benjamin Grierson's Epic 1863 Civil War Raid Through Mississippi*. El Dorado Hills, CA: Savas Beatie, 2108.

———. *Shiloh: Conquer or Perish*. Lawrence: University Press of Kansas, 2014.

———. *The Siege of Vicksburg: The Climax of the Campaign to Open the Mississippi River, May 23–July 4, 1863*. Lawrence: University Press of Kansas, 2021.

———. "Ulysses S. Grant and the Art of War." In *Grant at 200: Reconsidering the Life and Legacy of Ulysses S. Grant*, Chris Mackowski and Frank J. Scaturro, eds. El Dorado Hills, CA: Savas Beatie, 2023, 37–46.

———. *The Union Assaults at Vicksburg: Grant Attacks Pemberton, May 17–22, 1863*. Lawrence: University Press of Kansas, 2020.

———. "Victory at Any Cost: The Yazoo Pass Expedition." *Journal of Mississippi History* 67, no. 2 (Summer 2007): 147–166.

———. "'A Victory Could Hardly Have Been More Complete': The Battle of Big Black River Bridge." In *The Vicksburg Campaign: March 29–May 18, 1863*, Steven E. Woodworth and Charles D. Grear, eds. Carbondale: Southern Illinois University Press, 2013, 173–193.

Smith, Walter George. *Life and Letters of Thomas Kilby Smith, Brevet Major-General United States Volunteers, 1820–1877*. New York: G. P. Putnam's Sons, 1898.

Soman, Jean Powers, and Frank L. Byrne, eds. *A Jewish Colonel in the Civil War: Marcus M. Spiegel of the Ohio Volunteers*. Kent, OH: Kent State University Press, 1985.

Stephenson, George M. "Logistics of the Vicksburg Campaign." *Army Logistician: The Official Magazine of United States Army Logistics* 15, no. 4 (July–August 1983): 26–29.

Stoker, Donald. *The Grand Design: Strategy and the U. S. Civil War*. New York: Oxford University Press, 2010.

Stone, Mary Amelia (Boomer). *Memoir of George Boardman Boomer*. Boston: Press of Geo. C. Rand & Avery, 1864.

The Story of the Fifty-fifth Regiment Illinois Volunteer Infantry in the Civil War, 1861–1865. Clinton, MA: W. J. Coulter, 1887.

Strong, William E. "The Campaign Against Vicksburg." In *Military Essays and Recollections: Papers Read Before the Commandery of the State of Illinois, Military Order of the Loyal Legion of the United States*, 4 vols. Chicago: A. C. McClurg and Company, 1894, 2:313–354.

Supplement to the Official Records of the Union and Confederate Armies, 100 vols. Wilmington, NC: Broadfoot Publishing Company, 1994.

Sweetman, M. A. "From Milliken's Bend to Vicksburg." August 22, 1895, *National Tribune*.

Symonds, Craig L. *Joseph E. Johnston: A Civil War Biography*. New York: Norton, 1992.

Thomas, Emory M. *Robert E. Lee: A Biography*. New York: W. W. Norton & Company, 1995.

Thorndike, Rachel Sherman, ed. *The Sherman Letters: Correspondence Between General and Senator Sherman from 1837 to 1891*. New York: Charles Scribner's Sons, 1894.

Tilley, Nannie M., ed. "Letter of Judge Alexander M. Clayton Relative to Confederate Courts in Mississippi." *Journal of Southern History* 6 (1940): 392–401.

Townsend, Mary Bobbitt. *Yankee Warhorse: A Biography of Major General Peter Osterhaus*. Columbia: University of Missouri Press, 2010.

"Troops in the Battle of Port Gibson." *Confederate Veteran* 23, no. 5 (May 1915): 205.

Trowbridge, Silas T. *Autobiography of Silas Thompson Trowbridge, M.D.* Carbondale: Southern Illinois University Press, 2004.

———. *Autobiography of S. T. Trowbridge, M.D.* N.p.: n.p., 1872.

Tucker, Phillip Thomas. *The Forgotten "Stonewall of the West": Major General John Stevens Bowen*. Macon, GA: Mercer University Press, 1997.

———. *Westerners in Gray: The Men of and Missions of the Elite Fifth Missouri Infantry Regiment*. Jefferson, NC: McFarland & Company, 1995.

Tunnard, W. H. *A Southern Record: The History of the Third Regiment Louisiana Infantry*. Baton Rouge: n.p., 1866.

van Creveld, Martin. *Supplying War: Logistics from Wallenstein to Patton*, 2nd ed. Cambridge: Cambridge University Press, 2004.

Van Dorn, Robert J., and Daniel A. Masters, eds. *The 57th Ohio Veteran Volunteer Infantry*. Perrysburg, OH: Columbian Arsenal Press, 2021.

Walke, Henry. *Naval Scenes and Reminiscences of the Civil War in the United States, on the Southern and Western Waters During the Years 1861, 1862 and 1863*. New York: F. R. Reed, 1877.

War of the Rebellion: A Compilation of the Official Records of the Union and Confederate Armies. Washington, DC: Government Printing Office, 1880–1901.

Warner, Ezra J. *Generals in Blue: Lives of the Union Commanders*. Baton Rouge: Louisiana State University Press, 1964.

———. *Generals in Gray: The Lives of the Confederate Commanders*. Baton Rouge: Louisiana State University Press, 1959.

Welsh, Jack D. *Medical Histories of Union Generals*. Kent, OH: Kent State University Press, 1996.

Whaley, Elizabeth J. *Forgotten Hero: General James B. McPherson*. New York: Exposition Press, 1955.

White, Ronald C. *American Ulysses: A Life of Ulysses S. Grant*. New York: Random House, 2016.

Wilkin, Jacob B. "Vicksburg." In *Military Essays and Recollections: Papers Read Before the Commandery of the State of Illinois, Military Order of the Loyal Legion of the United States, Volume 4*. Chicago: Cozzens and Beaton Company, 1907, 215–237.

Williams, John Melvin. *"The Eagle Regiment," 8th Wis. Inf'ty Vols.: A Sketch of Its Marches, Battles and Campaigns From 1861–1865 With Complete Regimental and Company Roster, and a Few Portraits and Sketches of Its Officers and Commanders*. Belleville, WI: Recorder Print, 1890.

Williams, Kenneth P. *Grant Rises in the West: From Iuka to Vicksburg, 1862–1863*. Lincoln: University of Nebraska Press, 1997.

Williams, T. Harry. *Lincoln and His Generals*. New York: Alfred A. Knopf, 1952.

Williams, T. J. "The Battle of Champion's Hill." In *Sketches of War History, 1861–1865*. Cincinnati: The Robert Clarke Company, 1903, 5:204–212.

Willison, Charles A. *Reminiscences of a Boy's Service with the 76th Ohio, In the Fifteenth Army Corps, Under General Sherman, During the Civil War, By That "Boy" at Three Score*. Menasha, WI: The George Banta Publishing Company, 1908.

Wilson, Harold S. *Confederate Industry: Manufactures and Quartermasters in the Civil War*. Jackson: University Press of Mississippi, 2002.

Wilson, James Harrison. "A Staff Officer's Journal of the Vicksburg Campaign, April 30 to July 4, 1863." *Journal of the Military Service Institution of the United States* 43, no. 154 (July–August 1908): 93–109.

———. *Under the Old Flag: Recollections of Military Operations in the War for the Union, the Spanish War the Boxer Rebellion, Etc.*, 2 vols. New York: D. Appleton and Co., 1912.

Winschel, Terrence J. "The Absence of Will: Joseph E. Johnston and the Fall of Vicksburg." In *Confederate Generals in the Western Theater: Essays on America's Civil War*, 4 vols. Lawrence Lee Hewitt and Arthur W. Bergeron Jr., eds. Knoxville: University of Tennessee Press, 2010, 2:75–92.

———. "Applicability in the Modern Age: Ulysses S. Grant's Vicksburg Campaign." *Journal of Mississippi History* 80, nos. 1 and 2 (Spring/Summer 2018): 35–47.

——. "Fighting Politician: John A. McClernand." In *Grant's Lieutenants: From Cairo to Vicksburg*, Steven E. Woodworth, ed. Lawrence: University Press of Kansas, 2001, 129–150.

——. "The Guns at Champion Hill (Part II)." *Journal of Confederate History* 6 (1990): 94–105.

——. *Triumph and Defeat: The Vicksburg Campaign*. Mason City, IA: Savas Publishing Company, 1999.

——. *Triumph and Defeat: The Vicksburg Campaign, Volume 2*. New York: Savas Beatie, 2006.

——. "The Vicksburg Campaign." In *The Cambridge History of the American Civil War*, 3 vols. Aaron Sheehan-Dean, ed. Cambridge: Cambridge University Press, 2019, 1:246–268.

Winschel, Terrence J., ed. *The Civil War Diary of a Common Soldier: William Wiley of the 77th Illinois Infantry*. Baton Rouge: Louisiana State University Press, 2001.

Wood, D. W. *History of the 20th O. V. V. I. Regiment, and Proceedings of the First Reunion at Mt. Vernon, Ohio, April 6, 1876*. Columbus, OH: Paul and Thrall, Book and Job Printers, 1876.

Wood, Wales W. *A History of the Ninety-fifth Regiment Illinois Infantry Volunteers, From Its Organization in the Fall of 1862, Until Its Final Discharge from the United States Service, in 1865*. Chicago: Tribune Company's Book and Job Printing Office, 1865.

Woodworth, Steven E. "The First Capture and Occupation of Jackson, Mississippi." In *The Vicksburg Campaign: March 29–May 18, 1863*, Steven E. Woodworth and Charles D. Grear, eds. Carbondale: Southern Illinois University Press, 2013, 96–115.

——. *Jefferson Davis and His Generals: The Failure of Confederate Command in the West*. Lawrence: University Press of Kansas, 1990.

——. *Nothing but Victory: The Army of the Tennessee, 1861–1865*. New York: Knopf, 2005.

Woodworth, Steven E., and Charles D. Grear, eds. *The Vicksburg Campaign: March 29–May 18, 1863*. Carbondale: Southern Illinois University Press, 2013.

Wynne, Ben. *Mississippi's Civil War: A Narrative History*. Macon, GA: Mercer University Press, 2006.

Yeary, Mamie. *Reminiscences of the Boys in Gray, 1861–1865*. Dallas: Wilkinson Printing Company, 1912.

Young, John Russell. *Around the World with General Grant: A Narrative of the Visit of General U.S. Grant, Ex-President of the United States, to Various Countries in Europe, Asia, and Africa, in 1877, 1878, 1879. To which are Added Certain Conversations with General Grant on Questions Connected with American Politics and History*. New York: American News Company, 1879.

INDEX